Mississippi: A Hist

Mis...

A History

00

Visit us on the World Wide Web at www.harlandavidson.com

Library of Congress Cataloging-in-Publication Data

Busbee, Westley F.
  Mississippi : a history / Westley F. Busbee, Jr.
      p. cm.
  Includes bibliographical references and index.
  ISBN 0-88295-236-6 (hardcover : alk. paper) — ISBN 0-88295-227-7 (pbk. :
alk. paper)
  1. Mississippi—History. I. Title.
  F341.B93 2005
  976.2—dc22

                              2004025954

Cover photograh: Bay Springs Lake by Ian L. Barker,
Camera i, © Ian L. Barker 2003
Cover design: DePinto Graphic Design

Manufactured in the United States of America
08 07 06 05 1 2 3 4 MG

CONTENTS

List of Illustrations

PREFACE AND ACKNOWLEDGMENTS

As the twenty-first century begins to unfold, observers express contrasting opinions about the future of Mississippi. Optimists point out that the state's natural and human resources combined with recent educational and economic advances will contribute to a new progressive era. Pessimists counter that the state remains at or near the bottom of the fifty states in several important categories, including per capita income, adult literacy, and public health—and that lingering racial discord dampens hopes for real progress. While neither side is completely right, a competent assessment of future prospects requires a good understanding of the past. How and why did all of us who call Mississippi home get where we are? What past mistakes might we hope to correct and what innovative approaches might we take to enhance the state's future? These questions are addressed in the pages that follow.

This text, the first survey history of Mississippi ever developed for the undergraduate reader, is an assimilation of information gleaned from a multitude of sources, both secondary works—including journal articles, textbooks, biographies, and monographs—and primary sources—including government documents, newspapers, diaries, personal papers, interviews, and business records and reports. Except for the chapters dealing with the final decades of the twentieth century, which contain the findings of considerable original research, this text relies primarily on a careful examination of existing studies of Mississippi history. Years in development, this book features original maps and tables as well as a number of photographs, selected sources by chapter, a selected bibliography of Mississippi history (useful for anyone wishing to research further any aspect of our state's past), an appendix, and a full subject index. While all these features are intended to enhance the reader's experience, the central purpose of this book is to recount and interpret Mississippi history at a level appropriate for advanced students.

After many years of teaching Mississippi history at the college level with no appropriate textbook available, I decided to try to fill that void, to meet my own and my students' needs and, hopefully, those of other instructors and students. While the assignment of selected readings in various and diverse sources remains a desirable method of instruction, this book provides a common base of information for students pursuing knowledge and meaning in the study of their state's past.

Because so many people have encouraged and assisted me during the long process of preparing this text, I refrain from an attempt to catalog a long list of names. Such a compilation would include many colleagues and students at Belhaven College, numerous other persons interested in Mississippi history, professional historians as well as laypersons, and of course many librarians and archivists. Nevertheless, I could not have persevered without the involvement of several key individuals and groups.

Special thanks go to President Roger Parrott and Provost Daniel C. Fredericks of Belhaven College, who gave me continuing support including a sabbatical in 2002. Professors Paul R. Waibel and Stephen Philips in our Department of History and Political Science were steadfast in their interest and assistance. The staff of the Warren A. Hood Library at Belhaven was always ready and willing to help me find sources, many in distant locations. Heartfelt appeciation goes to Margaret B. Root, our Reference Librarian, who compiled the index. I received immeasurable encouragement, including valuable research assistance, from students in my Mississippi history and historiography courses over the past thirty-five years. They made countless trips to the Mississippi Department of Archives and History, where they found useful sources and leads to information that I would hardly have discovered as a lone researcher.

The Mississippi Department of Archives and History staff—particularly Anne Lipscomb Webster—was always helpful; needless to say, their incredibly well administered and extensive collections are indispensable for any major study of the state's history.

Two scholars with considerable experience teaching Mississippi history read the initial manuscript and provided substantive criticisms and recommendations. Dr. Dennis J. Mitchell, presently chair of the Division of Arts and Sciences and professor of history at Mississippi State University–Meridian and formerly professor of history at Jackson State University, made suggestions for additional sources and textual revisions. Dr. Charles Smith, professor of history and political science at Mississippi College, improved the organization of the manuscript and recommended the inclusion or expansion of coverage of several significant persons and events in the Mississippi story.

For his constant support, advice, optimism, and patience, I am especially thankful to Andrew J. Davidson of Harlan Davidson, Inc. His keen editing skills were surpassed only by his "brutally frank" questions and comments, all directly on target, based on his wide-ranging knowledge of American history, and all aimed to produce a readable, informative text. Also crucial to the book's quality, production editor Lucy Herz exhibited her amazing expertise in assembling the various facets of this book.

Finally, my wife and children deserve my heartfelt gratitude. Without their backing, of course, it would have been impossible for me to undertake this project. Carol read every word and made innumerable corrections and suggestions. She gets the ultimate credit for its successful completion because of her unrelenting help and encouragement, as well as her ability to understand and communicate the book's importance. Our three children, Westleyan, Jenny, and Brad, grew up listening to their parents' conversations about Mississippi history. Although they now have their own careers and families and reside in lands distant from my native state, they never failed to inquire about my progress and to give whatever assistance I needed.

Westley F. Busbee, Jr.
Jackson, Mississippi
January 1, 2005

CHAPTER ONE

Mississippi: The Name and the Place

THE STATE NAME

Meeting at a little Methodist Church in the heat of July and August 1817, a group of white frontiersmen had to decide what to call their state on the eve of its admittance into the United States of America. They debated whether to adopt a European name, like Washington or Columbia, or retain the Native American phrase already in use. The majority preferred the second option, to keep the name "Mississippi," an expression that had originated in the Muskhogean language, dialects of which were spoken but not written by most Indian tribes in the region. The phrase, which originally may have sounded more like "Meechee Seepe," was used by the Choctaws and other native peoples to mean "great river" or "father of waters." The French explorer and Jesuit missionary Jacques Marquette in 1672 translated the words he heard the Indians say as "Mitchisipi," and Franciscan friar Louis Hennepin in 1698 recorded the same as "Mechasipi" in a book describing his journeys with the French explorer La Salle. But credit goes to a British traveler, Daniel Coxe, for first spelling the name nearly in its final form when, in 1722, he published it as "Missisipi" in a description of his family's land claims in North America.

CLIMATE AND PHYSICAL GEOGRAPHY

When Spanish explorers first entered the Mississippi area in the 1540s—almost seventy years before the English colonists founded Jamestown in Virginia—they found a land virtually covered with forests. Some 460 years later, at the start of the twenty-first century, more than half of the state's land remains forested.

Located in a transitional zone between the tropics to the south and cooler climates to the north, Mississippi has long fostered abundant plant life (flora) and animal life (fauna). The state's average annual precipitation is 52 inches with little seasonal variation, ranging from about 50 inches in the northern counties to about 60 inches along the Gulf Coast. Along with such abundant rainfall, the state experiences high relative humidity rates, averaging above 70 percent but even higher in the summer.

Mississippi is one of the nation's warmest states, with an average annual temperature of 62° Fahrenheit. During the relatively short winters the average temperature is 48°, ranging generally from 42° in the north to 52° in coastal counties. Through the long summers the average temperature statewide is about 81°, but daytime temperatures routinely exceed 90°. Mississippi has a famously long grow-

ing season, extending from April through October in the northern counties, with at least 200 frost-free days, and from March through November along the Gulf Coast, with at least 270 frost-free days.

Borders

Before Mississippi entered the Union as the state with its current borders, the Mississippi Territory comprised the present-day states of Mississippi and Alabama as well as portions of present-day Florida and Louisiana. The land area within the present state is 47,914 square miles, ranking Mississippi thirty-first in size among the fifty states. The shape of the state is basically rectangular, with the longest distance from the Tennessee border to the Gulf Coast (north to south) about 350 miles, and the longest distance from the Alabama border to the Mississippi River (east to west) about 180 miles. Located in the center of the Gulf South region of the United States, between 30° and 34° north latitude and 88° and 91° west longitude, the state has both natural and geometric boundaries. On the west, the Mississippi and the Pearl rivers separate Mississippi from Arkansas and Louisiana. On the south, the eastern portion of the state reaches the Gulf of Mexico, and the western portion extends to 31° north latitude, which is the border with Louisiana. Mississippi borders Tennessee on the north and Alabama on the east. The latter borderline runs from the junction of Bear Creek and the Tennessee River southward to the northeast corner of Wayne County, and then southward to a point on the Gulf about ten miles east of the mouth of the Pascagoula River.

Land Surface

Located in the East Gulf Coastal Plain, a physiographic region of the southern United States, Mississippi's terrain varies relatively little. The land ranges from flat plains to rolling hills to slight elevations (in the northeast), but most of the land surface lies less than five hundred feet above sea level. Even the high points in the northeast reach only about eight hundred feet above sea level, with the highest point, Woodall Mountain in Tishomingo County, reaching 806 feet. In the central part of the state the elevations range from three hundred to five hundred feet, and in the south, near the coast, the land slopes from thirty feet down to sea level.

Soil Regions

The character of the soil varies in Mississippi and may be divided into ten major regions. (See map of Soil Regions, opposite.)

The Tennessee or Tombigbee Hills in the northeast is a region that features the highest elevations in the state, averaging 650 feet; it is drained by the Tennessee and Tombigbee rivers. Except in the river bottoms, the soil of this region is primarily a reddish, sandy, and infertile loam.

The Black Prairie lies west of the Tennessee Hills and forms a crescent, stretching from the Corinth area southward through the Macon vicinity and eastward into Alabama. This region, which ranges about twenty-five miles in width, has a relatively flat surface and lies several hundred feet lower than the surrounding regions. It is drained by the Tombigbee and its tributaries. Because its dark and fertile soil makes excellent farm- and pastureland, this region attracted cotton planters and their African slaves early in the state's history.

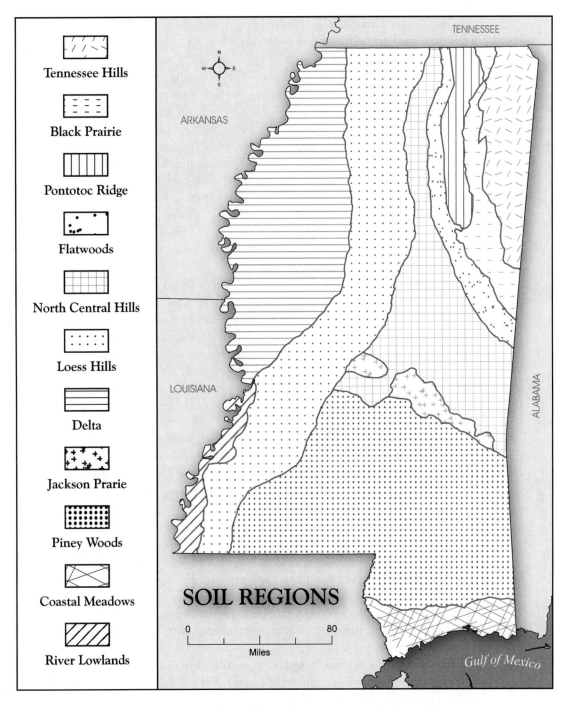

SOIL REGIONS

Legend:
- Tennessee Hills
- Black Prairie
- Pontotoc Ridge
- Flatwoods
- North Central Hills
- Loess Hills
- Delta
- Jackson Prarie
- Piney Woods
- Coastal Meadows
- River Lowlands

0   80
Miles

The Pontotoc Ridge, west of the Black Prairie, extends from Tennessee southward to the West Point area; its elevation ranges from four hundred to six hundred feet in remarkable contrast to the surrounding flatlands. Reddish clay and sandy loam compose the region's soils, and although they can sustain crops, they tend to erode easily.

The Flatwoods region, west of the Pontotoc Ridge, is only about ten miles wide but extends from Tennessee southward through Kemper County. Its clay soils are not well suited for farming.

The North Central Hills (also known as the Sand-Clay Hills) is a much larger area west of the Flatwoods that extends from Tennessee southward through Leake County in the central part of the state and eastward through Lauderdale and Clarke counties and into Alabama. This region forms a large plateau ranging from four hundred to six hundred feet high, with most of it lying within the Pearl and Big Black river watersheds. Its soil is a mixture of reddish sand, clay, and loam and is very susceptible to erosion. The bottomlands of the region, however, contain very rich soil. In Lauderdale, Kemper, and Neshoba counties, located in the southern zone of the plateau, the terrain becomes quite hilly in places.

The Loess Hills (also known as the Bluff Hills) is a region located west of the North Central Hills that forms a narrow belt extending from Tennessee southward through the state. Bordering the Delta to the west, the Loess Hills is named for the color and nature of the soil, a pale, fertile material, but one that tends to run shallow and erode and exhaust easily. Most of this region lies within the watersheds of the Big Black and Yazoo rivers.

The Delta (also known by geologists as the Yazoo Basin or the Mississippi–Yazoo Alluvial Plain) lies between the Yazoo River and the Loess Hills on the east and the Mississippi River on the west. About eighty miles at its widest point, the Delta extends roughly two hundred miles from Memphis's Chickasaw Bluffs to Vicksburg's Walnut Hills. A floodplain, the Delta is composed of alluvial deposits. Basically flat and dark, the soil is a mixture of sand, silt, and clays. Thanks to its level topography and rich soil, the Delta is the largest and most productive agricultural region in the state.

The Jackson Prairie is a narrow strip in the center of the state, extending from the vicinity of Madison County generally southeastward through Clarke County. The flat and undulating lands, containing areas of dark lime soils like those found in the Black Prairie, are well suited for farming and livestock concerns. This region is drained by tributaries of the Pearl and the Pascagoula rivers.

The Piney Woods, an extensive region covering most of south Mississippi, extends southward from the Jackson Prairie to within twenty miles of the Gulf Coast and westward from Alabama to the Loess Hills near the Mississippi River. The relatively high and rolling terrain ranges from two hundred to five hundred feet above sea level and lies within the Pearl and Pascagoula river watersheds. Its soils of red and yellow sandy loams are not very fertile, but the region produces longleaf and other types of pine trees in great abundance—the vast forests that underlay the development of Mississippi's important lumber industries in the twentieth century.

The Coastal Meadows, a region along the Gulf Coast, is about twenty miles wide, relatively flat, and contains fine sand and sandy loams that support some timber but very little farmland.

Major Rivers

The river systems of Mississippi played a significant role in the state's history, providing avenues of transportation and communication well before the colonial period. And because they provided the means for importing supplies and exporting farm produce, navigable rivers enabled European and then American settlers to

Mississippi River at Natchez. Courtesy of Westley F. Busbee, Jr.

populate and develop interior regions. Before the railroad revolution, the rivers were the main arteries of commerce in the state. Today riverbottoms and swamps still compose about 16 percent (7,560 square miles) of Mississippi's total land area.

The Mississippi River, the western border of the state, is naturally first among the state's rivers in size and importance, having provided the main avenue for exploration, trade, and transportation since the very beginning of the state's history. A number of major rivers enter the Mississippi, draining the western part of the state.

The Yazoo River and its tributaries form the most important watershed located wholly within the state. This system begins in the northwestern portion of the state, where it is formed by the union of the Tallahatchie and Yalobusha rivers, and flows about 190 miles southwestward, entering the Mississippi River at Vicksburg. Its main tributaries are the Coldwater and the Sunflower rivers.

The Big Black River flows more than three hundred miles in a southwesterly direction from the state's north central area and enters the Mississippi in the vicinity of Grand Gulf, about twenty-five miles south of Vicksburg. Farther south,

The Homochitto River provides a watershed for the extreme southwestern corner of the state.

The Pearl River, the longest internal river, meanders nearly five hundred miles from north central Mississippi southward to the Gulf Coast, forming the border with Louisiana south of 31° north latitude.

The Tombigbee River, in the northeast, was connected by canal with the Tennessee River in the 1980s. The Tombigbee provides an important watershed and avenue of transportation as it flows into Alabama then southward to the port of Mobile.

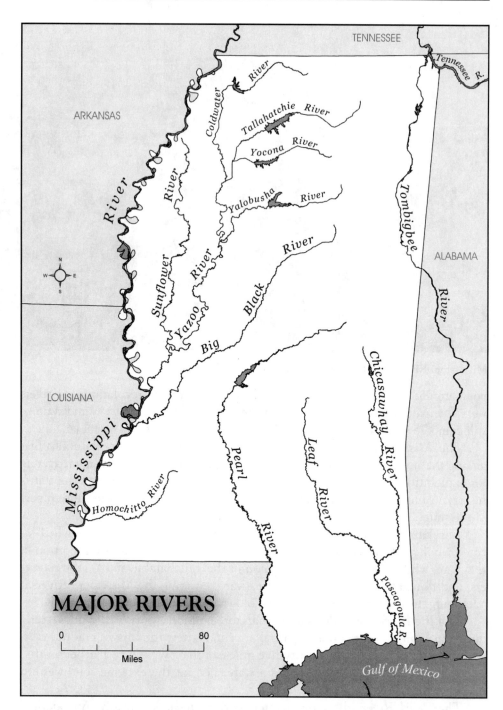

MAJOR RIVERS

The Pascagoula River, formed by the confluence of the Leaf and Chicasawhay rivers, drains the southeastern part of the state and empties into the Gulf at the port city of Pascagoula.

THE INFLUENCE OF GEOGRAPHY ON HISTORY

As indicated in following chapters, the state's geographic features have influenced the course of Mississippi's social, cultural, economic, and political history. For example, during the antebellum period the western soil zones attracted farmers who wished to grow cotton, a highly labor-intensive crop, so slavery grew faster there than in all other areas except for portions of the Black Prairie. In the decades following the Civil War, when the construction of levees along the Mississippi River lessened the threat of flooding, the Delta became the most important agricultural region of the state. Supplying the demand for labor on the massive cotton-producing farms, African Americans (former slaves and their descendants) were more numerous there than in most other regions. Most eastern counties, on the other hand, were not as productive agriculturally; thus relatively fewer African Americans, almost all of whom engaged in some form of agriculture for their livelihoods, resided there. A notable exception to this pattern was the large number of black residents in Clay, Lowndes, and Noxubee counties within the Black Prairie.

Signs of sectionalism, caused in part by geographic differences, became increasingly evident in the nineteenth century. Because the greatest concentrations of antebellum slave-owning planters resided in western counties, this region tended to produce many of the state's economic and political leaders well into the twentieth century. Eastern counties, which had greater proportions of small nonslaveholding farmers, tended to support "populist" causes in the post–Civil War decades. Sectional differences were equally stark between the southern and northern counties. For example, beginning as early as the 1830s and continuing through the twentieth century, leaders from these geographic regions disputed such issues as legislative apportionment and the location of state educational institutions.

One of the clearest manifestations of regional sectionalism in the late nineteenth and early twentieth centuries was the political party rivalry between "Bourbon" Democrats, based in Delta and other western counties, and Populists, strongest in the eastern counties. Often influenced by geographic circumstances, these groups battled to protect their divergent interests on such important matters as state regulation of corporations, restrictions on suffrage, the means of selecting judges, and the distribution of public school funds.

Some areas of the state experienced only gradual growth and would not wield significant influence in the state's economic and political life until the twentieth century. One example is the Piney Woods region, the influence of which awaited the development of the timber and petroleum industries. Another late bloomer, the Tennessee Hills, experienced increased economic importance only after the advent of projects by the Tennessee Valley Authority in the 1930s and the construction of the Tennessee-Tombigbee Waterway thereafter.

Partly because of its regional distinctiveness, the Delta fostered a particularly advanced cultural milieu in the twentieth century. There, African Americans overcame poverty and racial discrimination to produce original musical genres like the blues, and nationally acclaimed authors, both black and white, penned works remarkable in their quantity, quality, and variety. Even with their black population majorities, the Delta counties were dominated politically by white conservatives through the mid-twentieth century. But beginning with the civil rights movement of the 1960s, these same counties emerged as liberal strongholds. Meanwhile, during the last half of the twentieth century, eastern Mississ-

Cedar swamp. Courtesy of Kirk Irwin.

ippians increasingly supported conservative Republicans, thus reversing that region's long tradition of Democratic populism.

SELECTED SOURCES

Kelley, Arthell, "The Geography," in Richard Aubrey McLemore, ed., *A History of Mississippi*, 2 vols. (Hattiesburg: University & College Press of Mississippi, 1973), 1: 3–23.

McKee, Jesse O., "Evolution and Distribution of Mississippi's African American Population: 1820–1990," *Mississippi Journal for the Social Studies* 6 (1995): 1–7.

———, et al., *Mississippi: Portrait of an American State* (Montgomery, Ala.: Clairmont Press, 1995).

Mississippi Official and Statistical Register (various dates).

Parker, Joseph B., ed., *Politics in Mississippi*, 2d ed. (Salem, Wisc.: Sheffield Publishing Company, 2001).

Prenshaw, Peggy W. and Jesse O. McKee, eds., *Sense of Place: Mississippi* (Jackson: University Press of Mississippi, 1979).

Rowland, Dunbar, *History of Mississippi: The Heart of the South*, 4 vols. (Chicago-Jackson: The S. J. Clarke Publishing Company, 1925), vol. 1.

CHAPTER TWO

Two Worlds Collide:
Spanish Explorers and American Indians

The First Mississippians

When a small band of Spaniards wandered into the land we now know as Mississippi in 1540, they found a substantial number of native peoples whom they mistakenly identified as "Indians," following the precedent set by Christopher Columbus. Who were these Native Americans, and from where did they come? Notwithstanding the fascinating creation stories the Indian peoples told to succeeding generations and to Europeans who finally recorded them, the real answer, though incomplete and not without disagreement, is based on investigations of artifacts and early written and oral accounts by archaeologists, historians, and other scholars. These studies reveal that the earliest inhabitants of Mississippi were the descendants of numerous generations of peoples whose cultural development had passed through four major prehistoric epochs, beginning with their migrations from northeastern Asia to Alaska (across the frozen Bering Strait) and then to all other regions of the Americas.

During the Paleo-Indian Period (about 12000 to 8000 BC) small bands of nomadic hunters and gatherers reached the present-day southeastern United States. There they began to form transitory, seasonal settlements and make pottery in the Archaic Period, which extended into the first millennium BC. Late in the Archaic, family groups came together in organized villages, began mound building, and improved their hunting and tool-making skills.

Attracted by the region's favorable environment, increasing numbers of native peoples settled in present-day Mississippi during the Woodland Period (about 1000 BC to AD 1000). By this time large bands began to establish permanent residential settlements and more complex tribal organizations, which allowed them to make significant cultural advances. They constructed monumental earthworks (including burial mounds), practiced agriculture, developed trade networks, and made technological advances including the creation of distinctively decorated ceramic pottery and highly useful cultivation tools and weaponry.

These patterns continued through the Cole Creek transitional era and into the Mississippian Period (AD 1000 through the 1600s), producing in present-day Mississippi numerous large villages characterized by their inhabitants' increasing reliance on agriculture and even more complex political, economic, social, and religious organizations. Archaeologists refer to this time as the "Temple Mound" period in recognition of the great rectangular mounds on which the Indians constructed temples and other important structures. One such structure, Emerald Mound near Natchez, is the second largest mound of this culture.

By the sixteenth century as many as 200,000 native Mississippians lived in politically organized units known as chiefdoms. These societies were typically located in river floodplains, with temple mounds as their centers. They were overseen by chiefs, who may have exercised both political and religious authority but whose positions depended primarily on sufficient agricultural production. But it was not inadequate supplies of food that rapidly turned the Native American world upside down: it was the arrival of Europeans.

THE SPANISH INCURSION

In what at first appeared to be an inauspicious attempt to find a new, shorter sea route for Spanish ships to sail from Europe to Asia, Christopher Columbus in fact discovered a "New World" in 1492. Following Columbus's first voyage to the Americas, Spain sent successive expeditions to explore and conquer most of the Western Hemisphere. While Hernán Cortez and Francisco Pizarro respectively subdued the Aztec Indians of Mexico and the Incas of Peru, reaping incredible treasures of gold and silver, other Spanish conquistadors sought similar riches and a fabled water passage to Asia, the so-called Strait of Anián, by exploring along the coast of the Gulf of Mexico. Juan Ponce de León, Alonso Alvarez de Pineda, and Pánfilo de Narvaez led such expeditions, venturing into the present-day southeastern United States. Even though these explorers made useful maps of the coastline and saw a great river that flowed into the Gulf (possibly the Mississippi but probably the Mobile River), the Spanish crown temporarily suspended further efforts in the region, favoring instead to concentrate their efforts on exploiting other, more-promising parts of the Americas.

Hernando de Soto

Notwithstanding the apparent failure of these expeditions, stories told by the survivors (particularly Alvar Núñez Cabeza de Vaca's colorful account of his adventures with Narvaez in 1527) stimulated interest among other Spaniards to seek their fortunes in North America. One such explorer was Hernando De Soto. An experienced conquistador, De Soto was commissioned by King Charles I of Spain (who was also Holy Roman Emperor Charles V) to explore the region known as Florida in return for a share of the gold, silver, pearls, and other riches that might be found there. With the titles of Governor and Captain-General of Cuba and Florida, De Soto launched the expedition from Havana in the spring of 1539 with more than six hundred well-equipped soldiers, a number of clergymen and artisans, at least two hundred horses, and extensive supplies, including hundreds of pigs for food.

Although the promise of riches motivated them, the Spaniards justified their expedition into other peoples' lands by expressing their intention to spread the Christian gospel among the Indians, whom the Catholic Spanish considered "heathens" in need of salvation. Indeed, the newcomers routinely treated Native Americans they encountered cruelly, often without cause. Nonetheless, many Indians were initially friendly toward the white invaders, whom they might have perceived as potential new allies or trading partners. Those who met De Soto, however, were badly deceived by the Spaniard, who intentionally misled them to

DeSoto's men placing their dead leader's body in the Mississippi. Library of Congress. LC-USZ62-17898.

believe that he had come as a friend. Soon thereafter De Soto and his men took hundreds of Indians as captives before slaughtering them.

After wandering about in the present-day southeastern states for more than a year without having found any gold or other precious materials, De Soto sent orders for his ships to return to Havana, stock up with additional supplies, and then rejoin him at Pensacola Bay. In the meantime, De Soto and his remaining land party advanced southward towards the Gulf Coast. On the way they met disaster.

The Battle of Mabila In October 1540, while journeying through present-day Alabama, De Soto and company encountered and initially befriended Chief Tuscaluza (or Tuscaloosa), apparently with the design of capturing him.[1] The plan failed, however, because the chief was not fooled and discreetly summoned numerous Indian warriors in the region to concentrate for an attack on the Spaniards at Mabila (or Mauvilla), an Indian town in present-day Clarke County, Alabama, about twenty-five miles north of the confluence of the Alabama and Tombigbee rivers. The Spaniards eventually prevailed and then burned the town, but the victory proved costly. More than 2,500 Indians and nearly 100 Spaniards died, and hundreds more were wounded, including De Soto himself. The battle

1 It is likely that Tuscaluza ruled over a chiefdom that would later be called the Mobile tribe. Spanish chroniclers described the Indian chief as a gigantic black man, and they speculated that Indians of this coastal region appeared to be black because they spent so much time in sea-going activities, including saltwater fishing. With an estimated population of some 7,000 persons in the sixteenth century, the Mobilians' descendents may have been absorbed by the Choctaws. According to some sources, the name Tuscaluza means "Black Warrior" in Choctaw dialects. De Soto's motive was to hold the chief as a hostage to guarantee his party's safe passage through the territory. *De Soto Chronicles*, Volume 2, Book 3, Chapter 24.

also cost the Spanish invaders horses, equipment, and supplies considered indispensable for the expedition.

After the battle De Soto had to discontinue his southward march. After a long delay for recovery and reorganization, he turned northwestward, refocusing his troops' attention on finding wealth. He decided that meeting the supply ships at Pensacola, only about a six-days' march away, so soon after the Mabila catastrophe might dissuade his battle weary and disappointed men from undertaking any further inland exploration. The destruction of a collection of pearls—the only "riches" the tired Spaniards had managed to collect—in the fires at Mabila also may have influenced De Soto's decision.

Northeast Mississippi In mid-December 1540 De Soto entered Mississippi, crossing the Tombigbee River north of present-day Columbus, probably near Aberdeen but possibly as far north as Amory (Cotton Gin Port). Through the winter months he camped near a large Chicaça village in the area of present-day Pontotoc and Lee counties. Tired of the mistreatment at the hands of the Spanish interlopers, the Chicaças (probably ancestors of the eighteenth-century Chickasaws) attacked De Soto's quarters near the present-day towns of Pontotoc or Tupelo in March 1541. Killing at least twelve men but possibly as many as forty, the Indians destroyed or confiscated weapons and other essential supplies, including about fifty horses and hundreds of hogs. As a result of these losses, which only compounded those the expedition had suffered at Mabila, De Soto could not resume his search for riches to the northwest until late April.

The Mississippi River Traveling across northern Mississippi, De Soto again attacked Indian villages, whether or not the inhabitants resisted him. By now the Spaniards were driven primarily by their desperate need for food; earlier objectives of discovering great wealth must have seemed illusory. On May 8, 1541, De Soto's now small, bedraggled band arrived at the Mississippi River in present-day Tunica County, the location of the Quizquiz chiefdom.[2] The Spaniards built rafts and small boats and crossed the river in spite of the appearance of numerous, well-organized, and heavily armed Indian warriors on the opposite bank and in canoes on the water. For several months the Spaniards explored areas west of the river, in present-day Arkansas, but once again failing to discover gold or other treasures and fearing the Indians, De Soto's men began to lose the last shred of hope and demanded that the expedition turn back southeastward. But in May 1542, before De Soto made it back across the Mississippi, which he had named El Rio de la Florida, he succumbed to a fever and died. His men buried him in the great river.

The Spanish Exit Following the death of their leader, the surviving Spaniards determined to leave the Mississippi territory. After trying but having failed to reach Mexico overland, they returned to the Mississippi River and built boats that they used to float downstream. Some of them managed to reach Vera Cruz on the Mexican coast late in 1543. Following the Spaniards' exit, there is no documented evidence of any major European presence in the Mississippi territory until the arrival of the French about 130 years later.

2 There has been controversy among scholars over the exact location of De Soto's discovery of the Mississippi River, including claims extending as far north as Memphis, Tennessee, and as far south as Friars Point (Coahoma County).

Consequences of the Invasion   De Soto's invasion of Mississippi clearly failed to produce riches for Spain, but more significantly it wreaked dramatic and long-lasting damage to the local Indian peoples and their cultures. In Mississippi and across southeastern North America, Native Americans suffered severely from the cumulative effects of the Spanish legacy. Heretofore unknown diseases contracted from European men and their domesticated animals spread from village to village and passed to succeeding generations. As tribal elders fell victim to devastating epidemics, much of their societies' accumulated knowledge died with them, thus weakening the chiefdoms' viability. Moreover, high mortality rates among the youth, the other most susceptible group, not only demoralized the survivors but reduced the number of food producers and drastically lowered their future reproduction opportunities.

Massive depopulation and resulting cultural upheavals, therefore, produced vastly different Indian societies by the late seventeenth century, when the first French explorers arrived in Mississippi. According to some estimates, the native population by that time had dropped to about 40,000 persons, only 20 percent of the number living in the area at the time of first contact with Europeans. Moreover, an entirely different configuration of chiefdoms or "tribes" had emerged—culturally complex societies composed of refugees from collapsing chiefdoms as well as other ethnic groups introduced through occasional contact with European traders and their African slaves.

AMERICAN INDIANS OF MISSISSIPPI IN THE LATE SEVENTEENTH CENTURY

Subsistence Tactics

Although American Indian peoples in late seventeenth-century Mississippi were not necessarily homogeneous, they did share many practices and dialects. Their horticultural skills had advanced sufficiently to produce a great abundance of food. French explorers claimed the Indians had forty-two different recipes featuring corn or maize, their major crop. The Indians also harvested numerous other crops including squash, various beans and peas, potatoes (including "sweet potatoes"), peanuts, tomatoes, pumpkins, melons, and tobacco. For their meat they hunted and killed various animals, the most important game being deer, bear, bison, and fish. After consuming the meat, they used other parts of some animals as material to construct clothing, shelters, and weapons. Other food sources included the many varieties of naturally growing berries, nuts, and roots.

Culture

Based on their agricultural achievements, the native inhabitants gradually developed the requisites of what Europeans considered civilized society, including permanent villages and buildings, ritualized religious practices, governmental structures and procedures, military organizations, and commercial activities. Although there is no evidence of a written language, the tribal elders transmitted orally their history and legends, which included folktales about the tribes' creation, their migrations, as well as their accumulated technical knowledge and religious beliefs. By observing lunar cycles the elders were also the time or calendar keepers, dividing each year into four seasons and keeping records of passing years

Model of a Natchez Indian house. Courtesy Westley F. Busbee, Jr.

or "winters." The green corn dance performed in the spring or early summer heralded the new year of provisions provided by the gods.

Religion

Virtually every aspect of Indian life was integrated with their religious beliefs and practices. Most groups worshiped major and minor deities with the sun, usually the preeminent one, often represented by a sacred fire maintained and guarded by village priests. They also observed numerous lesser gods and spirits, which could possess both good and evil traits and powers. The Indians credited these deities as the causes for all human events and natural phenomena. Such explanations for life and concepts of an afterlife led them to perform elaborate funerals and burial practices that included long periods of mourning, usually done by women designated for that duty.

Society

Most tribes were divided into two classes, with each class subdivided into clans. Ancestry in each clan was traced through the women's families. Although adultery was strictly forbidden, polygamy was an accepted practice. There was usually a careful division of labor based on gender, with males and females having specific duties.

Typically, the Indians of Mississippi lived in square, rectangular, or round houses; vertical wooden poles formed walls that were plastered with mixtures of grass, twigs, and clay. In the case of round houses, the walls supported dome-shaped roofs made of sloping limbs thatched with various kinds of vegetation such as small branches, twigs, split cane, and grass. The earthen floors of such structures were covered with mats of straw, grass, or animal hides.

Before they obtained cloth from the Europeans, Indians wore garments made mainly of animal hides, with style and coverage depending on temperature, season, or activity. Typically, men preferred leggings made of deerskin (called buckskin) attached over a belt at the waist, while women wore buckskin dresses, some of which had fringes or painted decorations. Men often wore nothing on their feet, unless weather or travel required otherwise, but women usually wore moccasins of deerskin.

Other characteristics of American Indian society as described by the European observers included the men's preference to wear no facial hair, sometimes plucking even their eyebrows—this at a time when almost all European men had beards or mustaches. Indian men and women often styled their long, straight hair according to their tribe's particular fashion, sometimes adorning their locks with such colorful decorations as beads, tufts of bison hair, or porcupine quills. Finally, the men might mark their faces and skin with paint (red being a favorite color) or with tattoos made with charcoal. Dancing was an important activity and traditionally had a special purpose, such as celebrating the harvest or preparing for the hunt or warfare. The sundry medical practices of the Indians included drinking teas, made from sweet gum and various herbs, and the sweating and bleeding of ill persons.

Warfare   It appeared to the Europeans that the chief occupation of the Indians was warfare, as intertribal conflicts occurred frequently. As a sign of loyalty to their chieftains, the warriors sometimes consumed dog meat. Prior to battle they ate venison to make themselves swifter and avoided consuming bison and fish, which they believed would make them weak and slow. Eating while running apparently demonstrated that good warriors were always alert and on guard.

Government and Law   Each village had its own council of elders that supervised most local matters, including political and religious activities. For broader issues of security, warfare, and relations with other tribes, all of the villages or towns of the tribe formed a confederation or nation governed by one or more great chiefs and a council of elders.

Traditions or customs of the tribes, clans, and individual families constituted the law, which forbade certain actions and prescribed acceptable social behavior. Violators of major crimes, including murder, theft, and adultery, were judged by clan councils and could be punished publicly or privately. Family members of a murder victim, for example, were expected to kill the guilty person or members of his family should the murderer escape punishment. Public whippings, torture, and ostracism might also be imposed on perpetrators of lesser crimes.

Economy   According to custom, all land claimed by a tribe was shared by its members. Although the Indians did not develop the practice of private, individual ownership of land, each tribal member did exercise the privilege of occupying and using certain areas. While most necessities were derived from nature through hunting, gathering, and farming, Mississippi Indians, like all Native Americans by the late seventeenth century, traded regularly with other tribes or

The legend of Chata and Chickasa, which has many variations, provides interesting insight into the Choctaw and Chickasaw beliefs about their origins. Led by the two brothers, the band migrated from some undetermined western area, transporting their ancestors' bones and following a route designated by a sacred pole which was set into the ground each night. On the following sunrise they continued the pilgrimage in the direction that the pole leaned, led by a mysterious white dog that guarded the pole. Upon arriving in the area of the headwaters of the Pearl River in present-day Winston County, Mississippi, they discovered that the sacred pole had settled permanently and perpendicularly and that the white dog had died. At that point in east-central Mississippi, Chata declared that after forty-three years they had found a permanent home. His brother Chickasa, however, continued northward with his followers to become founders of the Chickasaw tribe. There were several explanations for the separation, including a disagreement about the location, a casting of lots, and a flood causing Chickasa's group to become lost. The Choctaws buried their bones and constructed Nanih Waiya ("leaning hill"), which became their religious and political center. Other versions relate that the band found the mound already in existence, a small hill leaning towards the river. Scholars now maintain that the mound dates from the first century BC during the early Woodland Period. Historian Dunbar Rowland's measurements of the mound in 1914 were 150 feet east to west by 60 feet north to south. Photograph of Nanih Waiya courtesy of Amanda B. Williams.

might obtain wanted goods through plunder or warfare. A common feature of intertribal commerce was the exchange of slaves—enemy warriors or civilians captured in raids or battle.

This virtually self-sufficient way of life was disrupted and ultimately destroyed by the Europeans. In addition to the devastation and upheavals European diseases brought, Indian peoples began to desire then gradually became dependent on European tools, weapons, and alcoholic drink. Now these former subsistence hunters, farmers, and warriors began to trade their products, including captive persons, for European articles, but through this increased contact with the newcomers they also acquired and helped spread a new wave of European viruses that included smallpox, measles, and venereal disease—all unknown in the Americas before first contact. These factors combined to help destroy some of the smaller tribes before 1800.

MAJOR TRIBES

The Natchez

Three groups, the Natchez, the Choctaws, and the Chickasaws, composed most of the total Indian population of Mississippi by the late seventeenth century. The Natchez tribe of perhaps 4,500 persons inhabited the southwestern region, south of the present-day town of Natchez in Adams County. In order to protect themselves and organize their society, they lived in string of villages concentrated along St. Catherine's Creek. Their principal population center was Grand Village (or White Apple Village), located about twelve miles from Natchez.

Religion   Although the Natchez, like most other tribes, were polytheistic, the worship of the sun as the supreme god was fundamental to their culture. Another important aspect of their religion was the belief in life after death. To appease the gods the members of the ruling class, which included the priests, would occasionally practice human sacrifice. For example, when an important member of the tribe died, a number of other people were killed so that the deceased would have assistants in the next life. The burial rituals were elaborate and included the building of ceremonial mounds to contain the bones of the dead. Located atop a platform mound and measuring about twenty feet wide by forty feet long, the temple might contain a sacred fire. According to Natchez legends, if the priest charged with maintaining the flame failed to do so, he might face execution.

Society   Socially the Natchez were divided into two groups: the noblemen (Suns) who had all the power, and the common people (Stinkards) who did all the work. Each group was further subdivided into several clans. Women held the highest social positions among the Suns. They were favored as heirs and inherited their families' possessions and status; within their clans each family's ancestry was traced through the female line, or matrilineally. Perhaps to lessen discontent among the lower classes, Natchez custom provided commoners some opportunity for advancement by requiring that one of the wives of each Sun be a member of the Stinkard class.

Government   The tribe was governed by a chief, the "Great Sun," his wife, their families, the council of elders, the priests, and other nobles, all of whom claimed to be descendants of the sun god. Based on this belief of divine right the chief exercised supreme authority, although his power could be checked by that of his wife and her clan through whom he had acquired his position. His decisions could also be influenced by the tribe's elders, who were respected for their wisdom and leadership, especially in matters of warfare. In practice, however, the tribe tended to accept the chief's authority absolutely, for loyalty to the chief and bravery in battle were key considerations for determining the males' status in the tribe. In the Natchez's custom of matriarchal lineage, the Great Sun's successor was usually his nephew—his eldest sister's son, known as the "Little Sun."

THE CHOCTAWS

The Choctaws formed the largest tribe, with as many as 20,000 people inhabiting forty to fifty independent villages scattered throughout the central section of present-day Mississippi. The area around their great mound, Nanih Waiya, appears to have been an important population center and the site of their principal council meetings. Located in present-day southern Winston County on the headwaters of the Pearl River, the mound stands about 20 feet high with a base measuring about 100 feet by 218 feet. According to legend, it had political as well as religious significance.

Society

Like the Natchez, the Choctaws divided themselves into upper and lower classes; there was limited social segregation, however, as members of the different clans intermarried, a practice known as exogamy. Families were closely knit, and parents exercised strict control over their children. Sexual immorality was strictly prohibited. Farming and various social activities were preferred to warfare, resulting in a population much larger than that of the other Mississippi tribes.

Notwithstanding their relatively peaceful lifestyle, for recreation and physical fitness the Choctaws participated in the very popular but violent game of *ishtaboli*. Known as the "Little Brother of War," the game, similar to modern-day lacrosse, was played on a large field with goalposts at each end. Two teams with evidently no limit on the number of players competed to drive a deerskin ball into their respective goals. Each player used two *kapucha*, hickory sticks with strips of raccoon-hide forming cup-like pockets on one end. Although there were strict rules, enforced by the elder males, players could use almost any means to stop an opponent or to score a point, resulting in an extremely physical and brutal contest that often resulted in serious injury.

Government   Although most government was local, conducted by the village elders, the Choctaws recognized at least three great chiefs who had administrative duties for different geographic areas throughout most of central Mississippi. Not only was the Choctaw nation's political power divided, but it was further limited by the presence of village chiefs (*mingos*), their assistants (*tichoumingos*), wartime chiefs known as "Red Chiefs," and numerous clan council members. Unlike the absolutism of the Natchez rulers, the Choctaws tolerated more individual freedom. In their relations with the European colonists, the Choctaw leaders sometimes befriended the French; later they supported the forces of the United States in wars against other Mississippi tribes.

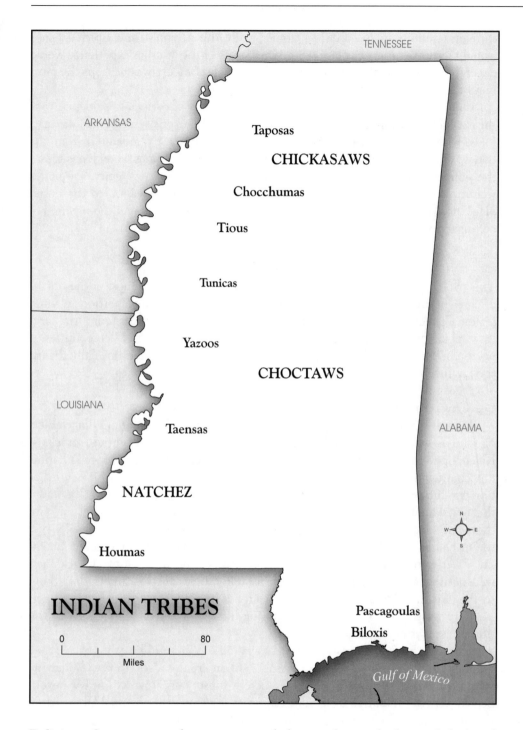

TENNESSEE

ARKANSAS

Taposas

CHICKASAWS

Chocchumas

Tious

Tunicas

Yazoos

CHOCTAWS

LOUISIANA

Taensas

ALABAMA

NATCHEZ

Houmas

INDIAN TRIBES

Pascagoulas

Biloxis

0   80

Miles

Gulf of Mexico

Religion Concepts regarding creation and ultimate fate, and religious beliefs and practices generally, did not appear as elaborate among the Choctaws as they did in Natchez society. The Choctaws did, however, preserve an oral folklore about a supreme deity who created their ancestors from the earth at Nanih Waiya. According to their legend, to that mound every person would return after death. Another story held that after death a person's outer spirit or soul would remain temporarily to oversee affairs in his physical home, while the person's inner spirit (*shilup*) would journey to another place where the nature of the afterlife experience would depend on the person's conduct in his physical life. Bravery was perhaps the most important trait required for admission to the "Happy Land."

One of the Choctaws' elaborate burial customs also reveals evidence that they valued religious concepts. Bodies of deceased persons were placed on scaffolds, where they remained until the flesh could be easily separated from the bones. Then, after the bone pickers' work was done, the bones were deposited in the village bone house. When the bone house was filled to capacity, the bones were placed in coffins and then transferred in a formal procession to the burial place, where they formed a pyramid. Finally, earth was placed over the pyramid of coffins to form a mound.

THE CHICKASAWS

This tribe had a population of about 4,000 persons, controlled most of the northern area of the present-day state, and their villages extended into portions of what is now Tennessee and Alabama. Seventeenth-century Europeans found the largest Chickasaw settlements clustered in the area of Pontotoc and Lee counties in northeast Mississippi. In the colonial era the Chickasaws sometimes allied with the English to fight against French expansion into their territories.

Government and Society

Like the other tribes, the Chickasaws were ruled by a number of village chiefs or mingos who were advised by councils composed of family groups or clans. Rulership was based more on military might than divine right, and successful military commanders often exercised greater authority than did chiefs, whose jurisdiction was limited to internal village affairs. Unlike the Natchez and the Choctaws, the Chickasaws preferred to practice warfare over sustenance agriculture, and they were superior to other tribes in the art of war. Noting their fighting skills, historian Dunbar Rowland described them as "the warlike, unconquerable Chickasaws." After the Europeans were established in North America, the Chickasaws were active in attacking smaller tribes, enslaving their captives, and trading them to the British colonists. A significant factor in their military prowess and high mobility was their breeding of outstanding horses, probably descendants of the horses lost by the De Soto expedition.

The Chickasaws were divided into social classes, but unlike other tribes, they did not permit marriages between members of different classes. In the Chickasaw villages lower-class women were completely subservient to men and were expected to perform all household duties, gardening, and other manual labors while the men held tribal councils, fought battles, blazed trails, and hunted food. Upper-class women, however, enjoyed a higher social standing, partly because through them family lineages and inheritances were determined.

Religion

Like the Choctaws, the Chickasaws' interest in religion was not as pronounced as that of the Natchez. The Chickasaws identified their supreme deity as a spirit in the skies, visible in the sun, lightning, and other natural phenomena, and vital in their military activities. There was some idea that one's earthly behavior would have consequences in an afterlife, and their belief in life after death was reflected in one of their burial practices. Deceased persons were buried in the sitting position facing the rising sun, and males were interred along with their favorite weapons and hunting gear.

MINOR TRIBES

The remaining Indian peoples composed scores of tiny tribal groups. The Biloxis and the Pascagoulas, for example, occupied the coastal region. In the southwest below Natchez, the Houmas lived along the Homochitto River. In the Yazoo River valley resided several small tribes, including the Chocchumas (or Chakchiumas), who occupied lands between the territories of the Chickasaws and Choctaws. Too weak to withstand the attacks of the larger and stronger tribes, the Chocchumas were virtually exterminated in the mid-eighteenth century. Other minor tribes in the area were the Taposas, the Tious, the Yazoos, and the Tunicas. Those smaller tribes not destroyed in warfare or forced to merge with the Chickasaws or the Choctaws moved west across the Mississippi River after the British took Mississippi from the French in 1763. According to the Pascagoula story, after a final battle the few survivors joined hands and marched into the river singing the tribe's death song.

CONCLUSION

The substance of the Native American world was undercut by the European intrusion of the mid-sixteenth century, after which fundamental and wide-ranging changes ensued. In their struggle to survive, the Indian peoples of Mississippi adapted to the changing circumstances by resorting to wars of resistance and developing new trade networks, diplomatic relationships, and military alliances. Ultimately, though, they could not hold on to their traditional lifeways or their lands. Even though almost all of Mississippi's native inhabitants would either be destroyed or forcibly removed from the land by the 1830s, their rich culture would persevere and have a lasting influence on the state's history.

SELECTED SOURCES

Bigelow, Martha M., "Conquistadors, Voyageurs, and Mississippi," in Richard Aubrey McLemore, ed., *A History of Mississippi*, 2 vols. (Hattiesburg: University & College Press of Mississippi, 1973), 1: 90–109.

Bond, Bradley G., *Mississippi: A Documentary History* (Jackson: University Press of Mississippi, 2003).

Carson, James Taylor, *Searching for the Bright Path: The Mississippi Choctaws from Prehistory to Removal* (Lincoln: University of Nebraska Press, 1999).

Galloway, Patricia, *Choctaw Genesis, 1500–1700*, Indians of the Southeast series, Theda Perdue and Michael D. Green, eds. (Lincoln: University of Nebraska Press, 1995).

Hudson, Charles, and Carmen Chaves Tesser, eds., *The Forgotten Centuries: Indians and Europeans in the American South, 1521–1704* (Athens: The University of Georgia Press, 1994).

Marshall, Richard A., "The Prehistory of Mississippi," in Richard Aubrey McLemore, ed., *A History of Mississippi*, 2 vols. (Hattiesburg: University & College Press of Mississippi, 1973), 1: 24–68.

McKee, Jesse O., *The Choctaw*, Indians of North America Series, Frank W. Porter, III, ed. (New York: Chelsea House Publishers, 1989).

———. "The Choctaw: Self Determination and Socioeconomic Development," in *American Indians: A Cultural Geography*, 2nd ed. Thomas E. Ross, Tyrel G. Moore, and Laura R. King, eds. (Southern Pines, N.C.: Karo Hollow Press, 1995), 165–178.

McKee, Jesse O., and Jon A. Schlenker, *The Choctaws, Cultural Evolution of a Native American Tribe* (Jackson: University Press of Mississippi, 1980).

O'Brien, Greg, *Choctaws in a Revolutionary Age, 1750–1830* (Lincoln: University of Nebraska Press, 2002).

Publications of the Mississippi Historical Society. Numerous articles by H. S. Halbert and other writers.

Rowland, Dunbar. "Did De Soto Discover the Mississippi River in Tunica County, Mississippi?" *Publications of the Mississippi Historical Society*, Centenary Series 2: 144–148.

———. *History of Mississippi: The Heart of the South*. 4 vols. (Chicago-Jackson: The S. J. Clarke Publishing Company, 1925), vol. 1 contains colorful accounts of various Indian legends.

———. "A Second Chapter Concerning the Discovery of the Mississippi River by De Soto in Tunica County, Mississippi." *Publications of the Mississippi Historical Society*, Centenary Series 2: 158–164.

Trigger, Bruce G., and Wilcomb E. Washburn, eds., *North America*, Vol. 1, *The Cambridge History of the Native Peoples of the Americas* (Cambridge: Cambridge University Press, 1996).

Wells, Mary Ann, *Native Land: Mississippi, 1540–1798* (Jackson: University Press of Mississippi, 1994).

CHAPTER THREE

French Colonies

Colonial Louisiana

At the end of the seventeenth century, France began to establish the first permanent European settlements in the lower Mississippi River valley. This vast region, called Louisiana by French explorers who claimed it for King Louis XIV, encompassed the present-day states of the south-central United States. Thus the Gulf Coast states of Alabama, Louisiana, and Mississippi share the historical accounts of the early European settlers in colonial Louisiana. And because the Mississippi area was just one district of the huge colony until French control ended there in 1763, the story of Mississippi during this period is actually one about Louisiana as well.

The government of King Louis XIV regarded Louisiana as an expansion of New France, the official name of its Canadian colony. Jacques Cartier had first explored the Gulf of St. Lawrence and claimed the region for France as early as the 1530s. Because he found neither a "northwest passage" to Asia nor gold and silver, the French suspended efforts to establish colonies in Canada—a decision strikingly similar to the one Spain made about the same time following De Soto's fruitless expedition in the lower Mississippi region. But almost a century later, promises of big profits in the fur business revived France's interest in Canada. Trappers and merchants quickly advanced from Quebec southwestward along the St. Lawrence River, seeking to benefit from Europeans' raging demands for beaver-fur hats and other fashionable apparel made of North American animal pelts.

Initial French Exploration

Marquette and Joliet

Prompted by such commercial appetites, which coincided with the French crown's desire to expand New France to other parts of the North American continent and to find the illusive Northwest Passage to Asia, a wealthy Canadian merchant hired explorers to scout for new fur-trapping lands along the "great river" in the west. The first effort to trace the Mississippi's route was undertaken in 1673 by a small party led by Louis Joliet, a Canadian businessman and explorer, and Father (*Pere* in French) Jacques Marquette, a Jesuit missionary. The duo traveled from the Great Lakes region southward along the Mississippi River to its confluence with the Arkansas River. By the time they reached this point they had determined that the Mississippi flowed neither into the Atlantic Ocean nor into the Pacific Ocean but instead into the Gulf of Mexico. They had also become fearful that their small party could not protect itself against potential attacks by Indians

Marquette and his men descending the Mississippi. Library of Congress. Lot 4409-A (R).

and possibly the Spanish farther south. In order to avoid such dangers and preserve for future expeditions the information they had gathered, Marquette and Joliet returned to their Canadian base.

La Salle's First Expedition

Within a few years King Louis XIV commissioned Robert Cavelier, Sieur de la Salle, to explore the western regions of Canada and the Mississippi River for the purposes of enlarging French colonial holdings in North America and discovering a route to Mexico. The king was persuaded to launch this project by his minister of finance, Jean Baptiste Colbert, who desired to check Spanish and British expansion in the region. The plan was to establish French bases along the Mississippi River and on the Gulf of Mexico as the southernmost extensions of New France. La Salle was chosen to lead the colonization effort because he had already exhibited military and administrative abilities in Canada and he was a member of the Jesuit Society, the Roman Catholic order that had participated in most European expeditions to the Americas. In addition, he was able to finance the expedition in return for a guaranteed share of any land and riches he might discover.

From a base in the Great Lakes area, La Salle and his loyal assistant, Henri de Tonty (or Tonti), in February 1682 led their expedition into the Mississippi River, which La Salle named the Colbert River in honor of the French minister of finance. Tonty, nicknamed "Iron Hand," had hired a blacksmith to fashion an iron hook to replace his right hand, which he had lost in a grenade explosion as a young man. The La Salle party included a Franciscan priest, twenty-three Frenchmen, and roughly an equal number of Indians, including women and children. In early March they reached the confluence of the Mississippi and Arkansas rivers, near the present-day town of Rosedale, Mississippi, where they formed a makeshift fort for protection against a potential Indian raid. Continuing southward, they observed various Indian tribes, including the Chickasaws, Choctaws, and Natchez. They visited the Natchez villages and estimated that this tribe had about three thousand warriors and that they were good farmers.

"Louisiana"

La Salle's party reached the mouth of the Mississippi in early April 1682, where they formally claimed for King Louis XIV the entire river valley or "Louisiana," allegedly with the consent of local Indians and "upon the assurance that we have received from all these nations that we are the first Europeans who have descended or ascended the River Colbert. . . ."[1] As if to ward off suspicions about the veracity of these assertions, the priest conducted a worship service and erected a cross symbolizing that the king's most important goal in this land was the spread of Christianity. An official declaration was prepared regarding the importance of the Church, and a column was erected to display the name of the king, the date, and the emblems of French authority.[2]

La Salle's Second Expedition

La Salle returned to Canada and then sailed to France in September 1683, where he reported to the crown his discoveries and arranged a larger expedition to "Louisiana." In July 1684, he sailed with about four hundred men and a fleet of four ships with the objective of entering the Mississippi River from the Gulf, founding a colony, and continuing to explore and claim the region for France. La Salle's ships, however, sailed past the mouth of the Mississippi and eventually landed on the Texas coast. From there the party attempted to find the river by marching overland. This plan proved fruitless, and the expedition became lost as it wandered through southeast Texas. Finally, La Salle was killed mysteriously—some say at the hands of his frustrated, even mutinous men—in March 1687.

Henri de Tonty

In the meantime, another party led by Henri de Tonty was descending the river from the north to meet La Salle. Tonty traveled all the way to the mouth of the river, visited with various Indian tribes along the banks, including the Choctaws, and left a letter for La Salle that, remarkably, would be delivered to Pierre le Moyne, Sieur d'Iberville, the leader of France's next colonizing efforts in the region, nearly fourteen years later. Late in 1687 Tonty met some of the survivors of La Salle's expedition who had probably reached

René Robert Cavalier, Sieur de La Salle, proclaiming the French Empire in America. Library of Congress. LC-USZ62-15933.

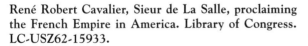

1 Quoted in Dunbar Rowland, *History of Mississippi: The Heart of the South*, 4 vols. (Chicago-Jackson: The S. J. Clarke Publishing Company, 1925), 1: 122–125.
2 In his later writings Franciscan friar Louis Hennepin claimed to have discovered the mouth of the river in 1680, two years before La Salle.

the Mississippi River and then moved northward, recrossing the river from time to time into what is now the Mississippi Delta. They were en route to Canada in order to return home to France. But because they did not report the death of La Salle to Tonty, he again explored along the river in 1690 trying to learn of the expedition's outcome. According to Mississippi historian Dunbar Rowland, Tonty's many explorations along the lower Mississippi made him "an important agent in founding and solidifying the French interests at and near the mouth of the Mississippi."

INTERNATIONAL RIVALRIES

The efforts to plant French colonies along the lower Mississippi were deferred by the European War of the League of Augsburg in the 1690s. Known as King William's War in North America, this conflict was fought primarily in Canada between forces of France and Great Britain, with Spain in alliance with the British. Following the Treaty of Ryswick, which ended the conflict in 1697, the colonial rivalries between France, Spain, and England for North America intensified.

Although their claims in Canada and the Mississippi River valley as far south as the Gulf of Mexico were tacitly recognized in the treaty, the French government continued to worry about the appearances of Spanish and British colonial expansion. In 1698 Spain, which at this time was still considered the dominant power in the Americas, built a fort at Pensacola Bay, anticipating that the French might expand their colonial claims from the Mississippi eastward along the Gulf Coast. In the spring of the following year English physician Daniel Coxe, whose family had received a royal land grant in the lower Mississippi valley, sailed into the mouth of the Mississippi and traveled upstream about one hundred miles. There he encountered a French boat commanded by Jean Baptiste le Moyne, Sieur de Bienville. After being summarily informed by Bienville that France had already taken possession of the Mississippi River area, Coxe withdrew.

IBERVILLE'S LEADERSHIP

The Le Moyne Brothers

The most recent basis for Bienville's contention was the founding of France's first colony in the Mississippi area by Bienville's older brother, Pierre le Moyne, Sieur d'Iberville, early in 1699. The Le Moyne brothers were natives of Montreal, Canada, and at the time of their expedition Iberville was already an experienced soldier in his mid-thirties, while Bienville was only about twenty years of age. With his experience in the colonial wars and the backing of his aristocratic family in Canada, Iberville succeeded in securing a commission from the crown to establish a colony in "Louisiana."

The project was part of a plan recommended to King Louis XIV by the Minister of Colonial Affairs, the Comte de Pontchartrain, who wished to confirm the work of La Salle and Tonty. It proposed the establishment of a line of bases along the Mississippi River and on the present-day Gulf Coast, which would form a connection between France's North American colonies in Canada and Santo Domingo and other islands in the Caribbean. Such a crescent-shaped string of settlements would, it was hoped, strengthen France's territorial claims and obstruct the northward and westward expansion of Spanish and British colonies.

Biloxi: The First Colony

In late October 1698 Iberville's small fleet of two frigates and two smaller ships sailed from Brest, France, with a company of marines and about two hundred settlers. Several women and children (probably the families of Canadian soldiers), various artisans, and clergymen, including Father Anastase Douay who had traveled with La Salle's first expedition, were among these original colonists. After a long and difficult sea passage the party arrived in the Gulf of Mexico in January 1699. The fleet was unable to land along the Florida Gulf coast because of the presence of the unfriendly Spanish bases at Apalachicola and Pensacola. So, after sailing along the coast westward past Mobile Bay, the party eventually entered the harbor north of Ship Island. Finally, on February 13, after a journey of more than three months, they went ashore at present-day Ocean Springs, or *Vieux Biloxy* (Old Biloxi).

The Mississippi River Rediscovered

Because the Biloxi Indians appeared friendly and helpful and the harbor provided protection for his ships, Iberville decided to use this area as the base from which he would search for the Colbert River and select a location for the settlement. He sent one group eastward, while he moved westward with a company that included Bienville, Father Douay, and Jean de Sauvole de la Villantry, an army officer. On March 2, 1699, Iberville and his men found the mouth of a great river they believed was the Colbert, the river the Indians called "Mississippi." The next day Father Douay performed mass in which he thanked God for the rediscovery.

With help from the Bayougoula Indians, Iberville's group explored northward along the river and found evidence that they had in fact located the river that La Salle had named Colbert and claimed for France. After passing the *Baton Rouge* (Red Stick) that marked the boundary between the territories of the Bayougoula and Houma tribes, they found Indians who possessed French-made clothing, axes, and knives—the gifts left by Tonty. In return for an axe, they acquired from the Mongoulacha tribe the letter that Tonty had written and left for the missing La Salle in the mid-1680s. The Indians also possessed a prayer book that had belonged to one of La Salle's men.

Fort Maurepas

After failing to find a satisfactory location for the first permanent settlement on the river, Iberville returned to the Biloxi area, where he ordered the construction of Fort Maurepas. Following the construction of the fort in the spring of 1699, Iberville returned to France for more colonists and supplies. He left the colony under the command of Sauvole and instructed Bienville to continue exploring the country.

Bienville's Discoveries

Eastward from Biloxi, Bienville explored the Pascagoula River and Mobile Bay areas. To the west he found and named the Bay of St. Louis, revisited Lake Pontchartrain, which had been discovered earlier during Iberville's exploration, and reached the Colbert River near the future location of New Orleans. From there Bienville traveled downriver, and in September 1699 he encountered

Jean Baptiste Le Moyne, Sieur de Bienville. Courtesy Louisiana State Museum.

Daniel Coxe's ship. Although the accounts of this confrontation differ, the outcome was as mentioned: after each party declared its rights in the region, the British ship withdrew. On their return eastward Bienville's party found pearls in shells—which Indians used as tools to carve out their canoes—in a river that the French named the "River of Pearls" or the Pearl River.

Except for those few pearls, Bienville's exploration during the late summer and fall of 1699 failed to produce any evidence of wealth for the colony. Moreover, Commander Sauvole experienced very difficult times as the small settlement at Biloxi struggled to survive the spread of diseases and shortages of food and essential supplies. The colony's existence now hinged on the reinforcements and provisions that were finally supplied by the return from France of Iberville in early January 1700.

Bienville Succeeds Iberville

Soon after his return, Iberville resumed his travels in the Colbert River, primarily to plan the building of a new fort to thwart British encroachments. His efforts were aided by the arrival of Tonty and a company of Canadians, which manifested the connection between France's colonial holdings from Quebec to the Gulf of Mexico. After this expedition, Iberville again returned to France in late May 1700. When Sauvole died of yellow fever in late August 1701, Bienville returned from his fort-building duties on the Colbert and took command. Iberville returned from France in March 1702, but he was ill; thus Bienville actually retained practical control of the colony.

Fort Louis at Mobile

Before Iberville's final departure from Louisiana in late April 1702, he ordered the construction of a fort on the Mobile River and removal of the colony there to be nearer the Spanish base at Pensacola. This decision was caused by the imminent outbreak of another European war, the War of Spanish Succession, in which France and Spain allied against Great Britain. While Iberville conducted diplomatic relations with the Spanish governor and the local Indian chiefs, Bienville handled the practical operations of building Fort Louis and moving the colonists from Biloxi in the spring of 1702.

THE BIENVILLE ERA, 1702–1743

The Death of Iberville

On his departure that spring Iberville considered the colonial project a failure because no mineral wealth had been found, even though there had been great expenditures in the building of forts along the coast and on the Colbert River. Despite his poor health, he attempted to return to the colony in 1706 but died aboard ship off the coast of Cuba. His "Louisiana" colony—now based at Mobile—was already under the control of his brother Bienville, who would continue as the true leader of French Louisiana for the next forty years.

The War of Spanish Succession

In the first decade of his command, 1702 to 1712, Bienville encountered serious troubles, including intracolonial controversies, conflicts between colonists and local Indians, and problems arising from the war with Great Britain. France's involvement in the War of Spanish Succession (known to the British in North America as Queen Anne's War) was primarily in Europe and Canada, so the Louisiana colony escaped direct military action. The British navy, however, patrolled along the Gulf Coast, launching attacks against France's ally, Spain, at Pensacola, and occupying Dauphin Island in Mobile Bay, which was undefended by the French. Toward the end of the war, the French government determined that the Louisiana colony was a liability and new leadership and investments were needed there.

The Crozat Failure

Late in 1712, King Louis XIV granted to a wealthy French merchant named Anthony Crozat a charter with a commercial monopoly in Louisiana for fifteen years. Crozat never visited the colony but sent Antoine Laumet de la Mothe Cadillac to serve as the first governor of Louisiana. Already known as the founder of the colony of Detroit a decade earlier, Cadillac arrived at Mobile in 1713 after the Treaty of Utrecht had ended the War of the Spanish Succession. By the terms of that treaty France had lost no territory in the Louisiana colony but had ceded to Great Britain vast regions of Canada, including Acadia, from which the French Acadians (known later as "Cajuns") would later migrate to Louisiana.

In this period the French were beginning to use the informal name "Mississippi" for the Louisiana colony, probably because of the popular usage of the Indian phrase as the name for the river. Bienville served as lieutenant governor, but he had continuing conflicts with Governor Cadillac, whose administration ended late in 1716. About one year later, after failing to realize any return on his investments for five years, Crozat returned Louisiana to the French government.

Fort Rosalie and Disputes with the Natchez Indians

During the Crozat period, Lieutenant Governor Bienville completed the construction of Fort Rosalie at present-day Natchez and started a French settlement there by 1716. Located on the site that Iberville had chosen during his second trip upriver, the fort was named in honor of the wife of the Comte de Pontchartrain. Bienville gained experience in dealing with the Natchez Indians during a dispute involving their alleged killing of four or five French Canadians, an episode that almost wrecked the project. The trouble occurred after the French soldiers arrested an Englishman who was accused of trading with the Natchez Indians. Given the continuing international competition for territory in the Mississippi Valley, French authorities prohibited dealings between the Indians and interlopers from other European colonies. They feared, for example, that a British trader might sell Indians weapons in exchange for deerskins and entice them to turn against the French settlers. As the prisoner was being taken to Mobile he somehow escaped and was killed. The Natchez Indians blamed the French for murdering their English friend and took revenge by killing the Canadian traders.

Now Governor Cadillac determined that the Natchez had to be punished, but he declined to take action himself. He had already treated this tribe with contempt earlier when he had traveled upriver seeking silver mines and refused to visit the Natchez and smoke the calumet (peace pipe) with them. Possibly reflecting his personal dislike of Bienville—caused by Bienville's rejection of the proposal to marry Cadillac's daughter as well as his jealousy of Bienville's popularity among the colonists—the governor decided to send Bienville into the Natchez country with a small force of forty-five soldiers.

The lieutenant governor, however, deceived the Natchez by making them believe he had a larger force. Through crafty negotiations with several chiefs whom he held as hostages, Bienville managed to persuade the Natchez to surrender for execution the persons guilty of killing the Canadians. He also required the Natchez to provide materials and labor to build Fort Rosalie. Soon after this triumph, Bienville became involved in a series of major transitions in the colony's administration.

The Mississippi Company

Following the commercial failure of Crozat in 1717, a joint-stock company enterprise organized by John Law, a Scottish adventurer, acquired a charter to operate the Louisiana colony for twenty-five years. Law's Mississippi Company had greater authority and more extensive financial goals than had Crozat's enterprise. Although the colony's estimated population was only about seven hundred persons, the company promised to its shareholders great profits in the fur trade, gold and silver discoveries, and slave trading. During its five-year existence the company brought about three thousand African slaves into the colony.

Except for a brief interlude early in 1717, the Mississippi Company employed Bienville as governor (or commandant) of the Louisiana colony. Company leaders preferred to concentrate their efforts in the Natchez area, partly because of its location and the demand there for slaves to clear land for agriculture. Bienville, however, decided in 1718 to begin the construction of the future capital at the site of New Orleans. But before this plan could be completed, major changes occurred in the colony's organization.

Following a brief war between France and Spain in 1719, which resulted in France's annexation of Spanish Pensacola for two years, the colony's council agreed with Bienville to move temporarily the colonial capital from Mobile back to the Biloxi area. It was located at the site of present-day Biloxi rather than the original site at Old Biloxi (Ocean Springs). Then, in 1721, news arrived from Paris that John Law's "Mississippi Bubble" had burst: the Company's inflated stock had collapsed and its charter had been transferred to the parent company, the Company of the Indies.

New Orleans

These transactions in France ruined many investors there but had little practical effect within the colony, which experienced population and economic

Indians of several nations, New Orleans, 1735, as pictured by Alexandre deBatz. The Louisiana Collection, State Library of Louisiana, Baton Rouge, Louisiana.

growth. After Governor Bienville moved the capital of Louisiana to New Orleans in 1722, the French government established nine districts for the administration of civil and military affairs in the colony. Three of the most important districts were located in Mississippi: Biloxi, Natchez, and Yazoo.

A Second Episode with the Natchez

One of the most difficult tasks Bienville faced was resolving problems with the Natchez Indians. He had been successful in 1716, but as the French population increased around Fort Rosalie and along St. Catherine's Creek, further conflict was inevitable. In 1723 when the soldiers stationed at the fort tried to punish the Natchez for killing three French settlers, things got out of hand. Bienville brought in seven hundred troops and threatened to slaughter the Natchez and burn their villages. An enraged Bienville even demanded the head of the chief before he would order the army to withdraw. The gross mishandling of this situation, which would have dire consequences later, along with a series of natural disasters that year, contributed to Bienville's suspension as governor by the French government from 1726 to 1734.

Governor La Périer and the Natchez Massacres

The administration of Bienville's successor, Boucher de la Périer, a distinguished naval officer, began favorably as the population expanded and agricultural production increased. This economic prosperity, however, was soon jeopardized by the new governor's failure to deal satisfactorily with the Natchez Indians. The result was the most terrible disaster of the French colonial period in Mississippi.

When the Sieur de Chepart, commander of the forces at Fort Rosalie, ordered the Natchez to move from White Apple Village, the center of their traditional homeland, so that French settlers could take the land, the Indians rebelled. On November 28, 1729, Natchez warriors with Chickasaw aid massacred about 145 men, 36 women, and 56 children residing in Fort Rosalie and the nearby settlements. In addition, they took a number of captives, so that the total number of colonists lost in the attack was about three hundred out of the total French and African population of about seven hundred persons.

Governor Périer carefully planned to punish the Natchez. In January 1730 the French force was joined by warriors from the Choctaws and other Indian allies. After a siege of the fort, which was still held by the Natchez with their prisoners, there followed a period of negotiations. In February, just before the release of the prisoners, the Natchez slipped away during the night, and many of them crossed to the west bank of the Mississippi. There they constructed a fort to defend themselves against the expected French attack. Acquiring heavy artillery and reinforcements, Périer's forces pursued the Natchez, finally crushing them in January of 1732. Virtually the entire Natchez tribe was exterminated. Most of the tribemembers were killed or captured and taken to New Orleans, where they were shipped away to Santo Domingo as slaves. A small number escaped to the Chickasaws for protection.

The End of Company Control

The conflicts with the Natchez and other problems during the administration of Governor Périer greatly increased the costs of maintaining the colony, which forced the struggling Company of the Indies to surrender its charter. In the spring of 1732 the government of King Louis XV took control of the colony and made major changes in its administrative structure. Now the French colony of Louisiana became a vastly larger province that stretched all the way up to and included the Illinois settlements, but it was now freed from the control of Canada.

Simultaneously, ominous conflicts began with the British. In the 1730s King George II of Great Britain reorganized the Carolina colony and established the new proprietary colony of Georgia. The charter of this new British colony declared that its western border extended all the way to the Mississippi River. After 1732, therefore, a large region of Louisiana, including the Mississippi area, was claimed by Great Britain.

The Chickasaw Wars

When Bienville was restored to the office of colonial governor by 1734, he faced the problem of dealing with the British efforts to advance their claims against France in the Mississippi area. Led by General James Oglethorpe of Georgia, the British began making alliances with various Indian tribes in the area, including the Chickasaws, who had provided aid and refuge for the Natchez during the wars with France. Using the Chickasaws' refusal to comply with Bienville's demand that they release the Natchez refugees, the governor declared war and invaded northern Mississippi.

Bienville organized two armies for the invasion: one army composed primarily of Frenchmen and Illinois Indians (led by Chief Chicago) attacked from the north through the Memphis area, while Bienville's force, composed of French troops and Choctaw warriors, arrived from the south by way of the Tombigbee River. With aid and encouragement from British colonists from Georgia, the Chickasaws were successful in dividing the two French armies and defeating both of them. The battle of Ackia or Tupelo in 1736 was such a humiliating defeat for Bienville that the French feared the northern portions of Mississippi and Alabama would be lost to the British and their Chickasaw allies.

In an attempt to regain control in the Chickasaw country, Bienville organized another campaign in the spring of 1739. Now the northern and southern forces of the French armies came together for an assault at Chickasaw Bluffs, on the east side of the Mississippi River near the site of present-day Memphis. This contingent included French troops from Louisiana and Canada, various Indian allies, and African slaves. Through the summer months Bienville constructed Fort Assumption on the Wolf River at Memphis as his base of operations. At this point the Chickasaws offered to negotiate a truce on the mistaken belief that the invaders greatly outnumbered their own warriors. But the treaty of March 1740 was not much of a victory for the French. The Chickasaws retained control over their own land, although they did promise not to interfere with French movements along the Mississippi.

FINAL YEARS OF FRENCH RULE IN MISSISSIPPI

Governor Vaudreuil, 1743–1753

After this campaign, which had failed to suppress the Chickasaws, Bienville retired, and in May 1743 he left the colony and spent the rest of his life in Paris, where he died in 1767. His successor was Philippe de Rigaud, Marquis de Vaudreuil, who took office in 1743 and served as governor for a decade. Like his predecessors, the new governor found himself immediately burdened with the daunting tasks of subduing the "unconquerable" Chickasaws and defending his colony against the British, who were now engaged in yet another international conflict with France—the War of Austrian Succession (known to the British in North America as King George's War). To worsen matters for the colonists, by this time the Chickasaws had developed the strategy of dividing the Choctaw nation and attracting many of them into an alliance with the British. Nevertheless, by 1750 Vaudreuil's forces, assisted by the pro-French Choctaws, were able finally to crush the pro-British Choctaw faction after killing their leader, Chief "Red Shoes," whose headquarters lay in the area of present-day Jasper County.

To punish the Chickasaws for their role in trying to divide the loyalties of the Choctaw nation and to overcome their successes against Bienville's armies in the campaigns of the 1730s, Vaudreuil launched another campaign in 1752. His invasion route, like Bienville's in 1736, was the Tombigbee River from Mobile to Cotton Gin Port. Although the French army destroyed villages and crops, the attack failed to conquer the Chickasaw nation.

Governor Kerlerec and The French and Indian War, 1753–1763

Vaudreuil's failure to conquer decisively the Chickasaws led to his dismissal as colonial governor. He was succeeded in 1753 by Louis Billouart de Kerlerec, the colony's last governor. The most important event of Kerlerec's administration was the French and Indian War, known as the Seven Years' War in Europe. In the North American theaters of this worldwide conflict the British ultimately defeated France and its Spanish ally. Because most of the French troops in the Louisiana colony were required to serve in other areas during the war, Governor

Kerlerec had to depend primarily on Indian allies for defense of the colony. In this endeavor he organized extensive, formidable alliances, which included the Choctaws and other tribes in present-day southeastern states. But before he could test his new forces against the British, the war ended.

The End of the French Period

The Treaty of Paris of 1763 ended the French and Indian War; it also ended the French period in Mississippi history. The terms of the accord required France to surrender its long-held colony of Louisiana in the lower Mississippi Valley. The territory west of the river and the city of New Orleans were ceded to Spain pursuant to a secret agreement of 1762, and the territory east of the river, which included the future state of Mississippi, was ceded to Great Britain. Spain also lost its Florida colony to the British.

FRENCH COLONIAL LIFE

Church and State

During the sixty-four years that France controlled the Mississippi area, government was virtually a military dictatorship, and there was no separation of church and state. The Roman Catholic Church was the religion established by the government, and the practice of all other religions was strictly forbidden. The governor exercised absolute military and civil authority and was assisted by a superior council that had legislative, administrative, and judicial authority. The first code of law, which was established by Bienville in 1724, was designed to maintain rigid control over the lives of the colonists. This code included laws that have been described as Mississippi's first slave or "black code" because they included many regulations for slave owners and slaves.

Slavery

The Mississippi Company had begun selling African slaves into the colony in 1719. Bienville's Black Code prohibited slaves from possessing any type of weapon or forming any kind of gathering or assembly. Owners' treatment of their slaves was carefully prescribed, including their responsibilities to provide Christian instruction and physical care for their human property. They also were expected to control and discipline their slaves by inflicting physical punishments, though certain unusually brutal practices were prohibited. The Code forbade owners from selling separately husbands, wives, and children under fourteen years of age in slave families. It allowed owners to free some or all of their slaves, who would then have the same rights and privileges as other French colonists.

But as the African population of the colony grew, rising to almost 3,400 in 1731 and to about 6,000 by the end of the French period in 1763, the administration established increasingly restrictive guidelines. For example, to keep slaves in subjection and at the same time exert more control over Indians, colonists sometimes paid bounties to Indians for returning runaway slaves.

The Population

With wide demographic variations, colonial Louisiana was inhabited by three diverse groups of people, the French colonials, African slaves, and the American

Indians. The struggle to survive in this frontier outpost of the French empire, not to mention achieve a profitable economy, produced fluid relationships ranging from mutual reliance to racial tensions and conflicts. A major, persisting problem for the colony in its early years was how to attract European settlers. Although the administration did not offer political or religious freedom, it did promise generous land grants to immigrants, and propaganda in France promised prospective colonists riches in silver and gold, tobacco production, and other natural resources.

Such enticements were ineffective until the 1720s, however, due to subsistence uncertainties, tenuous markets, and fragile alliances with mobile and sometimes restive Indian tribes, who resorted to raids and to warfare in defense of their lifeways and cultures. Determined to populate the colony in spite of all such obstacles, the French government resorted to the forced exportation to Louisiana of convicts, vagrants, orphans, and even insane persons. Another program provided free passage and land to persons who would agree to work as indentured servants for a number of years after arrival in the colony. Still, population growth was slow, and by the late 1720s some 2,500 indentured servants and 2,000 slaves composed the majority of the colony's approximately 6,000 inhabitants. New Orleans was the fastest growing area, with a total of about 1,600 persons as early as the mid-1720s. In succeeding decades, as the pace of European immigration increased, the population ratios between whites, blacks, and Indians changed. The French colonists' rising numbers along with their stricter legal and sometimes extralegal controls over the two latter groups laid foundations for a future plantation system.

Agriculture and Trade

Having found no silver, gold, or other precious materials, the settlers turned to farming and trading in animal furs and skins. Attempting to produce commodities that could be shipped to France in return for wanted manufactured goods, colonists experimented with several crops, including silk, rice, indigo, lumber, and tobacco. While none of these enterprises achieved the expected level of success, the deerskin trade became a viable business. Overall, however, the colony's economy proved unstable, especially after the collapse of the Mississippi Company, when the paper currency lost its value and prices became greatly inflated. Because of these money problems, colonists continued to trade in Spanish dollars even after their use was outlawed.

Conclusion

The French colonial effort in Mississippi was, ultimately, a failure. The reasons include the inability to establish a reliable and prosperous economy, governmental instability, and less than peaceful relations with certain Indian tribes. All of these colonial problems reflected France's internal problems during the eighteenth century and, consequently, its failure to compete successfully with the British for the North American colonies. Notwithstanding its material failure, however, the French period provided a significant cultural legacy for the future state of Mississippi.

Selected Sources

Bond, Bradley G., *Mississippi: A Documentary History* (Jackson: University Press of Mississippi, 2003).

Carson, James Taylor, *Searching for the Bright Path: The Mississippi Choctaws from Prehistory to Removal* (Lincoln: University of Nebraska Press, 1999).

Elliott, Jack D., Jr., "The Fort of Natchez and the Colonial Origins of Mississippi," *Journal of Mississippi History* 52 (August 1990): 159–197.

Galloway, Patricia, *Choctaw Genesis, 1500–1700*, in Indians of the Southeast Series, Theda Perdue and Michael D. Green, eds. (Lincoln: University of Nebraska Press, 1995).

Howell, Walter G. "The French Period, 1699–1763," in Richard Aubrey McLemore, ed., *A History of Mississippi*, 2 vols. (Hattiesburg: University & College Press of Mississippi, 1973), 1: 110–133.

O'Brien, Greg, *Choctaws in a Revolutionary Age, 1750–1830* (Lincoln: University of Nebraska Press, 2002).

Rowland, Dunbar, *History of Mississippi: The Heart of the South*, 4 vols. (Chicago-Jackson: The S. J. Clarke Publishing Company, 1925), vol. 1.

Usner, Daniel H., Jr., *Indians, Settlers, and Slaves in a Frontier Exchange Economy: The Lower Mississippi Valley Before 1783* (Chapel Hill: The University of North Carolina Press, 1992).

Wells, Mary Ann, *Native Land: Mississippi, 1540–1798* (Jackson: University Press of Mississippi, 1994).

CHAPTER FOUR

The British Period, 1763–1781

BRITISH WEST FLORIDA

Following its victories in the French and Indian War, the government of Britain's King George III organized the territory acquired from France and Spain on the Gulf of Mexico into two new colonies. The area east of the Apalachicola River was named "East Florida," while the region from the Apalachicola to the Mississippi became "West Florida." In 1763 the initial northern borders for the new colonies were the Georgia boundary and 31° north latitude for East and West Florida respectively. Within a year, however, the British government extended the northern border of West Florida to 32° 28' north latitude (the confluence of the Yazoo and Mississippi rivers at present-day Vicksburg) in order to include Natchez and other interior settlements. The Chattahoochee and Apalachicola rivers formed the eastern border. (See map: Mississippi Territory, 1798–1817, p. 56.)

THE BRITISH GOVERNORS

Governor George Johnstone, 1764–1767

Until the arrival of the first royal governor, the British military oversaw the colony and supervised the transfer of authority from France in the west and Spain in the east. By early September 1763, a month after a British army battalion arrived at Pensacola, the capital of West Florida, the Spanish had departed. Later that fall British troops occupied Mobile but experienced more difficulties there with the transfer of control from France.

After about a year of military rule, the first British governor arrived in Pensacola to assume office. The young naval officer, George Johnstone, was evidently illsuited for the task of taking control of the new, expansive colony, and his tenure was brief. Nevertheless, he began the work of organizing the colony's first civil government by appointing a council to assist him and the first judicial officials, including a number of justices of the peace and judges for a court of pleas, a supreme court, and a vice-admiralty court. Because there was no representative assembly, the governor and his council made the first laws for the colony.

Known for his rather aggressive and stubborn personality, Johnstone, a native of Scotland, had problems from the beginning in his relations with the military commanders, particularly Captain Robert MacKinen in Pensacola and Major John Farmar in Mobile. Unlike the French colonial system, civil and military jurisdictions in the British colonies were separated. The situation became so serious that the London government had to intervene early in 1765, declaring that the

View of the Fort of the Natchez.

Fort Panmure at Natchez. Courtesy Courtesy Mississippi Department of Archives and History.

governor should administer civil affairs only, while the garrison commanders had exclusive jurisdiction in military matters. The latter sphere was considerable, given the unsettled conditions and the need to provide protection for the newly acquired colony.

It was important that the civil and military officials resolve their differences, because the British Board of Trade had directed that they take the lead among all the colonies in implementing the Proclamation Line of 1763 regarding relations with Indian tribes. Subsequent to this directive, the British held two congresses with the Indians in 1765 to develop friendly relations, make trade agreements, determine boundaries, and acquire additional land for the colony.

From the beginning of the colonial era, the Europeans' belief that their race was naturally superior to nonwhite peoples shaped their relations with the American Indians. But their attempts to make slaves of the Indians failed, for the Indians did not accept an inferior status and refused to comply with European demands for servile labor. Relations between the two peoples, complicated by internal rivalries within each group, were usually based on mutual distrust. Their associations ranged widely from ones of guarded friendliness to suspicious dealings and outright hostility.

Although there were occasional instances of genuine friendship (and intermarriage), the two societies remained socially segregated and interacted only when circumstances seemed to make contacts mutually beneficial. The Indians of Mississippi possessed certain commodities that the Europeans desired, including

land, tribal warriors who could be valuable military allies, and deerskins and bea-
ver pelts that brought handsome prices in European markets. The Europeans, on
the other hand, had products that the Indians wanted, including firearms and ammunition, cloth for blankets and clothing, iron utensils for cooking, and alcoholic
drink.

So the European and Indian peoples maintained an uneasy coexistence, trading goods, land, and military arrangements. But when one side broke deals in fact
or in perception, the other side might retaliate, setting off a chain reaction of re-
crimination and violence. Accusations of trickery or abuse by white traders or
trappers, for example, might cause Indians to raid European settlements, while reports of thievery by Indians in one place might provoke settlers to attack Indian
villages in another. Even if the leaders on both sides preferred to maintain peaceable relations, they were often drawn into local outbreaks of violence, each one
blaming the other for having started the trouble.

Some of the British goals were achieved at the Mobile Congress in late March
1765, in which Governor Johnstone and other leaders negotiated a treaty with
representatives from the Chickasaw and the Choctaw tribes. The accord contained the Indians' first cession of land: areas in the lower Tombigbee River, the
Mobile area, and the coastal zone south of 31° north latitude from Mobile to the
Mississippi River. It also included agreements on punishments for certain crimes,
trade regulations, and specific prices that traders were allowed to charge Indians
for particular items. Some prices were fixed in pounds of deerskin: for example,
one gun cost sixteen pounds of deerskin; forty bullets cost one pound; a knife, one
pound; and twenty strands of beads, one pound. The selling of intoxicating beverages to Indians was prohibited. No such positive results, however, were produced
in the second congress, which met at Pensacola with the Creek Indians.

Because of the British tradition that allowed colonists some share in their
own government, many West Florida residents complained about the royal
governor's arbitrary rule. They petitioned the Board of Trade and the governor's
council demanding the formation of a representative assembly, which would be
composed of white men (subjects of King George III) who owned large tracks of
land. Although the first assembly was elected in November 1766, Governor
Johnstone remained unpopular and was finally dismissed early in 1767. Besides
his imperious behavior in general and his quarrels with the military, he had failed
to maintain peaceful relations with the Creeks, against whom he unwisely attempted to initiate a war.

Lieutenant Governor Browne, 1767–1769

Following Johnstone's removal, Lieutenant Governor Montfort Browne conducted the duties of governor for about two years. The two most important accomplishments of his brief administration were improved relations with the Indian tribes and increased attention to the western section of the colony. Browne
was the first West Florida leader to support enthusiastically the development of
the Natchez area. In the year following the Treaty of Paris, British troops had occupied and repaired Fort Rosalie, which was renamed Fort Panmure. In 1766
Browne had traveled to the Natchez area and had reported very favorably on the
potential of the region. Based on his personal observations, he recommended that

British governor Elias Durnford and his wife. Courtesy Mississippi Department of Archives and History.

a town be planned on the site, and he persuaded the British government to maintain a military regiment there. Ten years later the town of Natchez was officially organized, and in 1777 the surrounding region—extending from the present-day Vicksburg area southward to 31° north latitude—became an administrative subdistrict of the West Florida colony.

Browne's tenure ended in 1769 when John Eliot arrived to take control as the new governor. In April, however, during his council's proceedings against Browne, who had been charged with embezzlement, Governor Eliot committed suicide. Later that year Browne was removed from his position as lieutenant governor, and Elias Durnford was appointed governor.

Governor Elias Durnford, 1769–1770

Having already served as surveyor general and member of the governor's council in West Florida, Durnford was a well-known and popular man. During his one-year term as governor, he presided over the continuing trials of former lieutenant governor Browne, but Durnford's chief concern was the mounting discord with Indians. In an attempt to address the situation, the assembly passed a law in 1770 to regulate trade relations between the colonists and the Indians. In agreement with Browne's earlier reports, Governor Durnford also recommended the development of western settlements in the colony. When Peter Chester became the new governor in August 1770, Durnford served as a member of his council.

Governor Peter Chester, 1770–1781

With more than twenty years of experience as a British army officer, Chester was the most successful governor of West Florida, although his long tenure would culminate in Great Britain's loss of West Florida to Spain in 1781. On taking office he was instructed that the most important matters were Indian affairs, improvement of the assembly's performance, and development of the Mississippi region.

To address the Indian difficulties, which arose primarily from abuses by colonial traders, Governor Chester appointed commissioners to handle disputes with the traders, who were required to obtain licenses and obey the colonial trade regulations. He also called for congresses in 1771 and 1772 in which grievances were discussed. As a result of these actions, Indian relations improved during Chester's administration.

In response to problems related to the assembly, the governor decided virtually to eliminate its activity. He called only two sessions during his tenure and, in order to maintain control, he refused to specify the duration of the assembly members' terms. There were only two sessions, as mentioned, in 1771 and in 1778, but neither conducted any business before the governor adjourned it. In 1778, for the first time, the Natchez District had representation in the brief assembly. The other election districts included Manchac, Mobile, and Pensacola. The West Florida colonial government, therefore, did include a representative assembly, but it was totally subordinate to the royal governor and did not have the power exercised by assemblies in the older British colonies.

Regarding the development of the western regions of the colony, Governor Chester was optimistic about the potential cultivation of various crops, including rice, indigo, hemp, and corn. He observed the favorable climate, the fertile soil, the timber resources, and the easy access by river navigation. He developed plans for westward expansion, including settlements in the Natchez area, which he figured would stimulate immigration and trade. To accomplish his goals, Chester sent a request to the British Colonial Office in London for additional military regiments to provide assistance for settlers, defend them against potential Indian raids, and generally maintain law and order.

The governor's efforts resulted in the beginning of major permanent settlements with increasing numbers of immigrants from the older colonies of Georgia, South Carolina, and Virginia. Inducements for migration to the Natchez District included generous land grants, assistance for transportation, and even temporary supplies. During Governor Chester's first four years in office, the population of the Mississippi region rose to roughly three thousand settlers. British West Floridia's other population centers were Pensacola, Mobile, and Manchac. One estimate of the colony's total population in 1774, excluding Indians, was nearly five thousand inhabitants including about 1,200 slaves.

SOCIAL AND ECONOMIC LIFE

In the brief, two-decade British period farming and trade continued as the bases of economic life. The slave population remained relatively static because farmers grew no major cash crops. In this period before the invention of the gin, which greatly facilitated the separation of the lent from the seed, the production of cotton was impractical. Instead, most farmers cultivated indigo, tobacco, and other crops, but they found that livestock and lumber were more profitable products. With the growing number of land grants attracting settlers to the region, mercan-

River scene showing a keelboat. Courtesy Mississippi Department of Archives and History.

tile and shipping businesses developed along the Mississippi River and its tributaries. In general, however, the Mississippi section of British West Florida still remained a primitive frontier region.

In this setting the pioneers expressed seemingly little interest in organized religion or education. The Church of England was the established church and most residents were nominally Anglican. But unlike the French, the British administration granted religious toleration to other Christian religions—even to the French Catholics who remained in the colony. Because of the sparse population, there were very few churches and only two Anglican clergymen, one in Mobile and the other in Pensacola. Existing church buildings were inadequate, and no evidence exists of any churches having been constructed during the British period. The first clergymen in the Mississippi area of the colony arrived during the 1770s. Samuel Swayze, a Congregationalist (later Presbyterian) missionary who traveled from New Jersey to the Natchez area, formed the first Protestant church in present-day Mississippi.

There were virtually no formal educational opportunities in the colony. No school building had been constructed as late as 1772. Private tutoring, church schools, and informal home schooling provided the only educational activities that transpired. The colonial government made no provision for families who were unable to pay for their children's education.

THE AMERICAN REVOLUTION

West Florida was one of several British colonies in North America that did not contemplate joining the thirteen "United States" declaring independence in 1776. Many inhabitants of the colony were British soldiers or sailors or veterans who had received land grants from the king. Then, during the American Revolution, many "Tories" (persons declaring loyalty to the British crown or otherwise refusing to join the rebellion) from Georgia, the Carolinas, and Virginia moved to the Mississippi area. In the Natchez District, for example, leading royalists included persons like William Dunbar and Anthony Hutchins. A veteran of the French and Indian War, Hutchins arrived from South Carolina in 1774 to occupy his two thousand acres, and four years later he represented the Natchez District in the colonial assembly. Many prominent residents of this colony, therefore, opposed the war for colonial independence, and if it had not been for the ensuing struggle for control of the Mississippi River, they would not have become involved in it at all.

The first event of the American Revolution that affected Mississippi directly was the rather bizarre string of raids conducted in 1778 by James Willing, a former resident of Natchez acting as a secret agent of the Continental Congress. Leading a force of about one hundred men, Willing plundered and confiscated property in Natchez and other areas. The properties of important British loyalists, such as Anthony Hutchins's plantation, were particular targets of the raid. After the forays Willing and company transported to New Orleans any supplies that might be useful to the American army. At New Orleans, the sympathetic Spanish authorities provided various additional military stores and helped transport all the goods to American bases on the upper Mississippi and Ohio rivers.

In response to the raids Governor Chester sent militia reinforcements to Fort Panmure in late 1778 and early 1779. Within a few months, however, he had to withdraw the entire garrison to defend against a more dangerous threat. In 1779 Spain joined France in the alliance with the fledgling United States, and a large Spanish force commanded by Bernardo de Gálvez, the governor of Louisiana, attacked Baton Rouge in late September.[1] The result was that the British had to surrender not only Baton Rouge but the other posts in the region, including Fort Panmure at Natchez. After Gálvez went on to capture Mobile in March 1780 and Pensacola in May 1781, British rule in West Florida ended.

Spanish occupation of Natchez began in October 1779 and continued throughout the remainder of the war. Some of the residents, prompted by their loyalty to Britain and fears of property confiscation and religious persecution by the Spanish military, attempted an uprising in 1781. Their opportunity came while Gálvez's principal military forces were on the Gulf Coast, hundreds of miles away. Believing that Gálvez would not succeed at Pensacola, leaders of the pro-British faction in Natchez, including Captain John Blommart and Anthony Hutchins, obtained approval for their rebellion plan from the British military commander in Pensacola. The insurgents were advised that British troops and supplies were being sent to support them and that they should recapture Fort Panmure. The courier delivering this message arrived in Natchez with a small band of Choctaw warriors led by "Chief" Folsom, a white man who had married a Choctaw woman. With this promise of support from Pensacola, the British loyalists attacked Fort Panmure in April 1781.

With only one cannon in their arsenal, they failed to capture the fort by force but used trickery to persuade the Spanish to surrender without a fight. Having intercepted a letter from a Spanish sympathizer, which had initially reported the weakness of the rebels, the loyalists altered it to read that the fort would be destroyed by an explosion of gunpowder unless the Spanish garrison withdrew. Within a few weeks, however, the British takeover collapsed when Spanish rein-

---

1 Spain entered the war against Britain in 1779, not as a genuine ally of the United States but because Spain saw the opportunity to recover the Floridas from Britain.

forcements arrived simultaneously with the news that Pensacola had indeed fallen to Gálvez. Natchez was re-occupied by a combined force of French, Indian, and Spanish troops in late June 1781, and a month later Colonel Don Carlos de Grand Prè became commandant of Fort Panmure.

Spain had achieved its war aim of recovering the Floridas, which it had lost to Britain twenty years earlier. The Treaty of Paris in 1783, which ended the American Revolution, returned to Spain not only eastern Florida but also the former British colony of West Florida. The northern border in this area was set at 31° north latitude, even though Spain had occupied and held Natchez and other posts north of that line since 1779. Now residents of the Natchez District found themselves in a peculiar situation: according to the treaty they were within the jurisdiction of the United States, but in fact they were subject to Spanish rule, which would continue there until 1798.

SELECTED SOURCES

Bettersworth, John K., *Mississippi: A History* (Austin, TX: The Steck Company, 1959), 86–101.

Carson, James Taylor, *Searching for the Bright Path: The Mississippi Choctaws from Prehistory to Removal* (Lincoln: University of Nebraska Press, 1999).

Fabel, Robin F. A., *Bombast and Broadsides: The Lives of George Johnstone* (Tuscaloosa: University of Alabama Press, 1987).

———, *Colonial Challenges* (Gainesville: University Press of Florida, 2000).

———, *The Economy of British West Florida, 1763–1783* (Tuscaloosa: The University of Alabama Press, 1988).

Kynerd, Byrle A., "British West Florida," in Richard Aubrey McLemore, ed., *A History of Mississippi*, 2 vols. (Hattiesburg: University & College Press of Mississippi, 1973), 1: 134–157.

O'Brien, Greg, *Choctaws in a Revolutionary Age, 1750–1830* (Lincoln: University of Nebraska Press, 2002).

Rowland, Dunbar, *History of Mississippi: The Heart of the South*, 4 vols. (Chicago-Jackson: The S. J. Clarke Publishing Company, 1925), 1: 253–289.

Wells, Mary Ann, *Native Land: Mississippi, 1540–1798* (Jackson: University Press of Mississippi, 1994).

CHAPTER FIVE

Spanish Rule, 1781–1798

THE BOUNDARY DISPUTE

Following the American Revolution, Spain continued to occupy the Natchez region. In justifying their new claim to the area the Spanish cited their military conquests during the war and their rejection of treaty provisions between Great Britain and the United States fixing the northern border of West Florida at 31° north latitude. The newly formed United States also claimed the Natchez District, which lay north of that border and thus in territory the United States had acquired from Great Britain, as confirmed in the Treaty of Paris of 1783. Still, Spain countered that because the British had not actually controlled Natchez at the end of the war, they had not the legal authority to cede the area to the United States or to any other nation. To complicate matters further, the State of Georgia also continued to claim the area as the westernmost part of Georgia's colonial charter.

In spite of the conflicting claims, for almost two decades Spain controlled the lower Mississippi River, including Natchez and other settlements in Mississippi. Not only did Spain regularly tax products shipped down the river to New Orleans, but in 1784 it closed that port to U.S. trade. During the years prior to the founding of the United States Constitution, when the government of the new republic operated on the restrictive Articles of Confederation, Congress attempted to remove Spain from the Natchez District and secure free navigation on the lower Mississippi through diplomatic means. It authorized Secretary of Foreign Affairs John Jay to achieve those objectives in negotiations with Don Diego de Gardoqui, the Spanish charge d'affairs. Notwithstanding his experience in diplomacy, representing the United States in Spain during the Revolution and at Paris for the treaty negotiations, Secretary Jay failed to accomplish his mission. Meeting with Gardoqui in New York, the United States capital at that time, Jay accepted Spain's exclusive control of the lower Mississippi River and the Natchez District in return for certain commercial opportunities with Spain. Finding these terms unacceptable, Congress refused to ratify the Jay-Gardoqui Treaty in 1786.

SPAIN MAINTAINS CONTROL

Spain's efforts to maintain control in Mississippi were implemented by the successive governors-general of Louisiana and West Florida, headquartered in New Orleans. Following Governor Bernardo de Gálvez's departure in 1786, Esteban Miró served as the top official until 1792, when Francisco Luis Hector de Carondelet took control. The last Spanish governor-general to exercise authority in the Natchez District was Manuel Gayoso de Lemos, who took office in 1797.

North America, 1873

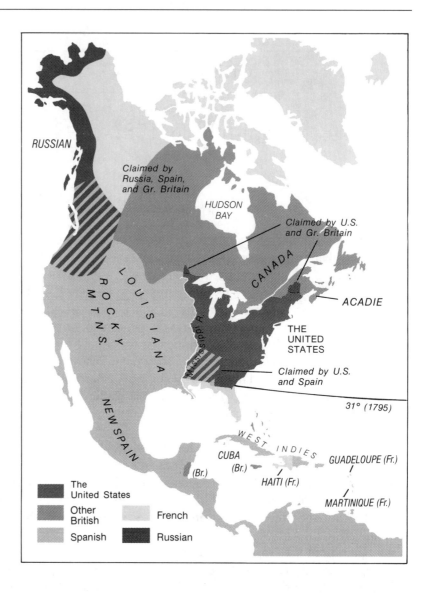

The strategy all these Spanish administrators employed was to win the friendship of both the British inhabitants and the Indian tribes of Mississippi in order to promote a movement for the secession of the area from the United States. General James Wilkinson, who had served in the United States Continental Army during the Revolutionary War, played an instrumental role in these efforts during the 1780s.

In an attempt to extend and strengthen their control in the region, in 1791 the Spanish constructed Fort Nogales at Walnut Hills, the future site of Vicksburg. Because of its strategic location on a high point (later known as Fort Hill) overlooking the river, this post was more useful than the Natchez fort in Spain's efforts to control traffic on the Mississippi River. They erected another fort, Bayou Pierre, in the Grand Gulf area to protect settlers against attacks from hostile Indians. This policy of expansion was continued by Governor-General Carondelet, whose treaties with the Chickasaws led to the establishment of a fort at Chickasaw Bluffs near the future site of Memphis. During the mid-1790s Spanish authorities stationed at this fortification stopped and inspected all descending river boats and thereby exercised tight control of the lower Mississippi. By the late 1790s, Spanish territorial claims extended from the Natchez area northward beyond Memphis.

To defend its holdings in the Natchez District, Spain relied on a permanent military force, the Louisiana Infantry Regiment, which numbered about 1,500 soldiers, and a squadron of gunboats on the river. Because the army was responsible for protecting the entire Louisiana and West Florida areas, it was reinforced in times of crisis by regular troops from Mexico and Cuba and by members of the Natchez militia. Although this Spanish colonial military was never seriously challenged, it did thwart several potential disasters. Its presence, for example, helped prevent pro-French uprisings and invasions during the early 1790s, when Spain was at war with France. It also helped stop British schemes to invade Spanish territory from the north, the encroachment of land-company speculators from Georgia and South Carolina, and doubtless some Indian raids.

In dealing with the Indians, however, treaties were more helpful to European settlers than were military forces. Following the practice of the French and the British colonial administrations, the Spanish officials negotiated a series of treaties with Indian tribes at Mobile and Pensacola in 1784. By the Treaty of Natchez in 1792 the Choctaws ended their objections to the location of Fort Nogales by selling that tract to Spain. The following year the Treaty of Nogales formed an alliance among Spain, the Chickasaws, Choctaws, Creeks, Cherokees, and other local tribes.

SPANISH ADMINISTRATION IN NATCHEZ

Beginning with Gálvez, the governors-general in New Orleans appointed commandants to exercise civil and military authority in the Natchez area. Among the most important commandants were Carlos de Grand Prè (1781–82 and 1786–92), Esteban Miró, who served in Natchez briefly in 1782 and later became governor-general, Francis Bouligny (1785–86), and Don Manuel de Gayoso (1789–97), who afterward was appointed governor-general and oversaw Spain's withdrawal from Mississippi.

Gayoso was a native of Portugal, the son of a Spanish diplomat and a Portuguese woman. His superior education, including proficiency in English and several other languages, had prepared him for a career in civil and military affairs. At forty-two years of age he was chosen by the Spanish crown to defend and improve the empire's outpost at Natchez. On his extensive land grant near the town, he developed a plantation and constructed a personal residence, "Concord," which would become the model for later "antebellum" mansions in the area. Scholars consider Gayoso a major contributor to the beginnings of the antebellum Natchez culture.

During the twenty years of their rule, the Spanish virtually imposed martial law in Natchez, and dismantled the British traditions of representative government and jury trials. The commandants simply issued laws or edicts, usually after consultation with the wealthy property owners. When civil disputes or crimes occurred, the cases were heard and decided by the Spanish commandants or their officers. These officials theoretically followed the tenets of the Spanish colonial law code, but they sometimes made practical adjustments to accommodate influential British settlers in order to gain their cooperation.

Population Growth and Land Grants

By 1785 the Natchez District, which was part of the Spanish colonies of Louisiana and West Florida, had a population of about 1,100 white persons, 900 African slaves, and uncounted numbers of Indians. St. Catherine's Creek and Cole's Creek were the locations of the earliest communities in the vicinity of Fort Panmure at Natchez, which was the most populated part of the colonies except for New Orleans. The town of Natchez itself was planned by Gayoso and featured six east-to-west streets intersected by seven others running parallel to the river. It was here that prosperous planters began to build imposing homes and import European furniture, beginning the tradition of the antebellum Natchez mansions. Another community was begun in the Vicksburg area around Fort Nogales.

Most Europeans in the Natchez District were British; some French families had remained, but there were very few Spanish settlers. Although the usual freedoms experienced under British rule had been discontinued by the Spanish military regime, the authorities occasionally looked the other way in order to attract colonists. Free land was granted to immigrants who met certain conditions, including a willingness to clear the land, build roads, and plant certain kinds of crops. The Spanish land grants ranged from 240 to 800 acres. Around Natchez more than 250,000 acres had been granted by 1792, and the population had swelled to more than 4,000 persons. When Spanish rule ended in 1798, the population had increased to 4,500 whites and 2,400 blacks.

Rosalie, an antebellum home in Natchez. Courtesy Westley F. Busbee, Jr.

Even as Spain was issuing numerous and large grants of land in the Natchez District, the State of Georgia made grants in the same region, based on its claim of ownership dating back to its original colonial charter. Viewing the Spanish presence as an illegal occupation, the Georgia state legislature in 1785 organized Bourbon County in the Natchez area and sent commissioners to distribute land grants. Even though the Spaniards impeded the Georgia land agents' activities, four years later the Georgia legislature sold 10 million acres in the area to the South Carolina Yazoo Company. This huge expanse extended from the mouth of Cole's Creek, north of Natchez, to 33° north latitude and eastward to the Tombigbee River. In the same year the legislature sold another tract of more than 11 million acres, located north of the South Carolina purchase, to the Virginia Yazoo Company for $93,741. In 1795 a Georgia law authorized the sale of approximately half of what is now Mississippi and Alabama to three other land speculation companies. When it was discovered the next year that many of the legislators held stock in the companies, the new legislature repealed the law, even though some of the land had already been sold.

Economic Life

The Spanish government provided various types of economic assistance to the settlers struggling to begin profitable farming operations. From the beginning, the government protected the colonists from their British creditors, and later, in response to debtors' petitions, Spanish officials lowered interest rates and allowed extensions on loan repayments to merchants. In its effort to encourage the production of tobacco as a successful cash crop in the colony, Spanish officials established a warehouse in Natchez and purchased most of the tobacco grown in the region. Temporarily prosperity ensued, for the typical tobacco farmer could harvest as much as 2,000 pounds per acre with the assurance that the government would buy it for as much as 10 dollars per 100 pounds.

This business reached its peak in the late 1780s when about 1.5 million pounds of tobacco were produced. But tobacco failed to become the staple crop because the strain of the plant grown in Mississippi was inferior in quality to those produced in the United States, and because the Spanish price support had created an artificial market, ultimately resulting in oversupply and falling prices.

As tobacco production declined to about 75,000 pounds in 1792, many farmers turned to the cultivation of indigo, a plant used as a source for dye. Indigo growers could hope to harvest an average of 150 pounds an acre, which they could sell for as much as 2 dollars per pound. By 1792, however, indigo production also reached its peak, at about 35,000 pounds. It, too, failed as the farmers' mainstay because its production was expensive, the crop was susceptible to insects and disease, and the market for the crop was never stabilized. Moreover, growing indigo in the 1790s was harmful to laborers and the environment.

Cotton finally became the major crop after Daniel Clark and David Greenleaf introduced Eli Whitney's cotton gin into Mississippi in the mid-1790s. Thereafter the production of cotton increased rapidly; by 1797 the planter William Dunbar was harvesting 20,000 pounds annually. Later Dunbar developed the square bale as the most efficient way to handle and ship cotton. Soon the cotton business—from planting to selling and transporting—became so universal in Mis-

William Dunbar (1750–1810) was born and educated in Scotland. At the age of twenty-one he traveled to the American colonies, and after a brief sojourn in Philadelphia he began a plantation in British West Florida. Later Dunbar established "The Forest," his plantation near Natchez. In addition to his successful farming pursuits, Dunbar engaged in other interests including scientific experiments, politics, and exploration. He made a number of practical proposals and inventions relating to the production and use of cotton, including the idea of manufacturing cottonseed oil and the screw press to form square cotton bales. After the establishment of the Mississippi Territory, Dunbar served as a judge and a member of the legislature. Recognizing his scientific expertise, President Thomas Jefferson in 1804 appointed Dunbar to join George Hunter in an exploration of the present-day Arkansas region (then part of the newly acquired Louisiana Purchase). During this excursion, which coincided with the beginning of the Lewis and Clark expedition, Dunbar kept a detailed journal of Indian life, fossils, plants, and other features of the area, including the first description of the hot springs. According to some scholars, Dunbar's versatile accomplishments made him Mississippi's first "Renaissance Man." Portrait courtesy Mississippi Department of Archives and History.

sissippi that gin receipts gained acceptance as currency. In addition to cotton, tobacco, indigo, corn, and other farm crops, livestock was an important aspect of the area's economy.

Directly related to this agricultural economy was the growth of the slave trade. The peculiar institution had commenced during the French period, but the Spanish encouraged it by offering additional land to settlers who agreed to bring slaves with them into the colony. Before long most of the leading planters and government officials participated in the slave trade, a practice widely accepted throughout the colony. The numbers of enslaved black persons increased from about 500 in 1784 to as many as 2,400 in the late 1790s, at which time the selling price for an adult African slave ranged from $300 to $400. Records reveal only one slave uprising during the Spanish period, one that was quickly suppressed by Grand Prè in the mid-1790s.

Social Life

Although most settlers were small farmers, the ready availability of land and laborers and the assistance of the Spanish government allowed a number of enterprises to expand into large plantations during the Spanish period. At one such cotton plantation, Springfield, the home of Thomas Green near Natchez, Andrew Jackson and Rachel Donelson Robards were married in 1794.

During these years most settlers displayed an inconsiderable interest in religion. The Roman Catholic Church once again was the established church: a 1783 proclamation ordered that all prospective immigrants had to be (or claim to be)

Roman Catholics; and a royal decree in 1792 required that the Catholic clergy conduct all baptisms and marriages in the colony. But because most settlers were Protestants, such religious laws were not usually enforced, unless non-Catholics worshiped in public without permission. John Bolls, a Presbyterian elder, was arrested following a public service, and for the same reason an Episcopal minister, Adam Cloud, was taken as a prisoner to New Orleans. Richard Curtis, a Baptist minister, had to leave the colony in 1795 after declaring his belief that God's law, which was an authority greater than Spanish edicts, justified his public preaching. In spite of the occasional efforts by the Spanish governors to suppress their beliefs and worship services, Protestants managed to organize several churches. The Swayze family had already begun the first Presbyterian churches, while Richard Curtis founded the first Baptist church, Salem, in 1791.

The Catholic Church and the Protestant ministers provided the only educational opportunities for the children of the colony. Except for the church schools, no formal educational institutions existed, and most children received instruction in proportion to their parents' own levels of education.

SPAIN'S WITHDRAWAL

Spain's failure to maintain control of the Natchez District ultimately resulted from several interrelated developments. First, the secessionist strategy failed to win widespread support among the inhabitants. Second, the Spanish crown was encountering serious diplomatic and financial problems at home because of its unsuccessful wars with France. Finally, under its new Constitution of 1787, the federal government of the United States had grown stronger.

A resolution of the boundary controversy was finally achieved during the presidency of George Washington. In October 1795 Thomas Pinckney, U.S. minister to Great Britain acting as special envoy to Spain, signed an agreement with the government of King Charles IV. In Pinckney's Treaty or the Treaty of San Lorenzo El Real—named for the historic monastery near Madrid where the negotiations transpired—Spain finally accepted the 31° north latitude line as the boundary between the United States and Spanish West Florida along the Gulf Coast. The treaty also granted to United States citizens the unfettered right to ship their products all the way down the Mississippi River, to deposit them at New Orleans, and to reship them in ocean-going vessels. In addition, they would be exempt from paying export duties to Spain for a period of three years.

But the dispute did not end immediately. Even after the United States Senate ratified the treaty in May 1796, Governor-General Caron-

Baron de Carondelet. From the holdings of the Carondelet family, Madrid. Courtesy Louisiana State Museum.

delet saw evidence that Spain might retain control in Mississippi. The Washington administration had other urgent problems to solve, including the "Whiskey
Rebellion" in western Pennsylvania and the outbreak of warfare with Indians and
their British allies in the Northwest Territory. Carondelet, therefore, delayed for
as long as possible making any plans to implement the treaty's provisions. It was
not until February 1797 that the U.S. commissioner, Andrew Ellicott, arrived to
survey the border with the assistance of William Dunbar, who was employed by
Spain for the project. When disagreements about jurisdiction quickly developed
between Ellicott and Natchez Commandant Gayoso, the settlers took sides. Many
big landowning planters and merchants sided with Ellicott, while the small farmers and debtor class favored Gayoso because Spain had provided them economic
relief.

Gayoso's position was strengthened when in April 1797 Piercy S. "Crazy"
Pope arrived in Natchez with troops to take possession of the fort for the United
States but instead became involved in disputes with Ellicott. Riots broke out
when a Baptist minister verbally attacked Spain and the Roman Catholics. Then
minister John Hannah was physically assaulted by Irish residents and was arrested
by Commandant Gayoso, who had initially allowed him to preach. In the unrest
that followed two groups emerged: the wealthy "City" party composed of creditors
who supported Ellicott, and the "Country" party composed of small farmers and
debtors sympathetic with Spanish rule.

It was during this crisis that Gayoso left Natchez to assume the office of governor-general of Louisiana in New Orleans. The new commandant was Stephen
Minor, a friend of both Ellicott and Gayoso. Nevertheless, order was not restored
until the arrival of United States Army Captain Isaac Guion late in 1797. Assert-
ing his authority over Ellicott and Pope and their respective followers, Guion
forced Spain to evacuate Natchez and Nogales by the end of March 1798. At last,
the three-year-old Treaty of San Lorenzo was implemented; Governor-General
Gayoso formally surrendered Natchez and the other areas north of 31° north latitude, and the United States took possession. Within a month the U.S. Congress
established the Mississippi Territory, and the first territorial governor, Winthrop
Sargent, arrived in August with General James Wilkinson, who took command of
the fort.

Selected Sources

Bettersworth, John K., *Mississippi: A History* (Austin, Texas: The Steck Company,
    1959).

Carson, James Taylor, *Searching for the Bright Path: The Mississippi Choctaws from
    Prehistory to Removal* (Lincoln: University of Nebraska Press, 1999).

DeRosier, Jr., Arthur H., "William Dunbar, Explorer," *Journal of Mississippi History*
    25 (July 1963).

———, "William Dunbar: A Product of the Eighteenth Century Scottish Renais-
    sance," *Journal of Mississippi History* 28 (August 1966).

Dunbar, William, *Life, Letters and Papers of William Dunbar*, Comp. Mrs. Dunbar
    Rowland (Jackson: Press of the Mississippi Historical Society, 1930).

Holmes, Jack D. L., *Gayoso: The Life of a Spanish Governor in the Mississippi Valley, 1789–1799* (Baton Rouge: Louisiana State University Press, 1965).

———, "The Provincial Governor-General: Manuel Gayoso de Lemos," in Gilbert C. Din, ed., *The Spanish Presence in Louisiana, 1763–1803*, Vol. 2, Louisiana Purchase Bicentennial Series in Louisiana History (Lafayette, La.: Center for Louisiana Studies, University of Southwestern Louisiana, 1996).

———, "A Spanish Province, 1779–1798," in Richard Aubrey McLemore, ed., *A History of Mississippi*, 2 vols. (Hattiesburg: University & College Press of Mississippi, 1973), 1: 158–173.

O' Brien, Greg, *Choctaws in a Revolutionary Age, 1750–1830* (Lincoln: University of Nebraska Press, 2002).

Weber, David J., *The Spanish Frontier in North America* (New Haven: Yale University Press, 1992).

Wells, Mary Ann, *Native Land: Mississippi, 1540–1798* (Jackson: University Press of Mississippi, 1994).

CHAPTER SIX

The Territorial Period, 1798–1817

THE FIRST STAGE OF TERRITORIAL GOVERNMENT

On April 7, 1798, President John Adams approved an act of Congress that established the Mississippi Territory and provided for the territorial government. The inhabitants would not directly participate in their governance until at least five thousand free men of voting age resided in the territory. In the meantime, the president appointed and Congress approved five officials—a governor, a secretary, and three judges—and empowered them to make laws for the territory and appoint all civil and militia officers.

Borders

The law's description of the new territory's borders required a settlement of Georgia's western claims, because it made the Chattahoochee River—more than four hundred miles east of the Mississippi River—the border between that state and the new territory. The northern border of the Mississippi Territory ran from the juncture of the Yazoo and Mississippi rivers eastward; the southern border was 31° north latitude, the United States border with Spanish West Florida; its western border was the Mississippi River. The territory's neighbors, therefore, were Spanish Louisiana on the west and southwest, Spanish West Florida on the south, Georgia on the east, and on the north unorganized lands claimed by the U.S. government but still held and occupied by Indian tribes. Acting with no apparent consideration of the ownership rights of the Indian nations, in 1804 Congress added the northern tracts to the territory. Then, in 1810, President James Madison added West Florida, having seized this area from Spain. During the seven years prior to statehood, therefore, the Mississippi Territory included all of the present-day states of Mississippi and Alabama. (See map, Mississippi Territory, p. 56.)

Natchez

As capital of the territory until 1802, Natchez was the largest town in Mississippi. Still, in fact, a small frontier community, it benefited from the presence of its fort, its location as a key trading post on the Mississippi River, and as the southwestern terminus of the Natchez Trace, Mississippi's first road, and early roads from Georgia. Natchez's two contrasting sections accommodated very different types of people. Designed by Spanish Governor-General Manuel Gayoso in the previous decade, Natchez proper ("On-the-Hill") comprised stores, ware-

NATCHEZ UNDER-THE-HILL, MISSISSIPPI.

Natchez "Under-the-Hill." Courtesy Mississippi Department of Archives and History.

houses, professional and government offices, and some elegant residences, while Natchez "Under-the-Hill," at the river's edge, served as a meeting place for travelers, including the sometimes rowdy boatmen known collectively as "Kaintucks" (whether they came from Kentucky or elsewhere). Taverns and saloons with free-flowing alcoholic drink, gambling, fist and gun fighting, and prostitution came to characterize "Under-the-Hill." Indeed, the rough and tumble conditions there may be compared to those of the "wild west," for at the time Natchez was the nation's (south) west, and this part of the town certainly had the reputation of being wild!

Governor Winthrop Sargent, 1798–1801

Winthrop Sargent, the first to assume the office of territorial governor, was a Federalist who had served as secretary of the Northwest Territory, where he had become a wealthy land speculator with ambitions for the governor's title there. During his three-year tenure in Mississippi, Sargent and his assistants ruled arbitrarily, favoring the small merchant-creditor class and treating most other residents as if they were soldiers under his command. The latter element of small farmers and debtors, led by the families of Anthony Hutchins and Thomas Green, including Cato West, tended to favor the Jeffersonian Republican party, which opposed the Federalists locally and nationally. This group agitated against Sargent, demanding a greater voice in public affairs and a change in the administration.

Political considerations notwithstanding, Sargent began the process of organizing the territory into counties and appointing officials to enforce the first laws,

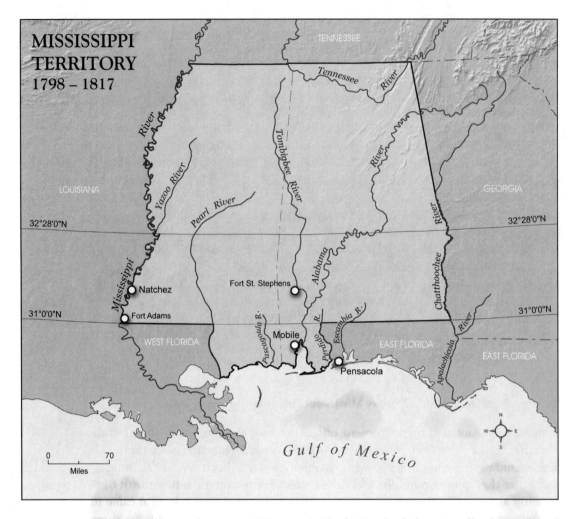

MISSISSIPPI
TERRITORY
1798 – 1817

harsh regulations known as "Sargent's Codes," which he initially decreed and then drafted with the aid of the secretary and the judges. The first counties, Adams and Pickering, were formed in the Natchez region. In 1800 Washington County was created in the country east of the Pearl River in present-day Alabama. County sheriffs, justices of the peace, and coroners were among the first local officers appointed. Another of the governor's critical but difficult responsibilities in this frontier environment was organizing a territorial militia. Sargent's foremost problem, however, involved the new territory's relations with the Indians, a matter complicated by the alleged actions and policies of the Spanish officials in Louisiana and West Florida.

Following their withdrawal from the Natchez district, the Spanish governors-general in New Orleans were accused by Mississippi officials of encouraging the Choctaws to resist U.S. authority by raiding settlements in the Mississippi Territory. And from the moment he took office Sargent was apprehensive about reports that—in violation of the Treaty of San Lorenzo—Spain continued to interfere with free trade on the lower Mississippi River. The governor feared that such allegations, if true, might cause the United States to declare war against Spain, or against France should that nation, now controlled by Napoleon Bonaparte, regain

The transformation of disconnected Indian trails into a continuous though rough wilderness road from Nashville, Tennessee, to Natchez began in the early years of the territorial period. First suggested in a publication by an Englishman, Francis Bailey, who had experienced the difficult and perilous journey, the road was needed to facilitate immigration from eastern states. It was demanded, moreover, by the growing numbers of interior farmers, lumbermen, and trappers, who floated their products down the rivers to markets but often returned home on foot or horseback along Indian trails. Constructing the trace was a daunting task due not only to the enormous physical challenges but also to uncertainties and dangers of trespassing through vast regions belonging to Indians from whom permission for passage was difficult if not impossible to obtain. Notwithstanding these many obstacles, travel increased out of necessity and gradually a number of rather crude inns or stands were built—about twenty by 1820—to provide shelter and food for travelers and their animals. The most prominent stands were at Mount Locust (above) and Red Bluff.

Samuel Mason, a Virginia native who traveled with his three sons to Kentucky and then into the Mississippi area, led a band of robbers and river pirates that sometimes included other notorious cutthroats like Wiley "Little" Harpe and Samuel Mays. After several years of disrupting travel on the Trace, the latter couple double-crossed Mason and killed him for a $500 bounty (though some sources say $2,000). Another account reported that Mason's wife denied that the head brought back by Harpe and Mays belonged to her husband, who escaped finally to Canada. In any case, when territorial officials of Jefferson County early in 1804 identified Harpe and Mays as gang members themselves, their reward was the gallows rather than the money. According to one story, their heads were mounted on poles along the Trace to discourage other outlaws. Though very real and extremely dangerous and intrusive at the time, the varying accounts of the outlaws on the Natchez Trace became legends and would served as the basis for entertaining tales best exemplified by Eudora Welty's Robber Bridegroom published in 1946 and still the basis for popular plays and comic musicals. Photographs: (top) Mount Locust, courtesy Mississippi Department of Archives and History; (bottom) Natchez Trace, courtesy Westley F. Busbee, Jr.

Louisiana. A war with either nation, Sargent worried, would threaten the very existence of the newly organized Mississippi Territory, situated as it was on the exposed southwestern frontier of the new nation.

Another complicated issue involved conflicting titles to land as a result of previous grants made by the governments of France, Great Britain, Spain, and the State of Georgia. During the territorial period, various agents of land companies arrived to enforce their claims, while Spain was attempting to lure Mississippi inhabitants to emigrate into Louisiana or Texas, the northern province of Mexico, by offering them free land or other incentives.

THE SECOND STAGE OF TERRITORIAL GOVERNMENT

The problem that proved fatal to Governor Sargent's administration, however, was the opposition from the Hutchins-Green faction, which launched a vicious campaign to disrupt the militia and the courts. By 1800 this popular movement led by the Republican element had produced a change in the territory's form of government, although the governor opposed it and the official population requirement had not been attained. Led by Cato West, this "country" party selected Narsworthy Hunter to present their complaints against Sargent and their petition for a change in the territorial government to the United States Congress.

With the support of Tennessee Congressman William Charles Cole Claiborne and other Republicans, the Congress authorized the establishment of a bicameral territorial legislature. The territory's new house of representatives would have nine members elected by qualified voters. The legislators had to be "free male inhabitants," U.S. citizens, three-year residents of the districts they represented, and owners of at least two hundred acres of land. Voters had to meet basically the same requirements, except the residency and property qualifications were lowered to two years and fifty acres respectively. The upper house, a five-member legislative council, would be appointed by the president of the United States from ten nominations submitted by the territorial house of representatives. In the first election only 306 men voted, but they elected eight Republican representatives, including Hutchins, Green, and West. Ignoring Sargent's protests, the representatives assembled and chose Hunter as the territory's delegate to Congress.

Following the Republican party victories in the congressional and presidential elections of 1800, Governor Sargent journeyed to Washington to defend his record and to try to persuade the new president, Thomas Jefferson, to reappoint him as territorial governor. But Jefferson refused and appointed instead William C. C. Claiborne, a twenty-six-year-old Virginia native, who was, as mentioned, representing Tennessee in the House as a Jeffersonian Republican.

GOVERNOR WILLIAM C. C. CLAIBORNE, 1801–1803

Although Governor Claiborne attempted to pursue a moderate course and reduce political dissension at the outset of his tenure the legislature took actions that clearly expressed Republican partisanship. Sargent's laws were rewritten, and several new counties were created. Adams County, the base of Federalist party strength and the most populous part of the territory, was divided; the southern part became the new county of Wilkinson. Existing Pickering County was re-named Jefferson, and another new county, Claiborne, was organized to the north of Jefferson. In 1802 the town of Washington, just a few miles northeast of Natchez, became the territorial capital. To encourage immigration into this part of the territory, the Republican-controlled U.S. Congress opened a federal land office at Washington and established Fort Dearborn nearby. Following the death of Narsworthy Hunter, the territorial legislature chose Thomas M. Green as Mississippi's delegate to Congress.

Reaction to the Republican partisans led to a revival of the Federalist party in Natchez, and Governor Claiborne found it difficult to please either faction in his efforts to solve the territory's problems. Nevertheless, by 1803 he had settled some of the conflicting land claims, and pursuant to his recommendation the U.S. Congress enacted a land law by which the State of Georgia's interests were satis-fied and persons with titles to land in Mississippi received proper validation. The law also provided for the establishment of land offices at Washington to serve the western district and at St. Stephens to manage the eastern district. As a result, fur-ther progress could be made in settling other land claim disputes, inhabitants could validate their property titles, and new immigrants could easily purchase land at federal offices.

Directly related to the land issues was the maintenance of peaceable relations with the Indians. Another task was protecting trade on the Mississippi River and on the Natchez Trace. Indeed, in light of Spain's continuing interference with river trade and an increasing incidence of thievery on the Natchez Trace by the notorious Mason gang and other outlaws, Claiborne strengthened the territorial militia. Following France's acquisition of New Orleans from Spain in 1801, United States commerce became vulnerable on the lower Mississippi.

The Louisiana Purchase, 1803

Meanwhile, tumultuous conflicts in Europe further shaped the lower Missis-sippi area. In 1801 Napoleon Bonaparte, the "first consul" and soon to be emperor of France, forced Spain to cede its Louisiana colony to France. Then in 1803, he sold this territory to the United States for the amazingly low sum of $15 million. Governor Claiborne and General James Wilkinson were sent by President Jeffer-son to New Orleans to represent the United States in the transfer of the territory. Thereafter, Claiborne remained in New Orleans and became the governor of the Orleans Territory in 1804. His position in Mississippi was temporarily occupied by the territorial secretary, Cato West, who served as acting governor until the next governor arrived.

GOVERNOR ROBERT WILLIAMS, 1805–1809

Although President Jefferson appointed Robert Williams as the next governor in March 1805, Williams did not arrive in Mississippi to assume the office until May 1806. A former congressman from North Carolina, Williams was familiar with the situation in Mississippi, having served as territorial land commissioner in the western district since December 1803. During his tenure as governor, the territory experienced population growth and controversy. In the eastern areas, and in the

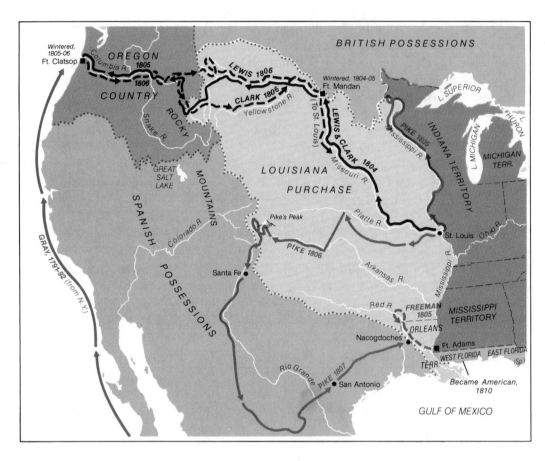

The Louisiana Purchase and Explorations of the Far West.

Pearl and Tombigbee river valleys, new settlements were established and a new federal judicial district was created by Congress. Judge Harry Toulmin emerged as the leader of this interior part of the territory.

Major reasons for the increase in migration to Mississippi at this time were the United States' acquisition of the vast Louisiana Territory in 1803 and the Choctaw Indians' cession of land to the Mississippi Territory in 1805. (There had been an earlier cession in 1801 by the Treaty of Fort Adams, which extinguished the Choctaws' claims to land in the Natchez region.) By the so-called first Choctaw Cession of 1805 the south-central area of Mississippi became available to settlers who could purchase land from the federal government.

Property owners in the southern part of the territory, meanwhile, were increasingly interested in taking possession of Spanish lands south of the border (31° north latitude). Leaders of this movement were the Kemper brothers, Reuben, Nathan, and Samuel, who had immigrated from Virginia and settled in Wilkinson County. The Kempers went so far as to advocate armed resistance against the Spanish in West Florida, and in 1804 they gathered supporters and launched an assault on the fort at Baton Rouge. Their efforts to overthrow Spanish rule in West Florida would continue throughout Williams's administration.

From the beginning of his administration Governor Williams was confronted by intense squabbling among the various political factions, including the Federalists and divergent groups within the Republican party. Evidently frustrated with such partisanship, Williams soon departed on a trip to his home state of North Carolina. In his absence territorial secretary Cowles Mead served as acting governor.

The Burr Affair

It was at this point that a most remarkable episode occurred. In January 1807 former U.S. vice president Aaron Burr and his band of adventurers arrived at Bayou Pierre near Bruinsburg, a river town in Claiborne County. Acting Governor Mead suspected that Burr and General James Wilkinson—current governor of the Louisiana Territory—were involved in a conspiracy against the United States. The suspicion held that Burr and his associates were conniving, possibly with foreign assistance, to separate regions in Mississippi and Louisiana from the United States and establish an independent nation under their own control. Accordingly, Mead ordered the territorial militia, a force of 275 men commanded by Major Ferdinand L. Claiborne, the younger brother of former governor Claiborne, to capture Burr.

Burr, who apparently had managed to garner support among some Mississippians, voluntarily surrendered to the militia at Bayou Pierre in late January, with the stipulation that he would stand trial in the territory. Many Federalists tended to support Burr, believing that the true nature of his mission was to acquire additional territory for the United States; however, Judge Thomas Rodney, who had also served as land commissioner, was determined to prosecute Burr as a traitor. At a critical time in the process, Governor Williams returned from North Carolina and disagreed with the strong action that Mead had taken against Burr. In February 1807 in Washington, Mississippi, a pro-Federalist grand jury found Burr guilty of no crime.

The following month, however, in the area north of Mobile, Burr was again arrested and this time taken to Richmond, Virginia, where he stood trial in federal circuit court; again he was found not guilty. The presiding judge was Chief Justice John Marshall, who favored the Federalist party philosophy in general but accepted the Republicans' principle of strict constitutional interpretation in this case and dismissed the charge of treason.

As the Burr affair intensified political factionalism in the territory, Mead took the lead in forming a faction to oppose Governor Williams. This group included the Green family as well as George Poindexter and Ferdinand L. Claiborne. In 1807 the legislature elected Poindexter as territorial delegate to Congress, and Mead and Ferdinand Claiborne were elected to the territorial legislature. Poindexter presented petitions to Congress criticizing Governor Williams's administration, while Mead led the opposition strategy in the legislature.

In spite of these moves in Washington, D.C., and in Washington, Mississippi, Williams survived and was appointed to a second three-year term in 1808. But in the territorial elections of 1808 the anti-Williams candidates (known as the "country ticket") won a majority in the legislature, which elected Ferdinand Claiborne as speaker of the house and reelected Poindexter as the delegate to Congress. Controversy regarding the governor extended even to the judiciary, as Superior Court Judge Rodney favored his opponents, while Judge Harry Toulmin in the eastern district remained loyal to Williams. Burdened by such mounting opposition among territorial leaders, Governor Williams finally decided to resign,

Governor David Holmes. Courtesy Mississippi Department of Archives and History.

and President Jefferson appointed David Holmes of Virginia to take the position in March 1809.

GOVERNOR DAVID HOLMES, 1809–1817

The fourth territorial governor of Mississippi was born in Pennsylvania but grew up in western Virginia. He was a lawyer and had been appointed by President Jeffereson to the United States House of Representatives, where he served for twelve years. Unlike the previous governors, Holmes was a popular leader who was able to reduce the factionalism within the territory. Serving during the final years of the territorial phase, he presided over rapid population growth, the acquisition of the Gulf Coast, the traumas of the War of 1812, and Mississippi's transition to statehood.

When Holmes first arrived in Mississippi he encountered several developments that made political unity easier to achieve. One was that many of the older political leaders were retiring from public affairs. Another factor was the increasing awareness that harmony would help Natchez maintain its control of the territory, which might be threatened by the rapid population growth in the eastern (Alabama) regions. Finally, outside dangers forced political unity.

As the belligerent nations in Europe's Napoleonic wars began to threaten U.S. commercial shipping, the national government took steps to protect America's maritime rights. But the various embargos of the Jefferson and Madison administrations caused economic depression in Mississippi: denied ready export markets, planters faced rapidly falling cotton prices. The prevailing sentiment as expressed by territorial delegate George Poindexter and others was that the federal government should use military action against Great Britain rather than the commercial sanctions, which were damaging the territory's economy.

One reason for this hostile attitude toward Great Britain was the existing British land claims in the territory, which created problems for some land sales. Another factor was the suspicion among Mississippians that British agents were encouraging Indian recalcitrance, especially among the Creek Nation in the eastern areas.

THE ANNEXATION OF WEST FLORIDA

Another problem for the Holmes administration was the situation in Spanish West Florida, where officials had decreed harsh penalties against Mississippi settlers who crossed the border. Moreover, in their efforts to protect West Florida against U.S. interests, the Spanish imposed heavy taxes on trade through the port at Mobile and cultivated close relations with the Creeks and other Indian nations.

These policies failed to change the impression in the United States that Spain would soon be unable or unwilling to retain West Florida following Napoleon's conquest of Spain in 1808. Consequently, President Madison authorized Governor Claiborne of the Louisiana Territory to communicate formal messages of encouragement to U.S. citizens who had been resisting Spanish rule in the Baton Rouge area. When General George Mathews was directed to arrange a peaceful surrender of West Florida to the United States, the Spanish commandant allowed the inhabitants to hold a convention in September 1810, evidently hoping the delegates would choose to remain loyal to Spain. But instead of averting problems for Spain, the convention planned the capture of the Spanish fort at Baton Rouge. Following the seizure of the fort, which was not effectively defended, the convention declared the independence of the "State of Florida" and named Fulwar Skipwith as president.

Governor Holmes was involved in these events and sent militia companies to the border. He hoped West Florida would be immediately annexed and the entire area would become part of the Mississippi Territory. However, "President" Skipwith and the leaders of the rebellion in the Baton Rouge area desired separate statehood or annexation by the Louisiana Territory. In October 1810 President Madison issued a proclamation that seemed to settle the question of West Florida's destiny. It officially annexed the region along the coast from the Mississippi River to the Perdido River. Because the president's position was that this area had been part of the Louisiana Purchase of 1803, he instructed Governor Claiborne to take possession of it; however, Madison also notified Governor Holmes to occupy the area if Claiborne failed to do so.

As a result of these directives, both Claiborne and Holmes arrived in St. Francisville with militia troops, symbolizing the U.S. annexation of West Florida. But this occupation was at first limited to the western area, while the region east of the Pearl River, particularly Mobile, remained under Spanish control. Late in 1810 Reuben Kemper, who had been a leader in West Florida since the earliest rebellions, went to Fort Stoddert to arrange the occupation of Mobile. This effort failed, for when the Spanish officials refused to surrender the town, Kemper and the militia officers could not get the authority and support they needed to take it by force.

The issue of whether West Florida would be incorporated into Louisiana or Mississippi was finally decided through a compromise in early 1812, when Poindexter persuaded the Congress to divide the area at the Pearl River. Therefore, the region between the Pearl and the Perdido rivers would join the Mississippi Territory, while the region west of the Pearl would become a part of the new State of Louisiana.

THE WAR OF 1812

Another key event affecting Mississippi was the U.S. declaration of war against Great Britain in June 1812. Although the official cause was the mistreatment of American sailors by the British navy on the high seas, different motivations fueled anti-British sentiment in Mississippi. Having failed to occupy Mobile, Mississippians led by George Poindexter in Congress strongly favored the war on the conviction that it would lead to the completion of the Florida annexation. Another important related cause was apprehension about potential conflicts with Indian tribes supported by Britain and Spain.

According to legend, the famous Indian leader Tecumseh had "prophesied" an earthquake would occur in mid-December 1811, a signal for all Indians to join together against the Europeans who had stolen their lands. Without arguing how much truth if any is contained in the story, the historical fact is that on the eve of the war, a series of earthquakes that began on December 16, 1811, and continued through February 7, 1812, were among the most violent quakes in U.S. history. The New Madrid earthquakes, so-called because the epicenter was near New Madrid, a small community in the southeastern region of the Missouri Territory, were felt in varying degrees over more than 1 million square miles but had the greatest impact in the Mississippi River valley. Scientists believe that had the Richter scale been in use at that time, each of the three greatest shocks would have measured greater than 8.0.

According to various "eyewitness" recollections, five towns in three states disappeared, islands vanished in the Mississippi River, the course of the river changed, new lakes formed, and "the river flowed backward for a brief period." Large areas of land sank and rose, and extensive forests were destroyed, but because of the sparse population in the region, human injuries and fatalities were relatively few.

Residents of the Natchez area reported to the Natchez Weekly Chronicle *that the series of shocks caused a "tremulous motion of the earth and buildings," stopped clocks, damaged some houses and their contents, destroyed trees, and forced the Mississippi and other rivers to rise and fall rapidly. A New Orleans writer speculated that if the earthquake had not been caused by "The Comet" [Halley's?], then "the skake [sic] which the Natchezians have felt may be a mysterious visitation from the Author of all nature, on them for their sins . . . [for] wickedness and the want of good faith have long prevailed in that territory. Sodom and Gomorrha would have been saved had three righteous persons been found in it—we therefore hope that Natchez has been saved on the same principle."* The Louisiana Gazette and Daily Advertiser, *December 21, 1811, http://asms.k12.ar.us/armem/richards. For further information on the New Madrid earthquake, see Norma Hayes Bagnall,* On Shaky Ground: The New Madrid Earthquakes of 1811–12, Missouri Heritage Readers Series, *ed. Rebecca B. Schroeder (Columbia, MO: University of Missouri Press, 1966.)*

The arrival of a renowned Indian leader only exacerbated these concerns. The chief of the Shawnee Indians and friend of the British, Tecumseh, had come into the Mississippi area to persuade the Chickasaws, Choctaws, Creeks, and Seminoles to form a confederation against the United States. He was most successful with the Creeks, who were already on friendly terms with the Spanish in Florida. In Mississippi, therefore, the War of 1812 was mainly a conflict with the various Indian tribes rather than one simply against Great Britain.

Early in the war General James Wilkinson was ordered to occupy West Florida east of the Pearl River, where the Spanish had remained notwithstanding President Madison's annexation proclamation. In mid-April 1813, regular United States Army troops under Wilkinson took Mobile, and the Spanish withdrew to Pensacola. Governor Holmes visited Mobile to extend the territorial government into the area. He recommended that Judge Harry Toulmin preside over the judiciary there. Holmes expressed concern about the British using Pensacola as a base of operations to supply the Creek Indians. Without success he requested assistance from the United States Army, which was now under the command of General Thomas Flournoy, who had replaced Wilkinson.

The first battle between the Creeks and the territorial militia occurred on July 27, 1813, at "Burnt Corn Creek" in the southeastern region of the territory. The volunteer militia, under the command of James Caller, ambushed a force of Creeks known as the "Red Sticks" who were returning from a visit to Pensacola. With the military supplies they had secured at Pensacola, the Creek warriors not only defended themselves against the surprise attack but routed the militia.

To strengthen defenses in the Alabama River area the commanding general of the Mississippi militia, Ferdinand L. Claiborne, sent a force of about five hundred volunteers to assist the regular army. In late August a portion of the militia force under the command of Major Daniel Beasley was defending a stockade called Fort Mims when the "Red Sticks" took revenge for the ambush at "Burnt Corn Creek." The Creeks massacred at least 250 people, including soldiers and women and children who had sought refuge there. Major Beasley was accused of negligence for having failed to anticipate the attack.

Governor Holmes responded to the Fort Mims disaster by sending to Fort Stoddert about two hundred cavalry troops under the command of Major Thomas Hinds. The governor himself accompanied militia troops to Fort Stoddert in late October. The Mississippians received invaluable support in November when Tennessee militia general Andrew Jackson and about 2,500 Tennessee volunteers entered the Alabama area. In November Jackson's forces defeated the "Red Sticks" near Talladega and then cooperated with the Mississippians in an all-out campaign against the Creek Nation.

In late December 1813 Claiborne's troops captured and burned a Creek village called "Holy Ground" on the Alabama River. They killed about thirty warriors, but most of the town's inhabitants managed to escape across the river. Claiborne was unable to take advantage of this victory because his men were unwilling to continue for want of proper winter provisions. In this battle, Choctaw warriors under the leadership of Chief Pushmataha fought alongside the Mississippi militia. Pushmataha would continue to render his services to the United States during the War of 1812.

At a sharp turn on the Tallapoosa River known as "Horseshoe Bend," the Creeks were finally crushed in late March 1814. Jackson continued to subdue all Indian resistance, and in August he forced the Creek Nation to surrender about half their lands to the United States. In September Jackson, now a U.S. major general in command of regular army troops, repulsed the British attack on Mobile, ending the war in Mississippi. From there Jackson, accompanied by Colonel Thomas Hinds's Mississippi cavalry, known as "Hinds' Dragoons," occupied Spanish Pensacola. Jackson and Hinds then reported to New Orleans for the defense of that city against the mighty armed forces of Great Britain.

The Battle of New Orleans

After a British fleet of fifty ships carrying more than 10,000 men had destroyed a small American fleet, the British landed their troops and began the march across the swampy ground toward New Orleans. The British attacked the city a number of times, but each time the American defenders, outnumbered more than 2 to 1, forced them to withdraw. Finally, in the last attack, on January 8, 1815, Andrew Jackson's army dealt the British a smashing blow, inflicting more than 2,000 casualties while suffering only 71. Although the Treaty of Ghent ending the war had been signed in Belgium by U.S. and British agents on Christmas Eve, 1811, word of the signing had not arrived in time to prevent the bloodshed at New Orleans. So, with that stunning victory, the new nation had survived its hardest test and a new national hero, in the person of Andrew Jackson, had been born.

ECONOMIC CONDITIONS

The War's Results

The successful defense of the southwestern United States against the British and the triumph over the Creek Indians brought major gains to the Mississippi Territory. Among them were the annexation of the Gulf Coast zone, particularly Mobile, the acquisition of about 20 million acres of Creek lands east of the Tombigbee River, and the guaranty of free navigation in the lower Mississippi River. The result was a rapid influx of settlers and a rise in the price of cotton at the New Orleans market to eighteen cents per pound, more than double the average price of the past five years. The postwar years, therefore, promised prosperity and growth to the territory.

Population Growth

After the war migrants from other parts of the United States flowed into the territory, occupying the land (especially the Creek territory) even though they did not in many cases have clear legal title to it. In short, the availability of so much cheap land and the prospects of high cotton prices were irresistible attractions for thousands of people seeking new opportunities on the southwestern frontier.

In the first two decades of the nineteenth century most immigrants settled in Natchez and the western counties rather than in the eastern (present-day Alabama) districts of the territory. Between 1801 and 1811 the number of inhabitants in the west rose from almost 8,000 to more than 31,000. The number of slaves increased from about 3,000 to almost 15,000, a faster rate of growth (400 percent) than that of the whites, and slaves represented about 48 percent of the western population in 1811. Counting the eastern (Alabama) settlers, who numbered more than 6,400 whites and 2,600 slaves, the total population of the territory approached 42,000 in 1810, almost five times greater than the number in 1800.

By 1810 population growth had caused the formation of several new counties in the west, including Amite, Franklin, and Warren counties and Madison County in the northeastern region of the territory. By 1816 the following seven additional counties had been organized in the Mississippi portion of the territory: Greene, Hancock, Jackson, Lawrence, Marion, Pike, and Wayne.

While the population of the territory had increased steadily in the decade before the War of 1812, it grew at a much faster rate in the immediate postwar years. By 1816, the year prior to Mississippi's admission to statehood, the total population had jumped to about 75,000 persons. The greatest growth in this period occurred in the Alabama areas, primarily in Washington County along the lower Tombigbee River and in Madison County along the Tennessee River. By 1820 the total number of inhabitants in the east was almost 147,000, an increase of almost 138,000 since 1810. The number of slaves increased to almost 48,000, one-third of the total population. The growth in the Mississippi portion of the territory was substantially less, rising to 75,448 persons, of which 44 percent were slaves.

POLITICS

During the war the decline of the Federalist party was paralleled by the emergence of new factional alignments within the Jeffersonian Republican party, splits based on personalities, economic issues, and sectional rivalries. In Mississippi, one of the most dramatic examples of such Republican dissensions was the longtime feud—personal and political in nature—between editor Andrew Marschalk and George Poindexter. Marschalk, a Federalist who had shifted into the Republican party, published one of the territory's first newspapers, the *Mississippi Herald,* in Natchez. Among his many withering attacks on Poindexter, perhaps the most severe was the allegation that Poindexter was a coward, because as a militia officer at New Orleans in 1812 he had fled the field before the battle ended. After Poindexter announced that he would not to be a candidate for a fourth term in Congress, the legislature stunned him in 1813 when it elected William Lattimore over Cowles Mead, Poindexter's political ally and hand-picked successor.

In 1814 Lattimore, also a Republican, championed the cause of the landholders who were behind in their payments (to the government or banks). He also called for the Congress to address the land title controversies with the Yazoo Land Company and British speculators. In March 1814 Congress finally settled the Yazoo matter by compensating the claimants $5 million from the public land sale proceeds; however, uncertainties about the British claims lingered. But Lattimore's most significant accomplishment in Congress would be the formation of the State of Mississippi, a goal that Poindexter had failed to achieve. In fact, the movement for statehood became the most important postwar issue.

SELECTED SOURCES

Bagnall, Norma Hayes, *On Shaky Ground: The New Madrid Earthquakes of 1811–12,* Missouri Heritage Readers Series, ed. Rebecca B. Schroeder (Columbia, Mo.: University of Missouri Press, 1966).

Carson, James Taylor, *Searching for the Bright Path: The Mississippi Choctaws from Prehistory to Removal* (Lincoln: University of Nebraska Press, 1999).

Haynes, Robert V., "The Formation of the Territory," in Richard Aubrey McLemore, ed., *A History of Mississippi,* 2 vols. (Hattiesburg: University & College Press of Mississippi, 1973), 1: 174–216.

———, "James Willing and the Planters of Natchez: The American Revolution comes to the Southwest," *Journal of Mississippi History* 37 (February 1975): 1–40.

————, "The Road to Statehood," in Richard Aubrey McLemore, ed., *A History of Mississippi*, 2 vols. (Hattiesburg: University & College Press of Mississippi, 1973), 1: 217–250.

Lowery, Charles D., "The Great Migration to the Mississippi Territory, 1798–1819," *Journal of Mississippi History* 30 (August 1968): 173–192.

O'Brien, Greg, *Choctaws in a Revolutionary Age, 1750–1830* (Lincoln: University of Nebraska Press, 2002).

Remini, Robert, V., *The Battle of New Orleans: Andrew Jackson and America's First Military Victory* (New York: Viking Press, 1999).

CHAPTER SEVEN

The New State, 1817–1832

PROGRESS TOWARDS STATEHOOD

For years before the War of 1812 most people in various parts of the Mississippi Territory had advocated statehood. They had disagreed, however, on whether the new state should include the entire territory or some portion of it. The more populous Natchez District had favored the former plan, while the sparsely settled eastern settlements had demanded a division of the territory. These perspectives were virtually reversed after the war because of the population growth in the eastern areas, where vast tracts of land became available to settlers following Indian cessions in 1814 and 1816.

Although the prewar movement for statehood had been actively supported by many prominent citizens, it had been delayed for several reasons. Land owners in the territory, because of their relatively limited numbers, feared that significantly higher taxes would be imposed upon them in order to fund the expenses of organizing and administrating a new state. Another reason for delay was the prevailing sentiment among many leaders that the persisting land grant controversies should be settled prior to the state's formation. But the most important obstacle was the disunity between the western and eastern sections of the territory. The eastern inhabitants had originally requested a division of the territory, because they believed their interests would not be fairly represented in the state government. The easterners further reasoned that the Natchez area, where the capital would be located, was too far away, this at a time when transportation and communication were slow, difficult, dangerous, and expensive.

Favoring the westerners' wishes, however, territorial delegate George Poindexter had proposed to Congress in 1810 the admission of the whole territory. The measure had failed because the lack of agreement within the territory provided an excuse for congressmen from northeastern states to oppose it. The following year, therefore, Poindexter had introduced a resolution to form a state that would have included the southern half of the territory and West Florida. His plan to include West Florida would prevent that region from becoming a part of the Louisiana Territory, and it would add significantly to the population of the proposed state. Following the failure of Poindexter's efforts, the circumstances of the War of 1812 had required a virtual suspension of the movement for statehood.

Early in 1815, territorial delegate William Lattimore renewed the effort. By this time some of the obstacles had been removed—the Yazoo land claims had been settled and the population of the territory had increased significantly. In December 1816 the census results showed that the Mississippi Territory contained

75,512 persons, of whom 45,085 were free white people, 356 were free people of color, and 30,061 were slaves.

In February 1815 Lattimore introduced a bill to authorize the territory to write a state constitution. Favorable action by Congress was delayed by differences of opinion on the old question of whether the territory should be divided. To express their sentiments on the issue, territorial leaders assembled in October at the home of John Ford on the Pearl River in Marion County (near present-day Columbia). The host, a Methodist minister and South Carolina native, was widely known as one of the region's earliest settlers. The so-called Pearl River Convention was composed of delegates from most regions of the territory, but it was controlled by the easterners, who now favored the admission of the whole territory. The convention sent Judge Harry Toulmin to Washington to express its position and work with Lattimore in Congress. But the two Mississippians were unable to cooperate because Lattimore favored a division plan that would form the new state in the western half of the territory.

Late in 1816 the territorial legislature approved by a close vote the petition of the "Pearl River Convention" and sent a request to Congress calling for the admission of the whole territory. Contrarily, the large minority, composed primarily of westerners, sent to Congress its counterproposal for admittance of a divided territory. Ultimately Lattimore chose to introduce a bill to authorize the western counties to call a constitutional convention. His decision, which appeared to disagree with the majority opinion in the territory, resulted from his own identification with the west and from his understanding of the greater likelihood of getting the Congress to approve the admission of the smaller state. Lattimore had learned that for political purposes the southerners in the United States Senate would favor carving two slave states rather than one out of the large territory in the southwest.

Federal Legislation

Three steps were required for the territory to become a state. First, an enabling act (with accompanying legislation if needed) had to be passed by the United States Congress and approved by the president. Second, pursuant to this legislation, a territorial convention had to write a constitution for the prospective state. Finally, this constitution had to be accepted by both houses of Congress.

Early in 1817 the legislation for Mississippi was expedited by southern members of Congress who, though outnumbered by northerners in the House, wanted to preserve the sectional balance in the Senate by maintaining an equal number of slave and free states. The enabling act for Indiana, a free state, had been adopted in December 1816, upsetting the balance, so the admission of Mississippi as a slave state would restore it. The enabling act for Mississippi passed the United States Senate in January and the House of Representatives in February and was signed by President James Monroe on March 1, 1817. This act made provision for the admission of the western part of the Mississippi Territory to statehood and for the organization of the eastern part as a new territory (Alabama). A second measure described the border dividing the territory: it would begin at the point where Bear Creek emptied into the Tennessee River and follow a straight line directly south to the northeastern corner of Wayne County (which was also the northwestern corner of Washington County in present-day Alabama). From that point

Home of John Ford, site of the "Pearl River Convention." Courtesy Mississippi Department of Archives and History.

the border would turn slightly southeastward to avoid severing the eastern portion of Wayne County and reach the Gulf Coast at a point about ten miles east of the mouth of the Pascagoula River.

This division of the territory reflected a compromise between the demands of easterners, who wanted to push the line as far west as the Pearl River, and westerners, who favored the Tombigbee River. Needless to say, leaders in neither part of the territory were completely satisfied with the boundary as determined by Congress. Poindexter and Cowles Mead, along with others in the west, blamed Lattimore for "losing" the important port town of Mobile. Lattimore, however, had seen the need to accept the compromise in order to propel the statehood movement.

THE CONSTITUTIONAL CONVENTION OF 1817

Pursuant to the enabling act, the qualified voters in the western part of the territory were indeed authorized to elect delegates to a constitutional convention. Participants in this process (voters and delegates) had to be free white males, at least twenty-one years of age, and have resided in the territory for at least one year and paid county or territorial taxes. The document they drafted had to establish a state government republican in form and in harmony with the Constitution of the United States.

Mississippi's first constitutional convention met for six weeks, from July 7 to August 17, 1817, in the town of Washington near Natchez. The forty-eight delegates, who were elected to represent the fourteen counties, assembled in the small Methodist Church on the campus of Jefferson College. The membership was evenly divided between the Mississippi River counties and the Piney Woods counties, so sectional disagreements arose. For the most part, however, the convention was not characterized by profound political differences. All delegates were Jeffersonian Republicans, almost all of them were big landowners, and several had held high positions in the territorial government. Without objection they elected Governor David Holmes to preside as president of the convention.

Despite this apparent homogeneity, the deliberations began under contentious circumstances. Many of the delegates resented bitterly the loss of Mobile and other settlements along the Tombigbee River to the new Territory of Alabama that Congress had organized. George Poindexter's motion to adjourn the convention until Congress could be persuaded to extend the state's boundaries failed on a vote of thirty-two to fourteen. Another interesting decision concerned the name of the new state. Cowles Mead's proposal that it should be named "Washington" received seventeen votes, while "Mississippi" received twenty-three votes.

How to determine representation for the legislature became the greatest controversy. Delegates from the sparsely populated eastern counties wanted the state senate apportioned equally among the counties. Some delegates from the Mississippi River counties, home of the largest plantations, wanted to count slaves in determining representation for both houses. The heated debate led to a motion by David Dickson of Pike County to suspend the convention and therefore statehood. This crucial motion lost in a tie vote of twenty-three yeas to twenty-three nays. The representation issue was finally settled through a compromise that house representation would be based on the free white population, but each county would have at least one member. Representation in the senate would be based on "free white taxable inhabitants," which was a victory for the populous western counties, where a greater proportion of the white population owned large, taxable tracts of land.

The acknowledged leader of the convention was George Poindexter of Wilkinson County. He chaired the committee to draft the proposed constitution, and the document finally adopted was mainly his work. The committee submitted its proposal to the convention on July 17, and after it was debated and amended, the constitution was adopted on August 17. All present delegates except Cato West signed it.

THE CONSTITUTION OF 1817

The controlling influence of the aristocratic Natchez element was reflected in a number of provisions in the constitution. Natchez was designated as the capital of the new state, and there were high qualifications for suffrage and officeholding. Except the governor and lieutenant governor, all executive and judicial officers were elected by the legislature. There were no limits on the number of terms an officeholder could serve. The amendment process was intended to be very difficult in that another convention was required to make changes to the constitution. These provisions notwithstanding, there was really nothing innovative about Mississippi's first constitution for it was quite similar to the constitutions of other southern states. The convention did not submit its proposed constitution to the voters for approval but sent it directly to President James Monroe.

The Declaration of Rights

The provisions of the twenty-nine sections in the first article of Mississippi's constitution were much like the bills of rights in other state constitutions and that in the Constitution of the United States. They guaranteed to white "freemen" the basic freedoms of religion, speech and press, assembly, protection from unreasonable searches, due process and trial by jury in criminal and civil cases, and the right to possess arms for defense.

The Legislature

Adhering to the principle of the separation of powers, the constitution divided the authority of the state government into three distinct departments: legislative, executive, and judicial. Intended to be the most powerful branch of the state government, the legislature, named the "general assembly," consisted of the house of representatives and the senate. Representatives were elected for one-year terms and had to be U.S. citizens, at least twenty-two years old, residents of the state for at least two years, and owners of at least 150 acres of land or real estate worth at least $500. The house of representatives had exclusive authority to originate all revenue bills and impeach state officials.

State senators were elected for three-year terms, but their terms were staggered, with one-third of the senate being elected annually. Candidates for the senate had to be U.S. citizens, at least twenty-six years old, residents of the state for at least four years, and owners of at least three hundred acres of land or real estate worth at least $1,000. The senate had the responsibility of trying impeachments.

The Executive

Given the unpleasantness Mississippians had experienced with some of the territorial governors and following the tradition of the era, the convention intended to limit the powers of the executive branch. It was composed of the governor—"the supreme executive power," lieutenant governor, secretary of state, treasurer, and auditor. The governor and lieutenant governor were elected by the voters for two-year terms. To qualify for either office candidates had to be U.S. citizens for at least twenty years, at least thirty years of age, residents of the state at least five years, and owners of at least six hundred acres of land or real estate worth at least $2,000. The governor's powers and duties included commanding the state's militia, approving or vetoing bills passed by the general assembly, enforcing the laws, granting reprieves and pardons, and appointing persons to fill unexpected vacancies in the general assembly. The other executive department officials were elected by the legislature.

The Judiciary

The judicial branch was composed of a supreme court, superior courts, inferior courts, and the office of the attorney general. The general assembly was directed to divide the state into judicial districts and to appoint from four to eight supreme court judges who would serve "on good behavior" or until they reached sixty-five years of age. These supreme court judges would hold biennial sessions of the superior courts in each county. The legislature was also required to establish a system of inferior courts, including chancery, circuit, probate courts, and justices of the peace.

Suffrage

The suffrage qualifications were quite restrictive. In order to vote, a person had to be a U.S. citizen, a free white male at least twenty-one years of age, a resident of the state for at least one year and of his county or voting district for at least six months, and either a member of the state militia (unless excused from militia service) or a state or county taxpayer.

Slavery

The constitution explicitly protected the institution of slavery. The state government was prohibited from emancipating slaves without the slave owner's consent, and persons entering the state, immigrants as well as visitors, were allowed to bring their legally owned slaves in with them. While the general assembly was authorized to require humane treatment of slaves, it was not required to provide slaves full due process in criminal prosecutions, except trial by jury in capital cases.

Church and State

The principle of the separation of church and state was not clearly asserted in the new constitution. In an attempt to assure impartiality, the constitution protected the freedom of worship and prohibited ministers from holding the offices of governor, lieutenant governor, or legislator. On the other hand, it contained provisions that explicitly endorsed religion. For example, no person who denied the "being of God or of a future state of rewards and punishments" would be eligible for any state office. And the document declared religion, along with morality and knowledge, "necessary to good government, the preservation of liberty, and the happiness of mankind."

FORMAL ADMISSION TO STATEHOOD

In early December 1817 the United States Congress approved the proposed constitution and adopted a joint resolution admitting Mississippi as the twentieth state on equal terms with the original states. President Monroe signed the resolution on December 10, 1817, and within a week the state's two senators and one representative were officially installed in Congress. Such a prompt installment of the congressmen had been made possible because, anticipating a favorable reaction by the national government, Mississippi's political leaders had held the first state elections in September and the first General Assembly had already met in Washington, Mississippi. By the end of the year, pursuant to the state constitution, the capital was moved to Natchez, the state's largest and most important business center.

Although Natchez already had been deemed the new state capital, a yellow fever epidemic in that town had forced the government to meet in Washington temporarily. The first General Assembly, which had convened in early October 1817, was composed of eight senators and twenty-three representatives. This group decided that the annual sessions of the state legislature would begin in January in Natchez and that the annual elections would be held in August. From time to time thereafter the legislature changed the times and sometimes even the places for legislative sessions. For example, as early as January 1821 it decided to assemble in November of each year, and in November of 1821 the second session of that year met in Columbia.

GOVERNOR DAVID HOLMES, OCTOBER 1817–JANUARY 1820

David Holmes, who had served ably as territorial governor since 1809, was elected first state governor without opposition. Duncan Stewart defeated Cowles Mead to become lieutenant governor, and George Poindexter was unopposed in his election to the U.S. House of Representatives. In October 1817 the General Assembly elected Walter Leake and Thomas Hill Williams as the state's first senators. Williams, a lawyer from North Carolina, had held several key positions in the territorial government and had been a delegate to the 1817 constitutional convention. He served in the U.S. Senate until March 1829.

The Holmes administration was devoted primarily to organizing the state's governmental structure pursuant to the Constitution of 1817 and to establishing new public and private institutions. After the executive and legislative departments were in place, the General Assembly organized the judiciary and selected judges for the Supreme Court and the inferior courts. The Bank of Mississippi was changed from a private to a state institution with a charter extending to 1840 and its capitalization was increased to $3 million. In 1818 the legislature chartered an important private institution, Elizabeth Female Academy. It was located in Washington near Jefferson College, the private military academy for men that had been established by the Territorial General Assembly in 1802.

GOVERNOR GEORGE POINDEXTER, JANUARY 1820–JANUARY 1822

In the August 1819 gubernatorial election, Congressman Poindexter defeated General Thomas Hinds. Incumbent Governor Holmes's two-year term, which had begun in October 1817, was extended by the legislature to January 1820 so that succeeding administrations would commence at the beginning of the year.

State Laws
The most important contribution Poindexter made as governor was the first codification of the state's laws. Upon his recommendation, the legislature authorized the governor to prepare the code. Soon after his term expired, the "Poindexter Code" was adopted by a special session of the General Assembly in June 1822. A century later, in 1925, historian Dunbar Rowland asserted that "The Poindexter Code has been the foundation of all the codes of the State of Mississippi." In another effort to improve the administration of the law, Poindexter recommended and the legislature established in 1821 the superior court of

chancery with jurisdiction over matters of equity, which included noncriminal cases relating to controversies over inheritance, land, debts, and divorce settlements.

The Anti-Bank Movement

Deeply concerned that the Bank of Mississippi's power to regulate the currency and thus control prices would damage the economy generally and hurt small farmers specifically, Governor Poindexter launched an attack against the institution, demanding the removal of exclusive state privileges from the bank's charter. Although the legislature did not immediately act, Poindexter's position would eventually win approval, reflecting the emerging hostility to state (government-controlled) banks among the Democratic Republicans (known later as the Jacksonian Democrats).

The Acquisition of Choctaw Land

Population increases generally and the movement of settlers into Indian-held lands prompted the national government to obtain title to Choctaw lands. The Choctaws had previously made two major land cessions: in the Treaty of Fort Adams of 1801, which included the Natchez District; and in the Treaty of Mount Dexter of 1805, which included a large area in the south-central section of the Mississippi Territory. A large portion of the latter cession became part of Wayne County when it was formed in 1809.

Now, in October 1820, in the Treaty of Doak's Stand, the Choctaw Indians ceded about one-third of their remaining lands to the United States. This vast area of more than 5 million acres in the central part of the state that constituted approximately one-sixth of the state's entire land area. Several of the earliest counties created within the region were Bolivar, Copiah, Hinds, Holmes, Madison, Rankin, Simpson, Washington, and Yazoo. (See map: Indian Land Cessions, p. 83.) In return for this cession the Choctaws were promised a huge track of about 13 million acres in the Arkansas Territory west of the Mississippi River. The negotiations occurred at Doak's Stand, a tavern located on the Natchez Trace near the Pearl River in the southeastern corner of present-day Madison County. The United States was represented by Andrew Jackson and Thomas Hinds, and the Choctaws were represented mainly by Chief Pushmataha.

Governor Poindexter recommended that proceeds from the sale of this Choctaw land that the federal government remitted to the state be used to finance a program of internal improvements. But primarily because of disputes about land titles in Arkansas, implementation of the Doak's Stand Treaty was delayed. Finally, adjustments were made in the Choctaw Treaty of 1825, an agreement between Chiefs Pushmataha and Mushulatubbee and Secretary of War John C. Calhoun in Washington, D.C.

While these negotiations were occurring, and before the Choctaw land was officially acquired, the legislature took steps to organize this cession. In 1821 two huge new counties were formed: Hinds and Monroe. Initially Hinds County comprised an enormous area in the central and western region, but it would soon be divided into other counties, such as Yazoo and Copiah, which were created in 1823. Monroe County was organized on the Tombigbee River in the northeast region of the state and included the town of Columbus, which was incorporated early in 1821.

The inhabitants of Monroe County quickly responded to Governor Poindexter's appeals for schools. In his 1821 message to the legislature, he called for an educational or "literary" fund to be used for the "education of the poor" in each county. Using the proceeds from leases of sixteenth-section or school lands, in 1821 Columbus established Franklin Academy, the first "free" (public) school in the state. The British colonial practice of reserving the sixteenth section (a one-square-mile parcel) of each township (a six-square-mile area containing thirty-six sections) for the support of public education had been established by the U.S. Congress in the Land Ordinance of 1785 and the Northwest Ordinance of 1787. Later, as the United States expanded westward, Congress required new territories and states to use the same land survey system, including the obligation to reserve sixteenth-section lands for educational purposes.

The Selection of Jackson as the Capital

Soon after the Treaty of Doak's Stand, the legislature voted in January 1821 to move the capital away from the Natchez area to a site nearer the center of the expanding state. A commission composed of Thomas Hinds, William Lattimore, and Lieutenant Governor James Patton was charged with determining a location within twenty miles of the state's geographic center and on a navigable river. After considering the upper Big Black area, they chose Le Fleur's Bluff, on the Pearl River and only ten miles from the Natchez Trace. The commissioners presented their report to the legislature on November 20, 1821. The legislature responded promptly and favorably and ordered Hinds, Lattimore, and Peter A. Van Dorn to survey and plan the town.

The new capital city was named in honor of the national hero, General Andrew Jackson, and the county was named for General Thomas Hinds, who had served with Jackson during the War of 1812 and gained fame at the Battle of New Orleans. The surveyors completed their work in 1822, and settlers were sold lots at bargain prices with two years to pay, provided they built homes or businesses on their parcels by November of 1831. A small, two-story brick building was constructed to serve as the capitol at the corner of Capitol and President streets, and the legislature assembled there for the first time in December 1822. This transfer of the state government to Jackson occurred during Governor Walter Leake's first year in office.

Governor Walter Leake, January 1822–November 1825

In 1821 U.S. Senator Walter Leake was elected as governor. He had been a territorial judge for ten years and a delegate to the 1817 constitutional convention before going to the Senate. David Dickson gained election to the office of lieutenant governor. When Leake resigned from the Senate in 1820 to become a candidate for governor, the legislature elected former governor David Holmes as his replacement. The contest for the state's one seat in the U.S. House of Representatives proved more controversial. Christopher Rankin, who had succeeded Poindexter in 1820, overcame a challenge by his predecessor (and former governor) in the election of 1822, because of Rankin's early identification as a "Jackson

Democrat," public misgivings about the "Poindexter Code," and Lieutenant Governor Dickson's opposition to Poindexter.

Leake was the first governor to be reelected for a successive term, defeating two well-known and experienced political leaders, David Dickson and William Lattimore, in the 1823 election. Because Governor Leake died during his second term, it is interesting that Dickson chose not to run for reelection as lieutenant governor, and instead Gerard C. Brandon was elected to that office. Brandon was born on a plantation near Natchez while the region was still under Spanish control. A planter who was educated as a lawyer, he had served as a delegate in the constitutional convention of 1817.

At the time of the Marquis de Lafayette's visit to Natchez in April 1825, which was considered one of the greatest social events of the decade, the governor was unable to welcome personally the French general, who was widely acclaimed for his role in the American Revolution. After Governor Leake died at his home, Mt. Salus, near present-day Clinton, on November 17, 1825, he was succeeded by Lieutenant Governor Brandon, the first Mississippi native to serve as governor. Brandon completed the remaining weeks of Leake's term and then resumed the office of lieutenant governor in January 1826, when David Holmes became governor for the second time.

Governor David Holmes, January 1826–July 1826

In the 1825 election Senator Holmes, former territorial governor and the state's first governor, won in a landslide victory over opponent Cowles Mead. Brandon's reelection as lieutenant governor was significant, as he would soon assume the office of governor again, this time upon the unexpected early retirement of Holmes.

The Case for Internal Improvements

In his second, although brief, administration Holmes continued his predecessor's policies of supporting internal improvements, including the building of roads and improving river transportation in the frontier regions. His inaugural address included such recommendations as prohibiting the importation of slaves for trading purposes and beginning a state program of education. All the early governors followed Holmes's example in their appeals for action in several important areas of the new state's development. They virtually always mentioned the need for educational opportunities, internal improvements, the further acquisition of Indian lands, banking improvements for more economic opportunities, and, later, the defense of slavery. Exceptions to these themes were disagreements about strategies on banking and currency matters and the slavery issue, as well as the usual political controversies.

The Slavery Issue

William Haile was elected in 1826 to fill the vacancy in the U.S. House of Representatives caused by the death of Christopher Rankin. Prior to his election, Haile served in the state house of representatives and authored a committee report on the question of slavery, an issue that was beginning to be discussed nationally with much passion among those for and against it. Evidently the subject had not been suddenly introduced in the Mississippi legislature, for as early as 1822 the body had moved to prohibit the immigration of free black persons into the state.

Haile's report, the recommendations of which were adopted by both houses of the General Assembly in 1826, represented a stage in the evolution of Mississippi's reaction to the abolition movement. It declared that the right of property in slaves was sacred and inviolate; "however great may be the national evil of slavery and however much we may regret it, circumstances over which we have no control [presumably the state's heavy reliance on the labor-intensive crop of cotton] have rendered it inevitable, and places it without the pale of legislative authority." The report opposed all forms of emancipation, even in other states, arguing that such action would excite the hopes and prospects of persons remaining in slavery and create a spirit of discontent and insurrection that would endanger white citizens. "The Southern states who suffer and are compelled by circumstances to endure the evil, ought to be the best judges of the remedy; and as soon as they can concur in any expedient for their relief it will be time enough to adopt it."[1]

Holmes's Exit

When Holmes's health failed, causing him to resign in July 1826 and retire to his family's home in Virginia, Lieutenant Governor Brandon again succeeded to the governor's office and completed Holmes's term. He succeeded in retaining that position in the gubernatorial election of 1827.

GOVERNOR GERARD C. BRANDON, JULY 1826–JANUARY 1832

Major Issues

A Jacksonian Democrat, Brandon echoed his party's platform by favoring the disestablishment of the national bank, which was, according to the Jacksonians, a monopolistic instrument controlled by northeastern financial interests. The governor particularly objected to the national bank's plan to establish a branch in the state, holding that the institution would deter state and private banking operations. Brandon also supported the Jacksonian policy of removing all remaining Indian tribes from the state. As a native of Adams County and, like other governors in this era, a big landowner and slaveholder, he generally favored the interests of the old Natchez District. He opposed "protective" tariffs (import duties imposed by the national government for the purpose of protecting domestic manufacturers), arguing that they raised costs paid by Mississippi planters who imported farm implements, furniture, and other products. But Brandon favored internal improvements, and during his administration a state Board of Internal Improvements was created. Like Holmes, he favored prohibiting the importation of slaves for the purpose of trade. This latter position reflected not only the early nineteenth-century Mississippians' apologetic attitude for the "necessary evil" but, paradoxically, their growing uneasiness about the possibility of slave insurrections.

1 Haile's committee report as quoted in Dunbar Rowland, *History of Mississippi: The Heart of the South,* 4 vols. (Chicago-Jackson: The S. J. Clarke Publishing Company, 1925), 1: 547.

The legislature agreed with Brandon's opposition to the U.S. Congress' tariff act of 1828, known as the "tariff of abominations," and adopted resolutions declaring the state's objections to the high protective tariff. Pursuant to the governor's recommendations, the state's literary fund was revived to support education, and several laws were enacted to encourage primary and higher education. The constitution was amended in 1829 to authorize the trustees of sixteenth-section lands to establish schools in townships, using revenue from the sale or rent of such land. Unfortunately, there is no evidence that these actions resulted in any significant progress for public education in the state.

Presidential Election of 1828

Presidential candidate Andrew Jackson visited Mississippi in January 1828. During the wildly popular ex-general's visit, several leading moderates were temporarily converted to Democrats, including William L. Sharkey, Governor Brandon, and George Poindexter. (Poindexter had not supported Jackson in 1824, and he would desert him soon after the 1828 election.) In November Jackson received 6,714 votes in Mississippi to only 1,674 for President John Q. Adams. Jackson won every county with larger majorities than he had gotten in his unsuccessful and controversial run for the White House in 1824.[2] Evidently support for Adams in the state had decreased markedly during his administration; only in the Natchez District did he receive significant support.

Dancing Rabbit Creek

As the second governor elected to a successive term, Brandon presided over several major controversial transitions in the early history of the state. Following the lead of President Jackson's federal policy of Indian removal, Governor Brandon and the legislature called for the extension of state law into Choctaw and Chickasaw lands and for the final expulsion from Mississippi of these nations. The Choctaws, therefore, found themselves with the choice of moving to lands west of the Mississippi River or submitting to state law. After the tribe's leaders in a turbulent council resisted compromise, the majority was persuaded by David Folsom and Greenwood Leflore to accept the inevitable. Led by Leflore, who was recognized as chief, the Choctaws finally agreed to negotiate with President Jackson's representatives, Secretary of War John Eaton and John Coffee. The meeting occurred in September 1830 at Dancing Rabbit Creek in present-day Noxubee County. The treaty provided for the Choctaws to surrender all their remaining lands in return for an area west of the Mississippi River, to which they were required to move within the next three years. Each Choctaw family that chose to remain in the state would receive 640 acres of land and become subject to state and federal law. (See map: Indian Land Cessions, p. 83.)

2 In 1824 Adams had received 1,694 votes, while Jackson had won 3,234 votes. In the congressional election of 1828 Representative Haile was opposed by Thomas Hinds and David Dickson. Hinds was elected primarily because of his direct associations with Andrew Jackson. In this period the state was represented in the United States Senate by Thomas Hill Williams (since 1817) and by Powhatan Ellis, an enthusiastic Jacksonian, who was chosen to fill the vacancy caused by Holmes's resignation in 1825. (See Appendix for Antebellum Representatives and Antebellum Senators.)

Greenwood Leflore. Courtesy Mississippi Department of Archives and History.

Greenwood Leflore, the son of Louis, a French trader from Canada and founder of the "French Camp" stand on the Natchez Trace, and Rebecca, who had French, English, and Choctaw ancestors, played a colorful role in Choctaw and Mississippi history. Unlike Chiefs Pushmataha and Mushulatubbee, who acquiesced to the Choctaws' land cessions but continued to defend and promote their people's traditions, Leflore and his ally Folsom embraced European culture in return for substantial rewards. While Mushulatubbee migrated along the "trail of tears" to the western Indian Territory after signing the treaty at Dancing Rabbit Creek, Leflore chose to remain and received more than 2,500 acres of land in the Delta (future Leflore County) where he became a prosperous slaveholding planter residing at his mansion, "Malmaison," and won election to the state legislature.

As a result of the Treaty of Dancing Rabbit Creek, the central area of the state, composing about one-third of the total square land mileage of Mississippi, was opened to white settlers. During Brandon's second administration, therefore, the legislature extended its jurisdiction over these Indian lands, following the pattern of Georgia in that state's controversy with and ultimate forced eviction of the Cherokee Indians.

The Planters' Bank

Related to the opening of these vast new lands, another major event of Brandon's second administration was the change in state banking practices. In

---

Although Pushmataha (ca. 1764–1824) is well known in the state's history—his portrait hangs in the Mississippi Hall of Fame at the Old Capitol Museum in Jackson—little is known about his early life. Born probably near present-day Noxubee County, in east central Mississippi, he became a legendary deer hunter and warrior and was given the name Pushmataha, which means "a messenger of death" or one whose weapon "is fatal in war or hunting." Though his parents were probably not members of the upper class, he came to be recognized as a Choctaw chief in his mid-thirties due to his successes in warfare and his possession of unusual spiritual pow-

ing and reasoning skills, Pushmataha represented his people with wisdom and foresight in critical relations with other Indian tribes and the United States. He has been described as a leader who desired to preserve his traditional Choctaw culture but also understood that fundamental changes were required for his people's very survival. Such a unique comprehension of his place in history helps to explain his military and diplomatic roles in the first quarter of the nineteenth century. Picture courtesy Mississippi Department of Archives and History.

1830 the legislature chartered the "Planters' Bank of the State of Mississippi" in Natchez and authorized that two-thirds of its capital would be reserved for state funds. This action represented a transfer of the state's resources from the old Bank of Mississippi to the new Planters' Bank. The former institution's conservative policies had restricted the amount of currency in circulation, while the new bank would be expected to satisfy the fast-growing demand for easier access to capital. The long-lasting banking monopoly had finally been broken, and other financial institutions began to organize and start operations. Another major reason for the change was the wealthy state leaders' desire to compete favorably with (and undercut if possible) the branch of the national bank that was about to open in Natchez.

Jacksonian Politics

The state's leading congressmen in the early 1830s were Senators George Poindexter and John Black and Representative Franklin E. Plummer. To fill the vacancy caused by the death of Senator Robert H. Adams, Poindexter was appointed by Governor Brandon in July 1830, an action affirmed by the legislature later that year. Senator Poindexter, who soon rose to the office of president pro tempore, became a bitter political opponent of President Jackson, disagreeing on the bank issue and the nullification controversy. The number of pro-Jackson congressmen from Mississippi increased, however, when Senator Black was chosen to succeed Powhatan Ellis in 1832, Representative Plummer was elected in 1830 to succeed Thomas Hinds, and Representative Harry Cage became the state's second member of the House in 1833 as the result of the population report in the 1830 census. (See Appendix II: Members of the U.S. Congress, 1817–1861.)

Population Growth

During the Brandon years the state's population increased rapidly. The 1830 census reported a total of 136,621 inhabitants, including 70,443 whites and 66,178 blacks. (Indians were not counted.) These numbers represented an 81 percent increase in total population since 1820. In this decade the slave population doubled, while the number of whites rose by 67 percent. Along with the additional land and growing population, the state witnessed the early beginnings of a revolution in transportation—the building of railroads. In 1831 the legislature chartered the first railroad company in the state, the West Feliciana Railroad Company, which would run twenty-nine miles from Woodville, Mississippi, to St. Francisville, Louisiana.

GOVERNOR ABRAM M. SCOTT, JANUARY 1832–NOVEMBER 1833

Sectionalism

One of the pains of growth, sectionalism, became a factor in the 1831 election campaign. The main differences emerging between the old Natchez District and the new areas involved the banking situation and calls for a new constitution. In the gubernatorial race Abram M. Scott, a planter from Wilkinson County on the Mississippi, very narrowly defeated several opponents from the interior counties, including future governors Hiram G. Runnels and Charles Lynch.

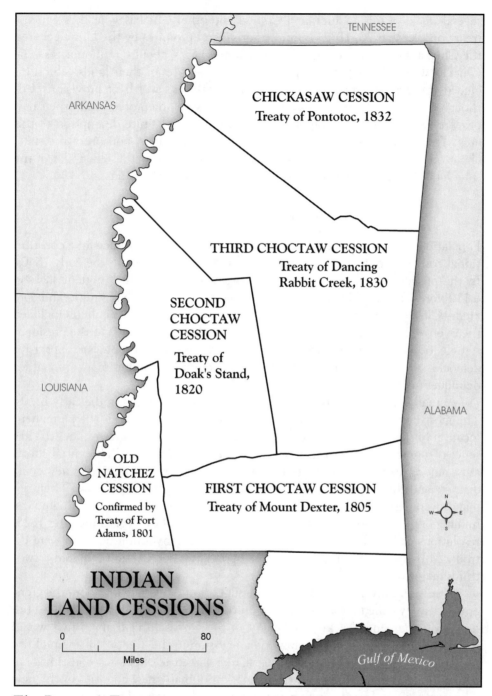

CHICKASAW CESSION
Treaty of Pontotoc, 1832

THIRD CHOCTAW CESSION
Treaty of Dancing
Rabbit Creek, 1830

SECOND
CHOCTAW
CESSION

Treaty of
Doak's Stand,
1820

OLD
NATCHEZ
CESSION

Confirmed by
Treaty of Fort
Adams, 1801

FIRST CHOCTAW CESSION
Treaty of Mount Dexter, 1805

TENNESSEE

ARKANSAS

LOUISIANA

ALABAMA

INDIAN
LAND CESSIONS

0   80
Miles

Gulf of Mexico

The Pontotoc Treaty

Demands for a new constitution gained momentum as a result of the Treaty of Pontotoc, which removed the last Indian tribe from Mississippi during Scott's first year as governor. The Chickasaws had begun negotiations with President Jackson's commissioners in 1830 under the same terms that had been offered the Choctaws. In September 1832 John Coffee met with the Chickasaw council on Pontotoc Creek in the southeastern area of present-day Pontotoc County. After several weeks of talks, Chief Levi Colbert and other Chickasaw leaders signed a treaty on October 20, 1832. In return for several promises by the United States, the Chickasaws agreed to cede their remaining lands, about 6 million acres. The Chickasaws would receive the proceeds from the sales of their lands, which included the expenses of their removal and one-year's worth of provisions. Although they were also given assurances of ownership and protection in their new property west of the Mississippi River, there was no definite description of this area. This Chickasaw cession included the entire northern portion of the state, about one-sixth of the total land area of Mississippi. Now the remainder of the state had opened for settlement. (See map: Indian Land Cessions, p. 83.)

THE CONSTITUTION OF 1832

Population growth in these areas further contributed to the crusade for a constitutional convention, as did the surge of Jacksonian Democracy in the early 1830s. In the presidential election of 1832, Mississippi voters gave President Jackson 6,110 votes to only 791 for National Republican (soon to be Whig) candidate Henry Clay. Earlier evidence of the rising support for Jacksonian policies included the overwhelming support they received from Mississippi voters in the presidential elections of 1824 and 1828. Another early example of popular support for democratic reforms was the 1824 legislature's action to prohibit imprisonment for delinquent debtors.

Actually, the movement for a new constitution had begun in the early 1820s. The most important reasons for it were the disagreements about the permanent location of the capital, the demands for various democratic reforms, and the absence of a practical amending process in the 1817 constitution. The initial efforts arose among leaders in the frontier areas, who called for the creation of new court districts and the reapportionment of representation in the legislature. Their demands were resisted by the conservative river counties, which had dominated the framing of the existing constitution. In every session of the legislature after 1825, resolutions calling for popular referendums on the convention question were introduced but defeated, in part because approval for such action required a two-thirds majority vote.

Finally, in November 1830, with the support of Governor Brandon, the General Assembly called for a referendum on the issue. The major factor behind the move was the general acknowledgment of the far-reaching changes that would soon result from the final Choctaw Indian cession in the Treaty of Dancing Rabbit Creek. Now even the western legislators agreed to support a constitutional convention, to be held prior to the formation of many new counties in the new Choctaw cession. Interestingly, some easterners also changed their position; hoping to wait until the number of convention delegates from their region greatly increased, perhaps even putting them in control, they attempted in vain to defeat or delay action.

In the general election of August 1831 the voters favored holding the constitutional convention by a wide margin. The only significant opposition came from the Tombigbee area and the Piney Woods. In the gubernatorial campaign that year the convention proposal was a major topic but not a contentious issue, given its widespread popular support. Pursuant to the election results, in December the General Assembly ordered the election of convention delegates in August 1832 and the convocation of the convention on September 10 in Jackson.

The Constitutional Convention

In the campaigns for convention membership the candidates took sides on several controversial topics including the judiciary, qualifications for voting and officeholding, legislative reapportionment, internal improvements, and the slave trade. Judicial reform was perhaps the hottest issue, particularly the method of selecting judges. The conservative candidates (known as "aristocrats") wanted the legislature to continue appointing judges, while the more democratic candidates demanded judicial elections. A group called the "whole hogs" wanted the popular election of all judges, while the "half hogs" preferred the election of lower court judges but the appointment of supreme court judges by the governor with senate approval.

The majority of the forty-six delegates who assembled in Jackson from September 10 through October 1832 to draft the state's second constitution were interested in implementing democratic reforms that would change substantially the rather conservative structure of the Constitution of 1817. In general the delegates from the western counties were the most conservative, delegates from counties in the northeastern and recently acquired Indian lands the most "democratic," with the Piney Woods delegates about equally divided. Some of the state's political leaders were not present for various reasons, including Seargent S. Prentiss, William L. Sharkey, Robert J. Walker, Franklin E. Plummer, and Henry S. Foote. The most prominent delegates in attendance were Governor Brandon, John A. Quitman, and Stephen Duncan. Occupations reported by the delegates included twenty-four lawyers, sixteen planters, and eight physicians. About one-half of the convention membership (twenty-four) had experience in the legislature, but only five of them had served in the 1817 constitutional convention.

The convention elected P. Rutilius R. Pray of Hancock County as president and organized five major committees. The Bill of Rights Committee was chaired by Nathan G. Howard of Rankin County, the Executive Department Committee by Cicero Jefferson of Jefferson County, the Judicial Department Committee by John A. Quitman of Adams County, the Legislative Department Committee by Governor Brandon of Wilkinson County, and the General Provisions Committee by John F. Trotter of Lowndes County.

The Constitution

Although the convention retained the basic structure of the 1817 constitution, it made a number of fundamental alterations in the operation of state government.

General Provisions   Some of the significant changes in the constitution's general provisions included the following:

- The right of adult white males to participate directly in state and local government was significantly expanded: there would be no property ownership requirements for voting or holding office; the suffrage qualification of paying taxes or serving in the state militia was eliminated; and although voters still would have to reside in the state at least one year, their minimum residence in voting districts was shortened from six to four months.

- All officials except U.S. senators would be elected by direct, popular vote. All state officers would be elected for a term of two years except judges, U.S. senators, state senators, and the attorney-general. No official would be elected for life or for tenures "during good behavior."

- The state capital would remain at Jackson until 1850, when the legislature would determine the permanent location.

- The process of amending the constitution was simplified somewhat. Instead of requiring new conventions to make changes, the legislature was authorized to propose amendments by a two-thirds vote and submit such proposals to the voters for approval by a simple majority.

- The sections protecting the institution of slavery remained unchanged, with the proviso, however, that the importation of slaves into the state as merchandise for sale would be prohibited after May 1, 1833.

- The legislature was authorized to pass laws to prevent dueling and to exclude from public office persons who engaged in duels after 1832.

- The section excluding "ministers of the Gospel" from the offices of governor, lieutenant governor, and membership in the legislature was deleted, while the other provision regarding religion remained unchanged.

- A new provision required a two-thirds majority vote of the legislature to approve expenditures for internal improvements—one of the few victories of the conservative delegates.

- Another new provision, of which conservatives approved, required that any borrowing on the state's credit would have to be authorized by two-thirds majority votes in two successive legislatures.

The Legislature   The new constitution contained the following changes regarding the legislature:
- The house of representatives and the senate would be designated as the *Legislature* rather than the *General Assembly*.

- State elections would occur in November rather than in August, and the legislature would have biennial rather than annual sessions.

- The minimum age for representatives was lowered from 22 to 21 years, but the residency requirements were left unchanged. The property-holding requirements were deleted.

- Representatives' terms were extended from one to two years. The number of representatives, determined by required regular reapportionments based on census reports, had to be at least thirty-six but not more than one hundred.

- The minimum age for senators was raised from 26 to 30 years, but the residency requirements remained unchanged. The property-holding requirements were deleted.

- Senators' terms were lengthened from three to four years, with one-half of the senate elected every two years. The size of the senate had to be at least one-fourth but not more than one-third of the number of representatives.

The Executive   The new constitution contained the following changes regarding the executive branch:

- Except for the removal of property requirements, the qualifications for the governorship remained the same. The governor could still succeed himself but could not serve more than four years in any six-year period.
- The office of lieutenant governor was abolished; if the governor could not complete his term, the order of succession would be first the president of the senate and then the speaker of the house of representatives.
- The governor's power to pardon now would require consent of the senate.
- Other executive officers appointed by the legislature, including secretary of state, auditor, and treasurer, would be elected for two-year terms.

The Judiciary   Changes regarding the judicial branch were the most controversial. The committee presented two opposing reports. Against the objections of Chairman Quitman, the convention decided on the popular election of all judges for specified terms. The delegates' final vote on the constitution reflected the strong disagreement on this issue. Indeed, ten delegates who voted against approving the new constitution were all opponents of judicial elections; five hailed from the Piney Woods counties, the other five from the western Mississippi River counties. The other important changes in the judiciary included the following:

- No judge would serve for life or on "good behavior," but instead for definite terms.
- The *Supreme Court* was renamed the *High Court of Errors and Appeals* and would be composed of three judges who would serve six-year terms. Each judge would be elected in one of the three supreme court districts that the legislature would establish, and their elections alternated so that one judge would be elected every two years.
- The legislature was authorized to create circuit court districts and additional chancery court districts. The circuit court judges would be elected within their districts for terms of four years. The chancellor would be elected statewide for a term of six years.
- In each county a probate court judge would be elected for a term of two years.
- The only eligibility requirement for judges was age, except the probate court judges for whom no minimum age was specified. The high court judges and the chancellor had to be at least 30 years of age, and the circuit court judges at least 26 years old.
- The attorney general would be elected statewide to a four-year term, and district attorneys would be elected in their respective districts; the legislature was directed to prescribe their terms.

Assessment   Mississippi's Constitution of 1832 has been hailed as the most democratic constitution in the South during the era of Jacksonian democracy—a period when most states were making constitutional reforms. Such a characterization, however, must be qualified by the document's stalwart maintenance of the institution of slavery. The new "democratic" provisions did not apply to nearly one-half of the state's population—more than 66,000 enslaved persons. For whites, however, the new constitution did provide opportunities for greater political participation, important examples of which include the less-complicated amending procedure, the extension of suffrage, the imposition of term limits, the elimination of property-owning requirements for all officeholders, and the popular election of all judges. The latter provision, which, as mentioned, created so much controversy among the convention delegates, may have been the most radical, as Mississippi was the only state in the period to adopt this practice.

CONCLUSION

Within the first fifteen years of its history as a state, Mississippi experienced major changes. The vast interior lands were taken from the Choctaws and Chickasaws who were virtually removed from the state. The population increased rapidly in the northern and eastern regions where new counties were organized. The opening of these lands along with the improvements in transportation and the growth of the cotton market produced a sharp rise in the number of black slaves. These developments altered the state socially and economically and forced political reform and government restructuring as reflected in the Constitution of 1832.

Except for the president and the secretary of the convention, the delegates did not sign their completed work. Even though it appeared that a majority of the state's voters favored the democratic character of the new constitution, the convention did not require a popular vote for its approval. Without delay, the new constitutional order was launched: elections were held in December 1832 for the next legislature, which assembled in January 1833, and elections for other state and county officials were scheduled for May 1833.

SELECTED SOURCES

Bentley, Marvin, "The State Bank of Mississippi: Monopoly Bank on the Frontier (1809–1830)," *Journal of Mississippi History* 40 (November 1978): 297–318.

Carson, James Taylor, *Searching for the Bright Path: The Mississippi Choctaws from Prehistory to Removal* (Lincoln: University of Nebraska Press, 1999).

Constitution and Form of Government for the State of Mississippi, 1817.

The Constitutions of Mississippi as Originally Adopted (University, Miss.: Bureau of Governmental Research, 1982).

Drake, Wilbourne Magruder, "The Framing of Mississippi's First Constitution," *Journal of Mississippi History* 29 (November 1967): 301–327.

Fortune, Porter L., Jr., "The Formative Period," in Richard Aubrey McLemore, ed., *A History of Mississippi,* 2 vols. (Hattiesburg: University & College Press of Mississippi, 1973), 1: 251–283.

Haynes, Robert V., "The Road to Statehood," in Richard Aubrey McLemore, ed., *A History of Mississippi,* 2 vols. (Hattiesburg: University & College Press of Mississippi, 1973), 1: 242–250.

Kidwell, Cara Sue, *Choctaws and Missionaries in Mississippi, 1818–1918* (Norman: University of Oklahoma Press, 1995).

O'Brien, Greg, *Choctaws in a Revolutionary Age, 1750–1830* (Lincoln: University of Nebraska Press, 2002).

Rowland, Dunbar, *History of Mississippi: The Heart of the South,* 4 vols. (Chicago-Jackson: The S. J. Clarke Publishing Company, 1925, vol. 1). This source provides extensive biographical information for the leading delegates in the constitutional conventions.

Weems, Robert C., "Mississippi's First Banking System," *Journal of Mississippi History* 29 (November 1967): 386–408.

CHAPTER EIGHT

Antebellum Politics

Political parties in the United States had their beginnings in the 1790s. The first parties were the Federalists, led originally by Alexander Hamilton, and the Republicans, supporters of Thomas Jefferson. During Mississippi's territorial stage, the Jeffersonian Republicans virtually controlled the national government (except the Supreme Court) under the leadership of Presidents Jefferson (1801–09) and James Madison (1809–17). The Federalist party began to lose its appeal during the War of 1812, and following the Hartford Convention of 1814, it no longer competed with the Jeffersonian Republicans on the national level.

At the time of Mississippi's admission into the Union, therefore, the Jeffersonian Republican party was dominant. Its control was not seriously challenged during the administrations of James Monroe (1817–25) and John Quincy Adams (1825–29). Thus, during the territorial period as well as the formative years of statehood, the Jeffersonian Republican party became deeply entrenched in Mississippi politics.

Beginning with the presidential election of 1824, however, divisions began to develop within the party nationally. President Adams and Secretary of State Henry Clay were recognized as leaders of the "National Republicans," while Andrew Jackson, the most popular candidate in 1824, became the leader of the "Democratic Republicans." Most Mississippi voters favored Jackson in each of his three presidential campaigns from 1824 through 1832. In this era of rapid state expansion the ideals of "Jacksonian Democracy" were widely accepted, as demonstrated in the Constitution of 1832.

During Jackson's first term, 1829–33, new political party alignments emerged, and new labels were adopted. The "Democratic Republicans" became the Democrats, and their opponents became the Whigs. Although most Mississippians remained loyal to Jackson and considered themselves Democrats, many others who had supported the National Republicans, including leading merchants, bankers, and planters, now had reason to join the Whig party. During the antebellum decades, therefore, a strong two-party system persisted in Mississippi: Democrat and Whig candidates competed actively for offices at every level.

TRANSITIONS FOLLOWING THE CONSTITUTION OF 1832

Before beginning its biennial sessions in 1834, as provided by the new constitution, the legislature met in January 1833. Some of its actions were intended to facilitate the transition from the old to the new constitutional structure of state government. It scheduled the 1833 state elections for May instead of the regular time in November. Because the new constitution abolished the office of lieutenant governor, the senate elected a president, Charles Lynch, a Whig, who would become the successor to the governor in case of a vacancy. Lynch had been an unsuccessful candidate for governor in 1831.

In late February 1833 the legislature appropriated $95,000 for the construction of a new state house, and $10,000 to build a residence for the governor. Both buildings would not be occupied for several years—the capitol in January 1839 and the governor's home in January 1842. The costs of construction greatly exceeded the original appropriations, rising to about $400,000 for the capitol and to about $50,000 for the governor's home plus $4,000 appropriated in 1842 for furnishings.

In the May 1833 election Governor Scott barely lost in his bid for reelection to Jacksonian Democrat Hiram G. Runnels. One month later, in June, "lame duck" Governor Scott died of cholera, necessitating that the senate president, Charles Lynch, assume the office of governor until November 1833, when the legislature could meet in extraordinary session. At that time Lynch resumed his senate seat, and Governor-elect Runnels was inaugurated, although he was not constitutionally scheduled to take office until January 1834. This early inauguration would create an irregularity at the end of his two-year term.

THE NULLIFICATION CONTROVERSY

A major states' rights dispute that affected Mississippi politics was the nullification movement in South Carolina. That state's 1832 resolution to nullify the federal tariff acts of 1828 and 1832 was condemned by President Jackson, who threatened with the support of Congress to enforce the tariff through the use of military force if necessary. In 1832 the South Carolina legislature, controlled by the so-called "Nullies," called for a state convention to consider the tariff issue. The convention declared that the tariffs were null and void and that South Carolina would secede from the Union should the United States government attempt to enforce the tariffs. President Jackson issued a proclamation against nullification and mobilized the U.S. Army and Navy. Although Senator Henry Clay managed to secure the passage of a compromise tariff act in 1833, some Mississippi Democrats decided to support the nullification principle of state sovereignty and oppose the position of their party leader, President Jackson.

Now this "Nullifier" faction joined with the Whigs to form an unusual political alliance. Except for their mutual dislike of Jackson, albeit for different reasons, they agreed on few other issues. Although Senator Poindexter split with Jackson on this and other policies, Mississippi's acting governor, Charles Lynch, advised the legislature to take no nullification action. During the 1830s the Whig-Nullifier combination was often able to challenge successfully the Jacksonian Democrats in statewide political contests.

GOVERNOR HIRAM G. RUNNELS, NOVEMBER, 1833–NOVEMBER, 1835

Governor Runnels called a special session of the legislature for January 1835, because the body needed to choose a U.S. Senator. Poindexter's term would expire in March 1835, and the Congress would assemble in December, prior to the next

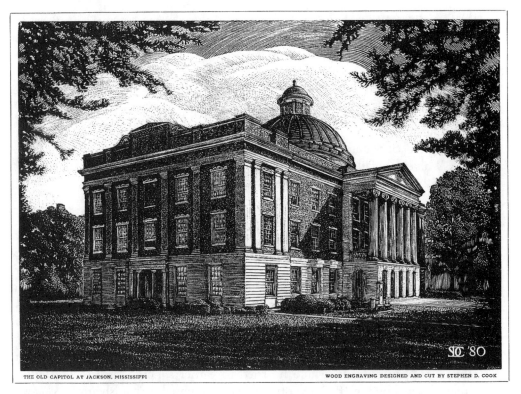

THE OLD CAPITOL AT JACKSON, MISSISSIPPI   WOOD ENGRAVING DESIGNED AND CUT BY STEPHEN D. COOK

The Old Capitol. Wood engraving designed and cut by Stephen D. Cook. Collection of the Old Capitol Museum, Mississippi Department of Archives and History.

regular session of the legislature in January 1836. The ensuing fight between the Whig-Nullifier faction, which favored Poindexter's reelection, and the Democrats, who supported Robert J. Walker, was a classic example of Mississippi's partisan politics in the antebellum era. The contest pitted a powerful, anti-Jackson incumbent U.S. senator against an outspoken pro-Jackson planter-lawyer. By blocking action in the boisterous special session, the Whigs prevented the election of Walker, causing a vacancy in one of Mississippi's Senate seats until a newly elected legislature could act to fill it. The Whig-Nullifiers won clearer victories in the elections of David Dickson to the U.S. House of Representatives, a disputable majority in the legislature, and Charles Lynch to the governor's office.

THE EXTRAORDINARY INTERIM OF GOVERNOR JOHN A. QUITMAN

Because of the early inauguration in 1833, Governor Runnels's two-year term expired in November 1835 instead of January 1836. The result was a rather strange irregularity in the orderly succession of the executive department. Governor-elect Lynch, who had acted as governor following Governor Scott's death in 1833, was not scheduled to take office until January 1836. The office of lieutenant governor had been abolished, and the president of the senate had died. Who would serve as governor from November until January?

The secretary of state called the senate into session to elect a president who would act as governor during the interim. That body selected John A. Quitman, a leader of the Nullifiers. His message to the legislature in its regular biennial session of January 1836 was an ambitious state paper that attacked the anti-slavery propaganda and anti-slavery legislation in Northern states. Quitman's fiery defense of the institution of slavery and each state's sovereign authority over it prompted some historians to label him the father of secession in Mississippi.

GOVERNOR CHARLES LYNCH, JANUARY 1836–JANUARY 1838

Although the Whigs elected Congressman Dickson and Governor Lynch, the Democrats in the 1836 legislature finally managed to capture Poindexter's vacant seat in the U.S. Senate. In a hotly contested election Jacksonian Democrat Robert J. Walker prevailed. Only after five ballots did Walker receive the required majority by the narrowest margin—forty-four out of eighty-four votes.

Support for Texas

One event on which all parties could agree in 1836 was support for the Texans' struggle for independence from Mexico. Mississippians had played an early role in the story. Dr. James Long, who had settled in Mississippi following his service as a medical officer with Andrew Jackson during the New Orleans campaign, led a small expedition from Natchez to east Texas in June 1819. Aiming to resist Spanish authorities and secure an area for settlement by U.S. citizens, Long and his armed force occupied the areas of Nacogdoches and Galveston and declared an independent republic. Soon thereafter, Long returned to Mississippi then moved to New Orleans, where he tried to garner support for a second effort, which he launched in 1820. Eventually overtaken by the Spanish army, Long was taken to Mexico and executed. These filibustering[1] campaigns coincided with the outbreak of Mexico's successful revolution against Spain (1821), and they represented the beginnings of American migration into Texas, which culminated in the Texas Revolution against a newly independent Mexico.

Mississippians' support for the 1836 Texas Revolution that established "the Lone Star Republic" of Texas was expressed in several ways. Led by John A. Quitman and a brother of Samuel Houston, small companies of volunteers organized but did not arrive in Texas in time to join the decisive battles, although individual Mississippians were actively involved in them. Quitman would later distinguish himself in the War with Mexico and become engaged in questionable filibustering campaigns of his own. Demonstrating support for the Texans, several groups in Mississippi contributed money to help defray the rebels' military expenses and the costs of organizing the new government. Senator Walker's resolution favoring United States recognition of Texas as an independent republic was adopted by the U.S. Senate early in 1837.

Political Party Competition

While there appeared to be consensus between the parties on the Texas question, on other issues the political partisanship continued. In the 1836 presidential election, Mississippi's popular vote split evenly between Democrats and Whigs, but its electoral votes went to Jackson's successor. Vice President Martin Van

---

1 The term *filibuster* has two different usages. In the present context it refers to persons such as James Long—military adventurers who, without legal authority, try to commandeer land either for personal gain or to bring it under the control of their home governments. The other meaning is a politician who employs obstruction tactics to try to prevent the passage of legislation.

Buren, a Democrat, won 9,979 votes, while Hugh L. White, a Whig from Tennessee, received 9,688 votes.

The political landscape remained unsettled as the state's population continued to expand, and new counties were formed in the Chickasaw lands. The Democratic party made significant gains in 1837, when ten of its candidates in north Mississippi won elections to become new members of the state house of representatives. But in spite of such Democratic party successes, supported further by Samuel J. Gholson's victory over John A. Quitman for the U.S. House of Representatives, the Whig party persisted. In a series of fiercely contested and officially challenged congressional elections, Whigs Seargent S. Prentiss and Thomas J. Word unseated the Democratic incumbents in 1838.

GOVERNOR ALEXANDER G. McNUTT, JANUARY 1838–JANUARY 1842

In the gubernatorial election of 1837, Democrat Alexander G. McNutt defeated Whigs Jacob B. Morgan and John A. Grimball. It was during McNutt's first administration that the state government finally occupied the new capitol. The legislature first met there in January 1839, although the final completion of the building took another year. After his reelection in 1839, McNutt was the first governor inaugurated in the capitol. In that election the Democrats used the banking controversies to help Governor McNutt defeat the Whig candidate, Edward Turner. Democrats also recaptured the two congressional seats, sending Albert G. Brown and Jacob Thompson to the U.S. House of Representatives in 1839.

But these Democratic victories did not yet signal the end of the Whigs. In 1839 the Whigs were strong enough in the legislature to elect John Henderson as a U.S. Senator. And the following year Mississippi voters favored Whig presidential candidate William Henry Harrison over President Martin Van Buren by a margin of 19,518 to 16,976 votes. It was, however, the last Whig victory in Mississippi for a presidential candidate.

Expanding Population, Slavery, and Sectionalism

The census of 1840 reported the state's total population at 375,651, including 179,074 whites and 196,577 persons of color. During the 1830s, therefore, Mississippi witnessed a remarkable increase of 175 percent overall, with whites gaining by more than 100,000 persons (a 154 percent gain) and blacks by more than 130,000 (a 197 percent gain). Now, for the first time, enslaved blacks outnumbered whites, composing about 52 percent of the total population—the gap would continue to widen in the coming decades.

With this rapid growth of population in the newly organized Choctaw and Chickasaw counties, the state's north-south sectional rivalry in-

Governor Alexander G. McNutt. Courtesy Mississippi Department of Archives and History.

tensified. This sectionalism, however, involved more than geographic differences: it was related to the pattern of political alignments within the state. The new counties usually elected Democrats, while the Whigs were stronger in the older counties in the south and southwest. The competition between the Democratic north and the Whig south had already been demonstrated in the abortion of the 1835 special legislative session following the addition of the Choctaw counties. Two years later there had been a similar but unsuccessful attempt led by Seargent S. Prentiss when the Chickasaw county representatives entered the legislature. In 1841 the legislature decided on a north-south sectional vote of 58 to 57 that the newly proposed University of Mississippi would be located in Oxford instead of Mississippi City on the Gulf Coast. (The university was chartered in 1844 and opened in 1848.)

The Union Bank Bonds Controversy

During McNutt's administrations a banking controversy arose that would have economic and political implications in Mississippi for many years. Supported by Democrats and opposed by Whigs, President Jackson's successful attack on the national bank followed by his attempt to curb runaway inflation had resulted in the Panic of 1837. Jackson's Specie Circular of 1836, which ordered the U.S. Treasury Department to accept only gold and silver as payment for public land, caused growing numbers of people across the nation to exchange their paper notes for specie. As the demand mounted, many banks failed, leaving individuals and businesses holding deflated and virtually worthless paper money. Construction companies had to suspend operations, land speculators lost fortunes, and unemployment soared.

In an attempt to cope with the crisis in Mississippi, the legislature in 1838 chartered the Union Bank. As required by the constitution, two successive legislatures approved the bill establishing the bank, with a capital stock of $15 million. Because the sale of Union Bank stock shares was slow, the legislature determined to "prime the pump" by enacting a Supplementary Act in 1838, which was passed in a single vote in the same session of the legislature. This act authorized the state to issue $5 million in bonds and to use the revenue to purchase bank stock. The state was obligated to redeem the bonds' principal plus interest at a 5 percent annual rate. Governor McNutt approved the legislation, and former Governor Runnels was elected president of the Union Bank.

But instead of helping to solve the state's financial problems, this banking legislation only added to them. Beginning in November 1838, the proceeds from the bond sale were invested in Union Bank stock, enabling the bank to make loans to its customers.[2] But when this activity did not appear to improve economic conditions immediately, debtors in Mississippi blamed banking institutions in general and the Union Bank in particular for their continuing distress.

Beginning with the 1839 election, the Democrats became identified with this "anti-bank" sentiment and used it to reelect Governor McNutt. Although he had approved the Union Bank legislation during his first administration, McNutt be-

2 The bonds were sold to the Philadelphia, Pennsylvania, bank of Nicholas Biddle, former president of the Bank of the United States.

gan to attack the bank and questioned the legality of the bond sales. In 1840, with the support of the legislature, the governor announced that the Union Bank charter was forfeited. In the following year he attempted to have the bonds repudiated, but the legislature would not agree. McNutt argued that the Supplementary Act of 1838, which had authorized the bond issue, was unconstitutional because it had not been passed in two successive sessions of the legislature. He further claimed that the bonds had been sold below par, which was a violation of the law.

In the state elections of 1841 the Democrats and Whigs took sides on the banking controversy. Following McNutt's lead, the Democrats held that the bonds were illegally issued, did not constitute a legal obligation, and should not be paid. The Whigs disagreed, claiming that the debt was a "legal" obligation underwritten by "valid" bonds. They recommended instituting a direct (poll) tax as the means for payment.

By this time the composition of the Whig party was changing. The old Nullifier faction had gradually disintegrated, and most of these former Whig allies were now in the Democratic party. The bond controversy, however, produced a new coalition between the Whigs and the "Bond-Payer Democrats." Disagreeing with the "regular" or "anti-bond" Democrats, the Bond-Payers advocated the redemption of the bonds, even though there were valid questions about the legality of the bond issue. To them the question of legality was less important than the moral obligation, because, they argued, the state had accepted the money and had turned it over to the bank.

GOVERNOR TILGHMAN M. TUCKER, JANUARY 1842–JANUARY 1844

The Union Bank bonds question, therefore, remained the principal campaign issue in the next two state political campaigns. In 1841 the anti-bond Democrats prevailed against the Whigs and their allies, the "Bond-Payer Democrats." Tilghman M. Tucker defeated the Whig candidate, Judge David O. Shattuck, by a rather close margin, and the Democrats also won majorities in both houses of the legislature. Tucker, like his predecessor, favored repudiating the bonds, while his Whig opponents campaigned for payment.

Being the first governor to occupy the recently completed governor's mansion on Capitol Street, Tucker inherited a financial situation an observer described as "most embarrassing and distressing." To make matters worse for the state's credit rating, however, the governor promptly recommended and the legislature acted in February 1842 to repudiate officially the state's obligation to redeem the Union Bank bonds. The vote along party lines was 16 to 10 in the senate and 54 to 37 in the house. With such an anti-bond (or anti-bank) majority in the legislature, repudiation seemed to be the order of the day. And although there was no question about the legality of other bonds issued for the Planters' Bank, the legislature failed to appropriate funds for their payment as well. The state never paid the holders of the Union Bank or Planters' Bank bonds.[3] Defaulting on these debts had mixed results for Mississippians. Most folks had little sympathy for the

3 In 1990 law suits were filed in federal court by descendants of families that purchased the bonds, demanding their redemption plus accumulated interest! Needless to say, perhaps, they were unsuccessful. The present-day Mississippi Constitution (adopted in 1890) explicitly prohibits the bonds' redemption. See *Constitution of the State of Mississippi*, 1890, Section 258.

The governor's mansion on Capitol Street. Courtesy Westley F. Busbee, Jr.

wealthy, out-of-state bondholders and thought not paying them would only save the state money. What they did not seem to understand, of course, was that repudiation would have long-lasting negative effects on their standard of living. It seriously impaired the state's fiscal reputation, and for many decades thereafter investors identified Mississippi with too much risk.

GOVERNOR ALBERT G. BROWN, JANUARY 1844–1847

These actions did not end the bond controversy, which continued to be an economic and political issue in the 1840s. It continued to divide the Democrats who refused to nominate Governor Tucker for reelection in 1843 and chose instead Albert G. Brown.[4] The anti-bond Democrats won the election as Brown defeated the Whig candidate, G. T. Clayton, and former U.S. Senator Thomas Hickman Williams, a "Bond-Paying Democrat."[5]

4 Brown had one of the most impressive political careers in Mississippi's antebellum era. He served in the state house of representatives from 1836 to 1839 and presided as speaker of the house. After one term in the U.S. House of Representatives (1839–41), he served as circuit court judge until 1844, when he became governor. Before his second term as governor expired, he was again elected to the U.S. House and served three more terms. In 1845 he became U.S. senator and continued in that office until Mississippi seceded from the Union in January 1861.
5 Not to be confused with former Senator Thomas Hill Williams who died in 1840, Thomas Hickman Williams (1801–51) served only a few months in the Senate and then became a leader in the founding of the University of Mississippi, serving as its secretary and treasurer and gaining recognition as the "Father of the State University."

National Issues

It was during Brown's administration that national events began to influence politics as much as state economic controversies. In the presidential election of 1844, Democrat James K. Polk, whose party favored the annexation of Texas and Oregon, defeated Whig Henry Clay by a decisive margin of 25,126 to 19,206 votes in Mississippi. During the campaign, leaders like Brown, Walker, Quitman, and newcomers Jefferson Davis and Henry S. Foote joined together to support Polk and the Democratic party platform's Texas plank. The Whigs' support for Clay was led by Congressman Prentiss, but he could not overcome Clay's equivocation on the question of admitting Texas to the Union. Still, the Whigs carried some of the southwestern counties, where politics were dominated by the conservative, slaveholding planters.

Following the Democratic party's presidential victory, Governor Brown gained reelection in 1845 by a landslide. Winning a greater margin than any previous gubernatorial candidate, he received two times the number of his opponents' combined votes. During Brown's second administration a major national event that many Mississippians enthusiastically supported was the War with Mexico, which began as a result of the United States annexation of Texas in late February 1845.

State Politics

In state politics the legislature elected Henry S. Foote and Jefferson Davis to the U.S. Senate. With the support of Brown and Congressman Jacob Thompson, Foote won over former Governor McNutt and John Quitman. Foote and Davis had campaigned together for Polk in 1844, but in the Senate their friendship turned to open hatred, personally and politically.

In 1846 Mississippi's congressional representatives, the number of whom had been increased to four because of the state's rapid population growth, were elected in separate districts for the first time. This change provided only one district in the southern region, which was now outnumbered by the central and northern areas, and served to intensify the north-south sectionalism already extant in Mississippi. Another accommodation of the state's growth was the reapportionent of the legislature, which increased in size to include ninety-seven representatives and thirty-two senators.

The Question of Education

In state affairs Governor Brown is now best known for his efforts to establish more schools in Mississippi. Perhaps the most notable event during his first administration occurred in 1844 when the legislature chartered the University of Mississippi, which began its first academic session four years later. Brown also fulfilled his reelection campaign promise to support a program of public edu-

Governor Albert G. Brown. Courtesy Mississippi Department of Archives and History.

cation. Acting on his recommendation, the legislature passed an act in 1846 to establish a system of "common schools" in Mississippi. The law, which had bipartisan support, authorized the county boards of police to levy special taxes for the support of education. Such tax levies, however, had to be approved by a majority of the "heads of families" residing in each township. Because of popular opposition to additional taxation, Brown's plan for public education failed. Another reform effort proved unsuccessful when the legislature defeated a measure for the establishment of a "lunatic asylum" in Jackson.

Unfortunately, leading Mississippians evidently were more interested in national events—the War with Mexico and the subsequent crusade to protect the institution of slavery and expand it into the newly acquired western states and territories—than they were in making the sacrifices required to initiate a system of public education in their own state.

The Slavery Question

In fact, beginning in the mid-1840s, politics in Mississippi and other southern states would be virtually dominated by the national debate on whether slavery could be excluded from territories that would be acquired from Mexico after the war. For the first time in almost a decade, banking was no longer a major political issue. By this time no state banks were open for business, and no new banks were chartered by the state during the antebellum period. Mississippi residents had to rely on commission merchants and brokers as well as banks chartered in other states.

An outspoken defender of slavery, Joseph W. Matthews, ran as the Democratic nominee for governor in 1847. A. B. Bradford was the candidate of the Whig party, which by now had the reputation for favoring banks and internal improvements and for being moderate if not compromising on the question of slavery in the West. The results indicated clearly the priorities of Mississippians: Matthews was elected by a two-to-one margin.

SELECTED SOURCES

Biographical Directory of the United States Congress, 1774 to Present (Washington, D.C.: Government Printing Office, 2003, http://bioguide.congress.gov).

Biographical Directory of the United States Congress, 1774: Bicentennial Edition (Washington, D.C.: United States Government Printing Office, 1989).

Bridgeforth, Lucie Robertson, "Mississippi's Response to Nullification, 1833," Journal of Mississippi History 45 (February 1983): 1–22.

Coleman, James P., "Two Irascible Antebellum Senators: George Poindexter and Henry S. Foote," Journal of Mississippi History 46 (February 1984): 17–27.

Gonzales, John Edmond, "Flush Times, Depression, War, and Compromise," in Richard Aubrey McLemore, ed., A History of Mississippi, 2 vols. (Hattiesburg: University & College Press of Mississippi, 1973), 1: 284–309.

Historical Statistics of the States of the United States: Two Centuries of the Census, 1790–1990, comp. Donald B. Dodd (Westport, Conn.: Greenwood Press, 1993), Population.

Jordan, Daniel P., "Mississippi's Antebellum Congressmen: A Collective Biography," *Journal of Mississippi History* 38 (May 1976): 157–182.

Lucas, Philip M., "To Carry Out Great Fundamental Principles: The Antebellum Southern Political Culture," *Journal of Mississippi History* 52 (February 1990): 1–22.

Moore, John Hebron, "Local and State Governments of Antebellum Mississippi," *Journal of Mississippi History* 44 (May 1982): 104–135.

Rowland, Dunbar, *History of Mississippi: The Heart of the South*, 4 vols. (Chicago-Jackson: The S. J. Clarke Publishing Company, 1925), 1: 574–650.

CHAPTER NINE

Antebellum Life

"FLUSH TIMES"

Life in antebellum Mississippi changed rapidly in some ways and very little, if at all, in others. A number of interrelated factors contributed to the state's growth in the early 1830s, a period sometimes labeled "flush times" because of the somewhat precipitous, if partly artificial, economic expansion followed by sudden financial troubles in the Panic of 1837. The most important catalysts were land availability, population growth, cotton production, transportation improvements, and monetary resources that appeared reliable but were in fact tenuous.

The Availability of Farmland

As described in the previous chapter, vast tracks of land were opened for settlement as a result of the cessions of land by the Choctaw and Chickasaw nations. Acreage became available to farmers at low prices on easy credit terms. Facilitating the business of land sales, speculators garnered large profits, some of which were invested in various emerging enterprises within the state.

Throughout the antebellum period almost every family arriving in Mississippi settled in a rural area, and urban places experienced virtually no population increases through the 1830s. In 1840 only 3,612 persons, less than 1 percent of the total population, were described as urban inhabitants, while agricultural workers constituted more than 37 percent of all inhabitants. Even after the nominal increases during the following two decades, when the urban population climbed to 20,689 persons, the state's population was still 97.4 percent rural.

Population Growth

Attracted by the availability of relatively inexpensive farmland, great numbers of white farmers along with their black slaves entered the state. In the 1820s the population increased by 81 percent, rising to 136,621 persons, and based on this growth the state's membership in the U.S. House of Representatives was increased to two representatives. The population rose to 375,651 during the 1830s, an increase of 175 percent, and again the number of congressional representatives was doubled. Although the population growth rate slowed somewhat in the 1840s, the 1850 census reported 606,526 persons, an increase of more than 60 percent. The state now elected five representatives to the House, a number that would remain constant until after the Civil War. In 1860 the population was 791,305, an increase of 30 percent during the previous decade.

TABLE 9.1 Farm Sizes in 1860

ACRES	NUMBER OF FARMS	PERCENT
<10	563	1.5
10–19	2,516	6.8
20–49	10,967	29.6
50–99	9,204	24.9
100–499	11,408	30.8
500–999	1,868	5.1
1000>	481	1.3
TOTAL	37,007	100.0

SOURCE: *University of Virginia Geospatial and Statistical Data Center, United States Historical Census Data Browser (fisher.lib.virginia.edu/census).*

Slave Population

Throughout the antebellum decades the rate of growth for blacks exceeded that for whites. In 1820 33,272 black persons lived in Mississippi, about 44 percent of the total population, and all but about 500 of them were slaves. During the 1820s the total number of blacks increased by almost 100 percent, reaching a total of 66,178, while the free black population remained constant. The greatest increase in the slave population occurred during the 1830s, when their number rose by almost 200 percent, resulting in a total of 196,577 persons, 52 percent of the state's total population.

In the last two antebellum decades there was a steady increase in the slave population. In the 1840s the number of blacks increased by about 58 percent, reaching 310,808, and during the final antebellum decade their rate of growth was about 40 percent. At the beginning of the Civil War, therefore, the total number of blacks was 437,404, including less than 800 free blacks and representing about 55 percent of the total population. The rise of the slave population during these decades was due in part to natural reproduction, but another important reason was Mississippi planters' continuing purchases in the vigorous albeit temporarily outlawed slave trade, which was fueled by the planters' dreams of wealth and power.

Cotton

The most powerful motivation for buying slaves was the landowners' need for laborers who could be used to produce cotton, a crop that promised the greatest cash profits but one that required great amounts of cheap labor to grow and harvest. Most white Mississippians accepted a colonial-type economic system. Rejecting agricultural diversification, they sold their farm crops to outside markets and purchased manufactured commodities from Northern and foreign producers. Prior to the emergence of cotton as the chief crop in the first decade of the nineteenth century, farmers had attempted to grow a variety of crops. Tobacco had been the principal cash crop around Natchez in the 1780s, but when the demand for Mississippi tobacco declined during the 1790s, planters turned to indigo without much success. By 1807 cotton had become the chief crop of the Natchez region.

Picking cotton. Courtesy Mississippi Department of Archives and History.

Although there was already a market for cotton, its production was not profitable because the tedious process of removing seeds from fiber by hand cost three to four times as much as the costs of planting and harvesting the crop. Soon after the introduction of the cotton gin began to solve this problem in the 1790s, a better variety of cotton, one known as Mexican cotton, was introduced into Mississippi. According to legend, Walter Burling, an agent for General James Wilkinson, had smuggled this type of cottonseed into Natchez hidden in Mexican dolls. Whatever its origin, large planters like Rush Nutt, a physician, improved this new strain of cotton to produce an even finer version called "Petit Gulf." These developments soon produced an enormous demand for cotton—and for more slaves to work for a growing number of planters.

Transportation

The development of the state's interior lands, however, depended on the development of various means of transportation. Indian paths, which also were traveled by the earliest settlers, became the first roads. The best-known such trail was the aforementioned Natchez Trace, which linked Natchez with settlements in northeast Mississippi and in Tennessee. During the Territorial era the Chickasaws allowed the federal government to use the trace as a post road and agreed to treat travelers through their territory in a friendly manner, but sojourners on the trace were often victims of highwaymen like the notorious gang led by Samuel Mason.

An extension of the Natchez Trace, a road known as Gaines' Trace, connected Cotton Gin Port (present-day Amory) on the Tombigbee River to Col-

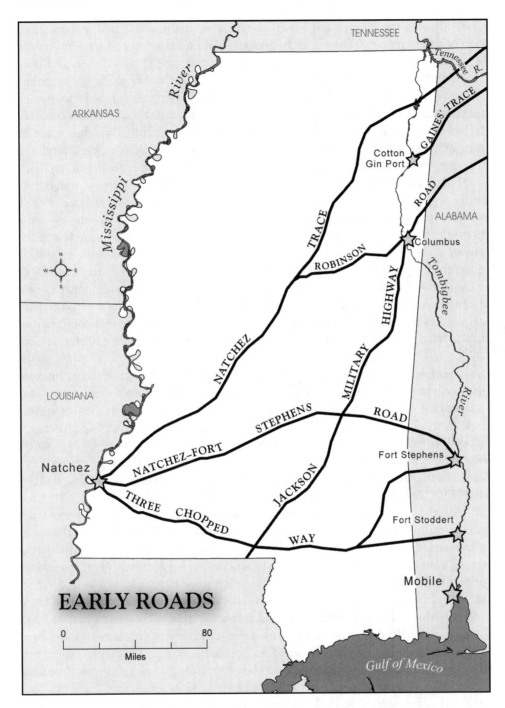

EARLY ROADS

0 ———————— 80
Miles

bert's Ferry (present-day Muscle Shoals, Alabama) on the Tennessee River. An-other early road was the "Three Chopped Way," so-called because it was originally marked in 1807 with three notches carved on trees along the way. It extended from Milledgeville, Georgia, to Fort Stoddert (in present-day Alabama) and then westward to Natchez. Parallel to this road, the Natchez–Fort Stephens Road was completed in 1811 as the first wagon road to connect two settlements within the Mississippi Territory.

Following the War of 1812 the federal government authorized the construction of a military road, known as the Jackson Military Highway, so that in times of war troops could be moved rapidly through the territory. The road extended from Columbia, Tennessee, southwestward through Muscle Shoals and diagonally across central Mississippi and into Louisiana. In 1820 Robinson Road was opened for travel and would serve for many years as the only direct route from Columbus to Jackson. It connected the Jackson Military Highway and the Natchez Trace by way of present-day Louisville in Winston County and Doak's Stand and the Choctaw Agency in present-day Madison County. (See map: Early Roads, p. 103.)

For the most part, these early roads were no more than narrow, rough, dirt trails or paths, and virtually no care was given to their maintenance. While wealthy planters often traveled in their own carriages, most people used the horse-drawn stagecoaches that ran between the scattered towns in the state. Heavy rains and flooding could quickly turn these muddy roads into impassable quagmires, and in the absence of bridges, travelers had to find ferries or fords to cross rivers and creeks. Travel was exceedingly slow, difficult, and dangerous; for example, in the late antebellum era a trip from Jackson to Oxford could require about forty hours. Moreover, the conveyance of farm equipment and commodities to and from remote, interior areas was so cumbersome as to be prohibitive in time and costs.

The fastest and safest mode of transportation was still by river boats, including keelboats, but until the introduction of steamboats, passenger travel by water was limited. In 1812 a revolution in transportation occurred when the first steamboat in the Mississippi Territory, the *New Orleans*, began transporting passengers as well as freight from Natchez to New Orleans. After the War of 1812 a new boat, the *Enterprise*, also began to make regular trips, and by 1817 Henry Shreve had constructed a special steam-powered river boat, a broad vessel with a shallow draft that could navigate interior rivers and their branches.

Another revolution in transportation occurred in the 1830s when more than twenty railroad companies were chartered in Mississippi. While many of these enterprises failed to overcome the difficult and expensive task of constructing tracks, a number of short lines operated successfully. All of the early railroads were primarily designed for short hauls of cotton within the state and to help conduct local banking transactions, even though some of them, like the Mobile and Ohio and the Mississippi and Tennessee, had interstate plans. The state's first railroad company, the West Feliciana, a twenty-seven-mile line connecting Woodville in Wilkinson County with St. Francisville, Louisiana, on the Mississippi River, was the first railroad to cross the state boundary line and the first to use what became the standard track gauge throughout the United States—four feet, eight and one half inches between rails. Built almost entirely by slave labor, these early rail lines transported wood-burning locomotives capable of towing only a few cars, yet they represented a major potential means for hauling heavy agricultural products from interior farms to markets on rivers.

Finances

To pay the costs of railroad construction and maintenance and to buy land, slaves, and farm equipment, most Mississippians had to borrow money. Except

Port Gibson Bank, Port Gibson, Miss., Erected 1840

Port Gibson Bank Building, 1840. Courtesy Mississippi Department of Archives and History.

during "flush times" in the 1830s, when banking institutions became their principal financial sources, farmers depended on commission merchants or "factors." Usually a northern man residing in New Orleans, the factor advanced money to planters who pledged their future crops as collateral and contracted to pay the factor for other expensive but essential services, such as storing, selling, and transporting the crop, as well as arranging purchases of manufactured goods from northern and European sources.

Until 1833 there were only three banks in Mississippi—two state banks and a branch of the national bank in Natchez. Competing with the state banks, a branch of the United States Bank established at Natchez in 1831 provided the most credit for Mississippians during "flush times," loaning $3.7 million by 1833. After President Andrew Jackson vetoed legislation rechartering the national bank in 1832 and then withdrew government funds from it the next year, the federal treasury began to make deposits in "pet banks," so called because they were chosen allegedly as rewards for political support—a practice of the Jacksonian "spoils system." One million dollars in federal funds were deposited in each of the two state banks, the Planters' Bank and the newly chartered Agricultural Bank. Another state bank, the Union Bank, was chartered in 1838; however, this institution soon failed, and the state legislature, as mentioned, repudiated the bonds that had been issued to buy stock in the bank.

In the meantime, many private banks were chartered, beginning a period of "wild cat banking." The number of such banks increased from five to twenty-four, and loans in paper notes flowed freely. By the time President Jackson attempted to restore financial order in the Specie Circular of 1836, which required gold and silver coin rather than paper currency for public land payments, some $7 million worth of paper money circulating in Mississippi was at least ten times greater in face value than specie capital available. This wild inflation finally caused the collapse of "flush times," as thousands of small farmers, suddenly unable to exchange worthless notes for coin, lost their property and left the state. In many instances creditors arriving to collect at farmhouses found only crude notes marked "GTT" (Gone to Texas). But farmers were not the only victims of the Panic of 1837. Most banks had to suspend specie payments and forfeit their charters by 1840. Except for two institutions—one in Yazoo City and another in Holly Springs—every private bank quickly became insolvent, forfeited its charter, and shuttered its doors. The days of banking in Mississippi were over for many decades to come.

THE SOCIAL STRUCTURE: WHITES

Poor Whites

Regardless of whether economic conditions were good or bad, farming continued as the basic way of life in antebellum Mississippi, and agricultural interests permeated the entire culture. In 1860 a large number of poor whites lived and worked on small farms of a few acres or made their living from working land they did not own. Inhabiting backwoods regions of inferior farmland, like the Piney Woods and the central and northeastern hills, these people cultivated just enough food to survive and engaged in such occasional chores as lumbering, herding hogs and cows, hunting, and fishing. But the absence of wealth may not have been the sole criterion for this class, which was often described by other whites and even blacks as "white trash" and which was later stereotyped as lazy and dangerous—people like William Faulkner's fictional Snopes family.

Yeoman Farmers

The delineation between poor whites and the middle or yeoman class was not always clear, particularly in a frontier society characterized by masses of families without noticeable wealth. By 1860 less than half of all white families had risen to the level of affording to own even one slave. An important indication of the yeoman rank, however, was its stable, land-owning, agricultural way of life. This group encompassed persons who owned about twenty to one hundred acres they worked without slaves, as well as a few larger farmers who were slaveholders. Composing the majority of white families in the state, yeomen held varying social and political interests. Out of economic and social aspirations, many of them occasionally identified with the planters' interests, but the smaller farmers usually supported evangelical churches, the Jacksonian Democrats, and later the secessionists. The upper yeomen, some of whom owned more than five slaves and as many as several hundred acres of land, often took more conservative positions, in tight alignment with the planter classes.

Planters

At the top of the white social structure were the planters, large farmers who held more than twenty able-bodied slaves. The large majority of this class formed a middling group, wealthy planters who owned fifty or fewer slaves and sometimes held political interests closer to those of the upper yeomanry than to those of the large planters. Reigning above small planters and all other classes, the elite plant-

TABLE 9.2 Slaveholders in 1860

NUMBER OF SLAVES	NUMBER OF SLAVEHOLDERS	PERCENT OF ALL SLAVEHOLDERS
All Slaveholders		
1–5	14,498	46.9%
6–9	5,061	16.4
10–19	5,489	17.7
20–29	2,322	7.5
30–39	1,143	3.7
40–49	755	2.4
50–69	814	2.6
70–99	545	1.8
100–199	279	0.90
200–999	37	0.12
TOTAL	30,943	100
Non "Planter" Slaveholders		
1–5	14,498	47%
6–9	5,061	16
10–19	5,489	18
TOTAL	25,048	81
All "Planters"		
20–29	2,322	7.5%
30–39	1,143	3.7
40–49	755	2.4
50–69	814	2.6
70–99	545	1.8
100–199	279	0.90
200–299	37	0.12
1000>	0	0
TOTAL	5,895	19
Small "Planters"		
20–29	2,322	7.5%
30–39	1,143	3.7
40–49	755	2.4
TOTAL	4,220	13.6
Elite "Planters"		
50–69	814	2.6%
70–99	545	1.8
100–199	279	.9
200–299	37	0.12
1,000>	0	0
TOTAL	1,675	5.4

SOURCE: *University of Virginia Geospatial and Statistical Data Center, United States Historical Census Data Browser (fisher.lib.virginia.edu/census).*

ers operated the largest plantations, some of which comprised one thousand or more acres. Composing about 5 percent of all slaveholders, the members of this highest order owned more than fifty slaves, although only nineteen planters owned more than three hundred slaves in 1860. The elite planters were concentrated in the most desirable agricultural regions along the Mississippi River, primarily the Natchez district, while the smaller planters cleared lands in the interior areas.

Though the planter class was small numerically, altogether composing less than 20 percent of all slaveholders and only about 1 percent of all white families in 1860, it dominated the state's political, economic, and social life. With the advantages of wealth and education, planters influenced local elections, controlled county boards of police and typically served as judges, legislators, and governors. Notwithstanding the appearance of democratic processes, other classes usually deferred to the men most empowered by land and slave ownership, particularly in local affairs, in which a strict hierarchical order was accepted.

Claiming physical mastery and personal honor as their most cherished virtues, planters as well as men aspiring to attain that status in society accepted the *code duello*, a set of dueling rules most recently formulated in eighteenth-century Ireland. Even after the proscription of dueling in the Constitution of 1832, prominent men continued the practice, sometimes traveling across state borders or to islands in the Mississippi River in order to "defend their honor."

The list of notable duelists includes Governors Henry S. Foote, Hiram G. Runnels, and Alexander McNutt; Congressmen William M. Gwin, Sergeant S. Prentiss, and William A. Lake (who was killed by Henry C. Chambers, his opponent in the campaign for the Confederate Congress in 1861); supreme court judges Isaac Caldwell and Joshua Childs; newspaper editors, and other well-known persons such as Jim Bowie, who dueled in Natchez with his now-famous "Bowie knife" in 1827. A law enacted in the 1840s declared that a person could be charged with murder if he made dueling arrangements within the state and then caused his antagonist's death in a duel outside Mississippi's jurisdiction. An example of dueling as a part of antebellum society is revealed in a recently discovered manuscript by William Faulkner, "Sons of the South," in which one of the principal characters, antebellum planter Colonel Robert Louis McAlister, dies in a duel with a prominent banker who had won more than seventy-five such contests.

THE SOCIAL STRUCTURE: AFRICAN AMERICANS

Most black persons in antebellum Mississippi were slaves who had arrived from other southern states where their parents and grandparents had been slaves. Because foreign trade in slaves had been prohibited by Congress in 1808, few of them came directly from Africa, although smuggling did occur from time to time. Slaves were brought into Mississippi primarily from regions of Virginia, Maryland, and other Atlantic coast states, where their numbers exceeded the demands for slave labor on old tobacco plantations. In the early nineteenth century many planters migrated to the southwest, taking their slaves with them. Beginning in the 1820s, however, a growing majority of relocated slaves were bought by traders in the Upper South and then taken to the Lower South, where they were resold.

Slave traders marched men, women, and children—often enchained and inadequately clothed—overland in caravans (known as "coffles") down the Natchez Trace into Mississippi or, less often, transported them by ships and river boats to New Orleans, Natchez, or other port cities. The traders sold their human cargo in markets at Natchez (the largest), Vicksburg, Jackson, and most other towns throughout the state. What a seller might expect to get for a slave at auction depended on the sex, age, health, and skill of the person for sale as well as shipping expenses, the going prices for cotton, and other timely considerations. Generally the price a healthy slave commanded at market ranged from an average of $500 in 1830, $800 in 1850, $1,200 in 1860, with men priced slightly higher than women. Advertisements in newspapers routinely announced various types of "Negroes" available for sale at the markets, including fieldhands, mechanics, and house servants skilled in cooking and washing and ironing.

It is difficult to exaggerate the extent of the slaves' ordeal in this experience. To arrive at the most opportune time for brisk sales—late winter and early spring, when planters had cash on hand, and diseases like malaria and yellow fever were less prevalent—traders moved the slaves during the winter season. The mean duration from original purchase to final sale was 106 days, although walking overland from Richmond, Virginia, to Natchez could be accomplished in about seven weeks. The slaves obviously endured considerable physical discomfort in these forced migrations, but these hardships were temporary for people accustomed to similar privations and hard labor. The most profound consequence, one that had lingering effects, was the emotional agony of being uprooted from homes, family members, and friends. Forced separations of spouses and of children from their parents caused scars that would not soon heal. In the 1930s Smith Simmons, a former slave in Mississippi, recalled his childhood experiences for the Works Progress Administration interviewers:

> I never heared anybody say what year I was born. . . . My father Charles and my mother Calline was both from North Carolina. . . . In them days there wasn't no money paid for work. Everybody worked for their owner for their keep. The clothes we had wasn't nothing to brag on. The children wore shirt tails the year round. When the weather was cold, they put one on over the other. The children didn't wear shoes neither winter or summer. Their foots would crack open from the cold if they went outside in bad weather. The grown folks had good shoes cause they had to go outside to work. . . . My white folks . . . didn't have no overseer or driver. . . . Master looked after everything hisself. . . . [He] blowed the horn at daylight for the field hands to get up. . . . At sundown the work stopped. . . . None of the slaves on our place could read and write. None [of] them knowed so much as the A. B. C. There wasn't no body to teach them. Old Miss and Old Master couldn't so much as write their own name. . . . We didn't know much about religion. There wasn't no church to go to, and we never as much as heared about the Bible or Baptizings. . . . It was very seldom a slave ever ran off. My oldest brother tried that once. He was caught by the patrollers and brought back so quick he never tried that no more. My father lived on a different place from us. My master didn't own him.
>
> Quoted in Bradley G. Bond, ed., *Mississippi: A Documentary History* (Jackson: University of Mississippi Press, 2003), 70–72.

PICTURES OF THE SOUTH—NEGRO QUARTERS ON JEFFERSON DAVIS'S PLANTATION.—[SKETCHED BY A. R. WAUD.]

"Negro Quarters" on Jefferson Davis's Plantation. Courtesy Mississippi Department of Archives and History.

Although about two-thirds of all slaveholders owned fewer than ten slaves in 1860, almost two-thirds of all slaves in Mississippi worked on plantations. While most slaves were manual laborers in the fields, some were skilled workers such as blacksmiths, mechanics, or carpenters, while others were household servants. On larger plantations their lives were controlled by an established hierarchy, including the owners, stewards, who acted as administrative agents for the planters with extensive holdings, overseers, who managed the labor force and related operations, and drivers—usually slaves themselves—who directed the routine work of the field gangs.

Historians have long debated the treatment of slaves and the profitability of slave labor. Scholars in the late twentieth century led by historians like Kenneth M. Stampp disputed the optimistic interpretations by Southern historians like Ulrich B. Phillips and others. Historian Eugene D. Genovese has argued that slaves were primarily "cultural" rather than economic capital for slaveowners and that the institution actually retarded the overall economic development of the South. Slave labor, according to this view, was inefficient and stunted industry. The slave-master relationship was mainly one of paternalism complicated by race issues, resulting in the paradox of simultaneous kindness and cruelty. Robert William Fogel, Stanley L. Engerman, and other historians reject this interpretation and portray slaveholders as businessmen who used slaves more for economic than for cultural reasons. Planters' paternalistic expressions of affection merely indicated their appreciation for slaves' productivity. In spite of their political and social conservatism, planters were keen capitalist who exploited slave labor primarily for profit.

And in spite of evidence that many masters showed humane concern for slaves, providing them with the essentials—lodging, clothing, food, and some medical care—the fact remains that the entire system was based on whites' belief that blacks were inherently inferior to them and must remain subordinate.

Viewed essentially as chattel that had to be controlled for the benefit of the owner, slaves were subjected to varying degrees of abuse in violent as well as subtle forms.

Slave Laws

With the increasing number of slaves, the growing demand for cotton, and the abolitionist movement gaining momentum in the Northern states, whites in Mississippi went on the defensive, which resulted in more numerous instances of severe corporal punishment and forced slave family separations. An even clearer reflection of whites' growing need to feel completely in control of their slaves and all black people was the changes in the state's slave laws, which became increasingly restrictive during the antebellum decades. While slaves charged with capital offenses were still subject to the same laws as white persons, they were hardly treated as equals by the authorities. They were not allowed to testify in a trial involving a white person, and they could not serve on juries. Slaves could not leave their owner's property without permission, and it was a high felony for any person to incite or aid slaves to run away or rebel. Slaves now were prohibited from undertaking private enterprises or any outside jobs or occupations, entering into contracts, owning property, possessing weapons or ammunition, marrying, or receiving an education. Activities such as preaching and meeting in groups were denied to slaves unless they had proper approval of whites and careful supervision. Whites who violated slave laws, for example, by teaching slaves to read and write, could be fined and imprisoned. Slaves who disobeyed their masters, physically assaulted whites, or tried to run away were punished severely by the injured white person or the civil authorities. Such punishments included whipping, branding, imprisonment, and even death. In the late 1850s the High Court of Errors and Appeals opined that because of slaves' intermediate status between unthinking animals and white people in the natural order, state laws were intended to perpetuate the institution of slavery.

During the early decades of the nineteenth century, many whites who questioned the morality of the institution and feared slave insurrections favored laws prohibiting the slave trade. Pursuant to the Constitution of 1832, the legislature did indeed outlaw the importation of slaves into Mississippi for the purpose of sale or trade. But as economic and political changes occurred, the earlier apologetic, "necessary evil" sentiment was replaced by the attitude that slavery was a "positive good," and a brisk trade in slaves continued despite the prohibition, which was formally repealed by 1846.

Free Blacks

Due to the strict state laws impeding slave emancipations and free black immigration, there were never more than about 1,400 free blacks in the state during the antebellum period. On the presumption that all "persons of color" were slaves, laws required free blacks to obtain and frequently renew at considerable expense certificates of registration from local courts. Because of restrictive laws as well as social ostracism, many free blacks moved out of the state. While most of them went to Northern states, more than five hundred free blacks emigrated to Africa under the auspices of the state Colonization Society, which was formed on the model of the national society. Their colony in present-day Liberia was named Greenville for the town of that name in Mississippi.

In spite of laws either prohibiting or obstructing them from entering the state, possessing weapons, attending schools, conducting most business activities, practicing most crafts, and socializing with whites, some free blacks had successful careers as businesspeople and farmers. The best-known example was William Johnson of Natchez (1809–51), a slave-owning black man who also owned several barbershops and engaged in a variety of other businesses. Like Johnson, most free blacks were mulattoes—persons born to slave women and white men, usually their owners—who were sometimes given their freedom and some property in their fathers' wills. Because they were required by law to work in urban places, the majority of free blacks resided in counties with larger towns, like Adams and Warren counties.

Before state restrictions were tightened in the decades before the Civil War, as many as forty-five free blacks in Mississippi owned slaves. William Johnson owned at least three slaves and as many as three thousand acres of land. He was murdered in a land dispute, but his murderer, another free black man, was acquitted, primarily because state law prohibited the black witnesses to the crime from testifying in court.

EDUCATION

White leaders not only erected legal barriers against educating slaves and free blacks, but they failed to provide a workable school system for the white population. Public officials' expressions of concern about the absence of educational opportunities for white children resulted only in sporadic, piecemeal action. Ex-

Jefferson College. Courtesy Westley F. Busbee, Jr.

cept for private tutors, church and home schools, and a few private academies, the only significant educational institution opened prior to statehood was Jefferson College, a private school for wealthy white males in the town of Washington near Natchez.

Chartered in 1802, Jefferson College's opening was delayed for nine years due to inadequate financial support and disputes over its location. Financial exigencies and a tempestuous relationship with the state legislature continued to plague the institution throughout the antebellum period, and wartime hardships finally forced its closure in 1863. Jefferson College offered preparatory studies as well as college degrees, with courses ranging from elementary subjects to those in the classical languages and military science.

The first college chartered by the state legislature was the Elizabeth Female Academy in 1818. It was named for Miss Elizabeth Roach, who designated gifts of land and buildings to the Mississippi Conference of the Methodist Episcopal Church for a school of higher education for white women. The academy, which was located one-half mile from Washington and continued operations until 1843, was one of the first colleges in the United States at which women could earn advanced degrees. In 1858 Mississippi Methodists established another women's school, Whitworth College, in Brookhaven as the successor to the Elizabeth Female Academy.

Among the more than two hundred private and church-sponsored academies that existed during the antebellum period, Franklin Academy at Columbus and Hampstead Academy at Mount Salus (present-day Clinton) had the longest tenures. Franklin Academy, chartered in 1821 as the state's first "free school," continues as a public elementary school. Hampstead Academy, which was established in 1826, was the foundation for present-day Mississippi College, the state's oldest existing institution of higher learning. Although initially intended for white males, the college offered a "female department" until 1850 and had the distinction of being the first private institution in the United States to grant collegiate degrees to women in 1831. After experiencing private, community, state, and Presbyterian leadership, the college was transferred to the Mississippi Baptist Convention in 1850.

Another church-supported institution, Oakland College in Claiborne County, was founded by the Presbyterians in 1831; after closing during the Civil War its campus became the setting for Alcorn College during the Reconstruction period. A number of other colleges had temporary tenures before the Civil War, including, for example, Sharon College for women in Madison County and Centenary College for men in Rankin County, both supported by the Methodists. After having suspended operations during the Civil War, the former institution was renamed Madison College and continued until 1874. In 1845 Centenary was moved to Jackson, Louisiana, and later to its present-day location in Shreveport.

Except for Jefferson College and Mississippi College, which received only limited and erratic governmental assistance, the only state-supported educational institution was the University of Mississippi at Oxford, which was established by the legislature in 1844 for white males.

Notwithstanding the considerable number of academies and colleges, only a tiny minority of whites were able to obtain an education beyond the rudimentary skills. In 1850 about 6,600 students, just 5 percent of all white persons aged five to nineteen years, were enrolled in the state's 171 academies and other private schools. These institutions were staffed by approximately three hundred teachers, an average of less than two per school and an overall student-teacher ratio of twenty-two to one. At the college level only 862 students were enrolled in eleven colleges staffed by a total of forty-five professors.

Efforts to create a comprehensive system of public schools for the masses of white children were unsuccessful due to the unwillingness of white landowners to pay additional taxes as well as the mismanagement and sometimes fraudulent handling of educational funds by state and county officials. Although federal laws designated for public education the income derived from the lease of sixteenth-section lands and from the so-called Chickasaw lieu land, these funds were diverted to other interests, invested unwisely, and generally proved to be ineffective in supporting schools. The state's "Literary Fund" was woefully inadequate, and the legislature's numerous education laws—about 125 measures passed between 1825 and 1860—provided little if any state revenue, gave full responsibility and control to county school boards, and required a majority of county property owners to approve taxes to finance their respective county's schools.

In spite of the number of public schools reported, there were in fact few educational opportunities for the vast majority of young persons in antebellum Mississippi. The state outlawed teaching blacks to read and write and failed to provide adequate schools for whites. In the decade prior to the Civil War, the number of public schools rose from 782 to 1,116, and enrollments increased from almost 19,000 to 31,000 pupils. Although these numbers represent 16 percent of school-age whites in 1850 and 22 percent in 1860, enrollment did not necessarily indicate regular attendance. There was neither curriculum uniformity, teacher certification standards, school accreditation criteria, nor equality in the distribution of school funds. Great disparities existed among counties, as only a few communities supported public education, while most were either unwilling to, unable to, or both. The result was short sessions averaging three months, mostly one-teacher schools, unqualified teachers, inadequate facilities, and few if any textbooks. Most pupils were fortunate to receive instruction in the basic skills of reading, writing, and arithmetic, and few were introduced to the classical curriculum available to the wealthy minority whose families could afford to send them to the private academies. The great majority of white and all black children would have to wait until the 1870s for formal educational opportunities.

RELIGION

Most antebellum Mississippians were not only unschooled, but they were also unchurched. In spite of the "bible belt" reputation the state would later earn, the majority of early-nineteenth-century folks were not active in churches. In 1817 only one of every twenty white adults was a church member, but on the eve of the Civil War the ratio had risen dramatically, to one-third, as a result of the Great Revival movement. Increasing numbers of blacks and whites were attracted by evangelistic revivals and camp meetings that became widespread in the 1830s. Although only partial statistics are available for blacks' church affiliations, there is sufficient evidence to conclude that substantial numbers of slaves were involved in religious activities, forming their own independent—sometimes hidden or "invisible"—churches, attending whites' worship services, or receiving "religious instruction" from their owners.

The evangelical denominations attracted the greatest number of adherents, black and white. By the end of the antebellum era, Methodists and Baptists claimed about three-fourths of all church members, followed by Presbyterians and other groups including Episcopalians, Roman Catholics, Disciples of Christ, Lutherans, and Jews. All but the latter three religious bodies began their organizations during the territorial period or earlier.

Due to its broad appeal through circuit-riding preachers and popular camp meetings, the Methodist Church was the largest denomination in the antebellum era. Its Mississippi Conference reported 1,846 white and 389 African American members in the year of statehood. Membership rose rapidly in the following decades, reaching totals of more than 60,000 members, including 11,000 African Americans, in 606 churches by 1860.

Located primarily in small rural communities, independent Baptist churches formed local associations and resisted statewide organization until the formation of the state convention in 1836. The number of Baptists grew dramatically thereafter, rising from about 5,000 members in 107 churches to more than 41,000 members in 529 churches on the eve of the Civil War. With its congregational form of church structure, less formal worship services, and rejection of educational requirements for preachers, this evangelical denomination attracted more blacks than did the other church bodies. By 1860 slaves may have composed as much as one-third of the total Baptist membership in the state.

Presbyterians developed churches as increasing numbers of Scots-Irish immigrants arrived in the territory. Under the leadership of missionaries and pastors like James Swayze, Joseph Bullen, and James Smylie, the Mississippi Presbytery was formed in 1816. By 1835, when the Synod of Mississippi was established, there were twenty-four Presbyterian churches with average memberships of about thirty-five persons. The Presbyterian Church, which grew steadily but at a slower rate than the other evangelical groups, reported 148 congregations and about 7,100 members in 1860. Reasons for this denomination's failure to match the growth rate of the Methodists and Baptists included its rigid seminary requirements for ministers, strict Calvinist doctrine, and appeal primarily to well-educated residents.

Another Presbyterian body, the Cumberland Church, which arrived in the state in the 1830s, modified the mainline church's teachings, emphasizing revivalism and ordaining circuit-riding preachers who were not required to have seminary degrees. Appealing to a different set of people, the Cumberland Presbyterians established sixty churches in northern counties by 1860. Two other small protestant denominations that entered the state late in the period were the Disciples of Christ (the Christian Church), which organized twenty-four churches by 1860, and the Lutherans, who had only nine churches. Other than the African-based religions still practiced by some of the slaves, the only notable non-Christian group was the Jews, who organized their first congregations in Vicksburg, Natchez, Jackson, and other large towns beginning in the 1840s.

The oldest established churches in Mississippi were the Roman Catholics and the Episcopalians, who had small albeit influential adherents in the antebellum period. Originally introduced to the region in the sixteenth century by the Spaniards, the Catholic Church virtually disappeared in Mississippi following Spain's withdrawal in 1798. Not until the 1840s did the newly created Diocese of Natchez receive its first bishop, and by 1860 there were only seventeen Catholic churches, located primarily in the larger towns. Dating from the British Period, the Episcopal Church was banished by the Spaniards in the 1790s, and not until the mid-1820s did it recover sufficiently to organize its first Diocese in the state. Attracting wealthy planters, merchants, and professionals, most of the twenty-five Episcopal congregations in 1860 were in the Natchez area and along the Gulf Coast.

The most dramatic antebellum religious development was the rise of revivals and camp meetings. Evangelicals rebelled against the exclusive society of wealthy aristocrats and their alleged promotion of worldliness, sometimes characterized as the "hospitality" culture. Revival preachers delivered animated sermons warning that the fires of hell were waiting for people who partook of the elite's lifestyle, which sometimes included gambling, consuming alcoholic drink, dancing, attending the theater, reading secular materials, and wearing fancy attire and jewelry. Such proclamations were particularly intense at annual camp meetings conducted by Methodists and Baptists. Sometimes continuing as long as one week, these gatherings attracted hundreds of people—both black and white, slaves and slave owners—who spent their time listening to preachers, testifying, praying, undergoing emotional conversions, and generally socializing. It was not unusual for worshipers "in the spirit" to exhibit vivid emotional, even physical, expressions such as shouting, weeping, running, jumping or dancing, and falling to the ground as if struck unconscious.

Another significant aspect of this phenomenon was the emergence of a distinctive African American religious identity that influenced and was influenced by evangelical Christianity. Despite slaveholders' apprehensions, blacks formed independent churches with their own black preachers, a practice that persisted notwithstanding increasingly restrictive state laws. In many evangelical churches blacks and whites worshiped together, although in the last decade before the Civil War white leaders began to require blacks to sit in back pews or galleries or to attend separate services. The latter practice was usually preferred by blacks, as it gave them more independence to incorporate their own traditions, music, and expressions of worship.

Finally, it was the abolition movement and the persisting fear of slave insurrections that produced fundamental changes in the evangelical churches. After struggling for decades to resolve contradictions between biblical principles of Man's equal worth in God's sight with the enslavement of brothers and sisters in Christ, white ministers began to use scripture to defend the institution of slavery. Although there were a few exceptions, most white men of the cloth in the antebellum era ultimately convinced themselves that declarations of their race's supremacy were not only comforting amidst rumors of slave unrest but also theologically justifiable. In some cases reflecting and in others shaping proslavery sentiments in their communities, pastors preached the old doctrine of "slaves obey your masters." And their messages had a powerful influence among white church members: in the mid-1840s the Methodists and Baptists severed relations with their respective Northern denominations and formed Southern organizations. The Presbyterian schism occurred in 1861.

Selected Sources

Barnett, Jim, and H. Clark Burkett, "The Forks of the Road Slave Market at Natchez," *Journal of Mississippi History* 63 (Fall 2001): 169–187.

Berlin, Ira, *Slaves without Masters: The Free Negro in the Antebellum South* (New York: W. W. Norton & Co., Inc., 1974).

Berry, Trey, "A History of Women's Education in Mississippi, 1819–1882," *Journal of Mississippi History* 53 (November 1991): 303–319.

Bond, Bradley G., *Mississippi: A Documentary History* (Jackson: University Press of Mississippi, 2003).

Bridgeforth, Lucie Robertson, "Medicine in Antebellum Mississippi," *Journal of Mississippi History* 46 (May 1984): 82–107.

Davis, Dernoral, "A Contested Presence: Free Blacks in Antebellum Mississippi, 1820–1860," Mississippi History Now, An Online Publication of the Mississippi Historical Society, mshistory.k12.ms.us/features.

Fogel, Robert William, and Stanley L. Engerman, *Time on the Cross: The Economics of American Negro Slavery* (Boston: Brown, Little and Company, 1974).

Galloway, Patricia, ed., *Native, European, and African Cultures in Mississippi, 1500–1800* (Jackson: Mississippi Department of Archives and History, 1991).

Genovese, Eugene D., *Roll, Jordan, Roll: The World the Slaves Made* (New York: Random House, 1974).

Historical Statistics of the States of the United States: Two Centuries of the Census, 1790–1990, comp. Donald B. Dodd (Westport, Conn.: Greenwood Press, 1993), Population.

Hogan, William Ransom, and Edwin Adams Davis, eds., *William Johnson's Natchez: the Ante-Bellum Diary of a Free Negro* (Baton Rouge: Louisiana State University Press, 1951).

———. *The Barber of Natchez; Wherein a Slave Is Freed and Rises to a Very High Standing; Wherein the Former Slave Writes a Two-Thousand-Page Journal About His Town and Himself; Wherein the Free Negro Diarist is Appraised in Terms of His Friends, His Code, and His Community's Reaction to His Wanton Murder* (Baton Rouge: Louisiana State University Press, 1973).

Huffman, Alan, *Mississippi in Africa: The Saga of the Slaves of Prospect Hill Plantation and Their Legacy in Liberia Today* (New York: Gotham Books, 2004).

Lucas, Aubrey K., "Education in Mississippi from Statehood to the Civil War," in Richard Aubrey McLemore, ed., *A History of Mississippi*, 2 vols. (Hattiesburg: University & College Press of Mississippi, 1973), 1: 352–377.

Moore, John Hebron, "Economic Conditions in Mississippi on the Eve of the Civil War," *Journal of Mississippi History* 22 (July 1960): 167–178.

———, "Railroads of Antebellum Mississippi," *Journal of Mississippi History* 41 (February 1979): 53–82.

Olsen, Christopher J., *Political Culture and Secession in Mississippi: Masculinity, Honor, and the Antiparty Tradition, 1830–1860* (New York: Oxford University Press, 2000).

Pillar, James J., "Religious and Cultural Life, 1817–1860," in Richard Aubrey McLemore, ed., *A History of Mississippi*, 2 vols. (Hattiesburg: University & College Press of Mississippi, 1973), 1: 378–419.

Rutledge, Wilmuth S., "Dueling in Antebellum Mississippi," *Journal of Mississippi History* 26 (August 1964): 181–191.

Scarborough, William K., "Heartland of the Cotton Kingdom," in Richard Aubrey McLemore, ed., *A History of Mississippi*, 2 vols. (Hattiesburg: University & College Press of Mississippi, 1973), 1: 310–351.

Sparks, Randy J., "Mississippi's Apostle of Slavery: James Smylie and the Biblical Defense of Slavery," *Journal of Mississippi History* 51 (May 1989): 89–106.

———, *Religion in Mississippi*, Vol. 2, Heritage of Mississippi Series (Jackson: University Press of Mississippi for the Mississippi Historical Society, 2001).

Wright, Donald R., *African Americans in the Early Republic, 1789–1831* (Wheeling, Ill.: Harlan Davidson, Inc., 1993).

CHAPTER TEN

Mounting Sectional Strife

MISSISSIPPI AND THE WAR WITH MEXICO

The cause for the war between the United States and Mexico in 1846 had arisen shortly after Texas declared its independence in 1836. Although the Republic of Texas had gained formal recognition by the United States, Great Britain, and France, Mexico had never accepted the Treaties of Velasco, which Generals Sam Houston and Antonio López de Santa Anna had signed, and it continued to claim the province of Texas as its sovereign territory. Indeed, Mexico threatened war in the event the United States annexed Texas. Thus, when Congress did just that in early 1845, war was virtually unavoidable.

For many years Mississippians had supported the annexation of Texas. Their motivations stemmed from: early efforts to foster American settlements in Mexican Texas, as demonstrated in the Long Expedition of 1819; volunteers who fought alongside the Texans in the revolution in 1836; the desire to have an additional slave state in the Union; the migrations of kinfolk and friends to Texas; and personal investments in the "Lone Star Republic" made during the 1830s.

Based on these strong and longtime interests, Mississippians overwhelmingly approved Congress's declaration of war against Mexico in 1846, and thousands responded to Governor Brown's call for troops. Three Mississippi Regiments participated in the conflict, and hundreds of the volunteers lost their lives in combat or as a result of disease.

In September 1846 at Monterrey, an important fortress town in northeastern Mexico, Colonel Jefferson Davis and an infantry regiment known as the "Mississippi Rifles" led in the fighting under the command of Brigadier General John A. Quitman, who became Mississippi's most famous military leader in the war. Mississippians were also outstanding in General Zachary Taylor's successful assault against Mexican leader Santa Anna at Buena Vista in February 1847. This battle, fought around a small village near Monterrey in northern Mexico, was one of the turning points in the war. Davis, who was wounded at Buena Vista, earned distinction as a military commander.

After the battle of Monterrey, Quitman was transferred to General Winfield Scott's army, which had landed on the Mexican coast at Vera Cruz and was organizing for an advance on Mexico City. When the United States Army occupied the capital city, Quitman was appointed military governor and was later promoted to the rank of Major General by Congress.

The Wilmot Proviso

Early in the war the question of slavery in the territories that likely would be acquired from Mexico was raised in Congress. In August 1846, Representative

David Wilmot of Pennsylvania introduced an amendment to an appropriation bill that would have prohibited slavery in any territories taken from Mexico as a result of the war. Although the so-called Wilmot Proviso never became law, the fiery debates it spawned in Congress—with opponents clearly lining up on a proslavery (North) versus antislavery (South) axis—would have important consequences in Mississippi.

The California Question

By the treaty of Guadalupe Hidalgo, which formally ended the war in February 1848, the United States acquired from Mexico vast territories, including California, and the Rio Grande River was declared the southern border of Texas. (Before the war, Mexico had claimed that the Nueces River, some 150 miles north of the Rio Grande, was its border with Texas.) After the war, the application by California for admission to the United States as a state without slavery (a "free state") caused another round of heated sectional debate throughout the nation. In Mississippi leaders of both parties strongly opposed California statehood, fearing that both houses of Congress would soon be controlled by Northern (antislavery) interests.

GOVERNOR JOSEPH W. MATTHEWS, JANUARY 1848–JANUARY 1850

The War with Mexico was in its final phases when Joseph Matthews was elected governor of Mississippi in 1847, and the ensuing sectional controversies dominated his administration. A farmer from Marshall County in the northern part of the state, Matthews had very little formal education but was an unpretentious and popular person, sometimes referred to as "Joe the Well Digger," apparently a reference to his earlier life in Alabama. His prior political experience was limited to terms in each house of the legislature; he was serving his second senate term when he won the office of governor.

Rebutting the principle of the Wilmot Proviso, Matthews declared in his inaugural address that it was unconstitutional to make the prohibition of slavery a condition for a new state or territory, and that the institution of slavery enjoyed guaranteed protection by the United States Constitution and was a right reserved by the individual states. He furthermore implied that Congress's violation of the Constitution in this matter could mean the secession of Mississippi from the Union. "This is a momentous question; one on which is suspended the existence of this happy confederacy."[1]

Domestic Issues

In the midst of mounting controversies related to the outcome of the War with Mexico, Mississippians also faced several domestic issues. Matthews was the first governor to express the belief that the state should redeem the Planters' Bank bonds. He recommended that revenues generated by land sales, rather than through tax increases, could repay the bondholders as well as fund a program of internal development, which might include river navigation improvements and

1 Quoted in Dunbar Rowland, *History of Mississippi: The Heart of the South*, 4 vols. (Chicago-Jackson: The S. J. Clarke Publishing Company, 1925), 1: 698–699,

railroad building. Although the legislature adopted these proposals, Matthews's optimistic economic predictions fell flat due to crop failures and low cotton prices, along with a string of unusually severe natural disasters including floods and an outbreak of cholera.

Even with the evidence that former Governor Brown's plan for public education had failed, the legislature of 1848 responded weakly by adopting rather makeshift and piecemeal measures for schools in some counties. These actions made no significant progress toward the creation of a uniform, state-supported system of education. In fact, local schools still had to rely on tenuous sources of revenue—special taxes that required approval by county voters and leases of sixteenth-section lands or other designated lands.

The legislature did, however, record a measure of success in the founding of two charitable institutions. In 1848 the lawmakers established an institute for the blind by creating a board of trustees, appropriating funds, and providing property for a building in Jackson. A "lunatic asylum" or "insane hospital" (accepted phrases of the day) was also created that year for the state's indigent mentally ill, who were not at the time being treated humanely. Funds for building materials, contracts for convict labor, and land in Jackson were appropriated for the institution.

Heightened concern for public health emerged early in 1849 when the southwestern region suffered a cholera epidemic, which mostly victimized slaves. Beginning in New Orleans late in 1848, the epidemic spread northward along the Mississippi River by means of steamboats and flatboats, taking victims on plantations in the Natchez area by the spring of 1849. On some plantations hundreds of slaves died, for whites were the first to receive medical attention. Eventually, the disease took as many as three thousand lives in Mississippi.

The Elections of 1848

Such challenging state problems, however, did not eclipse the current national debate about slavery and state rights. With these questions looming on the political horizon, Mississippian voters were almost evenly divided between the two parties in the presidential election of 1848. Democrat Lewis Cass received 26,537 votes, while the Whig candidate, General Zachary Taylor, who won the presidency, got 25,922 votes in Mississippi. In the congressional elections, however, Democrats won all four seats in the House of Representatives.[2]

A Sectional Crisis

The division in presidential politics, however, was not reflected in the state's response to South Carolina Senator John C. Calhoun's appeal for united Southern opposition to a compromise that would allow California to join the Union as a free state. In May 1849, Democrats and Whigs met in Jackson to discuss this proposal. With Governor Matthews and Judge William L. Sharkey (a Whig) presiding, the group issued strong statements against the admittance of California

---

2 The congressmen were incumbents Albert G. Brown, Winfield S. Featherston, and Jacob Thompson; newcomer William McWillie defeated Whig incumbent Patrick W. Tompkins. (See Appendix II.) In the Mississippi legislature the Democrats outnumbered Whigs 20 to 10 in the senate and 62 to 36 in the house.

and the principle of the Wilmot Proviso and called for a statewide convention in October.

Agreeing with Calhoun's advice that Southern states should band together and cooperate in this time of crisis, the October Convention, chaired by Sharkey, nominated delegates to attend a convention of all slave states, which was scheduled to assemble in Nashville, Tennessee, in June 1850. That meeting's purpose was to agree on a Southern strategy for resisting the actions of Congress. Although the Whig leadership was reluctant to agree that the decision should necessarily be secession, that option appealed strongly to many Mississippians, as demonstrated in such publications as the "Chronicles of the Fire-Eaters of the Tribe of Mississippi." Written anonymously (by "Seraiah the Scribe," probably a journalist), this document contained humorous, Old Testament-type expressions that aimed to shape public opinion. Composed of such influential men as John A. Quitman, as well as prominent spokesmen from other Southern states, the so-called fire-eaters fiercely and unreservedly demanded secession as the only means of preserving states' rights and the institution of slavery. Seraiah wrote, for example:

> For behold the day cometh and is even now at hand that ye must rise in your might and your strength and show unto the tribes of the North, even the Yankees and the Free Soilers, that ye are a great and mighty people, and then none can withstand you, yea not even the tribes of the Yankees, the people of all nations, nor the rest of mankind.

For more excerpts see John K. Bettersworth, *Mississippi: A History* (Austin, Texas: The Steck Company, 1959), 222–26.

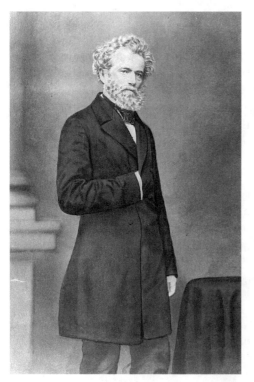

GOVERNOR JOHN A. QUITMAN, JANUARY 1850–FEBRUARY 1851

This explosive sectional crisis dominated the election campaigns of 1849. When Governor Matthews announced his decision not to run for reelection, the Democrats unanimously nominated John A. Quitman, who had gained favorable recognition in Mississippi and throughout the South for his role in the War with Mexico and his position on state sovereignty. A native of New York, he had arrived in Natchez in 1821 to practice law. He was elected to the legislature in 1827 and was a "Nullifier" when, as president of the senate, he succeeded Governor Runnels and served as governor from November 1835 to January 1836. He served as

Governor John A. Quitman. Courtesy Mississippi Department of Archives and History.

chancellor of the state and as judge of the High Court of Errors and Appeals. In 1848 Quitman was seriously considered for the vice-presidential nomination by the Democratic party's national convention, and in his final years he would represent the state in the U.S. House of Representatives.

For their part, the Whigs nominated Luke Lea, supported President Taylor, defended the institution of slavery, but issued amiable statements of confidence that conflicts would be resolved without any states having to resort to secession. In this political environment, Democrats swept the elections of 1849. Quitman was elected governor by a wide margin, and Democrats won majorities in both houses of the legislature.

Secession Proposals

Following Matthews's farewell address and Quitman's inaugural, both of which recommended that Mississippi should consider secession (without actually using the word) if Congress adopted the Wilmot Proviso doctrine and compromised on California, the Democratic majority in the state legislature adopted resolutions opposing antislavery bills in Congress and the admission of California as a free state. The legislators also approved sending a delegation to the Nashville Convention and voted to pay its expenses. In case the state needed to take action as a result of decisions made in Nashville or to defend its sovereignty against unacceptable congressional actions, the legislature appropriated $200,000 and authorized the governor to call a state convention.

The Nashville Convention

It was clear, therefore, that early in 1850 there was excitement about whether Mississippi would participate in a secession movement. In June delegates from Mississippi and eight other Southern states attended the Nashville Convention. Disagreeing with the fire-eaters' secessionist proposals, Judge Sharkey was elected president of the convention. With the moderates of both parties composing the majority, the delegates resolved that slavery must be protected everywhere but that the controversy in the Western territories might be settled by extending the Missouri Compromise line to the Pacific.[3] After the Congress finally passed the Compromise of 1850 in September (admitting California as a free state), a smaller group reconvened the Nashville Convention, denounced the Compromise, and appealed to the South to secede.

Responses to the Compromise of 1850

The responses in Mississippi to the Compromise of 1850 were dramatic, prompting political realignments and a rush toward secession. Led by Senator Foote, many Mississippians, including most Whigs and some Democrats, organized the "Union Party." They preferred to give the Compromise of 1850 a chance to resolve the sectional strife. Foote had been actively involved in formu-

3 Congress had established the Missouri Compromise line at 36° 30' north latitude extending across the Louisiana Territory as part of the legislation admitting Missouri into the Union as a slave state in 1820. The law had prohibited slavery north of the line, except in Missouri. In 1850 Congress did not adopt the Nashville Convention's proposal to extend the line through the recently acquired California territory to the Pacific Ocean.

lating the legislation that admitted California as a free state but also included a so-called "popular sovereignty" provision that allowed voters in the other territories acquired from Mexico to decide the question of slavery for themselves. Another part of the Compromise contained a new and stricter Federal Fugitive Slave Law that authorized federal marshals to capture persons alleged to be runaway slaves and without legal proceedings return them to persons who claimed to be their owners. The Union Party, led by Whigs who wished to maintain the Union through compromise, was denounced by a new "State Rights Party" composed of Democrats who favored secession and had the support of Senator Davis, the state's other congressmen, Governor Quitman, and most of the legislature. In a special session summoned by Quitman late in 1850, the legislature called for a state convention in the fall of the following year to consider secession.

Although it appeared in 1850 that Mississippi would indeed secede from the United States, events in 1851 took a different turn. In February Governor Quitman resigned following his indictment by a federal grand jury for his alleged involvement in the Narcisco Lopez expedition to Cuba in 1850. Quitman had been accused of violating federal laws by supporting the expedition in order to promote slave trading and the annexation of Cuba as a slave state. For the remainder of Quitman's term, two presidents of the senate served as acting governors in succession: John Guion until November, when his senate term expired; then James Whitfield until January 1852.

In the meantime Quitman, who ultimately was acquitted by the federal court in New Orleans, returned home to lead the campaign for the September election of delegates who would favor secession in the upcoming state convention. But he was opposed by Senator Foote, who successfully argued the case of union and compromise. Quitman and Foote went beyond political debate and actually had a fist fight during the campaign. When the Unionists won 57 percent of the votes in the convention election, Quitman withdrew his candidacy for governor, and the states'-rights Democrats nominated Davis.

GOVERNOR HENRY S. FOOTE, JANUARY 1852–JANUARY 1854

The division among Mississippi voters on whether to accept the Compromise of 1850 was illustrated clearly in the 1851 gubernatorial election. In a very close contest Foote defeated Davis by a margin of only 999 votes, and the Unionists (Whigs and Union Democrats) gained control of the state house of representatives. Responding to Governor-elect Foote's recommendations, the state convention in November resolved that most Mississippians preferred compromise within the Union instead of secession and, quite possibly, civil war.

Domestic Affairs

In retrospect it may seem that national events overshadowed state affairs in the 1850s, but in fact there was a temporary lull in sectional tension during Foote's administration. With the hope that the Compromise of 1850 would settle once and for all the apprehension over the extension of slavery in the West, Mississippi looked forward to a decade of economic growth. By now the state's total population had increased to 606,526, including 295,718 whites and 310,808 non-whites. The 1840s, therefore, had witnessed an increase of more than 61 percent for the total population, roughly 65 percent for whites and 58 percent for blacks.

Revival of Sectional Conflict

Events outside the state, however, revived the conflicts that would eventually lead to secession. Among the earliest problems was the Northerners' resistance to the enforcement of the 1850 Fugitive Slave Law. Not only was there open defiance of the law in the North, where abolitionist sentiment ran high, but some Northern state legislatures enacted "Personal Liberty Laws" that, according to Mississippians and other Southerners, made the federal law virtually unenforceable. These laws, declared unconstitutional by the U.S. Supreme Court in 1859, extended the right of habeas corpus and jury trials to persons arrested as fugitive slaves.

In the presidential election of 1852 the Democratic party candidate, Franklin Pierce, known for his pro-Southern sympathies, defeated Whig nominee Winfield Scott, former U.S. Army general and hero of the War with Mexico. In Mississippi the Democrats won smashing victories as Pierce received 26,876 votes to only 17,548 votes for Scott. Former Mississippi Senator Jefferson Davis, who led the campaign for Pierce, was appointed secretary of war, while Democrats in the legislature chose Albert G. Brown to represent the state in the Senate.

GOVERNOR JOHN J. McRAE, JANUARY 1854–NOVEMBER 1857

Although significant numbers of voters in the 1853 elections still appeared to support compromise, the states'-rights Democrats continued to gain ground. Democrat John J. McRae won the gubernatorial contest by a comfortable margin, defeating Frank M. Rogers, the Whig Unionist.

Domestic Developments

In spite of the renewal of sectionalism during his administration, McRae promoted state improvements by obtaining appropriations for various projects, especially the construction of railroads. Before McRae left office, trains were running through Jackson to New Orleans on the Great Northern Railroad and through Meridian to Mobile on the Mobile and Ohio Railroad. Concerned about the status of education, he urged the legislature to appropriate more money for public schools. In 1854 the legislature established an Institute for the Deaf in Jackson. Another important accomplishment of the McRae years was the completion and adoption a new state law code in 1857.

The Ostend Manifesto

On the national scene the political storm continued to brew, which would not only cause a basic change in party alignments but also lead to more serious, even bloody, conflicts between pro- and antislavery factions. In 1854 newspapers published the "secret" Ostend Manifesto, an ultimatum that had been drafted in Belgium by Pierre Soulé of Louisiana and other U.S. diplomats, demanding that Spain sell Cuba to the United States. Mississippians, like most Southerners, strongly favored the acquisition of Cuba, but most Northerners did not and accused the Pierce administration and the South of plotting to go to war with Spain in order to extend slavery and acquire additional slave states.

The Kansas-Nebraska Act

In 1854 Congress organized two additional western territories, Kansas and Nebraska, with the provision that the inhabitants of each territory would determine by popular vote whether to legalize slavery. Most Democrats in Mississippi favored this plan because it provided an opportunity for the formation of slave states north of the Missouri Compromise line. Some southern Democrats and most Whigs, however, opposed the Kansas-Nebraska Act, warning that it would simply lead to more conflicts. The position of the latter group proved to be correct, for civil war soon broke out between the pro- and anti-slavery settlers in Kansas.

Decline of the Whigs

The revival of sectional agitation caused the disintegration of the national Whig party, which struggled to survive by reorganizing and joining with other groups to form the American party, which was also called the "Know-Nothing" party in Mississippi and other states. At the same time in 1854 many Northern Whigs helped to organize the new Republican party, which would oppose the proslavery Lecompton Constitution in Kansas and blame proslavery Southerners in general for the series of deadly conflicts then raging in "Bleeding Kansas." In Mississippi, the political effect of sectional controversies was that Democrats would overwhelm the old Whigs in future elections.

In 1855 Governor McRae was reelected, defeating the "Know-Nothing" candidate, Charles D. Fontaine, a former Democrat. During McRae's second term the situation in Kansas worsened, the further bloodshed deepening the North-South division and producing radical political changes. The national Democratic party now began to divide along sectional lines, with Southerners denouncing John Brown and other prominent abolitionists and demanding admittance of Kansas into the Union under the proslavery Lecompton Constitution.

The Brooks-Sumner Affair

The violence even spilled into the Senate in 1856 after Senator Charles Sumner, a Republican from Massachusetts, insulted an absent colleague, Senator Andrew Pickens Butler of South Carolina, in a speech Sumner made on the floor of the Senate. A few days later a relative of Butler, Representative Preston Brooks, took revenge by physically attacking Sumner as he sat at his desk in the Senate chamber. According to some observers, Mississippi Representative William Barksdale assisted Brooks by holding his coat while the latter proceeded to beat the Massachusetts senator over the head with his cane. Barksdale had been elected as a states'-rights Democrat after the 1850 census results gave the state an additional (fifth) seat in the House.

Elections of 1856

Mississippians again had reason to hope for a resolution of the conflict when Democrat James Buchanan was elected president in 1856, defeating John C. Fremont, the Republican, and Millard Fillmore, the nominee of the Whig remnant, the American party. Buchanan sided with the southern Democrats' position on Kansas and won a large majority of Mississippi votes, 34,457 to 24,191 for Fillmore. Mississippi Whigs could not maintain political unity, and many of them actually supported Buchanan. Moreover, in a significant congressional contest that year Democrat Lucius Quintus Cincinnatus Lamar was elected to the U.S. House of Representatives, defeating Whig James L. Alcorn, who would later serve as a Republican governor during the Reconstruction period.

At the beginning of President Buchanan's administration there were favorable signs for Mississippi and the South. Jacob Thompson of Mississippi became secretary of the interior, and former secretary of war Jefferson Davis reentered the

U.S. Senate. The Supreme Court's ruling in the *Dred Scott* case (1857) seemed to validate the South's interpretation of the Constitution regarding the status of slavery in the West. In that decision the high court ruled that Congress could not ban slavery in the territories. President Buchanan appointed Mississippian Robert J. Walker, former U.S. Senator, as governor of the Kansas territory. Walker, however, soon resigned because he disagreed with the president on the validity of the Lecompton Constitution, which he correctly determined had not received approval by a lawful majority of the voters.

Jefferson Davis. Courtesy Mississippi Department of Archives and History.

GOVERNOR WILLIAM McWILLIE, NOVEMBER 1857–NOVEMBER 1859

In the state election of 1857 (held in October as provided by constitutional amendment in 1856) Democrat William McWillie overwhelmed Edward M. Yerger, the American party candidate. In hindsight, the results of the elections of 1856 and 1857 had indicated the decline and virtual disappearance of the Whigs in Mississippi.

Except for news coverage of the Lincoln-Douglas debates in the 1858 Illinois campaign for the U.S. Senate, sectional discord seemed to have abated during McWillie's first year as governor. In his inaugural address, he stressed the importance of developing the material resources of the state, the urgent need to build levees to protect the fertile bottomlands from flooding, and the building of additional railroads.

Impact of Harper's Ferry

Unfortunately such attention to state development was diverted when the brief quiet in sectional strife was shattered in October 1859 when John Brown, a radical abolitionist who had instigated the bloodshed in Kansas, raided a U.S. arsenal at Harper's Ferry on the Potomac River in western Virginia. While the event was relatively minor and had been quickly suppressed, Mississippi newspapers greatly exaggerated the story, helping to bring simmering fears of an abolitionist/slave insurrection to a boil. Now, disunionists in the state spread rumors of slave revolts, heightening the atmosphere of fear and even panic. Resolving to cooperate with other Southern states to stop prospective abolitionist attacks and slave uprisings, the legislature appropriated $150,000 to equip a state militia, which would be reorganized and prepared for action.

Not surprisingly, in the state elections of 1859 the key issue was, once again, secession. Candidates made campaign promises that in the event a Republican was elected United States president in the following year, they would lead Mississippi out of the Union. In the gubernatorial contest, Democrat John Jones Pettus, a disunionist disciple of John A. Quitman, totally overpowered Harvey W. Walter, the "Opposition" candidate. Finally, after a decade of talk about secession, the circumstances were ripe for Mississippi to leave the Union and, if necessary, fight to defend its own sovereignty.

Governor William McWillie. Courtesy Mississippi Department of Archives and History.

SELECTED SOURCES

Bond, Bradley G., *Mississippi: A Documentary History* (Jackson: University Press of Mississippi, 2003).

Brent, Robert A., "Mississippi and the Mexican War," *Journal of Mississippi History* 31 (August 1969): 202–14.

Broussard, Ray, "Governor John A. Quitman and the Lopez Expeditions of 1851–1852," *Journal of Mississippi History* 28 (May 1966): 103–20.

Gonzales, John Edmond, "Flush Times, Depression, War, and Compromise," in Richard Aubrey McLemore, ed., *A History of Mississippi,* 2 vols. (Hattiesburg: University & College Press of Mississippi, 1973), 1: 299–309.

Historical Statistics of the States of the United States: Two Centuries of the Census, 1790–1990, comp. Donald B. Dodd (Westport, Conn.: Greenwood Press, 1993), Population.

McCardell, John, "John A. Quitman and the Compromise of 1850 in Mississippi," *Journal of Mississippi History* 37 (August 1975): 239–66.

Moore, Glover, "Separation from the Union, 1854–1861," in Richard Aubrey McLemore, ed., *A History of Mississippi,* 2 vols. (Hattiesburg: University & College Press of Mississippi, 1973), 1: 420–446.

Phillipps, Adrienne Cole, "The Mississippi Press's Response to John Brown's Raid," *Journal of Mississippi History* 48 (May 1986): 119–34.

Rowland, Dunbar, *History of Mississippi: the Heart of the South,* 4 vols. (Chicago-Jackson: The S. J. Clarke Publishing Company, 1925), 1: 649–773.

Tyson, Raymond W., "William Barksdale and the Brooks-Sumner Assault," *Journal of Mississippi History* 37 (May 1964): 135–40.

CHAPTER ELEVEN

Secession and Civil War

John Jones Pettus, November 1859–November 1863

The state Democratic Convention of 1859 adopted a resolution favoring immediate secession should a Republican party candidate win the presidential election of 1860. Meanwhile, the Democratic candidate for governor, John J. Pettus, described as "a grim, abrupt," stubborn, tobacco-chewing man, made secession the main issue in the campaign and won the office by a wide margin. Indeed, 77 percent of the voters favored Pettus and his pro-secession position, and two years later (in 1861) after the state had withdrawn from the United States, joined the Confederate States, and entered the war, Pettus won reelection without significant opposition.

At the beginning of the Civil War, Mississippi's total population stood at 791,305, including 353,899 whites and 437,404 black slaves and other persons of color. Even though for the first time in the state's history the rate of population growth had slowed during the 1850s—a decade of increasing sectional strife—the total number of inhabitants had still increased by more than 30 percent. The enslaved black population had experienced a greater rate of growth than the white population—more than 40 percent for slaves to less than 20 percent for whites.

Presidential Election of 1860

Because of the widespread fear of slave insurrection and talk of secession in the wake of John Brown's raid on Harper's Ferry in October 1859, the presidential election of 1860 became the major political event during Pettus's first year as governor. The Democratic national convention assembled in April in Charleston, South Carolina, where the north-south division within the party surfaced as soon as the delegates began to debate the party platform. The Mississippians present favored a proposal by Alabama delegate William L. Yancey (a well-known fire-eater) that the federal government was required to maintain positive protection for the institution of slavery. The platform committee approved Yancey's proposition; the convention majority, however, adopted a different proposal, one that had the backing of Senator Stephen A. Douglas, leader of the party's Northern wing. The Douglas platform attempted to evade the issue by calling for adherence to the Supreme Court's decision in the *Dred Scott* case as well as standing by the popular sovereignty solution for determining the legality of slavery in the new western states and territories. In other words, settlers in each territory would be the proper parties to determine whether slavery should be allowed or prohibited.

In protest to the Douglas position, which fell far short of the guarantees they sought, the Mississippi delegates joined Yancey and other Southern state delegations and walked out of the Charleston convention. When the Democrats reassembled in June in Baltimore, Maryland, the seceding Southern delegates returned but again withdrew to meet separately in Baltimore and later in Richmond, Virginia.

While the Northern Democrats went on to nominate Douglas and Herchel V. Johnson of Georgia to head the presidential ticket, the Southern wing of the party in Richmond nominated John C. Breckinridge of Kentucky for president and Joseph Lane of Oregon for vice president. Their platform took the position that neither the settlers in a given territory nor Congress had the authority under the Constitution of the United States to exclude slavery.

Two other parties nominated candidates for the presidency in 1860. The Republicans nominated Abraham Lincoln and adopted a platform that opposed the extension of slavery but sanctioned the states' authority to control their own institutions. In other words, while they were against the spread of slavery, they acknowledged its legality in the states where it already existed. For their part, the Constitutional Unionist party, a fusion of Whigs who had been called Americans or Know-Nothings in 1856, nominated John Bell of Tennessee and Edward Everett of Massachusetts.

As far as Mississippians were concerned the issue of slavery remained paramount in the election. They believed the Republicans, and even the Northern Democrats to some extent, were determined to undermine the institution. While none of the parties officially declared any intention to abolish slavery, they did substantially disagree over how the Constitution should be interpreted on the question of congressional authority in the West.

Laboring under the anxieties fueled by the Harper's Ferry raid and with the secessionist resolutions still ringing in their ears, Mississippians cast 39,962 votes for Breckinridge, 24,693 for Bell, and only 3,579 for Douglas. Nationally, Lincoln, who received a plurality of the popular votes (40 percent) but a majority of the electoral votes (59 percent), won the election, and the young Republican party made significant gains in the Congress. Now, of course, Mississippi's political leaders moved toward secession.

SECESSION

As soon as the presidential election results were known in Mississippi, Governor Pettus summoned the legislature into extraordinary session for the purpose of ordering the election of delegates to a state convention to consider secession. There was no question about the governor's and most legislators' sentiment on the question. In its regular session earlier that year the legislature had already passed preparatory measures, including Pettus's recommendation to appropriate $150,000 for weapons and ammunition. After calling for the "secession" convention, the legislature voiced support for South Carolina's decision to secede (which had occurred on December 20, 1860) and began preparations for Mississippi's possible exit from the United States.

When the convention met in Jackson on January 7, 1861, it chose William Barry as its president and Lucius Q. C. Lamar as chairman of the committee to draft an ordinance of secession. In the debate on the question, the following

Introduced to the secession convention by a group of white women, the Bonnie Blue flag, a solid blue rectangle with a large white star in its center, was accepted and raised over the capitol as the emblem for the newly established Mississippi Republic. On January 26, 1861, a magnolia image on a white field was added to the Bonnie Blue flag, and this newly formed "Magnolia" flag became the state flag when Mississippi joined the Confederacy on March 27, 1861. Although the Bonnie Blue flag had a brief tenure, it was destined to have long-lasting fame because of the song named for it, written and initially sung by vaudevillian Henry McCarthy in Jackson. It became one of the most popular battle songs of the Confederacy. As late as 2001, the Bonnie Blue flag and the Magnolia flag were both considered as replacements for the current state flag, which dates from 1894 and contains the stars and bars of the Confederacy in its canton corner. Secession symbols courtesy Mississippi Department of Archives and History.

propositions were offered but rejected: (1) oppose secession because private property would be protected more effectively within the Union; (2) postpone action to see what other slave states would do; and (3) postpone action and present the question to the voters in a referendum.

On January 9, 1861, the ordinance of secession was approved by a vote of eighty-four to fifteen and signed by all but one delegate. It provided that the union between the State of Mississippi and the other states was dissolved. The convention also revised the state constitution to form an independent republic, reorganized the military system and provided for defense, and established a postal service. Then it selected delegates to the convention of southern states, which was to convene in Montgomery, Alabama, in February. During the following days Mississippi's senators and representatives withdrew from Congress, recognizing their state's new independent status and hoping that military conflict could be avoided. Lamar had withdrawn in December 1860 to prepare for the secession convention. The other four representatives left on January 12, Senator Brown two days later, and Senator Davis on January 21, after delivering a speech appealing for peace but warning against the use of force by the United States.

After conventions in six other states had also adopted secession ordinances, the Montgomery convention drafted a constitution for the "Confederate States of America" and elected Jefferson Davis as provisional president and Alexander H. Stephens of Georgia as provisional vice president.

THE CIVIL WAR, 1861–65

Mississippians learned that war had begun in April 1861, when Confederate forces commanded by General Pierre G. T. Beauregard fired on Fort Sumter, a United States military outpost in the harbor of Charleston, South Carolina. Following the Union regiment's surrender of the fort, President Lincoln issued a call for 75,000 volunteers to suppress the Southern states' rebellion. Governor Pettus immediately ordered Mississippi volunteers to help defend Virginia and other Confederate states against invasions by the armed forces of the United States.

From the outset of what proved to be the most horrific conflict in the nation's history, the United States was superior to the Confederacy in troops and resources. The former had the advantages of many more industrial factories and munitions makers, a far more extensive network of railroad lines, and a vast merchant marine and navy, with which they soon blockaded the Southern coasts. And while the Confederacy did have many capable and experienced military leaders, many of whom had served with distinction in the United States Army before secession, throughout the war it suffered shortages of essential supplies. Such was certainly the case in Mississippi. Private individuals offered to help the cause by contributing cotton, sugar, gunpowder, weapons, and other provisions. Some railroad companies transported troops and supplies free of charge. But with no ammunition factory or federal arsenal in the state, Mississippi troops went without adequate weaponry. In addition, most soldiers had to furnish not only their own weapons but also uniforms, horses, and other equipment and supplies.

Ship Island and the Gulf Coast

Because President Lincoln declared a naval blockade of the Confederate coastline on April 19, 1861, the first combat in Mississippi took place along the Gulf Coast. Located about ten miles from the coastline at Biloxi, Ship Island had long attracted the federal government's attention as a strategic site for a military base, and the Army Corps of Engineers began the construction of a fort there on the eve of the Civil War. But the workers were civilians, and no Union forces were present to stop a small Confederate garrison from occupying the island in June 1861. The Confederates withstood a brief attack by the U.S.S. *Massachusetts* in July but evacuated the island in September 1861. Three months later Union troops from New England took control of

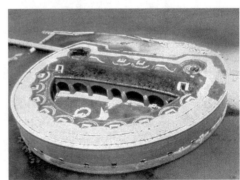

Fort Massachusetts, Ship Island. Courtesy Mississippi Department of Archives and History

Ship Island and completed the construction of Fort Massachusetts. From this base Union army and naval forces then launched raids along the Mississippi coast. On April 3, 1862, one such attack on Biloxi destroyed considerable property. Later a Federal force of 1,200 men attacked a Confederate camp at Pass Christian. It was also from Ship Island that Federal troops and ships began attacks on New Orleans in 1862. Later in the war Ship Island served as the location of a prisoner-of-war camp.

Shiloh and Corinth

While these events occurred in Mississippi's coastal counties to the south, more ominous military developments unfolded in the extreme northern part of the state. The battle at Shiloh on April 6–7, 1862, occurred in Tennessee just across the state border, roughly twenty miles north of Corinth, Mississippi. Shiloh proved to be an early turning point in the Civil War because its outcome opened northern Mississippi to immediate invasion, which led to the United States' most important victory in the western theater, the siege and capture of Vicksburg in the following year.

United States' strategy in the West was to gain control of the Mississippi River, thus dividing the Confederacy vertically and cutting off its western sources of supplies. To accomplish this goal, Union General Ulysses S. Grant's army planned to take control of the northern regions along the river and march southward, while United States Navy Admiral David Farragut's fleet moved northward up from New Orleans.

In February 1862 Grant opened his campaign by capturing two Confederate forts near the Tennessee-Kentucky border, Fort Henry on the Tennessee River and Fort Donelson on the Cumberland River. Grant's forces then moved along the Tennessee River through Tennessee towards the border of Mississippi.

On April 6, 1862, at Pittsburg Landing on the Tennessee River, Grant encountered a Confederate army commanded by General Albert Sidney Johnston. The Confederates, 40,000 strong, had moved up from Corinth and surprised the Federal troops. The two-day battle was fought around Shiloh Church near the banks of the Tennessee River.

On the first day of the engagement the Confederates drove Grant back to the river, but after the death of Johnston, they suspended the offensive. During the night the Union army was reinforced by the arrival of the force under General Don Carlos Buell, and the next day the Federals drove the Confederates, under General Beauregard and Mississippi General Earl Van Dorn, from the battlefield, forcing them to retreat to Corinth. The fighting around Shiloh had left more than 3,400 dead and 16,500 wounded Union and Confederate soldiers, making it the single bloodiest battle ever fought in the Americas to this date; but by the time the Civil War ended three years later, the battle of Shiloh would rank seventh in casualty numbers.

In late May the Confederates fell back southward from Corinth to Tupelo, leaving Union forces in control of the junction of the Mobile and Ohio Railroad and the Memphis and Charleston Railroad at Corinth. Reeling from the reports of the major setback in his home state, President Jefferson Davis, known for his detailed management of Confederate military leadership and strategy, named General Braxton Bragg to replace General Beauregard as commander in Mississippi.

The Vicksburg Campaign, 1862–1863

Following their victories in western Tennessee and northeastern Mississippi in the spring of 1862, Union forces were poised to undertake one of the most important campaigns of the Civil War. The conquest of Vicksburg would accomplish one of President Lincoln's basic strategies—gaining full control of the Mississippi River. Both Lincoln and Davis understood the critical importance of Vicksburg which, positioned on high bluffs at a horseshoe-shaped bend in the river, surrounded by virtually impassable swamps and rough terrain, and fortified with heavy artillery, stood as the strongest Confederate fortress along the Mississippi.

With Vicksburg as their ultimate objective, during the spring of 1862 the Union army captured key points along the Mississippi River in the vicinity of Memphis, including Island Number Ten, and occupied Memphis without much resistance in early June. In the meantime, Admiral Farragut and General Benjamin F. Butler took control of New Orleans and the lower Mississippi River, including Baton Rouge and Natchez in May.

The First Attack on Vicksburg

During the summer of 1862 Farragut made the first Union assault on Vicksburg. Even with reinforcements from Memphis, the Federal gunboats were unable to score substantial hits because of the town's strong defensive position on the high bluffs. In July Confederate ships, such as the ironclad *Arkansas*, inflicted enough damage on the Union fleet to force its withdrawal. The next month Confederate General John C. Breckinridge marched southward from Vicksburg in the hope of recovering key points along the river. While he failed to retake control of Baton Rouge, he succeeded in extending Confederate control from Vicksburg down to Port Hudson, Louisiana. Therefore, the failure of the Union forces' first effort to take Vicksburg left them to devise other tactics.

Grant in North Mississippi

While the United States Navy was shelling the town from the river, there were delays in the Union army's land campaign to approach Vicksburg from northeast Mississippi. After Shiloh, Union General Henry Halleck had come down to Pittsburg Landing and assumed command of the combined armies of Grant, Buell, and Major General John Pope, the latter having recently smashed the Confederate defenders on Island Number Ten near the Kentucky-Tennessee border. Now Halleck directed his primary attention on a mission to capture Chattanooga, Tennessee. In response, Confederate General Bragg moved his Army of the Mississippi up to Chattanooga and then into Kentucky, while General Sterling Price's forces remained in northeastern Mississippi.

In mid-September 1862 Halleck was called to Washington, and Grant resumed command of the Union forces in northern Mississippi. Grant's plan was to make two approaches on Vicksburg: his army would move southward through Holly Springs, Oxford, Grenada, and Jackson and advance on Vicksburg from the

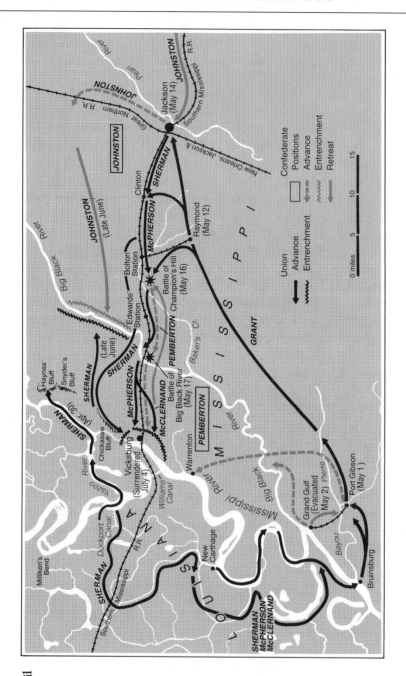

The Vicksburg Campaign, April to July 1863.

A native of Philadelphia, Pennsylvania, John Clifford Pemberton (1814–81) was a graduate of the U.S. Military Academy (West Point) and a veteran of the War with Mexico. Probably due to the influence of his Virginian wife and years of service in the South before the Civil War, he decided to side with the Confederacy. In spite of his preference for administrative rather than combat duties, and notwithstanding controversies that developed during his first command in South Carolina, where suspicions arose that a Northern-born general could not be trusted, Pemberton was given the most difficult Confederate task, the defense of Vicksburg. Although he was accused of treachery after the surrender, in fact Pemberton was outnumbered and outmaneuvered by Grant and was caught between conflicting orders from Davis and Johnston. Still, he managed to extract concessions from a general who was already widely known as "Unconditional Surrender" Grant. Agreeing to surrender on July 4 (for which Southerners would never forgive him), Pemberton got paroles for his soldiers and permission for his officers to retain their weapons, uniforms, and horses. Despite a reduction in rank and a ruined reputation, he continued to serve the Confederacy throughout the remainder of the war.

Nathan Bedford Forrest (1821–77), arguably the most successful Confederate warrior, did not acquire his skills at West Point or any other formal school, for that matter. Born in Bedford County, Tennessee, he moved with his struggling family to Marshall County, Mississippi, where at sixteen years of age he became the sole provider for his widowed mother and his younger siblings. Through hard work and the ingenuity that characterized his later military and business career, Forrest gained success and even wealth. By the time the Civil War began, he owned a cotton plantation and slaves in west Tennessee and had successful business interests in Memphis. He joined a Confederate cavalry company in June 1861 and rose through the ranks from private to lieutenant general by 1865. He and his soldiers finally surrendered along with Lieutenant General Richard Taylor's army in May 1865, the last Confederate troops east of the Mississippi to lay down their arms. Famous for his daring cavalry exploits, par-

ticularly the tactic of the flank attack, Forrest preferred to describe his forces as "mounted foot soldiers," men "who quickly dismounted to fight then fiercely pursued the enemy." He explained his military philosophy in simple terms: "War means fighting, and fighting means killing" and "Get there first with the most men." Although he regained financial prosperity after the war, farming and serving as president of a railroad company in Memphis, Forrest's reputation suffered from his leadership role (Grand Wizard) in the Ku Klux Klan and persisting accusations that he and his troops had massacred black Union soldiers at Fort Pillow on the Mississippi River above Memphis in 1864. Photographs courtesy Mississippi Department of Archives and History.

east, while another force would descend the Mississippi River and attack from the north. He believed that these actions would divide the Confederates and thus weaken their defenses.

By mid-October Grant's forces had defeated the Confederates under Price and Van Dorn. After failing to control Iuka and regain Corinth, the Confederates prepared for Grant's invasion into central Mississippi by placing Van Dorn at Holly Springs and making General John C. Pemberton responsible for the defenses at Jackson and Vicksburg.

Nevertheless, the indefatigable Grant occupied Holly Springs in mid-November, forcing the Confederates to withdraw through Oxford to Grenada. But Grant's progress was halted in mid-December by reports that Confederate General Nathan Bedford Forrest and his cavalrymen were destroying railroad lines in west Tennessee. Then, on December 20, the Union force in Holly Springs was surprised by an attack from General Van Dorn's cavalry. Because this raid destroyed most of Grant's supplies, and Forrest had wrecked the railroad by which more supplies could be brought in, Grant on December 21 began to pull back toward Tennessee. Thus, this first part of Grant's plan to take Vicksburg ended in failure.

The Second Attack on Vicksburg: Sherman on the River

As Grant's army withdrew from Holly Springs, Pemberton ordered troops from Grenada to Vicksburg because of reports that Union forces were being transported by steamboats down the Mississippi from Helena, Arkansas. This activity on the river was the first phase of the second part of Grant's plan in 1862. In late November he ordered General William T. Sherman to take command of the troops raised by General John McClernand and stationed in Memphis and Helena and launch an amphibious assault on Vicksburg from the Yazoo River.

By December 26 when Sherman entered the Yazoo, Pemberton had received reinforcements. The Confederate force of about 9,000 soldiers defended the high bluffs against a Union army about 30,000 strong, attacking from the swamps on the north. The Confederates suffered only about 200 casualties, while the Union forces lost about 2,000 men in this "Chickasaw Bayou" campaign. By January 2, 1863, the Union had failed in this second attack against Vicksburg.

Grant on the River

In January 1863 Grant changed his plans. He moved his army to the Mississippi River and joined forces with Sherman to begin another campaign from Milliken's Bend, a base about twenty miles upriver from Vicksburg. The advantage of this plan was that with Union Admiral David D. Porter's gunboats in control of the river above Vicksburg, Grant could depend on steamboats to supply his army.

For more than two months Grant tried in vain to move his army across the Mississippi and through the swamps, bayous, and dense forests of the Delta to the higher ground around Vicksburg. The Confederates retarded his progress by blocking the channels with fallen trees and debris. When the Union forces tried to dig a canal across a hairpin turn in the river, a sudden rise in the water level destroyed their work and forced Grant to abandon the idea of attacking Vicksburg from the north.

Grant's Southern Campaign

By late March 1863 Grant rejected the options of launching the assault on Vicksburg across the river or returning to Memphis to resume the overland invasion. Instead he decided to move the army southward through Louisiana and then cross the river into Mississippi for a campaign from the south. In April he marched from Milliken's Bend south to New Carthage about twenty miles below Vicksburg. After nightfall on April 16 Admiral Porter began to run his gunboats and transports by Vicksburg to provide transportation for Grant to cross the river. Despite suffering heavy damage from the Confederate batteries, Porter's fleet succeeded in reaching its rendezvous with Grant.

In the meantime Grant created diversions in the Delta. He also ordered Colonel Benjamin Grierson to begin a cavalry raid through central Mississippi. Leaving La Grange, Tennessee, on April 17, Grierson swept through the length of Mississippi and reached Baton Rouge on May 2. Finally, on April 29, Porter attacked Grand Gulf, and the next day began transporting Union troops and canons across the river to Bruinsburg several miles south of Grand Gulf.

Confederate General Joseph E. Johnston now ordered General Pemberton, who commanded the forces at Vicksburg, to move his army out of the city to confront Grant. But without certain knowledge of Grant's intentions, Pemberton moved slowly. He finally realized that instead of marching north to Vicksburg, Grant was moving northeastward through Port Gibson and Raymond towards Jackson. Now Confederates discovered that the Union army was between Pemberton and Johnston, preventing their uniting to stop Grant.

On May 1, near Port Gibson, the Confederates under General John S. Bowen could not repulse Grant and his army, and the next day the Union forces occupied the town. As this victory secured Grant's position on the Mississippi, the Union army continued its march into the state, passing through Rocky Springs and Utica towards Raymond. There on May 12 the Confederates, outnumbered about three to one, could not stop Grant's drive towards Jackson.

The Union army forced Johnston to evacuate Jackson on May 14, 1863. But instead of remaining in control of Mississippi's capital, Grant turned his army westward towards Vicksburg without delay. He met the Confederates near Edwards at the battle of Baker's Creek or Champion's Hill on May 16. Unable to deter the enemy, the Confederates fell back to the Big Black River. The next day Pemberton's forces, outnumbered by Grant's army and unable to get reinforcements from Johnston, had no choice but to retreat across the river and back to Vicksburg. The battle of Champion's Hill is considered by some scholars as the most important battle of the Civil War because it determined the fate of Vicksburg. It was remembered as a savage struggle, literally "a hill of death." (See map: The Vicksburg Campaign, April to July 1863, p. 136.)

The Surrender

After the Union army tried unsuccessfully on May 19 and 22 to break through the Vicksburg defenses in the rough terrain, Grant decided on May 25 to besiege the town and starve its inhabitants into submission. During the six-week siege, soldiers and civilians became increasingly weak, sick, and desperate, finally compelling Pemberton to surrender the town, which was finally occupied by Grant's army on July 4, 1863.

Not only did the fall of Vicksburg demonstrate that the United States now controlled the Mississippi River, thus dividing the Confederacy, but it also resulted in the destruction of a major Confederate army along with the loss of hundreds of cannon and enormous amounts of other military equipment. In addition, Vicksburg would henceforth be used as a base for further Union invasions into the state.

Sherman's Marches, 1863 and 1864

After the capture of Vicksburg, Grant sent Sherman back to reoccupy Jackson on July 17, 1863. Without giving significant resistance, Confederate General Johnston withdrew to Brandon.

After Sherman returned to Vicksburg, he was assigned the mission of moving Union troops from northern Mississippi to Chattanooga, Tennessee, where they were needed to oppose General Bragg, who had defeated the Union army at Chickamauga in September 1863. In spite of Confederate cavalry operations under the command of General James R. Chalmers along the Memphis and Charleston Railroad in northern Mississippi, Sherman completed his march and participated under Grant's command in the victory at Chattanooga, which drove Bragg into northern Georgia late in November 1863.

Early in 1864 Sherman moved back to Vicksburg and began another march eastward across the state. This time his objective was Meridian, a key railroad junction and the most important town in the state still under Confederate control. Encountering only minor cavalry resistance, he easily reentered Jackson on February 5. Two days later he crossed the Pearl River and entered Brandon. (It was in crossing the Pearl River, when Sherman purportedly uttered his famous declaration, "War is hell.") From there he took Morton and finally Meridian on February 14. General Leonidas Polk offered little resistance in defense of the town and withdrew to Demopolis, Alabama.

Once in Meridian, Sherman wasted no time in destroying the railroad facilities and tracks along the Mobile and Ohio as far south as Quitman. Late in February he marched back to Vicksburg. In the meantime, a Union force under the command of General William Sooy Smith, which had marched out of Memphis to join Sherman at Meridian, was repulsed by General Nathan Bedford Forrest near West Point.

Sherman's Meridian Campaign was, in retrospect, a dress rehearsal for the strategy and tactics he employed during his invasion of Georgia and the Carolinas later in 1864 and early in 1865. In Mississippi he covered more than 370 miles, letting his soldiers live off the land—which included simply taking desired crops, livestock, and other supplies from local farms and plantations—wrecked the railroads, and destroyed enormous amounts of property. The only opposition was provided by the Confederate cavalry, which raided intermittently. The most effective cavalry commander was Forrest, who was based in northeast Mississippi when Sherman began his famous march across Georgia.

Brice's Crossroads and Nathan Bedford Forrest

As he invaded northern Georgia in the spring of 1864, Sherman determined to protect his supply lines in Tennessee against Forrest's cavalry raids. He ordered

Brice's Crossroads. Courtesy Mississippi Department of Archives and History.

the Union forces in the Memphis area to find and destroy Forrest, long a thorn in his side, in northeast Mississippi. Union troops commanded by General Samuel D. Sturgis and General Grierson met Forrest near Brice's Crossroads on June 10, 1864. Although he was outnumbered, Forrest stopped the Union forces and drove Sturgis back towards Memphis.

Still concerned about his supply lines, in early July Sherman directed General A. J. Smith to confront Forrest in northern Mississippi. To prevent the Confederates from reinforcing Forrest, General Henry Slocum's Union troops moved out of Vicksburg to occupy Jackson for the fourth time. Then from there Slocum campaigned in the Grand Gulf area. In the meantime, in pursuit of Forrest, Smith destroyed most of Ripley and advanced through New Albany towards Pontotoc. But near Pontotoc, Smith turned towards Tupelo and established a strong Union position there on the Mobile and Ohio Railroad. Even though Forrest's counterattack at Tupelo proved unsuccessful, Smith decided to withdraw towards Memphis. In his pursuit of Smith, Forrest was wounded but refused to withdraw from the campaign.

Through August 1864 the fierce fighting between the forces of Forrest and Smith continued in northern Mississippi. As the Union troops were about to take Oxford, Forrest led a daring cavalry raid with about 2,000 troops to Memphis, surprising the Union army there. This raid forced Smith to give up Oxford and return to Memphis by the end of August. In the remaining months of the war there were scattered cavalry actions as the Union forces attempted to destroy those railroad lines still being used to transport supplies for Confederate General John B. Hood's futile invasion of Tennessee following his defeat at Atlanta.

THE CIVIL WAR HOMEFRONT

The Peace Movement and Politics

The initial, overwhelming support for secession and the war faded fast as the bloody conflict brought staggering human casualties, the destruction of millions of dollars of property, and the resulting deprivations and disruptions of ordinary life. As the conflict wore on, a growing number of white Mississippians, particularly small farmers in the northeastern hill counties and in the Piney Woods region, even began to demand an end to the war. In some quarters by 1863 antiwar feelings were strong enough to produce resistance to state and Confederate authorities. The best-known example of the latter extreme occurred in Jones County, where opposition to conscription was led by Newton Knight, a small farmer from neighboring Jasper County who deserted a Mississippi battalion, objecting to "a rich man's war and a poor man's fight." Going even further, Knight formed a small band that conducted sporadic guerrilla raids against Confederate cavalrymen searching for deserters. The legend of Jones County's "secession" from the Confederacy and the formation of a separate "Republic of Jones" with Knight as president was based primarily on stories told and embellished by war veterans in the postwar decades. Even though the myth appears to be without any solid historical basis, its persistence reveals the presence of antiwar sentiment as well as continuing confusion about race relations.[1]

Another indication of a mounting desire for peace was revealed in the elections of 1863. Because Governor Pettus, who represented the fire-eating secessionists, was ineligible for a consecutive third term, his close political ally and an outspoken prowar Democrat, Reuben Davis, was expected to be Pettus's successor. Davis was opposed by Charles Clark, a Delta Whig who had opposed secession in the 1850s but supported the war once it came, rising to the rank of brigadier general in the state and Confederate armies. A veteran of the War with Mexico, Clark had served in the state legislature from Jefferson County and from Bolivar County after 1856. He had been wounded in combat at Shiloh and again seriously at Baton Rouge and was a prisoner of war in New Orleans until his release early in 1863. During the gubernatorial campaign he was on crutches, still recuperating from war wounds. A third candidate was Unionist Absalom West, another antisecession Whig who represented the peace movement. Clark's election along with the results in the legislative elections were viewed as victories for the conservatives who were turning away from the fire-eater mania of earlier years. The new governor had an aristocratic bearing that contrasted him dramatically with the rough-edged Pettus, but as a wounded combat veteran and recently released prisoner of war, Clark was committed to continuing the fight. With a sharp state rights bent, however, he experienced serious conflicts with Confederate President Davis, with whom Pettus had enjoyed relatively cordial relations.

Even before the newly elected officials could take office, the orderly administration of state and local government, including the criminal justice system and the maintenance of official records, had become difficult if not impossible, depending on the area and proximity of military action. Early in 1863 Governor Pettus had left Jackson, and the legislature had followed him to Enterprise, a small town south of Meridian. After the Union army's destructive occupations of Jackson transformed the town into a "Chimneyville," the state government sought refuge by moving about the eastern counties, settling temporarily in Meridian, Macon, and Columbus.

1 This legend is the subject of James Street's novel *Tap Roots*.

The Slaves' Role

Although they had no voice in the elections, the majority of the black inhabitants of Mississippi consistently opposed the Confederate effort, even if giving the appearance of loyalty. Composing 55 percent of the state's total population in 1860, slaves were forced to support the war by continuing their labors on the plantations and farms or by directly participating in the war. Many thousands of black men and women were compelled to perform various types of manual labor for white troops, including but not limited to building fortifications, digging trenches, cooking meals, driving draft animals, and serving as all-around servants for Confederate officers. But with the Union army's incursions into Mississippi and President Lincoln's issuance of the Emancipation Proclamation on January 1, 1863, rising numbers of slaves began to demonstrate their true desire for freedom by leaving their masters' farms and armies. Indeed, at least 17,000 African Americans from Mississippi eventually took up arms and fought for the Union.

Economic Conditions

The war virtually destroyed the state's economy, which, of course, had depended primarily on farmland, slave labor, and the production of cotton. During the war "King Cotton" was dethroned, as farmers across Mississippi had no way to get their crops to market, and great amounts of cotton were destroyed or confiscated by both the Union and Confederate forces. By 1864 production had dropped to less than 10 percent of the 1861 crop.

Prompted by Confederate soldiers' desperate need for foodstuffs as well as concerns about cotton farmers trading with the enemy, the legislature in 1863 levied a tax on cotton seed. In response to these and other measures discouraging cotton planting, prohibiting private trading of the commodity, and promoting crop diversification, farmers devoted more attention to the production of food crops, particularly corn, sweet potatoes, rice, and sorghum. These efforts, however, were hampered by natural and human obstacles, including severe droughts, floods along the Mississippi River, and foraging and plundering by opposing armies as well as by roving bands of deserters. Other problems confronting farmers were military impressment of farm equipment and draft animals and tenuous labor forces.

Even if farmers managed to plant and harvest food crops during the war, unreliable transportation severely limited their ability to get them to markets or to Confederate armies. At the beginning of the war, eight railroad lines had operated only about 870 miles of track in the state, and by 1863 the Union armies controlled or destroyed portions of tracks and depots on all the key lines. By that time, moreover, the United States also controlled all the state's river and coastal ports as well as the major towns. Union army occupation and naval blockade also would have prevented the transportation of manufactured goods, if there had been any to transport. Despite efforts to encourage the development of industry during the 1850s, Mississippi still ranked next to last among all states in the value of manufactured products. The leading industries, lumber and textile mills, had increased in number before the war and were expected to help supply military needs, but most mills had to close or were destroyed during the war.

The state's financial condition grew increasingly hopeless. In the absence of solvent banks and available capital, the state government attempted to raise

The only president of the Confederate States of America, Jefferson Davis visited his home state in December 1862 in response to Governor Pettus's appeal for help in lifting public morale, which was showing signs of deterioration. Davis visited Vicksburg and Grenada and addressed the legislature in Jackson. The following year he sent reinforcements requested by Pettus during Grant's siege of Vicksburg. But the president's relationship with Mississippi changed dramatically once Governor Clark took a state's-rights position and insisted on controlling troops drafted into service.

After the war Davis was imprisoned for two years at Fort Monroe, Virginia, during which time he was accused of helping to plan the assassination of President Lincoln and indicted for treason. In December 1869, more than two years after his release on a bail bond for $100,000, Chief Justice Salmon P. Chase presiding over the federal circuit court in Richmond, Virginia, opined that the Fourteenth Amendment exempted Davis from further prosecution, and no further action was taken in the case. After traveling with his wife, Varina, to Canada and Europe, and finally recovering his plantation, Brierfield, south of Vicksburg on the Mississippi River, Davis chose to retire at Beauvoir, a home on the Gulf Coast near Biloxi. There he wrote several articles and books, including The Rise and Fall of the Confederate Government, *which he completed in 1881. Throughout his retirement years, spent primarily on the Gulf Coast, he symbolized the "Lost Cause," refusing to request amnesty and defending to the end the Constitutional right of states to secede from the Union. Eighty-nine years after his death in 1889, a joint resolution passed by the Congress and signed by President Jimmy Carter restored posthumously full rights of United States citizenship to Jefferson Davis, effective December 5, 1868. Photograph: Jefferson and Varina Davis. Courtesy Mississippi Department of Archives and History.*

money and obtain supplies through three main methods: borrowing by issuing bonds, issuing paper notes, and raising property taxes (in cash and in kind). None of these efforts was successful, however, for the state's credit was already weak, paper currency became virtually worthless (as there was little collateral in specie), the crops were unreliable, and few farmers could pay their tax bills or paid them with inflated state or Confederate currency. The outcome was that the state treasury accumulated an indebtedness of about $9 million in outstanding bonds and could not rely on state banks, most of which failed.

Social Disruption

In such dire economic circumstances most families found their lives dramatically changed. As mentioned, when the war started most white Mississippians were small farmers who owned few if any slaves and generally formed a class that ranked socially and economically below the slaveholding planters but above poor

Civil War battle re-enactment. Courtesy Mississippi Development Authority/Division of Tourism.

whites and blacks. The relatively comfortable existence of this large class of whites was undercut by wartime exigencies that forced all inhabitants, regardless of rank or race, into a struggle for survival and a departure from ordinary social and cultural activities.

Except for army camps where religious "revivals" occurred as clergymen traveled among the troops, most churches in Mississippi experienced declining attendance, and many of them lost their pastors and discontinued regular services. Instead of customary church attendance, many communities held prayer meetings led by white women, who sometimes declared that the decline of religious interests caused the state's distress and considered "prayer the most powerful of all weapons."

Educational institutions suffered a similar fate as enrollment at the university and other colleges dropped to almost no students or faculty members. Male students formed military companies and left their campuses, which often served as military hospitals. Two of the state's oldest schools, Jefferson College and Oakland College, permanently closed during the war. While some of the schools for females remained opened, attendance declined and regular operations were severely restricted due to financial and military exigencies. The state had no system of public schools, but in counties not exposed to warfare local schools were maintained by volunteers for teaching and social functions. Literary pursuits, which had been a significant feature of the state's antebellum society, were curtailed during the war. Almost all of the state's two hundred printers closed their shops, and most of the seventy-three newspapers suspended publication or were forced to relocate, if they were able to escape military destruction.

Women on the Homefront

As white and black men marched off to war, women faced burdens of farming and providing food and other essentials for their families' livelihood, as well as contributing to the war effort. Some white women were required to manage their slave laborers, who appeared loyal at first but became distracted or even absent as the fortunes of war fulfilled their dreams of freedom. Numerous wartime diaries described the ingenuity of mothers, wives, sisters, and daughters who found ways to overcome wartime deprivations by making inventive substitutions for scarce commodities like coffee and tea and by making clothing and accomplishing other arts of makeshift.

Traditional accounts of the war experience focused on activities of men in combat, but recent studies have revealed that women may have contributed as much as men did to the overall struggle. Not only did they hold together a torn social fabric at home, but women also participated directly in military action and indirectly in providing essential material and psychological support. A few women disguised themselves as men to serve as soldiers, while others acted as spies for the armies. A greater number of white women, some of whom were aided by slave women, formed "needle regiments" to make uniforms and other articles of clothing and flags for the troops. In many communities women formed hospital associations to gather food and medical supplies and served as nurses for wounded and dying soldiers. Writing letters, poems, songs, and prayers, white women expressed their love and support for individual soldiers as well as for the cause—secession and slavery.

THE WAR ENDS

Signals of the war's end began to arrive in April 1865 with the surrenders by Generals Robert E. Lee in Virginia and Joseph E. Johnston in North Carolina. Closer to home, General Richard Taylor, who commanded the Confederate troops in Mississippi and neighboring states, surrendered his army in southwest Alabama on May 4. A few days later President Jefferson Davis was captured near Irwinville, Georgia, and the last Confederate army, under the command of General Kirby Smith in the Trans-Mississippi theater, surrendered in western Louisiana on May 26.

As the Confederacy crumbled in the spring of 1865, the people of Mississippi found themselves in a desperate situation. Government on every level had collapsed, occupying "Yankee" troops remained in the state, and farms, roads, churches, and towns lay in a shambles. There was extreme poverty among the masses of both races. The white male population had been decimated during the four years of warfare. Almost all adult, able-bodied white men—about 78,000—had participated in the "Lost Cause" and more than one third of them did not return home. This loss constituted about one-fourth of the total number of white males fifteen years of age and older in 1860.

With the war over, and the Confederacy defeated, Mississippians were not only short on basic sustenance, but they were confused about the future. How would they recover economically? What would the federal government require of the state politically? How would the slavery question be settled? These and many other unanswered questions were further complicated by events in Washington,

D.C., as Vice President Andrew Johnson of Tennessee succeeded to the presidency following the death of President Lincoln at the hand of an assassin in mid-April 1865. Would Johnson change Lincoln's plans for reconstructing the states of the former Confederacy?

Notwithstanding the occupation of Mississippi by Federal troops, Governor Charles Clark attempted to continue civilian government by calling for a convention to address the situation. The United States Army, however, refused to recognize his authority, and on May 22, 1865, Clark surrendered to U.S. General Embury D. Osband. Mississippi, like the other Confederate states, now came under military rule and awaited President Johnson's plan for reconstruction.

Selected Sources

Ballard, Michael B., *Pemberton: A Biography* (Jackson: University Press of Mississippi, 1991).

———. *Civil War Mississippi: A Guide* (Jackson: University Press of Mississippi, 2000).

Bearss, Edwin C., "The Armed Conflict, 1861–1865," in Richard Aubrey McLemore, ed., *A History of Mississippi*, 2 vols. (Hattiesburg: University & College Press of Mississippi, 1973), 1: 447–491.

Berlin, Ira, Joseph P. Reidy, and Leslie S. Rowland, eds., *Freedom's Soldiers, The Black Military Experience in the Civil War* (New York: Cambridge University Press, 1998).

Bettersworth, John K., "The Home Front, 1861–1865," in Richard Aubrey McLemore, ed., *A History of Mississippi*, 2 vols. (Hattiesburg: University & College Press of Mississippi, 1973), 1: 492–541.

Bettersworth, John K. and James W. Silver, eds., *Mississippi in the Confederacy* (Jackson: Mississippi Department of Archives and History, 1961).

Bond, Bradley G., *Mississippi: A Documentary History* (Jackson: University Press of Mississippi, 2003).

Bynum, Victoria E., *The Free State of Jones: Mississippi's Longest Civil War* (Chapel Hill: The University of North Carolina Press, 2001).

Cheseborough, David B., "Dissenting Clergy in Confederate Mississippi," *Journal of Mississippi History* 55 (May 1993): 115–30.

Darst, W. Maury, ed., "The Vicksburg Diary of Mrs. Alfred Ingraham" (May 2–June 13, 1863), *Journal of Mississippi History* 44 (May 1982): 148–79.

Historical Statistics of the States of the United States: Two Centuries of the Census, 1790–1990, comp. Donald B. Dodd (Westport, Conn.: Greenwood Press, 1993), Population.

James, D. Clayton, "Mississippi Agriculture, 1861–1865," *Journal of Mississippi History* 24 (July 1962): 129–41.

Kondret, Nancy R. "The Romance and Reality of Defeat: Southern Women in 1865," *Journal of Mississippi History* 24 (July 1962): 129–41.

Rowland, Dunbar, *History of Mississippi: the Heart of the South,* 4 vols. (Chicago-Jackson: The S. J. Clarke Publishing Company, 1925), 1: 774–903.

Winter, William F., "Mississippi's Civil War Governors," *Journal of Mississippi History* 51 (May 1989): 77–88.

CHAPTER TWELVE

Reconstruction in Mississippi

PRESIDENTIAL RECONSTRUCTION, 1865–1867

Historians refer to the first phase of post–Civil War Reconstruction as "presidential" because it was implemented by President Andrew Johnson. Some forty-four days after he assumed office, President Johnson issued a proclamation on May 29 providing guidelines for the readmittance into the Union of the former Confederate states. Following the reconstruction procedures that President Lincoln had initiated during the war, Johnson offered amnesty to persons who would take an oath of loyalty to the United States, but there were exceptions. Denied this generous offer were those who had held high civil or military offices in the Confederacy and those who had owned property worth $20,000 or more in 1860. These individuals could obtain amnesty only by petitioning the president directly. But as it became generally known during the course of the first year that Johnson intended to grant amnesty to every applicant, many of the antebellum and wartime leaders qualified to participate in the new state government.

William L. Sharkey

To oversee the program of reconstruction in Mississippi, Johnson appointed as provisional governor William L. Sharkey, a Union Whig who, as mentioned, had

been prominent in state affairs before the war. In addition to helping the military administer the amnesty program, Sharkey's task was to organize an election of delegates for a state constitutional convention. Working promptly, the provisional governor called for the election on July 1, 1865, and the delegates met in Jackson on August 14.

The Constitutional Convention of 1865

In this first postwar election, the old Union Whigs experienced a victory over the state's secessionist Democrats. The convention, which included seventy-one Whigs and only eighteen Democrats, determined to restrict its focus on the president's main require-

William L. Sharkey. Courtesy Mississippi Department of Archives and History.

Congress created the Freedmen's Bureau in March 1865 and then expanded its operations over President Johnson's veto in February 1866. The president appointed a commissioner, General Oliver O. Howard, to manage the agency and ten assistant commissioners to implement its programs in the former Confederate states. As part of the War Department, the Freedmen's Bureau worked closely, but often awkwardly, with the military, and most members of its staff were army officers.

In Mississippi the first assistant commissioner was Colonel Samuel Thomas, who opened a Bureau office in Vicksburg in June 1865. His successors served both as Bureau assistant commissioners and military commanders: General Thomas J. Wood beginning in April 1866, General Alvan C. Gillem beginning in January 1867, and, finally, General Adelbert Ames in March and April 1869, when the agency ceased operations in Mississippi. The assistant commissioners appointed soldiers as well as some civilians as local agents throughout the state. Ultimately the quality of the Bureau's service depended on the performance of these agents, whose extensive duties included issuing essential provisions to destitute black and white refugees, regulating the terms of labor contracts between former slaves and white employers, making sure the freedmen received just treatment from their employers and in all legal proceedings, and assisting blacks families by encouraging marriage ceremonies, educational programs, and the adoption of orphans.

Colonel Thomas's statement to Congress in 1865 illustrates the kind of opposition the Bureau encountered in Mississippi: "Wherever I go—the street, the shop, the house, or the steamboat—I hear the [white] people talk in such a way as to indicate that they are yet unable to conceive of the Negro as possessing any rights at all. . . . [They] will cheat a Negro without feeling a single twinge of their honor. To kill a Negro they do not deem murder; to debauch a Negro woman they do not think fornication; to take the property away from a Negro they do not consider robbery. The people boast that when they get freedmen affairs in their own hands, to use their own classic expression, 'the niggers will catch hell.' The reason for all this is simple and manifest. The whites esteem the blacks their property by natural right, and however much they may admit that the individual relations of masters and slaves have been destroyed by the war and *the President's emancipation proclamation, they still have an ingrained feeling that the blacks at large belong to the whites at large, and whenever opportunity serves they treat the colored people just as their profit, caprice or passion may dictate."*

(See Records of the Assistant Commissioner for the State of Mississippi, Bureau of Refugees, Freedmen, and Abandoned Lands, 1865–69; and Bureau of Refugees, Freedmen and Abandoned Lands in 39 Cong., 1 Sess., Senate Exec. Doc. 2 (1865); placed online by Stephen Mintz at the University of Houston at http: chnm. gmu. edu/courses/122/recon/ thomas.htm)

Overleaf: Photograph of Black Refugees, 1897. Courtesy Mississippi Department of Archives and History.

ments for readmission to the United States: to annul the ordinance of secession and abolish slavery. The delegates made no substantive changes in the structure of state and local government and excluded deliberation on the pressing economic problems and related questions about the former slaves' new status. In that vein the convention refused to consider President Johnson's proposal to Governor Sharkey that suffrage be extended to black property owners, even though it was suggested that such action might weaken the "Radical" Republicans in the United States Congress who opposed Johnson's program. The so-called Radical Republicans were members of that party who had fervently supported the abolition of slavery before the war and now sought full civil rights for African Americans.[1]

With such a narrow agenda, the convention completed its work within eleven calendar days. In addressing the two principal requirements, the delegates did not appear to accept willingly the war's verdict. They repealed but did not annul the 1861 ordinance of secession, and they declared that slavery had been destroyed and would no longer exist in the state. Such wording as well as the convention's reticence on the new position of freedmen aroused criticism among blacks in the state and Republicans in the United States Congress.

State Elections of 1865

Despite the convention's lukewarm attitude and the negative reaction to its decisions, President Johnson accepted the new state constitution, and elections were scheduled for October 2, 1865. The time was not right, however, for the critical selection of the state's first postwar leadership, including congressional representatives, the governor, legislators, judges, and the numerous county and local officials. Indeed, there was uncertainty about the new labor arrangements, and the year's harvest did not look good. Would the newly freed persons work on plantations and farms for wages, as tenants, or would they leave the state altogether? People were unclear about what appeared to be conflicting jurisdictions among the Freedmen's Bureau (the federal agency assigned the task of assisting the former slaves in their transition to freedom), the military, and an incoming group of state and local officials. Of particular significance was the fact that by

1 President Lincoln's wartime Emancipation Proclamation had freed slaves only in areas "in rebellion against the United States," and the proposed Thirteenth Amendment abolishing completely the institution would not be ratified until December 1865.

this time most of the United States soldiers (about 13,000) in Mississippi as the occupying force were black. False rumors began to circulate about the freedmen starting a race war, and in some places white militia groups organized and actually skirmished with U.S. troops.

In this atmosphere most candidates for office in the 1865 elections promised to support measures that would control the former slaves. They did not, however, agree on the extent of regulation. Some favored harsh laws which would give blacks no civil rights or legal equality, while moderates called for protecting blacks and warned that Congress would refuse to admit Mississippi's congressional representatives and senators if the freedmen were officially denied all civil rights. Some newspaper editorialists warned that refusing minimal rights would strengthen the case of the Radical Republicans. Generally, the old Whigs preferred the milder course.

Amidst all the rhetoric about the status of freed persons, the most important campaign issue somehow became who was to blame for secession and the war. Whigs placed the responsibility squarely on the Democrats. A caucus of Whig delegates in the constitutional convention selected a slate of conservative candidates, including Benjamin G. Humphreys for governor. A planter in Sunflower County, Humphreys had been a Union Whig prior to secession, but during the war he had served as a Confederate brigadier general. Humphreys's opponent was William S. Patton, a Union Democrat from Meridian.

The election results confirmed the voters' preference for conservative Whigs as opposed to the secessionists Democrats or the unconditional Unionists. Humphreys was elected and his party won a majority in the legislature. In addition all congressional elections resulted in Whig victories, and the legislators elected Whig leaders Sharkey and James Lusk Alcorn to the United States Senate. But on arriving in Washington, these persons were denied seats in the Congress, for it did not accept President Johnson's reconstruction program, questioning its leniency in general and state leaders' attitudes regarding the rights of the freed persons in particular. Following this action, which was also taken against persons elected to Congress in other ex-Confederate states, Congress established the Joint Committee on Reconstruction to examine conditions in the Confederate States.

The Black Code

Governor Humphreys and other state, county, and town officials would continue to hold office through 1867, but some of their actions gave the appearance that the state intended to avoid certain consequences of the war. From its beginning on October 16, 1865, the new government's authority was somewhat clouded. Not only was the state unrepresented in Congress, but the Freedmen's Bureau and the United States military was still a constant presence.

One of the first and most important matters addressed by the legislature was the status of the freedmen. Contrary to its formal title, the "Act to confer Civil Rights on Freedmen," the so-called Black Code denied blacks virtually all rights of citizenship. A vagrancy law was designed to enforce the requirement that all black males enter into labor contracts. "All freedmen, free Negroes, and mulattoes" under eighteen years of age were forced to become "apprentices" under the control of white employers—usually former slave owners. Black persons were not allowed to own guns or serve as ministers without the proper licenses. Stiff punishments including imprisonment were imposed for "disturbance of the peace" and a comprehensive list of behaviors that could be broadly interpreted by white law officers. The only "civil rights" in the code were carefully qualified: freedmen were allowed to testify in court, but only when they were parties in the case; and they could own property but could not rent or lease rural property.

The new legislature adopted the Black Code in late November 1865; it was the first such postwar measure in the South. Although the legislators evidently viewed it as rather moderate, the Freedmen's Bureau agents, as well as some white leaders, denounced the code as an attempt to resurrect slavery. By early 1867, toward the end of Presidential Reconstruction, the legislature repealed many features of the Black Code but retained the restrictive vagrancy law. While black Mississippians saw their long-awaited freedom now being taken back, they had little opportunity to react publicly. They expressed disappointment and anger behind closed doors, a practice deep-rooted in lifetimes of bondage, except when individuals occasionally reported to Bureau agents complaints of cruelty and injustice. Even then, however, blacks feared that the response might be one of retaliation instead of relief, for many of the agents were local white men. Finally, postwar conditions prevented blacks from leaving the state, an option that only became available years later.

Economic Conditions

Most Mississippians were not as concerned about political and racial questions as they were about their own personal economic situation and the problems of making a living. Economic recovery was extremely slow because it depended on farming. And although they understood the importance of agricultural diversification, most farmers, desperate to realize some cash for their hard work, continued to place their hopes on cotton. With little or no money, they simply turned to the crop that could get them loans, and one with which they were most familiar. Moreover, the price of cotton on the New Orleans market was high in 1865, but dependence on cotton proved to be a mistake. The crops of 1865 and 1866 were limited and hardly brought economic recovery. Even with the assistance of the United States military and the Freedmen's Bureau, by 1867 many farmers were virtually destitute.

Despite some signs of recovery by 1869, optimism was short-lived as farmers still failed to diversify and increasingly began to rely on the crop-lien system. In this system farmers mortgaged their future cotton crops in order to obtain essential supplies. But the consequence of the practice was that most farmers fell even deeper into debt when the harvest failed to raise enough money to satisfy their debts. Thus, for whites as well as blacks, the immediate postwar years were times of extreme economic hardship, agricultural depression, and an atmosphere of hopelessness.

The problems facing farmers were exacerbated by the near total disruption of transportation and commercial activities in the wake of the war. The costs of repairing railroad tracks, facilities, and equipment were paralyzing, and some of the heavily indebted railroad companies were now taken over by Northern operators. Although a number of new railroads were chartered in the state, many of the counties and towns that helped to finance them could not pay their bondholders, and very little new rail construction was actually accomplished. Like the railroads, most towns tried to rebuild after the war only to find their progress stalled by commercial sluggishness.

CONGRESSIONAL OR "RADICAL" RECONSTRUCTION, 1867–1876

The second and final phase of Reconstruction is called "congressional" or "radical" because Congress, now controlled by Radical Republicans, dismantled President Johnson's program (extending even to impeachment of the president) and instituted a totally different reconstruction plan for the former Confederate states. The Radicals' motivations ranged from purely political and economic interests to humane concerns for the former slaves. Though the real reasons for their actions may be debatable, there is no question about what the Republicans saw in Mississippi and other ex-Confederate states: the same white power structures that had existed before the war had regained control, and they refused to accept the results of the devastating and costly Civil War. They further saw black people subjected to a system similar to slavery, one called peonage by some witnesses. The Radicals aimed, therefore, to establish new state governments, open to blacks but not to unrepentant whites, that would implement their party's policies, including civil rights for the former slaves.

Military Re-occupation and New Voter Registration in 1867

Winning overwhelming majorities in both houses of Congress in the 1866 elections, the Radical Republicans adopted a series of laws ending Presidential Reconstruction and reestablishing military rule in Mississippi and other Southern states. In March of 1867 two Military Reconstruction Acts were passed over President Johnson's vetoes. Major General Edward Ord was given the duty of implementing these laws in the Mississippi-Arkansas District.

The military's first duty was to reregister voters who would then elect a state constitutional convention in November 1867. This new voter registration included all adult black males and excluded many white leaders now ineligible to take the "test oath" of consistent loyalty to the United States Constitution. Prior to the November election, therefore, the total number of registered voters in Mississippi comprised about 137,000 men, of whom 58 percent were African American.

The Mississippi Republican Party and Its Opposition

The organizers of the first Republican party in the state were Northerners, known derisively as carpetbaggers, white Mississippians, the so-called scalawags, and African American ministers and school teachers. The "carpetbaggers," including United States soldiers, Freedmen's Bureau agents, businessmen, and missionaries, were motivated by personal economic designs as well as genuine interests in equal rights for the former slaves. The scalawags comprised former Democrats and old Whigs who speculated that the best opportunity for progress in the state, given the current political situation, was through cooperation with the Republican party. Though small in number, their leaders included prominent businessmen, physicians, and planters like James Lusk Alcorn and Robert W. Flour-

Notable African Americans elected from Mississippi to the United States Congress during Reconstruction were Republicans Blanche K. Bruce (1841–98) and John R. Lynch (1847–1939). Born to a slave and her white master in Virginia, Bruce served as sheriff of Bolivar County before the legislature elected him to the United States Senate in 1874. He was the second African American Senator from any state—after Revels—and the first to serve a full term (1875–81). Lynch, whose father was a Louisiana planter who had emigrated from Ireland, represented Adams County in the legislature from 1869 to 1873, where he served as the state's youngest speaker of the house of representatives. After two terms in the United States House of Representatives (1873– 77), Lynch failed to win a third successive term but successfully contested the election results of 1880 and served again from 1882 to 1883, taking the seat of James R. Chalmers, a white Democrat. Remaining active in the Republican party, Lynch held several federal posts later in the century, served as a U.S. Army captain in the Spanish-American War, and while practicing law in Washington, D.C., and Chicago, wrote The Facts of Reconstruction, *a defense of Republican leadership in Mississippi. Photograph of Blanche K. Bruce courtesy Mississippi Department of Archives and History.*

noy. The third group included leaders of the African American community, persons like Blanche Kelso Bruce, a school teacher, and African Methodist Episcopal ministers James D. Lynch and Hiram Rhodes Revels, who rallied the former slaves to support the Republicans.

To oppose this Republican organization, white conservatives, now a minority of the registered voters, tried various political strategies. First, several Democratic party leaders formed a "Reconstruction" party, which would appear to accept Congress's requirements in order to allure black support. As this plan failed to materialize, former Whigs tried an opposite maneuver. Resurrecting the old "Constitutional Union" label, they vigorously resisted Congressional Reconstruction, even to the extent of refusing to vote in the convention election. By doing so they hoped to forestall the convention, which could not assemble without the participation of a majority of all registered voters.

The Election of 1867

The election in November 1867 was to determine whether the newly registered voters favored a convention. If so, then delegates would be elected, but if not, the process would be suspended and the military would continue to govern the state. The conservative whites' boycott strategy not only failed to block the convention, but it also resulted in the election of a large Republican majority.

The Constitutional Convention of 1868

The convention, which conservative whites would later characterize as the "Black and Tan Convention," assembled in Jackson on January 7, 1868. It was composed of 97 delegates, including 79 Republicans, 17 "conservatives," and 1 whose party is unknown. All but one of the eighteen African American delegates were Republicans. The convention leaders favored a constitution with "radical" provisions, and they succeeded in converting the moderate majority. Beroth B. Eggleston, a moderate Republican from Lowndes County, was elected convention president, though he appointed leading Radicals as committee chairmen. A carpetbagger, Eggleston had been a merchant-farmer in Ohio and had served as a brigadier general in the Union Army.

Although it did not change the basic structure of state government, the Constitution of 1868 included several significant adjustments. Its bill of rights contained several new sections: the protection of married women's property rights; duelists were excluded not only from public office but also from suffrage; government funds were to be withheld from any public institution—except public schools—that discriminated among citizens; the institution of slavery was prohibited; and the state's withdrawal from the "Federal Union" was forbidden. The African American delegation tried in vain to include a section guaranteeing equality in public accommodations.

One apparent inconsistency was the bill of rights' prohibition of any religious test as a qualification for public office and the contradictory requirement in the general provisions (retained from the previous constitution) that no officeholder could deny "the existence of a Supreme Being." Another section of the general provisions prohibited lotteries.

The new constitution nullified the 1861 ordinance of secession, fully repudiated all debts contracted to support the Confederate cause, and denied any compensation to former owners for the emancipation of slaves since 1861. Although the state was prohibited from pledging its credit or buying stock in corporations, it was not enjoined from subsidizing railroad companies. For the promotion of internal improvements, sections were added directing the legislature to create a board of public works and the office of commissioner of immigration and agriculture.

Both houses of the legislature would be apportioned according to the number of qualified voters rather than total population. The governor's term was extended from two to four years with no restrictions on reelection, and he was empowered to appoint all judges and militia officers with the consent of the senate. The convention restored the office of lieutenant governor, who would also act as the president of the senate and have the same qualifications and terms as the governor. The title of the high court of errors and appeals was changed to the supreme court, vacancies on which would be filled by the governor.

The most controversial and radical actions of the convention were its decisions about qualifications for officeholding and suffrage. All former Confederate civil and military leaders were excluded from holding public office. The right to vote was extended to all adult males except those who were excluded from registration by the "test oath" of 1867. An additional requirement was an oath admitting "the political and civil equality of all men." These suffrage provisions would have the effect of disfranchising thousands of white men in the state.

The convention's most constructive achievement was the establishment of a state system of public education. At first controversial, the article on education was finally approved after virtually all groups agreed not to require racially integrated schools. The article directed the legislature to establish schools for all children between the ages of five and twenty-one years. The system would be administered by an elected superintendent of public education, a board of education composed of the secretary of state, the attorney general, and the superintendent, and by county superintendents and boards of education.

To finance the schools, the legislature was instructed to establish a "common school fund" from various sources of revenue including state land sales, poll taxes, and other taxes. Agricultural colleges were to be established "as soon as practicable."

The Election of 1868

After more than four and one half months of deliberations, the convention finally adjourned on May 18, 1868, and General Alvan C. Gillem called for an election to approve the proposed constitution, and at the same time to elect the officials who would serve according to its provisions. To oppose the new constitution and preserve white supremacy, Democrats and Whigs now joined together under the Democratic party label. For their candidate for governor they chose Benjamin Humphreys, who was still occupying the governor's mansion as a last vestige of Presidential Reconstruction. When he began to campaign against the Constitution of 1868, however, Humphreys was removed from his now futile position by General Irvin McDowell, who served briefly with Gillem commanding the Federal troops occupying Mississippi.

The Republicans nominated convention president Eggleston for governor but experienced divisions within their ranks. Some moderates disliked some of the constitution's radical provisions, while African Americans were displeased that none of their leaders, like James Lynch, had been nominated for an office.

Despite the presence of the United States military, the Ku Klux Klan and other white supremacist groups used subtle as well as direct, even violent, acts of intimidation to prevent African Americans from voting. One widely employed tactic, for example, was to record the names of blacks who voted so that they could be fired by their employers. The result was that in a close contest the Democrats succeeded in defeating the acceptance of the new constitution. Therefore, the state would continue under the military administration of General Gillem, who appeared to sympathize with the Democrats.

Even in their dismayed reaction to the outcome of the election, the Republicans could not unite. Following the national elections of 1868, in which Ulysses S. Grant, the Union hero of the Civil War, was elected president, two opposing delegations of Mississippi Republicans visited Washington, D.C. President-elect Grant, who was known to favor a magnanimous policy of Reconstruction toward the South, favored the moderate group. In April 1869 the president persuaded Congress to approve a plan resubmitting the constitution to the voters of Mississippi in November. This time, however, the proscriptive clauses (those excluding former Confederate civil and military officers from voting and holding office, for example) would have to be approved separately.

Hiram Revels (1827–1901) was born in North Carolina a free black. After attending seminaries in Ohio and Indiana, he became a minister in the African Methodist Episcopal Church at the age of twenty-three. During the Civil War he helped recruit black soldiers in Maryland and served as chaplain for black troops in Vicksburg. After establishing a school for freedmen in St. Louis, Missouri, Revels moved to Natchez in 1866. John R. Lynch, who encouraged the minister to enter politics, recalled that one of Revels's eloquent prayers opening a legislative session was so powerful that he soon became the Republican members' favorite candidate for the United States Senate. After Reconstruction, Revels served as president of Alcorn College (1876–82) before returning to full-time ministry in Holly Springs. Photograph courtesy Mississippi Department of Archives and History.

The Election of 1869

In the following months the moderate Republicans organized a National Union Republican party with support from the Grant administration. For governor they nominated Louis Dent, brother-in-law of President Grant. But when this group became increasingly conservative, Grant announced that he would support the regular Republican party, which had agreed to oppose proscription and radicalism in order to bring their party back together. They nominated scalawag James Lusk Alcorn for governor, carpetbagger Ridgely C. Powers for lieutenant governor, and moderate black James Lynch for secretary of state. This group was supported by General Adelbert Ames, who had replaced Gillem as district commander.

With the backing of President Grant and General Ames, a large turnout of black voters, and many whites refusing to participate, the election in November 1869 was complete victory for the regular Republicans. The constitution's unpopular provisions were removed, Alcorn received two-thirds of the gubernatorial vote, and the Republicans won big majorities in the legislature and the entire delegation to the U.S. House of Representatives. A wealthy planter, Alcorn had served in the antebellum legislature and in the secession convention and had been elected (but not admitted) to the U.S. Senate by the 1865 legislature. He had been a Union Whig who had originally opposed secession but had finally voted for the ordinance.

James Lusk Alcorn. Courtesy Mississippi Department of Archives and History.

Readmission to the Union

The new legislature convened on January 11, 1870, and quickly completed the requirements of Congressional Reconstruction. It ratified the Fourteenth and Fifteenth amendments to the United States Constitution and elected to the United States Senate Hiram Revels, a black minister from Natchez, and General Adelbert Ames. A compromise was made on these elections, with Revels being elected for the short term that would end in March 1871. After Congress restored Mississippi to its "proper relations" with the Union in February 1870, and President Grant ended military rule in the state, the legislature met again for Alcorn's inauguration.

The Alcorn-Powers Administration, 1870–1874

In his inaugural address, Alcorn promised to support legal equality for blacks and appealed for cooperation with the small white farmers who, he judged, had been ignored by the antebellum Democrats. Still, his words failed to convert most white conservatives, who attacked him as a Republican who had accepted the Radicals' entire racial agenda. Pursuant to the legislature's previous agreement, Alcorn's tenure would end in March 1871, when he entered the Senate. Lieutenant Governor Powers would then assume the office of governor and serve out the four-year term.

Administrative Changes

Using the new constitutional authority, the governor appointed judges—usually scalawags—who were experienced lawyers with favorable reputations. Except for a few justices of the peace who were elected in their county districts, all judicial positions were held by whites. In fact, conservative whites' allegations that the Republican party and its African American members would soon attain complete control and use their power to destroy the state's white traditions proved unfounded. Although the military commanders had earlier appointed a number of blacks to local offices, during the Alcorn-Powers administration most counties elected conservative white Democrats. Indeed, in 1871 thirty-nine counties were controlled by Democrats and thirty-four by Republicans. Moreover, the conservatives' accusations of excessive taxation, extravagant spending, and fraudulent behavior in predominately black counties were greatly exaggerated.

Economic Conditions

There were signs of improving economic conditions in the early 1870s. Land values increased, railroad services improved, and larger cotton crops were harvested. The Alcorn-Powers administration's promotion of crop diversification was supported by leading businessmen who warned against the antebellum single-crop economy. To encourage manufacturing businesses in the state, the legislature in 1872 enacted a measure allowing tax refunds for firms that made only small profits.

Public Education

Pursuant to the new state constitution, the legislature in 1870 established a state system of public education that required separate schools for black and white pupils. However, even a segregated system, the only acceptable one for whites who refused to have their children attend school with blacks, had a difficult beginning. The initial enrollment in 1870 amounted to only about 24 percent of the total number of children between the ages of five and eighteen years. In all, some 66,000 students enrolled in about 3,000 schools. They were taught by 3,600 teachers, including only 400 African Americans. For various reasons there was widespread white opposition to the public schools. Some wealthy whites objected to the "mingling" of children from different social ranks, even within all-white schools, while other groups disliked the idea of paying higher taxes that the new school system might require. Although most whites did not appear to oppose education for blacks in general, they objected to a public school system organized by Republicans, who could use it to indoctrinate pupils and to justify higher taxes.

The Ku Klux Klan

The most unfortunate indication of such opposition was the rising membership of the Ku Klux Klan in the 1870s. Masked men, usually riding in the night, wrecked school buildings and intimidated teachers. Growing violence by the Klan was so widespread that the United States Congress appointed a special joint committee of inquiry. As part of the state government's efforts to destroy the Klan, Governor Alcorn in July 1870 approved a law imposing severe punishments

Facsimilie of Ku Klux Klan "Warning" in Mississippi during Reconstruction—put in evidence before a Congressional Committee. Picture Collection, The Branch Libraries, The New York Public Library, Astor, Lenox and Tilden Foundations.

"Dam Your Soul. The Horrible *Sepulchre* and Bloody Moon has at last arrived. Some live to-day to-morrow "*Die.*" We the undersigned understand through our Grand "*Cyclops*" that you have recommended a big Black Nigger for Male agent on our nu rode; wel, sir, Jest you understand in time if he gets on the rode you can make up your mind to pull roape. If you have any thing to say in regard to the Matter, meet the Grand Cyclops and Conclave at Den No. 4 at 12 o'clock midnight, Oct. 1st, 1871.

"When you are in Calera we warn you to hold your tounge and not speak so much with your mouth or otherwise you will be taken on surprise and led out by the Klan and learnt to stretch hemp. Beware. Beware. Beware. Beware.
(Signed)   "PHILLIP ISENBAUM,
                                                                                       "*Grand Cyclops:*
                                                                    "JOHN BANKSTOWN
                                                                    "ESAU DAVES.
                                                                    "MARCUS THOMAS.
                                                                    "BLOODY BONES.

"You know who. And all others of the Klan."

on the perpetrators. But such action was ineffectual. A major incident occurred in Meridian in March 1871, resulting in the deaths of at least twenty-five African Americans. The violence broke out in the courthouse when a crowd of gun-packing white men killed the "carpetbagger" judge, three black men on trial for arson, as well as several African Americans in the courtroom audience. The self-styled vigilantes, who boasted Klan membership, then rampaged through the town for three days. This widely reported riot showed that the state had failed to curtail racial violence and helped convince Congress to subject Klan activities to federal jurisdiction in the Enforcement Act of 1871.

Divisions in the Mississippi Republican Party

The Republican party's main problem was its composition of distinct factions with differing objectives. Carpetbaggers and scalawags distrusted each other, while African Americans were disheartened by such disunity. Alcorn tried but failed to reconcile the competing groups. For example, his veto of a railroad bill in 1870 was designed to appease but instead offended each faction. The bill would have given Northern businessmen more power in local communities, and it prohibited racial segregation on railroad cars.

Alcorn versus Ames

This factionalism was best illustrated in the gubernatorial election of 1873 between United States Senators Ames and Alcorn. Having served only two and one half years in the Senate, Alcorn entered the race for governor against his colleague, Ames, who had two years remaining in his Senate term. Disagreements between these two Republican leaders had begun earlier in the presidential election of 1872. Alcorn and the scalawags had allied with the "Liberal" Republicans who supported Democratic presidential candidate Horace Greeley over the reelection of President Grant.

In 1873 the regular Republicans refused to nominate for reelection incumbent Governor Powers, who was Senator Alcorn's choice for the office and nominated instead Senator Ames. Following this decision, Alcorn declared his own candidacy. Generally, scalawags and conservatives supported Alcorn, while carpetbaggers and African Americans voted for Ames. There were, however, important exceptions to this alignment: for example, Ames supporters included many conservative former Whigs and some conservative Democrats like John M. Stone, the president pro tempore of the senate who would later succeed Ames. The Democratic party leaders, meeting in Meridian, declined to nominate candidates, apparently favoring Alcorn.

The outcome was a big victory for Ames, who received 58 percent of the total vote. Another consequence was the election of a number of African Americans, including Lieutenant Governor Alexander K. Davis, Speaker of the House I. D. Shadd, nine state senators, and fifty-five representatives. All of the black officeholders were Republicans, and their party won two-thirds of the senate and house memberships. Other key black officials were Secretary of State James Hill, Superintendent of Education T. W. Cardoza, and Commissioner of Immigration and Agriculture Richard Griggs. Conservative Democrats bemoaned what they considered to be an excessive number of blacks in office and warned that they would soon completely dominate the state. Such propaganda in the years following the election of 1873 produced more cooperation among most whites, who began to focus on defeating all Republicans in the future. To them one evidence of the urgency of overthrowing the Republicans was the legislature's action to raise the tax rates to the highest levels in state history.

The Vicksburg Riots

To make matters worse for the Ames administration, several racial crises diverted attention from reforms needed to improve the state's economy. A major outburst of violence occurred in Vicksburg, where African Americans controlled the governments of the city as well as Warren County. Attempting to remove them from office, a county grand jury composed of white men in 1874 indicted Sheriff Peter Crosby, a Union army Civil War veteran, and other black officials for such crimes as bribery and theft of public funds. After a white gang decided to take the law into their own hands, storming into Crosby's office and taking over the courthouse, armed conflict broke out between blacks, determined to oust the insurgents, and whites, just as resolved to take power. When the smoke finally cleared, both sides reported scores of casualties, including at least two whites and twenty-nine blacks shot dead.

In December 1874 Governor Ames, the former general, intervened in the affair, trying to suppress the violence and restore Sheriff Crosby to his office. Appealing without success to President Grant for military intervention in Vicksburg, the governor promised Crosby that state assistance was on its way. To fulfill his pledge, Ames called the legislature into special session. That body renewed the call for federal troops and adopted special legislation related to the riot; the metropolitan police law established a military police department in Warren County under the governor's control. Adding further muscle, the legislature enacted the Gatling Gun law, authorizing the state to supply guns to the police and to the state militia. In spite of these actions, including enough national attention to cause a congressional investigation, Crosby ultimately resigned and was replaced by a white sheriff.

THE END OF RECONSTRUCTION

The "Tax Payers' Convention"

The Ames administration's inability to ameliorate the state's continuing difficulties caused many of his moderate supporters to abandon him and turn to the Democrats. Economic hardships, punctuated by higher taxes, and whites' fear of a race war and black domination were the two major reasons for the Democratic party's resurgence in 1875. In the month following the Vicksburg riots, a "Tax Payers' Convention" met in Jackson. The convention demanded tax reforms and warned that steps had to be taken to reduce racial tensions in the state. The actual outcome of the meeting, however, was the inception of a plan to end the Republicans' control of the state. In short, conservative white Democrats in Mississippi—like their counterparts in other states under reconstruction—resolved to take back political power.

The "First Mississippi Plan"

When the legislature failed to respond positively to the "tax payers" grievances, the Democrats began aggressively to organize statewide. Their state convention in August 1875 designed a strategy to win the state elections in November. Known later as the "First Mississippi Plan," the scheme boiled down to keeping African Americans away from the polls, stuffing ballot boxes, destroying or altering Republican ballots, and the willingness to use any other means necessary to take and retain power.

An outbreak of racial violence in Clinton on September 4, 1875, played into the Democrats' hands, as they used it to incite fear among whites of a looming race war. In addition the newspapers regularly reported incidents of racially motivated violence in the state. Now Democrats warned that peace could be achieved only by returning the state to white control. After Ames's request for federal troops to oversee the election was refused by President Grant (because of the political sentiment in the North against continuing federal intervention in the South), the governor called upon the militia temporarily. As election day approached, however, he dismissed the militia, believing that Democratic leaders would keep their promises to refrain from further provocations and promote an orderly election process.

Not surprisingly, the opposite course of action ensued, as whites used intimidation including physical violence to prevent thousands of African Americans from voting. They literally forced many other black voters to cast ballots for Democrats. While it was a shameless travesty of justice, no one could deny that the "Mississippi Plan" worked, as the 1875 election resulted in an overwhelming victory for the white Democrats, who won controlling majorities in both houses of the legislature and elected most county officials.

"Redemption"

Early in 1876, the Democrats moved quickly to impeach Republican officials, charging them with bribery, theft, unconstitutional acts, and other violations of law. The house of representatives impeached Lieutenant Governor Davis, who was convicted by the senate and removed from office. Superintendent of Education Cardoza and Governor Ames resigned following their impeachment in the house but before the senate could take action. With the office of lieutenant governor already vacant, the successor to the governor's office was the president pro tempore of the senate, John M. Stone.[2] By the end of March 1876 the entire executive branch was controlled by white conservative Democrats. Soon the judicial branch was also brought under that party's influence, as Governor Stone made appointments to fill vacancies on the expiration of judges' terms. During the course of 1876, therefore, all three branches of state government were "restored" to the white Democrats. But their so-called "redemption" of the state would depend on what actions, if any, the federal government might take in response.

THE HAYES-TILDEN COMPROMISE

The success of the "First Mississippi Plan" was confirmed by the settlement of the disputed presidential election of 1876. In the compromise involving twenty con-

2 Stone served the remainder of Ames's term and was reelected for a full term (1878–82). In1889 he was elected for another term.

tested electoral votes, the Democrats in Congress, led by Southerners including newly elected Senator Lucius Quintus Cincinnatus Lamar of Mississippi, agreed to accept the election of Republican Rutherford B. Hayes and sacrifice their candidate, Samuel Tilden, in return for certain guarantees. Among them was a promise by Hayes, which he kept, to withdraw the remnants of Federal troops from the South, to appoint a Southerner to his cabinet, and to recommend federal funds for improvements in Southern states. These policies, particularly the troop removal, symbolized the end of Reconstruction in Mississippi and the other former Confederate states, all of which would remain under the control of the Democratic party for the rest of the nineteenth and almost all of the twentieth century.

SELECTED SOURCES

Bell, Frank C., "The Life and Times of John R. Lynch, 1847–1939: A Case Study," *Journal of Mississippi History* 38 (February 1976): 53–68.

Bond, Bradley G., *Mississippi: A Documentary History* (Jackson: University Press of Mississippi, 2003).

Currie, James T., "The Beginnings of Congressional Reconstruction in Mississippi," *Journal of Mississippi History* 35 (August 1973): 267–286.

Ellem, Warren A., "Overthrow of Reconstruction in Mississippi," *Journal of Mississippi History* 54 (May 1992): 175–201.

Harris, William C., *The Day of the Carpetbagger: Republican Reconstruction in Mississippi* (Baton Rouge: Louisiana State University Press, 1979).

———, *Presidential Reconstruction in Mississippi* (Baton Rouge: Louisiana State University Press, 1967).

———, "The Reconstruction of the Commonwealth 1865–1870," in Richard Aubrey McLemore, ed., *A History of Mississippi*, 2 vols. (Hattiesburg: University & College Press of Mississippi, 1973), 1: 542–570.

Humphrey, George D., "The Failure of Mississippi Freedmen's Bureau in Black Labor Relations, 1865–1867," *Journal of Mississippi History* 45 (February 1983): 23–37.

Libby, Billy W., "Senator Hiram Revels of Mississippi Takes His Seat, January–February, 1870," *Journal of Mississippi History* 37 (November 1975): 381–394.

Mann, Kenneth Eugene, "Blanche Kelso Bruce: United States Senator without a Constituency," *Journal of Mississippi History* 38 (May 1976): 183–98.

McNeily, J. S., "Climax and Collapse of Reconstruction in Mississippi," *Publications of the Mississippi Historical Society*, 12: 283.

Nieman, Donald G., "The Freedmen's Bureau and the Mississippi Black Code," *Journal of Mississippi History* 40 (May 1978): 91–118.

Sansing, David G., "Congressional Reconstruction," in Richard Aubrey McLemore, ed., *A History of Mississippi*, 2 vols. (Hattiesburg: University & College Press of Mississippi, 1973), 1: 571–589.

Scales, Lura, "Mississippi Public Schools, 1870–1876," Master's Thesis, 1970, Mississippi College.

Thompson, Julius, *Hiram R. Revels, 1827–1901: A Biography* (New York: Arno Press, 1982).

Timberlake, Elise, "Did the Reconstruction Give Mississippi Her Public Schools," *Publications of the Mississippi Historical Society*, 12: 72.

CHAPTER THIRTEEN

Bourbons and Populists

DEMOCRATIC PARTY SUPREMACY

Beginning with their overthrow of the Republican leaders in 1876, the Democrats steadily expanded their grip on the state. The last important Republican holdouts were U.S. Senators James L. Alcorn and Blanche K. Bruce, an African American. But when Alcorn's term ended in 1877, his position was taken by L. Q. C. Lamar who had been overwhelmingly elected by the legislature in 1876. Voters that year favored Democratic presidential candidate Tilden by a wide margin and elected Democrats to all six seats in the House of Representatives. Thus, except for Senator Bruce, whose term would end in 1881, the entire Mississippi delegation to Congress was composed of Democrats.

The key reason for the Democrats' success was their disfranchisement of African Americans and their use of the race issue to convert white Republicans to their party. The 1876 vote was a portent of this trend: only about one-third of the total number of votes cast went to Republican candidates. In the following decades—indeed for generations—the Republican party would be increasingly perceived as the "black man's party." It continued to nominate candidates in local elections and occasionally in statewide contests; however, as new state laws virtually eliminated African American suffrage, particularly following the adoption of the Constitution of 1890, Republicans ceased to be a meaningful factor in state politics.

L. Q. C. Lamar. Courtesy Mississippi Department of Archives and History.

THE BOURBONS

The leading Democrats in Mississippi, those who had "redeemed" the state from Republican rule, were known as Bourbons. In general they were aristocratic conservatives who were reluctant and sometimes unwilling to accept the social and political results of the Civil War. Most Bourbon political bosses had been Democrats before the war, and many of them had served as Confederate officers. Favoring the disfranchisement of virtually all blacks and even some whites, they actually restored some aspects of the antebellum social order. In these traits they were occasionally likened to the French royal family, with its "fleur-de-lis" emblem, that had been overthrown during the French Revolution but had returned to power after the fall of Napoleon in 1815.

And despite the Mississippi Bourbons' maintenance of a "lily white" Democratic party, as practical businessmen they understood that some changes to the old economic order would benefit the state they controlled. Thus they supported conservative capitalists who wanted to diversify the state's economy and attract outside investments, dollars to fuel business growth, including railroads and industrial manufacturing. To achieve these goals they were willing to make financial deals with Northern businessmen, and in this respect were often viewed as friends of big business and unsympathetic towards the plight of small farmers. This image cost the Bourbons politically, as various agrarian or "populist" organizations began to demand reform.

Always the pragmatists, however, the Bourbons understood what was required to retain political control and accomplish their financial goals. Theirs was the delicate balance of satisfying the masses of small farmers, cooperating with the federal government, and promoting national reconciliation, even while presiding over a society that clearly maintained white supremacy in the social and political order.

GOVERNORS JOHN M. STONE AND ROBERT LOWRY, 1876–1896

Prominent representatives of Bourbon leaders in the late nineteenth century include two governors and three U.S. senators. After assuming office on the resignation of Governor Adelbert Ames in March 1876, John M. Stone, a former school teacher, a Confederate veteran, and state senator from Iuka in Tishomingo County, was elected to a full term in 1877. Then, following Robert Lowry's two terms as governor, Stone was elected again in 1889 and served as governor during the years of constitutional change, finally leaving office in 1896.

As the first "Redeemer" governor, Stone sought to reduce state expenditures, lower taxes, and promote industrial and railroad development. Some of his actions, however, aroused opposition among the agrarians—populist groups of small farmers. For example, as a fiscal conservative, he opposed currency inflation by the federal government—which in this era included the issuing of "greenbacks" and raising limits on silver coinage to get more money in circulation. In 1878 he further alienated the agrarians by vetoing a bill to regulate railroads. But more appealing to some populists was Stone's support for public education; during his first administration the legislature founded the Mississippi Agricultural and Mechanical College (later Mississippi State University) over which Stone presided as president after his final term as governor.

Perhaps the most conservative Bourbon leader, Governor Lowry (1882–90) continued Stone's pro-business agenda, although the state's public debt rose during Lowry's two terms. In 1884 he vetoed a bill for state regulation of the railroads but then approved a different, weaker measure that created a railroad commission, the three members of which the governor would appoint. Illustrating his resistance to government intervention in private business, Lowry appointed as the first chair of the new commission former governor Stone, who shared Lowry's conservative philosophy and had vetoed a similar bill six years earlier. Nevertheless, the new railroad commission, the forerunner of the state highway commis-

African American convicts at work. Courtesy Mississippi Department of Archives and History.

sion of the twentieth century, was a turning point in governmental regulation of interstate commerce.[1]

Governor Lowry consistently opposed a convention to rewrite the state constitution, primarily because he disagreed with the populists' demands for reforms. One urgently needed action that Lowry's administrations failed to accomplish was the termination of convict leasing, an atrocious practice that increased rapidly in the 1880s. The system forced prisoners, primarily black men, to labor in miserable conditions subject only to the capricious whim of the leaser. Because of discriminatory laws, a prejudiced judicial system, and their impoverished circumstances in general, blacks greatly outnumbered whites in the state's jails. Thus, by leasing convicts to big planters in return for revenue, a practice not unlike that of "hiring out" slaves in antebellum times, Mississippi, like a number of other southern states, was in fact virtually resuming the institution of slavery.

OTHER BOURBON LEADERS

On the national level the voice and face of Mississippi Bourbons were the state's officials in Washington, D.C. Among those leaders, Senators L. Q. C. Lamar, James Z. George, and Edward C. Walthall exerted the most clout in state and federal politics. Lamar, who moved up from the House to the Senate in 1877, had an illustrious career. A native of Georgia, he had practiced law in Oxford, Mississippi, before his election to the U.S. House of Representatives in 1856. He had resigned from Congress in December 1860 to become a member of the secession convention. Following military and diplomatic service in the Confederacy, he had served as a delegate to the constitutional conventions of 1865 and 1868 before becoming the first Mississippi Democrat elected to Congress during Reconstruction. While a member of the House of Representatives (1873–77), he had helped design the Mississippi Plan of 1875.

---

1 In *Stone v. Farmers Loan and Trust Co.* (1886) the U.S. Supreme Court upheld the Mississippi railroad commission law generally but ruled that the state's regulatory power was limited and that portions of the law violated the due process clause of the Fourteenth Amendment. The following year the U.S. Congress enacted the Interstate Commerce Act, establishing a federal commission to regulate railroads.

In contrast to his early partisan activities, Lamar's post-Reconstruction career was characterized by national statesmanship. His eulogy for Senator Charles Sumner in 1874 and his leadership in the compromise of 1877 helped identify Lamar as a genuine supporter of North-South reconciliation. In his moving speech before the crowded chamber of the U.S. House of Representatives, Lamar said in part:

> Charles Sumner in life believed that all occasion for strife and distrust between the North and South had passed away, and there no longer remained any cause for continued estrangement between those two sections of our common country. . . . Shall we not, while honoring the memory of this great champion of liberty, this feeling sympathizer with human sorrow, this earnest pleader for the exercise of human tenderness and heavenly charity, lay aside the concealments which serve only to perpetuate misunderstandings and distrust, and frankly confess that on both sides we most earnestly desire to be one—one not merely in political organization; one not merely in community of language, and literature, and traditions, and country; but more and better than all that, one also in feeling and in heart?
>
> . . . .
>
> Would that the spirit of the illustrious dead, whom we lament today, could speak from the grave to both parties to this deplorable discord, in tones which would reach each and every heart throughout this broad territory: My countrymen! know one another and you will love one another.

The first Mississippian to serve in a president's cabinet after the war, Lamar was appointed secretary of the interior by President Grover Cleveland in 1885. Two years later Cleveland appointed him a justice on the United States Supreme Court, a position Lamar held until his death in 1893.

Lamar's career illustrated the Bourbon's realistic political approach. By helping to heal the sectional wounds created by the war, he secured for Mississippi and the South federal funds for internal improvements. On national currency matters, he went against popular sentiment in the state and followed the conservative Bourbon line by voting against the Bland-Allison Silver bill in 1878 (see p. 168–69). He was an advocate for the railroads and specifically supported the construction of a projected transcontinental line that would connect the South with California.

Lamar and James George had strikingly similar careers. They were born within a year of each other in Georgia, but George's family had moved to Mississippi first, while he was still a child. Both men were lawyers and both had health problems that interfered with their military pursuits. After serving together in the secession convention, they entered into the service of the Confederacy. George rose to the rank of brigadier general of Mississippi troops, while Lamar withdrew from military service in 1862 as a lieutenant colonel. During Reconstruction George helped reorganize the Democratic party, and as its chairman in 1875 he played a critical role in the plan to overthrow the Republicans. He served briefly as chief justice of the state supreme court before being elected to the U.S. Senate,

Ethelbert Barksdale, influential editor of the *Jackson Clarion*. Courtesy Mississippi Department of Archives and History.

succeeding Senator Blanche Bruce in 1881. George and Lamar were Senate colleagues until 1885, when Lamar entered President Cleve-land's cabinet. George would be reelected two times and served in the upper house until his death in 1897.

In contrast to other Bourbon leaders, Senator George backed many of the agrarian proposals, including currency expansion, state regulation of railroads, and civil service reform. Therefore, in spite of his identification with the Democratic party aristocracy, he received steady support from the agrarian constituency. Unlike most other Bourbon Democrats, George favored calling the state constitutional convention of 1890 and was a leader in writing the new document. His support for such populist causes, however, did not erase George's Bourbon label. In 1892 the Farmers' Alliance nominated Ethelbert Barksdale, influential editor of the *Jackson Clarion* and a Democratic party leader who promised tighter regulation of railroads, to challenge, albeit unsuccessfully, Senator George's reelection by the legislature.

Edward C. Walthall of Holly Springs, perhaps the most aristocratic Bourbon, had served as a district attorney before participating in the war and rising to the rank of major general. In 1885 Governor Lowry appointed Walthall to fill the vacancy in the Senate caused by Lamar's resignation. Walthall was subsequently elected to that office and continued in the Senate until 1894, when he resigned due to illness. A year later, however, Senator Anselm J. McLaurin became a candidate for governor, and Walthall reentered the Senate, serving until his death in 1898.

Having been a lawyer who represented the railroads, Walthall was unable to gain as much support from the agrarians as did Senator George. Walthall disagreed with the disgruntled farmers' groups on some important issues; for example, he opposed calling the 1890 constitutional convention, predicting that the disfranchisement of black voters would not solve the race question. On the other hand, he supported many reforms favored by the populists, including the Interstate Commerce Act, the Sherman Anti-Trust Act, and the free coinage of silver.

THE POPULISTS

Notwithstanding their consolidation of power, several threats to the Bourbons' dominant political "machine" arose during the last three decades of the nineteenth century. Internal dissensions were occasionally disruptive, as seen for example in Ethelbert Barksdale's opposition to Lamar, particularly on the Bland-Allison silver matter. But the most serious challenge came from the populists, a loosely aligned group of small farmers and progressive third-party advocates. While they wanted political changes that would weaken Bourbon dominance, abolish convict leasing, and prohibit alcoholic beverages, the populists' principal concerns were economic in nature. They demanded financial reforms that included a more flexible currency, one with more silver coins and paper notes in circulation, which would help debt-ridden small farmers and artisans. Another proposition they supported was the "sub-treasury plan," a program designed to protect farmers against falling commodity prices by allowing them to obtain federal loans secured by stored crops. But the populists' paramount interest related to strict governmental controls over big corporations, upon which most folks depended for their very livelihoods. They demanded regulations that would stop railroads from engaging in price-fixing schemes that not only charged farmers exorbitant rates for transporting their products but discriminated in favor of big shippers and against small farmers. The populists called further for public supervision of banks, particularly to prevent them from charging unfairly high interest rates on loans that farmers needed in order to buy land, mules, plows, seed, and other equipment and supplies essential to their operations.

The birth of the populist movement came during Reconstruction with the creation of the Patrons of Husbandry, known casually as the "Grange," a fraternal order of farmers that had begun in the midwestern states. The founder, Oliver H. Kelley, helped organize chapters of the Grange in Mississippi during the early 1870s. At first nonpolitical, Grangers met to discuss improved farming methods and to devise various cooperative programs, through which they could band together to buy and sell in bulk at substantial savings. Then, coming together to defend themselves against the threatening practices of powerful railroads and banks, Grangers increasingly adopted overtly political strategies in the following decade. Many small farmers in the state joined the Farmers' Alliance movement and associated with the Greenback party, both precursors of the national People's party, known as the Populist party, which would be officially established in 1891.

This movement undertook its first major political campaign in 1881 when various independent populist opponents of the Bourbon Democrats fused with the Republican and Greenback parties, hoping to serve as a viable "third-party" choice for voters like themselves who felt ignored by the ruling Bourbon "Redeemers." Under the banner of the Greenback party, these groups came together to nominate for governor Benjamin R. King, a former Whig, who received most blacks' votes but lost

Meeting place for the Grangers in Vicksburg. Courtesy Mississippi Department of Archives and History.

white support because of the party's association with the Republicans and blacks. The result was a landslide victory for Robert Lowry, the Bourbon Democrat, and the virtual disappearance of the Greenbackers in the state, although on the national level the "Greenback-Labor" party in 1884 nominated for vice president Mississippian Absalom M. West, a former Whig and president of the Mississippi Central Railroad.

Notable agrarian leaders who formed the Populist party in Mississippi included Thomas P. Gore, the sightless orator from Webster County, and Rufus K. Prewitt of Ackerman. Although they were elected to the state legislature and to the U.S. House of Representatives as Democrats, farmers Clark Lewis of Noxubee County and Joseph H. Beeman of Scott County were active members of the Farmers' Alliance and campaigned as supporters of its platform.

Perhaps the most widely recognized and definitely the most outspoken Mississippi Populist was Frank Burkitt, of Okolona, editor of the *Chickasaw Messenger*. Frequently donning an old Confederate uniform and a wool hat, Burkitt promoted the Grange and the Farmers' Alliance, blasted the Bourbons, supported Populist candidates, and demanded a new state constitution. "The Wool Hat," his widely read pamphlet, became the emblem of agrarians throughout the South. Burkitt was elected to the legislature in the 1880s but would fail in his congressional campaign of 1892, receiving 39 percent of the vote, and in his 1895 gubernatorial bid against Anselm McLaurin, attracting only 27 percent.

The Demand for a New State Constitution

Beginning in the 1870s, leaders of the agrarian movement crusaded for a new state constitution. Their goal was the disestablishment of Bourbon political authority, which they blamed for economic and social hardships, including unfair practices by creditors and corporations, unsatisfactory progress in public education, the cruelty of convict leasing, and even the misuses of alcohol and gambling.

African Americans experienced the greatest grievances, suffering not only from financial woes but also from the state's racist practices. White officials used both legal and illegal means to control and intimidate blacks, including "fusion" political strategies and gerrymandering, early "Jim Crow" laws, "bulldozing" (using threats and bullying), and, most barbaric of all, lynching. As the state's total population increased from 1,131,597 in 1880 to 1,551,270 in 1900, the number of blacks rose faster than the number of whites, amounting to about 59 percent of the total population. This formidable segment of the populace was a potential source of votes for Populist candidates, provided however that it remained enfranchised.

The Populists, therefore, demanded reforms to alleviate the problems experienced by small farmers, both black and white. They wanted greater popular involvement in state and local government, including the election (not the appointment) of judges, which they believed would lead to the enactment of various economic and social reforms. Their ideas were opposed by Bourbon Democrats like Governor Lowry, who feared increasing involvement of the masses, including African Americans, and warned that constitutional changes could cause the renewal of federal interference in state affairs. Using the race issue, therefore, Bourbon Democrats frustrated Populists' chances of winning elections and getting meaningful reforms into a new constitution. A divided white vote, the Bourbons forcefully argued, would lead to "Negro domination" as in the "dark days" of Reconstruction.

Following the defeat of bills authorizing a constitutional convention in several successive legislatures, the movement for a new constitution culminated in the late 1880s. Finally a bill passed ordering an election to determine whether the state's voters favored a convention. Even though the bill was blocked by Governor Lowry's veto, the voters were given the same opportunity to decide the question during the 1889 state elections.

In the campaign Bourbon leaders took different stands: Senator George spoke in favor of a convention; Senator Walthall opposed it; and gubernatorial candidate John Stone refrained from taking a position but promised to support the voters' decision. Also aware of political realities, the Populists understood that success depended on their making compromises with the Bourbons, primarily on the question of black suffrage.

The turning point came when the Bourbons, led by George and Stone, made a deal with the Populists. If the latter group would agree to include black suffrage restrictions in the new constitution, then Stone would support legislation for the convention. Following his election, Governor Stone kept his word and approved a bill ordering an election of delegates to a constitutional convention in 1890. Most legislators from western counties, where African Americans outnumbered whites, voted against the bill. Except for legislators from the northeastern counties, most representatives and senators from the white counties in the eastern sections, the seat of the Populists' support, favored the bill.

Following the election of delegates late in July 1890, the convention assembled in Jackson on August 12 and continued through October. All but four of the 134 delegates were Democrats, and there was only one African American, Isaiah T. Montgomery of Mound Bayou, who also was one of only three Republican members. The delegates included 57 lawyers, 48 farmers, and 8 planters.

Isaiah Montgomery (1847–1924) was born and raised as a slave at Davis Bend in Warren County on a plantation owned by Joseph E. Davis, older brother of Jefferson Davis. Schooled under the tutelage of his father, Benjamin T. Montgomery, who had received an education as a slave in Virginia prior to being sold to Davis, Isaiah was given increasing responsibilities in his master's business affairs. After the war the Montgomery family contracted to buy the Davis property, which they managed until the early 1880s when Isaiah opened a store in Vicksburg. In the meantime Isaiah's growing interest in creating a separate colony for African Americans led to his involvement in a brief and futile exodus to Kansas in 1879 and culminated in his establishment of Mound Bayou in Bolivar County in 1887. On the issue of suffrage he supported the 1890 constitution's literacy requirements, explaining that he preferred ignorance rather than race as a reason for disfranchisement, reasoning that blacks could overcome the former barrier but not the later. Photograph courtesy Mississippi Department of Archives and History.

Judge S. S. Calhoon of Jackson was elected president, defeating Robert C. Patty of Noxubee County. Perhaps the most influential member, Senator George, led the committee that proposed the critical suffrage provisions.

THE CONSTITUTION OF 1890

The Right to Vote

A principal purpose for the convention—setting new qualifications for voting—was the most controversial issue. Delegates from counties in which blacks composed the majority population wanted strict voting requirements including literacy and property owning, while those from white counties favored moderation, so that fewer whites would be disfranchised. The final package on suffrage, however, would have the effect of disfranchising most blacks as well as many whites. In order to qualify to vote, one now would have to be a resident of the state for at least two years (instead of six months) and in the voting precinct for at least one year (instead of one month in the county). To register, a person now was required to give a "reasonable interpretation" of any portion of the state constitution that a local election official might ask him to read or read to him. In addition, voters had to register at least four months prior to election day, and they had to provide proof that they had paid the annual poll tax and other taxes for the past two years. Finally, persons convicted of certain crimes were disqualified. This entire scheme to disenfranchise African Americans has been called by some historians "the Second Mississippi Plan."[2]

Bill of Rights and General Provisions

The new constitution did not significantly alter the general structure of state government as prescribed by previous constitutions. Several changes in the Bill of Rights and the General Provisions, however, revealed the convention's intention to alter fundamentally the substance of the Reconstruction constitution of 1868. Section 6 included a new provision emphasizing state sovereignty (which would be used in the 1960s to resist federal civil rights requirements). Although the section prohibiting the state's withdrawal from the United States was retained (Section 7), a new provision directed the legislature to provide pensions for indigent Confederate veterans and their widows (Section 272).

A number of alterations were craftily designed to obstruct or deny certain rights to African Americans and other persons. Section 12 guaranteeing the right to bear arms contained a new clause allowing the legislature to "regulate or forbid carrying concealed weapons" (measures that might be selectively enforced by white lawmen). The new bill of rights omitted several sections in the 1868 document that had intended to protect the civil rights of persons without property or education. Of particular significance was the deletion of sections excluding property ownership as a qualification for jurors and officeholders, banning property and educational qualifications for suffrage, and guaranteeing citizens' equal rights

2 One strategy to accomplish the dilution of the African American vote but at the same time broaden the white electorate was the extension of suffrage to white women, an idea supported by Populist reformers inside and outside the convention, but one which was too far ahead of the times.

of travel on public conveyances. Alternatively, Section 264 was inserted to mandate that all jurors meet the new suffrage requirements and pass educational tests. Section 263 expressly prohibited marriages between whites and African Americans, including "mulattos," who were defined as persons having "one-eighth or more of negro blood." The protection of married women's property rights was modified somewhat in Section 94, which allowed the legislature to regulate contracts between spouses.

Several new provisions concerning religion were also added. Section 18 prohibiting religious tests for officeholders was extended to forbid the exclusion of "the Holy Bible from use" in public schools. In Section 265 of the general provisions the requirement that officeholders believe in "a Supreme Being" was retained, but Sections 269–70 voided all bequests of estates to religious denominations.

The Legislative Department

Members of both state houses would be elected to serve four-year terms. A representative had to be at least twenty-one years old, a qualified voter, and resident of the state for at least four years and of his county for at least two years. A senator had to be at least twenty-five years old and otherwise fulfill the same qualifications as a representative. The legislature was reapportioned with 13 additional representatives from the white counties. The number of representatives could not be fewer than 100 or exceed 133, and the senate had to have at least 30 members but not more than 45.

The regular sessions of the legislature would convene in even-numbered years beginning on the first Tuesday after the first Monday in January. Appropriations bills had to be passed by at least three fifths of the members present and voting in each house. Section 258 retained the old limitations on the use of the state's credit and the prohibition on the payment of the Union and Planters' bank bonds. Any portion (or line) in such bills could be vetoed by the governor. But, by a two-thirds majority vote in both houses, the legislature could override a veto and enact laws without the governor's approval. Moreover, the legislature had some control over the executive and judicial officers through the power of impeachment.

The Executive Department

Both the governor and lieutenant governor had to be at least thirty years old, qualified voters, citizens of the United States for at least twenty years, and residents of the state for at least five years. They would be elected to serve four-year terms, and the governor could not be reelected for a succeeding term. The governor had to receive a majority of both the electoral votes and the popular votes. Because electoral votes were divided among the counties according to the number of their representatives in the house, the Populists and white counties gained more control in gubernatorial elections. If no person received both required majorities, electoral and popular, then the house of representatives would elect the governor from among the top two candidates.

While the governor was limited by the no-successive-term clause, he did exercise several important responsibilities. His legislative duties included making recommendations to the legislature, signing or vetoing bills, and calling the legislature into special session. His judicial powers included pardoning convicted criminals and making appointments to fill temporary vacancies in the courts. His executive authorities included his positions as commander-in-chief of the state military forces and as chief law enforcer, as well as his powers of appointment and removal.

The lieutenant governor presided as president of the senate, and in case of a vacancy in the office of governor, he succeeded to that position. Unlike the governor, the lieutenant governor was not prohibited from succeeding himself in office.

The other members of the executive branch were the secretary of state, the state treasurer, and the state auditor, who were elected by the voters and served four-year terms. The treasurer and auditor were banned from immediate reelection to the same office. All these officers had to be at least twenty-five years of age and citizens of the state for at least five years.

Executive officers on the county level were the sheriffs, coroners, tax assessors, and surveyors. They served four-year terms, and except for the sheriffs, they were eligible for immediate reelection. Sheriffs had the general responsibility of enforcing laws and collecting taxes.

The Judicial Department

Next to the suffrage issue, the most controversial matter concerned the selection of judges. It was in their effort to return to an elective judiciary that the Populists lost their biggest battle in the convention on a final vote of 36 yeas to 55 nays. Under the new constitution, all judges would continue to be appointed by the governor with the advice and consent of the senate. The supreme court, which had appellate jurisdiction, would continue to comprise one judge from each of the three supreme court districts. The supreme court judges would serve nine-year terms with one judge being appointed every three years. They had to be at least thirty years old and practicing attorneys and citizens of the state for at least five years.

Circuit and chancery court judges would serve four-year terms in districts established by the legislature. They had to be at least twenty-six years old, practicing attorneys, and citizens of the state for at least five years. Basically, the circuit courts had original jurisdiction in civil and criminal cases, while the chancery courts' jurisdiction included equity matters and other cases involving various family controversies and property disputes. District attorneys would serve four-year terms in each circuit court district, and the manner of their selection and their duties were to be prescribed by the legislature.

Qualifications for the state attorney general were the same as those for the circuit and chancery court judges. Also having a four-year term, the attorney general would be elected at the same time and in the same manner as the other executive officers of the state; he could be reelected to successive terms.

On the county level, a board of supervisors had jurisdiction over the roads, ferries, and bridges. It was composed of one member elected by the voters in each of five districts. The supervisors had to be residents and property owners within their districts. Within each supervisor's district at least one justice of the peace had jurisdiction over minor controversies—those not exceeding $200.00, petty misdemeanors, and lesser crimes for which the punishment was limited to a fine or imprisonment in the county jail. The justice of the peace would be elected by the voters within his district for a four-year term. The only qualification for this officer was that he had to be a resident of the district for at least two years.

The Populist Scorecard

Despite their role in obtaining the new constitution, the outvoted Populist delegates scored only two of their major goals. Article seven included restrictions on corporations, especially the railroads. The legislature was authorized to charter all corporations and to tax the property of all private corporations that operated for pecuniary gain. Local governments were prohibited from buying stock in or making loans to railroads or other corporations. The legislature was directed to enact laws regulating railroad practices and charges and supervising railroad businesses. This article, moreover, contained specific restrictions on railroads and other corporations.

Another reform supported by the Populists was the abolition of the state's practice of leasing convicts to businesses and individuals beginning in 1895. This provision, however, did not apply to county prisoners, who could still be leased out to persons or corporations in the county where they were convicted. Moreover, the legislature could authorize the state's employment of penitentiary convicts for work on public roads, levees, and state lands. The committee on penitentiary affairs recommended the removal of the state penitentiary from Jackson and the use of that property for the future construction of a new capitol building.

The Populist delegates had ambivalent positions on the issue of public education. Generally favoring learning opportunities for farmers' children but opposing county taxes for schools in towns and state funds for colleges, they were ultimately displeased with most of the convention's actions. Article 8 on education contained important additions and alterations in three areas. First, an explicit requirement for racially segregated schools was added in Section 207. Second, greater emphasis was placed on the state's duty to provide adequate funding. Deriving from poll taxes, optional county or district school taxes, and the state's general fund, the "common school fund" had to pay the costs of maintaining schools in each district for at least four months each year. The legislature was ordered to oversee the income from sixteenth-section lands, including income from lands in the "Choctaw purchase" and the "Chickasaw school fund," which was reserved for public schools. The state funds would be distributed among the school districts in proportion to the number of educable children in each district. Third, the legislature was required to provide institutions for the education of deaf and blind persons and to support the state's institutions of higher education, specifically the Agricultural and Mechanical College (later Mississippi State University) and Alcorn Agricultural and Mechanical College (later Alcorn University).

On November 1 the final draft of the Constitution of 1890 was adopted by a vote of 104 to 8. Populists Frank Burkitt and Thomas Gore voted against the completed constitution, objecting to the literacy requirements for suffrage, the omission of an elective judiciary, and the convention's failure to submit the constitution to a popular vote. To facilitate the transitions following the adoption of the new constitution, the convention provided for the incumbent governor's term, which would have expired in January 1894, to extend to January 1896. Other state and county officials would serve out the terms to which they had been elected.

One of the most immediate and tangible results of the new constitution was the substantial reduction in the numbers of African American voters. Beginning in 1892 the so-called "Second Mississippi Plan" succeeded in excluding blacks from the state's political processes and the result would be the advancement of "Jim Crow" legislation segregating the races.

THE POPULIST PARADOX

In the last decade of the nineteenth century the most attractive candidates for political office were persons who appeared to favor regulations for railroads and other big businesses, an expansion of the currency, and more direct, popular participation in public affairs. Although the Populists fulfilled these prerequisites, they could not break the hold of the Democratic political machine. They failed to elect governors and congressmen, and while they succeeded in many legislative and local elections, the Populists remained a small minority party. In the presidential election of 1892, Democrat Grover Cleveland won about 90 percent of the state's popular vote. Four years later the Populist party candidate William Jennings Bryan (who was defeated nationally by Republican William McKinley) won a similar landslide vote in Mississippi. But what seemed to be a big Populist victory in the state was only an illusion, because the Democratic party had also nominated Bryan as its candidate that year; thus voting for Bryan the Populist was the same as voting for a Democrat!

This paradox of having the most popular positions but losing most elections was caused by the Populists' failure to change the Democrats' image as "redeemers" of the state from the Republicans' Reconstruction regime. Cynically, but deftly, using the color line, Democrats excluded African Americans from the party and warned that electing Populists would result in black rule, given that race's majority in the state. Other major obstacles were that the Democrats controlled most of the state's newspapers and, more important, the election apparatus. Each county executive committee of the Democratic party decided on how and when candidates would be nominated.

STATE FINANCIAL DIFFICULTIES

The financial panic of 1893 and collateral economic difficulties should have given the Populists their best opportunities for success. Experiencing serious shortages in tax revenues, the administration of Governor Stone resorted to questionable if not illegal financial devices. Following the legislature's action authorizing the issuance of interest-bearing paper bills, the United States Treasury Department intervened, and in September 1894 federal agents arrested Governor Stone along with the state treasurer and the state auditor. Although these officials were never indicted, the incident called attention not only to the extent of the state's financial distress but also its alleged mishandling of public affairs.

Looking for scapegoats some observers, including many Populists, blamed the monetary shortfalls on the state's increased levels of spending for public education. Pursuant to requirements in the new constitution, appropriations had risen by more than 300 percent, jumping to more than $920,000 by the mid-1890s. In 1896 state legislators considered but did not pass a bill that would have segregated tax revenues for public schools; similar to an unsuccessful proposal in the constitutional convention, this plan designated for African American schools only the income from taxes paid by African Americans.

Compounding the state's financial woes, several natural disasters and epidemics struck Mississippi in the 1890s. The decade began with a major flood of the Mississippi River that inundated large areas of the Delta, and it ended with severe outbreaks of yellow fever and typhoid.

Governor Anselm McLaurin, 1896–1900

Following an unusually long term as governor, extending from 1890 to 1896 as mandated by the new constitution, Stone was succeeded by Anselm McLaurin, a member of the Democratic machine. In the election of 1895 McLaurin defeated Frank Burkitt, the Populist, by an overwhelming vote of 46,873 (73 percent) to 17,466. The new governor, a native of Brandon in Rankin County, had served as a captain in the Confederate army. After the war he had practiced law and had represented Rankin County in the state house of representatives and in the 1890 constitutional convention. The legislature had elected McLaurin to fill United States Senator Walthall's seat in 1894–95. Following his term as governor, McLaurin was returned to the United States Senate, where he served until his death in 1909.

Financial Priorities

One of the main goals of the McLaurin administration was to end the state treasury deficit and balance the budget by raising the rates of ad valorem taxes (determined by the assessed value of property being taxed) and by resisting additional expenditures. An interesting example of the unusual frugality of the administration was the secretary of state's order to remove the costly telephones from the state capitol. Anticipating better financial conditions, legislators expressed an interest in the construction of a new capitol building. Over the governor's opposition, in 1896 the senate passed a bill appropriating $1 million for a new building on the site of the state penitentiary. The house of representatives, however, voted to reduce the appropriation by 50 percent and to have the structure remain in the existing location. A stalemate occurred when the two bodies failed to concur on the amount of the expenditure and the location. In a special session called by Governor McLaurin in 1897, the senate finally agreed with the house's new plan to issue $750,000 in bonds to cover the expense of erecting a new capitol, but the governor vetoed the bill. Thus, the proposed building would have to wait for a new administration in 1900.

The Spanish-American War, 1898

The most important event of McLaurin's administration was the United States' declaration of war against Spain in the spring of 1898. Mississippians strongly supported the war for Cuba's independence, sympathizing with the Cubans' wretched living conditions and mistreatment by the Spanish authorities, as described by the newspapers of the day. Three regiments of volunteers were organized at Camp Pat Henry near Jackson, and another regiment mustered at Columbus. Only the latter force, however, actually rendered service in Cuba, this at the conclusion of the war.

Unfortunately the war may have given some state officials the opportunity to practice graft. McLaurin was accused of various questionable practices, including nepotism and excessive use of his pardoning powers. And in this era of mounting support for the temperance movement, the governor's critics charged him with drunkenness, an allegation he publicly admitted.

McLaurin's term coincided with the end of the century and the beginning of a new era in Mississippi. The last Confederate veteran to serve as governor, McLaurin would be succeeded by a new generation removed from direct involvement in the Civil War. Indeed, the new leadership's enthusiastic support for the war effort against Spain symbolized in some ways an acknowledgment of the state's return to full allegiance to the Union.

The Triumph of "Jim Crow"

Such allegiance must have been easier for white Mississippians in view of certain rulings by the United States Supreme Court. In *Plessy* v. *Ferguson* (1896) the court essentially validated Mississippi's legal system of racial segregation by deciding that states could require separate facilities for blacks and whites as long as they were equal, the so-called "separate but equal" doctrine. Two years later, the court in *Williams* v. *Mississippi* upheld provisions of the 1890 constitution that were being used to deny African Americans certain civil rights, particularly the right to become registered voters. With such sanctions, state officials would persist in the maintenance of so-called Jim Crow laws for decades to come. The *Jim Crow* term began to be used in antebellum times when white minstrel entertainers painted their faces to resemble black people, creating derogatory and stereotypical images of black inferiority. As a practical matter, these Jim Crow laws guaranteed white supremacy and second-class citizenship for African Americans. The persistence of this "unreconstructed" attitude was reflected in the adoption of a new state flag in 1894 that contained the Confederate battle flag.

GOVERNOR ANDREW HOUSTON LONGINO, 1900–1904

The state began the new century under the leadership of Andrew H. Longino. A native of Lawrence County in south Mississippi, he earned the bachelor of arts degree at Mississippi College in 1876 and then studied law at the University of Virginia. He served in the state senate from 1880 to 1884, and was appointed chancery court judge in 1894. While still serving in that office, he was elected governor in 1899, defeating Rufus K. Prewitt, the nominee of the People's party (Populist), by a landslide vote of 42,273 to 5,007. Following his term as governor, Longino would continue in public office, serving as judge in Hinds County.

The Primary Election Law of 1902

Longino was the last governor to be nominated by the convention method. In his inaugural address he supported legislation for direct primary elections to nominate party candidates. With his sponsorship and the support of Populists, Republicans, and some Democrats in the eastern sections of the state, the legislature adopted the primary election law in 1902. This measure finally broke the Bourbons' control of the Democratic party, because it enabled their opponents to participate in the selection of all party nominees.

In the old convention process the Democratic party bosses—usually the Bourbons—actually hand-picked the party's nominees. The new law required all nominations be made in the primary elections, beginning in 1903. The primary would be held on the first Tuesday after the first Monday in August. If no candidate won a majority of the total vote, then a second primary would be held three weeks later between the two candidates receiving the largest number of votes. The general election was held on the first Tuesday after the first Monday in November.

Because the primary election law did not change the fact that Democratic party continued to dominate Mississippi politics in the early twentieth century, its nominees were virtually assured of being elected to office in the general elections of November. The primaries, therefore, became the actual contests in which the officeholders were chosen. Originated by the "Second Mississippi Plan" of 1890 and maintained by the legal and extralegal exclusion of blacks from the Democratic party as well as from the ballot box, this feature of the so-called "solid South" would continue until the 1970s.

Other Developments during Longino's Administration

Economic conditions at the turn of the century had improved since the panic of 1893. By the end of Longino's term, the state treasury had a positive balance, and investments of outside capital had risen to about $73 million, almost three times the amount invested during the McLaurin years. Notwithstanding such indications of economic progress, the Longino administration's most enduring accomplishments were several state symbols and institutions. In 1900 the legislature approved the selection of the magnolia as the state's official flower. That same year $1 million was appropriated for the construction of a new capitol. Located on the site of the state penitentiary, which was moved to Parchman in the Delta, the capitol was designed by architect Theodore C. Link and completed in July 1903. The Department of Archives and History was established in 1902 under the direction of Dunbar Rowland. On the Gulf Coast the Jefferson Davis residence, "Beauvoir," was opened as a home for disabled Confederate veterans and their widows and began receiving state appropriations in 1904.

Intrastate Sectional Disputes

Not unlike the earlier Bourbon-Populist conflicts, political disputes between the state's eastern and western counties continued during the Longino administration. One such controversy involved the method of distributing state funds for public schools. Simultaneously, the historic north-south sectional conflicts were revived by early-twentieth-century population growth in the southern part of the state. Along these lines a struggle developed concerning the apportionment of legislative seats, always a thorny issue. For purposes of maintaining regional parity in the legislature, Section 256 of the Constitution of 1890 divided the state into three geographic areas and guaranteed a minimum number of legislators from each section. An amendment to Section 256 in 1900 realigned the sections to reflect the population shifts. The new divisions were the northeastern, the central and southern, and the western counties.

The End of Bourbonism

The final collapse of Bourbon predominance came at the end of Longino's term. Anticipating the emerging "progressive" crusade, state leaders began to favor anti-trust laws, the unlimited coinage of silver, and the popular election of United States senators. The movement to tighten state supervision of railroads and other businesses gained momentum, and in 1902 an insurance department was established to enforce stricter state regulations. A new generation of voters, disillusioned with the old-style leadership, was ready for a complete break with the recent political past.

SELECTED SOURCES

Bond, Bradley G., "Edward C. Walthall and the 1880 Senatorial Nomination: Politics of Balance in the Redeemer Era," *Journal of Mississippi History* 50 (February 1988): 120.

————, *Mississippi: A Documentary History* (Jackson: University Press of Mississippi, 2003).

Clark, Eric, "Legislative Apportionment in the 1890 Constitutional Convention," *Journal of Mississippi History* 42 (November 1980): 298–315.

————, "Regulation of Corporations in the Mississippi Constitutional Convention of 1890," *Journal of Mississippi History* 48 (February 1986): 31–42.

Coleman, James P., "The Mississippi Constitution of 1890 and the Final Decade of the Nineteenth Century," in Richard Aubrey McLemore, ed., *A History of Mississippi*, 2 vols. (Hattiesburg: University & College Press of Mississippi, 1973), 2: 3–28.

Constitution of the State of Mississippi, 1890.

Cresswell, Stephen, *Multiparty Politics in Mississippi, 1877–1902* (Jackson: University Press of Mississippi, 1995).

Faries, Clyde J., "Redneck Rhetoric and the Last of the Redeemers: The 1899 McLaurin-Allen Campaign," *Journal of Mississippi History* 33 (November 1971): 283–298.

Halsell, Willie D., "The Bourbon Period in Mississippi Politics, 1875–1890," *The Journal of Southern History* 11 (1945): 519–546.

Kirwan, Albert D., *Revolt of the Rednecks, Mississippi Politics: 1876–1925* (Lexington: University of Kentucky Press, 1951).

Loewen, James W., and Charles Sallis, eds., *Mississippi: Conflict and Change* (New York: Random House, 1974), Chapter 10.

McMillen, Neil R., *Dark Journey: Black Mississippians in the Age of Jim Crow* (Urbana: University of Illinois Press, 1989).

Revels, James G., "Redeemers, Rednecks, and Racial Integrity," in Richard Aubrey McLemore, ed., *A History of Mississippi*, 2 vols. (Hattiesburg: University & College Press of Mississippi, 1973), 1: 590–621.

United States Bureau of the Census, Urban and Rural Population: 1900 to 1990.

Upchurch, Thomas Adams, "Why Populism Failed in Mississippi," *Journal of Mississippi History* 65 (Fall 2003): 249–276.

Wharton, Vernon L., *The Negro in Mississippi, 1865–1890* (Chapel Hill: The University of North Carolina Press, 1947).

CHAPTER FOURTEEN

Into the Twentieth Century: Economic and Social Trends

I receive from the landlady seeds tools stock
credit for food and usable living quarters
· ·
My shack has cardboard windows
A kitchen without knives
· · · · · · · · · · · · · · · · · · [1]

ECONOMIC CONDITIONS

A Population of Farmers

As Mississippians entered the new century and approached their centennial of statehood, they could review past economic and social trends and anticipate future developments. As they had for generation after generation, most families continued to work the land following the Civil War, and farming remained the predominant way of life into the twentieth century. Politicians and private citizens made efforts to improve the state's economy and raise living standards by diversifying crops and developing industry, but progress towards these goals was slow and generally unsuccessful.

One of the most significant trends of the post–Civil War era was the increasing number of small farmers. One quarter of a century after the conflict, 95 percent of the state's total population lived in rural areas, and 72 percent of all employed persons worked on farms. Composing about 59 percent of the state's total land area, were 114,318 farms averaging 122 acres in size. In the century's last decade the number of farms rose by 93 percent and the average farm size fell to only 83 acres. Now, most families either operated their own small farms, worked small units of land on larger farms or plantations as tenants (renters or sharecroppers), or labored as hired hands on plantations.[2]

The Burden of Indebtedness Sharecropping, basically the practice of providing labor in return for supplies and the use of farmland, evolved in the years following the Civil War. The former slaves, as well as many landless whites, agreed to "share" a certain percentage of the profits on their cotton crops with the landowner as payment for occupying his land. At first beneficial to both parties, the

---

1 Ellen Gilchrist, "Sharecropper," as quoted in Dorothy Abbott, ed., *Mississippi Writers: Reflections of Childhood and Youth*, vol. 3, *Poetry* (Jackson: University Press of Mississippi, 1988), 103.
2 On the eve of the Civil War there were about 37,000 farms averaging 370 acres.

A typical African American sharecropper's shanty. Courtesy Mississippi Department of Archives and History.

sharecropping system soon reduced tenants, particularly the blacks, to a kind of bondage not unlike slavery. How did this condition occur?

All tenants, even most small landowning farmers, had to borrow money early in the year, using mortgages on their land or the crop lien system, which was formalized by the agricultural lien law of 1876. This law authorized the landlord and the furnishing merchant (often the same person) to take liens or mortgages on crops to guarantee that they would be repaid by tenants to whom they routinely loaned money and furnished necessities. Then the tenants struggled to pay their debts at harvest time. But because the amount of cash income from the sale of crops was difficult to predict and often insufficient, the tenants were often forced to pay debts with portions of their crops. The latter practice was more likely for tenants who not only incurred debts for farming operations and rents but also had to provide their own buildings, mules, equipment, seed, and other necessities.

Unable to buy their own property, numerous black and white families made various arrangements to farm parcels of land belonging to planters. Some of these persons paid rent in cash, depending on the size and quality of the land they rented and the amount and types of equipment they supplied for themselves. But most of these renters became sharecroppers who lived on the planter's land with dwellings, water and fuel, and all farm equipment and supplies being provided by the landowner. Whether renting or sharecropping, however, all tenants were forced to borrow money or obtain personal necessities on credit from furnishing merchants—often their landlords—who took high-interest liens on the anticipated crops.

After the harvest when the accounts were settled, tenants often found themselves deeper in debt than when the growing season had begun, a cycle that obviously continued year after year. Rising numbers of the state's population, including virtually all African Americans, therefore, became captives to rising indebtedness and victims of other burdensome practices by the dominant creditor class.

Daily life in this era was difficult. Farming was backbreaking work at which most people barely eked out a living. In an era before the advent of modern machines, appliances, automobiles, and public water and electric utilities, the standard of living for most people would be hardly imaginable for a twenty-first-century person. Methods of producing crops had not changed for generations, and the mule remained the main work animal. The average price per pound of cotton in December 1890 was only 8.8 cents, and the average yield per acre was 198 pounds. The average cotton farm, therefore, produced only about $2,100 annual gross income.

The Persistence of Cotton   In spite of efforts to diversify crops in the post–Civil War years and the decline in cotton prices, farmers stubbornly relied on cotton as their main crop, often a requirement of their landlords. In 1890 more than 60 percent of all acreage producing primary crops was devoted to cotton. Other principal crops were corn (34 percent), oats, hay, and sweet potatoes. Relatively new sources of farm income included vegetables and livestock.

Attempts to Modernize   The failure to adopt progressive practices was due in part to farmers' lack of education generally and their unawareness or suspicion of new scientific methods in particular. Fertilizers, for example, were available, but most farmers considered them a waste of time and money, because they had had no reliable knowledge about their uses. The legislature took important steps toward reducing such resistance to change with the founding of agricultural and mechanical colleges at Alcorn and Starkville and the creation of state agricultural experiment stations. To help educate farmers these stations, beginning at Starkville in 1888, published bulletins on topics such as fertilizers, insects, livestock diseases, and the importance of developing water resources and improving farm-to-market transportation by constructing gravel-surfaced roads.

It was a particular insect that compelled Mississippi farmers to accept the practical value of applying scientific methods to agriculture. Traveling some sixty miles per day, the boll weevil had moved out of Mexico, across Texas and Louisiana, arriving near Natchez in 1907. Within three years, it had covered virtually all of Mississippi, devastating cotton farms and causing financial ruin in thousands of families. Threatening to wreck the state's economy from top to bottom, the boll weevil triggered panic among farmers, politicians, and businessmen. A new agricultural experiment station was established in the Delta, and scientists published circulars about the insect and locations of heaviest infestation. But they found no effective solutions, as some desperate farmers dusted or sprayed cotton plants with largely ineffective insecticides and others even attempted to catch weevils in traps! Pushed by the crisis, farmers now had no choice but to recognize the importance of implementing scientific techniques. Farmers' Institutes, fore-runners of the twentieth-century Cooperative Extension Service, offered programs on wide-ranging topics such as crop diversification and livestock production. Information was also disseminated through agricultural training programs in public schools and agricultural high schools.

Industrial Growth

Although politicians and business leaders promoted industrial development in the decades following the Civil War, there was no consistent state policy until the crisis of the Great Depression in the 1930s. Between 1880 and 1900 there were increases in the number of manufacturing establishments and in the value of finished products, but these numbers do not reveal much genuine industrial growth. Capital investments in cotton and woolen mills climbed to $3.5 million in the 1890s, and opportunities for nonfarm jobs gradually increased in some counties. The largest textile mills were located in three areas: on the border of Copiah and Lincoln counties at Wesson; in Clarke County at Enterprise; and in newly created Alcorn County at Corinth. Other expanding industries were cottonseed oil mills and lumber mills.

Overall, however, no major new industries were established. Although industrial growth quickened in the 1890s and the century ended with about 4,800 "factories," almost all of them were small shops and mills that employed five or fewer workers. Moreover, it was remarkable that in a cotton-producing state only nine major textile mills were in operation in 1890. The total number of factory employees rose to only about 16,000 persons in 1890 and climbed to a mere 26,000 by the turn of the century. Capital investments were similarly sluggish, reaching $15 million in 1890 and then rising to almost $36 million in 1900.

Thus, in spite of the Bourbon Democrats' pro-industry strategies, the state remained overwhelmingly agricultural at the end of the nineteenth century. Although the gross value of manufactured commodities as a percentage of farm production increased from 26 percent in 1890 to 45 percent in 1900, Mississippi ranked thirty-eighth nationally in gross value of industrial products and thirty-ninth in average number of workers in plants. More than 92 percent of the state's population was rural, making Mississippi the fourth most rural society in the nation.

Factors Opposing Industry   Many reasons underlay this slow industrial development. The state's agricultural heritage and the educational deficiencies of its overwhelmingly rural population fostered a persistent attitude that corporations were evil and people should earn their living from the land. This sentiment was reflected in the Constitution of 1890, which placed extensive restrictions on corporations, particularly the railroads, and in anti-industry legislation during subsequent decades. Laws limiting the amount of land that nonresident corporations could acquire and the state's adverse property-tax structure slowed industrial growth.

The Lumber Industry   Because forest land, next to farmland, was the state's major natural resource, lumbering became an important business in last decades of the nineteenth century, especially as railroads began to penetrate the vast interior areas of virgin forests. Other favorable factors were the increasing demand for

One Perfect Pine Tree 185 Years Old – 6 Cuts Below The Limb, Scaling 9,005 Feet, Grown On The Gloster Lumber Company Holdings, Gloster, Amite County, Miss.

"One perfect pine tree, 185 years old." Courtesy Mississippi Department of Archives and History.

longleaf pine timber in northern states, the proximity of timber lands and lumber mills to ports, the low costs for timber lands, and favorable geographic factors—flat or gently rolling land, and a climate that allowed for year-round work. Just after the turn of the century more than 60 percent of the state's industrial workers were lumbermen, and about half the value of all manufacturing came from this business.

The fastest growing lumbering operations were located along railroads and primarily in the Piney Woods and Delta regions. Because most Mississippians still believed that all land should be farmed and that clearing the great forest lands required excessive expenditures, northern investors moved into the state to buy hundreds of thousands of acres and start lumber businesses. The number of sawmills increased from 295 in 1880 to 608 in 1899, but the biggest growth came in the next decade, with 1,761 mills in operation mills by 1909. Capital investments in lumbering increased from just $1 million in 1880 to almost $11 million in 1899 and jumped to almost $39 million in 1910. Sawmills produced more than one billion board feet of lumber in 1899 and doubled that volume in the following decade. By 1910 the gross revenues from the lumber industry approached $43 million. By 1915 Mississippi ranked third among lumber-producing states, and production reached a record high in 1925 with more than three billion board feet. This thriving business, however, dropped fast with the coming of the Great Depression, which just happened to coincide with the exhaustion of the "first forests." By 1932 there were only 257 saw mills producing 500 million board feet, numbers that compared to those of 1889.

Transportation

The turn of the century witnessed increasing commercial activity along the Gulf Coast, with the establishment of canning factories for shrimp and oysters and with the opening of the Gulfport harbor as an official port of entry in 1904. New railroad construction and improvements of inland waterways facilitated commerce in other regions; however, in these years before the rise of the automobile, when most commercial traffic was borne by water and rail, there was little progress in the improvement of internal roadways. Appeals by private business groups for better roads as well as legislative enactments encouraging county road commissioners to construct and maintain roads yielded no noticeable results.

Inadequate Roads   The absence of a reliable system of public roads, therefore, was a fundamental obstacle to economic growth. Before the World War I years a tangled web of unplanned and unmapped local roads centered around county seats and other scattered places like cotton gins and warehouses and lumber yards. The two main impediments to road improvement were local county supervisor control rather than state supervision and the absence of tax revenues for road building and maintenance. The result was a haphazard system of local roads that was incomplete and poorly maintained. Roads did not necessarily connect with routes in other counties or even with those in other districts within the same county. They were impassable during floods or winter months and bridges were extremely unsafe or nonexistent.

In this setting of provincialism and isolation, most of the state's major products, cotton and lumber, had to be transported by river and rail. Farm and industrial developments in interior regions, therefore, had to wait for railroad construction, which was frequently retarded by the restrictive policies of state and local governments. Until the 1920s, road conditions remained so bad that the average cost for farmers to get their crops to market was a large percentage of the price (as much as one-sixth in some places) that they were paid for those products. Finally, as the 1920s progressed, the state's newly established highway commission would receive sufficient authority and funding to begin the construction and maintenance of a state system of roads.

Rivers   Rivers, of course, provided the oldest means of transportation for farmers and businesses in the state, and the first settlements were located near the banks of the major rivers and their tributaries. Bales of cotton were delivered on river boats from the Delta and the Loess Hills regions along the Yazoo, the Big Black, and Mississippi rivers to New Orleans. Farmers in the Black Prairie region shipped their products to Mobile along the Tombigbee River, and lumber barons in the Piney Woods floated log rafts down to the Gulf along the Pearl and Pascagoula rivers. As invaluable as water transportation was, however, it did not reach the state's expanding population in remote regions.

Railroads   Trains had some major advantages over river boats because the rail lines could extend to interior areas far from the riverbanks. In the late nineteenth and early twentieth centuries the railroads were also much more useful than the undeveloped and unreliable roads. Despite such obvious benefits, however, the development of rail lines was dilatory for many decades. Although numerous charters were issued before the Civil War, only four major railroad companies were well established by 1861. Even these lines were incomplete and lacked interstate connections, and most of them were destroyed during the war. During Reconstruction the trend was to build north-south lines to connect the Gulf Coast with the Ohio River and the city of Chicago and from these main lines to extend lateral branches into cotton and timber lands. Beginning in the 1870s fragmen-

Steam engine, a "cotton train." Courtesy Mississippi Department of Archives and History.

Ein Baumwollentrain

tary antebellum railroads began to merge with the Illinois Central (IC), which also built new lines within the state. The IC finally completed its uninterrupted connection between New Orleans and Chicago in 1889.

In eastern Mississippi there was not as much progress in the development of railroads, which would eventually connect with Mobile and northern markets. William C. Falkner (great grandfather of William Faulkner, who added the "u" to his surname) started the Ripley Railroad Company in northeast Mississippi but failed to achieve his plan of connecting lines in Tennessee with the Gulf and Ship Island Railroad, although the latter line was completed from the coast to Hattiesburg in the 1890s. This line and other small companies would finally consolidate into the Gulf, Mobile and Ohio Railroad in 1938 but would not connect Mobile with Chicago until 1947.

Several east-west railroads attempted to link the Mississippi River with Alabama cities such as Birmingham. They included the Alabama and Vicksburg, which ran through Meridian and Jackson generally along present-day Interstate 20, and the Columbus and Greenville in the general path and vicinity of present-day U.S. Highway 84. In the south the New Orleans and Texas Pacific Railroad ran through the Piney Woods and later became the Southern Railroad. By 1880 the Louisville and Nashville had extended its line from Mobile to New Orleans, 141 miles along the Gulf Coast.

Railroad track mileage expanded at a rapid rate, rising from about 990 miles of disconnected lines in poor condition in 1870 to about 3,000 miles in the 1890s and then to more than 4,300 miles at the height of railroad commerce in 1910. After World War I there was a steady decline in operative track mileage, as many local short lines failed due to changes in the economy and the emergence of automobiles and trucking businesses. In the 1920s railroads, which had been the state's basic and essential means of transporting freight and passengers, became increasingly obsolete for local traffic. The remaining major railroads were the IC, the Southern, the Gulf, Mobile and Ohio, and the Louisville and Nashville. Most of the business of these surviving larger systems involved transporting freight and passengers through the state and made relatively minor contributions to the state's economy.

New Opportunities for an Education

The Beginnings of a Public School System

Mississippians' struggle to raise their standard of living involved not only the search for economic improvements but also the desire to give their children better educational opportunities. The first state system of public education began during Congressional Reconstruction and maintained racially segregated schools until federal intervention during a "second reconstruction" nearly a century later. Article 8 of the Constitution of 1868 required the legislature to establish "a uniform system of free public schools . . . for all children between the ages of five and twenty-one years." As mentioned, the entire school system was to be supervised by an elected state superintendent and a state board of education—composed of the superintendent, the secretary of state, and the attorney general—which managed the school funds and appointed the original county superintendents. A school district was organized in each county, with separate districts for towns of five thousand or more residents. Each district was expected to maintain one or more schools for at least four months each year.

The first state superintendents of education were Henry R. Pease (1869–73) and Thomas W. Cardoza, an African American who was impeached and removed from office by the white "Redeemer" Democrats in 1876. During the first decades of the state school system, few children attended class regularly, and many never even entered the schoolhouse doors. Most parents, uneducated themselves, did not appreciate the value of schooling, but even those who did needed their children at home to help work the farm. Still other families could not afford to transport their children to schools that might be many miles away. By 1876, when Reconstruction ended, the average monthly attendance was only 38 percent of all the state's educable children. Even with this small proportion in class, the number of students per teacher was often excessively high, particularly in black schools.

By 1890, 60 percent of all school-age youths were enrolled in school, including two-thirds of all white and 55 percent of all black children on the rosters, though many were not present regularly. Because school-age blacks greatly outnumbered their white counterparts, their actual enrollment numbers were higher, but black pupils had fewer teachers. The result was that while each black teacher was responsible for instructing an average of 57 enrolled students, the student-teacher ratio in white schools was 35 to 1. After two decades, therefore, the faculties in most school districts were still too small and inadequately trained, the result of meager teacher salaries and the shortage of qualified persons available to teach.[3]

The first schools were financed primarily by revenues realized from public land sales, fines counties collected for violations of the law, the sale of certain state licenses, and special taxes. These proceeds were supposed to be divided pro rata among all educable children, but the early disbursements proved to be scanty and inequitable in distribution. Although 59 percent of the state's educable children were African Americans in 1890, most of the education funds went to white schools. There were two related reasons for these delinquencies: first, public sentiment opposed taxes for public education in general and for black schools in particular and, second, large portions of the funds went to white schools in the populous, black-majority counties, where very few blacks attended school. Less populous white-majority counties became increasingly unhappy with their relatively small shares of the education funds, because they reported higher numbers of students in regular attendance.

The Second Phase   Although most of the basic provisions for public education were retained in the Constitution of 1890, that document included two fundamental changes. Section 206 authorized the levying of additional state and county taxes, and Section 207 required separate schools for whites and blacks, a practice already well established. Under the new constitution the state superintendents of education, unlike the governor, could be reelected for successive terms. Governors, however, exerted considerable influence through their authority to fill vacancies upon the resignation of a superintendent. During the six de-

3 In 1890 there were 332,037 school-age African Americans, 226,649 school-age whites, 3,221 "colored" teachers, and 4,289 white teachers.

cades following the adoption of the Constitution of 1890, the superintendents with the longest tenures were initially appointed to office. In 1898 Governor Anselm McLaurin appointed Henry L. Whitfield, who would then be elected two times and serve until his resignation in 1907.

General Funding and Teachers' Salaries   A continuing obstacle to the advancement of public education was inadequate funding, a condition further exacerbated by growing political disagreements about how the meager school funds should be distributed. The financial source for public education was the "common school fund," which included poll-tax revenues, sixteenth-section funds, appropriations from the state treasury, and local tax revenues. But state spending for education was too little and its growth was too slow. In the mid-1890s the total annual sum was $616,000, only about $1.11 per student.

Nevertheless, political leaders continued to bemoan the overall costs of the school system and even tried to ban the use of white taxpayers' money for black schools. The latter efforts were mostly for political purposes, for such appropriations had been negligible for decades, and the legislature usually approved funds only when they were required to match grants given by out-of-state philanthropies.

After an intense geographic controversy involving the demand for more state funds for schools in white counties, the legislature in 1900 accepted Governor Andrew H. Longino's proposal to replace the pro rata method. By a large majority the voters approved a constitutional amendment requiring that school funds be distributed on the basis of actual school attendance. But even this issue had racial overtones. State school funds had been allotted among counties or districts on a basis of the total number of educable children. Because western counties with larger African American populations had greater total numbers of children, they received a larger percentage of the state money. Even so, these funds were spent mainly for white children, as many black children did not actually attend school. Claiming that their smaller shares were unfair, representatives of eastern counties demanded a different distribution formula.

The problem of too few qualified teachers, mainly due to low salaries and inadequate facilities, remained unresolved under the old "Bourbon" rule. Through the 1890s the average annual teacher salary in the most populous counties was less than $300 for white instructors and less than one-half that amount for their black counterparts, while in the smaller counties the monthly salary was as low as $16 for sessions of three to four months. With the ascendance of a new, "progressive" generation of leaders, however, state support for education gradually increased, but mostly for whites.

Public Higher Education

In the half century following the Civil War only a tiny number of white and black youths had access to a baccalaureate-level education within Mississippi. The war severely crippled or permanently closed all institutions of higher learning, and in the ensuing decades five state-sponsored colleges would provide opportunities for a limited number of students. At Oxford the University of Mississippi, "Ole Miss," reopened in 1865 with an enrollment of fewer than 200 stu-

The Lyceum at the University of Mississippi. Courtesy Westley F. Busbee, Jr.

dents, and that number rose to only 260 by 1900. Originally intended for white males, UM began to admit white women in 1882. The initial curriculum in the arts and sciences had expanded to include a school of law in 1854—the nation's fourth state-supported law school—as well as schools of education, medicine, pharmacy, business, and graduate studies in the first decade of the twentieth century. UM was also the first institution of higher learning in the state accredited by the Southern Association of Colleges and Schools (SACS), in 1895.

Alcorn College at Lorman (present-day Alcorn State University) was founded for African American males during Reconstruction in 1871, and was reorganized seven years later as Alcorn Agricultural and Mechanical College. The institution first admitted women in 1895 and had an enrollment of 425 students by 1900. Like other "land-grant" A&M colleges, Alcorn initially required students to work on the farm or in shops as part of the curricula and emphasized vocational training.

The State Agricultural and Mechanical College (present-day Mississippi State University) was founded in 1878 at Starkville for white males. By 1900 the college had a healthy enrollment of 516 students and offered three areas of study—agriculture, engineering, and textiles.

The largest college enrollment in 1900 was reported by the Industrial Institute and College at Columbus (present-day Mississippi University for Women), which was established in 1884 as the nation's first public institution of higher learning for women. It provided general education courses and training in the industrial arts for 700 students.

Holly Springs was the setting for several efforts to provide higher education for African Americans, but most of these schools survived only temporarily. A "State Normal School," which received some state support, was established in the post–Civil War decades. The school's purpose was to prepare teachers, but it had to limit its enrollment to about 200 students in 1900, for it had only three full-time faculty members. The status of the school changed in 1905 when the Mississippi Conference of the Colored Methodist Episcopal Church opened the Mississippi Industrial College, a private school for blacks that survived into the late 1980s.

Private Colleges

Most college students during this era attended the dozens of church-sponsored institutions, only eight of which, including Mississippi Industrial College, would remain in operation through the twentieth century. With the longest history of continuous operation of all collegiate institutions in the state, Mississippi College in Clinton had been founded in 1826. Sponsored by the Mississippi Baptist Convention since 1850, the college enrolled white males.

Interestingly, the earliest postwar private colleges were organized for African Americans. In 1866, during the first phase of Reconstruction, the Freedman's Aid Society of the Methodist Episcopal Church founded a church school for African Americans in Holly Springs. Its name was changed from Shaw University to Rust University in 1882, honoring supporters and leaders in the Society. Titled Rust College in 1915, the institution was the first college in the nation established for African Americans and ranked as the second oldest private college in Mississippi.

In 1869 the American Missionary Association of New York organized a school for African Americans in an area just north of Jackson near the border of Hinds and Madison counties. The state chartered the institution as Tougaloo University in 1871; in 1916 the name was changed to Tougaloo College.[4]

The Natchez Seminary for African American students, organized in 1877 by the American Baptist Home Mission Society of New York, was moved to Jackson in 1882 and renamed Jackson College (present-day Jackson State University) in 1899 to reflect the broader curriculum. Following financial difficulties during the Great Depression and flagging private support, the college temporarily closed.

During the latter stage of Reconstruction, Blue Mountain College in Tippah County of northwest Mississippi was founded in 1873 by the Mark Perrin Lowrey family. It operated as a private school for white girls until 1920, when its ownership was transferred to the Mississippi Baptist Convention.

Three other church-supported, liberal arts colleges began in the late nineteenth and early twentieth century. Belhaven College had its origin in three private schools founded for white females—the Mississippi Synodical College of the Presbyterian Church, which was founded in Holly Springs 1883, the McComb Female Institute, and Belhaven College for Young Ladies in Jackson. In 1911 the Central Mississippi Presbytery named the school Belhaven Collegiate and Industrial Institute, and four years later the title Belhaven College was adopted by the board of trustees. The college began to admit male students in the mid-1950s.

---

4 Tougaloo is a Native American term meaning "where three creeks meet."

First Presbyterian Church in Brandon. Courtesy Westley F. Busbee, Jr.

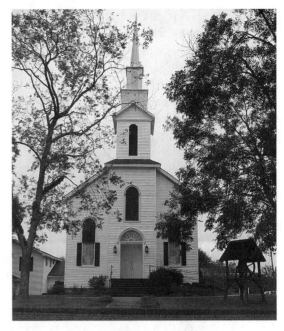

Inaugurated in 1890 as an institution for white males, Millsaps College in Jackson was originally endowed by a gift from Reuben Webster Millsaps, which was matched by contributions from other Mississippi Methodists. Another church-sponsored college began in 1912 for white women when the state Baptist Convention opened the Mississippi Women's College south of Hattiesburg (present-day William Carey College). In the mid-twentieth century both Millsaps and William Carey became co-educational institutions.

While gradual advances in educational opportunities resulted in rising literacy rates among whites, disparities in state support for white and black schools produced no such improvement for African Americans. In 1900 about one-third of the total population (blacks and whites) of the state was illiterate. Eight percent of white adults were illiterate, but almost half of all black adults, 105,331 persons, could not read or write. In the following decade the white illiteracy rate declined slightly while the number of illiterate blacks ten years of age or older rose to almost 260,000 persons. A sizeable portion of the state's adult population, therefore, was unable to read newspapers, not to mention the works of such notable late-nineteenth-century Mississippi novelists as Sherwood Bonner of Holly Springs and William C. Falkner of Ripley (the twentieth-century writer's great grandfather), or such historians as J. F. H. Claiborne.

RELIGIOUS LIFE

Because Chapter Twenty-one describes religious life in Mississippi, this section explains briefly three key developments that reflected social life in the late nineteenth and early twentieth century: the emergence of separate African American churches; the rise of Christian fundamentalism; and the advent of the social gospel.

Black Churches

It is likely that the bible was the book read by most people in this era, although most African Americans had to depend on their ministers' competencies. Racial segregation was virtually perfected in the state's religious denominations. Separate black churches emerged during Reconstruction, when white congregations began to deny full membership to the former slaves and, at the same time, many African Americans desired to control their own church organizations. A "Colored Conference" was formed for Methodists in 1867, and a General Missionary Baptist Association created in 1873 included 327 churches and almost

30,000 members. Ministers like Hiram Revels, the first African American member of the U.S. Senate, held important political positions, and their churches became centers for the freedmen's social and political education.

With African Americans composing a majority of the state's population, the number of black church members rose faster than and exceeded the number of white congregants. Between 1906 and 1936 total black church membership more than doubled, reaching 781,000 persons, of which number more than 40 percent were Baptists.

Pentecostals

Another significant trend in the state's religious life was the rapid growth of Pentecostal groups, which included several small denominations such as the Assemblies of God, the Churches of God, and various Holiness and Pentecostal churches. Early in the twentieth century increasing numbers of black and white Christians left the mainline denominations and moved into these fundamentalist, charismatic churches. Most of these congregations emphasized an emotional conversion experience, which might involve receiving the gift of the Holy Ghost, speaking in tongues, and commitment to a "sanctified" lifestyle untainted by worldliness. Their worship services were characterized by impassioned and spontaneous preaching, testimonies, music, and even healing services. There were virtually no formal requirements for ministers except having received "the call" of God.

Due to the informality and autonomy of many of these churches, membership numbers are difficult to establish. By 1936 the white Assemblies of God, which began in 1899 at Magnolia, had founded twenty-seven churches, and the black Church of God in Christ had at least ninety churches.

The Social Gospel

While the different religious groups tended to disagree about whether their churches should become involved in political and social issues, in the late nineteenth century many churches began to preach the "social gospel." Evangelicals and fundamentalists were willing to disregard their insistence on church-state separation in order to accomplish certain social reforms they considered necessary; highest on their list was the temperance movement. Support from religious leaders like Methodist Bishop Charles B. Galloway and others helped secure a statewide prohibition law in 1908, and ten years later Mississippi was the first state to ratify the Eighteenth Amendment to the United States Constitution, which banned the "manufacture, sale, or transportation of intoxicating liquors" in the entire nation.

News of the famous 1925 Scopes "monkey" trial in which John Scopes, a high school biology teacher in Dayton, Tennessee, was found guilty of illegally teaching the theory of evolution, encouraged Mississippi religious groups to intensify their efforts to outlaw such instruction in public schools. After the legislature rejected a bill similar to the Tennessee law, the state superintendent of education issued an anti-evolution order to teachers. Sponsored by a Church of God minister, a measure prohibiting the teaching of the theory of human evolution passed in 1926 and was approved by Governor Whitfield, even though Chancellor

Alfred Hume of the University of Mississippi and other educators urged him to veto it.

THE PUBLIC HEALTH

Private Care

One positive aspect of the social gospel was the effort by many churches to establish agencies devoted to the improvement of Mississippians' health. Several denominations provided hospitals and orphanages, and church leaders called for the expansion of public health programs. The need for improvements in health care had been critical for decades. Due to the climate and lifestyles, Mississippians historically suffered outbreaks of such endemic diseases as yellow fever, malaria, tuberculosis, influenza, pellagra, and hookworm. The number of deaths caused by tuberculosis and typhoid fever in the first decade of the twentieth century exceeded those resulting from the widespread epidemics of yellow fever and small-pox in the 1890s.

With limited state assistance or supervision until the end of the nineteenth century, most Mississippians seeking medical treatment had no choice but to rely on the services of local practitioners of folk medicine, country "horse-and-buggy" doctors, and unlicensed practitioners. In critical cases poor people sought care in the few charity hospitals located in larger towns like Natchez, Vicksburg, Jackson, and Meridian. Such institutions were sponsored locally, as no state-supported charity hospitals were founded until the first decades of the twentieth century. Throughout the nineteenth century there were very few private hospitals, but between 1890 and 1920 about sixty small hospitals were established around the state. These facilities, operated by physicians, civic groups, or churches, mostly treated white patients—although some of them did offer segregated sections for blacks and a few others were designated as "colored hospitals." An example of a typical private hospital was Rush's Infirmary in Meridian, which was founded in 1915 by Dr. James H. Rush. Among the church-sponsored hospitals, the King's Daughters, a Seventh-Day Adventist women's organization, established nine facilities, including at least two small infirmaries for African Americans in the Delta. In 1902 the Baptists began the Hunter-Shands Hospital in Jackson, the forerunner of the Mississippi Baptist Hospital.

State Programs

Public concern about epidemic diseases, high rates of infant and maternal mortality, as well as poor health conditions in general was the major impetus for the founding of the State Board of Health in 1877. Initially the Board was a small body of physicians appointed by the governor to make recommendations and nominate county health officers. These local officers enforced the Board's policies for the prevention and containment of contagious diseases and reported sanitary conditions in public places.

In succeeding decades the state's involvement in public health care gradually expanded. In 1882 the legislature established a board of medical censors in each congressional district to examine the qualifications of applicants to practice medicine, and ten years later a law authorized the State Board of Health to examine applicants. In the early twentieth century the state established a number of charity hospitals and extended public support for health-related assistance to persons with sight, hearing, and psychiatric impairments.

Appropriations were increased for the state's antebellum institutions for the blind, for the deaf, and for the "State Lunatic Asylum," which was renamed the State Insane Hospital in 1900. All three facilities were located in Jackson until the 1920s, when the legislature appropriated $2.5 million to move the State Insane Hospital to Rankin County and construct new facilities on a site named Whitfield in honor of the governor. After delays caused by the Great Depression, the new hospital would finally open in 1935 and would be known as "Whitfield," although its official name was the Mississippi State Hospital. In 1882 a similar institution, the East Mississippi State Insane Asylum, was founded in Meridian. Renamed the East Mississippi State Hospital in 1928, it would serve as a custodial facility until the 1950s, when treatment services began.

Another new state facility established in this period was the Tuberculosis Sanatorium hospital in Simpson County, which operated under the jurisdiction of the State Board of Health. Dr. Henry Boswell, the principal supporter of the project, was appointed superintendent of the hospital in 1916 and served forty years in that capacity.

Accomplishments

An evaluation of improvements in Mississippi's pubic health at the turn of the century yields a mixed report. Among the many examples of progress was the cooperation among the State Board of Health, the United States Health Service, and Baptist orphanages, in which medical experiments led to the discovery of the causes of and cures for pellagra. These studies in 1915 helped to prove that pellagra, responsible for nearly 1,200 deaths that year alone, was not a contagious disease but instead resulted from dietary deficiencies that could be easily rectified to prevent further occurrences. By 1937 the Board of Health would report remarkable success through its immunization program and other advances in the prevention and treatment of typhoid fever, smallpox, diphtheria, malaria, and tuberculosis.

Notwithstanding these accomplishments, in some categories the state's health conditions paled in comparison to those in the rest of the nation. For example, the 1922 infant mortality rate in Mississippi was an incredibly high 64.6 per 1,000 live births, and the maternity mortality rate stood at 6.8 per 10,000 live births. These rates were more than two times the national averages.

SELECTED SOURCES

Bigelow, Martha M., "Mississippi Progessivism," *Journal of Mississippi History* 27 (May 1965): 202–205.

Bond, Bradley G., *Mississippi: A Documentary History* (Jackson: University Press of Mississippi, 2003).

Clark, Thomas D., "Changes in Transportation," in Richard Aubrey McLemore, ed., *A History of Mississippi*, 2 vols. (Hattiesburg: University & College Press of Mississippi, 1973), 2: 274–311.

Coleman, James P., "The Mississippi Constitution of 1890 and the Final Decade of the Nineteenth Century," in Richard Aubrey McLemore, ed., *A History of*

Mississippi, 2 vols. (Hattiesburg: University & College Press of Mississippi, 1973), 2: 3–28.

Cresswell, Stephen, *Multiparty Politics in Mississippi, 1877–1902* (Jackson: University Press of Mississippi, 1995).

Giles, William Lincoln, "Agricultural Revolution, 1890–1970," in Richard Aubrey McLemore, ed., *A History of Mississippi*, 2 vols. (Hattiesburg: University & College Press of Mississippi, 1973), 2: 177–211.

Griffith, Reuben W., "The Public School, 1890–1970," in Richard Aubrey McLemore, ed., *A History of Mississippi*, 2 vols. (Hattiesburg: University & College Press of Mississippi, 1973), 2: 392–414.

Gunn, Jack Winton, "Religion in the Twentieth Century," in Richard Aubrey McLemore, ed., *A History of Mississippi*, 2 vols. (Hattiesburg: University & College Press of Mississippi, 1973), 2: 477–491.

Harrell, Laura D. S., "Medical Services in Mississippi, 1890–1970," in Richard Aubrey McLemore, ed., *A History of Mississippi*, 2 vols. (Hattiesburg: University & College Press of Mississippi, 1973), 2: 516–569.

Hickman, Nollie W., "Mississippi Forests," in Richard Aubrey McLemore, ed., *A History of Mississippi*, 2 vols. (Hattiesburg: University & College Press of Mississippi, 1973), 2: 217–223.

Jenkins, Robert L., "The Development of Black Higher Education in Mississippi (1865–1920)," *Journal of Mississippi History* 45 (November 1983): 272–86.

Kirwan, Albert D., *Revolt of the Rednecks, Mississippi Politics: 1876–1925* (Lexington: University of Kentucky Press, 1951).

McLemore, Nannie Pitts, "The Progressive Era," in Richard Aubrey McLemore, ed., *A History of Mississippi*, 2 vols. (Hattiesburg: University & College Press of Mississippi, 1973), 2: 29–58.

McLemore, Richard Aubrey, "Higher Education in the Twentieth Century," in Richard Aubrey McLemore, ed., *A History of Mississippi*, 2 vols. (Hattiesburg: University & College Press of Mississippi, 1973), 2: 415–445.

McMillen, Neil R., *Dark Journey: Black Mississippians in the Age of Jim Crow* (Urbana: University of Illinois Press, 1989).

Mississippi Official and Statistical Register [various dates].

Mississippi Statistical Abstract [various dates].

Rogers, Ralph J., "The Effort to Industrialize," in Richard Aubrey McLemore, ed., *A History of Mississippi*, 2 vols. (Hattiesburg: University & College Press of Mississippi, 1973), 2: 233–249.

Rowland, Dunbar, *History of Mississippi: The Heart of the South*. 4 vols. (Chicago-Jackson: The S. J. Clarke Publishing Company, 1925), vol. 2.

Sparks, Randy J., *Religion in Mississippi*, Vol. 2, Heritage of Mississippi Series (Jackson: University Press of Mississippi for the Mississippi Historical Society, 2001).

United States Bureau of the Census. Statistical Abstract of the United States [various dates].

University of Virginia Geospatial and Statistical Data Center. United States Historical Census Data Browser. http://fisher.lib.virginia.edu/census/.

CHAPTER FIFTEEN

Progressive "Rednecks"

THE BEGINNING OF PROGRESSIVE REFORMS

In the new century rising demands for political and economic reforms ushered in an era of progressivism, corresponding to the national movement. In Mississippi the failure of the Populists to compete successfully with the Democrats combined with the old Bourbon machine's inability to satisfy the state's agrarian interests produced this new political phenomenon. A new generation of "progressive" politicians, therefore, accepted the Democratic party label but advocated a new brand of populism. To get elected, the "progressive" politicians had to proclaim their defense of the small farmers, embrace policies that discouraged big corporate interests, and, unfortunately, espouse the principle of white supremacy.

Governor James K. Vardaman, 1904–1908

Born in Texas, where his father had moved before the Civil War because of financial difficulties, young James Kimble Vardaman had returned to Mississippi

with his family after the conflict. In the early 1880s he had practiced law and edited a newspaper in Winona before moving to Greenwood. As a member of the state house of representatives from 1890 to 1896, Vardaman had been one of only three members from the Delta who favored calling the constitutional convention. After serving as speaker in 1894, he waged an unsuccessful bid for the governorship in 1895. His dual professions of lawyer and editor were interrupted in the following years, as he served as a major in the Spanish-American War. Shortly thereafter, he ran again for governor in 1899. Vardaman was not, however, an easily discouraged man, and he used his newspaper and his political campaign platforms to promote the state's adoption of primary elections for the nomination of party candidates.

With the advantage of mounting anti-Bourbon sentiment and the implementation of the new pri-

Governor James K. Vardaman. Courtesy Mississippi Department of Archives and History.

mary election law, Vardaman finally won the Democratic party's nomination for governor in 1903. After receiving a plurality of the votes in the first primary contest with Edmund F. Noel and Populist Frank A. Critz, Vardaman then defeated Critz in the second primary by a vote of about 53,000 to 46,000.

The Politics of Race   Adding a new twist on the old Populist strategy, "progressive" Democrats such as Vardaman played the race card in order to win elections and retain the support of the virtually all-white electorate. Then, once in office, they generally pursued the old Populist agenda—now known as "progressivism." Although he was a recognized figure in the Democratic party, Vardaman was no friend of the Bourbon establishment, and in supporting most of the Populist causes he portrayed himself as the champion of the small white farmers against the monied interests of the railroads and other big corporations.

He did, however, see the political advantage of making race a major political issue, and extreme racial pronouncements were major features of Vardaman's political technique. Known in some circles as the "Great White Chief," he proclaimed the doctrine of white supremacy and declared that the Mississippi Democratic party was the "white man's party." Arguing that blacks were inherently inferior, indolent people, he renewed the old proposal that the allocation of state funds to the separate black and white schools should be based on the actual sum of the taxes paid by the persons of each race.

After a nationally covered visit by President Theodore Roosevelt to LeRoy Percy and other wealthy planters in the Delta, Vardaman made Roosevelt an issue in the 1903 election.[1] He viciously attacked the Republican president's appointment of a black postmaster in the state and his invitation of Booker T. Washington to the White House. Then, in his inaugural address, Vardaman denounced the Fourteenth and Fifteenth amendments to the United States Constitution, which extended the rights of citizenship to African Americans. He went on to say: "The nation should correct this error, this stupendous solecism, and now is the time to do it. . . . The Southern people should take the initiative. They are familiar with all the facts; they alone are capable of informing the world of the profound, God-stamped, time-fixed and unalterable incompetence of the Negro for citizenship in a white man's country."

Reform Measures   His racist vitriol notwithstanding, Vardaman's actions as governor did not always match his extreme rhetoric. In the area of public education, however, he favored the termination of state funding for black schools, an action the legislators were unwilling to take. During his administration appropriations for public education increased by almost 20 percent and teachers' salaries by almost 30 percent, but such funding was slanted heavily in favor of white schools. In 1904 he supported the legislature's creation of a state textbook commission, which would require textbook publishers to submit competitive bids in the selection process of books for the public schools, but the commission was also charged with adopting materials that promoted white supremacy and racial segregation.

For greater efficiency in the operation of the numerous scattered schools, legislation was enacted initiating the future trend of school district consolidations.

1 When Roosevelt refused to shoot a captive bear during a hunt in the Delta, the nation's newspapers reported the incident and began to use the term "Teddy Bear," which would become Roosevelt's symbol in the 1904 presidential election.

Public execution of African American [B]ill Mack, 1909. Courtesy Westley F. Busbee, Jr.

To oversee the state system of public schools, Vardaman selected capable leaders but ones who demonstrated a firm commitment to segregation. For example, when Superintendent of Education Whitfield resigned in 1907 to become president of the Industrial Institute and College in Columbus, the governor appointed Joseph N. Powers, who would be elected twice and serve as superintendent until 1914.

Another aspect of the reform agenda was related to the state penal system. Legal loopholes in the 1890 constitution allowed private landowners to continue their exploitation of convict laborers through convict leasing. After a 1906 legislative committee investigation uncovered continuing abuses, the penitentiary control board was replaced with a penitentiary commission. With three elected members and a superintendent appointed by the governor, the new commission was directed to reform the system of convict farm labor, which would be confined to state-owned lands.

Corporations   Though he probably would not have liked the comparison, Vardaman tried to be as aggressive in "trust-busting" as President Roosevelt. Always claiming to be the defender of the "common people," the governor proposed legislation that would tax and otherwise strictly regulate various large corporations, including insurance companies, utilities, and banks. Vardaman demanded increased supervision of the railroads by the state Railroad Commission, or in the alternative, direct government ownership of railroad companies. Deeming many of the governor's recommendations as excessively antibusiness, even socialistic, the legislature often refused to cooperate. Instead of enacting Vardaman's proposed privilege tax on major landowning corporations, the legislators passed a bill that would have accomplished the opposite result. The governor vetoed the measure, arguing such would promote Northern firms, particularly lumber companies, and hinder Mississippi small farmers and businesses from acquiring land. One important agreement between the executive and legislative departments, however, resulted in the creation of the state Department of Agriculture.

Vardaman's Political Future   Hoping to continue the "progressive" reforms that he had begun, Governor Vardaman supported the candidacy of Edmond F. Noel in the gubernatorial election of 1907. At the same time he attempted to win the party's nomination for the U.S. Senate but was narrowly defeated by John Sharp Williams, an eight-term congressman from Yazoo City.[2] Vardaman was again unsuccessful in 1910 but was elected two years later and served in the Senate from 1913 to 1919, when his bid for reelection failed. Never one to step aside following defeat, Vardaman campaigned for a fifth time for the U.S. Senate in 1922 but without success. Throughout all these years, however, he remained a force in state politics.

Governor Edmond F. Noel, 1908–1912

The Campaign of 1907   Among the six gubernatorial candidates in the Democratic primary of 1907 (which actually determined the next governor because general elections by now were merely a formality in Mississippi), the leaders were Edmond F. Noel and Earl Leroy Brewer. During the campaign Noel called attention to his youthful poverty and declared that Brewer received the backing of the railroad companies. Noel, the leader in securing the primary election law in 1902 and a long-time supporter of judicial elections, promised to continue Vardaman's reform program, declaring that he favored higher taxes on the railroads and a reapportionment of the legislature. A native and lifetime resident of Holmes County, Noel had served in both houses of the legislature and as army captain during the Spanish-American War. For his part, Brewer also claimed to be a friend of the small farmers, and he insisted that the railroads were actually backing Noel. An important issue of the campaign was statewide prohibition of the sale of alcoholic beverages, and Noel, a strong supporter of prohibition, charged that Brewer was the candidate of the saloon managers. Each candidate, however, pledged not to use "liquor money" in his campaign and tried to outdo the other in proving himself a champion of the people against the corporations.

After some controversy, including the report that more votes were counted than the number of registered voters, the secretary of state declared that Noel and Brewer would enter the second Democratic primary. With Governor Vardaman's support probably making the difference, Noel won the nomination by only about two thousand votes.

Progressive Reforms   As governor, Noel not only kept his pledge to continue the program advanced by the Vardaman administration, but he accomplished more than had his predecessor. Enjoying a more cooperative legislature, Noel approved a series of reform measures, including the statewide prohibition of the production and sale of intoxicating liquors, a labor law protecting children and other

2 A lawyer and cotton planter, Williams had received an excellent education at the University of the South, the University of Virginia, and the University of Heidelberg in Germany. He was elected eight times to the U.S. House of Representatives, serving from 1893 to 1909. Thereafter he was elected to the Senate two times, serving from 1911 to 1923. In all, he served in the U.S. Congress for thirty years.

prolabor legislation, a pure food law, and appropriations for the construction of a state charity hospital in Jackson. Through county health officers the state Board of Health expanded its objectives from controlling to preventing epidemics and communicable diseases. When President Theodore Roosevelt called for a National Conservation Congress in 1908 to discuss the conservation of the nation's natural resources, Noel represented the state and was elected the first president of that body. The following year he served as a member of the president's National Conservation Commission, formed to promote the expansion of the national forest system.

Some of the most urgently needed reforms undertaken by the Noel administration involved providing aid to farmers who were experiencing the onset of the infestation of boll weevils in their cotton crops and of disease-spreading ticks in their livestock. In 1908 the legislature requested federal aid to promote scientific farming methods, particularly crop diversification. A state Livestock Sanitary Board was established to assist farmers in treating and preventing animal diseases. Finally, county boards of supervisors were authorized to organize county departments of agriculture and appoint county commissioners who would facilitate the delivery of information and services available from the state Department of Agriculture, various departments at the state A&M College in Starkville, and several branch experiment stations.

Education   Under Noel, a number of improvements in public education also were accomplished, including the creation of a board of trustees for the state's universities and colleges and the establishment of the state's first college to train white teachers. With the backing of the governor and leading educators like Henry Whitfield, the legislature in 1910 chartered the Mississippi Normal College, forerunner of the present-day University of Southern Mississippi. Located in Hattiesburg, the college opened in 1912 with eighteen faculty members and about two hundred students.[3] Renamed the State Teacher's College in 1924, five years later it received accreditation from the Southern Association of Colleges and Schools.

Addressing local needs, the legislature authorized county supervisors to levy property taxes for school purposes, provided a majority of voters in the respective counties approved the taxes and the schools conducted classes at least seven months each year. These tax revenues could be used to help defray the costs of student transportation, the construction, maintenance, and repair of school buildings, and teachers' salaries. Other legislation provided free transportation of students to and from schools and encouraged the consolidation of rural school districts. The latter plan was specifically promoted through legislation passed in 1908 that authorized counties to establish agricultural high schools, institutions that provided boarding for students and required hands-on farm work and vocational classes in addition to the traditional curriculum. Within a decade about fifty of these institutions had been organized, but as school consolidation progressed and transportation improved, many agricultural high schools began to be

3 Over opposition from legislators from other parts of the state, Hattiesburg was chosen as the site partly because the city and the county offered $250,000 plus the cost of utilities, the Mississippi Central Railroad agreed to extend a line to the location, and the Newman Lumber Company donated a section of land for the campus.

replaced by traditional ones, while others became bases for the new "junior colleges" in the 1920s.

Politics   The death of Senator McLaurin late in 1909 produced an intense political struggle that would have lasting consequences for the state. Reminiscent of the old Populist versus Bourbon contests, an issue arose over the nomination of the Democratic-party candidate, to be chosen by the legislature, to complete the remaining three years of McLaurin's term in the Senate. Former governor Vardaman announced his candidacy but was opposed by LeRoy Percy, a powerful Delta planter and lawyer. In a prolonged "secret caucus" early in 1910, the Democratic legislators voted 87 to 82 to nominate Percy. Following the marathon process (two months), state senator Theodore G. Bilbo of Poplarville, a Vardaman backer, reported that he had been given a bribe of $645 by the Percy people. Bilbo claimed that he had accepted the money in order to expose the corruption of Vardaman' s enemies. Not only did Bilbo escape punishment by the senate for this violation, but he used the affair to gain recognition as a populist-type leader who would crusade against the aristocratic elements in the Democratic party. Thus began Bilbo's successful campaign for the office of lieutenant governor in the following year.

Governor Earl Leroy Brewer, 1912–1916

The Elections of 1911   Earl Leroy Brewer, the man who had lost the controversial and close election of 1907, ran unopposed in the Democratic-party gubernatorial primary of 1911. A native of Carroll County, Brewer had practiced law in Yalobusha County and served in the state senate from 1896 to 1900. At the time of his gubernatorial campaigns, Brewer lived in Clarksdale in Coahoma County.

The elections of 1911 resulted in significant victories for supporters of the emerging Vardaman-Bilbo coalition, the so-called rednecks. The term *rednecks* as a political label probably originated when supporters of Vardaman wore red neckties and called themselves "rednecks" following Senator Percy's July 4, 1910, speech in which he use the term to describe some rowdy backers of his opponents. Thereafter, the rednecks embraced the term and the trademark red ties to emphasize their status as or sympathy with ordinary white farmers who worked in the fields under the hot sun.

Having gained notoriety in the bribery episode, state Senator Theodore Bilbo won the lieutenant governor's election, and Vardaman won by a wide margin the primary nomination for the U.S. Senate, defeating Senator Percy and C. H. Alexander. Getting their revenge for the "secret caucus," which had chosen Percy in 1810, the rednecks in the 1912 legislature—with Lieutenant Governor Bilbo presiding as president of the senate—had the privilege of officially electing Vardaman to succeed Percy. In the same year the newly elected state officials took office, Democratic party nominee Woodrow Wilson won the presidency under a banner of reform, and an era of progressive reforms was in full momentum on the national and state levels.

Social and Economic Measures   Calling for harmony among contentious political and sectional groups, Governor Brewer approved considerable legislation to ameliorate some of the state's social and economic problems. Aiming for better health conditions, a Bureau of Vital Statistics was established in 1912 to register births and deaths, and in 1914 a Board of Nurse Examiners was created. The child labor law was strengthened, and to provide enforcement legislators created an office of factory inspector within the state Board of Health. In 1915 Governor Brewer pardoned several prisoners who volunteered to participate in a medical experiment to discover the cause of pellagra. Under the supervision of the United States Public Health Service, the study confirmed that the disease was curable through dietary corrections.

Pressure resulting from the rising number of bank failures and perhaps the attention given to banking reforms by President Wilson's administration resulted in major financial legislation. Considered by some contemporary observers the most important reform of the Brewer administration, a law in 1914 created a state Banking Department that included a Board of Bank Examiners. The objective was to require sound practices and guarantee deposits.

The legislature increased appropriations for public education and in 1912 initiated a program of teacher licensing for college graduates who met the requirements of certain courses in education. The Board of Trustees for Higher Education was expanded to nine members and given additional responsibilities. The biggest increase in spending by the 1914 legislature was its biennial appropriation of $3.3 million for public schools.

Judicial Reforms After several unsuccessful attempts to resume the elective judiciary since the 1890 convention, in 1912 a constitutional amendment for the popular election of circuit and chancery court judges was finally approved. At the time the state judiciary comprised seventeen circuit court districts and ten chancery court districts. Two years later additional amendments provided for the election of the three supreme court judges, one from each geographic district, the terms of which were reduced from nine to eight years. Another amendment to Section 31 of the constitution provided that nine or more jurors, instead of all twelve jurors, could return the jury's verdict in civil suits.

Initiative and Referendum   Efforts to establish initiative and referendum, which were considered by conservatives as radical processes for direct, popular participation in government, caused prolonged controversy. Initiative allows voters, by petition, to propose laws and constitutional amendments which then are adopted or rejected in a general election. Also by petition, referendum permits voters to demand that laws already enacted be placed on the ballot for acceptance or repeal by the voters. Ultimately the legislature voted to add an initiative and referendum provision to Section 33 of the constitution. Because the popular vote on the issue was 19,118 to 8,718 in favor of the proposed amendment, the legislature placed it in the state constitution in 1916. The state supreme court upheld the amendment, and the initiative feature was used to propose a constitutional amendment in 1922. But that same year the supreme court reversed its position, and the initiative and referendum provision was deleted from the constitution. The justices, who were among the first members of the newly elective judiciary, were motivated in part by concerns that the processes could have the effect of weakening the state's policy of white supremacy.[4]

4 This issue would be resurrected in the early 1990s related to interests in a state lottery, term limits, and other actions that could not pass through the regular legislative process. In 1992 the constitution was amended allowing voters to propose constitutional amendments.

Governor Theodore G. Bilbo. Courtesy Mississippi
Department of Archives and History.

Governor Theodore G. Bilbo, 1916–1920

The Election of 1915   In the first Democratic party primary in 1915, Lieutenant Governor Bilbo won the nomination for governor, receiving about one thousand votes more than the combined votes of the four other candidates. Born near Poplarville in Pearl River County in 1877, Bilbo had served in the state senate from 1908 to 1912. Eight years after the completion of his first term as governor, he would be elected to a second term (1928–32) and would thereafter serve in the U.S. Senate from 1935 until his death in 1947. Bilbo authored *Take Your Choice: Separation or Mongrelization,* which advocated that African Americans be returned to Africa. The Senate denied him readmission in 1947 and began an investigation of his 1946 reelection campaign. Lee M. Russell, a political ally of Bilbo, was elected to the office of lieutenant governor in 1915.

Former governor Brewer's program of providing various state services was accelerated by the Bilbo administration. Even though the state house of representatives was under the leadership of Speaker Martin Sennett Conner, a political critic of the governor, the legislature responded favorably to most of Bilbo's proposals. Indeed, it passed numerous notable reforms, some of which had been Populist proposals introduced as early as the Vardaman administration.

Social Programs   In 1916 a state sanatorium for tuberculosis was founded near Magee with Dr. Henry Boswell as superintendent. A state charity hospital was established in Laurel, and Bilbo recommended that other such institutions be created in other sections of the state. Enacting an earlier proposal to encourage the rehabilitation of wayward youths by placing them in institutions separate from common jails, the legislature established an industrial training school for juveniles at Columbia.

In 1918 Mississippi was the first state to ratify the Eighteenth Amendment to the United States Constitution, prohibiting "the manufacture, sale, or transportation of intoxicating liquors." Prohibition, which had already been adopted by the state legislature, would continue in Mississippi for decades after the repeal of the Eighteenth Amendment in 1933.

Support for the Public Schools   Bilbo was more successful than previous governors in getting substantial increases in appropriations for public schools. The system was administered by Superintendent Willard F. Bond, who was appointed by the governor in 1916 and remained in office for two decades. That same year a school code commission and an illiteracy commission were established, and in 1918 the legislature enacted a compulsory attendance law. The state program to certify teachers was improved, and following the enactment of the Smith-Hughes

Act by Congress in 1917, the legislature officially accepted federal funds to help pay salaries for vocational teachers in agricultural high schools. The voters overwhelmingly approved a constitutional amendment in 1919 establishing county school funds derived from poll taxes to support academic sessions of at least four months. To help fund longer sessions, counties were allowed to adopt additional taxes. State monies would be distributed according to the number of educable children in each county, but legislature was authorized to make additional appropriations to equalize public school terms throughout the state.

Assistance to Farmers   Intending to provide further state assistance to farmers, the legislature adopted a statewide, compulsory dipping-vat law to exterminate the plague of cattle ticks (an action that the governor would later regret). The faculty of the animal husbandry department at the State A&M College and scientists at the state agricultural experiment station convinced Bilbo and a majority of the legislators that the success of the livestock industry, judged essential to the future growth of agriculture in Mississippi, required the eradication of ticks that transmitted "Texas fever," a fatal disease that had spread rapidly to herds of cattle throughout the state. A voluntary program of dipping cows in large vats filled with chemicals had already started, but many farmers, suspicious of new-fangled ideas—some fearing that the chemicals would kill their cows—and objecting to the time and expense the process required, refused to participate. Now, the new law required them to dip all cattle, horses, mules, and other livestock every fourteen days at such times and places determined by a government inspector, who supervised the dipping procedure. Other measures included cholera vaccinations for hogs and a state plant board to help prevent the spread of crop diseases. Finally, as farmers were now becoming more dependent on trucks and the number of personal automobiles in the state and the nation was increasing, greater attention was given to road improvements, including the creation of a State Highway Commission, which had been proposed originally by Governor Brewer.

The First State Highway Commission   Three related factors finally prompted state action to improve overland transportation—the intolerable road conditions, the growing market for lumber and other products during World War I, and the new availability of federal aid to help fund the cost of road construction. The Bankhead Act of 1916 provided federal funds for road building and maintenance but required states to appropriate matching funds and place the supervision of public roads in a state highway department rather than in the hands of county governments. Acting on the recommendations of newly installed Governor Bilbo, the legislature established the State Highway Commission in 1916, and the governor personally certified to the federal government that the state would fulfill the additional requirements to receive federal monies for road building and maintenance.

A public relations campaign to garner political support for the program was launched by Attorney General Ross A. Collins and Highway Commission Chairman J. M. McBeath, both of Meridian. Their efforts were greatly enhanced by wartime demands for the transportation of weapons, supplies, and personnel. Even in these circumstances, however, overcoming the basic obstacles of county opposition to centralized state control and insufficient state revenue proved to be a slow and difficult struggle.

Top: Capitol Street in Jackson.
Bottom: Street scene in Gulfport. Photographs courtesy Mississippi Department of Archives and History.

The State Tax Commission   Another agency, the State Tax Commission, was created in 1916, partly to implement a plan to equalize property taxes. The equalization program passed over vigorous opposition in some counties (especially those in the Delta) where the assessments were still as low as $1 per acre. Although the Tax Commission's implementation of the law had the effect of raising taxes in only sixteen counties, the new property valuations, including big increases on public utilities, amounted to an overall increase in revenue of at least $163 million between 1915 and 1917. But any anticipation of continuing rises in tax revenue ended with the legislature's enactment of Bilbo's tax reduction proposal in 1917.

Administrative Actions   Except for its unwillingness to adopt Bilbo's call for a constitutional convention, the first such recommendation by a governor in the twentieth century, the legislature agreed with his other recommendations for administrative changes and additions.[5] They included the termination of the fee basis for most county officials and the creation of a host of new state agencies, among the most important of which were the Highway and Tax commissions, as described above; a Board of Pardons, which would remove that power from the governor and significantly reduce the number of pardons; a Board of Law Examiners, a Board of Pharmacy, and a Game and Fish Commission.

WORLD WAR I

Plans for an exposition at Gulfport to celebrate the state's centennial were interrupted by the outbreak of world war in Europe in 1914. The exposition buildings were used instead as naval training stations after the Congress declared war against Germany in April 1917, and they housed a veterans' hospital after the war. Other principal centers for military activities in Mississippi included Camp Shelby near Hattiesburg, the largest army training station, Payne Field near West Point, an aviation base, and Pascagoula, a shipbuilding center.

The first volunteers for military service were members of the First Mississippi Infantry, who were called into service in 1916 for the Mexican border action. A year later the United States' entry into the European war required additional troops, including members of the national guard who were organized into infantry, cavalry, artillery, and engineer units. Local selective service boards registered almost 345,000 men and called into service more than 45,000, including more than 24,000 African Americans. During the course of the war a total of about 58,000 Mississippians served in the United States military.

Thousands of other persons undertook wartime duties. Women throughout the state formed committees of national defense that promoted food production and conservation. Under the supervision of the state Cooperative Extension Service, home demonstration agents in each county organized canning clubs, such as the "girl's tomato clubs," and encouraged "war gardening." As part of the effort women signed pledges that promised, "One can for the Government." Families observed the government's request to refrain from eating particular foods on certain days in order to conserve food for the army. Other wartime activities included

5 Two of his stated purposes for a convention were to revise the tax structure and to alter the legislature's apportionment formula to give more representation to southern counties.

The War Memorial in Jackson. Courtesy Westley F. Busbee, Jr.

volunteer work through the American Red Cross, chapters of which included persons of all ages and races who performed such services as making bandages and clothing, practicing first aid, and assembling boxes and other supplies for the soldiers. Drives for financial support through the purchase of Liberty Loan Bonds and War Saving Stamps produced more than $80 million in Mississippi during the war. One Mississippi historian observed that while the Spanish-American War had restored the state to the Union "more completely than a thousand reconstruction acts," the First World War made Mississippians conscious of their membership in the world community.

The Decline of Progressivism

Despite the successes of Bilbo's administration, the rednecks suffered some reversals in 1918. Senator Vardaman's opposition to the United States involvement in the war was a key reason for his failure to gain reelection. Pursuant to the Seventeenth Amendment to the United States Constitution, which was ratified in 1913, United States senators now were elected by the voters of each state rather than by the legislatures. Senator John Sharp Williams was reelected without opposition in 1916, but two years later Senator Vardaman was defeated by Congressman Byron Patton "Pat" Harrison, who received 56,715 votes to 44,154 for Vardaman.[6] To succeed Williams in the House of Representatives, five candidates entered the campaign, including Governor Bilbo. In the first and second primaries in 1918 the governor ran second to Paul B. Johnson, a circuit court judge from Forrest County. Bilbo claimed that he had been "crucified on a cross of ticks," blaming his defeat on farmers' opposition the compulsory feature of the dipping-vat law.

In retrospect, such developments indicated the beginning of a conservative shift in the attitudes of most voters. Even though Bilbo and some of his allies

6 Harrison, a native of Copiah County, taught school, practiced law, and served as district attorney before moving to Gulfport in 1908. He served in the House of Representatives from 1911 to 1919 and in the Senate from 1919 until his death in 1941. Harrison represented the state in Congress for a total of thirty years.

would be elected to leadership positions in the 1920s, the era of the "progressive rednecks" was waning. In hindsight, it is not that easy to say whether their programs were progressive or regressive. If compared to similar social and economic reforms in other states, one could say that, yes, they were progressive. In the Mississippi setting, however, gross racial inequities impeded meaningful progress for most of the state' s citizens, and a final answer to the question had to depend on the direction state leaders took in the next decade.

Selected Sources

Bond, Bradley G., *Mississippi: A Documentary History* (Jackson: University Press of Mississippi, 2003).

Buchanan, Minor Ferris, *Holt Collier: His Life, His Roosevelt Hunts, and the Origin of the Teddy Bear* (Jackson: Centennial Press of Mississippi, Inc., 2002).

Cobb, James C., *The Most Southern Place on Earth: The Mississippi Delta and the Roots of Regional Identity* (New York: Oxford University Press, 1992).

Green, A. Wigfall, *The Man Bilbo* (Baton Rouge: Louisiana State University Press, 1963).

Holmes, William, "James K. Vardaman: From Bourbon to Agricultural Reformer," *Journal of Mississippi History* 31 (May 1969): 97–115.

———, "James K. Vardaman and Prison Reform in Mississippi" *Journal of Mississippi History* 27 (May 1965): 229–236.

Kirwan, Albert D., *Revolt of the Rednecks, Mississippi Politics: 1876–1925* (Lexington: University of Kentucky Press, 1951).

McCain, William D., "The Triumph of Democracy, 1916–1932," in Richard Aubrey McLemore, ed., *A History of Mississippi*, 2 vols. (Hattiesburg: University & College Press of Mississippi, 1973), 2: 59–96.

McCorkle, James L., Jr., "Cotton, War, and Mississippi, 1914–1915," *Journal of Mississippi History* 45 (May 1983): 90–115.

McLemore, Nannie Pitts, "The Progressive Era," in Richard Aubrey McLemore, ed., *A History of Mississippi*, 2 vols. (Hattiesburg: University & College Press of Mississippi, 1973), 2: 29–58.

McMillen, Neil R., *Dark Journey: Black Mississippians in the Age of Jim Crow* (Urbana: University of Illinois Press, 1989).

Morgan, Chester M., *Redneck Liberal: Theodore G. Bilbo and the New Deal* (Baton Rouge: Louisiana State University Press, 1985).

Rowland, Dunbar, *History of Mississippi: The Heart of the South* 4 vols. (Chicago-Jackson: The S. J. Clarke Publishing Company, 1925), vol. 2.

CHAPTER SIXTEEN

A New Era, The 1920s

Hoping to continue their brand of progressivism, the rednecks campaigned hard in 1919. What they discovered that year and in the succeeding decade was that voters' support for their progressive programs had declined and that the level of opposition they faced from conservative officeholders had grown. Even with Bilbo's endorsement, Lieutenant Governor Lee M. Russell encountered strong opposition in the gubernatorial election.[1] In the first primary Russell received 48,348 votes, about 9,000 more than Oscar G. Johnston, a conservative from Coahoma County, but not enough for a majority. Other candidates, including former governor Andrew H. Longino and Attorney General Ross A. Collins attracted several thousands of votes each. Russell won the second primary by a vote of 77,427 to 69,565 for Johnston. Homer H. Casteel won the nomination for lieutenant governor, narrowly defeating John F. Frierson in the second primary.

Governor Lee M. Russell, 1920–1924

Interestingly, Russell's inaugural address contained many of Bilbo's farewell address proposals. For example, he called for the ratification of the Nineteenth Amendment to the United States Constitution for women's suffrage, increased appropriations for public education, a program for hard-surfacing highways, the use of convict labor to manufacture brick for state construction projects, conservation of natural resources, and the establishment of additional charity hospitals. Russell disagreed, however, with Bilbo's recommendation for selling the governor's mansion and instead favored renovating the historic building.

Population Trends   The post–World War I years was a time of change and challenge for the state. The 1920 census reported a total population of 1,790,618 persons, a decrease of about 6,500 since 1910. Almost 87 percent of the state's inhabitants lived in rural areas. African Americans still composed the majority of the population, outnumbering whites by about 100,000, but their numbers were declining as the great migration of Southern blacks, including Mississippians, to Northern cities was beginning. Rejecting both Booker T. Washington's position of accommodation and W. E. B. Du Bois's call for resistance, an increasing number of Mississippi blacks chose to escape the degradations of "Jim Crow" simply by leaving the state.

1 Russell was a lawyer from Lafayette County. Prior to his election in 1919, he had served in the state house of representatives (1908–10), in the state senate (1912–16), and in the office of lieutenant governor.

Woman Suffrage   One significant change was the extension of suffrage to women. Notwithstanding the recommendations by Bilbo and Russell, the legislature refused to approve the Nineteenth Amendment; instead, it proposed to extend to women the right to vote in an amendment to the state constitution. Even though the federal amendment became effective in August 1920, the voters rejected the legislature's proposal in the November general election. Incredibly, Mississippi was the last state to ratify the Nineteenth Amendment, not taking this action until 1984.

Social Programs   Although Governor Russell was not as successful as previous governors in getting many of his major proposals enacted, the legislature's appropriations for educational and welfare purposes during his tenure set new records. State spending rose for public schools and colleges, for charity hospitals (including the approval of three new ones), for the Tuberculosis Sanatorium, and for an institution to houses and treat the mentally ill, which was established at Ellisville. Constitutional amendments required at least a four-month school year, authorized a poll tax of $2 on both men and women for education purposes, and provided pensions for Confederate veterans or their widows.

Russell's recommendations for changes in higher education were only partly successful, but landmark legislation in 1922 provided the basis for a state system of junior colleges. The legislature rejected the plan to move the University of Mississippi from Oxford to Jackson in the process, but in 1920 it voted to raise appropriations for the woman's college in Columbus, changing its name from the Industrial Institute and College to the Mississippi State College for Women.

Economic Conditions   The Russell administration saw the beginning of a decade of economic troubles. There were declines in cotton acreage due in part to the inexorable boll weevil and in prices for cotton and other farm products. The number of factory workers dropped in the 1920s, this after an increase in the preceding decade. One important reason for the latter trend was the decline of the sawmill businesses as timber resources began to diminish—this at a time when the state's vast pine forests were not being replenished through reforestation practices. A fundamental cause of the downturn, however, was the state's unfriendly policy towards corporations. For decades the Populists' regulatory legislation had increasingly discouraged outside investors, and any hopes for a diverse economy including more industry remained unfulfilled.

Noting the unfavorable economic conditions, Governor Russell offered a series of remedies, none of which was particularly innovative nor altered the state's negative business stance. His recommendations for transportation improvements and a public utilities commission fit with the traditional emphasis on helping farmers rather than promoting industry. He asked the legislature to place main roads under the control of the state Highway Department instead of the county supervisors. To pay for highway construction and maintenance Russell proposed issuing bonds and levying a two cents per gallon tax on gasoline.

Except for its rather ineffective attempt to reorganize the Highway Department, the legislature rejected most of the governor's ideas. Instead, it loosened restrictions on land ownership by corporations and proposed several constitutional amendments to address the problems. An amendment in 1920 enlarging the county supervisors' authority over roads, including the power to contract with businesses, was defeated by the voters. Other amendments provided for the election of levee commissioners and abolished the office of county treasurer.

Politics   Thanks to the Nineteenth Amendment, women voted for the first time in Mississippi in the presidential election of 1920, which swelled the total number of votes cast, from 64,448 in 1912 to 82,351 in 1920; the turnout jumped to 112,438 voters in 1924. Nationally the 1920 Republican-party nominee, Warren Harding, defeated Democrat James Cox in a landslide. But in Mississippi, Cox (who opposed Prohibition and supported the United States joining the League of Nations) won 84 percent of the votes. Harding, who received more than 60 percent of the national popular vote, got less than 12,000 votes in the state.

This outcome illustrated Mississippi's ongoing participation in the South's unwavering allegiance to the Democratic party. President Woodrow Wilson, a Democrat, had proposed the League of Nations idea in his Fourteen Points address during World War I and had succeeded in getting a provision for the organization written into the Treaty of Versailles in 1919. But his desperate struggle to obtain the Senate's ratification of the treaty failed, primarily because such approval would mean United States membership in the League of Nations. The isolationist-minded Republican majority in the Senate spearheaded the opposition, demanding changes in the document that the president refused to accept. Although some Democrats joined the opponents of the League, Senators John Sharp Williams and Pat Harrison of Mississippi remained loyal to Wilson.

In the 1920s dissensions began to appear among the Populists (now known as Progressive Democrats). Most early-twentieth-century political leaders had once been Vardaman disciples, but now a new generation of politicians, like future governors Henry L. Whitfield and Martin Sennett "Mike" Conner, began to stray from the Populist fold. When Senator John Sharp Williams retired in 1922, Bilbo refused to support Vardaman's effort to return to the U.S. Senate. Vardaman led in the first primary but was defeated in the runoff by Congressional Representative Hubert D. Stephens,[2] who received 52 percent of the vote. This 1922 election involved women candidates for Congress for the first time in the state's history. Belle Kearney entered the Senate race, receiving more than 18,000 votes, and Mrs. J. E. Arnold received 2,500 votes in the Fifth Congressional District, where former state attorney general Ross Collins was easily elected.

An event in 1922 that had serious political ramifications was the lawsuit against Governor Russell. In the complaint, a former secretary demanded $100,000 from Russell for breach of promise and seduction. The trial in federal court at Oxford in December 1922 ended in favor of Russell, but the publicity it generated damaged his image and ended his political career. The indefatigable Bilbo, however, tried to benefit from his nefarious role in the event. After violating a subpoena to appear as a witness in the trial, Bilbo was found in contempt of court in April 1923, sentenced to thirty days in jail, and fined $100. He served ten days of his sentence and, as was his practice, used the occasion to launch his next political campaign.

2 Stephens, a lawyer from New Albany, had served in the U.S. House of Representatives from 1911 to 1921. He would continue in the Senate until 1935, having been defeated for reelection by Bilbo.

MISS BELLE KEARNEY
Candidate for the United States Senate

The state's leading advocates for women's rights in the late nineteenth and early twentieth centuries, Belle Kearney and Nellie Nugent Somerville, had similar backgrounds and social agendas but different ways of accomplishing their goals.

Carrie Belle Kearney (1863–1939) was born "a slaveholder's daughter" near Flora in Madison County, where she was educated in the local public school, the Canton Female Institute, and the Normal School in Iuka. Early in her brief school-teaching career, she met Frances Willard, national president of the Woman's Christian Temperance Union (WCTU), who was visiting Mississippi in 1889. Thereafter, Kearney devoted her life to the causes of temperance and woman's suffrage, traveling internationally as a professional speaker for women's rights. In the South she began to use the "negro problem" to promote suffrage for white women whose vote, she proclaimed, would maintain white political supremacy. The first woman to serve in the state senate (1924–28), Kearney chose not to run for reelection.

A member of the Mississippi Hall of Fame, Nellie Nugent Somerville (1863–1952), was born on a plantation in the Delta near Greenville. After completing the course of studies at Whitworth College in Brookhaven, she earned a college degree at Martha Washington College in Abingdon, Virginia, in 1880. Upon returning home, Nellie Nugent married Robert Somerville in 1885 and became the mother of four children. Unwilling to limit herself to the woman's traditional role, Somerville began to engage in social reform first through missions programs of the Methodist Church then, following Frances Willard's Mississippi trip in 1889, through the WCTU and the Woman Suffrage Association. Serving as president of local and state chapters of both organizations, Somerville devoted decades to the causes of women's and children's rights. She became the best-known crusader in

Mississippi for women's right to vote, expressing her views through speeches, letters to editors, brochures and leaflets, and finally in politics. In 1923, Somerville was elected as the first woman member of the state house of representatives. Photographs courtesy Mississippi Department of Archives and History.

Governor Henry L. Whitfield, 1924–1928

The Elections of 1923   The leading candidates for governor in 1923 were Bilbo, Mike Conner, Lester Franklin, Percy Bell, and Henry L. Whitfield. In the first primary Whitfield received a large plurality of the votes, and he went on to defeat

Bilbo by a comfortable margin in the runoff. Dennis Murphree was elected lieutenant governor, defeating Hernan D. Money, a lawyer who had been closely associated with his father, former U.S. representative and senator Hernando de Soto Money (a cousin of Vardaman).

During the campaign of 1929 Bilbo promised extensive programs of social and economic reform, but he could not overcome opposition from the recently enfranchised women voters, who disapproved of his behavior during the Russell trial. On the other hand, most women voters respected Whitfield, who had been a popular school teacher, state superintendent of education, and president of Mississippi State College for Women. Moreover, many women objected to Bilbo's alleged involvement with Governor Russell in the termination of Whitfield as president of the state women's college in 1920.

Opening the voting booths to women, therefore, began to produce significant repercussions in Mississippi politics. This early era of woman suffrage witnessed the election of women to the legislature for the first time, Nellie Nugent Somerville of Washington County and Belle Kearney of Madison County. Leaders in the woman's suffrage movement and activists in the temperance movement, Somerville and Kearney entered the state house of representatives and the senate respectively in 1924.

New Economic Policies   Inheriting a troubled economy, Whitfield recommended new policies that were friendlier to corporations. Legislation enacted under Whitfield encouraged railroad consolidation, promoted the manufacture of cotton products, and repealed state limits on landholding by large corporations. Significant revisions in the tax laws increased revenues and enabled the state to

Women's Christian Temperance Union parade. Courtesy Mississippi Department of Archives and History.

improve its system of transportation and attract business investments. The governor's program improved the assessment process and lessened the tax burden on land from almost 70 percent of the state's total revenue to about 59 percent. With the addition of various new excise levies, including inheritance and privilege taxes, net increases in state revenues not only balanced the budget but provided the means to fund internal improvements.

Emphasizing the critical need for better highway maintenance and new construction, the legislature raised taxes on gasoline. In response to the governor's call for more-responsible policies regarding the states' forests, the legislature established the state Forestry Commission in 1926 to oversee the management and preservation of Mississippi's forests. In addition, a ten-year tax exemption was allowed on land dedicated to the cultivation of new trees. Although conservation minded, Whitfield's program ultimately would contribute to a major revival of the state's slumping lumber industry.

An Early Depression   Unfortunately, the state's dominant business activity, agriculture, experienced no such revival. After a brief period of higher cotton prices caused by the rising demands during World War I, farmers saw a sharp decline in the early 1920s; indeed, for Mississippi farmers, the Great Depression of the 1930s began a decade early. As a result of the precipitous drop in the price of a pound of cotton from 38.5 cents in the spring of 1920 to 9.8 cents in April 1921, many farmers could no longer pay their debts. To make matters worse, a heavy boll-weevil infestation caused cotton production to plummet to a low of 604,000 bales, with an average yield per acre of only 97 pounds, in 1923. Even though farm income already was inadequate, even worse conditions and lower cotton prices lay ahead.

The financial difficulties Mississippi farmers experienced were exacerbated by their inability to acquire modern equipment and the resulting trend of having to cultivate an increasingly smaller number of acres. By 1920 there were only 667 farm tractors in operation in the state—roughly 1 for every 405 farms—while about 523,000 horses and mules still worked on the farms. Between 1890 and 1930 the number of farms more than doubled, rising to 312,663, as their average size decreased to only 55 acres.

And farmers found few opportunities for escape into other occupations, notwithstanding the efforts of the Whitfield administration to attract job-providing industries to the state. Lieutenant Governor Murphree's project of advertising the state's advantages to the nation by the means of a "Know Mississippi Better" train helped to attract several companies, including several furniture manufacturers and the Borden Milk Company. But, evidently, this rolling display of the state's "opportunities, possibilities and resources" could not overcome its distinct disadvantages. Two obstacles, for example, were the dilatory efforts of the state Highway Commission and the relatively late arrival in Mississippi of widespread electric power and natural gas resources.

Not until the 1920s did small, local electric power businesses begin to consolidate. In 1923 the Mississippi Power and Light Company (MP&L) was formed in central and western areas with 10,200 customers and 157 miles of lines, and by 1925 the Mississippi Power Company was organized to serve about 5,500 customers in the Gulf region.

Natural gas became widely available to households and businesses even later, for only two gas fields had been discovered by 1930, and delivery of natural gas remained difficult and expensive. The first field discovered, near Amory in Monroe County, supplied Amory, Tupelo, and Aberdeen by 1926, and the Jackson field began to supply Hinds and Rankin counties in 1930.

Social Policies   As part of his plans for economic development and educational improvements, Whitfield was the first governor since Reconstruction to advocate better relations between the races. The former college president reminded the legislature that public education was the state's largest business. Demanding quality and efficiency, he remarked that in his judgment too many people were attending college, and that colleges and universities were "carrying too much dead weight" among their students. In an action that appeared contradictory to the governor's call for higher academic standards but was in fact a popular response to the widely publicized Scopes trial in Tennessee, the legislature, as mentioned, passed a law in 1926 prohibiting the teaching of the theory of human evolution in public schools.

On Whitfield's recommendation, the legislature passed a number of measures to expand teacher education programs. In 1924 it authorized the establishment of the state's second school for white teachers, Delta State Teachers College. The legislature's selection of Cleveland as the site for the college was influenced by substantial contributions from the town and Bolivar County, including property, the agricultural high school buildings, free electricity and water, insurance policies, and cash payments to help defray the initial costs of operation. With Governor Whitfield and Superintendent Willard Bond serving as ex officio members of the first board of trustees, the college opened in 1924 with eleven faculty and staff members and ninety-seven students.

An action that would remain controversial for the next six years involved the State Insane Hospital. In 1926 the legislature voted to move the institution from Jackson to Rankin County. To oversee the project and sell the existing facilities and property in north Jackson, a commission composed of the governor, the superintendent of the State Insane Hospital, and other three members appointed by governor was established.

Politics   In 1924 Senator Pat Harrison was reelected, easily defeating former Governor Earl Brewer. There were no seriously contested congressional elections, as seven incumbents were returned to office, and one new congressional representative was elected to succeed Benjamin G. Humphreys, who died in 1923. Because the outcome in the state was taken for granted, there was little interest in the presidential election. Democrat John Davis received almost 90 percent of the vote, while Republican Calvin Coolidge (who won the national election, retaining the high office to which he had ascended when, as vice president, he had become president on the death of President Warren Harding in August 1923) got only 8,500 votes in Mississippi. Two years later all eight incumbents in the U.S. House of Representatives were returned to office.

Governor Whitfield's death on March 18, 1927, changed the state's political landscape. He was succeeded by Lieutenant Governor Murphree, who had previously announced that he would run for reelection as lieutenant governor. After assuming the governor's office, however, Murphree changed his mind and announced that his name would be on the ballot for governor instead. In the meantime, his leadership was sorely tested.

THE 1927 FLOOD

In spring of 1927 the great Mississippi Valley flood occurred in the Delta as the river flowed over and through the levees, covering almost 1 million acres of farmland. Displacing nearly 200,000 persons, mostly African Americans, destroying thousands of homes and other buildings, work animals, livestock, and poultry, the flood was the greatest natural catastrophe the state and the nation had experienced.

In "Flood Song,"[3] Hodding Carter, the Pulitzer Prize winning author and editor of the *Greenville Delta Democrat-Times*, wrote about the river's victory despite frantic work on the levee by blacks and whites:

> Ol' Mississip's a-rarin',
> She's growlin' and she's swearin'.
> Ain't that a body floatin' in the light?
> She's reachin' out an' snatchin'
> Cause she's gonna raise a ruckus tonight.
> Jesus Marster, but these bags is heavy,
> Cain't stop no river with san'.
> Heave up, boys, and pile 'em on the levee.
> Us is flirtin' with the Promised Lan'.
> . . . .
> Ol' Mississip's a-rumblin'
> Cain't you see them san' bags tumblin'?
> She don't care if you's nigger folks or white.
> An' when she starts to spillin'
> She's ready for a killin'.
> She's raisin' her a ruckus tonight.[3]

After his experiences as chairman of local relief programs in Greenville, William Alexander Percy described the flood's destruction in his autobiography, *Lanterns on the Levee*, in which he writes, "The 1927 flood was a torrent ten feet deep the size of Rhode Island; it was thirty-six hours coming and four months going...." To cope with the emergency, Percy asked Governor Murphree to send the national guard to the Delta. According to Percy, the tragic and deadly flood did, at least, generate two positive lessons for the state: that enough salmon (or other fish) in the diet helped eliminate the disease of pellagra, and the value of raising alfalfa as a fall crop. The former discovery occurred after the Red Cross distributed canned salmon as rations for the refugees. Secretary of Commerce Herbert Hoover, who supervised the federal rescue and relief program, proposed the alfalfa idea and provided free seed to destitute farmers who had lost their spring and sum-

3 Hodding Carter, "Flood Song," as quoted in Dorothy Abbott, ed., *Mississippi Writers: Reflections of Childhood and Youth*, vol. 3, *Poetry* (Jackson: University Press of Mississippi, 1988), 69–70.

Opposite: Scenes of the 1927 flood. Courtesy Mississippi Department of Archives and History.

mer crops. Thereafter, Delta farmers adopted alfalfa as the best crop for hay and found that it served as a general fertilizer and soil enhancer as well.

But there were other consequences that affected the future of the state and the nation. The exploitation of African Americans by the national guard during the crisis would cause even higher numbers of them to leave the Delta in search of favorable opportunities in Northern cities. The guardsmen refused to evacuate black laborers, many of whom had come to the Delta from other parts of the state to work the 1927 cotton crop. Bending to the demands of the white planters, who worried about the availability of future workers as well as the likelihood that the cost of labor might increase if blacks were allowed to leave, the national guard maintained concentration camps, forcing blacks to live and work in miserable conditions and, at the same time, keeping labor agents from entering to offer them opportunities for employment elsewhere.

Moreover, black leaders began to question their traditional loyalty to the Republican party, now under the leadership of President Coolidge. They were disappointed by Secretary Hoover's failure to stop the mistreatment of blacks and the pattern of favoring white over black refugees in the administration of relief. Hoover spent about two months in the state and, notwithstanding black Republicans' criticisms of his performance in Mississippi, used the national publicity of his "humanitarian" efforts to become the Republican presidential nominee in 1928.

Finally, in some ways the federal government's direct assistance in the flood's aftermath served as a paradigm for future New Deal programs. One lasting example was the creation of the United States Corps of Engineers' Waterways Experiment Station in Vicksburg, a flood-prevention project that offered government jobs to Mississippians.

GOVERNOR BILBO'S SECOND ADMINISTRATION, 1928–1932

The Election of 1927

Theodore G. Bilbo's campaign for the election of 1927 had begun immediately after his defeat by Whitfield four years earlier. His record of scandalous behavior as well as his intense populism aroused strong opposition to the ex-governor, particularly among the Delta politicians and many newspaper editors, such as Frederick Sullens of the *Jackson Daily News*. Not to be outdone, Bilbo had started a rival publication in Jackson, the *Mississippi Free Lance*. His rivals in the campaign included Governor Murphree, Mike Conner, and Albert C. Anderson. Bilbo won a large plurality of the votes in the first Democratic primary and received 52 percent of the votes in the runoff to defeat Murphree. The contest for the office of lieutenant governor was even closer, with Bidwell Adam of Pass Christian defeating Mark P. L. Love by only 514 votes in the second primary. Mississippians by now had become so accustomed to the Democratic party's political monopoly in the state that they accepted its primaries as the final elections, and few voters even bothered (or remembered) to participate in the general election, which was merely a formality.

The governor's optimistic inaugural address indicated no expectation of the looming economic crisis that would strike during his administration. Indeed, he predicted an era of great prosperity, making recommendations similar to the programs he had advanced during his first administration. Then, in an action that would affect Bilbo's entire administration, the house of representatives in January 1928 elected by a wide margin Thomas Bailey as speaker, even though the new governor opposed his selection. As speaker, Bailey and his powerful committee chairmen organized the house to resist Bilbo's programs.

Education Issues

The hostile legislature proceeded to reject many of Bilbo's plans for education, including the creation of a state printing plant to reduce the cost of providing school books to children as well as for the publication of government documents. But the 1928 legislature did authorize some of the governor's education proposals, such as the establishment of a Board of Architecture, a Commission for the Blind, and a Junior College Commission. It also enacted a law requiring eight-month terms for the public schools, and it approved bond issues to fund the institutions of higher learning.

Such accomplishments, however, were overshadowed by the governor's efforts to implement fundamental reforms in higher education as presented in the "O'Shea Study," a report that had been initiated by Governor Whitfield. Based on progress achieved in the State of Wisconsin, the plan recommended the creation of a state system of higher education that would run more efficiently, raise academic quality, and provide opportunities to a greater number of white students. Governor Bilbo proposed consolidating the state's colleges with the University of Mississippi (UM), which under the plan would be moved to Jackson. The new system, as well as the public schools, would be overseen by an eight-member state Board of Education whose members would be appointed by the governor for terms of eight years. No governor would be able to appoint a majority of the board's members, as they would be appointed to staggered terms.

Although the future of the state's educational system would have greatly benefited by the adoption of this plan, it was defeated, mainly because of effective lobbying by University Chancellor Alfred Hume and rather dramatic opposition expressed by UM faculty members and students. Among other arguments, opponents of the plan accused Bilbo of seeking revenge for the academic community's political support for Dennis Murphree, his opponent in the 1927 election. Failing to get the adoption of his recommendation, Governor Bilbo in 1930 persuaded the trustees of four colleges to replace their presidents with persons who would favor his ideas. New presidents were chosen for the State Teachers College at Hattiesburg, the University of Mississippi at Oxford, the Agricultural and Mechanical College at Starkville, and the State College for Women at Columbus. The governor then ordered the dismissal of 179 faculty and staff members among whom he suspected opposition. In response to these severe and overtly political actions, the Southern Association of Colleges and Secondary Schools suspended the accreditation of these four Mississippi institutions; not until 1933, during the Conner administration, would their accreditation be reinstated. Delta State Teachers College escaped this academic setback, because its trustees had successfully resisted Bilbo's intervention efforts. Alcorn Agricultural and Mechanical College also was not affected, as it had not yet received accreditation.

Recent studies of this affair invalidate the traditional view that Bilbo's plan and his subsequent "purge" were entirely without merit. On the contrary, his intentions for the most part were positive and in line with what other states were doing at the time to modernize their systems of higher education.

Highways

Bilbo had greater success in his campaign to begin a modern highway program, building on the efforts of his first administration and two key accomplishments of the Russell and Whitfield years. With the promise of millions of federal aid dollars and an increasing number of automobiles in the state, a turning point had come in 1922. After rejecting a similar proposal two years earlier, the voters, now including women, had ratified an amendment to Section 170 of the state constitution, which now placed public roads under state rather than county control. In actions just as revolutionary in their implications, the legislature had finally made substantial provision for road revenues by levying taxes on the purchase of gasoline.

Following these successes and the flow of federal funds to Mississippi, the state Highway Department initiated plans to improve and maintain the state's public highways. The highway commissioners announced that all routes connecting with federal highways would be numbered in conformance with national policy. For example, east-west highways were even numbered, like Highway 80 connecting Meridian with Jackson and Vicksburg, and north-south routes were given odd numbers, like Highway 49 connecting Jackson and Hattiesburg. The progress made in road building in the 1920s, however, was interrupted by the Mississippi River flood of 1927.

Throughout his second term Bilbo repeatedly recommended the construction of hard-surfaced roads and the reorganization of the state Highway Commission. In campaign speeches he suggested the appropriation of state funds and the use of convict labor for the construction and operation of brick manufacturing plants that would produce bricks with which to pave roads. Commenting on the efficiency of his plan, Bilbo explained that after the top surfaces began to wear, the bricks could be turned over on their other sides!

After his highway proposals met rejection, Bilbo called two special sessions of the legislature to reconsider them. Faced with the threat that federal highway funds might be discontinued, the legislature in 1929 approved the recommendations by Horace Stansel, a civil engineer. The "Stansel law" approved a hard-surfacing program of concrete roads, added engineers and other technical specialists to the Highway Department, and expanded the total state highway mileage to six thousand miles. Legislation in 1930 gave the state Highway Commission complete authority over state highways and provided for three popularly elected commissioners, one from each supreme court district, to serve four-year terms.

The Junior College Movement

Agricultural High School Beginnings   An example of the progressive endeavors undertaken during this era was the state's effort to make post-secondary education more available financially and geographically for high-school graduates. Interested in providing more convenient and affordable access to post-secondary edu-

"The Arbors" on the campus of Jones County Junior College. Courtesy Jones County Junior College.

cation, local leaders proposed the use of agricultural high school facilities for college courses. As early as 1921, some first-year college classes were offered at the Pearl River County Agricultural High School in Poplarville. The following year the legislature authorized all agricultural high schools that were not located near existing state colleges to extend their curriculum through the first two years of college studies—in effect, the thirteenth and fourteenth grades.

The Hinds County Agricultural High School in Raymond immediately began to offer college freshman courses, and in the following years similar programs began in other agricultural high schools, including the Harrison-Stone-Jackson school at Perkinston (later named Mississippi Gulf Coast Community College) in 1925, Holmes County at Goodman in 1925, Sunflower County at Moorhead (Mississippi Delta Community College) in 1926, Tate County at Senatobia (Northwest Mississippi Community College) in 1926, Jones County at Ellisville in 1927, Kemper County at Scooba (East Mississippi Community College) in 1927, Copiah-Lincoln at Wesson in 1928, Newton County at Decatur (East Central Community College) in 1928, and Pike County at Summit (Southwest Mississippi Community College) in 1929.

With the backing of Governor Bilbo, who had been a supporter of the Pearl River County school, the legislature appropriated $80,000 to support these "people's colleges," and it established a state Junior College Commission to oversee them in 1928. In the following years the number of students attending these institutions increased faster than the number enrolled at senior colleges due to lower costs and closer proximity to students' residences.

CONCLUSION

For Mississippi the first three decades of the twentieth century were years of some progress, albeit limited and tainted. Reforms were accomplished in several social areas, including public education, public health, child labor, and convict labor. Voters were given access to the nomination process and allowed to elect judges. White male leaders, however, retained absolute control, denying political access to African Americans and resisting woman suffrage. The all-white Democratic party continued to dominate the state, and the general elections remained essentially meaningless. The legislature refused to approve the Nineteenth Amendment to the United States Constitution, and the state was forced to open the polls to women only after the amendment was ratified by the required number of other states.

The state's economic situation withered. Political expediency retarded agricultural diversification and industrial growth, because officeholders had to favor the interests of farmers and oppose those of big businesses in order to win elections. Not until the Whitfield administration did the legislature begin to remove some restrictions on corporations and promote industrial development. Although most politicians recognized the critical need to improve roads and highways, little progress was made, due in part to county supervisors' unwillingness to surrender their local control.

Though at times it appeared that sweeping social, economic, and political improvements were being made, all of them benefited the white population primarily, and African Americans were only indirectly or incidentally affected, if at all. Governors' racist views—sometimes in the extreme—were shared in varying degrees by most political leaders, and they permeated the various "progressive" programs. It would have been difficult for Mississippi to make progress in any case, but with more than half of its inhabitants in a state of subordination and second-class citizenship, genuine advances were virtually impossible.

SELECTED SOURCES

Barry, John M., *Rising Tide: The Great Mississippi Flood of 1927 and How It Changed America* (New York, N. Y.: Simon & Schuster, 1997).

Bond, Bradley G., *Mississippi: A Documentary History* (Jackson: University Press of Mississippi, 2003).

Cobb, James C., *The Most Southern Place on Earth: The Mississippi Delta and the Roots of Regional Identity* (New York: Oxford University Press, 1992).

Green, A. Wigfall, *The Man Bilbo* (Baton Rouge: Louisiana State University Press, 1963).

Hataway, Marsha Perry, "The Development of the Mississippi State Highway System, 1916–1932," *Journal of Mississippi History* 28 (November 1966), 286–303.

Kirwan, Albert D., *Revolt of the Rednecks, Mississippi Politics: 1876–1925* (Lexington: University of Kentucky Press, 1951).

McCain, William D., "The Triumph of Democracy, 1916–1932," in Richard Aubrey McLemore, ed., *A History of Mississippi*, 2 vols. (Hattiesburg: University & College Press of Mississippi, 1973), 2: 59–96.

McLemore, Nannie Pitts, "The Progressive Era," in Richard Aubrey McLemore, ed., *A History of Mississippi*, 2 vols. (Hattiesburg: University & College Press of Mississippi, 1973), 2: 29–58.

McMillen, Neil R., *Dark Journey: Black Mississippians in the Age of Jim Crow* (Urbana: University of Illinois Press, 1989).

Morgan, Chester M., *Redneck Liberal: Theodore G. Bilbo and the New Deal* (Baton Rouge: Louisiana State University Press, 1985).

Prince, Vinton M., "The Woman Voter and Mississippi Elections in the Early Twenties," *Journal of Mississippi History* 49 (May 1987), 105–14.

Rowland, Dunbar, *History of Mississippi: The Heart of the South*, 4 vols. (Chicago-Jackson: The S. J. Clarke Publishing Company, 1925), vol. 2.

Sansing, David G., *Making Haste Slowly: The Troubled History of Higher Education in Mississippi* (Jackson: University Press of Mississippi, 1990).

Swain, Martha H., Elizabeth Anne Payne, and Marjorie Julian Spruill, eds., *Mississippi Women: Their Histories, Their Lives*, foreword by Anne Firor Scott. (Athens: The University of Georgia Press, 2003).

Taylor, A. Elizabeth, "The Woman Suffrage Movement in Mississippi," *Journal of Mississippi History* 30 (February 1968), 1–34.

Young, James B., and James M. Ewing, *The Mississippi Public Junior College Story: The First Fifty Years, 1922–1972* (Jackson: University Press of Mississippi, 1978).

CHAPTER SEVENTEEN

The Depression Years

MISERY SETS IN

The End of the Bilbo Administration, 1928–1932

The major event that Governor Bilbo had confronted during his first term (1916–20) was the Great War (the popular term for World War I); in his second administration (1928–32) he faced the Great Depression. While the former period had been one of important accomplishments, the latter one was unproductive and troublesome, even tragic, for the state as well as the nation.

Bilbo's second term may be divided into two distinct phases. In the first half he attempted to resume his old policies of the "progressive era," as explained in the previous chapter. But in the second half the governor struggled to understand and find solutions for the economic crisis. Throughout both parts of his administration, political conflicts between Bilbo and the legislators, especially the house of representatives, prevented the adoption of most proposals offered by the governor.

Economic Problems Even before the onset of the nationwide Great Depression, most Mississippians had fallen hopelessly into debt, with no dependable sources for financial relief. Many persons employed in nonfarm work began to lose their jobs in the late 1920s, but the majority of the population lived in rural areas, where gardens and farms could produce most necessities of life. The problem facing small farmers was their inability to satisfy mortgage payments and other debts, thereby losing their property and having to join the ranks of the tenants and sharecroppers. State assistance through the Agricultural Service Department and the Rehabilitation Commission, which was created in 1928 to provide assistance to inhabitants of the flooded counties, did little to alleviate the mounting economic troubles.

The need for greater relief in the deepening Great Depression persuaded many legislators to favor the holding of a special session late in 1930. There, they acknowledged the urgent need to deal with many serious problems, including the growing unemployment rate, farmers' distress—due in part to falling cotton prices and a drought that caused massive crop failures—money shortages, bank failures, and growing state government deficits. Although all assembled seemed to agree that the government had to provide some kind of relief in this situation, the legislators and the governor failed to reach any agreements because of their ongoing political feud.

In September 1931 Bilbo told another special session of the legislature that Mississippians simply could not afford to pay their taxes and faced the loss of their

"Common folks" during the Great Depression. Courtesy Mississippi Department of Archives and History.

land and homes. He predicted that soon there would be food shortages because not only had crops been damaged by the drought, but cotton prices had declined steadily and sharply, falling from a high of almost twenty-nine cents per pound in 1923 to less than six cents in 1931. As evidence of the decline in business activity, he announced that eighty-five banks had failed, the state had record numbers of unemployed people, and the state treasury's balance was dangerously low, with anticipated revenues about one-half the amount budgeted by the legislature. Bilbo emphasized that without immediate action, many state employees would not be paid.

Responding to the dire predictions and recommendations of the governor, the legislature adopted several measures. These included some tax-relief measures, the restriction of cotton acreage (a virtually unenforceable law), a $5 million bond issue for highway construction, and $6 million in bond issues to cover the state government's operating deficit. Finally, an Agricultural Board was established with a $1 million bond issue to make loans to farmers.

Population Trends   The 1930 census reported that the state's total population had risen to 2,009,821 persons, an increase of 12 percent during the 1920s. Most population growth (more than 120,000 persons) occurred in the rural areas, where 83 percent of all Mississippians still lived. There had been minor population increases in the state's urban places, which realized a growth rate of less than 4 percent. But a major change had occurred in the number of African Americans, who now composed only slightly more than 50 percent of the population. While the white population had risen by almost 17 percent, the black population had increased by only 8 percent. This trend in changing racial proportions would gain momentum in the following decades.

Politics   In the federal elections of 1928, Senator Hubert D. Stephens was re-elected, defeating Congressman T. Webber Wilson. Except for Wall Doxey, who defeated Congressman Bill G. Lowrey in the Second Congressional District, and Robert S. Hall, who succeeded Wilson in the Sixth, all incumbent Democratic congressmen were reelected. Because the state was taken for granted by the Democratic party, it was a surprise when many Mississippian voters seemed inclined to favor Republican presidential nominee Herbert Hoover in 1928. They were influenced by favorable publicity about his leadership in the flood relief programs the previous year and reluctance to support the Democratic candidate, Alfred E. Smith, a New Yorker and a Roman Catholic who favored ending prohibition. But the Republican threat was defused by Governor Bilbo, who cast doubt on whether Hoover's racial views were acceptable in Mississippi. The outcome in November was that Smith won the state by a vote of more than 124,000 to about 26,000. Nationally, however, Hoover won the election in a landslide, receiving more than 58 percent of the popular vote and 84 percent of the electoral vote. The reelection of Senator Pat Harrison in 1930 was no surprise.

Political controversies were especially bitter and personal through Bilbo's administration, as there was a series of ongoing incriminations and investigations. Prompted by Bilbo's accusations, in 1929 the legislature's investigation of Attorney General Rush H. Knox and the state Tax Commission resulted in Knox's impeachment by the house of representatives and his resignation. Then chairman of the Tax Commission, Lester C. Franklin, was impeached by the house but found not guilty by the senate in 1930. These tumults and other contentious affairs made positive progress difficult, but one project on which the governor and the legislators did agree was the adoption of a new code of laws for the state in 1930.

Unfortunately, the real victims of Bilbo's troubled administration were the thousands of people in the state struggling to earn a living. The voters' dissatisfaction was demonstrated in the election of 1931, in which only 19 of the 140 representatives were reelected, and the successful gubernatorial candidate was an arch political enemy of Bilbo.

Governor Martin Sennett Conner, 1932–1936

Martin "Mike" Conner was born in Hattiesburg in 1891, the son of a successful sawmill owner and the grandson of a Confederate army captain of Irish descent. A brilliant student, he completed his secondary education and earned the bachelors degree from the University of Mississippi in 1910, this before his nineteenth birthday. Two years later he graduated from the law school at Ole Miss with highest honors and then he went on to Yale University, where he earned the doctor of laws degree cum laude in 1913. He

Governor Martin Sennett Conner. Courtesy Mississippi Department of Archives and History.

returned to Mississippi to begin a law practice in Seminary, Covington County, and two years later in 1915, at age of twenty-four, he was elected to the legislature. The following year he was elected speaker of the house, a position he held for five successive legislative sessions.

The Election of 1931   Conner was elected governor on his third successive try for that office. He had launched his first gubernatorial campaign in 1923, placing third in the first Democratic primary. Four years later he had again come in third in the first primary, and Bilbo, who had refused to debate Conner in the campaign, won the election. In 1931 Conner finally succeeded, against future governors Paul B. Johnson, Sr. and Hugh L. White. Overcoming his second place to White in the first primary, Conner received 54 percent of the 315,608 votes cast, a record turnout for a gubernatorial election. Such an endorsement provided him the mandate to confront boldly the massive problems of the Great Depression. In the contest for lieutenant governor, Dennis Murphree was again elected, easily defeating incumbent Adam in the first primary.

Economic Crises   On taking office in 1932 Conner inherited a disastrous financial situation. The state government had lost its credit worthiness, there was an operational deficit of about $13 million, and the state's debt had swelled to more than $50 million, an increase of about 74 percent since 1930. And while the debt had swelled rapidly, state income had decreased, with tax assessments having fallen about $80 million since 1928. And because of the state's deplorable credit condition, few businesses were willing to sell to the state on credit.

A more serious problem was that most of the state's inhabitants lacked adequate monetary incomes. The annual per capita income in 1932 was a paltry $126, as small farmers were caught in a downward spiral of falling prices for their agricultural commodities and declining production. The price of cotton dropped to less than seven cents per pound, and yield declined to 149 pounds or less per acre. Composing the vast majority of the state's population, tenant farmers, sharecroppers, and small independent farmers, and the families thereof, quickly went from poor to destitute. Thousands of families lost their property because their crops did not bring sufficient money to pay their debts and taxes. By the middle of the decade, almost 40,000 family farms had been lost to foreclosure.

The economic crisis had a devastating effect on public education, since the state government was unable to provide adequate funds for teachers' salaries or the maintenance of school facilities. Teachers found that if they were able to get their salary certificates cashed at all, they could not expect to receive full value for them. In 1932 the average annual teachers' salary was $414, which represented a substantial decrease from previous years. The annual state expenditures on the public schools was less than $4 million, which equated to less than $20 per pupil. To make matters worse, four of the state's institutions of higher education had, as mentioned, lost their accreditation during the Bilbo administration.

Although the environment was one of widespread disillusionment about economic and political conditions, there was at least one positive report. The director of the state Board of Health, Felix J. Underwood, reported that during 1931 and 1932 birth rates were increasing and death rates were decreasing; the average life span in Mississippi had reached a new record of 59 years; and there were record high numbers of marriages and low numbers of divorces. Even this report, however, contained some negative news: there had been a surprisingly large number of deaths caused by smallpox, almost two thousand cases in the two-year period.

Conner's Sales Tax   In retrospect some observers recalled Conner's inauguration as a rehearsal for the inauguration of Franklin D. Roosevelt the following year. But to launch in Mississippi a "little New Deal," the governor had to solve the daunting obstacles of a state's treasury deficit and declining revenues. His first priority was to increase state income by means of imposing a sales tax, and thus the Emergency Revenue Act, known as the sales-tax bill, emerged as the major issue in the 1932 legislative session. The governor argued that a 3 percent tax on sales would lessen the tax burden on the owners of property and businesses, who were paying too large a share. In an attempt to weaken opposition among groups of merchants who believed the sales tax would hurt their sales, he described the tax as a "consumption" tax, and then he used the race issue, declaring that blacks, who composed about 50 percent of the population, received state services but paid little in property taxes. This proposed legislation, Conner explained, would broaden the tax base and produce immediate revenue.

Nevertheless, opposition to the sales tax, led primarily by merchants, was so strong and emotional that disorders occurred in the capitol building and threats were made on the governor's life. The bill's strongest supporters were groups interested in state schools and colleges, led by State Superintendent of Education Willard F. Bond, who mobilized their lobbying strategies. Their efforts were supported by Speaker Thomas Bailey and other powerful leaders in the house of representatives. Finally, and after lengthy and heated debates, the final bill providing for a 2 percent retail sales tax passed by a close margin. It was signed by Conner on April 26, 1932, and took effect on May 1.

Recovery Efforts   The law seemed to have the desired result, immediately producing much needed revenue and lessening the state's dependence on revenues raised through property taxes. Within the first six months the state garnered almost $1.2 million in tax revenues, and with the application of frugal business practices some financial stability was restored to state government. From the huge deficit in 1932, the treasury grew to a cash balance of more than $3 million four years later.

On the basis of this accomplishment, the Conner administration undertook various internal improvements. In 1932 the first homestead exemption legislation provided tax relief for homeowners whose property was valued at $3,500 or less. The governor's reforms at the state penitentiary raised morale generally, and the institution began to pay its own expenses instead of requiring state assistance. Another accomplishment was the reinstatement of accreditation for the institutions of higher learning in June of 1933. Conner assured the Southern Association of Colleges and Secondary Schools that the new board of trustees for the institutions would be independent and free from any governor's control. Representing a fundamental change in the state's governance of the institutions of higher learning, the existing boards were replaced with a single state board composed of two members from each supreme court district and three from the state at large, all with overlapping terms. The governor still made the appointments with the advice and consent of the senate, and he served as ex officio chairman; however, the new arrangement greatly reduced the governor's authority over the board.

The agricultural high school in Pearl River County. Courtesy Pearl River Community College.

Revenues from Governor Conner's sales taxes in 1932 and stricter accountability for the use of state school funds required by the "Kyle-Cook Budget Law" of 1936 helped preserve the school system in the Great Depression, but schools and teachers remained woefully short of financial support. When Superintendent Bond retired in 1936, annual state expenditures averaged only $69 per student, as compared to $250 nationally. But with assistance from the Public Works Administration, one of the federal relief agencies created by President Franklin D. Roosevelt's "New Deal," which gave the state monies to maintain school facilities, and other federal sources, the estimated expenditures rose from $41 million in 1934 to $62 million in 1941. Not until 1944, however, would the state establish a retirement program for public school teachers.

The governor was not so successful, however, in his effort to accomplish major administrative reforms. Like Bilbo before him and many a future governor, Conner recommended that the legislature acknowledge the many changes in society since 1890, note the demands facing a modern state government, and call a convention to write a new state constitution. But like so many legislatures throughout the twentieth century, this set of lawmakers rejected this proposal, preferring to retain the conservative document that favored their branch and limited the powers of the executive.

In his attempt to deal with the pain inflicted by the Great Depression, Conner recommended policies that would attract industry by encouraging the development of oil, natural gas, and other extractive commodities as well as the conservation of these and other natural resources. In addition he believed that better highways and a program of public relations would help change the state's image and promote tourism and other revenue-generating activities.

One type of tourist business, the "Pilgrimage" concept, began somewhat by accident and completely independent of state government in 1932 when Mrs. Balfour Miller of Natchez decided to invite Mississippi garden club members to visit her residence, Hope Farm, and other antebellum homes. Although deplorable roads, or the complete lack of roads, had made it difficult for Mississippi to attract many visitors, this annual affair would expand to other towns and bring increasing numbers of tourists into the state.

The New Deal in Mississippi

The state's struggle to overcome the effects of the Great Depression could not have approached even partial success without the aid of the federal government. "Necessity is the mother of invention," and dire financial conditions delivered rather revolutionary innovations. During the 1930s, traditional attitudes about the role of government were substantially altered on both the federal and state levels. As supporters of and participants in President Roosevelt's "New Deal," the governor and the state's congressional delegation, led by Senators Harrison and Stephens, were responsible for acquiring extensive economic and social relief. Harrison was a somewhat reluctant New Dealer, but as chairman of the powerful Senate Committee on Finance from 1933 to 1941, he played a key role in negotiating with Roosevelt and securing the passage of the president's programs.

By 1934 the Civil Works Administration (CWA) was established in each county of the state, providing federal jobs for about 58,000 persons who built and maintained roads and bridges, improved waterways, performed nursing services, and worked in many other projects. Mississippians also secured substantial help through the implementation of numerous other agencies, such as the Federal Deposit Insurance Corporation (FDIC), through which individuals' bank accounts could be federally insured, the Works Progress Administration (WPA), and the Civilian Conservation Corporation (CCC). While the WPA employed thousands of men to do construction work of all kinds, the agency's lasting legacy was its special social and cultural activities, including "professional" projects in art, music, theatre, and historical surveys and writing. In Mississippi nearly one-third of the agency's employees were women, as compared to the national average of about 18 percent. The CCC provided jobs for thousands of young persons on public projects, such as the construction of parks and the improvement and maintenance of roads and forestlands. In all, the state received about $50 million in federal assistance during the Conner years.

Most New Deal programs were designed to rescue farmers, who still composed more than two-thirds of the state's total population in 1930. The Agricultural Adjustment Administration (AAA; later known as the Agricultural Stabilization and Conservation Service) financed new conservation practices, stabilized commodity prices, and provided subsidies to farmers. The Rural Electrification Administration (REA) delivered electric power to many previously unserved areas, which not only helped to raise many farmers' standard of living but also enabled them to use many types of labor-saving equipment like refrigerators and milking machines. As a result, poultry, hog, and dairy operations now could expand. The

Soil Erosion Service (later called the Soil Conservation Service) increased the level and breadth of knowledge about the different types of soil found in the state, which resulted in more efficient and profitable usage of land. The Resettlement Administration (later known as the Farmers' Home Administration), provided affordable loans for the purchase of homes and other facilities. Further aid for farmers was available through the Federal Surplus Commodities Corporation and the Farm Security Administration.

WPA Sewing Room in Jackson. Courtesy Mississippi Department of Archives and History.

With support from the United States Department of Agriculture, the state's agricultural experiment stations were expanded, and the Delta Branch Station was soon regarded as "one of the world's outstanding agricultural and forestry research centers." These programs collaborated with the Cooperative Extension Service, about which one scholar writes, "no public agency, with the exception of public schools, has touched the lives of so many people within the state." Its basic objective was to provide an education for farmers and persuade them to accept new, scientific methods and create a new farming culture. As heirs of the Farmers' Institutes, Extension agents traveled throughout the state spreading information about new farming techniques, new crop varieties and breeds of livestock, and entirely new types of agricultural businesses.

Commenting on the significance of the New Deal, a Mississippi journalist recalled, "These federal agencies were as much a part of the daily lives of the people in this period as was the growing of cotton in Mississippi in the years preceding and following the Civil War." Notwithstanding monumental federal assistance, the people of Mississippi continued to suffer and fear total financial collapse. In spite of federal attempts to restore confidence, many people completely lost faith in the banks and resorted to different kinds of barter as money shortages worsened. On leaving office, Conner's main point was that recovery still depended on changing the national, negative impression of Mississippi. A major factor in accomplishing such a change, he stressed, would be the attracting of industry, a task undertaken during the administration of Governor Hugh White.

Politics   During the Great Depression the Democratic party only gained in strength. In the presidential election of 1932 the party's nominee, Franklin D. Roosevelt, won 96 percent of the state's popular vote. For the first time since 1916 Mississippi voted for the winner, as Roosevelt defeated President Hoover by receiving 57 percent of the nation's popular votes and 89 percent of the presidential electors. Pursuant to the census returns of 1930, the state lost one of its eight seats in the U.S. House of Representatives, and in the 1932 congressional elections all incumbents were reelected except James W. Collier of Warren County in the old Eighth District and Percy E. Quin of McComb, who died in February 1932 after having served the Seventh District since 1913. Lawrence Russell Ellzey of Wesson was elected to succeed Quin.

One extraordinary political event during the Conner years was the resurrection of the political life of Theodore G. Bilbo, who upon leaving the governor's office in 1932 had obtained a rather bureaucratic position in the United States Department of Agriculture through the assistance of Senator Pat Harrison. In 1934 Bilbo and Congressman Ross Collins challenged Senator Stephens. In the second Democratic primary Bilbo defeated incumbent Senator Stephens by a vote of 101,702 to 94,587. Once in the Senate, however, Bilbo refused to work harmoniously with his senior colleague, Senator Harrison; in fact, the two senators even declined to speak to each other in a feud that lasted through Harrison's final four years in office. The controversy was caused in large measure by Bilbo's resentment that Harrison controlled most patronage related to the New Deal agencies in Mississippi, particularly the AAA and WPA, and by their different stances regarding President Roosevelt's programs. In contrast to Harrison's vital yet guarded position, the junior senator backed the New Deal completely and enthusiastically. The notorious feud was dramatized nationally in 1937 when Bilbo cast the decid-

Governor Hugh Lawson White. Courtesy Mississippi Department of Archives and History.

ing vote for Alben William Barkley of Kentucky as Senate Majority Leader, thus denying the position to Harrison, his fellow Mississippian.

Governor Hugh Lawson White, 1936–1940

Back home in Mississippi, Hugh L. White was elected to succeed Governor Conner. A native of McComb, White was born in 1882, the son of Confederate Army Captain John James White who had founded a successful sawmill business. J. J. White had been active in the Presbyterian Church and the community and served as president of the McComb Female College, which later merged with Belhaven College in Jackson. After attending the University of Mississippi, where he played football, Hugh White entered his father's business and, at the age of twenty-eight in 1909, became president of the J. J. White Lumber Company. The company, moving from McComb to Columbia in 1912, expanded to include four sawmills and other businesses and hired more than one thousand employees.

A charismatic, outgoing man, Hugh White stood over six feet tall and weighed about 260 pounds. Like his father, he was not only successful in business but was involved in local affairs, serving three terms as mayor of Columbia. In honor of his parents, he constructed the J. J. White Memorial Presbyterian Church in McComb.

To persuade large industries in other states to locate factories in Columbia, he traveled to Northern cities promising business executives that Marion County would finance the construction of plant facilities and that prospective relocaters could expect to enjoy local tax exemptions and an adequate supply of affordable laborers. The major business that White managed to attract to his city was the Reliance Manufacturing Company of Chicago.

Thus, long before Hugh White campaigned for the high office of governor, he had won statewide recognition as the mayor of Columbia who had succeeded in increasing the number of factory jobs for the people of Marion County. His gubernatorial platform promised that he would accomplish for the state what he had done for Columbia; that is, his program of "balancing agriculture with industry" or the "BAWI" program. White would launch that effort and obtain the adoption of a meaningful homestead exemption law, among other reforms, despite suffering a heart attack that restricted his physical activity during the last year of his term.

The Election of 1935   In his first gubernatorial campaign in 1931, White had led the other candidates in the first Democratic primary, including Mike Conner, who had won the second primary to become governor. In 1935 White and a family friend, Congressman Paul Johnson, were the two leaders in a very close first primary, which Johnson won by only 728 votes. In the second primary, White's margin of victory was only slightly wider, as he received 51.7 percent of the votes. J. B. Snider, a journalist, was elected lieutenant governor, and other state officials included Greek Rice as attorney general, Walker Wood as secretary of state, Newton James as treasurer, J. C. Holton as commissioner of agriculture and commerce, and J. S. Vandiver as superintendent of education.

The people of Mississippi were told by their new governor what they already knew too well: they were still suffering the hardships of the Great Depression with widespread unemployment and money shortages. White held out three basic plans to improve conditions: first, launch a highway program that would facilitate commerce and business activity and provide employment opportunities; second, his BAWI program; and third, provide tax relief and stimulate the economy simultaneously by giving property-tax exemptions to homeowners.

White's Highway Program   Despite the considerable efforts of previous governors, the state government had been unable financially to provide significant appropriations for highway construction. Due to the efforts of the Highway Department director Edgar Douglas Kenna and Senator Pat Harrison, the Roosevelt administration increased the Public Works Administration funds for Mississippi early in 1936. Under the leadership of future governor Fielding L. Wright in the state house of representatives, state senator George Smith, and Horace Stansel, the state director of PWA, White's highway bill passed both houses without opposition.

Because the legislature agreed to White's recommendations regarding matching appropriations, the total amount available for highway building in 1936 was about $42.5 million. Two years later the legislature extended the program so, with added revenue from the new gasoline tax, the total funds for highways increased to about $100 million. The program produced dramatic results. The mileage of paved highways increased from less than one thousand miles (about 15 percent of the total miles of state highways) to about four thousand miles (65 percent). To handle traffic problems and, when called upon by the governor and local law enforcement agencies, respond to statewide emergencies and help enforce laws, the legislature in 1938 created the Mississippi Highway Safety Patrol, the state's first statewide police force.

Agricultural Diversification   Notwithstanding the problems derived from the lack of diversity in the kinds of crops farmers planted and the imbalance between agriculture and industry, long-held habits were difficult to change. Fortunately, some positive signs began to appear for suffering farmers with the harvests of 1936. In some areas the average per-acre production had increased to 306 pounds of cotton (a rise of almost 120 percent since the crop of 1932), more than 200 bushels of corn, and about 135 bushels of oats. Greater diversification resulted in Mississippi farmers cultivating more sweet potatoes, pecans, tung trees (which produced an oil used in paints and wood polishes), and other crops, along with an increase in the numbers of livestock, mainly cattle and hogs. Crop diversification also caused a reduction of cotton acreage by about one-third and an increase by two-thirds in the acreage for various food crops like grains.

BAWI   Agricultural diversification was only part of the answer for the state's economic recovery. Another requisite was industrial growth. In 1936 farmers' income amounted to about $185 million, while income from industrial jobs was only about $14 million. As mentioned, Governor White's plan to address this need was his "balance agriculture with industry" or BAWI program. Enacted by a special session of the legislature in 1936, BAWI authorized local governments to issue bonds for the purpose of constructing industrial plants. A substantial portion of this indebtedness would then be retired partly through revenue from rents paid by businesses using the facilities. Three commissions were established to implement the program: the Industrial Commission, known as the BAWI Board, to approve bond issues by counties or municipalities; the Advertising Commission, to promote the program's benefits, which included tax exemptions for industries locating in the state, and foster tourism; and the Planning Commission, to provide basic data for potential enterprises.

Although a few critics labeled BAWI as socialistic, and some bankers at first questioned its financial basis, the local bond elections revealed that by overwhelming majorities the voters supported the program. As new factory jobs became available, and the additional money in circulation improved economic conditions generally, the criticisms virtually disappeared. Within four years, twelve plants had been approved, and personal income from total manufacturing had jumped to $49 million. BAWI's most important accomplishment was attracting Robert I. Ingalls, the owner of an iron works company in Birmingham, Alabama, to start a shipbuilding business, the Ingalls Shipbuilding Corporation, in Pascagoula in 1938. Although less than $1 million in public bonds had been approved to attract this business, Ingalls produced more than $40 million in total wages by 1943, due to the demands of wartime. The greatest benefits of BAWI, however, would come later, because the program laid a foundation on which the state could build aggressively during World War II and afterward.

Homestead Exemption   Another stimulus to the stale economy was the homestead exemption law, enacted by a special session of the legislature in 1938. Homesteads with valuations up to $5,000 and comprising less than 160 acres of land were exempt from nearly all ad valorem taxes. This reform not only represented tax relief but encouraged homebuilding, which would have far-reaching economic repercussions.

Politics   During the late 1930s there were no deviations from the tradition of reelecting Democratic party incumbents. Easily surmounting the challenge by former Governor Conner, in 1936 Senator Harrison won his fourth consecutive election to the U.S. Senate. President Roosevelt was reelected, receiving 97 percent of Mississippi's votes, 61 percent of the nation's popular vote, and carrying all but two states, Maine and Vermont. In the congressional elections, six of the seven incumbents were reelected, and former representative Ross Collins, who had withdrawn for an unsuccessful campaign for the Senate in 1934, was returned to the House in 1936. Two years later all seven incumbent Representatives were reelected.

The Depression Continues   Notwithstanding Governor White's new programs and continuing federal aid, Mississippians continued to suffer serious hardships. Experiencing some improvements by the end of the decade, recovery seemed to be beginning with more employment opportunities, better highways, and a measure of property-tax relief. Throughout the state thousands of families for the first time got access to electric power through the efforts of the REA.

Various forms of taxation, however, still burdened Mississippians, particularly the poorest among them, with the sales tax and the poll tax falling equally on all families regardless of their ability to pay. The effort to repeal the poll tax, which had been used historically as an obstacle for black suffrage—since most blacks could not afford to pay it—was, unfortunately, blocked by the White administration. It was only with a cataclysmic event—the the Japanese bombing of Pearl Harbor which brought the United States into the greatest war in history—that Mississippi and the nation finally woke up from the economic nightmare of the Great Depression.

Selected Sources

Bond, Bradley G., *Mississippi: A Documentary History* (Jackson: University Press of Mississippi, 2003).

Clark, Eric C., "Legislative Adoption of BAWI, 1936," *Journal of Mississippi History* 52 (November 1990): 283–99.

Cobb, James C., *The Most Southern Place on Earth: The Mississippi Delta and the Roots of Regional Identity* (New York: Oxford University Press, 1992).

Emmerich, J. Oliver, "Collapse and Recovery," in Richard Aubrey McLemore, ed., *A History of Mississippi*, 2 vols. (Hattiesburg: University & College Press of Mississippi, 1973), 2: 97–119.

Green, A. Wigfall, *The Man Bilbo* (Baton Rouge: Louisiana State University Press, 1963).

McCain, William D., "The Triumph of Democracy, 1916–1932," in Richard Aubrey McLemore, ed., *A History of Mississippi*, 2 vols. (Hattiesburg: University & College Press of Mississippi, 1973), 2: 59–96.

McMillen, Neil R., *Dark Journey: Black Mississippians in the Age of Jim Crow* (Urbana: University of Illinois Press, 1989).

Morgan, Chester M., *Redneck Liberal: Theodore G. Bilbo and the New Deal* (Baton Rouge: Louisiana State University Press, 1985).

Mississippi Official and Statistical Register, 1935–1937.

Sansing, David G., *Making Haste Slowly: The Troubled History of Higher Education in Mississippi* (Jackson: University Press of Mississippi, 1990).

Scott, Roy V., *The Reluctant Farmer: The Rise of Agricultural Extension to 1914* (Urbana, Illinois: University of Illinois Press, 1970).

Swain, Martha H., "The Lion and the Fox: The Relationship of President Franklin D. Roosevelt and Senator Pat Harrison," *Journal of Mississippi History* 38 (August 1976): 333–59.

———, "A New Deal for Mississippi Women, 1933–1943," *Journal of Mississippi History* 46 (August 1984): 191–212.

Vogt, Daniel C., "Government Reform, the 1890 Constitution, and Mike Conner," *Journal of Mississippi History* 48 (February 1986): 43–56.

———, "Hoover's Reconstruction Finance Corporation in Action: Mississippi Bank Loans and Work Relief, 1932–1933," *Journal of Mississippi History* 47 (February 1985): 35–53.

Whatley, Larry, "The Works Progress Administration in Mississippi," *Journal of Mississippi History* 30 (February 1968): 35–50.

CHAPTER EIGHTEEN

A Rich Cultural Heritage

Its long-term failure to correct the deep inadequacies in its system of public education notwithstanding, Mississippi is the home state of many of the nation's finest artists and scholars, whether in literature, the visual or performing arts, or music.

LITERATURE

While it may well be that more Mississippians watch college football on television on any given Saturday than read a Faulkner novel throughout the entire year, the promotional spots those watching "Ole Miss" games see during time-outs boast more about the literary giants the university has turned out over its long history than its sports heroes. Indeed, the work produced by the state's writers in the twentieth century, both in terms of quantity and quality, is remarkable: considering education and poverty levels in the state and the size of the population, it is phenomenal. Across genres, Mississippi authors have received national acclaim as leaders in a "literary awakening" that began in the South after the turn of the twentieth century.

Critics' efforts to explain the factors underlying these accomplishments include two major proposals: the influence of change and that of place. The former factor involved major and sometimes explosive societal transformations, particularly regarding economics, politics, and race relations as well as the resistance to these sharp breaks with tradition. The latter factor, the influence of place, involved a growing interest in what was seen as a unique way of life in a setting where folks portrayed an idealized community and family life that was very often at odds with the tragic realities of poverty, ignorance, and the legacies of slavery. Another theory credits the lingering persistence of a traditional, rural, and somewhat isolated setting in which a slow-paced lifestyle allowed for quiet reflection, storytelling in the oral tradition, and the development of individual imagination and expression.

The following number of writers and works reveals the glaringly disproportionate literary output of the state's relatively tiny population. In 2002 the University of Mississippi Department of English's *Writers Page* listed a total of nearly two hundred recognized authors in four categories: fiction, nonfiction, poetry, and drama. All but twenty-four of these persons worked in the twentieth century, and more than half of them published in more than one genre. In a more exhaustive search for all twentieth-century authors, the Starkville High School Department

Top: Eudora Welty. Bottom: Margaret Walker
Alexander. Courtesy Mississippi Department of
Archives and History

of English's *The Mississippi Writers and
Musicians Project* compiled an extensive
list of at least 365 writers who produced a
total of roughly 1,247 publications comprising all genres. Due to the constraints
of space in this text, as well as the availability of ample reference sources for
interested students, the following list of
outstanding writers is, admittedly, lim-
ited, and only a few key figures in Mississippi's great literary
history receive commentary.

Fiction

The state's best-known literary accomplishments fall
in the category of fiction, and of the more than 120 best-
known authors listed in this genre by the University of
Mississippi Department of English in 2002, about 20 of
them published significant works in other categories as
well. Some of the most outstanding fiction writers were
Margaret Walker Alexander (1915–98), William Attaway
(1911–86), Larry Brown (1951–), Ellen Douglas (1921–),
William Faulkner (1897–1962), Richard Ford (1944–),
Ellen Gilchrist (1935–), John Grisham (1955–), Barry
Hannah (1942–), Greg Iles (1961–), Willie Morris
(1934–99), Walker Percy (1916–90), Patrick D. Smith

(1927–), Elizabeth Spencer (1921–), James Howell Street (1903–54), Richard
Wright (1908–60), Eudora Welty (1909–2001), Al Young (1939–), and Stark
Young (1881–1963).

Stark Young of Oxford, a leader of the so-called Southern Renaissance, wrote
numerous plays and novels. *So Red the Rose* (1934) was one of several historical
novels concerning plantation life in the Old South. The story describes the clash
between two ways of life, agrarian and industrial, and the collapse of the cotton
aristocracy. In "Not in Memoriam, but in Defense," which was written as the con-
cluding essay for the agrarian manifesto *I'll Take My Stand,* Young summarized the
philosophy of his fiction: although one could "never go back," there were "worth-
while things" in the old Southern way of life that should survive. Young's career
was honored at the "Oxford Conference for the Book" at the University of Mississippi in April 2003.

A quite different view of Southern life is presented by African American writers such as Richard Wright and Margaret Walker Alexander. For the first nineteen years of his life Wright struggled with poverty, family disruptions, and racism,
first in rural Adams County and then in Jackson and Memphis. Although his ma-

jor works (plays, novels, various nonfiction publications) were written in New York City, where he lived after a ten-year sojourn in Chicago, many of them were strongly influenced by his Mississippi heritage. The plight of a young African American, Bigger Thomas, living amidst poverty, violence, and racial oppression in Chicago is presented in the highly acclaimed novel *Native Son* (1940). Wright describes his own Mississippi experiences in *Black Boy: A Recollection of Childhood and Youth* (1945).

One of Wright's literary friends, Margaret Walker Alexander, chose to describe life in the mid-nineteenth-century South. In her novel *Jubilee* (1966) she relates the tumultuous experiences of African Americans during slavery, Civil War, and emancipation. Accomplished in poetry and other genres as well as fiction, Alexander in 1968 established the Institute for the Study of the History, Life and Culture of Black People. Among her many legacies is the Margaret Walker Alexander National Research Center at Jackson State University, where she served as professor of English for more than thirty years.

Many scholars consider another friend of Alexander, Eudora Welty of Jackson, one of America's best fiction writers of the twentieth century. In numerous short stories, novels, and essays, she painted a portrait of the ways Mississippians lived in the state's different places, ranging from the Delta to the Red Clay Hills to the Piney Woods, and all along the Natchez Trace. Her main subject, according to *One Writer's Beginnings* (1984), was human relationships. Welty's stories in *Curtain of Green* (1941) and *The Golden Apples* (1949) reveal the uniqueness of provincial home folk forced to make moral choices when facing local, yet universal, problems. But her wideranging novels did not always explore serious human relationships. For example, *The Robber Bridegroom* (1942), and *Losing Battles* (1970), among other of her novels, describe the comical rituals of everyday life in small rural communities and at family gatherings.

After formal schooling away from Jackson, Welty traveled the state during the Great Depression as a publicist for the Works Progress Administration. During this time she developed a keen interest in photography, which not only sharpened her writing skills but produced widely acclaimed exhibitions and publications. Nevertheless, the stories she typed in her upstairs room at home, rather than photographs taken on the road, brought Welty the Pulitzer Prize and membership in the French Legion of Honor, as well as many other major literary recognitions.

While Welty was still a student, another Mississippi short story writer and novelist was already attracting national attention. Towering above his state and national colleagues, William C. Faulkner of Oxford was ranked by one panel of experts as the second most influential Southerner in the twentieth century, behind only Martin Luther King, Jr., and ahead of Elvis Presley of Tupelo and the Reverend Billy Graham.

Considered by many critics as the "Shakespeare" of the century, Faulkner (changed from Falkner in 1924) is best known for his Yoknapatawpha series of fifteen novels published between 1929 and 1959. The place is a miniature county (actually Lafayette County), and the time is from the Civil War through the Great Depression. The stories portray the universal conflicts of honor versus

Rowan Oak, home of William Faulkner. Courtesy Westley F. Busbee, Jr.

greed, humanism versus materialism, universal principles displayed by the fictional Sartoris and Snopes families. Faulkner uses the Sartoris (good and bad) to represent the old slaveholding but now declining aristocrats and the Snopes to depict conniving, sharecropping, poor whites who burn barns, steal horses, and commit other evil deeds.

Faulkner's most notable novels include *The Sound and the Fury* (1927), *As I Lay Dying* (1930), *Absalom, Absalom!* (1936) *Intruder in the Dust* (1948), *A Fable* (1954), and *The Reivers* (1962), in which he employs a variety of writing styles: traditional narrative, stream of consciousness, flashbacks, and multiple narrators. His style of writing has drawn comparisons to the work of jazz musicians, his prose punctuated by the syncopated dialects of hillbillies, African Americans, and other Mississippi folk. His recurring themes include isolated community life, sexual tensions and miscegenation, social decadence, poverty, and racism.

Some scholars observe that Faulkner's ability to tell a "griping story," his original expressive language, and the moral significance of his works, underpin his greatness. In his 1950 Nobel Prize acceptance speech he said, "I Decline to Accept the End of Man. . . . there should be no room in the writer's workshop for anything but the eternal verities," which include "love and honor and pity and pride and compassion and sacrifice," the essential aspects, he believed, of human ability to prevail. Five years later he won the Pulitzer Prize and the National Book Award for *A Fable*, an allegorical tale of World War I, which Faulkner considered his masterpiece. Literary critics cite instead *Absalom, Absalom!* for that distinction.

Nonfiction

The largest number (146) of writers listed by the UM *Writers Page* published nonfiction works in a wide variety of fields, including biography, journalism, sociology, and history; however, at least half of them were also known for their work in other genres. Some prominent nonfiction writers who hailed from Mississippi include Stephen E. Ambrose, historian (1936–2002), Ida Wells-Barnett, journalist (1862–1931), Lerone Bennett, Jr., historian (1928–), John K. Bettersworth, historian (1909–91), Will D. Campbell, theologian, historian (1924–), Charlotte Capers, archivist, historian (1913–96), William Hodding Carter, II, journalist (1907–72), Turner Catledge, journalist (1901–83), Thomas D. Clark, historian (1903–), David L. Cohn, essayist, historian (1887–1960), David Herbert Donald, historian (1920–), William Ferris, folklorist, historian (1942–), Shelby Foote, historian (1916–), Dumas Malone, historian (1892–1986), Robert McElvaine, historian (1947–), William Alexander Percy, historian (1885–1942), and Dunbar Rowland, historian, archivist (1864–1937).

The son of Senator LeRoy Percy and member of one of the Delta's oldest planter dynasties, William Alexander Percy of Greenville was at heart a poet. His best-known work, however, was an autobiography that interpreted life in the Mississippi Delta, *Lanterns on the Levee: Recollections of a Planter's Son* (1941). The work describes the background and influence in the region of his family, his personal philosophy that virtue is an end in itself, and his observations of changes that seemed to have challenged traditional values. His close friend, David Cohn, presented a somewhat different version of Delta society in *Where I Was Born and Raised* (1948). Remarking that the "Delta" extends from the lobby of the Peabody Hotel in Memphis to Catfish Row in Vicksburg and that a person in the former location will eventually "see everybody who is anybody in the Delta," Cohn's work paints a complex albeit mythical social order of aristocrats guided by principles of noblesse oblige in their relations with poor whites and African Americans.

Born in radically different circumstances in 1903, Thomas D. Clark of Winston County earned a bachelor's degree at the University of Mississippi, a master's at the University of Kentucky, and the doctorate at Duke University in North Carolina. Countless thousands of students and readers of Southern history have benefited from his classes at the University of Kentucky and many other American and European colleges and universities, as well as from his more than thirty books and numerous articles and other publications. His contribu-

Dunbar Rowland. Courtesy Mississippi Department of Archives and History.

tions include such widely acclaimed studies of rural life in the South as *Pills, Petticoats, & Plows: The Southern Country Store* (1944) and *The Southern Country Editor* (1948). Clark's remarkable accomplishments include his leadership role in the Organization of American Historians, the Southern Historical Association, and many other professional organizations. When colleagues celebrated his centennial year at the 2003 annual meeting of the Southern Historical Association in Houston, Texas, the honoree displayed acuity, humility, and wit in recalling his scholarly experiences, which spanned the twentieth century.

But because his scholarship focused solely on Mississippi and he remained in his native state throughout his career, Dunbar Rowland may be considered the state's leading historian of the early twentieth century. Born in Oakland, Yalobusha County, during the Civil War, Rowland shifted from his law practice to the position of the state's newly established Department of Archives and History in 1902. More than three decades in that position, he produced numerous volumes and articles, including but not limited to such works as *History of Mississippi, The Heart of the South*; *Military History of Mississippi, 1803–1898*; *Mississippi Provincial Archives: French Dominion, 1749–1763*; *Mississippi: Comprising Sketches of Counties, Towns, Events, Institutions, and Persons, Arranged in Cyclopedic Form*; and *Jefferson Davis, Constitutionalist: His Letters, Papers, and Speeches*. As if the preponderance of these works was not enough, Rowland initiated the state's series of the Official and Statistical Register and was the first editor of the Publications of the Mississippi Historical Society.

Poetry

Although most Mississippi authors wrote poetry, their work in this genre received less national acclaim. Almost 120 poets listed by the UM *Writers Page* were prominent, but almost half of them gained more recognition for their publications in other fields. Some examples of the best-known poets were Margaret Walker Alexander (1915–98), James Autry (1933–), Charles Greenleaf Bell (1916–), Katherine Bellamann (1877–1956), Lerone Bennett, Jr. (1928–), Maxwell Bodenheim (1892–1954), Charlie R. Braxton (1961–), Jonathan Henderson Brooks (1904–45), Sarah Pauline Simmons Busbee (1917–), Jack Butler (1944–), Turner Cassity (1929–), Winifred Hamrick Farrar (1923–), Charles Henri Ford (1913–), Brooks Haxton (1950–), T. R. Hummer (1950–), Angela Jackson (1951–), Emory D. Jones (1944–), Etheridge Knight (1931–), Linda Peavy (1943–), Sterling D. Plumpp (1940–), Edgar Simmons (1921–79), John Stone (1936–), Jerry W. Ward, Jr. (1943–), Nagueyalti Warren (1947–), James Whitehead (1936–), Benjamin Williams (1947–), John A. Williams (1925–), and Otis Williams (1939–).

Striving to make Mississippians aware of the importance of writing and preserving poetry, a group of eleven women organized a state poetry society in 1932 at Belhaven College. Demonstrating students' and writers' expanding levels of interest, the society established three regional branches in the 1980s. Widely recognized for her literary accomplishments and leadership in the society, Winifred Hamrick Farrar of Meridian was appointed state poet laureate for life by Governor Cliff Finch in 1978. By the late 1990s the Mississippi Poetry Society reported a total membership of more than one hundred members, many of whom were published poets.

The common traits of the state's poets include the distinctive regional and racial voices, African Americans' reflections on yesteryear filled with paradoxes, whites' nostalgia for the pastoral past, a mixture of guilt and resentment over racial injustices and other tragedies, and memories of community, familial, and religious relationships. Although the work of the respective poets is diverse in style and content, influences of the state's cultural heritage tend to permeate most of it. In 1916 Maxwell Bodenheim, a native of Claiborne County who would attract attention as a novelist and playwright in Chicago and New York City, wrote the following "Poet to His Love."

> An old silver church in a forest
> Is my love for you.
> The trees around it
> Are words that I have stolen from your heart.
> An old silver bell, the last smile you gave,
> Hangs at the top of my church.
> It rings only when you come through the forest
> And stand beside it.
> And then, it has no need for ringing,
> For your voice takes its place.[1]

In "Heart Pine" (1993) and other poems Meridian native Sarah Pauline Simmons Busbee reminds readers of the importance of place, time, and values in Mississippi.

> "Heart pine," my father said, when letting go the house.
> We added on back then, did not tear out
> as she is doing now, to modernize.
> Three or four generations back folks valued quality, chose
> their planks from sawmills run by neighbors,
> pointing out the pieces, as blade arrested seeping sap.
> And what was built was there to stay.
> These boards refuse to yield to muscled crowbar, and
> stubborn nails will break before they bend.
> . . . .[2]

Similar memories are revealed in Turner Cassity's "Cane Mill," Winifred Farrar's "Remember Corn Fields?," and Ellen Gilchrist's "Sharecropper."

African-American voices, however, speak of different experiences, involving fond recollections tempered with feelings of umbrage and triumph. A recurring theme is the people's reliance on music as one way to make life tolerable through

---

1 See Louis Untermeyer, ed., *Modern American Poetry* (New York: Harcourt, Brace and Howe, 1919), poem number 128.
2 Pauline Simmons Busbee, *Heart Pine* (Brandon, Miss.: Encorenterprises, 1993), 3.

the dark times. In "Make'n My Music" Angela Jackson, a Greenville native writing in Chicago in the 1970s, recalls the spirituals of the "saint-tified folks" in her youth and that "my Black woman'hood ain't been noth'n but music."[3] Similar reflections are presented by Grenada native Otis Williams in "About the Blues":

> Use to stop by the Sanctified Church
> On my way home
> The Gospel Singin' made my soul shout
> The Spirit hit me
> The spirit was always live
> And Movin' in the Sanctified Church
> Like Christ was comin' in the mornin'
>
> . . . .

Another prevailing note is the struggle to overcome racial oppression. Margaret Walker Alexander's "For My People" was dedicated to past, present, and future generations of African Americans: ancestors "singing their slave songs . . . their blues and jubilees. . . ."; the Jim Crow generation's "memory of the bitter hours when we discovered we were black and poor and small and different and nobody cared and nobody wondered and nobody understood . . ."; folks who left the South to become "lost disinherited dispossessed and happy . . . tied and shackled and tangled among ourselves by the unseen creatures who tower over us omnisciently and laugh"; contemporary people "blundering and groping and floundering in the dark of churches and schools . . . distressed and disturbed and deceived and devoured . . . preyed on by facile force of state . . . by false prophet and holy believer . . . [but] standing staring trying to fashion a better way. . . ." She concludes,

> Let a new earth rise. . . .
> Let a second generation full of courage issue forth;
> let a people loving freedom come to growth.
>
> . . . .

In "Whitey Remembers," Emory D. Jones explores whites' reaction to the civil rights movement, and Nagueyalti Warren's "Mississippi Woods" speaks of the black folks' sacrifices, as expressed in the following verse:

> If woods could talk
> wonder what would they say.
> Would they give away southern secrets:
> tell of murders by knights in white sheets
>
> . . . .

3 Unless otherwise documented, the source for all poetry quoted in this chapter is Dorothy Abbott, ed., *Mississippi Writers: Reflections of Childhood and Youth*, vol. 3, *Poetry* (Jackson: University Press of Mississippi, 1988).

Warren's "Southern Memories" were about

Mississippi summer
delta sun burning black hot white memories
of lush green
rope bearing trees
bringing death to Black folk
who dared to live free.

Drama

In contrast to the large number of poets, there were relatively few prominent Mississippi dramatists, almost all of whom were also known for their work in other genres. Nonetheless, this group of writers produced a sizeable body of work that attracted national and even international acclaim. Some of the state's best-known playwrights include Beth Henley (1952–), Jim Henson (1936–90), and Thomas Lanier "Tennessee" Williams (1911–83). Many of the state's best-known fiction authors produced works subsequently presented on the theater stage, as films, and as television productions. Some prominent examples include works by Attaway, Faulkner, Grisham, Morris, Welty, and Wright.

Inspired by his childhood experiences in Mississippi, Tennessee Williams was regarded as one of the nations' greatest dramatists, having won Pulitzer Prizes for *A Streetcar Named Desire* in 1948 and *Cat on a Hot Tin Roof* in 1955. Henley's *Crimes of the Heart* and *The Miss Firecracker Contest* (both later made into films) won national acclamation and a Pulitzer Prize for the former play. Endesha Ida Mae Holland of Greenville won acclaim for her one-woman play, *Miss Ida B. Wells*, and her autobiographical *From the Mississippi Delta*. Jim Henson created the highly successful "Muppets," the puppet stars of public television's *Sesame Street* as well as their own feature-length films and videos. His character, Kermit the Frog, beloved by generations of children, was named for a close childhood friend in Leland.

An excellent source for substantive study of the state's twentieth-century literature is the *Mississippi Writers* series, published between 1985 and 1991 by the Center for the Study of Southern Culture at the University of Mississippi. The series includes anthologies of fiction, nonfiction, poetry, drama, and a summary anthology of all four genres. Volume one, *Fiction*, contains 66 works by 57 authors; volume two, *Nonfiction*, includes 72 nonfiction selections by 67 writers; volume three, *Poetry*, presents poems by 112 authors; and volume four, *Drama*, contains 18 selections from works by 20 dramatists. The final volume, *An Anthology*, includes 69 selections by 47 writers in the four genres. Each of the five volumes provides biographical sketches of the authors along with titles of their best-known works.

If, as mentioned, a significant portion of Mississippi literature revealed ordinary folks' efforts to cope with the frustrations of poverty, ignorance, and violence in an environment of bigotry and racial injustice, another recurrent theme was the people's dependence on music, particularly the blues and gospel, as a means of coping with, even fighting against, the many encumbrances of life in Mississippi.

Music

The state's literary accomplishments were paralleled by considerable contributions in music distinguished by the production of original genres. Like litera-

Blues singer "Son" (Rufus) Thomas. Courtesy Mississippi Department of Archives and History.

ture, music may be categorized, but each form is closely related to and influenced by the others. African Americans contributed directly to the evolution of several distinctive music styles, including spirituals, gospel, the blues, and jazz. The "Negro Spiritual" came from early African American churches as a form of rhythmic music that welcomed improvisation, expressed emotion, and encouraged participation. This form became popular in the twentieth century and influenced the emergence of "gospel singing" in black and white churches.

Gospel   Particularly among fundamentalist churches—whether Baptist, Holiness, or Pentecostal—gospel music gained widespread popularity in the twentieth century. The Reverend C. L. Franklin, father of widely acclaimed gospel singer Aretha Franklin, was a singing pastor in the Mississippi Delta before moving to a Baptist church in Detroit. Black groups like the Staple Singers and white quartets like the Blackwood Brothers attracted large audiences in churches and via records and the radio. In the mid-1920s, when commercial radio became available in the state, gospel music was among the most popular presentations on the air.

Blues   The merger of gospel with secular kinds of music, such as the work songs handed down through generations of slaves, sharecroppers, and even convict laborers, contributed to the rise of other distinctive musical genres, "the blues" and "rhythm and blues" early in the twentieth century. While guitarist Robert Johnson is widely hailed as the "king of the Delta Blues," the living "king of the blues," B. B. King, was first taught to play the guitar and sing in church by a "sanctified

Muddy Waters honored at the Delta Blues Museum. Courtesy Mississippi Development Authority/Division of Tourism.

preacher." According to some observers, blues artists might play at a club on Saturday night and then in church on Sunday morning. Dorothy Moore of Jackson, who began singing in The New Stranger Home Baptist Church Choir at the age of five, received wide acclaim in rhythm and blues, country and western, and gospel. Other Delta blues performers included John Lee Hooker (1917–2001), Rufus Thomas (1917–2001) of Cayce, Muddy Waters (McKinley Morganfield), W. C. Handy, known as the "father of the blues," and Charley Patton, who was recognized as the first great bluesman. In his explanation of the historical context and the content of the blues, James C. Cobb argues persuasively that the Mississippi Delta "was clearly the principal source of blues performers during the music's formative years."

Three Mississippians were recognized for their contributions in this genre by Lifetime Achievements Awards from the National Academy of Recording Arts and Sciences (purveyors of the "Grammy"). In 1987 B. B. King was described as "one of the most original and soulful of all blues guitarists and singers, whose compelling style and devotion to musical truth have inspired so many budding performers, both here and abroad, to celebrate the blues." Muddy Waters was acclaimed in 1992 as singer-composer-guitarist who pioneered the electric blues era and defined the Chicago blues sound, influencing "young English musicians (such as the Rolling Stones) and therefore the British rock revolution." John Lee Hooker, whose style was used by all white blues bands beginning in the early 1960s, was honored in 2000 for "his lengthy tenure as one of the prime architects of electric blues and boogie, who combined his Mississippi Delta roots with the urban intensity of his adopted home Detroit into a signature sound that influenced numerous young boogie/rockers, including the Rolling Stones, the Animals, ZZ Top, and Bonnie Raitt."

In his poem, "About the Blues," Otis Williams says only through experience can one understand the blues. "But they move me Like the Holy Ghost moves a sinner," [and it's a feeling that]

> Takes me back, way back
> Every hurt, every joy, ever tear I've shed
> Flashes across my Mississippi mind. . . .

Al Young writes in "The Blues Don't Change,"

> And I was born with you, wasn't I, Blues?
> Wombed with you, wounded, reared and forwarded
> from address to address, stamped, stomped
> and returned to sender by nobody else but you,
> Blue Rider . . . .

Melancholy and pride are blended in the music as expressed by poet Benjamin Williams:

> And Not Just in Sorrow
> was slavery endured by our fathers
> or the spirituals born
> only to give a voice to despair.
> And not just in sorrow
> have we aspired to greatness
> merging our jazz and blues
> into the fabric
> of human consciousness.

In "Blues and Bitterness," praising the jazz and blues of singer Billie Holiday and lamenting her untimely death, Lerone Bennett, Jr., describes her haunting voice and verse,

> I wondered why God made me.
> I wondered why He made me black.
> I wondered why Mama begat me—
> And I started to give God His ticket back.

Country   Another genre, the emergence of which paralleled the spirituals, was "country" music (also known in the early stages as "hillbilly"). Originating from early Celtic ballads, this style was influenced by and had some affect upon gospel, blues, and other types of music. Jimmie Rodgers (1897–1933), born near Meridian where he was known as the "Singing [railroad] Brakeman," was recognized as the "father of country music." His popular songs blended country, blues, gospel, and bluegrass. According to one writer, by writing and singing "songs that drew from the full spectrum of music that he knew, Rodgers was creating a truly American music and setting a precedent that would be followed by a number of the most progressive and influential figures in country music history."

Some of Mississippi's best-known country music performers include Paul Davis of Meridian, Mickey Gilley of Natchez, Faith Hill of Star, Charlie Pride of Sledge, LeAnn Rimes of Pearl, Marty Stuart of Philadelphia, Conway Twitty (Harold Lloyd Jenkins) of Friars Point, and Tammy Wynette of Tremont.

Rock and Roll   With a background in country music, with all its inclusiveness, and in church music—both the spirituals and gospel—Elvis Presley of Tupelo burst into the world of music in the 1950s with still another blend of music, one called "rock and roll." Two of his earliest recordings reveal the unique sound of this music: "That's All Right Mama" and "Blue Moon of Kentucky." These two were soon followed by even more popular songs, "Don't Be Cruel," "Hound Dog," "Love Me Tender," and "Heartbreak Hotel," Elvis's first number-one record, unveiled in 1956.

While Elvis was known as the "king" of rock and roll, Bo Diddley (Otha Ellas Bates McDaniels) of McComb has been dubbed the "father of rock and roll." Other prominent rock performers include the explosive Jerry Lee Lewis of Nesbit, the great Sam Cooke of Clarksdale, and the showman Ike Turner of Clarksdale. In 1999 Cooke was posthumously honored by the Recording Academy with a Grammy for the Lifetime Achievement Award for having delivered his "silky smooth gospel-inflected pop to both black and white audiences and [laying] the foundation for modern soul stirrers."

Classical   Revealing close relationships among the genres, many Mississippians wrote and performed in several different types of music. Others, however, were more accomplished in one genre; for example, Cassandra Wilson of Jackson in jazz, Kenneth Haxton of Greenville in classical, and Leontyne Price of Laurel and Lester Senter Wilson of Jackson in opera. In 1989 Price received the Recording Academy's Lifetime Achievement and was honored as the "'Stradivarius of Singers' and possessor of one of the most beautiful operatic voices." Lehman Engel of Jackson was a prolific composer of classical and other forms, including scores for many Broadway plays—such as the music for the original productions of *A Streetcar Named Desire* and *The Ponder Heart*. William Grant Still, born on a plantation near Woodville and educated at the Oberlin College Conservatory of Music, was an African American pioneer in symphonic and opera compositions.

In the mid-twentieth century growing numbers of Mississippians supported the cultivation of classical music. Beginning in Jackson in 1944, symphony orchestras were organized in several municipalities, providing performances by local as well as nationally acclaimed musicians and encouraging greater appreciation and study of classical music within the state. Forty-five years after its small beginning following a concert at Belhaven College, the Jackson Symphony Orchestra in 1989 became the Mississippi Symphony Orchestra, "in response to its growing influence statewide." An indication of such growth was increasing financial and volunteer support, which helped the orchestra expand its budget from $100,000 in 1968 to $1.3 million in 2002. With more diverse performances, including a "Pop series" and "KinderConcerts" in communities statewide, the Orchestra claimed to be "Mississippi's greatest cultural force."

Another indication of interest in classical music was the founding of several opera companies in cities such as Jackson, Hattiesburg, and Biloxi. The Mississippi Opera in Jackson commenced its fifty-ninth season in 2003.

Governor Winter with Eudora Welty, Leontyne Price, and Elise Winter. Courtesy Mississippi Department of Archives and History.

The Fine Arts

To the layperson it may seem that as in the case of Mississippi's poets who received less acclaim than writers in other literary genres, other of the state's numerous artists produced superior works yet generally received less national tribute than their counterparts in music and literature. Many of the state's outstanding artists, however, gained recognition after they moved away from the state, and to students of art history the contributions of Mississippians are as remarkable as those produced by artists in other field.

Societies and Events   Reflecting the steadily growing interest in art in Mississippi, early in the twentieth century a state art association and the first of many local and regional artistic societies were created. The mission of the Mississippi Art Association, which was initially organized in 1903 as an "art study club" by Bessie Cary Lemly of Belhaven College, was "to promote the original work of Mississippi artists, sculptors, writers, craftsmen, and workers in other artistic fields." According to its charter, the association's first priority "was to establish a permanent and monumental gallery and grounds, wherein the finest examples of the work of Mississippi artists and other artists may be shown, and where collections of art work may be accumulated and preserved." After almost seven decades, these aims were finally achieved with the opening of the Mississippi Museum of Art in Jackson.

Another important event was the founding in 1948 of an art colony at Allison's Wells, a hotel and spa in Madison County, under the leadership of John and Hosford Fontaine and Karl and Mildred Wolfe. There, an increasing number of participants gathered in biannual workshops to receive instruction from well-known artists. After the hotel was destroyed by fire in 1963, the colony reorganized as the Mississippi Art Colony and moved to Stafford Springs in Jasper County. Beginning in 1973 it conducted spring and fall workshops at Camp Henry Jacobs near Utica.

The Mississippi Arts Festival, which presented annual expositions in Jackson from 1964 through 1978, represented a major contribution to the state's cultural and social climate. Programs by prominent actors, dancers, and musicians, and exhibits of prestigious works of art attracted favorable national attention. Critics noted not only the superior quality of the festival's presentations but also the occasional inclusion of racially integrated audiences—this during the years of the state's strongest resistance to civil rights for blacks. Although the Mississippi Arts Festival closed due to mounting expenses and insufficient numbers of volunteer workers, it nonetheless served as a model for numerous local festivals that received grants from the state Arts Commission.

Collections and Museums   Notwithstanding their attendance at the festivals, African Americans until the 1960s were denied access to public art galleries, major art collections, and academic programs at the all-white universities and colleges. A meaningful step in the amelioration of this condition was the establishment of the first collection of contemporary art in Mississippi at Tougaloo College in the mid-1960s. With initial backing from New York artists, the collection received donations of funds and prestigious art works, principally abstract impressionist pieces, from an expanding circle of supporters.

Two major state repositories of art were the University Museums, established in the mid-1970s after the University of Mississippi acquired the thirty-seven-year old Mary Buie Museum in Oxford, and the Mississippi Museum of Art in Jackson. Numerous communities throughout the state organized art museums and galleries, all of which sponsored exhibitions and housed collections. Some examples include the Lauren Rogers Museum of Art in Laurel, founded in 1924; the Meridian Museum of Art, with origins in the 1930s; and the Kate Freeman Clark Art Gallery in Holly Springs, which opened in the 1960s. In 2002 the Ohr-O'Keefe Museum of Art in Biloxi became the second museum in the state to affiliate with the Smithsonian Institution in Washington, D.C. (The first one was the Old Capital Museum in Jackson, which became the state historical museum in 1961.) The Smith Robertson Museum and Cultural Center in Jackson opened in 1984 for the promotion of African American history and culture.

Artists[4]   A study of the hundreds of notable Mississippi artists reveals such names as Annette McConnell Anderson of Ocean Springs (1867–1964), Walter Inglis Anderson of Ocean Springs (1903–65), Marshall Bouldin of Clarksdale (1923–), Andrew Bucci of Vicksburg (1922–), Caroline Russell Compton of Vicksburg (1907–), Kate Freeman Clark of Holly Springs (1875–1957), Maude Schuyler Clay of Sumner, photographer (1953–), William Dunlap of Tupelo (1944–), Samuel Marshall Gore of Clinton, sculptor (1928–), Sam Gilliam of Tupelo (1933–), Theora Hamblett of Oxford (1895–1977), William Hollingsworth of Jackson (1910–44), Marie Atkinson Hull of Jackson (1890–1980), Bessie Carey

4 The list includes natives of the state as well as other persons who produced notable artistic works while residing in Mississippi. Unless otherwise indicated, painting was the primary medium for each artist listed. The best history of Mississippi art is Patti Carr Black, *Art in Mississippi, 1790–1980,* vol. 1, Heritage of Mississippi Series (Jackson: University Press of Mississippi for the Mississippi Historical Society and the Mississippi Department of Archives and History, 1998).

Lemly of Jackson (1871–1947), Betty McArthur of Columbus (1866–1944), John McCrady of Oxford (1911–68), Ed McGowin of Hattiesburg (1938–), Samuel "Sambo" Mockbee of Meridian, architect, (1944–2001), George E. Ohr of Biloxi, potter (1857–1918), James Seawright of Jackson (1936–), Mary Clare Sherwood of Vicksburg (1868–1943), Wyatt Waters of Clinton (1955–), William Woodward of Biloxi (1859–1939), and Karl Wolfe and Mildred Nungester Wolfe of Jackson (Karl, 1904–85).

Perhaps the best-known early-nineteenth-century artist was John James Audubon, who traveled down the Mississippi River to Natchez in the 1820s. After teaching art lessons at Elizabeth Female Academy and painting portraits, Audubon entered a career of studying and drawing and painting wildlife. He is perhaps best known for *The Birds of America*, a standard of natural history which included among many other painting, "Chuck-Will's Widow" (1822).

According to one critic, George Ohr, "the Mad Potter of Biloxi," was perhaps America's greatest potter. Beginning in the 1880s, he produced countless vessels of endless variety, including popular wares decorated with local scenes and ceramic vases in expressionistic forms. Not until the 1960s, long after his death, did his work begin to attract national acclaim. Today his pieces are prized by critics and collectors alike.

Walter Inglis Anderson was even more eccentric than Ohr but like the Mad Potter, Anderson did not live to see the widespread appreciation for his art. In the 1930s he began to suffer mental disorders, and during the final eighteen years of his life he withdrew from his wife and children to live alone in Ocean Springs. He spent most of that time camping primitively on Horn Island, some twelve miles off the coast, which he reached by rowboat. In this spartan setting he produced literally thousands of oil and watercolor paintings of birds, animals, fish, reptiles, and plant life.

Another master of watercolor lived a very different life. Marie Hull of Jackson earned a degree in music at Belhaven College, was a charter member and president of the Mississippi Art Association, and "became one of the most influential and respected artists in the state," according to art historian Patti Carr Black. As an expression of her belief in the importance of progress and change, Hull's art evolved during her long career, embracing varying subjects and techniques. She is best known, however, for watercolors of landscapes and still lifes, such as "Granada" (ca. 1929) which today hangs in the Mississippi Museum of Art.

Although accused of resisting the expressionist trends of "modern art," an accusation that he denied, painter John McCrady won national acclaim for his vivid colors of local scenes in Mississippi. Critics in the mid-1930s suggested that his contributions to art in the South were comparable to the effects the work of Faulkner had on Southern literature. In any event, the powerful influence of African American culture and religion in McCrady's works is palpable in his somewhat surreal "Evening Meal, Duck Hill, Mississippi" (1934) and "Judgment Day" (1938).

Theater and Dance

Theater   Achievements in literature, music, and the visual arts may have overshadowed those in the fields of theater and dance, but late in the twentieth century signs of growing interest in these activities finally emerged. Professional drama began in Mississippi in the mid-1920s with the formation of the Little Theater in Jackson. Organized in the mid-1950s, the Mississippi Little Theatre Association reflected the rising number of community theaters throughout the state. In the early 1970s the association was renamed the Mississippi Theatre Association, and more than forty community theaters were active members by the end of the century. Along the Gulf Coast fourteen local theaters advertised productions in 2002. In addition, most universities and colleges sponsored drama productions and offered academic studies in the field.

Dance   Like that in theatre, interest in professional dance came late to the state but advanced steadily during the final decades of the twentieth century. The first ballet companies were the Mississippi Gulf Coast Ballet and the Jackson Ballet Guild, both organized in the 1960s. A major event that stimulated interest was the USA International Ballet Competition, which came to Jackson in 1979. Under the leadership of Thalia Mara, the Mississippi Ballet International, Inc., was formed to produce the first event. In 1982 Jackson was designated by the United States Congress as the official location for the competition, which continued every four years thereafter.

Ongoing dance education and productions in the state were cultivated through the formation of Ballet Mississippi, representing a merger of the Jackson Ballet Guild and the Mississippi Ballet Theatre in 1983. In 1990 the state legislature commended Ballet Mississippi for its promotion of the dance form in Mississippi. Still another organization was Ballet Magnificat, founded by Kathy Thibodeaux as a Christian ballet company and school of arts in 1986. Interest in dance was also reflected in the growth of dance programs in the institutions of higher education. Belhaven College, for example, established a dance major in the 1990s that attracted scores of students from Mississippi, other states, and even foreign nations.

Financial Support

Except in rare situations—ones attracting wide, popular appeal and acclaim—"the arts" in Mississippi were hardly self-sustaining. Typically, more financial support came in the form of sponsors' donations and state government assistance than from sales of tickets and artworks. A turning point came, however, in the 1960s with the establishment of the National Endowment for the Arts, which made matching federal funds available to applicant artists in all the states. Subsequent to this federal action, the state legislature established and funded the Mississippi Arts Commission, the state's official grants-making agency. An increasing number of artists and organizations received grants in the following decades, and in 2002 the Commission announced that grants from state and federal funds as well as donations from the private sector had been sufficient to award monies to 104 teaching and performing artists. This impressive roster included six grants in dance, twenty-nine in dramatic and literary arts, thirteen in visual arts and crafts, and fifty-six in music.

CONCLUSION

One of the interesting paradoxes in the Mississippi experience was cultural richness in the midst of economic poverty, a paucity of educational opportunities, and racial inequalities. On the bright side, exposure to and involvement in the arts expanded significantly in the late twentieth century. Nevertheless, limited financial resources for education and cultural programs and low per capita incomes restricted access to the arts for the majority of the state's residents.

SELECTED SOURCES

Abbott, Dorothy, ed., *Mississippi Writers: An Anthology* (Jackson: University Press of Mississippi, 1991).

———. *Mississippi Writers: Reflections of Childhood and Youth*, Vol. 1, *Fiction* (Jackson: University Press of Mississippi, 1985).

———. *Mississippi Writers: Reflections of Childhood and Youth*, Vol. 2, *Nonfiction* (Jackson: University Press of Mississippi, 1986).

———. *Mississippi Writers: Reflections of Childhood and Youth*, Vol. 3, *Poetry* (Jackson: University Press of Mississippi, 1988).

———. *Mississippi Writers: Reflections of Childhood and Youth*, Vol.. 4, *Drama* (Jackson: University Press of Mississippi, 1991).

Black, Patti Carr, *Art in Mississippi, 1790–1980*, Vol. 1, Heritage of Mississippi Series (Jackson: University Press of Mississippi for the Mississippi Historical Society and the Mississippi Department of Archives and History, 1998).

———, and Marion Barnwell, *Touring Literary Mississippi* (Jackson: University Press of Mississippi, 2002).

Busbee, Pauline Simmons, *Heart Pine* (Brandon: Encorenterprises, 1993).

Chapman, C. Stuart, *Shelby Foote: A Writer's Life* (Jackson: University Press of Mississippi, 2003).

Cobb, James C., *The Most Southern Place on Earth: The Mississippi Delta and the Roots of Regional Identity* (New York: Oxford University Press, 1992).

Dawidoff, Nicholas, "The Spirit of Jimmie Rodgers," *In the Country of Country: People and Places in American Music* (New York: Pantheon Books, 1999, in *New York Times* on the Web: Books. www.nytimes.com/books).

Kiger, Joseph C., "Cultural Activities in the Twentieth Century," in Richard Aubrey McLemore, ed., *A History of Mississippi*, 2 vols. (Hattiesburg: University & College Press of Mississippi, 1973), 2: 492–515.

Lloyd, James B., *Lives of Mississippi Authors, 1817–1967* (Jackson: University Press of Mississippi, 1980).

Mason, Nina, and Charlene Barr, comps., *History of the Mississippi Poetry Society Inc., 1932–1995* (Privately published by The Mississippi Poetry Society, Inc., 1995).

Maurer, Christopher, *Fortune's Favorite Child: The Uneasy Life of Walter Anderson* (Jackson: University Press of Mississippi, 2003).

Mississippi Art Colony (www.msartcolony.com).

Mississippi Arts Commission (www.arts.state.ms.us).

Mississippi Museum of Art (www.msmuseumart.org).

Mississippi Symphony Orchestra (www.msorchestra.com/history).

Prenshaw, Peggy W., and Jesse O. McKee, eds., *Sense of Place: Mississippi* (Jackson: University Press of Mississippi, 1979).

The Recording Academy [Grammy] (www.GRAMMY.com).

Rouse, Sarah A., "Literature, 1890–1970," in Richard Aubrey McLemore, ed., *A History of the Mississippi*, 2 vols. (Hattiesburg: University & College Press of Mississippi, 1973), 2: 446–76.

Shirley, Aleda, Susan M. Glisson, and Ann J. Abadie, eds. *Mississippi Writers: Directory and Literary Guide* (University of Mississippi: The Center for the Study of Southern Culture, 1995). This source contains basic facts about 130 Mississippi authors.

Starkville [Mississippi] High School Department of English, *Mississippi Writers and Musicians Project* (shs.starkville.k12.ms.us/mswm/MSWritersAndMusicians). This site also includes artists.

Sutton, Cantey Venable, ed., *History of Art in Mississippi* (Gulfport, Miss.: The Dixie Press, 1929).

Swain, Martha, Elizabeth Anne Payne, and Marjorie Julian Spruill, eds., *Mississippi Women: The Histories, Their Lives,* Foreword by Anne Firor Scott (Athens: The University of Georgia Press, 2003).

University of Mississippi Department of English, *The Mississippi Writers Page* (www.olemiss.edu/mwp).

CHAPTER NINETEEN

The World War II Era

Another World War Begins

During the 1930s the world went back to war, first in Asia as the Japanese invaded China and other countries and then in Europe as the German armies of the totalitarian dictator Adolf Hitler occupied Austria, then Czechoslovakia, then Poland. By September 1939 the greatest conflict in human history was well underway, but the United States would remain officially neutral for two more years. In Mississippi, decisions about political leadership during this challenging period were, not surprisingly, made in the Democratic party primaries, held in August 1939.

Governor Paul Burney Johnson, 1940–1944

The Elections of 1939   The three leading gubernatorial candidates were well-known politicians Thomas L. Bailey, speaker of the house of representatives, former governor Martin Conner, and Paul B. Johnson, former circuit court judge and congressman from Forrest County. In the first primary Johnson received a large plurality, 103,099 votes, far ahead of the second place candidate, Conner. Johnson went on to win the second primary with 55 percent of the votes. Dennis Murphree was nominated in the first primary and returned to his old office of lieutenant governor.

The election marked Johnson's third attempt to reach the governor's office. Eight years earlier he had not survived the first primary, finishing third behind Conner and Hugh L. White, and in 1935 he had led in the first primary but then lost to White in the runoff. A native of Scott County, Johnson had practiced law in Hattiesburg where he had served as city court judge. Then, following nearly a decade as circuit court judge, he won election to the U.S. House of Representative in 1918, defeating Governor Bilbo. After two terms in Congress, Johnson had declined to run for reelection in 1922 and returned to his law office.

Governor Paul Johnson, Sr. Courtesy Mississippi Department of Archives and History.

In the 1939 campaign, Johnson pledged to expand the homestead exemption law, to reduce other kinds of taxes, to improve rural roads, and to make improvements in public education, including providing free textbooks. Amidst the continuing hardships of the Great Depression, he endorsed President Franklin D. Roosevelt's New Deal programs and, like other politicians of the time, including his former friend Huey P. Long of Louisiana—the late governor and U.S. senator—Johnson favored expanding state welfare policies.

Accomplishments During the Johnson Administration   Steadily pursuing his goals, as governor Johnson managed to fulfill several of his campaign promises. His administration oversaw three major accomplishments, two of which stirred controversy. A fourth important achievement of the Johnson years, however, came from the legislature as a reaction against the governor. First, the 1940 legislature modified the existing homestead exemption law so that property valued at less than $5,000 would be completely exempt from taxation. A second relief measure, which affected an even greater number of people, provided free school books for all pupils in public and private schools. This program was considered the most noteworthy of his administration, for it not only represented considerable savings for thousands of Mississippi families but encouraged a greater number of children to attend school. Although some whites in the Delta were critical of the move because they feared free textbooks might somehow threaten segregation, the program received wide acclaim.

Two generations later, the governor's grandson, Pete Johnson, recounted an incident that illustrated not only the governor's personality but also his determination on this issue. While the bill was still being debated, a powerful legislator told Governor Johnson that he probably could get it passed, but that, if so,

> Catholic and black children were not going to be able to get free school books. My grandfather replied: "If one child in Mississippi gets a free school book, every child will get a free school book." The legislator rose to his feet, pointed and shook his finger at my grandfather and angrily said: "Well, if that's the way you want it, you'll be in for one hell of a fight." My grandfather jumped to his feet, took his coat off, stormed around to the front of the desk where the man was standing and, as they stood toe to toe, said, "Alright, by God, let's fight." [No fisticuffs ensued, but the point had been made.] [1]

The third measure was Governor Johnson's revision of the existing Balance Agriculture with Industry (BAWI) program, an action criticized by many of the governor's opponents, among whom Jackson newspaper editor Fred Sullens was the most vicious. The most notorious episode in Johnson's feud with Sullens was their fight in a Jackson hotel lobby. Again, Pete Johnson retold the story:

> On the day of the "assault," my grandfather was walking through the lobby of the old Walthall Hotel and as he walked by Mr. Sullens, who was sitting reading his paper, Mr. Sullens made a derogatory remark to him and that is all it took. My grandfather turned on Mr. Sullens and whipped him good with the cane,

1 Sid Salter, "Sunday Morning With Pete Johnson," *The Clarion-Ledger*, October 20, 2002.

even gave him a concussion. Mr. Sullens sued my grandfather for assault and battery, and my grandfather countersued for libel and slander. The jury concluded that Mr. Sullens deserved the whipping and that he did, in fact, libel and slander my grandfather, thereby awarding him $36,000. . . .[2]

The governor also triumphed over opposition in the legislature, which finally agreed to dismantle the BAWI Commission (formally titled Mississippi Industrial Commission) and establish a new agency, the Board of Development, principally a planning group without authority to continue the original program.

The fourth major action was a constitutional amendment in 1942 formalizing and strengthening the Board of Trustees of the Institutions of Higher Learning as part of state government. The legislature initiated the change following reports that Governor Johnson sought to influence the existing state board to effect personnel changes on college campuses. Judging that some changes at Mississippi Southern College were politically motivated, the Southern Association of Colleges and Secondary Schools placed this institution on probation and issued a warning to the other state institutions. In response to these difficulties, the legislature proposed the constitutional amendment to make the state institutions of higher learning more independent of political interference.

Upon approval by 90 percent of the voters the amendment added to the constitution Section 213a, which restructured the board and granted it full "management and control" authority. The new twelve-member board was composed of one person from each of the seven congressional districts, one from each of the three supreme court districts, and two from the state at large. The members were appointed by the governor with the advice and consent of the senate, but their twelve-year terms were staggered so that four members' terms expired every four years. The board elected one of its members as president and appointed a nonmember as Commissioner of Higher Education. The Commissioner gathered information, made recommendations, and acted generally as the board's agent in administering its policies.

Population Trends In spite of the new programs to attract industrial investments, the rate of urban growth had actually slowed during the 1930s, and more than 80 percent of the state's population was rural. The 1940 census reported a total population of 2,183,796, an increase of 8.7 percent since 1930. This rather sluggish rate of growth was caused primarily by the continuing emigration of African Americans, which resulted in their numbers falling below 50 percent of the state's total population for the first time in 110 years. The "Great Migration" of African Americans from Mississippi and other Southern states to Northern cities, which had begun during World War I and gathered momentum in the 1920s, was just beginning: it accelerated to an even greater pace during World War II.

Politics Except for the U.S. Senate race, 1940 held no interesting political campaigns. All seven of the state's congressmen gained reelection, and President Roosevelt was reelected for an unprecedented third term, receiving 96 percent of Mississippi's vote. Even though Hugh White had suffered a heart attack in 1939, which severely restricted his physical activity during the last year of his term as governor, he decided to challenge Senator Bilbo's reelection bid in 1940. In spite

2 Ibid.

of White's favorable record as governor, Bilbo prevailed by a wide margin in a relatively small turnout for the Democratic primary. This result was particularly notable because Senators Bilbo and Harrison were, as mentioned, personal enemies and unable to work together harmoniously. Bilbo even refused to support his colleague when Harrison was elected president pro tempore of the Senate in 1941. The outcome of the senatorial election may have been considered unfortunate by White and his supporters, but they could take some comfort in the fact that progress had been made in Mississippi during his administration. And, of course, there was always the possibility that he could be elected governor again at a later time.

Several significant changes occurred in the state's congressional delegation in the early 1940s. Four legends in twentieth-century Mississippi politics arrived on the scene. James O. Eastland, a lawyer and planter from Sunflower County in the Delta, took Senator Pat Harrison's seat and remained in the U.S. Senate for thirty-six years, rising to president pro tempore and chairing the powerful Committee on the Judiciary. New faces in the U.S. House of Representatives included Jamie L. Whitten of Tallahatchie County (northwest), who held office for fifty-three years; Thomas G. Abernethy of Chickasaw County (northeast), who served for thirty-one years; and W. Arthur Winstead of Neshoba County (east-central), who continued in the House for twenty-two years. Through the congressional system of seniority that promotes members on the basis of tenure, these Mississippi Democrats—along with Representative William M. Colmer of Jackson County (south) who served from 1933 to 1973—exerted far-reaching influence on national legislation.

Following the state elections of 1943, Governor Johnson, at the age of sixty-three years, suffered a heart attack and died on December 26. Lieutenant Governor Murphree served the final three weeks of Johnson's term. By this time economic conditions in the state had begun to improve, and they were certainly better than when Murphree last served as governor during the crisis of the 1927 flood. Indeed, at the end of Johnson's administration the state treasury had its biggest surplus in its history, almost $24 million. But the factors that underlay this recovery were not as much the results of federal and state programs as they were the demands generated by world war.

MISSISSIPPI AND WORLD WAR II

Pearl Harbor

On December 7, 1941, Mississippians began their Sunday pretty much as usual. By that afternoon—about the time many arrived back home from church services—their world had changed forever, for by then they had heard the news that the Empire of Japan had bombed Pearl Harbor, a United States naval base in Hawaii. Grim reports of the surprise attack continued into the evening, and folks who had radios found their living rooms crowded with neighbors, all anxious to hear the latest reports of the disaster. Japanese aircraft had sunk most of the U.S. Pacific Fleet and destroyed more than 150 American airplanes. Casualties rose to 2,300 military personnel killed and another 1,100 wounded. That night President Roosevelt called a meeting in which he informed the cabinet and some congressmen of the full extent of the tragedy, and the next day Congress declared war on

Soldiers marching on Capitol Street in Jackson. Courtesy Mississippi Department of Archives and History.

Japan. Three days later, Germany and Italy honored their treaty commitments to Japan and declared war on the United States.

Military Mobilization

While political campaigns still attracted some attention, Mississippians were far more concerned with their struggle to make a living and the adjustments required by the expanding world war. During Governor Johnson's first year in office almost 260,000 men between the ages of 21 and 35 registered with their local selective service boards, pursuant to the requirements of the new federal military conscription law. In the course of the war more than 267,600 Mississippians entered military service, including reserves of the National Guard, volunteers, and persons drafted in the selective service.

Throughout the state military training posts were established. Camp Shelby, an old World War I base that had been used by the National Guard, was reactivated in 1940; during the war its military population reached at least 75,000. Keesler Field, which housed roughly 69,000 personnel, was established at Biloxi for the training of pilots and mechanics in the Army Air Corps. Smaller posts in the state included Camp Van Dorn near Centreville, Camp McCain south of Grenada, and Foster Military Hospital in west Jackson. A number of army airfields were located in Greenville, Greenwood, Columbus, Jackson, Laurel, Meridian, as well as in other, smaller towns. A small naval base was constructed in Gulfport, and ordnance plants were established near Flora and Aberdeen. Certain facilities of the University of Mississippi and several state and private colleges were also used for military purposes.

A different kind of military base, the prisoner-of-war (POW) encampments, appeared in Mississippi in the summer of 1943, with the arrival of thousands of German and Italian soldiers who had been captured by the U.S. and British armies in North Africa. Four major camps—Clinton, Como, McCain, and Shelby—and fifteen branch camps housed the POWs until their release in 1946. At Camp Clinton the Germans, under the direction of the U.S. Corps of Engineers constructed a one-square-mile model of the Mississippi River basin, which the Corps hoped to use in planning for flood control. Depending on the location of their camps, most POWs worked in farm and forestry tasks throughout the state. The elite German officers were housed at Clinton where they received special privileges and liberties.

A mid-twentieth-century contrast in modes of transporation. Courtesy Mississippi Department of Archives and History.

Economic Changes

With the sudden growth of military camps and new industries, thousands of Mississippians went to work for wages higher than the Great Depression generation could have imagined. The best example of wartime business and employment growth was the Ingalls enterprise. As a part of the BAWI program, the town of Pascagoula had purchased an old World War I shipbuilding company and then leased it to Robert I. Ingalls in 1938. During World War II the Ingalls Shipbuilding Company became a leading producer of merchant ships, employing as many as 12,000 people. Thousands of Mississippians, seeking employment, or in some cases more income than they were earning from the farm or current job, headed for the shipyard. A school teacher in Meridian, for example, decided to take welding courses in his school's vocational department, leave the classroom, and commute each week to Pascagoula, a distance of nearly two hundred miles. Wartime needs also stimulated action on other existing BAWI proposals, and the state attracted more than 700 new factories, which created almost 25,000 new jobs.

Therefore, a combination of continuing New Deal programs, the exigencies of war, and state initiatives ushered into Mississippi a new economic era. The emergence of industrialism and urbanism paralleled the continuing decline of small farms and changes in the kinds of crops produced. During the war the agricultural population declined by almost 25 percent, and the number of farms fell by approximately 9 percent. Although the average farm size increased from 66 to 74 acres, most farms in 1945 were still smaller than 30 acres and operated by sharecroppers. In addition, the mule remained the principal source of power on Mississippi farms, although the appearance of the tractor would soon begin to reduce the number of these "tenants." Perhaps the most revolutionary event during the World War II years was the introduction on Delta farms of an improved mechanical cotton picker, a needed boost in production as part of the war effort. Mechanization soon enabled those farmers who could afford tractors and other machines to devote fewer acres to cotton but produce greater quantities of the crop and, in the meantime, increase livestock and poultry production.

While agricultural changes and wartime industrial development seemed to offer a brighter economic future for some people, most Mississippians saw only gradual, if any, improvement in their standard of living. More women began to take jobs in factories and, overall, the state's annual per capita income increased from $218 in 1940 to $605 in 1946. But even at that level, the average income for persons in Mississippi remained lower than that of people in the rest of the nation. Furthermore, the state did not make much permanent industrial progress, and Mississippi ranked last among all states in the number of private and government facilities related to wartime production.

Social Adjustments

Wartime conditions, moreover, were not always positive. In some communities rapid population growth caused shortages of housing and food. Schools, roads, and other public services like sanitation were not prepared to accommodate the flood of thousands of plant workers and their families. And the influx into the state of military personnel brought social inconveniences and challenges to traditionally accepted moral behavior and race relations. With the arrival of a great number of African American soldiers from the North, men whom white Mississippians assumed did not understand the South's Jim Crow system, some racial conflicts occurred—the main ones at Camps Van Dorn and McCain in the summer of 1943. At Centreville near Camp Van Dorn ugly verbal exchanges between white residents and members of a black regiment led to a brawl that finally ended with a local white law officer shooting to death a black private. After these incidents further trouble arose at the camp during a segregated dance party when white officers and soldiers blocked admission to black soldiers. A few weeks later, after whites at Starkville assaulted several black soldiers from Camp McCain, a

"Victory Gardeners." Courtesy Mississippi Department of Archives and History.

group of blacks retaliated by firing random shots into Duck Hill, a small community near the camp. A black soldier from Pennsylvania later recalled being stationed at Camp McCain and his experiences in nearby towns:

> In the restaurant they had the familiar signs colored and white, and the bathrooms was the same. A lot of us didn't know about the situation and it didn't filter in that we couldn't eat in certain places. We were in uniform too. We were only served in certain areas that was reserved for us and that was it. . . . They should have dropped the A-bomb on Mississippi.[3]

State and local governments responded to these and other problems by passing laws stiffening penalties for such violations as disorderly conduct, thievery, seditious speech and writing, and prostitution. In towns teeming with new residents, whether Mississippians seeking newly available jobs or outsiders affiliated with the military, the local authorities relaxed enforcement of the traditional "blue laws"—ordinances forbidding most businesses, including movie theaters, from opening on Sundays—and ignored prohibition and anti-gambling laws.

Despite the difficulties in adjusting to wartime mobilization, most Mississippians responded positively and patriotically to the nation's war in Europe and the Pacific. All across the state people sacrificed to buy war bonds, collect rubber materials and scrap metal, and faithfully observe rationing, the practice of limiting usage of certain foods like butter, sugar, and other commodities such as gasoline and tires. Hundreds of posters, like the one proclaiming "Rationing Means a Fair Share For All of Us," appeared on the doors and windows of corner grocery stores. Another popular poster, "Keep 'em Rolling, Pal . . . Produce for Victory," called on women—this one a model dressed in denim—to go to work for the war.

GOVERNOR THOMAS L. BAILEY, 1944–1947

The Election of 1943

Speaker of the House Bailey won the Democratic party's gubernatorial nomination in the August primary of 1943. The other leading candidates were former Governor Conner and Lieutenant Governor Murphree. In the first primary Conner led with 110,917 votes, while Bailey narrowly finished in second place ahead of Murphree by only 453 votes. The outcome of the second primary was a surprise, as Bailey attracted most of Murphree's supporters and defeated Conner by a vote of 143,153 to 125,288. Fielding L. Wright from Sharkey County was elected lieutenant governor, defeating Sam Lumpkin.

A native of Webster County, Bailey had been a school teacher before beginning a law practice in Meridian. A member of the state house of representatives from 1916 to 1940, he served as speaker during the last twelve years of his tenure. Drawing on his record in the legislature, Governor Bailey's initial concerns were reforms in public education and renewal of the BAWI program. As a former public school teacher, he recommended higher salaries for teachers and the creation of a retirement plan for them. He basically agreed with Governor Johnson's phi-

3 World War II Oral Histories, "The Agony of Victory, a Black Pittsburgh History Recalled," Carnegie Library of Pittsburgh, www.carnegielibrary.org/locations/pennsylvania/ww2/ww211.html.

Governor Fielding L. Wright. Courtesy Mississippi Department of Archives and History.

losophy of government and supported various state programs, including more assistance for senior citizens, a state hospital in Jackson, and appropriations to improve rural roads.

Key Reforms

In a period of dramatic change as World War II drew to a close, the Bailey administration accomplished several important reforms, the foremost being the resurrection of Governor White's BAWI program, which had been severely weakened in 1940. The legislature in 1944 established the Mississippi Agricultural and Industrial (A&I) Board and gave it virtually the same authority and direction that had characterized White's Industrial Commission of 1936. The new A&I Board combined the advertising and industrial activities of the previous commissions, and the law establishing this agency allowed communities to own and then lease property to manufacturing businesses. The necessary funds for acquiring this property came through the issuance of bonds, which had to be approved in local elections and the value of which could not exceed 20 percent of the assessed value of the property.

Significant advances were also achieved in the state's system of education. In 1944 a public school teachers' retirement plan was finally established, and in 1946 the legislature created in the Delta a separate vocational college for African Americans and approved the relocation of the two-year medical school from Oxford to Jackson, authorizing it to provide a four-year curriculum. Governor Bailey appointed Jackson M. Tubb in 1945 to fill the position of superintendent of education. Having the longest tenure of all holders of that office, Tubb would serve until 1968 and encounter the most dramatic events in the state's public school history—the approach of racial desegregation.

Another achievement was the 1946 appropriation of $5 million to improve county roads to help most Mississippians, who were still farmers living in rural areas. Other reforms included reorganizing the state penitentiary, improving the parole system, creating a civil service commission in larger towns, and beginning a program of forestry education. The state's credit was improved as surplus funds in the treasury were used to reduce indebtedness. Appropriations also were increased for needy senior citizens and dependent children.

Fielding Wright

After serving less than three full years, Governor Bailey died of cancer on November 2, 1946, and Lieutenant Governor Fielding L. Wright moved into the governor's office to complete the final year of Bailey's term. A special session of the legislature early in the next year cooperated with Wright on three of the four purposes for which it was called. First, the primary election laws were altered to shield the all-white state Democratic party from the civil rights trends of the national Democrats. In a nutshell, the changes were carefully designed to prevent African Americans from registering to vote, notwithstanding a ruling by the United States Supreme Court in Smith v. Allwright three years earlier that declared such practices, specifically the all-white primaries, unconstitutional.

A second major objective of former governor Bailey was achieved as substantial appropriations were designated for the faculties of public school teachers and junior colleges. Third, legislation was passed making the state eligible to receive federal funds for the school-lunch programs. Finally, the legislature balked, refusing to repeal the state's seven-year-old "black market" tax of 10 percent on the sale of "illegal products," i.e., "intoxicating liquors." (In one of the incredible paradoxes of the times, Mississippians voted for prohibition, state law banned the sale of alcohol, yet people bought alcohol illegally, and the state levied and collected the so-called black market tax from the bootleggers!)

Political Trends

Although there were signs of future changes in Mississippi's relationship with the national Democratic party, the state continued through this era to give overwhelming support to its nominees. By landslide proportions the state had voted for FDR in three presidential elections, and virtually without exception Mississippi's senators and representatives backed the president's domestic and foreign policies.

As the 1944 presidential election approached, however, Mississippi's political leaders at home and in Washington began to voice concerns about the Roosevelt administration's interest in advancing the civil rights of African Americans. As an expression of their opposition to such reforms, the state Democrats attempted a mini-revolt by choosing presidential electors who were not pledged to reelect Roosevelt. But this strategy succumbed to political reality—FDR's enormous popularity among Mississippi voters. Governor Bailey called a special session of the legislature that voted to delete the electors' individual names from the Democratic party presidential slate on the ballot, thus lessening the likelihood that a few maverick electors might vote for a presidential candidate other than Roosevelt. As a result of the device, in the general election voters who supported the Democratic party had to indicate their preference for the entire slate as a unit and, receiving 94 percent of the state's popular votes, all nine electoral votes were cast for the president and his vice presidential nominee, Harry Truman.

This election was a portent of long-lasting changes in the state's representation in Washington, as a new generation of Democrats, one that increasingly broke from the national party on civil rights issues, took office. The entry of Representatives Abernethy, Whitten, and Winstead (with Senator Eastland having just arrived) preceded the emergence of Representative John Bell Williams and Senator John C. Stennis. In the congressional elections of 1944 and 1946 all incumbents were reelected without significant opposition, except in the latter year when Williams, a lawyer and World War II veteran from Raymond, defeated Congressman Dan McGehee of Franklin County who had represented the Seventh District since 1935. Williams would continue in the U.S. House of Representatives until he resigned to become governor in 1968.

Another significant political event in 1946 was the reelection of Senator Bilbo, who had supported Roosevelt's New Deal programs but began to attract national attention with his extremely racist public statements. His calls for whites to use any means of intimidation including violence to prevent African Americans from voting were themes reminiscent of the Vardaman diatribes four decades earlier, and even the connivance of the "First Mississippi Plan" back in 1876. Three principal developments motivated Bilbo's outrageous behavior. First, the possibility that blacks would attempt to register and vote with federal protection pursuant to the Supreme Court's 1944 ruling in *Smith* v. *Allwright*, which, as mentioned, declared the white-only Democratic primary elections unconstitutional. Second, Bilbo needed a strategy to divert attention from charges made by his opponent Ross Collins that Bilbo had taken bribes from defense contractors during the war. And third, he planned to ride the publicity that he had attracted in 1945 by leading the successful Senate filibuster against the extension of Roosevelt's Fair Employment Practices Committee (FEPC). This agency, which had investigated complaints of discrimination and other unlawful practices in the war industries, was unpopular among Mississippi whites who feared widespread federal requirements for racial equality in the workplace.

Whatever his motivation, Bilbo's nasty rhetoric in the 1946 campaign backfired. After easily defeating four opponents in the first primary and encountering no opposition in the general election, he had to confront obstacles more potent than the voters. Not only did the Justice Department examine his racist tactics, but the Congressional War Investigating Committee gathered convincing evidence to support the bribery charges against him. Along partisan lines, a panel of five Senators—three Democrats and two Republicans—voted to exonerate him of the intimidation accusations, but he was not so fortunate when it came to the other criminal charges. In January 1947, when it appeared that he would be found guilty and that the Senate would refuse to admit him, Bilbo withdrew. A more serious reason for his departure was that he was ill with cancer of the mouth, which would end his life in August 1947.

The special election in November 1947 to fill the vacancy in the Senate had a rather unexpected result. Needing a plurality rather than a majority of the votes cast to win, six candidates entered the contest, including well-known politicians Ross Collins, Congressmen William Colmer and John Rankin, and Paul B. Johnson Jr., son of the late governor. John C. Stennis, circuit court judge from Kemper County, was elected with only 52,068 votes, 26.9 percent of the total turnout. Although not as prominent as most of his opponents, at forty-six years of age Stennis already had an admirable record of local accomplishments. After earning his law degree at the University of Virginia, he had served one term in the state house of representatives, five years as district attorney, and ten years as circuit court judge. He would be reelected to the Senate six times and serve until his retirement in 1989.

THE WAR AS A WATERSHED

The replacement of Bilbo with the relatively unknown Stennis was another indication of fundamental changes in postwar Mississippi. As the state's agrarianism began to make room for emerging towns, industries, and commerce, a new era dawned. At the same time the rising national concerns about the injustices suffered by African Americans were viewed warily by Mississippi whites who vowed to resist a "second reconstruction" by virtually any means.

Nevertheless, wartime employment and travel had introduced Mississippians to new ways of life. For the first time in the state's history, thousands of farming people turned to other occupations, anticipating greater prosperity and more leisure time than their ancestors had ever dared dream of. More than one quarter of a million young adult white and black Mississippians in military service had for the first time seen other parts of the United States and the world. Many veterans returned home with revised ideas about race relations, optimistic dreams of economic opportunities, an appreciation of the advantages afforded by an education, and, most important, an understanding that these goals were essentially interrelated.

Among them were African Americans, like Medgar Evers, Aaron Henry, James H. Meredith, and Amzie Moore, who not only had a new awareness of their race's historic condition but were willing to demand changes. In some instances these views were defended by young whites who also now questioned the state's "Jim Crow" system. Although such ideas were often unspoken or, if expressed at all, buried under the burdens of tradition and the forces of continuity, they represented monumental changes in the state's future. But occasionally their voices were heard, as in the career of Frank Ellis Smith, a white journalist, legislator, and congressman from Leflore County whose role is described in the next chapter.

Unfortunately, these postwar ideas of ending the state's discriminatory practices against African American workers and voters would be viciously opposed on every level for the next two decades. From the local police to state legislators and governors and even to the halls of Congress, white Mississippians would fight against irrepressible changes that had been launched by the experiences of World War II.

In the meantime, whether the result of having been emancipated from the fields by the mechanical cotton pickers, having gained more self-confidence as a result of military travel and experience, or refusing to remain in segregated subservience to whites, growing numbers of African Americans left their home state in the 1940s, and their exodus, the second phase of the "Great Migration," would continue in the following decades.

SELECTED SOURCES

Historical Statistics of the States of the United States: Two Centuries of the Census, 1790–1990, comp. Donald B. Dodd (Westport, Conn.: Greenwood Press, 1993), Population.

McMillen, Neil R., *Dark Journey: Black Mississippians in the Age of Jim Crow* (Urbana: University of Illinois Press, 1989).

———, ed., *Remaking Dixie: The Impact of World War II on the American South* (Jackson: University Press of Mississippi, 1997).

Mississippi Official and Statistical Register, 1945–1949.

Mitchell, Dennis J., *Mississippi Liberal: A Biography of Frank E. Smith* (Jackson: University Press of Mississippi, 2001).

Schmidt, William T. "The Impact of Camp Shelby in World War II and Hattiesburg, Mississippi," *Journal of Mississippi History* 39 (February 1977): 41–50.

Shea, William L., "The Enemy in Mississippi, 1943–1946," *Journal of Mississippi History* 41 (November 1979): 351–71.

Skates, John Ray, *Mississippi: A Bicentennial History*, The States and the Nation Series, James Morton Smith, ed. (New York: W. W. Norton & Company, Inc., 1979).

―――, "World War II and Its Effect 1940–1948," in Richard Aubrey McLemore, ed., *A History of Mississippi*, 2 vols. (Hattiesburg: University & College Press of Mississippi, 1973), 2: 120–139.

―――. "World War II as a Watershed in Mississippi History," *Journal of Mississippi History* 37 (May 1975): 135–141.

Woodruff, Nan Elizabeth, "Mississippi Delta Planners and Debates over Mechanization, Labor, and Civil Rights in the 1940s," *Journal of Mississippi History* 60 (May 1994): 263–84.

CHAPTER TWENTY

The Fifties

Postwar Transitions

The years following World War II witnessed major transitions in Mississippi. The total population declined by almost 5,000 persons during the wartime decade, resulting in the state's loss of one seat in the U.S. House of Representatives. African Americans continued to leave Mississippi in growing numbers, and many people who stayed, blacks and whites, moved from farms to towns. The 1950 census reported that since the last census in 1940 there were 106,000 fewer African Americans, who, at 45 percent of the population, no longer composed the majority. And for the first time in the state's history, noticeable growth was occurring in urban places, the residents of which rose from 20 to 28 percent of the total population. Personal income from nonfarm sources in 1950 was 3.4 times greater than it had been ten years earlier, and income from manufacturing establishments specifically was more than four times higher than the 1940 amount.

As a result of the increased industrial and commercial activity and more efficient farming, the state's annual per capita income jumped from $215 to $770 during the 1940s. Declining numbers and the increasing size of farms reflected the movement of sharecroppers away from the land and into other kinds of employment. In 1950 there were 40,000 fewer farms than in 1940, the average size of which rose from 66 to more than 82 acres. Nonetheless, most people still made their living on the state's more than 251,000 little farms, and due to more crop diversity and mechanization, agricultural workers' earnings tripled, reaching more than $385 million.

As incomes increased and more leisure time became available, a rising number of people pursued recreational activities (which are summarized further in Chapter Twenty-Four: The Social Environment). Now, Mississippians could devote more time to hunting and fishing, the favorite sports of most men in the state. But entire families became more involved in athletic events, both as participants and observers. High school and college games of football in the fall, basketball in the winter, and baseball in the spring and summer attracted thousands. The construction of country clubs gained momentum after World War II, but only a small number of relatively wealthy white families had the money or the time to engage in golfing and tennis at a club. "Bowling alleys" and dance halls provided more widespread entertainment, although many churches frowned on them as being "too worldly." Most folks, however, found no such restraint or obstacles of expense for the popular county fairs and performances by traveling circuses.

Left: Paramount Theatre in Jackson. Right: Rex Theatre "For Colored People." Courtesy Mississippi Department of Archives and History.

The era of television was just dawning in Mississippi, but most families now could afford their own radio set and spent evenings listening to such programs as the *Grand Ole Opry, Fibber McGee and Molly, The Life of Riley, The Shadow, Amos 'n' Andy,* and westerns featuring Roy Rogers and Dale Evans, Gene Autry, the Lone Ranger and Tonto, and Lash LaRue. Many of these cowboys made their way onto big screens in movie houses and at drive-in theaters in the larger towns, where folks from surrounding rural areas joined crowds of townspeople to pay a total of twenty-five cents per person to see the show and enjoy popcorn and a cold drink. People seeking newer productions paid more to see Elvis Presley in *Love Me Tender,* the film adaptation of two of Tennessee Williams's famous plays, *A Streetcar Named Desire* and *Cat on a Hot Tin Roof,* as well as other Academy Award winners like *From Here to Eternity.*

But the "big screen" now began to face competition in the form of television. Near towns with newly established television stations an increasing number of families paid relatively high prices for a TV set along with an outside antenna to watch programs based on some of the old radio favorites as well as the *Ed Sullivan Show, Walt Disney's Disneyland* (soon renamed *The Wonderful World of Disney*), *I Love Lucy, The Honeymooners,* and *Gunsmoke.* The networks also brought world news into Mississippi living rooms, with vivid glimpses of political and cultural scenes heretofore unavailable to most people in the state.

The transformations in Mississippians' lifestyles during the fifties, however, did not introduce meaningful changes in the practice of racial segregation. In entertainment arenas blacks and whites remained separated, as for example in the maintenance of the upstairs "colored" galleries in the movie houses and the practice of setting certain times, if any, for African Americans to attend fairs and other festivals. And even at athletic events the teams as well as the observers were either all black or all white.

Governor Fielding L. Wright, 1947–1952

The Election of 1947   A native of Rolling Fork, Sharkey County, Governor Fielding L. Wright had begun a law practice law there in 1916. He had been a member of both houses of the legislature and served as speaker of the house before his election to the office of lieutenant governor in 1943. His attainment of the governorship in 1947 was historic in several ways. First, he was in one sense the only incumbent to be reelected since the adoption of the 1890 constitution, which prohibited a governor from succeeding himself in office; as lieutenant governor, Wright had taken office after the death of Governor Bailey and had already served for more than a year. Second, he was also the first governor from the Delta since Earl Brewer and, third, Wright was the first governor since Bilbo (in 1915) to win the Democratic nomination in the first primary. Indeed, Wright received more votes (a total of 202,014) than all three of his opponents combined, although one of them, Paul B. Johnson, Jr., made a strong showing with 112,123 votes.

Progressive Programs   Postwar social and economic transitions contributed to new patterns in the state's political landscape. A new generation of leaders had emerged, as many members of the 1948 legislature were World War II veterans less than forty years of age, and most members of the house of representatives were freshmen. Responding to perceived opportunities of the new era and voters' demands for better jobs, roads, and schools, the legislature enacted a number of significant reforms. Actions related to economic improvements included the state's first workmen's compensation law in 1948, legislation extending the State Highway Commission's responsibilities and launching a new road construction program, and renewed emphasis on attracting industry through the BAWI program, which resulted in nearly two hundred projects and rapid growth of manufacturing jobs in the early 1950s.

Motivated by the pending federal threat to end legally imposed racial segregation in the public schools of every state in the nation, the Wright administration initiated a plan to reorganize the public school system and increase appropriations, particularly for black schools, which remained woefully inferior to white schools. Concerns about inadequate health care, caused in part by the shortage of physicians, prompted the 1950 legislature finally to approve the construction of the University of Mississippi's four-year medical school, a plan that had been authorized four years earlier. The facilities, which were located in north Jackson on the site of the old state insane asylum, would open in 1955. One major effort of Wright's administration, the reorganization of state government for more efficient operation, was left undone despite lengthy and expensive studies that produced recommendations for substantial reform.

Democrats and Civil Rights   While state leaders made important headway on the home front, they seemed increasingly preoccupied with defending Mississippi against certain federal policies, particularly the civil rights endeavors of President Harry S Truman's administration. Their attention to state affairs was sometimes overshadowed by these issues, as illustrated by portions of Governor Wright's in-

Poster for States' Rights Democrats ("Dixiecrats").
Courtesy Mississippi Department of Archives and
History.

ATTENTION
ALL STATES' RIGHTS, JEFFERSONIAN
DEMOCRATS
MASS MEETING
SATURDAY, MARCH 20
3:00 o'clock in the afternoon
COURTHOUSE
BELZONI

--KNOW THE DANGERS THAT CONFRONT US!
--HAVE A PART IN MISSISSIPPI'S PLAN OF ACTION!
HEAR GOVERNOR WRIGHT SPEAK
At the Mass Meeting Over
State-Wide Radio Network

ALL LOYAL MEN AND WOMEN
OF THE PARTY HAVE A JOB TO DO!
MISSISSIPPI STATE DEMOCRATIC PARTY, JACKSON, MISSISSIPPI

augural address. His warning to national Democrats that Mississippi was ready to take "drastic" action to remain "true to traditions of our party" was seconded by other prominent politicians who also had begun to consider making a break with the national party in order to resist civil rights programs. Among the key figures who championed the cause and helped design the state's strategy of resistance was Speaker of the House Walter Sillers, who had served in the house since 1916 and at this point was "probably the single most powerful political figure in state government," according to future Governor William Winter.

The Presidential Election of 1948   These state leaders began as early as February 1948 to develop a plan of action for that year's presidential election. First, Governor Wright addressed a mass meeting of more than five thousand white Mississippians, including the entire legislature. Resolutions were adopted by this assembly, attacking the civil rights program of the Truman administration and calling for a convention of "true white Jeffersonian Democrats." The governor then hosted a meeting of Democrats from ten Southern states to continue the discussion. Finally, the party's state executive committee adopted specific proposals that became the basis of the Southern strategy. Per the plan, every presidential elector had to be a staunch state's righter, and if the national convention of the Democratic party did not approve the states' rights position, then a separate Southern convention would be held to nominate candidates who would.

Formulation of the states' rights strategy was finalized in two events that occurred before the Democratic national convention assembled in Philadelphia, Pennsylvania. In May, prominent politicians from ten Southern states met in Jackson to hear from leaders like Governor Strom Thurmond of South Carolina and plan for the contingency of a separate convention of state's righters. The state Democratic party convention in June accepted this plan and chose presidential electors who pledged not to vote for any presidential candidate who supported civil rights. When the national convention did indeed approve a strong civil rights position, the entire Mississippi delegation, led by Governor Wright and Speaker Sillers, along with some of the Alabama delegates, walked out. Later, in Birmingham, Alabama, "States' Rights" Democrats, the so-called "Dixiecrats," convened to nominate Governor Thurmond for president and Governor Wright for vice president.

The presidential election of 1948 appeared to be a close contest between Republican candidate Thomas E. Dewey and President Truman who, unlike his Democratic predecessors, could not count on the support of a traditionally "solid

South." The strategy of the Dixiecrats was to garner enough electoral votes to force the final decision into the House of Representatives, where concessions would have to be made. Mississippi voters did their part, casting 87 percent of their votes for the Thurmond-Wright slate of electors, but they were joined by the electorate of only three other Southern states: Alabama, Louisiana, and Thurmond's home state of South Carolina. Although the Dixiecrat strategy failed, the election's outcome was significant in at least two major ways. First, the loyalty of the "solid South" had ended for the Democratic party, but, on the other side of the coin, Truman's surprise victory over the Republican Dewey meant that the Democratic party would no longer have to depend on the support of the South in future elections.

State Elections   Voicing support for the Dixiecrat position, in 1948 all seven U.S. congressmen and Senator Eastland were reelected without opposition. And there was nothing extraordinary about the congressional elections of 1950, except in the Third Congressional District, where two very different state legislators from the Delta campaigned to become the successor of longtime Congressman Will Whittington, who planned to retire. When Frank E. Smith of Greenwood narrowly and surprisingly defeated Oscar Wolfe of Bolivar County, the result was described as a victory of the small farmers over the aristocrats. In fact, Smith's election had more far-reaching significance: it was a break in the state Democrats' apparent unanimous opposition to civil rights. Smith, a thirty-two-year-old World War II veteran, later described by historian Dennis J. Mitchell as "a closet liberal and a secret integrationist," in 1950 defeated a sixty-year-old state's righter and ally of Speaker Walter Sillers and Governor Wright. During his six terms in the U.S. House of Representatives, Smith would continue Whittington's record of effective representation and gain a reputation for racial moderation. Before his election to Congress, Frank E. Smith had been a journalist, a legislative assistant to Senator John C. Stennis, and a member of the state senate from 1948 to 1950.

War in Korea   Political campaigns and routine affairs in the state were interrupted in early in the summer of 1950 by the beginning of the United States participation in the Korean War. After less than five years of peacetime, Mississippians again turned their attention to the demands of war. The lives of most people were affected as thousands of men in the National Guard were called into active service, many military facilities were reopened or expanded, and various wartime controls were reimposed.

Governor Hugh L. White's Second Administration, 1952–1956

The Election of 1951   In mid-June of 1951 farmers around the state were happy to get some rain. The weather bureau reported the likely end of forty-eight days of dry weather, "the worst spring drought in the history of the state."[1] Of lesser concern to most people was the choice of a candidate to support in the state's Democratic primaries in August of that year. They faced a lineup of eight names in the 1951 gubernatorial campaign, including former Governor Hugh L. White, Paul B. Johnson, Jr., Lieutenant Governor Samuel E. Lumpkin, Ross Barnett, and, for the first time, a woman, Mary D. Cain.[2] White and Johnson received the most votes

1 "Headline: 50 Years Ago," *Jackson-Clarion Ledger*, June 12, 2001.

2 Described as a "militant conservative" newspaper editor in Summit, Mary Cain was sometimes called "Hacksaw Mary" because of her defiance of federal laws.

in the first primary, and White, who had defeated Johnson's father in 1935, won the second primary by a close margin of 201,222 to 191,966 votes. White was only the second person to serve two full terms since the adoption of the 1890 constitution. Reflecting the breaks with tradition during this era, his election did not fit into the state's historic political paradigm.

Political Traditions   Ever since Reconstruction the Democrats had ruled Mississippi without serious challenges by other political parties or substantial disagreements among Democratic candidates on public policy issues. Instead, two major geographic sections had contended for control of state government and all the resulting economic benefits. The western section, described in various ways as the Delta, the river counties, or the "black counties," and the eastern and southern section, known as the "Hills," the "white counties," or the Piney Woods, were characterized by many fundamental differences.

Generally, the west had retained the largest number of African Americans but was controlled by white conservative aristocrats, those known as the Bourbons in the late nineteenth century. After "redeeming" the state from Republican rule during Reconstruction, this class for many decades had controlled state government (until the early twentieth century), promoting private business interests and blocking appropriations for public services. The "Hills" and Piney Woods regions, on the other hand, were inhabited by small farmers and poor whites and blacks, those who had favored the Populist then Progressive demands for government regulations on corporations and greater state spending for internal improvements. Supported by these interests, Governors Vardaman and Bilbo had finally overthrown the Deltans, but the struggle continued, with both sides appealing to racial issues. These competing interests had been evident in the patterns of voting for governor every four years until Hugh White. Although he hailed from the Piney Woods, most of his support came from the western counties. This anomaly resulted from White's emphasis on new economic developments and his successful BAWI program, which appealed to conservative business people.

The Threat to School Segregation   Notwithstanding White's reputation for progressive economic programs, his second administration was encumbered by a series of dramatic events involving public education. Governor White's first public explanation for urgent attention to this issue included the system's inefficient organization, woeful conditions of school facilities, and inadequate teachers' salaries, which averaged a paltry $1,534 per year, only 60 percent of the Southern states' average. The paramount, albeit initially unspoken, reason, however, was the threat of racial integration. Since the 1890s, state laws requiring segregation had been sanctioned by the "separate but equal" doctrine of the United States Supreme Court. But now that doctrine was being seriously challenged in the federal courts, and state leaders were painfully aware of the absence of equality between white and black schools. In other words, white Mississippi was in trouble even if the National Association for the Advancement of Colored People (NAACP) lawsuits were unsuccessful, because there were stark inequities in teachers' pay and in facilities.

The 1952 legislature, therefore, created a committee to study the situation and report measures for reorganization, and Governor White called a special session the next year to consider the committee's recommendations. Anticipating a decision in the federal courts on the segregation question, White acknowledged that the state had failed to maintain the equality requirement in the "separate but equal" doctrine. Regardless of the court decision, the governor explained, the state was obligated to achieve substantial educational equality for the races. Desperate to avoid desegregation at any cost, the house of representatives in 1953 took the radical action of proposing a constitutional amendment authorizing the legislature to abolish Mississippi's public schools, but the senate blocked the proposal, preferring to look for a more positive solution.

The legislature then undertook the two daunting tasks of reorganizing and equalizing the two separate school systems. Acting on the study committee's recommendations, the special session of 1953 provided for school district consolidations to make the overall organization more efficient. Its so-called equalization program included a building program to improve school facilities for blacks, equitable salaries for black and white teachers, and equal spending for school buses. The program was meant to signal an end to racial disparities in education, but in reality its costs required major increases in appropriations that were not immediately forthcoming.

Expecting an imminent decision by the Supreme Court, the regular session of the legislature in 1954 acted defensively rather than meaningfully regarding education. A twenty-five-member Legal Educational Advisory Committee, composed mainly of lawyers and educators, was created to communicate with other Southern states and consider courses of action pending the outcome of the case. In the meantime, the legislature withheld appropriations for its equalization program and adopted a wait-and-see policy.

It did not have long to wait. On May 17, 1954, the United States Supreme Court issued its unanimous ruling in *Brown v. Board of Education of Topeka, Kansas*, which overturned the "separate but equal doctrine" and declared unconstitutional racial segregation in public schools. Opposition to the decision was immediate and widespread, evoking denunciations by many prominent officials, including Governor White, Senator Eastland, Speaker Sillers, and Attorney General James P. Coleman. In July 1954, Robert B. Patterson and other white residents in Sunflower County founded the Citizens' Council to organize resistance to the high court's ruling.

Mississippi's elected officials became so preoccupied with this issue that they paid little attention to urgent state needs. A special session of the legislature met in September 1954 to consider the Legal Educational Advisory Committee's draft of the constitutional amendment that had been proposed by the house the previous year. The amendment would permit the legislature by two-thirds vote to abolish all public schools "as a last resort," allow individual localities to abolish public schools as they choose, and authorized the state to sell, rent, or lease school property to private individuals, and then pay each "educable" child's tuition to what would then essentially be private, segregated schools. Sadly, the legislature approved the amendment, and the virtually all-white electorate (with nearly all blacks still disfranchised) ratified it by a two-to-one majority in November 1954.

The final official actions on education during White's administration came in another special session, this one in January 1955. Refusing to accept the federal government's fiat regarding desegregation as inevitable, the legislature completed the work undertaken earlier to equalize the dual school systems by implementing its 1953 program. It made the additional funding for black schools take effect in the next budget year, a time that happened to coincide with the second *Brown v. Board of Education* ruling on May 31, 1955, which declared that all schools must be desegregated with "all deliberate speed." Even in the face of that decision, white Mississippians still clung to the belief that by taking steps toward equalization they could control the meaning of "deliberate speed" and prolong, if not avoid altogether, school segregation. But their confidence would soon receive a shock when President Dwight D. Eisenhower used military force to integrate the high school in Little Rock, Arkansas, in 1957.

Politics   Although the school integration issue dominated the public discussion during these years, other internal political problems demanded attention. Pursuant to the disappointing population report in the 1950 census, Mississippi, as mentioned, lost one of its seven seats in the U.S. House of Representatives, and the legislature was required to reapportion the congressional districts. After the usual sectional wrangling, the final solution in 1952 consolidated most of the counties comprised by the old First and Fourth Districts into a new First District. In the ensuing election Thomas G. Abernethy of the old Fourth District defeated John Rankin, who had served the old First District since 1921.

The Presidential Election of 1952

The anti–civil rights rhetoric permeated the campaigns and heightened tensions as the 1952 presidential election approached. The state Democratic Executive Committee determined that delegates to the national convention in Chicago would defend the doctrine of states' rights and that presidential electors would vote only for states' rights candidates. In June the state convention selected delegates who were committed to Senator Richard B. Russell of Georgia but who were not as combative and resolute as had been the 1948 delegation.

For two principal reasons many Democrats in the state did not want to repeat the unsuccessful 1948 "Dixiecrat" experiment. First, they had lost party patronage during the Truman administration; second, the 1952 national convention was less stringent on civil rights and nominated Governor Adlai Stevenson of Illinois for president and Senator John Sparkman of Alabama for vice president.

Nevertheless, the election of 1952 may be considered a turning point for political parties in Mississippi. For many decades the Republican party had been virtually inactive, except for patronage concerns during Republican administrations and the formalities of sending delegates to the party's national conventions. It was supported by very few whites and was controlled by Perry Howard, a lawyer who lived in Washington D.C. but maintained a legal residence in the state. In 1952 fundamental changes occurred. Howard's so-called "Black-and-Tan" group attended the Republican national convention, but it began to lose sway over Republicans in the state. Many Democrats, disenchanted with their own national party, now threw their support behind the Republican candidate, Dwight D. Eisenhower, the universally respected World War II general and hero. With the backing of leaders like former lieutenant governor Sam Lumpkin and Speaker Sillers, the "Democrats for Eisenhower" wrested control from Howard's faction.

Revival of a "New" Republican Party   Now, for the first time since Reconstruction, there was widespread white support for the Republican party in Mississippi in a presidential election. Eisenhower and vice presidential candidate Richard M. Nixon received almost 40 percent of the state's vote and 55 percent of the national vote. This election represented the beginning of the Republican party's revival in the state and the South, with the "new" Republican party becoming increasingly white, even as African Americans were now drawn to the postwar directions of the national Democratic party.

But the Republicans' true rise to power would take several more decades, as the Democratic incumbents continued to dominate the state. In the immediate aftermath of the 1954 *Brown* decision, Senator James O. Eastland was nominated for a third term, easily defeating Lieutenant Governor Carroll Gartin. In the 1954 general election there was only token Republican opposition to Eastland, and no challengers faced the six congressional incumbents.

The Race Issue   White's second administration witnessed the state's transition to an era in which racial issues predominated virtually every election and every official state-government consideration. In the previous six decades politicians had inflamed racial prejudices to get elected, but because the "Jim Crow" regime had effectively excluded blacks' from political, social, and economic opportunities without significant threats of federal intervention, race had not been a determinative political factor. In the 1950s, however, and notwithstanding the new economic opportunities of the immediate postwar period, state policymaking was dominated by the threat of "civil rights," a scenario reminiscent of the Reconstruction years. As a result, White's attempts to accomplish progressive reforms, as he had done during his first term, were eclipsed by the state's absorption with racial questions. While his primary legacy was his leadership in attracting industry, Governor White fully supported the state's resistance to racial integration, and future governors and most other state politicians would attract much more attention as rabid segregationists.

As if to confirm this new era of preoccupation with race, a leader of the NAACP, Gus Courts, was shot in Belzoni in 1955. But the incident that attracted the most attention during White's last year in office involved the brutal murder of a fourteen-year-old African American boy, Emmett Till, who had arrived from Chicago to visit family members in Leflore County. According to witnesses at that time, Till jokingly whistled at a white woman in the town of Money "to prove" to his Mississippi cousins that he had white girlfriends back home in Chicago. A few days later several white men entered the house of Till's great uncle, Moses Wright, during the night and kidnapped young Emmett. After a three-days' search county law officers found Till's horribly disfigured body in the Tallahatchie River. The funeral in Chicago and trial in Sumner, Tallahatchie County, Mississippi, attracted national news coverage. In September 1955 the two white men accused of the kidnapping and murder were acquitted by an all-white jury, despite the eyewitness testimony by Till's uncle and other blacks.

The Emmett Till episode had far-reaching consequences: it not only fueled the national civil rights movement but served as a harbinger of more racial violence in Mississippi. National coverage of the event raised concerns throughout the nation about violence against African Americans by whites in Mississippi and exposed via newspapers and television the disparities between Mississippi and the other states in the standard of living and illiteracy rates. Based on continuing and vivid recollections of Till's cousins and other witnesses, the United States Department of Justice reopened the Till case in 2004, working with local Mississippi authorities to pursue possible accomplices in the murder.

Governor James Plemon Coleman, 1956–1960

The Election of 1955   Just before the Till incident, the Democratic party primaries named the state's next governor. Five candidates entered the campaign in 1955, including Ross Barnett, Mary Cain, Attorney General Coleman, Paul B. Johnson, Jr., and former governor Wright. Although Wright was expected to secure a second full term, Johnson won the first primary and, surprisingly, the only first-time candidate, Coleman, came in second. In the second primary Coleman defeated Johnson, who was in his third campaign for governor, by a comfortable margin of 233,237 (56 percent) to 185,924 votes. There were no Republican candidates for state offices in the general election. This gubernatorial election further illustrates the breakdown of the state's traditional voting patterns. Wright, from the Delta, had won the 1947 nomination in the first primary, but in 1955 he finished third in the first primary. Although Coleman was from Choctaw County, in the "Hills" region, he received the Delta vote in his second primary victory over Johnson and ran unopposed in the general election.

Governor Coleman   After studying at the University of Mississippi, J. P. Coleman earned a law degree at George Washington University in Washington, D.C., where he served for several years as an assistant to Congressman Aaron L. Ford. Back at home as a lawyer in Ackerman, Coleman served eight years as district attorney in the Fifth Circuit Court District. In 1947 Coleman was elected circuit court judge, but he resigned in 1950 to accept an appointment by Governor Wright to the state supreme court. Within that same year he left the court to accept another appointment by the governor, this to fill the vacancy in the office of attorney general; in 1951 he was elected to that office without opposition.

Coleman considered himself "a practical segregationist" and took a moderate position on civil rights controversies. He argued that the state's best defense was careful legal actions rather than emotional rhetoric and irresponsible behavior. Such arguments did not, however, convert the intransigent proponents of white supremacy. These groups criticized Governor Coleman for refusing to support legislation that would obstruct federal investigations of alleged civil rights violations, for resisting efforts by legislators to ban the NAACP from the state, and for favoring the transfer of state property to the federal Veterans Administration for an inte-

Governor J. P. Coleman. Courtesy Mississippi Department of Archives and History.

grated hospital in Jackson. Coleman's record of consistently supporting Democratic party presidential candidates also aroused further suspicion among some of the state's aggressive segregationists. Another unpopular action by the governor came when he signed but expressed reservations about the legal efficacy of the legislature's declaration of the state interposition doctrine (similar to the old theory of state nullification), a document drafted to justify Mississippi's refusal to enforce certain federal civil rights laws.

The Maintenance of Racial Segregation   Although there was virtual unanimity among white leaders on the need to maintain segregation, two opposing concepts emerged about the state's best strategy. The most active and powerful group of radicals was the Citizens Council, which claimed to have thousands of members in most counties, including many influential political, business, and professional leaders who favored taking virtually any action necessary to block integration. A less extreme approach was taken by Governor Coleman, who came to be viewed as the voice of the moderates, a position that would increasingly be in the minority. Both groups, however, agreed with denunciations of *Brown v. Board of Education* in the so-called Southern Manifesto of 1956, which was signed by the state's entire congressional delegation.

Popular support for the radicals' agenda was augmented by the news media coverage of several civil rights incidents during Coleman's administration. In 1958 an African American native of Hattiesburg, Clyde Kennard, was denied admission to Mississippi Southern College, and he rejected Coleman's offer to pay his educational expenses in any other state. The same year Clennon King, a former professor at Alcorn A&M, was sent to the state mental hospital when he tried to register at the University of Mississippi. For his part, Governor Coleman was quoted by the newspapers saying that any black person who tried to attend a white school at this time was indeed a "lunatic." Another sensational event that reminded people of the Till case was the 1959 lynching of Mack Charles Parker in Poplarville, Pearl River County. A mob of hooded white men took Parker, a twenty-three-year-old black man accused of raping a white woman, from his jail cell and, after beating and shooting him, threw his body into the Pearl River. An all-white county grand jury failed to return an indictment in the case, although the identities of the perpetrators were well known in the community.

Bowing to the popular pressures of the times, Coleman approved the 1956 legislation establishing the Sovereignty Commission. Its twelve-member board included the lieutenant governor, the speaker of the house, the attorney general, state legislators, and others appointed by the governor, who served as chair. The commission's most important director was Erle Johnston of Forest, a journalist who had served as publicity director in the election campaigns of Fielding Wright in August 1947, John Stennis in November 1947, Senator Eastland in 1954, and Ross Barnett in 1955. Initially, the body's primary objective was to promote a better public image of Mississippi and, according to some observers, a temperate effort by Governor Coleman to prevent the potential escalation of racial violence. The character and purpose of the commission, however, would soon change during Governor Barnett's administration.[3]

3 The Commission was the successor of the 1954 Legal Educational Advisory Committee, which had planned Mississippi's initial resistance to integration.

Economic Policies   Trying to divert attention from the emotional issues of civil rights, Governor Coleman continued the economic policies of former governor White and launched other positive programs. BAWI was strengthened under the direction of Henry Maddox, who was appointed by Coleman as head of the A&I Board. Tax-exempt bonds were issued to build manufacturing plants, which were then leased to private corporations. Numerous small industries were started, providing employment opportunities in towns and communities throughout the state, as BAWI approached the potential anticipated when it was originally created by Governor White in the 1930s. By the late 1950s, the first $50 million in BAWI bonds had created 35,000 jobs with an annual payroll of $100 million.

With economic changes producing a larger urban population and more public services, such as electric power and natural gas, the Public Service Commission was given more authority to regulate public utilities. There was progress on significant public works projects like the Natchez Trace Parkway and the Tennessee-Tombigbee Waterway Development Authority.

Historical Interests   As a lawyer with broad experience in the local and state offices, Coleman understood the need to rewrite the Constitution of 1890, but, like earlier governors, he could not persuade the legislature to call a convention for that purpose. Other of his initiatives, however, met with more success. Exhibiting a keen interest in historical preservation, Coleman gave high priority to the restoration of the "Old Capitol," a project that had been delayed earlier, with the legislature in an uproar in the aftermath of the *Brown* cases. Now, however, Coleman convinced the legislature to appropriate sufficient funds and increase his authority in the state Building Commission. Working with Charlotte Capers, Director of the Department of Archives and History, the governor took the lead in the renovation of the capitol and the creation of a state historical museum. The projects were finally completed in 1961, shortly after Coleman had left the governor's office.[4]

Politics   Careful to use the appropriate campaign rhetoric opposing racial integration and supporting states' rights, the state's six members of the U.S. House of Representatives were reelected without significant opposition in 1956 and 1958. Senator Stennis, who had expressed his support for the "Southern Manifesto," was reelected in 1958 for a third term without opposition.

With the support of Governor Coleman and the state's congressional delegation, Democratic party presidential and vice presidential nominees Adlai Stevenson of Illinois and Estes Kefauver of Tennessee carried the state by a comfortable margin in 1956, receiving about 144,400 votes, 58 percent of the total turnout but a smaller proportion than the Democrats had received four years earlier. The opposition cast a total of 103,550 votes but they divided into three groups: electors pledged to President Eisenhower and Vice President Nixon received about 56,300 votes; independent, unpledged electors attracted about 42,950 votes; and the slate representing the remnant of the traditional Republicans in the state, the "Black and Tan Grand Old Party" drew only about 4,300 votes. Nationally, the

4 The Old Capitol had been used to house some departments of state government until the completion of the Woolfolk State Office Building in December 1949. Beginning in January 1950 the Old Capitol was occupied by the state Board of Health. The Coleman renovation also provided appropriations for the construction of new and separate facilities for the Board of Health.

Republicans were reelected by a wide margin of more than 57 percent of the popular vote and 86 percent of the electoral college.

Some forty years after Governor Coleman's term, former Governor William Winter recalled that "Coleman was a common sense man who . . . sought to develop consensus and bridge gaps between opposing forces. [He was] a man who used good judgment . . . and always . . . followed a moderate path in all his endeavors." In one of the state's most turbulent times, the beginning of the civil rights era, Coleman was the voice of moderation.[5] It is possible that Coleman, notwithstanding his rather unpretentious beginnings in rural Mississippi, was not as provincial as other political leaders. For several formative years he had lived in Washington, where he had worked in the Congress, studied law, and married a woman from Indiana. But Coleman's approach was too mild for most voters, and the election of 1959 brought into office a very different governor and increasingly turbulent times in Mississippi.

SELECTED SOURCES

Bond, Bradley G., *Mississippi: A Documentary History* (Jackson: University Press of Mississippi, 2003).

Historical Statistics of the States of the United States: Two Centuries of the Census, 1790–1990, comp. Donald B. Dodd (Westport, Conn.: Greenwood Press, 1993), Population.

Johnston, Erle, *Mississippi's Defiant Years 1953–1973: An Interpretive Documentary with Personal Experiences* (Forest, Mississippi: Lake Harbor Publishers, 1990).

Katagiri, Yasuhiro, *The Mississippi State Sovereignty Commission: Civil Rights and States' Rights* (Jackson: University Press of Mississippi, 2001).

McMillen, Neil R., *The Citizens' Council: Organized Resistance to the Second Reconstruction, 1954–64* (Urbana: University of Illinois Press, 1994).

———. *Dark Journey: Black Mississippians in the Age of Jim Crow* (Urbana: University of Illinois Press, 1989).

———. "Development of Civil Rights, 1956–1970," in Richard Aubrey McLemore, ed., *A History of Mississippi,* 2 vols. (Hattiesburg: University & College Press of Mississippi, 1973), 2: 154–176.

Minor, [Wilson] Bill, *Eyes on Mississippi: A Fifty-Year Chronicle of Change* (Jackson, Miss.: J. Prichard Morris Books, 2001).

Mississippi Official and Statistical Register, 1956–1960.

Mitchell, Dennis J., *Mississippi Liberal: A Biography of Frank E. Smith* (Jackson: University Press of Mississippi, 2001).

Skates, John Ray, Jr., *Mississippi's Old Capitol: Biography of a Building* (Jackson: Mississippi Department of Archives and History, 1990).

5 William F. Winter, interviewed by Peggy C. Case, in "Governor James Plemon Coleman: Mississippi's Voice of Moderation," A Paper for Historiography, Belhaven College, Jackson, Mississippi, November 30, 2000.

United States Department of Commerce, Bureau of Economic Analysis. *Regional Accounts Data: Annual State Personal Income. SA05 Personal Income by Major Source and Earnings by Industry—Mississippi, 1940, 1950* (www.bea.gov/bea/regional/spi/action.cfm).

Winter, William F., "New Directions in Politics 1948–1956," in Richard Aubrey McLemore, ed., *A History of Mississippi*, 2 vols. (Hattiesburg: University & College Press of Mississippi, 1973), 2: 140–153.

CHAPTER TWENTY-ONE

Religious Life

PERVASIVE ACKNOWLEDGMENT OF FAITH

After the essential matter of sustenance, most Mississippians expressed less inter-est in the arts and politics than they did in religious beliefs and practices. The so-ciety was always interwoven with religion, which directly and literally affected most people's daily lives. Throughout the twentieth century almost all adults were either members of or claimed affiliation with a religious organization. According to one study, an estimated 80 percent of white persons fourteen years of age and older were church members in the 1950s, and there was no reason to believe that the rate for African Americans was any lower. Forty years later an estimated 70 percent of the state's total population claimed religious affiliation, and although this proportion declined somewhat in the final decade of the twentieth century, a recent survey recorded that a scant 7 percent of all Mississippians reported no reli-gious affiliation, a rate lower than those indicated in all but two other states in the nation.

The Major Denominations

Baptists   Religious life in Mississippi is dominated by Protestant Christians, pri-marily the Baptists. Of the three leading Protestant groups that had seceded from

their respective Northern bodies before the Civil War, only the Southern Baptists retained their separate sta-tus throughout the twentieth century. This denomina-tion and other Baptists organizations were named by a large and rising majority of all persons reporting reli-gious affiliation. Early in the century African Ameri-cans outnumbered whites among the Baptists, but that ratio began to change after 1940, as their proportion of the total population declined and as many others of them were attracted to other denominations. By 1970 the estimated 931,000 Baptists included 531,000 whites and 400,000 blacks, although religious surveys identified even greater numbers of persons claiming af-filiation with the Baptists.

Chapel of the Cross, Madison County. Courtesy Missis-sippi Development Authority/Division of Tourism.

Bethel AME Church. Courtesy Mississippi Department of Archives and History.

The survey of "adherents" (adults and children) revealed a substantial growth of the white Baptists during the last decades of the twentieth century but did not contain conclusive data for African Americans. By 1990 there were almost 870,000 white Southern Baptist adherents, which represented one-third of the total population of the state, and the estimated number of black Baptist adherents was 324,000. The dominance of the Baptist church was revealed in a religious identification survey in 2001, which reported that 55 percent of all Mississippians considered themselves Baptists.

Methodists   Although the number of Methodists had approximated the number of Baptists in the late nineteenth century, thereafter the gap between the two denominations widened steadily. In 1968, some 123 years after their departure from the national body, Southern Methodists merged with the Evangelical United Brethren Church to form the United Methodist Church. In Mississippi the existence of separate conferences for African Americans ended in 1972, when a final merger brought all United Methodists under the jurisdiction of one state conference. But these unification movements did not contribute to the growth of the church. Not only did the number of black Methodists decline, but white membership did not rise significantly. Religious surveys, which did not include the historically black denominations, identified 184,000 Methodists adherents in 1970, representing 10 percent of the state's population; 240,325 adherents in 1990, about 9 percent; and 240,576 in 2000, about 8 percent.[1] A religious identification survey in 2001 reported that although the Methodists remained the second largest denomination in the state, only nine percent of all Mississippians claimed to be Methodists.

1 Official membership of the United Methodist Church was 187,013 in 1995 and 190,436 in 1999, representing an increase of less than 2 percent. Surveys indicated only 12,500 members of the African Methodist Episcopal Church in 1990, a decline of 57 percent since 1900.

Presbyterians   Until late in the twentieth century most Presbyterians belonged to the Presbyterian Church in the United States (PCUS), which had originated in the church's withdrawal from the national denomination in 1861. The Synod of Mississippi, which contained five presbyteries, experienced rather slow growth, reaching a membership of about 29,000 by 1950. During the 1960s the number of PCUS presbyteries was reduced to three and included separate white and black churches, with a total membership reaching almost 36,000 by the end of the decade.

A national reunion movement, which finally led to the formation of the Presbyterian Church in the United States of America (PCUSA) in 1983, did not please substantial numbers of Mississippi Presbyterians. Anticipating the reunion, various dissenting groups withdrew from the old PCUS and formed separate bodies, including the Presbyterian Church in America in 1973 and the Evangelical Presbyterian Church in 1981. Counting all divisions of the denomination, there were about 44,000 Presbyterians in the state in 1970, representing only 2 percent of the state's population. But that number declined in the following decades, as Presbyterians struggled with racial and other social issues involved with the mergers and divisions. In the last three decades of the century the denomination declined by 8 percent, with 41,700 adherents in 2000.[2]

Roman Catholics   The two oldest ecclesiastical bodies in Mississippi—founded in colonial times—were the Roman Catholic Church and the Church of England, which was organized as the Protestant Episcopal Church in 1789. Roman Catholic churches experienced steady growth in the twentieth century, rising from about 25,000 communicants in 1920 to almost 85,000 in 1970. During the last decade of the century the number of Catholic adherents rose from 95,000 to almost 116,000, representing about 4 percent of the state's total population. A survey in 2001 reported that 5 percent of all Mississippians identified themselves as Catholics. Unlike the other major denominations, the Catholic Church had not been divided by racial issues and had maintained integrated congregations. Throughout the twentieth century African Americans composed about 10 percent of all communicants.

Episcopalians   With a much smaller membership, the Protestant Episcopal Church experienced only gradual growth in the twentieth century. Remaining less than 1 percent of the state's total population, the number of Episcopal communicants increased from less than 3,000 in 1900 to about 17,000 in 1970. Renamed the Episcopal Church, USA, in 1967, the denomination led in the resolution of such issues as racial integration and women's ordination. By the end of the century its membership had risen to 21,124 communicants in 32 churches.

Churches of Christ   The fastest growing denominations in the twentieth century were the Churches of Christ and the Pentecostals. The former churches were conservative congregations that had withdrawn from the Christian Church in 1906. Beginning with only 3,155 members in churches mainly in northern counties, the Churches of Christ expanded rapidly in the following decades. According to estimates of religious affiliations, these churches had more than 43,000 members in 2000.

2 Official membership of the PCUSA in Mississippi declined to less than 14,000 in 2000. The PCA ended the century with about 1,000 more members than the PCUSA, having experienced some growth in its first two decades (15 percent) followed by losses in the 1990s (6 percent).

Pentecostals   A wide variety of Pentecostal-type churches grew at an even faster rate. Proclaiming themselves as "New Testament" evangelists, these fundamentalist groups attracted converts with their less formal styles of worship, including the singing of nontraditional music, emotional spiritual experiences, and literal biblical beliefs and practices. Their willingness to accept all believers as equals opened these churches to women preachers and, later in the century, biracial congregations. One survey reported that there were more than 52,000 adherents of these Pentecostal type churches in 1990 and more than 59,000 in 2000, representing more than 2 percent of the state's population. Another study found that all persons identifying themselves with these bodies composed nearly 6 percent of all Mississippians. The latter estimate may be the most accurate, because the former survey included neither the historically African American churches nor the United Pentecostal Church, which had grown to at least 183 local congregations at the end of the century.[3]

Other Religious Bodies   Among the numerous other Christian denominations in Mississippi, the following groups had the largest memberships by the end of the twentieth century: Lutherans, Seventh-Day Adventists, Salvation Army, Mennonites, and Greek Orthodox. Non-Christian bodies included the Jehovah's Witnesses, Mormons, Muslims, Jews, and Unitarian-Universalists.

Despite their relatively small numbers, some of these groups exerted an important influence on the state's culture. Jewish businesspersons, for example, were active in several key towns in which they had considerable economic and political clout. At the start of the twentieth century there had been seventeen Jewish congregations (synagogues) with 746 families; during World War II, 18 congregations served about 3,000 persons residing mostly in Delta towns like Greenville, Clarksdale, and Greenwood but also in Natchez, Vicksburg, Meridian, and Jackson. Until the 1960s, when anti-Semitism increased as part of the hostile reaction to the civil rights movement, the Jewish population remained static, but during the last decades of the century their numbers gradually declined to about 1,400.

THE SOCIAL GOSPEL

The many religious groups held inconsistent positions on and varying interpretations of the question of the separation of church and state. For example, on the maintenance of the state's traditional "blue laws" against conducting commercial activities on Sundays, most churches made certain allowances, sometimes giving in to the sake of convenience and economic exigencies. By the late twentieth century, even active churchgoers could be found filling their cars with gasoline, shopping for shirts at the mall, or buying groceries at the Wal-Mart at any given hour of the day on Sunday. An increasing number of people—whose grandparents had believed that laws should prohibit such "unbiblical" behavior—now justified the changes. Using the separation principle, they argued that secular authorities had no right to legislate in the spiritual realm. On the whole, however, most reli-

3 The great number and variety of independent Pentecostal and Charismatic congregations make numerical estimates of total membership difficult. The names of these churches included designations such as Apostolic, Bible, Deliverance, Evangelical, Fellowship, Jesus Name, New Life, Victory, Vineyard, and many others. Among the organized bodies were various Assemblies of God, Churches of God, Pentecostal Holiness, and United Pentecostal.

Church of Port Gibson. Courtesy Mississippi Development Authority/Division of Tourism.

gious people were willing to lower or entirely remove the historic "wall of separa-tion," depending on the issue at stake. On the other hand, they continued to de-mand state action against any practices they believed contrary to God's law.

Prohibition

Even after the national prohibition amendment to the U. S. Constitution was repealed in 1933, Baptists and other evangelical groups intensified their crusade against legalizing the sale (and presumably the consumption) of "intoxicating li-quors" in Mississippi. And they were successful for more than three decades, but not without the assistance of a powerful "unholy" alliance. Sheriffs and bootleg-gers had their own private reasons for supporting prohibition: many of the law-men took lucrative payoffs from the illegal operators, a relationship of mutual benefits. In 1952 a "special referendum" allowing the individual counties to de-cide whether or not to allow the sale of "intoxicating liquor" containing 4 percent alcohol was defeated by a vote of 140,700 to 80,800.

Finally, in 1966 the legislature passed the "Local Option Alcoholic Beverage Control Law" permitting voters in each county to decide the issue but clearly stat-ing that state policy still favored prohibition. Thirty-five years later, in 2001, among Mississippi's total of eighty-two counties, portions of three counties in addition to thirty-four entire counties, primarily in the eastern part of the state, were still "dry." Nevertheless, by this time the warehouse operated by the state Office of Alcoholic Beverage Control was depositing into the state's general fund an annual average of $36 million derived from the sale of alcohol and licensing fees.

Evolution

Religious groups also continued their fight against the teaching of the theory of human evolution in public schools. But the odds were against them. The state's

1926 anti-evolution law was not always strictly enforced, and a similar statute in another state was ruled unconstitutional by the United States Supreme Court in 1968. Nevertheless, the legislature, reflecting the strength of religious fundamentalism in Mississippi, refused to repeal the ban, which was finally overturned by the state supreme court in 1970.

Subsequently, there have been increasing public demands that the public schools' curriculum should include "creation science" to counterbalance the teaching of evolution. Denying the theory of evolution, creation scientists believe that scientific evidence proves that an "intelligent designer" created all of nature, including humans, at one point in time. Many of them, the so-called biblical creationists accept the book of Genesis as a literal account of creation.

School Prayers

Beginning in the early 1960s federal court decisions against the instructor-directed recitation of prayers in public school classrooms, auditoriums, or on athletic fields as required portions of school agendas produced strong reactions among Mississippians. And many of them continued the practice in order to demonstrate their belief that the "Godless" courts were denying religious freedom.[4] In 1993 Bishop Knox, the African American principal of Wingfield High School in Jackson, was dismissed after having defied state instructions and federal court rulings by allowing students to read prayers over the school's public address system. Public support for Knox was especially strong among black ministers and included that of the state NAACP president.

Three years later, most people in Pontotoc County expressed similar support for prayer in school but through negative means. When Lisa Herdahl, a white mother of six children—five of whom were enrolled in the county public school—objected to the school's practice of offering bible history classes and allowing students to pray over the intercom system and in classrooms, she encountered widespread hostility from the community. Public outrage reached an ever higher level of intensity and spread to other parts of the state after Herdahl filed a lawsuit in federal court, challenging the school's policies on the grounds that they violated her children's religious freedom. In 1996 federal district court judge Neal Biggers ruled in favor of Herdahl and ordered the school to discontinue classroom and intercom prayers as well as the bible history courses.

Without regard to race or church affiliation, widespread opposition to the bans on school prayers encouraged state legislators to pass a law in 2001 that permitted a "moment of quiet reflection" at the opening of each school day. Convinced that their religious teachings and practices should be included in school programs, many churches provided separate educational facilities for children, ranging from preschool nurseries and kindergartens through secondary schools. Three of the leading denominations, moreover, established and maintained colleges throughout most of the state's history.

Race Relations

In general, racial attitudes of white church leaders passed through three phases in the twentieth century. At the height of the "Jim Crow" era in the early

4 The initial case originated in New York and was decided in 1962 by the United States Supreme Court in *Engel v. Vitale*.

1900s the mainline denominations were willing to talk about the need for racial justice. In their view, however, such justice did not require any change in the total separation of black and white churches. Methodist Bishop Charles B. Galloway of Jackson led his church's campaign to improve inter-race relations, and groups within other white churches came together to assist black colleges and to lobby for increased state support for black public schools. But while these persons may have had noble intentions, ones easily extrapolated from biblical principles, their actions appeared paternalistic in the face of their continued acceptance of the practice of racial segregation and the doctrine of white supremacy.

During the second phase, that in the years following World War II, attempts by some white churches to promote better racial relations were undercut by the overwhelming support of the congregations for the 1948 Dixiecrat movement and the state's legal strategies to maintain the status quo. This stance was stiffened by whites' apprehension about the looming civil rights movement and their awareness that occasional biracial worship among Pentecostal groups might erode the widespread tradition of racially segregated churches. Reflecting these concerns, the legislature considered an overtly racist bill in 1956 that would have required integrated churches to pay property taxes. Although the measure was not enacted, four years later the legislature did pass a "church property law" that allowed any local congregation, on a two-thirds-majority vote of its adult members, to remove its church property from the national denomination's control through a petition to the appropriate chancery court. Having this option, local churches now

Galloway Memorial United Methodist Church. Courtesy Westley F. Busbee, Jr.

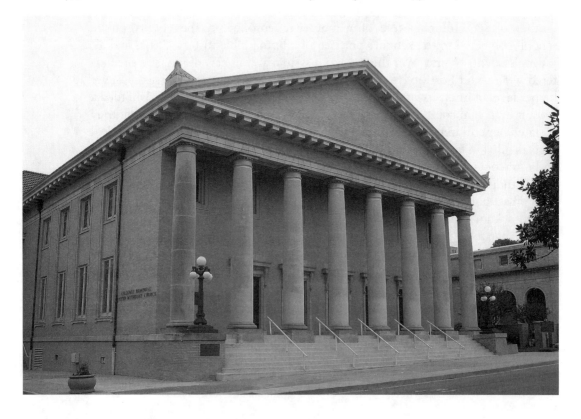

could virtually ignore mandates from their national governing bodies that required them to accept black members.

In spite of the major national denominations' official acceptance of desegregation in general, their local churches and state leaders spoke out against it. While they condemned acts of violence against African Americans and the burning of their churches, many Mississippi ministers justified racial segregation by referring to scripture, just as the defenders of slavery had done before the Civil War. A typical position was presented by the Reverend Dr. G. T. Gillespie, a Presbyterian, who used the Bible and the "curse of Ham" argument to justify segregation in his *A Christian View of Segregation*. Evidently this sentiment was widely shared in the 1960s, as most white Baptists were known to be supporters of the Citizens' Council and at least sympathetic with the goals of the Sovereignty Commission, the state agency organized to obstruct the civil rights movement.

White church members, however, were not unanimous in the practice of using religion as justification for segregation, and some "moderates" expressed their willingness to accept change. Catholic Bishop Joseph Brunini and other clergymen spoke out in favor of racial justice. Following controversies that included the resignation of Dr. W. B. Selah, minister of Galloway Memorial Methodist Church in Jackson, who favored accepting African American members, the church's board finally voted in 1966 to admit all persons regardless of race. The majority of white churches, however, continued to exclude blacks from their worship services.

The third phase began in the 1970s as the mainline denominations started to require the removal of racial barriers. Catholic and Episcopal churches were open to biracial membership and aggressively pursued racial reconciliation, while Methodists and Presbyterians moved more slowly by ending segregation in their church organizations—conferences and presbyteries—but by allowing local congregations within them to remain all-white for a period. But not even that level of progress was made by the state Baptist Convention, which refused to include black churches for decades. Most white church members, therefore, remained guilty of what theologian Reinhold Niebuhr called the "inevitable hypocrisy": that is, the failure to reconcile contradictions between the religious principles they espoused and the social inequities they advocated.

Racial Reconciliation

While all Christian denominations eventually claimed to support better race relations—they had little alternative given their claims of submission to biblical principles—the extent to which they practiced what they preached varied greatly. Black and white Baptists, for example, cooperated in supporting the Mississippi Baptist Seminary, an institution founded in 1943 in Jackson to serve black National Baptist students. In the 1970s the Southern Baptists created the Cooperative Ministries Program to foster connections with other denominations, particularly the National Baptists, although neither black nor white Baptists considered "cooperation" to mean genuine biracial worship, as evidenced by the fact that only about thirty black Baptist churches had joined and remained in the state convention by the end of the century. While most urban Southern Baptist churches in Mississippi would accept black members, there was perhaps only one genuinely biracial church in the state as late as the year 2000.

Perhaps the state's most prominent spokesperson for racial cooperation was John Perkins, who founded Voice of Cavalry Ministries (VOC) in 1964 in Mendenhall. An organization that promoted community economic and social programs and evangelical ministries for disadvantaged African Americans, the VOC was widely supported by white churches. Another organization that advanced reconciliation through practical biracial religious activities was Mission Mississippi, formed by black and white Christians in 1992.

Church Integration

Late in the twentieth century black and white Pentecostals and other fundamentalists began to challenge the tradition of segregation in worship. If they sometimes disagreed on social and political issues, their common spiritual experiences overshadowed such differences. Particularly in metropolitan areas, fundamentalists of all races came together for worship in democratically-run, autonomous churches that seemed to reflect the worldviews of their members more directly than the major denominations. Often African Americans entered the Pentecostal churches because the groups' message of hope cried out to the poor. Blacks and whites could be comfortable together in such congregations, which offered opportunities for leadership regardless of race or gender, and where strict moral teachings, emotional sermons, and lively, participatory music satisfied the spiritual needs of an increasing number of people. In 1994 a national conference of "Pentecostal Partners" based in Memphis issued a manifesto pledging not only to end segregation in congregations but to oppose racism in the communities outside the church.

Women's Role

Although traditionally women were the churches' leading advocates for the social gospel, they were excluded from ordination until the mid-twentieth century, when they finally began to gain acceptance as officers and ministers in the United Methodist Church, the Episcopal Church, the Presbyterian Church (U.S.A.), and various Pentecostal churches. Other denominations composing a large majority of the state's church membership, however, refused to ordain women as a principle of doctrine. One reason for the formation of the Presbyterian Church in America (PCA), for example, was that group's stand against the ordination of women. The Southern Baptist state convention in 1984 declared that women could not be ordained as ministers or pastors but ultimately left the decision to the individual churches. And in a few Southern Baptist churches in the state, women were elevated to pastoral positions. The prevailing biblical interpretation of the role of women lent support to the 1970s campaign against the "feminist movement" in general and the proposed but unsuccessful "Equal Rights Amendment" to the U. S. Constitution in particular.

Health Care

Interestingly, efforts to practice biblical teaching outside the walls of the church produced important advances in health care. By the late twentieth century the Baptists operated a comprehensive health system in the Jackson metropolitan area, which included a major hospital and several medical clinics, and they sponsored five other hospitals in other parts of the state. Examples of other denominations' contributions were the Methodists, who sponsored several hospitals, including the Wesley Medical Center in Hattiesburg and Mississippi Methodist Hospital and Rehabilitation Center in Jackson; the King's Daughters, a Seventh-Day Adventist women's organization that established three hospitals in the state; and the Catholics, who established St. Dominic-Jackson Memorial Hospital in Jackson and St. Catherine's Retirement Village in Madison County north of Jackson. One of the leading hospitals in the state, St. Dominic began in 1946 when the Dominican Sisters arrived to operate the Jackson Infirmary. Another agency, Catholic Charities, provided counseling, medical care, shelter and adoption services to needy pregnant women.

"Family Values"

The resurgence of fundamentalism in the late twentieth century paralleled the rising crusade supporting "traditional family values" and opposing abortion, homosexuality, and pornography. Without formal endorsement by the state's churches, the members of which were divided on such issues, and lacking most denominations' approval for their tactics, groups like Roy McMillan's "Christian Action Group" fought abortion and lobbied successfully for a law in 1986 requiring any minor seeking an abortion to have proof of consent of her parents or legal guardian. Mounting public sentiment on the issue resulted in several other measures to limit abortion in the state. Tighter restrictions on the procedure and abortion facilities passed over Governor Ray Mabus's veto in 1991, and a ban on "partial-birth" abortion became law in 1997. The legislature prohibited the expenditure of public funds for abortions, except in the cases of critical medical necessity or pregnancies caused by rape or incest, in 2002. And a law in 2004 imposed extensive reporting requirements on physicians, hospitals, and abortion clinics when abortions resulted in medical complications or death for the patient.

Donald E. Wildmon of Tupelo, a former Methodist minister, founded the American Family Association in the late 1970s to combat public displays of homosexuality, pornography, and other behaviors that he believed undermined traditional Christian values. The Mississippi Family Council lobbied for legislation protecting parents' rights to home-school their children, in favor of a school voucher program that would help defray the costs of a private-school education for those parents wishing to withdraw their children from the local public schools, and prohibiting same-sex marriages. The latter practice was banned in 1996 by the executive order of Governor Kirk Fordice and prohibited by law the following year. Other laws enacted at the end of the century (1997–2000) closely regulated the teaching of sex education in public schools, including parental consent, and required the newly created school nurse intervention program to promote sexual abstinence outside of marriage.

Gambling

Another troublesome issue for Mississippi religious groups was the introduction of casino gambling in the 1990s, a significant departure from the state's traditional values. After Governor Ray Mabus's effort to create a state lottery in 1989 encountered insurmountable opposition led by Baptists and other churches, the campaign to legalize gambling continued, focusing on economic arguments. Getting the support of leading businesspersons who also were notable in mainline churches proved a more successful strategy. In 1992 Governor Fordice signed a bill creating the Mississippi Gaming Commission and allowing counties on the Gulf Coast and along the Mississippi River to vote on whether to accept "dockside gambling."

The law's provision for local decisions made it difficult for churches to organize statewide opposition to the casino legislation. Also significant was that Governor Fordice's initial appointments to the Gaming Commission included respected Presbyterian elder and philanthropist Stuart C. Irby, Jr. After the opening of the first casinos in 1992, all churches issued public statements condemning gambling, pointing to the ill-effects of the activity on society, but some churches found themselves in a dilemma due to the economic impact of the businesses.

CONCLUSION

At the dawn of the twentieth-first century, Mississippi remained a "bible belt" state. The vast majority of the population was influenced by the evangelical and fundamentalist worldviews espoused by one or another church. Such traditionalism wrought both positive and negative results. Ironically, a few groups known for their narrow biblical interpretations and conservative political views made the most progress in achieving biracial congregations. They were not as progressive, however, in accepting racial equality in other aspects of public life. The large mainline churches, on the contrary, failed to achieve their stated ideal of integrated worship but supported societal efforts to improve relations between blacks and whites and to end racial discrimination in some but not all of its forms. Driven by the pervasiveness of religion, Mississippi continued to resist challenges to tradition, although economic and political exigencies caused some concessions to modernism, such as allowing the sale of alcoholic beverages and the legalizing of gambling. In this atmosphere, the most successful political candidates were those who identified themselves as church members and conservatives on social issues.

SELECTED SOURCES

American Religious Data Archive, *Religious Congregations* (www.thearda.com/RCMS/2000/State/28.htm).

American Religious Identification Survey, 2001, The Graduate Center of the City University of New York (www.gc.cuny.edu/studies/aris.pdf).

Curtis, Christopher K., "Mississippi's Anti-Evolution Law of 1926," *Journal of Mississippi History* 48 (February 1986): 15–30.

Gunn, Jack Winton, "Religion in the Twentieth Century," in Richard Aubrey McLemore, ed., A *History of Mississippi*, 2 vols. (Hattiesburg: University & College Press of Mississippi, 1973), 2: 477–491.

McAnally, Thomas S., "Gambling Creates Quandary for Church in Mississippi," *United Methodist News Service* (www.umns.umc.org/99/sept/472.htm).

Mississippi, Annotated Code of 1972.

Mississippi Official and Statistical Register [various dates].

Office of Research and Planning, The United Methodist Church, Mississippi Conference (www.gcom-umc.org/research/index/shtml).

Simms, L. Moody, Jr., "Theodore Dubose Bratton, Christian Principles, and the Race Question," *Journal of Mississippi History* 38 (February 1976): 47–52.

Sparks, Randy J., *Religion in Mississippi*, Vol. 2, Heritage of Mississippi Series (Jackson: University Press of Mississippi for the Mississippi Historical Society, 2001).

Stephens, Allen, Rankin County Baptist Association, interview by author, December 5, 2002.

The United Methodist Church (www.umc.org).

The United Methodist Church, Mississippi Conference (www.mississippi-umc.org).

The United Pentecostal Church International (wec.upci.org/churches).

CHAPTER TWENTY-TWO

The Second Reconstruction

Brown slapped the Board
And got our attention.
Boy,
You had been only
Southern scenery
Squatting in squalid shacks
That rimmed rows
Through which you dragged
Your autumn afternoons.
We thought
You'd keep your place
Forever.
. . . .[1]

THE ELECTION OF 1959

When the voters went to the polls in the summer of 1959, they were well aware of the election's consequences. They were quite possibly embarking on the journey that would lead to the end of Jim Crow. Few Mississippians, however, were aware that they stood on the eve of the "Second Reconstruction."

The leading candidates for governor in the Democratic party primary were Ross R. Barnett, Lieutenant Governor Carroll Gartin, and Charles L. Sullivan. Running for the third time, Barnett led the field by a narrow margin over Gartin, eliminating Sullivan, who ran third with a respectable number of votes. In the second primary most Sullivan backers turned to Barnett, who secured the election over Gartin with a comfortable 54 percent of the vote. Though widely respected and with experience in state office, Gartin was defeated mainly because his segregationist rhetoric was not as extreme as that of Barnett.

Paul B. Johnson, Jr., a candidate for lieutenant governor, and Evelyn Gandy, running for state treasurer, were both nominated by the party in the first primary. Although he was forced into a runoff, State Tax Collector William Winter was renominated. As usual all state officials won the general election without opposition.

1 Emory D. Jones, "Whitey Remembers," as quoted in Dorothy Abbott, ed., *Mississippi Writers: Reflections of Childhood and Youth*, vol. 3, *Poetry* (Jackson: University Press of Mississippi, 1988), 157.

The new governor, a native of Leake County, was the son of a Civil War veteran. Educated at Mississippi College and the University of Mississippi, Barnett had begun a law practice in Jackson in 1926. He was an admirer of Theodore Bilbo and his record of mixing populist ideas and racist campaign rhetoric. With no experience in public office, Barnett had entered the gubernatorial campaign in 1951 with a twenty-three-point program that promised "populist" reforms. Again in 1955 he had entered the race, this time pledging to promote economic growth and to oppose civil rights. In hindsight, Barnett's successful 1959 campaign was simply a more effective presentation of his "segregation forever" stand and ideas about attracting industry to the state.

POPULATION TRENDS

Three significant demographic trends that had begun in the 1940s continued into the 1960s: 1) overall population decline, 2) large-scale emigration of African Americans, and 3) urban growth. During the 1950s the 5.8 percent increase among whites was more than offset by the 7.2 percent drop among African Americans, whose proportion of the total population fell to 42 percent in 1960. The number of Mississippians residing in urban places rose by 10 percent in the 1950s, reaching almost 38 percent of the total population of 2,178,141.

The latter trend reflected the changing sources of workers' earnings, as wages derived from nonfarm industries increased even as those earned on farms declined. During the 1950s farm earnings fell by 24 percent, while earnings in nonfarm enterprises nearly doubled; by 1960 the ratio of farm to nonfarm earnings dropped from 39 percent to 15 percent. Although the state's overall per capita income rose to $1,237, an increase of 60.6 percent, this figure paled in comparison to the national average of $2,276 and ranked Mississippi last among all states.

GOVERNOR ROSS R. BARNETT, 1960–1964

Barnett's Economic Program

Although racial issues seemingly dominated Barnett's administration, the governor devoted considerable attention to the promotion of his economic development program. He took two approaches: first was his personal powers of persuasion, delivered on the more than thirty-five trips he made to other states to attract new industries; second was his appeals to the legislature to adopt business-attracting incentives. This plan was clear from the first moments of his administration, as the largest part of his inaugural address was devoted to plans for industrial expansion. Soon thereafter, the Agricultural and Industrial (A&I) Board sponsored and designed new programs to implement the governor's proposals.

The legislature took several legislative steps in 1960 to make the state more attractive to industries, especially those anticipating greater profits by paying low wages and dodging the hiring of unionized workers. A "right to work law" in the form of a constitutional amendment was approved by the voters in a special election, adding Section 198a "to guarantee that the right of persons to work shall not be denied or abridged on account of membership or non-membership in a labor union or labor organization. . . ." Despite its misleading title, the "right to work law" aimed to prevent labor unions from organizing in Mississippi. With relatively insignificant industry in their state's history, employers had rarely encountered even the possibility of dealing with unions. Except for an occasional formal demand for higher wages, limited hours, and better working conditions—as, for example, in the case of the resolution by the Gulfport Central Labor Union during the Great Depression—employees in the state, without the benefit of union support, were essentially voiceless. And Mississippi's business and political leaders wanted to keep it that way: they viewed organized labor as a threat not only to economic progress but to the social status quo.

The governor's so-called Industrial Bill of Rights, composed of forty-one laws, was adopted with stipulations providing for certain tax exemptions to businesses willing to relocate to the state, the construction of industrial parks into which businesses might move, job-training programs to improve the labor pool, and improvements in the state workmen's compensation laws. A special session of the legislature in 1961 lowered the rate of state income taxes and proposed a constitutional amendment authorizing further tax exemptions to encourage new manufacturers and utility enterprises. Another amendment empowered the legislature to provide for the sale or lease of certain sixteenth-section lands for industrial development. Now, for the first time, these lands could be sold, and the monies derived for their sale or lease could be used for purposes other than education.

These efforts resulted in several hundred new and expanded industrial plants, capital investments of more than $373 million, the creation of more than 40,000 new jobs, and a 39 percent increase in manufacturing earnings. In somewhat of a cultural landmark, thousands of women entered the wage-earning population for the first time—except during World War II, when masses of women had taken temporary, war-related jobs. Particularly in the clothing plants that sprang up in north Mississippi, many of these women were dropped off by their farming husbands, the so-called "go-getters," who would "go-get" them at the end of their shifts for the trip back home. The A&I Board reported in 1964 substantial progress in balancing the number of workers in agricultural and industry. The establishment of the Standard Oil Refinery in Pascagoula, with its more than 6,000 new jobs, was the single most important economic accomplishment. But the project for which Barnett was best remembered was the damming of the Pearl River to create the large reservoir north of Jackson. Although these achievements appeared positive, the reality was that by the end of this term in 1964 little progress had been accomplished in raising Mississippian's living standards, and the state continued to rank last in per capita income.

Civil Rights

Governor Barnett's industrial program was seriously limited in its potential contribution to the state's general welfare by the fierce public and private resistance to the nationally gathering civil rights movement, particularly its objectives to desegregate public facilities and register black voters. All the publicity surrounding economic growth was eclipsed by official state resistance to these objectives, and Barnett's election was widely perceived as a victory for the white racial zealots. The perception proved valid, as Mississippi entered the most racially intense period in the state's modern history. Within four months of Barnett's inauguration, a civil rights protest on the Gulf Coast escalated into a riot. In this incident,

Civil rights march in Hattiesburg. Courtesy Mississippi Department of Archives and History.

about forty-five African Americans went to the white-only part of a segregated beach, where they were attacked by angry whites; before it ended the violence had spread into Biloxi and left members of both races injured by gunshots.

Civil Rights Organizations

Organizations such as the National Association for the Advancement of Colored People (NAACP), the Congress of Racial Equality (CORE), and the Student Nonviolent Coordinating Committee (SNCC) spearheaded the civil rights movement in Mississippi and other states. Organized in 1909 by a group of social activists including Ida Wells-Barnett, a native Mississippian, the NAACP pioneered the struggle for racial justice throughout the nation. Over the decades this organization won key victories, including the landmark decision by the U.S. Supreme Court in *Brown v. Board of Education.* By mid-century its regional and branch offices had extended into Mississippi and other Southern states.

While the NAACP fought racism primarily through the courts, CORE took the fight for racial equality directly to segregated businesses and communities first in Northern states, then throughout the South. Created at the University of Chicago in 1942 as a decentralized organization composed mainly of white students, by the 1960s, as its chapters spread into the South, the membership had became predominately African American. CORE pioneered the strategy of nonviolent, direct action, using the tactics of "sit-ins" (literally sitting down in and refusing to move from segregated stores, bus stations, and other places of business), marches, and other protest activities to challenge on a person-to-person level all practices of racial discrimination. Many of the same methods were also employed by SNCC, an organization formed by black college students in North Carolina in

1960. Often in cooperation with other, larger civil rights bodies, SNCC sent students and other persons to Mississippi to participate in "sit-ins," "freedom rides," and voter-registration campaigns. The association adhered to its nonviolent, multiracial creed until the late 1960s, when its leaders began to call for "black power," a movement that stressed African American separatism and ultimately even called for the use of force if necessary to secure the freedom of blacks from white control.

Voter Registration   These organizations not only defied the segregation of public accommodations, but they also challenged the state's policy of excluding African Americans from voting. Sadly, that policy was still quite effective, as less than 2 percent of all adult blacks in Mississippi were registered to vote in 1960. In the previous decade attempts to break through the barriers had been undertaken by a number of black leaders including Amzie Moore, the Reverend George Lee, and Gus Courts in the Delta. In 1955 the latter two men had been gunned down—Lee fatally—by whites determined to stop their efforts for change. Violence, however, was not the only weapon in the white supremacists' arsenal. White businessmen, most of whom were members of the Citizens' Council (dubbed the "uptown Klan"), used economic intimidation against blacks who tried to register. In particular, banks and stores withheld credit, and landlords "cooked" their books to balloon debts owed by black sharecroppers interested in voting.

By 1961 whites' resistance to the activities of the civil rights' organizations had exploded into violent hostility throughout the state, beginning in southwestern counties where SNCC launched a voter registration campaign led by Robert Parris Moses, a twenty-year-old African American school teacher from New York who had earned a master's degree in philosophy at Harvard University. Moses's strategy was to cooperate with local NAACP chapters in starting schools that would prepare African Americans for the rigorous voter registration tests and then help them through the fearsome process of appearing before white officials at court houses to "interpret" the state constitution and satisfy the residency and poll-tax requirements. In Amite and Pike counties, where the Ku Klux Klan was stirring, the campaign met its strongest resistance, including not only the typical, petty harassments but bloody beatings of potential black voters in the streets by

white civilians as well as local policemen, arrests and imprisonments, and outright murders. In September 1961 a white man, reportedly a member of the state legislature, shot to death Herbert Lee, a black farmer and father of nine children, because Lee was helping African Americans register to vote in Liberty. On the streets of McComb, a crowd of whites taunted SNCC volunteers, then physically attacked Robert Zellnor, a white college student from Alabama. When Moses and others tried to shield Zellnor, they were beaten by the intervening police, arrested, and jailed.

Amzie Moore. Courtesy Mississippi Department of Archives and History.

Local opposition to the voter registration campaign was supported indirectly by official state action. Aiming to strengthen local authorities' already expansive powers to reject blacks' registration applications, the legislature proposed and the voters approved in 1960 a constitutional amendment adding Section 241a, which stated that "in addition to all other qualifications required of a person to be entitled to register for the purpose of becoming a qualified elector, such person shall be of good moral character." Newspapers reported that the amendment was designed "to Restrict Negro Voting."

"Freedom Riders" Instead of retreating before local and state resistance, various civil rights groups broadened and intensified their activities. Beginning in 1961 "freedom riders" sponsored by SNCC and CORE traveled by buses through the South for the purpose of desegregating various white-only public places and facilities. In Jackson they joined black students from Tougaloo College for a sit-in at the lunch counter of Woolworth's, a store on Capitol Street near the Governor's Mansion. After being harassed verbally and physically by a crowd of whites, the store manager declared that the store was closed for business, and the "outside agitators" left under police protection. Later, however, a number of the freedom riders were arrested on charges of disturbing the peace and other law violations and sent to the state penitentiary at Parchman after they refused to pay fines.

James Meredith One of the most dramatic and decisive events during the Barnett years began when an African American man named James Meredith tried to transfer from Jackson State College to the all-white University of Mississippi in 1961. Facing rejection through the University's interminable "delays" in processing his transfer request, Meredith, a native of Kosciusko and a United States Air Force veteran, pursued legal action in federal court. In June 1962, after sixteen months of litigation, the Fifth Circuit Court of Appeals overturned the federal district court and ordered the University of Mississippi to admit Meredith, ruling that the state had denied him admission only because of his race.

Committed to the maintenance of racial segregation, Governor Barnett invoked the doctrine of state nullification, interposing the state's sovereignty to stop Meredith from registering at Oxford. In a televised statement the governor called on all state officials to resist "the unlawful dictates of the federal government." In the meantime, however, Barnett, on a collision course with the federal government but desiring to save face in Mississippi, made an agreement by telephone with U.S. Attorney General Robert Kennedy: the attorney general would send federal marshals to carry out the court order and register Meredith, while Barnett would appear to condone any means of resistance to federal authority and refuse to authorize state authority to stop potential violence on the campus. But the plan backfired, as many whites took Barnett seriously and determined to stand by their governor. When the marshals escorted Meredith to Oxford in late September 1962, they met unruly white students, who were soon joined by larger numbers of outsiders, some carrying firearms.

On Sunday night, September 30, the situation became riotous, as the growing crowd actually attacked the federal marshals, who responded with tear gas. By the time peace was finally restored, this only after President John F. Kennedy sent fed-

Aaron Henry. Courtesy Mississippi Department of Archives and History.

eral troops to Oxford, including the federalized National Guard and regular army soldiers, two civilians had been shot and killed, 375 persons lay injured, including a number of federal marshals, and there had been extensive property damage on the University campus and in surrounding areas. Paradoxically, Barnett's invocation of state interposition was verbal only and not implemented through any physical resistance to federal authority by state law officers.

Meredith went on to graduate from the university in 1964, and he continued to participate in civil rights activities. During his "March Against Fear," a solitary walk from Memphis to Jackson in 1966, Meredith was wounded by a sniper's gunshot but recovered in time to complete the march, which had been joined by prominent leaders, including Martin Luther King, Jr., and Stokely Carmichael. After earning a bachelor of laws degree at Columbia University in 1968, Meredith turned to careers in business, writing and teaching and brief, unpredictable political ventures, including his staff position in the office of Senator Jesse Helms, the conservative Republican from North Carolina.

Hurdles for Voter Registration   While the university's integration was explosive enough, whites continued to react violently to the continuing efforts of civil rights groups to register black voters. With the support of SNCC, CORE, and the NAACP, by 1962 this movement had spread to key locations throughout the state. Two Mississippi black leaders in the NAACP were Aaron Henry, a Clarksdale pharmacist who served as state president, and Medgar W. Evers, state secretary.

In June 1963 the progress NAACP leaders and activists were making in the voter registration drive was dealt a major blow by the murder of Medgar Evers at his Jackson home. Evers, a World War II veteran and graduate of Alcorn A&M College, was killed by Byron de La Beckwith, a resident of Greenwood and an active member of the Citizens' Council. After two mistrials, both impaneled with all-white male juries, de La Beckwith remained free until 1994, when he was finally convicted of the crime and sentenced to life in prison. That term ended less than seven years later, for he died in January 2001 at the age of eighty.

The hard work and sacrifices of the NAACP, SNCC, and CORE volunteers notwithstanding, by the time of state elections in November 1963, fewer than 10 percent of the approximately 70,000 African Americans who had tried to register had been approved. In addition, the overall number of registered black voters stood at about 28,000, only 7 percent of the state's 400,000 African Americans of voting age. To protest the state officials' unremitting refusal to admit blacks to suffrage, the Council of Federated Organizations (COFO) mobilized a "freedom vote" in 1963, a mock election held throughout the state. About 82,000 blacks participated, electing "Governor" Aaron Henry and "Lieutenant Governor" Edwin King, a white chaplain at Tougaloo College. Such a demonstration, however, produced only fanciful results, and the hard truth remained that only federal intervention could break down Mississippi's racist suffrage policies.

Resisting these civil rights activities with dogged persistence, Governor Barnett relied heavily on the services of the Citizens' Council and the State Sovereignty Commission. Although it was a private organization, the Citizens' Council, under the leadership of William J. Simmons of Jackson, became an essential element of the Barnett administration. Indeed, its members garnered appointments to important offices in state government, including the supreme court and the Sovereignty Commission. The latter body helped pay—with state monies—for the Council's radio and television programs, and by late 1963, when such payments finally ended, almost $200,000 of the taxpayers' money had been spent for Council propaganda.

The Sovereignty Commission delegated to the Council most of its public relations activities and focused instead on investigating persons suspected of being involved in civil rights activities. Under the leadership of Erle Johnston, who became director in 1963, Sovereignty Commission agents traveled throughout the state and compiled lengthy typewritten reports on 250 organizations and tens of thousands of individuals, including civil rights workers and state officials. The agency's principal objective was to spy on and discredit any person or group associated with black voter registration, racial integration, or other civil rights activities.[2]

Politics   Under such conditions the state continued to reelect Democrats who spoke out against civil rights. In 1960 Senator James Eastland secured his fourth full term, easily defeating the Republican candidate Joe A. Moore. In the elections for the House of Representatives all six incumbents were reelected. Only John Bell Williams in the Fourth District (central and southwest Mississippi including Jackson and Natchez) and Arthur Winstead in the Fifth District (east central area including Meridian) faced challengers in the primary. In the general election Republicans participated only in the First and Third districts, where they garnered very few votes.

In presidential politics, however, the division among state Democrats—reminiscent of the 1948 Dixiecrat affair—portended future trends. Democratic party presidential electors (including former congressman Will M. Whittington) pledged to vote for John F. Kennedy and Lyndon B. Johnson, and that team received about 108,362 votes. Most Mississippi voters (116,248), however, preferred the party's "unpledged electors," sponsored by Governor Barnett with Charles Sullivan on the slate, representing their dissatisfaction with both national parties' coziness with civil rights. Republican electors pledged to vote for Richard Nixon and Henry Cabot Lodge, who received 73,561 votes. Nationally Kennedy and Johnson took the election by a narrow margin, but Mississippi's eight electoral votes went to Senators Harry F. Byrd of Virginia and Strom Thurmond of South Carolina.

2 After ten years of litigation in federal court, the files were finally opened to the public early in 1998 by United States District Court Judge William H. Barbour, Jr.

The reapportionment of congressional districts, which was required before the 1962 elections, illustrates the extent to which civil rights issues permeated virtually every aspect of life in the state. As a result of the 1960 census, Mississippi lost another congressional representative, and the legislature merged into one large new district most of the counties in the districts represented by Jamie Whitten in the northeast and Frank Smith in the Delta. To many observers, the action represented a transparent case of gerrymandering to oust Smith, who now had to face the perennial and powerful Whitten in the consolidated district. The 1962 contest between the two incumbents showcased not only the historic tension between the two geographic regions, the Hills and the Delta, but also the contrasting perceptions of Smith as a moderate Democrat who agreed too whole-heartedly with the national party and its "liberal" policies and Whitten as a states' rights Mississippi Democrat. As expected, Whitten defeated Smith in a landslide, receiving 62 percent of the votes.

A more difficult task was the reapportionment of the state legislature itself, which required a constitutional amendment. In a February 1963 special election the voters ratified the redistricting provision, increasing the size of the state senate from forty-nine to fifty-two members and reducing the membership of the house from 140 to 122.

Governor Paul B. Johnson, Jr., 1964–1968

The Elections of 1963 In the 1963 Democratic party primary the three leading candidates for governor were former governor Coleman, Lieutenant Governor Johnson, and Charles Sullivan. In a close contest Johnson finished first and faced Coleman in the second primary. Finally, in his third attempt (like his father before him), Johnson won the party's nomination for governor by a vote of 261,493 (57 percent) to 194,958. For the first time since Reconstruction, in the general election the Democratic party nominee for governor faced a formidable Republican challenger, Rubel L. Phillips. Although Johnson won with 62 percent of the vote, the outcome was significant in Mississippi's political history for at least two reasons. First, the high voter turnout (almost 400,000) was unusual in a general election, and second, a white Republican candidate was able to attract a substantial share of the votes cast (about 138,500).

The election, therefore, marked the growing interest of white Mississippi voters in the Republican party. Although he campaigned as a segregationist, Phillips may have had some difficulty in overcoming seemingly moderate statements he made in the mid-1950s when, as president of the state's Circuit Clerks' Association, he had complained about discriminatory voting laws. His campaign button in 1963, "K.O. the Kennedys! Phillips [for] Governor," proved to be an unfortunate slogan, as President John Kennedy was assassinated in Dallas, Texas, only weeks after the November election.

Johnson was the state's only governor to have a father who had held that office, and in 1941, during his father's administration, the younger Johnson's wedding ceremony had been conducted in the Governor's Mansion. A native of Hattiesburg, the new governor graduated from the University of Mississippi and had practiced law in his hometown and in Jackson. After serving as a Marine Corps officer in the Pacific during World War II, he served as Assistant United States Attorney for the Southern District of Mississippi, from 1948 to 1951. As lieutenant governor during the Barnett administration, he was a member of the A&I Board, the Building Commission, and the Sovereignty Commission, where, according to his own statement, "he was in the forefront of the constant fight to preserve and perpetuate Mississippi's basic and fundamental traditions."

In the first primary former lieutenant governor Carroll Gartin, who had been unsuccessful in the 1960 gubernatorial contest, led a field of five candidates seeking the office of lieutenant governor. He defeated State Treasurer Evelyn Gandy in the second primary, although the result was closer than expected, with Gandy getting about 48 percent of the vote. Like Johnson, in the general election Gartin faced a Republican opponent, Stanford E. Morse, Jr., whom he easily defeated. There were no Republican candidates in the other contests for state offices.

Civil Rights

Johnson's Role   During the gubernatorial campaign of 1963, Johnson portrayed himself as a strong opponent of racial integration, emphasizing his role as lieutenant governor in stopping at the "school house door" James Meredith's first attempt to enter "Ole Miss," an image that helped Johnson defeat Coleman, who was viewed as more moderate on the issue. But once in office, like Coleman, Johnson found practical politics and the exigencies of the times required he take a more temperate course. From the outset he seemed to understand that the state's future welfare depended on finding more reasonable solutions to the critical social problems than racial hatred and violence. Reflecting the large white majority, he personally opposed the federal civil rights laws but refrained from making strong public denunciations of them and pledges to resist their enforcement, as Barnett had done. Aiming to promote a more peaceful atmosphere during the initial integration of public accommodations and public schools, Johnson advised cooperation by local authorities. Because his public statements on the civil rights issues did not always match his actions or the lack thereof, some critics labeled the governor "ambivalent Paul."

The majority of the legislature was displeased with the governor's failure to follow in Barnett's footsteps, and it passed a resolution declaring that the (federal) 1964 Civil Rights Act was unconstitutional and calling on citizens to resist its enforcement "by all legal means." Other groups took even more radical positions. The Citizens' Council wanted to close all the public schools and organize boycotts of businesses that complied with the Civil Rights Act, and the Ku Klux Klan, which had been virtually dormant for decades but now claimed some 10,000 active members in the state, began to publish appeals for outright resistance.

Overcoming the Obstacles   Though Johnson's apparent acquiescence would continue to provoke its outspoken critics, an increasing number of influential voices endorsed a policy of moderation. Four interrelated developments underlay this trend, the first of which was a mounting federal assault on the state's discriminatory voting laws and practices, which included, for example, Congress' passage of the Civil Rights Act of 1964, the Voting Rights Act of 1965, and the ratification of the Twenty-fourth Amendment to the United States Constitution, which prohibited poll taxes as a requirement for voting in federal elections beginning in 1964. The Mississippi legislature took no action on the poll-tax amendment and never approved it. On the basis of noncompliance with these and other federal mandates, the United States Justice Department filed a growing number of lawsuits against the state, charging its officials with voter discrimination and employing other stratagem to maintain white supremacy and racial segregation.

The second development was the rising level of national interest in Mississippi's official racist policies and the ugly incidents of racially motivated violence, which only increased in number and intensity during Governor Johnson's administration. The best-known such event, which occurred only five months after the governor's inauguration, was the murder of three civil rights volunteers near Philadelphia in Neshoba County. The victims, all in their twenties, were Michael Henry Schwerner and Andrew Goodman, white CORE organizers from New York, and James Earl Chaney, a black native of Meridian. In June 1964 they drove from Meridian to investigate a reported church burning. On the way back to town the three were arrested without legitimate cause, jailed then released in Philadelphia, then murdered south of Philadelphia by a group of Klansmen that included members of the Neshoba County sheriff's department. After searching for more than a month, the Federal Bureau of Investigation finally located the bodies of the young men buried in a newly constructed earthen dam.

Following the failure of the county grand jury to indict the accused perpetrators, allegedly because the FBI refused to release pertinent evidence, a federal grand jury indicted nineteen men in 1967. After a ten-day trial in Meridian, an

Vernon Dahmer's property, firebombed by the KKK. Courtesy Mississippi Department of Archives and History.

Imperial Wizard of the Ku Klux Klan, Sam Bowers. Courtesy Mississippi Department of Archives and History.

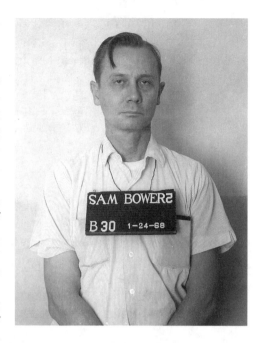

all-white male jury found seven of the defendants guilty of depriving Schwerner, Chaney, and Goodman of their civil rights, and federal judge Harold Cox sentenced the men to prison terms ranging from three years to ten years, Alton Wayne Roberts and the "imperial wizard" of the Klan, Sam Bowers, receiving the longest terms.

In another notorious incident, the Klan fire bombed in January 1966 the store and residence of Vernon Dahmer, an African American who had assisted in the black voter registration drive near Hattiesburg. Dahmer, a fifty-seven-year old native of Forrest County, was a successful businessman, an active member of the Shady Grove Baptist Church, and president of the county chapter of the NAACP. While trying to defend his family and property, Dahmer suffered fatal burns. Most of the Klansmen involved in the cowardly assault were arrested and prosecuted in state and federal courts, but Sam Bowers—not yet convicted in Meridian for the Neshoba County murders—who had ordered the Dahmer attack, escaped conviction in four mistrials. Thirty-two years later, in August 1998, Bowers was finally convicted of the murder and sentenced to life in prison.

The third development that finally forced Mississippi's government to take a more moderate stance on civil rights was a new awareness within the state that resistance would have negative economic consequences. White business leaders understood that federal money was necessary not only for economic progress but also for the maintenance of the public school system. Title VI of the Civil Rights Act made acceptance of desegregation a requirement for receiving federal assistance. Now, newspaper editors like Hodding Carter of the Greenville *Delta Democrat-Times*, Hazel Brannon Smith of the *Lexington Advertiser*, and Oliver Emmerich of the *McComb Enterprise-Journal* pointed out the folly of resisting federal civil rights laws and court orders. Also calling for peaceful compliance were organizations like the Mississippi Economic Council, local chambers of commerce, other business, church, judicial, and academic groups, and even the state association of sheriffs and law officers.

The fourth but perhaps the essential factor generating the three previous developments was the civil rights movement itself. Despite various conciliatory efforts by white groups and the somewhat ambivalent position of the governor, various civil rights organizations within the state intensified their activities. To continue the momentum of the previous year's "freedom vote," in 1964, COFO organized the "Mississippi Freedom Democratic Party" (MFDP) and planned a new campaign, known as the "Freedom Summer Project." During the Barnett years most of the civil rights groups had depended primarily on volunteers from other states, but beginning in 1964 an increasing number of Mississippi blacks became involved. One of the most outspoken representatives of this participation was SNCC activist Fannie Lou Hamer of Ruleville. With a background as a powerful speaker and singer in her Strangers Home Baptist Church, Hamer participated in Freedom Summer and attracted national attention as a leader in the MFDP, declaring on television, "I'm sick and tired of being sick and tired."

Remembering her contributions to the cause of freedom for African Americans, poet Otis Williams writes:

> She was nothin' special
> Jus' a Strong Black Mississippi Mother
> Made from the Mighty, majestic mold
> of
> Sojourner Truth
> . . . .
> It was freedom on her revolutionary mind
> Leadin' my people out of bondage
> Jus' like Moses
> And
> Befo' I be yo' Slave
> I be buried in my grave
> And go home to my Lord
> And be free[3]

Freedom Summer brought at least 750 college students into the state to strengthen the voter registration movement, help mobilize support for the 1964 elections, and, by attracting national attention, obtain greater federal intervention in Mississippi. The idea originated with SNCC leader Robert Moses and was then endorsed by David Dennis of CORE and Aaron Henry, state NAACP president. The agenda was to use primarily white, elite-college student volunteers to work in black community centers, teach in "freedom schools," and help organize the MFDP.

While many participants invoked Christianity as the movement's fundamental driving force, most white Mississippians were confident that God was on their side. Believing that the Freedom Summer project was an invasion by communists and other radicals to promote racial tension, local and state officials increased the number of law enforcement officers and imposed more severe penalties for disturbers of the peace. The result was the eruption of widespread violence as the young, idealistic crusaders confronted the realistic, often violent, circumstances of public and private resistance. According to CORE, the acts of violence perpetrated against the civil rights activists in Mississippi during the summer of 1964 included four murders, numerous beatings and shootings, roughly one thousand arrests, and the burning or bombing of about seventy churches, homes, or other buildings.

3 Otis Williams, "Fannie Lou Hamer," as quoted in Dorothy Abbott, ed., *Mississippi Writers: Reflections of Childhood and Youth*, vol. 3, *Poetry* (Jackson: University Press of Mississippi, 1988), 356.

It was almost cotton-picking time in 1917 when Fannie Lou Townsend was born to James Lee and Lou Ella Bramlett Townsend in Montgomery County, Mississippi. Her parents struggled to provide for the baby and her fourteen older brothers and five older sisters by sharecropping; her father also preached in Baptist churches while her mother worked as a "maid" for white folks. In 1919 the family moved to Sunflower County, where Fannie Lou grew up working in the cotton fields, going to school only occasionally through the sixth grade, and testifying and singing "This Little Light of Mine," "Precious Lord," and other gospel songs in church. She married Peter Hamer, a co-worker on the plantation near Ruleville where she was employed in 1944. After being physically threatened for trying to register to vote in

Elect
INFORMED

MRS.
Fannie Lou
HAMER
STATE SENATOR
District 11 – Post No. 2
BOLIVAR AND SUNFLOWER COUNTIES
NOVEMBER 2, 1971

1962, Fannie Lou Hamer became involved in civil rights activities, with which she integrated

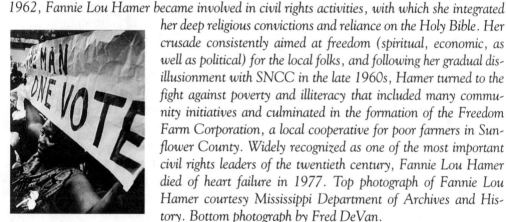

her deep religious convictions and reliance on the Holy Bible. Her crusade consistently aimed at freedom (spiritual, economic, as well as political) for the local folks, and following her gradual disillusionment with SNCC in the late 1960s, Hamer turned to the fight against poverty and illiteracy that included many community initiatives and culminated in the formation of the Freedom Farm Corporation, a local cooperative for poor farmers in Sunflower County. Widely recognized as one of the most important civil rights leaders of the twentieth century, Fannie Lou Hamer died of heart failure in 1977. Top photograph of Fannie Lou Hamer courtesy Mississippi Department of Archives and History. Bottom photograph by Fred DeVan.

The Mississippi Freedom Democratic Party   While there were differences of opinion concerning the mixed results of Freedom Summer, no doubt existed that the project benefited the Mississippi Freedom Democratic Party, which aimed to take control of the state Democratic party.[4] Leaders like Lawrence Guyot, a native Mississippian and graduate of Tougaloo College, Fannie Lou Hamer, Robert Moses, Aaron Henry, and David Dennis organized this new political party to parallel the structure of the regular state party. Their delegation to the national Democratic convention in Atlantic City, New Jersey, failed to gain recognition as the rightful representatives of Mississippi Democrats. Nevertheless, in nationally televised hearings the delegates declared that unlike the regular state Democratic party, which was racist, the MFDP was loyal to the national party platform and nominees for president and vice president.

4 Several scholars report that other positive results of Freedom Summer lay in the formation of new organizations, like the Delta Ministry, and in the arrival of scores of lawyers to investigate and report racial problems. The latter result may have been the most important cause for changes in race relations. Freedom Summer also helped to effect the ratification of the Twenty-fourth Amendment and the passage of the Civil Rights Act of 1964 and the Voting Rights Act of 1965.

Faithful to their declarations, in the 1964 presidential election the MFDP held its own unofficial "freedom election" in which President Johnson and the vice presidential nominee Hubert H. Humphrey got all but 17 of the 63,000 votes cast. Also claiming victory in this mock election were four MFDP candidates for Congress, including Aaron Henry and Fannie Lou Hamer. When Congress convened in the fall, more than one-third of representatives sided with the MFDP's challenge to the seating of the regularly elected congressmen from Mississippi. The incident produced more national publicity about the state's exclusion of African Americans from voting and officeholding, and John Bell Williams lost his congressional seniority because of his support for the Republican ticket in the presidential election.

In the 1964 Democratic party primaries Congressman Abernethy of the First District was nominated without opposition, and the other four incumbents easily defeated their challengers. The most significant contest was Fannie Lou Hamer's campaign against Congressman Whitten in the Delta. Receiving only 621 votes, the result of the flagging voter registration movement and continuing obstacles to black suffrage, Hamer nonetheless had called more attention to the need for federal voting-rights legislation.

The Emergence of the Republicans   During Governor Paul Johnson's administration Mississippi lost three major Democratic party leaders with the deaths of former governor White in 1965 and that of Lieutenant Governor Gartin and Speaker Sillers in 1966. This era also witnessed the emergence of a new Mississippi Republican party. Composed almost entirely of whites, the new Republicans attracted votes by portraying themselves as alternatives to longtime Democratic incumbents, whom they associated with the national party, and by echoing traditional Democratic support for economic and educational improvements and opposition to civil rights. A concomitant factor was the exodus of African Americans from the party, a trend that had begun in northern states during the New Deal era of the 1930s.

In 1964, for the first time in the twentieth century, most Mississippians voted for the Republican presidential candidate, casting roughly 356,500 votes (87 percent) for the electors pledged to Barry M. Goldwater and only about 52,600 votes for the Democratic electors pledged to President Johnson. While the Republican party mounted no challenge to Senator Stennis, who was reelected without opposition, nor to four of the Democratic congressmen, it did undertake a successful campaign in the Fourth District, where Winstead was defeated by Republican Prentiss L. Walker, a white businessman from Smith County who got 56 percent of the votes. Campaigning as a staunch segregationist, Walker became the state's first Republican congressional representative since Reconstruction.

Evidently encouraged by their successes in 1964, the Republicans fielded candidates in several congressional contests in 1966, though without a victory. For the Senate seat, the incumbent Eastland easily defeated two challengers in the Democratic party primary and received more than 65 percent of the votes in his victory over the Republican Walker and an Independent candidate in the general election. Except in the Fourth District, where Walker's seat was now open, the four Democratic incumbents were easily nominated in the first primary elections.

Attracting the most interest, Congressman John Bell Williams of the Third District defeated Edwin King, the civil rights activist at Tougaloo College, by a vote of 54,751 to 15,313, and in Walkers' Fourth District Democrat G. V. "Sonny" Montgomery of Meridian was narrowly nominated over three opponents.

And it was in the Fourth District, primarily composed of central and eastern counties, that the first Republican party primary in state history occurred. L. L. McAllister, Jr., won the GOP nomination, but he and his opponent together received a total of only 8,221 votes, and in November, Montgomery obtained more than 65 percent of the almost 80,000 votes cast to defeat McAllister (33 percent) and an Independent with ease. The Republicans also sent in challengers in the Second and Fifth districts, but the Democratic incumbents were reelected by wide margins.

African American Voters   Understanding that stubborn, sometimes violent resistance to black suffrage would not only threaten the state's economy but also its customary Democratic-party political monopoly, Governor Johnson and other white leaders by 1965 were privately recommending that local officials discontinue their traditional obstructive strategies. In addition, with the enactment of the federal Voting Rights Act of 1965 and the legislature's repeal of restrictive voting laws, which long had been used by county registrars against black applicants, the number of black registered voters increased rapidly, climbing to about 264,000 by 1968.

For African Americans the results of these changes came gradually. The first black county official since Reconstruction was elected in Panola County in 1966. The following year Congressman John Bell Williams, known as a staunch segregationist and states' rights spokesman, was elected governor, while about twenty-one blacks were elected to local offices, and Robert G. Clark, Jr., of Holmes County, the grandson of a slave, became the first black member of the state house of representatives in the modern era. In succeeding years the increasing numbers of newly enfranchised blacks would elect a rising number of African American candidates to local and state offices. And unlike their ancestors, who had been faithful to the Republican party of the Reconstruction era—the party of Lincoln and emancipation—they now transferred their allegiance to the national Democratic party, which had brought them a "Second Reconstruction" of civil rights.

Governor John Bell Williams, 1968–1972

The Elections of 1967   The state's acquiescence to civil rights may have begun during the administration of Governor Paul B. Johnson, Jr., but election outcomes in the late 1960s and early 1970s revealed only a gradual, reluctant acceptance of change. Seven Democrats entered the race for governor in 1967, including former Governor Barnett, James E. Swan, William L. Waller, Congressman John Bell Williams, and former State Treasurer Winter. The outcome of the first primary was that Winter emerged the leader, with about 222,000 votes, followed by Williams with about 198,000. In the second primary, however, Williams's record of opposition to civil rights legislation made him more attractive than Winter, whom the majority of white voters perceived as a moderate and a loyal national

Democrat. Williams, therefore, won the party's nomination, receiving 54 percent of the votes. In the general election he easily defeated Republican Rubel Phillips, who tallied only 30 percent of the votes.

The lieutenant governor's contest saw six candidates vying for the Democratic nomination, including Roy Herbert Black, Governor Johnson, Charles Sullivan, and Troy B. Watkins. Another name on the ballot was Byron de la Beckwith, the accused murderer of Medgar Evers, who received more than 5 percent of the total votes cast in the first primary. In the end, the leader was Sullivan, while Black edged Governor Johnson out of second place by a margin of only 122 votes out of almost 300,000 total votes cast for the two candidates. In the second primary Sullivan easily defeated Black to win the nomination.

John Bell Williams was a native of Raymond in Hinds County, where he had begun a law practice just before entering the United States Army Air Corps. He retired from active service in 1944, having suffered the loss of the lower portion of his left arm in an accident. After serving as prosecuting attorney for Hinds County for two years, he had won election to the U.S. House of Representatives in 1946. Twenty-seven years old at the time of his election, Williams had become the youngest Mississippian to serve in Congress, to which he was returned in ten succeeding elections before resigning in January 1968 to become governor.

Political Trends   To fill the vacancy in Congress created by Williams's resignation a special election was conducted in late February 1968. Charles H. Griffin, who had been Congressman Williams's assistant since 1949, was expected to win but encountered six challengers, including Charles Evers, the state NAACP executive secretary and brother of Medgar Evers. The somewhat surprising result was that Evers led Griffin by a vote of 33,706 to 28,927 but did not receive a majority of the total votes cast. In the runoff, however, Evers's supporters, a coalition of white moderates and African Americans, were able to attract only a third of the votes. Despite Griffin's victory, the contest appeared to be a turning point in recent state politics, as this campaign between a black and a white candidate had been conducted without inflammatory racial remarks. A change in the tone of state politics was beginning, albeit very slowly.

In June 1968, Mississippi voters were asked to nominate candidates for Congress as well as to ratify a state constitutional amendment providing for annual sessions of the state legislature. In an unusually close vote (98,842 for to 94,461 against) the amendment was approved, but there was nothing extraordinary about the congressional elections. In the primaries and the general election all five Democratic incumbents prevailed, and only one congressman met a Republican challenger in November. In the Fourth District, Republican Prentiss Walker, who lost in his 1966 campaign for the U.S. Senate, failed in his attempt to regain his seat in the House, now held by Montgomery. Griffin, meanwhile, was reelected without opposition.

Notwithstanding the rising number of African American voters in 1968, the state's regular delegation to the Democratic national convention included only three blacks among its forty-four members. On the grounds that the state party still practiced racial discrimination, the convention rejected the regular delegates and admitted instead the "Loyal Democrats," a biracial group pledged to support the party platform and its candidates. The regular party, subsequently, announced its support for Alabama Governor George C. Wallace, an outspoken and defiant segregationist.

In the 1968 presidential election Mississippi electors pledged to candidates Vice President Hubert H. Humphrey and Edmund Muskie received about 150,000 votes, while the Republican party electors pledged to Richard M. Nixon and Spiro T. Agnew won about 88,000 votes. But almost two-thirds of all Mississippians voting supported the American Independent party candidacy of Governor Wallace, who got about 414,000 votes. Wallace carried four other southern states as well, and nationally his 9.9 million votes prevented the major parties from winning a majority of the popular vote, but Nixon captured a sizeable majority of the electoral college. White Mississippians' vote in this election reflected the unrelenting opposition to racial integration, a stance symbolized by Wallace, who had once declared, "Segregation now! Segregation tomorrow! Segregation forever!" The election, moreover, occurred as public school integration was finally beginning in the state, with thousands of white families now sending their children to newly organized private schools.

The Republicans' only congressional primary in 1970 was conducted in the Third District, where Ray Lee won the nomination but received only 36 percent of the votes against Congressman Griffin in the general election. The other four incumbent representatives and Senator Stennis were reelected without facing Republican challengers.

The Vietnam War By this time unhappiness with national issues, like the United States' costly, frustrating, and seemingly fruitless efforts in the Vietnam War, a conflict that had been dragging on at this point for nearly a decade and had cost the nation the lives of many thousands of service men and women and billions of taxpayer dollars, influenced many voters. Mississippi lost 637 men and women in Vietnam, less than 10 percent of the total number of the state's veterans of the war. Among many decorated soldiers, Marine Corps Lance Corporal Roy M. Wheat, a native of Moselle, received posthumously the nation's highest military honor, the Congressional Medal of Honor, "for conspicuous gallantry and intrepidity at the risk of his life above and beyond the call of duty." In 2003 the U.S. Navy named its newest ship the USNS Lance Cpl. Roy M. Wheat in acknowledgement of the Mississippian's service in Vietnam. Further recognition of the state's contributions to the war came in the establishment of the Mississippi Vietnam Veterans Memorial in Ocean Springs.

During the war, however, Mississippians directed their attention mainly to battles on the homefront, particularly those involving the civil rights movement. And race even became a factor in attitudes toward the Vietnam War. Although antiwar sentiment did not rise to the levels it reached in other parts of the nation, the state was uncharacteristically reserved, even divided, in its commitment to the conflict. Many African Americans believed that they were "railroaded" into military service in disproportionate numbers, while privileged whites "dodged" the draft. In 1970 the city police fired guns at war protesters on the campus of Jackson State College, killing two students, wounding twelve, and damaging a dormitory building.

CONCLUSION

The road traveled by Mississippians during the administrations of Governors Barnett, Johnson, and Williams was a rough one strewn with many bloody obstacles. The theme of the journey was the clash of two unrelenting foes: whites' resistance and civil rights' insistence. The ultimate destination was removal of racial barriers to voting, holding office, and sharing equally public facilities. It was achieved in stages ranging from defiance by Barnett, acquiescence by Johnson, and pragmatism by Williams. But the racial alignments persisted. Growing numbers of whites forsook tradition and voted Republican, and African Americans turned away from the party of Lincoln to support the party of Lyndon Baines Johnson and his Great Society. Public schools in black majority districts witnessed the exodus of whites to private academies. But however shallow the state's conversion to civil rights, Mississippi had made progress, and the events of the era heralded times of transition.

SELECTED SOURCES

Andrews, Kenneth T., *Freedom is a Constant Struggle: The Mississippi Civil Rights Movement and Its Consequences* (Chicago: University of Chicago Press, 2004).

Blumberg, Rhoda L., *Civil Rights: The 1960's Freedom Struggle* (Boston: Twayne Publishers, 1984).

Bond, Bradley G., *Mississippi: A Documentary History* (Jackson: University Press of Mississippi, 2003).

Dittmer, John, *Local People: The Struggle for Civil Rights in Mississippi* (Chicago: University of Illinois Press, 1994).

"The Freedom Democratic Party, 1964: "The Right to Vote in Mississippi" (http://sunsite.berkeley.edu).

Henry, Aaron, with Constance Curry, *Aaron Henry: The Fire Ever Burning*, Margaret Walker Alexander Series in African American Studies (Jackson: University Press of Mississippi, 2000).

Historical Statistics of the States of the United States: Two Centuries of the Census, 1790–1990, comp. Donald B. Dodd (Westport, Conn.: Greenwood Press, 1993), Population.

Johnston, Erle, *Mississippi's Defiant Years 1953–1973: An Interpretive Documentary with Personal Experiences* (Forest, Miss.: Lake Harbor Publishers, 1990).

———, *I Rolled with Ross: A Political Portrait* (Baton Rouge, La.: Moran Publishing Corporation, 1980).

Katagiri, Yasuhiro, *The Mississippi State Sovereignty Commission: Civil Rights and States' Rights* (Jackson: University Press of Mississippi, 2001).

Lamis, Alexander P., *The Two-Party South* (New York: Oxford University Press, 1984).

Lee, Chana Kai, *For Freedom's Sake: The Life of Fannie Lou Hamer* (Urbana: University of Illinois Press, 1999).

Loewen, James W., and Charles Sallis, eds., *Mississippi: Conflict and Change* (New York: Random House, 1974).

McAdam, Doug, *Freedom Summer* (New York: Oxford University Press, 1988).

McMillen, Neil R., *The Citizens' Council: Organized Resistance to the Second Recon-struction, 1954–64* (Urbana: University of Illinois Press, 1994).

——, *Dark Journey: Black Mississippians in the Age of Jim Crow* (Urbana: University of Illinois Press, 1989).

——, "Development of Civil Rights, 1956–1970," in Richard Aubrey McLemore, ed., *A History of Mississippi*, 2 vols. (Hattiesburg: University & College Press of Mississippi, 1973), 2: 154–76.

Marsh, Charles, *God's Long Summer: Stories of Faith and Civil Rights* (Princeton, N.J.: Princeton University Press, 1997).

Mills, Kay, *This Little Light of Mine: The Life of Fannie Lou Hamer* (New York: E. P. Dutton, 1993).

Minor, [Wilson] Bill, *Eyes on Mississippi: A Fifty-Year Chronicle of Change* (Jackson, Miss.: J. Prichard Morris Books, 2001).

Mississippi, *Journal of the Senate*, 1964.

Mississippi Official and Statistical Register, 1960–1964; 1964–1968; 1968–1972; 1972–1976.

Mitchell, Dennis J., *Mississippi Liberal: A Biography of Frank E. Smith* (Jackson: University Press of Mississippi, 2001).

Newman, Mark, "Hazel Brannon Smith and Holmes County Mississippi, 1936–1964: The Making of a Pulitzer Prize Winner," *Journal of Mississippi History* 54 (February 1992): 59–87.

Payne, Charles M., *I've Got the Light of Freedom: The Organizing Tradition and the Mississippi Freedom Struggle* (Berkeley: University of California Press, 1995).

Simpson, William, "The Birth of the Mississippi 'Loyalist Democrat' (1965–1968)," *Journal of Mississippi History* 44 (February 1982): 27–45.

Skates, John Ray, *Mississippi: A Bicentennial History*, The States and the Nation Series, James Morton Smith, ed. (New York: W. W. Norton & Company, Inc., 1979).

United States Department of Commerce, Bureau of Economic Analysis, *Regional Accounts Data: Annual State Personal Income. SA05 Personal Income by Major Source and Earnings by Industry—Mississippi, 1940, 1950, 1960, 1964* (www.bea.gov/bea/regional/spi/action.cfm).

CHAPTER TWENTY-THREE

Times of Transition

Now we dial the phone
but Aunt Callie still yells into it
and ends every sentence with a question mark
as if she can't believe that all her words
can get through those little wires
But back then we stepped out and pointed our voices
across the hills
Whooooeeee

. . . .[1]

In the mid-twentieth century Mississippians entered a new technological age that foreshadowed transitions in virtually every aspect of their lives. The widespread distribution of fuels and electric power gave greater numbers of people access to modern devices, which they acquired for business improvements as well as for personal convenience and entertainment. This generation began to take for granted amenities that their grandparents had never experienced or even dreamed possible. Sweeping changes in lifestyles were realized with the arrival of new or improved machines, appliances, and vehicles. They included, for example, gas or electric kitchen stoves, ranges, and other appliances, inside plumbing facilities with access to public water utilities, improved and less-expensive radios, telephones, and a new contraption that would prove to be of momentous significance: the television set.

POPULATION TRENDS

Although high numbers of African Americans had, as mentioned, been leaving the state for decades, the most remarkable population trend during the 1960s was the sharp increase in the rate of African Americans emigration. By 1970 the white population had risen to 1,393,283, an increase of 10.8 percent, but the number of blacks had fallen to 887,206, a decline of 10.9 percent. The net loss of 100,000 African Americans during the racially turbulent 1960s lowered their proportion of the total population from 42 to 36.8 percent. The other significant trend was the accelerating movement of people into urban places, in which 44.5 percent of the total population resided by 1970, a gain of almost 7 percent since

1 James A. Autry, "Communication," as quoted in Dorothy Abbott, ed., *Mississippi Writers: Reflections of Childhood and Youth,* vol. 3, *Poetry* (Jackson: University Press of Mississippi, 1988), 3.

1960. Symptomatic of the state's failure to resolve its interracial strife and to diversify and advance its economy effectively, Mississippi's overall population growth virtually had stalled, and the 2,216,912 inhabitants reported by the 1970 census represented an increase of only 33,116 during the past three decades! (See Appendices IV and V.)

A New Economy

Agricultural Trends

The Mississippi Department of Agriculture and Commerce, headed by Commissioner Jim Buck Ross, reported that during 1968 revenues from sales of crops and livestock and from federal subsidies payments reached a record high of almost $1 billion. Of the total cash income roughly 20 percent came from each of the following markets: cotton, soybeans, meat (cattle, hogs, sheep), and poultry and eggs. Commissioner Ross believed these statistics indicated greater agricultural diversification than had existed even as late as the mid-1950s, when cotton had accounted for 57 percent of the state's farm income, processed meat 12 percent, poultry and eggs 9 percent, and soybeans 5 percent. Other positive signs included the emergence of new commercial crops like farmed fish, sweet potatoes and other varieties of vegetables, and particularly greatly increasing incomes derived from the sale of cattle and poultry, sales of which now ranked fifteenth and fifth in the nation respectively.

A New Farming Culture   Commissioner Ross was actually describing the emergence of a new farming culture in the state. Four interrelated factors had contributed to the transformation during recent decades: the expanding role of government, the demands of World War II, the application of new technologies, and the mass emigration of African Americans. The most obvious indicators of the new system included the decline of the sharecropper system, the replacement of unskilled laborers by machine operators, larger farming operations, new farming enterprises, crop diversification, and overall increases in agricultural production.

Labor Shifts   The total number of farmworkers had declined sharply since World War II. The biggest drop had occurred in the 1950s, when about 140,00 persons left the cotton fields, leaving the state or taking manufacturing jobs. During the following decade the number of farmworkers had remained relatively constant at about 124,000. Farm labor shifted from man and mule to tractors and harvesting machines, including the mechanical cotton-picker, products of the post–World War II technological revolution. By the 1970s the widespread use of increasingly powerful machines with various attachments performing virtually all tasks from planting through harvesting resulted in the production of cotton and some other crops with almost no hand labor. Now, in one day's work a two-row picker harvested as much cotton as 140 fieldhands. And a large tractor cultivated more land than several dozen mules with drivers.

Fewer but Larger Farms   The efficacy of the machines notwithstanding, their costs remained high, so small farmers found it difficult to compete with the larger, better-equipped planters. Having begun in the 1930s, a steady trend continued to see the number of farms decline, even as the state's total agricultural acreage remained constant. By 1970 the number of farms had dropped to 72,600, about 240,000 fewer than the 1930 number, and the average size of each unit had risen

Present-day cotton pickers in the Delta. Courtesy Westley F. Busbee, Jr.

from 55 to 220 acres. During these four decades African American farm owners declined by 36 percent, white owners by 19 percent. But a more revealing statistic was that while blacks composed more than half of the state's population through the 1930s and 37 percent in 1970, during this period they represented no more than 22 percent of all farm owners.

Crop Diversification   More knowledgeable about scientific and mechanical methods, farmers overcame the traditional adherence to crop farming exclusively. They now began to use less fertile lands more productively by developing livestock, dairy, and poultry enterprises. By the early 1970s the state reported seventy-four beef cows per thousand acres of farmland, first in the nation in that category, and more than twenty-five beef cattle per square mile, ranking among the top five states. Increasing numbers of farmers also turned to the production of broilers and eggs, and by the early 1970s the state was among the top five states in broiler production per year.

Crop diversification also lessened farmers' tenacious allegiance to cotton. Even though cotton remained the state's primary crop and its price rose to more than 40 cents per pound in the 1950s, Mississippi farmers had finally learned that raising other crops brought opportunities for increased profits. By 1969 cotton acreage dropped to 1.2 million acres, 61 percent less land devoted to the crop than in 1890. Rice acreage expanded from only 1,500 to more than 60,000 acres, mainly in the Delta with its suitable soil and water resources. Since before the Civil War, soybeans had been used mainly for hay (animal feed) and soil enrichment, but after World War II, due in part to the growing demand for the edible oil from the beans, the agricultural experiment stations developed better varieties of the crop. By the late 1960s farmers were using twice as much of their cultivated land for soybeans than for cotton. Corn acreage declined from more than 3 mil-

TABLE 23.1 Selected Farm Statistics, 1930–2000

	1930	1940	1950	1960	1970	1980	1990	2000
Number of Farms (thous.)	312.7	291.1	251.4	138.1	72.6	55	40	43
Average Size (acres)	55.3	6.6	82.3	134.7	220.4	265.5	325	258.1
Total Farm Acreage (mil.)	17.3	19.2	20.7	18.6	16.0	14.6	13	11.1
Total Net Income (mil. $)			$337.6	$233.8	$320.1	$701.6	$624	$949
Average Net Income ($)			$1,343	$1,693	$4,409	$12,756	$15,600	$22,070
Total Cash Receipts (mil. $)	$0.87				$1,038	$2,145	$2,292	$3,174
Livestock Products (mil. $)					$513	$892	$1,292	$2,143
Crops (mil. $)					$525	$1,253	$1,000	$1,031

SOURCES: *United States Department of Agriculture, National Agricultural Statistical Service. www.nass.usda.gov/ QuickStats. Mississippi Statistical Abstract, 1974, 1981, 1991; Mississippi Official and Statistical Register, 1972– 1976. Mississippi Department of Agriculture and Commerce, 2002. Statistical Abstract of the United States, 2001.*

TABLE 23.2 Farm Owners by Race, 1930–1969*
            (thousands)

YEAR	ALL	BLACKS	WHITES	%BLACK OWNERS
1930	86.1	22.7	63.4	26
1940	97.3	23.4	73.9	24
1950	120.8	28.9	91.8	24
1959	93.8	22.6	71.2	24
1969	66	14.5	51.5	22

Includes full and part owners.
SOURCE: *Mississippi Statistical Abstract, 1974, 483.*

TABLE 23.3 Selected Major Crops, 1890, 1969

CROPS	ACREAGE (THOUS.)			TOTAL PRODUCTION*			YIELD PER ACRE		
	1890	1969	CHANGE	1890	1969	CHANGE	1890	1969	CHANGE
Cotton	3,015	1,185	-61%	1,262	1,328	5%	.42 bales	1.12 bales	167%
Corn	1,690	318	-81	21,125	9,858	-53	12.5 bu	31 bu	148
Hay	66	619	838	85	996	1,072	1.3 tons	1.6 tons	24
Rice	1.5	60	3,900	6,579	2,520,000	38,204	438.6 lbs.	4,200 lbs.	858
Soybean		2,290			50,380			22 bu	

Units are bushels (thous.) for all except bales (thous.) for cotton, tons (thous.) for hay, and pounds (hundreds) for rice.
SOURCE: *United States Department of Agriculture, Census of Agriculture, www.nass, usda.gov/ census; William Lincoln Giles, "Agricultural Revolution, 1890–1970," in Richard Aubrey McLemore, ed., A History of Mississippi, 2 vols. (Hattiesburg: University & College Press of Mississippi, 1973), 2: 177–211.*

lion during the 1930s to 318,000 in the late 1960s, but the demands of the live-stock business would soon change that trend. Other new crops included tung trees, which, as mentioned, produced a useful oil for paint and finished wood products. The first tung trees were planted in the 1930s in south Mississippi around Poplarville. By 1958 tung oil production had reached a record high of 85,000 tons, but it declined in the late 1960s to only 2,000 tons. The business was seriously disrupted by Hurricane Camille in 1970, which destroyed hundreds of thousands of trees. Thereafter, farmers in the region turned to new and more prof-itable cash crops like sorghum grain, vegetables, and pecans.

Increased Production   Crop diversity complemented by mechanical and tech-nological applications resulted in greater farming efficiency and significant pro-duction increases. A major boost came in 1947 with the introduction of a new type of fertilizer, anhydrous ammonia, which farmers applied directly to the soil using new types of equipment. Another major boon arrived with the development of new kinds of insecticides to control the boll weevil and other pests and which could be sprayed efficiently and evenly from airplanes ("crop dusters"). Between 1890 and 1969, per-acre yields rose 167 percent for cotton and 285 percent for oats, resulting in greater production from less than half the cultivated acreage for each crop. Yields per acre jumped by 148 percent for corn, 675 percent for wheat, 111 percent for sweet potatoes, and 858 percent for rice. Among all crops the greatest total production came in wheat, hay, and rice, for which cultivated acre-age expanded significantly.

The value of agricultural products sold in 1970 was more than five times greater than the 1930 figure, with the fastest rises occurring in the 1950s and 1960s, during which total farm output had risen by more than 150 percent. In spite of this growth, however, income from farming could not keep pace with that of the rising industrial enterprises. During the 1960s, earnings by farmworkers had increased by 42 percent, but incomes of nonfarm workers had jumped by 122 per-cent, and the ratio of farm to nonfarm earnings had declined from 15 percent to 10 percent in 1970.

The Revival of Forestry

Another important sector of the economy, forestry-related businesses, re-bounded by the 1960s. According to the state Forestry Commission, the growing demand for forest products and the state's newly abundant resources created "the greatest industrial expansion in Mississippi history," with more than 1,200 plants and sawmills and other timber-related businesses contributing more than $800 million annually to the state's economy. This expansion had its origins in actions initiated as early as the Whitfield administration in the mid-1920s. Reversing an-tibusiness policies that had been in place for decades, the legislature had repealed restrictive land laws, encouraged railroad consolidation, and launched reforesta-tion programs.

Reforestation   Two essential elements in the forestry revival were land availabil-ity and reforestation. Until the 1930s the stubborn tradition of cultivating crops on cut-over forestland, the destructive effects of grazing swine and sheep, and fail-ure to manage wild fires had impeded progress in these areas. Interestingly, posi-tive change had finally begun during the years of the Great Depression. Vast tracks of forestland became available when a multitude of landowners, unable to pay mortgages and taxes, forfeited millions of acres in many counties to the state and federal governments. Major reforestation programs then began with the assistance of the Civilian Conservation Corps and the state Forestry Commission. Soon, six national forests were formed, and fire protection programs were launched within the state thanks to an influx of federal funds.

A big step in reforestation had come with the 1940 Severance Tax law, which repealed the old ad valorem tax on timber. Forest lands now had a lower tax assessment, with the timber being taxed only once it was cut and removed from the land. Even better, most of these tax revenues were returned to the counties from which the timber had come. A 1956 law increased this severance tax, and along with county taxes these timber revenues were used to expand fire protection to help protect more than 18 million acres of forest lands by 1970.

Growth of Forest-Related Industries   The forestry revival took off with the emergence of new (or "second") pine forests which, along with timber wastes, were used in the production of paper and fiber-board materials, processes initiated by the Dantzler family and William L. Mason in Laurel. Huge demands and high prices for lumber during Word War II attracted thousands of workers to lumbering jobs and employment in the burgeoning number of pulp and paperwood mills. Their work was facilitated by new mechanical equipment and processes including diesel trucks and other machines, which had replaced mules and oxen. Perhaps more important, using the gasoline-powered chain saw one man could fell as much timber in one day as two men with a cross-cut saw could in a week. The number of cords of pulpwood cut rose to 1.4 million in 1948, a 460 percent increase in just twelve years. It was estimated that in 1948 the forest industry provided jobs for 44 percent of all persons employed in manufacturing and 50 percent of that payroll.

In terms of personal income from manufacturing, the lumber and wood products industries ranked second only to textiles in the 1950s, and forestry and forest-related industries employed about one-half of the state's wage earners. By 1956 mills were paying about $32 million for cords of wood, and the value of paper products was about $50 million. The supply of the forest resources suddenly seemed inexhaustible; for the first time in memory the rate of timber growth exceeded the removal of trees. This trend reversal reflected profitability of the lumber business, which in turn drove the emphasis on reforestation and better land management. Every county in the state comprised a considerable stand of forest, ranging from 11 percent of the land in Sunflower to 86 percent in Stone, and more than 60 percent in forty other counties. Seventy-three percent of the Piney Woods region was timberland, while the only regions to see a decline in the 1950s were the Delta and the northeast. The overall increase was from 16 million acres in 1930 to more than 17 billion acres (57 percent of the state's total land area) in 1958.

Then, early in the 1960s, the development of the process of manufacturing plywood from pine revolutionized the lumber industry. That decade witnessed rapid growth, with additional pulpwood mills, furniture plants, plywood plants, and other related industries beginning operation. These businesses created thousands of new jobs and attracted hundreds of millions in investment dollars. Now,

The lumber industry. Top: NASA photo of Weston Lumber Company in Hancock County, 1928. Middle: Drying kiln at Hankins, Inc., in Tippah County. Courtesy Hankins, Inc. Bottom: Loaded logging truck. Courtesy Mississippi Loggers Association.

large, national and international corporations began to acquire older, local businesses. Georgia-Pacific Corporation of Atlanta, Georgia, bought the Fair Lumber Company at Louisville; the Weyerhaueser Corporation of Tacoma, Washington, bought the DeWeese Lumber Company at Philadelphia; the St. Regis Paper Company of the United Kingdom acquired the Crosby Lumber Company and built a large mill at Monticello; and, the International Paper Company, headquartered in Connecticut—probably the largest single landowner in Mississippi in the early 1970s—expanded its operations.

While lumber was still the largest finished product of the forest industries, the number of paperwood mills in the state also increased rapidly, consuming 48 percent of the timber harvested in 1959. In the 1960s larger sawmills began to replace smaller ones, responding to demands for timber and waste materials for use in the manufacture of paper and particle board. By the late 1960s the volume of timber cut in the state reached an all-time high of 3.3 billion board feet. The following year, however, lumbering activities were devastated by Hurricane Camille, which demolished trees through Hancock, Pearl River, Lamar, and other Piney Woods counties. It was estimated the storm laid waste to about 1.2 billion board feet of timber and about 900,000 cords of pulpwood. This volume of destruction equaled about two years' growth of timber in the state's "second forest" in fifteen counties.

Other Economic Trends

The Office of Federal-State Programs Observers in the 1960s may have been surprised that a state with such antagonism towards federal civil rights policies would pursue so aggressively various forms of assistance from the federal government. On the other hand, they may not have been surprised to learn that thanks to the state's racial prejudice, expressed officially through legislation and policies and private acts of violence, Mississippi saw its economy lag behind that of other states, received only small amounts of sorely needed federal aid, and failed to attract a great deal of capital investments from other sources. To address the situation, in 1968 Governor John Bell Williams established the Office of Federal-State Programs, appointing David R. Bowen as coordinator. With the responsibility of funding programs within the state with federal monies, the new State Office included divisions for Comprehensive Health Planning, Economic Opportunity, Law Enforcement Assistance, Manpower Training, the Governor's Committee on Employment of the Handicapped, as well as others. It also served as the state's Planning and Development Clearinghouse to review and coordinate all federal financial programs.

Industrial Progress In the late 1960s state leaders declared that the long-sought balance between agriculture and industry had finally been achieved. Success had been accomplished in part by a change in policy, as the state began to provide direct assistance to businesses, as opposed to the old BAWI strategy, which had allowed only local governments to borrow funds for industrial development. An example of the new pro-industry policy was the encouragement of economic research and development. The Agricultural and Industrial (A&I) Board was reorganized to comprise the newly created Marketing Council, through which the state would sell industrial products. Industrial acceleration during the administration of Governor Paul B. Johnson, Jr., had resulted in the founding or expansion of 549 plants and the creation of 38,631 new jobs. For the first time in Mississippi, industry was employing more people than agriculture, and by 1970 personal income from manufacturing was 20 percent of the state's total, while farm workers' income amounted to only 7 percent. More than 44,000 workers were employed in textile plants, more than 13,000 in furniture making, and almost 23,000 in lumber and wood products manufacturing.

Under the direction of Fred Bush, Joe Bullock, and Brad Dye during the 1960s the A&I Board had a total membership of twenty-five governmental and business leaders appointed by the governor and ten ex-officio members including the governor, lieutenant governor, speaker of the house, two senators, two representatives, and three other state officials. With origins in the BAWI program, the A&I Board expanded its duties from administering an industrial bond program and supervising the promotion of tourism to broader functions including the development of agricultural industries, the improvements of ports and harbors, and comprehensive public relations. In doing so it cooperated with a number of regional industrial development groups, utility businesses, and railroad companies.

Shipbuilding   One of the fastest growing industries in this period was shipbuilding. Ingalls, which had been building ships at Pascagoula since 1938, was employing almost 4,300 workers when the business was purchased in 1961 by Litton Industries, Inc., based in Woodland Hills, California. To expedite the transaction the legislature authorized public financing for the construction of a new shipyard to be leased to Litton. With voter approval, the local government furnished $1 million for the project, and in 1967 the state government made a lease agreement with Litton and then sold bonds to raise $130 million to build the facility, a debt that would be retired through lease payments by Litton. Following the completion of the building project in 1970, Litton received a United States Navy contract for more than $2 billion. By the end of the year the plant had ten thousand employees. Ultimately, Litton invested almost $95 million in this new project and almost $12 million in the older nuclear shipbuilding plant, also formerly a division of Ingalls.

The System of Transportation

Highways   While the availability of good highways might have been cited to attract new industry, their utter inadequacy proved to be a hindrance. As early as the 1930s, the major stimulus in the state's efforts to overcome transportation deficiencies was federal money. Funds received through the various New Deal programs rose to more than $40 million by 1937, and while the level of this funding increased, the actual costs for construction declined during the Depression years. Through the 1940s federal funds for highways and roads steadily increased, and by 1951 they totaled almost $107 million.

But even greater expenditures were required by the accelerating shift in commerce and travel from railroads to trucks and cars. By 1970 state roads were being used by almost 900,000 automobiles, more than 300,000 trucks, and almost 10,000 buses. For the first time in the state's history, all owners of motor vehicles manufactured or purchased after July 1, 1969, were required by law to apply for a certificate of title (owners of vehicles acquired earlier could apply voluntarily). In the months immediately after this law became effective, the Title Division reported processing about 1,500 applications daily.

To accommodate this transportation revolution, the state steadily increased its share in the costs for highway construction and maintenance. For example, from an incredibly small expenditure of $1,000 in 1917, the Highway Department reported that in 1969 the state's total investment in federal and state highways reached nearly $700 million, in addition to $205 million the state gave to construct or maintain the 14,000 miles of county roads. Between 1950 and 1970 the state highway system (not including county roads) expanded from 4,500 to 9,900 miles, of which 9,400 miles were paved, and 500 miles of which were four-lane highways. This progress was enhanced by construction of the new federal interstate highway system, which began in the 1950s but developed rather slowly in Mississippi. By 1970 about 530 miles of the planned 678 miles in the state had been completed, and 132 miles of interstates were under construction.

Water and Rail   While the transport of freight and passengers by trucks, buses, and automobiles steadily increased on an improving highway system, traffic on the other two traditional means of transportation, water and rail, underwent changes. Rivers and port facilities remained important avenues for heavy freight commerce, but passenger trains were fast disappearing and freight trains were principally used for long hauls. Small industries that had appeared back during the BAWI program depended more on the highways than the rails. An important exception to the withering railroad business was the Illinois Central which, with the most mileage in the state, continued to serve manufacturing plants, forestry-related activities, and agricultural enterprises. In addition to the Illinois Central's almost 2,000 miles of track, the Gulf, Mobile, and Ohio had 852 miles, and as many as ten small intrastate companies were still operating short lines in the late 1960s. But as early as World War II most towns no longer relied primarily on rail connections. By this time total railroad mileage in the state had declined to about 3,600 miles.

A rising volume of freight now was conveyed by water transportation, not so much on the state's rivers but through the state's port facilities. In 1968 the busiest port was the Jackson County Port Authority at Pascagoula, which received 344 ships carrying 12,721,000 tons of cargo, primarily bulk oil for the Standard Oil refinery and grain commodities, an increase of 7.5 percent over the previous year. Revenue derived from the port facilities for the repayment of state bonds amounted to more than $425,000, an increase of 47 percent over 1967.

Another major port, that of Gulfport, which had been owned by the city until its ownership was transferred to the state in 1961, had facilities valued at more than $11 million until hurricane Camille struck the Gulf Coast in 1969. The storm caused an estimated $6.6 million in damages to the Port of Gulfport, which, in the prior year, had handled a total of 820,000 tons of cargo, including bananas, forest and paper products, and fertilizer. After reconstruction, the port resumed operations as a leading port in the state.

Of the state's three Mississippi River ports, Vicksburg remained the busiest because of its location adjacent to the only river bridge between Memphis and Baton Rouge, major intersections of state and interstate highways, the confluence of the Yazoo and Mississippi rivers, and a depot of the Illinois Central railroad. Located in the Delta, with railroad and highway connections and facilities that included warehouses and an industrial park, Greenville served as a customs port of entry and the home base for many towing companies that operated more than 64 towboats and 120 barges. The port and harbor facilities of Natchez also featured warehouses, industrial parks, and highway and railroad connections.

Aviation   A new, twentieth-century means of transportation began in the state during World War I when Payne Flying Field was established at West Point. During World War II several air bases were constructed in the state, including two major pilot-training installations, Keesler Field at Biloxi and the Army Air

Gulfport-Biloxi International Airport. Courtesy Gulfport-Biloxi International Airport.

Field at Columbus. To promote aviation, in 1946 the legislature created the Aeronautics Commission, to which the governor appointed three commissioners, one from each supreme court district.

By the early 1970s three commercial airlines were increasing operations at airports in thirteen towns, including Jackson, Columbus, Tupelo, Laurel, Gulfport, Hattiesburg, and Greenville. Delta Airlines served Jackson and Meridian; Southern Airways, all thirteen airports; and Texas International, only Jackson. With state and federal aid amounting to $24.6 million, a total of sixty-seven public airports and eighty-six private ones were active in the state. The largest airport, serving the largest number of passengers and handling the greatest gross tonnage of freight, was Allen C. Thompson Field (known later as Jackson International Airport), which opened in 1963 in Rankin County near Jackson. In its first seven years the number of passengers boarding through Thompson Field increased from 105,623 to 260,000.

Energy and Communication Resources

Oil and Gas Production   All economic advancement depended in large measure on the availability of fuel, and by mid-century the production of petroleum and

natural gas production had become one of the state's fastest growing businesses. Since 1939, when oil was first discovered in Yazoo County, there had been a steady increase in productivity. By 1970 the state ranked ninth nationally in the volume and value of oil and tenth in natural gas production. During these three decades 5,200 oil-producing wells and 567 gas-producing wells had been drilled in the state.

In 1968 significant oil discoveries occurred in Clarke and Wayne counties, and early in 1969 the Shell Oil Company made an important discovery in Rankin County. The biggest producing oil fields by that year were in the counties of Yazoo, Lamar, Marion, Jasper, Jones, Lincoln, Adams, Pike, Smith, and Wayne. At this time, thirty-one counties were pumping oil or gas or both from a total of 100 wells.

An oil well in Jasper County. Courtesy Derek Zivney.

These operations employed more than 14,000 persons and were yielding annually more than 61 million barrels of crude oil and 136 billion cubit feet of natural gas. The total value of oil and gas production was $184.5 million, with an estimated annual contribution of $505 million to the state's economy.

During the 1960s the state's total consumption of natural gas from all sources doubled, rising to 360 billion cubic feet. This fuel was piped by municipal and privately owned distributors, like Mississippi Valley Gas Company in Jackson, to customers in more than 80 percent of the state's communities by 1970. In the following decade the number of customers rose to 353,000 residences and 40,000 commercial and industrial establishments.

Electric Power   Another vital source of energy was electricity. Acquired from the Tennessee Valley Authority (TVA) or otherwise generated in plants fueled primarily by gas and coal, electric power by the late 1960s was delivered by two types of public utilities, rural associations and municipalities, and two privately owned companies, Mississippi Power and Light (MP&L) and Mississippi Power. Most of the twenty-six locally owned and managed rural electric power associations and fourteen municipalities bought wholesale power from TVA. Established by the federal government in 1933 during the Great Depression, the TVA constructed dams and generating facilities along the Tennessee River that supplied electricity throughout northeast Mississippi and to other states as well. With substantial financial assistance from the federal Rural Electrification Administration, the electric power associations served 284,000 customers in more than three hundred communities covering thirty-five counties.

Responding to the growing demand for electricity in the changing economy, the two major private companies expanded rapidly. Since its beginning MP&L had invested $307 million to extend its services to more than 216,000 customers in forty-five western counties, and Mississippi Power had spent $219 million to enlarge its customer base to 132,000 in twenty-three southeastern counties. By 1970 virtually all Mississippians used in their homes, shops, and farms—and even took for granted—electric power, a source of energy that had not been available to most of them only four decades earlier.

Communications   Perhaps the most significant technological innovations of the mid-twentieth century came in communications. South Central Bell Telephone, formerly Southern Bell, increased its number of customers from 234,000 in 1956 to 451,000 in 1968. More than 32,000 other telephone customers were served by twenty-three independent companies in the state. Despite this expansion, which placed thirty-one telephones in the hands of every 100 persons and service in 62 percent of all households, Mississippi still lagged behind all other southern states.[2] Within the next five years, however, the number of telephones in service more than doubled.

By the early 1970s most folks had radios and regularly tuned into at least one of the state's 133 stations. Increasingly new automobiles and trucks came equipped with radios, but in the home, radios were gradually replaced as the main source of broadcast entertainment. Television came to Mississippi in the 1950s, and by 1970 nine TV stations were in operation. At first televisions were reserved

2 The national averages were 52 telephones per 100 persons and service for 88 percent of all households.

Governor William Waller. Courtesy Mississippi Department of Archives and History.

mainly for those families who could afford the relatively expensive equipment, usually including an outside antenna, and who lived within range of a broadcasting station. This new phenomenon, however, would expand rapidly and further revolutionize virtually every aspect of society. With the introduction of cable service and cost reductions for the television sets, increasing numbers of households managed to justify the extra expense.

Overall Economic Status

At mid-century Mississippi made steady albeit slow progress in attracting new industries and boosting agricultural production. By 1970 the state's overall per capita income had risen to $2,641, more than double the 1960 figure and three and one-half times higher than the 1950 amount of only $755. In spite of this growth, however, the per capita income was a mere 64.5 percent of the national average, ranking Mississippi behind all other states.

What caused Mississippi's low per capita income? The answer includes many leadership mistakes over the decades: for example, distrust of corporations in general and antibusiness policies in particular, resistance to agricultural diversification, failure to foresee the necessity of reforestation, and tardiness in transportation improvements. Other significant obstacles were related to the state's failure to address properly the persisting racial issues: for example, the high level of adult illiteracy, a symptom of an inadequate system of education; and the emigration of workers, primarily African Americans. Between 1950 and 1970, one-fifth of the 1950 population, about 454,000 persons, left the state. Preoccupation with civil rights issues, therefore, had seriously handicapped efforts to raise Mississippians' standard of living and help them keep pace with the economic progress made in other states.

A TRANSITION IN POLITICS

Governor William Lowe Waller, 1972–1976

Elections of 1971   In some ways the gubernatorial election of 1971 might be considered as a turning point in Mississippi politics. In this contest the voters actually rejected outspoken segregationist candidates and, for the first time since the Civil War, the leading contenders refrained from explicitly injecting race into the campaign. Other elements of the new political era included the election of African Americans and women to public office and the rise of the Republican party. The nation's ratification of the Twenty-sixth Amendment to the United States Constitution in July 1971 allowing persons eighteen years of age or older to vote was another factor. The Mississippi legislature did not approve the federal amendment but instead proposed a similar amendment to the state constitution, which was favored by 80 percent of the voters in the general election of 1972.

Of the seven Democrats who entered the gubernatorial contest the leaders in the first primary were Charles Sullivan with 288,219 votes and William L. Waller with 227,424 votes. A distant third place was taken by Jimmy Swan, a country music singer from Hattiesburg known as a white supremacist, who had been a candidate in 1967. In the second primary Waller won the nomination with 54 percent of the votes and then faced two very different independent candidates in the general election, Charles Evers and state circuit court judge Thomas P. Brady, an outspoken segregationist for the Citizens' Council in the 1960s. Waller easily prevailed, with Evers finishing second, with 22 percent of the votes, and Brady receiving a paltry total of less than 6,700 votes.

In the race for the office of lieutenant governor, William Winter was nominated in the first primary, defeating two other candidates including future governor Charles C. "Cliff" Finch. Winter, who faced no opposition in the general election, came to the office with twenty-four years of continuous experience in state government, before his unsuccessful gubernatorial campaign against John Bell Williams in 1967. A native of Grenada, Winter had served in the United States Army during World War II and the Korean War and, while still in law school, had been elected to the state house of representatives in 1947. Following two terms in the legislature, he had served as state tax collector (1956–64) and state treasurer (1964–68).

Governor Waller   Born in Lafayette County near Oxford, in the "Hills" region, Bill Waller served in the Korean War before practicing law in Jackson and serving two terms as district attorney in Hinds County. Illustrative of the ironies of state politics in this era, Waller managed to draw support from both factions of the changing Democratic party—the all-white "Regulars" and the "Loyalists," a coalition of the African American "Freedom Democrats" and moderate whites who supported the national party.

Although he had taken segregationist positions in the past, Waller now portrayed himself as a "populist," angling for support from African Americans. He had considerable name recognition among the former voters as the aggressive prosecutor of Medgar Evers's killer, Byron de la Beckwith, in 1964. On the other hand, Waller received key support from Senator Eastland, the godfather of the "Regular" Democrats and a nationally known arch enemy of civil rights. Eastland decided to favor Waller partly because of reports that Charles Sullivan, Waller's opponent, had "softened" on the race issue in order to get the backing of Aaron Henry, the African American leader of the state chapter of the NAACP, and the "Loyalist" Democrats. But Waller, apparently a better negotiator than Sullivan, managed to keep Eastland's support and win over the Loyalists as well by making private pledges to African Americans during the campaign. He promised to appoint blacks to certain offices, offer them positions on the party's state executive committee, and support a greater number of them as delegates to the national convention in 1972.

Recognized as the state's first governor to pursue actively the inclusion of African Americans and women in government, Waller established a Minority Advisory

Evelyn Gandy. Courtesy Mississippi Department of Archives and History.

Committee and a Status of Women's Commission. In 1974 he appointed Constance Slaughter-Harvey, an African American civil rights attorney, to the Minority Advisory Committee. Waller was also widely commended for his veto of funding for the Sovereignty Commission in 1973, thus acknowledging the end of legal segregation in the state.

Most of the state's executive department officials during Waller's term were incumbents, including Secretary of State Heber Ladner, Attorney General Albioun F. Summer, Superintendent of Education Garvin Johnston, Auditor Hampton King, and Commissioner of Agriculture and Commerce Jim Buck Ross. Bradford J. "Brad" Dye, Jr., a newcomer to an elected statewide position, was state treasurer, and Evelyn Gandy was commissioner of insurance. Gandy, a native of Forrest County, had practiced law in Hattiesburg before winning election to the state house of representatives in 1947. The first woman in Mississippi elected to statewide office, she also served terms as state treasurer (1960–64, and 1968–72) and as commissioner of public welfare during the administration of Governor Johnson.

The Congressional Elections of 1972   Even though Senator Eastland prevailed by relatively wide margins in his bid for reelection in 1972, for the first time in his long career he faced meaningful challenges. His two Democratic opponents managed to get 23 percent of the primary votes, and in the general election Republican Gil Carmichael of Meridian received 39 percent of the votes. Interestingly, Carmichael had won his party's nomination in a primary contest with James H. Meredith, whose name was known nationally as the first African American to integrate the state's educational institutions in 1962. The votes cast in that Republican primary totaled only 23,228, with Meredith receiving 21 percent. What was significant, however, was Carmichael's attack on the Regular Democrats, whom he blamed for the state's economic backwardness. Appealing to white and black voters as a businessman who would bring greater opportunities to all citizens regardless of race, Carmichael was accused of being too "liberal" by Eastland supporters.

Following the legislature's reconfiguration of the congressional districts in 1972, major changes occurred in the state's membership in the House of Representatives. Three Democratic party incumbents retired, including long-time Congressmen Abernethy and Colmer as well as Charles Griffin, who had succeeded John Bell Williams in 1968. Nine Democrats competed to replace Abernathy in the Second District (formerly the First), which now included the north central counties extending across the state from east to west. Former Congressman Frank Smith was edged out of the second primary by Tom Cook and David R. Bowen, and the party's nomination was won by Bowen, who had been the state coordinator of the Office of Federal-State Programs.

In the new Fourth District (formerly the Third), which extended from Hinds and Warren counties into the southwestern corner of the state, six candidates campaigned to replace Griffin. The leaders in the first primary were Ellis Bodron, the unsighted state senator from Vicksburg, and Walter Brown, the state representative from Natchez. In a close runoff, Bodron gained the nomination with 51 percent of the votes. For William M. Colmer's seat in the reconfigured Fifth District (now the southeastern counties, including the Gulf Coast) ten candidates entered the race. The leader in the first primary, state senator Ben Stone, went on to win the nomination, narrowly defeating Howard Patterson in the runoff.

Three of the five Democratic nominees faced strong Republican opponents in the general election. Bowen easily defeated Carl Butler, but Republicans Thad Cochran and Trent Lott were elected in the Fourth and Fifth districts respectively. Cochran, who received 48 percent to Bodron's 44 percent of the total vote, was helped by the independent candidacy of Eddie McBride, who got almost 12,000 votes. Lott won a more convincing victory, receiving 55 percent of the vote to defeat Stone. As a result, Mississippi would have three new, young congressmen who had not previously been elected to public office. And for the first time in almost a century, the state's congressional delegation would include two Republicans and only two returning Democrats, Jamie Whitten and Sonny Montgomery.

The Presidential Election of 1972   In what would later be known as a prelude to the Watergate scandal that finally forced the resignation of President Richard Nixon, the Republicans also achieved a significant victory in the presidential election of 1972. The uncovering of illegal activities—some of which occurred in offices in the Watergate building in Washington—that Nixon authorized during the campaign brought down his Vietnam-War embattled administration in 1974. But in 1972, Mississippi voters cast more than 505,000 votes, 78 percent for Nixon who won reelection in a landslide with 61 percent of the nation's popular votes and 97 percent of the electoral college. Democrats George McGovern and Sargent Shriver received only 126,782 votes in Mississippi.

The Congressional Elections of 1974   In the 1974 congressional elections all five incumbents were easily reelected. Montgomery faced no opposition in the primary or the general election, and Whitten had no difficulty with an independent challenger. In the other districts the contests were more interesting but not close. Democrat Bowen won 66 percent of the votes, winning over a Republican and an Independent, while Republicans Cochran and Lott prevailed by closer margins against Democratic and Independent challengers.

Governor Cliff Finch, 1976–1980
The Elections of 1975   Six Democrats participated in the 1975 gubernatorial primary, including Columbia lawyer Maurice Dantin, Jackson lawyer John Arthur Eaves, Cliff Finch, and Lieutenant Governor William Winter. In the first primary Winter emerged as the leader followed by Finch. The second primary played out like a rematch of their race for lieutenant governor four years earlier, but now the stakes were higher and the strategies taken different. Ultimately, as had happened so often in Democratic primaries for governor, the frontrunner met defeat in the second primary. Campaigning with a lunchbox and portraying himself as the candidate of the ordinary working people and his opponent as a "liberal," Finch won

the party's nomination by a comfortable margin, receiving 58 percent of the votes. In the general election Finch received 52 percent of all votes cast to defeat Republican Gil Carmichael and Independent Henry J. Kirksey, an African American candidate from Jackson.

In the Democratic primary for lieutenant governor the six candidates were led by Commissioner of Insurance Evelyn Gandy, State Treasurer Brad Dye, and Jim Herring, an attorney from Canton. The outcome of the first primary was very close among Gandy, the leader, Dye, and Herring. Gandy prevailed over Dye in the second primary, receiving 53 percent of the votes, and went on to defeat Republican Bill Patrick by a wide margin in the general election, becoming the first woman to serve as lieutenant governor of Mississippi.

The elections of 1975 were particularly significant because for the first time in the twentieth century Republican candidates participated in most statewide elections—all but the races for superintendent of public education and commissioner of agriculture and commerce. They also entered twelve state senate and twenty-eight house contests but won only two and three seats respectively. Interestingly, three of the five Republican legislators hailed from the predominately white Piney Woods county of Jones, including future federal judge Charles W. Pickering, who was elected to the senate. The newcomers elected to state executive offices—all Democrats—included Superintendent of Education Charles E. Holladay of Newton County, State Treasurer Edwin Lloyd Pittman of Forrest County, and Commissioner of Insurance George Dale of Jefferson Davis County.

Governor Finch   Cliff Finch was a native of Pope and had attended the public schools of Panola County. A veteran of World War II, he had earned a law degree at the University of Mississippi and practiced law in Batesville. After representing Panola County in the state house of representatives from 1960 to 1964, he served two terms as district attorney in Panola County. A new populist without the old racist baggage, Finch followed Governor Waller's example of appealing to minorities but went further in aggressively supporting the national Democratic party. He led the reunification of the "Loyalist" and all-white "Regular" factions in the state party, which had refused to cooperate in presidential elections beginning in 1964. Under Finch's leadership a united delegation led by co-chairs representing both races attended the Democratic national convention in 1976 and supported the successful nomination of Governor Jimmy Carter of Georgia. In July 1977 Governor Finch introduced President Carter during his visits to Jackson and Yazoo City.

The governor heightened his populist image through actions he declared would protect the interests of all working people, such as his efforts to avert a financial crisis involving the state's savings and loan associations and his support for legislation transferring control of sixteenth-section lands from county boards of supervisors to local boards of education and requiring leases at fair-market values. The governor's ambitions for national political office would lead him to enter the U.S. Senate race in 1978 and campaign as a presidential candidate in 1980. Occasionally appearing at construction sites wearing a hard hat and operating tractors during these campaigns, Finch attracted widespread attention but an insufficient number of votes.

White supremacists like Richard Barrett were outraged by the willingness of "scalawag Governor Finch" to accept and cooperate with African Americans.

Particularly objectionable to segregationists was the governor's selection of blacks for important positions and honors, including, for example, their appointment to membership in the traditional body of governor's "colonels." One such member was the Reverend John E. Cameron, pastor of Greater Mount Calvary Baptist Church in Jackson, who had been active in the 1960s civil rights movement at the side of Martin Luther King, Jr.

The Presidential Election of 1976 Finch's leadership contributed to the Democratic party's success in the presidential election of 1976. For the first time since 1956 the nominee of the national Democratic party won the state's seven electoral votes, although the victory was an extremely narrow one. Jimmy Carter received 381,309 votes (49.6 percent of all votes cast), while the Republican candidate, President Gerald Ford, got 366,846 votes (47.7 percent). Less than 3 percent of the state's votes were cast for the five independent candidates, including Lester Maddox, the former governor of Georgia known as a rabid segregationist, and Eugene McCarthy, the former U.S. Senator from Minnesota and leader of anti–Vietnam War groups. Nationally the election's outcome was as close as were the Mississippi results, with Carter winning 50 percent of the popular vote and 55 percent of electoral college.

The Congressional Elections of 1976 In contrast to the presidential election, Mississippi's congressional races aroused little excitement. Senator Stennis was nominated with 85 percent of the primary vote and ran unopposed in the general election. All five incumbent representatives were unopposed in the primaries, but in the general election, except for Whitten, they encountered a variety of candidates representing Democrats, Republicans, and third parties. Nonetheless, the three Democratic and two Republican incumbents all won landslide victories in their respective districts.

The Election of Senator Eastland's Successor Following Senator Eastland's retirement announcement, seven Democrats entered the party's first primary for the U.S. Senate in June 1978. The field included such prominent politicians as Governor Finch and former governor Bill Waller, along with former gubernatorial candidates Charles Sullivan and Maurice Dantin. The leaders were Dantin with 103,301 votes followed by Governor Finch with 98,662; in the second primary Dantin held his position and gained enough support to win the nomination with more than 65 percent of the votes.

In the general election, however, Dantin was unsuccessful against Republican Congressman Thad Cochran, who had won the party's nomination over state senator Charles Pickering. The presence of two independent candidates, Charles Evers and Henry Kirksey, defeated Dantin, as Cochran received 45 percent of the total vote, Dantin 32 percent, and Evers 23 percent. Significantly, the seat occupied by Eastland for thirty-six years would now belong to Mississippi's first Republican senator since 1881. This break with the past demonstrated not only the growing white support for Republican candidates but also the extent to which Mississippi Democrats relied on the African American vote. Absent Evers's candidacy, black voters would have united behind Dantin, guaranteeing him a big victory.

The Congressional Elections of 1978 In future elections the Democrats' tenuous biracial coalition would continue to threaten the party's chances for success.

An immediate example occurred in the following year. In the 1978 primaries for the House of Representatives, four incumbents were nominated, but in the Fourth District, the seat vacant due to Cochran's candidacy for the Senate, there was keen competition for the nomination in both parties. Of the seven Democrats who entered the race, the party nominated John Hampton Stennis, a state legislator and son of Senator Stennis. His Republican opponent in the general election was Jon Hinson, who had defeated three others for that party's nomination. Attracting most of the white voters, Hinson was elected with fewer than 52 percent of the total votes cast. The Democrats divided their support among Stennis (26 percent), Evan Doss, an independent African American candidate (19 percent), and two other independents. The other Republican congressman, Trent Lott, was reelected without opposition, and the three Democratic incumbents easily defeated their Republican challengers. The year, however, was significant for the state's Republican party, which had fielded candidates in every congressional district, retained their two seats in the House, and accomplished an historic victory for a place in the Senate.

Amendments to the State Constitution   Voters in this 1978 general election also approved several constitutional amendments designed to remove archaic provisions by repealing Section 19, which had prohibited dueling, Section 187, which had required railroads to pass through county seats, and Section 105, which had required a state decennial census. But the most important amendment, the repealing Section 207, which had required the maintenance of racially separate schools since 1890, was approved by 71 percent of the voters, including favorable majorities in every county. This result, however, was remarkable not in its passage, but rather because there was still a significant body of voters unwilling to express on the ballot their acceptance of an action already accomplished by federal law. Whether this vote was a portent of more strife or merely a reminder of a lingering resistance to change remained to be seen.

SELECTED SOURCES

Biographical Directory of the United States Congress, 1774 to Present (Washington, D.C.: Government Printing Office, 2003, http://bioguide.congress.gov.

Clark, Thomas D. "Changes in Transportation," in Richard Aubrey McLemore, ed., *A History of Mississippi*, 2 vols. (Hattiesburg: University & College Press of Mississippi, 1973), 2: 274–311.

Giles, William Lincoln, "Agricultural Revolution, 1890–1970," in Richard Aubrey McLemore, ed., *A History of Mississippi*, 2 vols. (Hattiesburg: University & College Press of Mississippi, 1973), 2: 177–211.

Hickman, Nollie W., "Mississippi Forests," in Richard Aubrey McLemore, ed., *A History of Mississippi*, 2 vols. (Hattiesburg: University & College Press of Mississippi, 1973), 2: 217–223.

Historical Statistics of the States of the United States: Two Centuries of the Census, 1790–1990, comp. Donald B. Dodd (Westport, Conn.: Greenwood Press, 1993), Population.

Lamis, Alexander P., *The Two-Party South* (New York: Oxford University Press, 1984).

Mississippi Official and Statistical Register, 1968–1972, 1972–1976, 1976–1980, 1980–1984.

Mitchell, Dennis J., *Mississippi Liberal: A Biography of Frank E. Smith* (Jackson: University Press of Mississippi, 2001).

Rogers, Ralph J., "The Effort to Industrialize," in Richard Aubrey McLemore, ed., *A History of Mississippi,* 2 vols. (Hattiesburg: University & College Press of Mississippi, 1973), 2: 233–249.

United States Department of Commerce, Bureau of Economic Analysis. *Regional Accounts Data: Annual State Personal Income. SA05 Personal Income by Major Source and Earnings by Industry—Mississippi, 1960, 1964, 1970* (www.bea.gov/bea/regional/spi/action.cfm).

CHAPTER TWENTY-FOUR

The Social Environment

RECREATION

Mississippians may have been interested in politics, but most people found that other pressing issues, such as jobs, places of residence, physical health, social relationships, and living conditions in general, demanded most of their attention. In their leisure time, if any, they looked for enjoyable and enriching activities that might lessen the anxieties of daily life. As economic and social circumstances in the state shifted rapidly during the late twentieth century, an increasing number of Mississippians began to participate in a wide range of pastime activities.

Such recreational pursuits included, for example, visiting one of the many public libraries. The state Library Commission developed fifty regional systems, many of which comprised a number of community libraries, covering the entire state and making books and other reading materials, audio recordings, videocassettes, and computers with Internet connections easily accessible to nearly every resident.

While reading appealed to a substantial number of people, more of them preferred outdoor forms of recreation, such as camping at a state or national park, boating and fishing in the many rivers, lakes, or the coastal waters of the Gulf, and hunting wildlife on private club property or public lands. The Department of Wildlife, Fisheries, and Parks (formerly the Game and Fish Commission) oversaw twenty-one lakes, encompassing a total of 5,111 acres and containing some 175 different species of freshwater fish. Large numbers of persons regularly visited the Gulf Coast for saltwater fishing, which might involve angling for redfish and speckled trout from piers or white shark, red snapper, and Spanish and king mackerel from boats.

Similarly, Mississippians found ample hunting opportunities, even if they could not afford to join a private club. The state contained more than 800,000 acres of game habitat in thirty-eight Wildlife Management Areas, touching every county. According to the Department of Wildlife, Fisheries, and Parks, "these areas offer unspoiled woodlands, fields and marshes filled with big and small game," including large populations of white-tail deer, wild turkeys, and ducks.

Whether one engaged in hunting and fishing or not, most family members either participated in or attended a variety of athletic activities—ranging from little league baseball and youth soccer programs to college and professional

University of Southern Mississippi–Jackson State University football game at Roberts Stadium in Hattiesburg, 1987. Courtesy University of Southern Mississippi. Photograph by King Photo.

events. Each season, hundreds of thousands of Mississippians attended football, basketball, and baseball games at local high schools and the state universities and private colleges. Avid sports fans far and wide faithfully followed their teams' performances via the newspaper, radio, and television, pulling for the "Braves" of Alcorn University, the "Tigers" of Jackson State University, the "Bulldogs" of Mississippi State University, the "Rebels" of Ole Miss, the "Eagles" of the University of Southern Mississippi, and the other college teams in the state.

Interested youths, dreaming of professional contracts someday, had a virtually endless list of models to emulate, depending on the sport, college, or professional team. In football, for example, they admired such legends as Charles Connerly and "Shorty" McWilliams in the 1940s, Eagle Day and Jackie Parker in the 1950s, Willie Richardson and Willie Brown in the 1960s, as well as Walter Payton, Archie Manning, Ray Guy, and Jerry Rice in succeeding years.

The state's hall of fame baseball players included men such as Clark R. "Dudy" Noble; Willie Mitchell, the first Mississippian to play in the major leagues (1919); James Thomas "Cool Papa" Bell and Bill Foster, both stars of the Negro National League as early as the 1920s; "Skeeter Webb," "Dizzy" Dean, David "Boo" Ferris, and Don Kissinger. Basketball greats included Margaret Wade, a tennis champion in college who later gained acclaim as a basketball coach, James "Babe" McCarthy, Bailey Howell, W. D. "Red" Stroud, Dot Murphy, Lusia Harris, and Purvis Short.

In other sports Mississippi produced champions such as Slew Hester in tennis, Hunter George Weddington and Mary B. Mills in golf, and Ralph H. Boston and Larry Myricks in track and field. Boston, a world record holder in the long jump, won medals in three successive Olympic Games in the 1960s, and Myricks began a four-time Olympian stint in the same event in the 1970s and 1980s.

Finally, beginning in the 1990s, an increasing number of people expanded their seemingly unquenchable desire for "gaming" by taking up gambling at the newly established casinos along the Gulf Coast and Mississippi River.

POPULATION TRENDS

Population Growth

After the Civil War the population of Mississippi grew rapidly, from 828,000 persons in 1870 to more than 1.5 million in 1900, an increase of 87 percent. But in the twentieth century increases were small in comparison to other states. The first decennial census to report a decline in the state's history was in 1920, when it was revealed that Mississippi had lost 0.4 percent since 1910. Relatively small increases between 1920 and 1940 gave the state a population of 2,183,796, but during the next three decades it experienced virtually no growth. The 1970 census reported 2,216,912 residents, a net increase of only 33,116 in thirty years, but in the last three decades of the century the population rose by 28 percent, reaching 2,844,658 persons in 2000.

Mississippi's ranking fell from twentieth in 1900 to thirty-first in 2000, with the pace of national population growth (14 percent) almost twice that of the state (6.4 percent). Among the many important results of this relatively slow growth was that the state's number of representatives to the Congress declined by 50 percent (from eight to four) in the twentieth century through the 2000 census.[1]

The Racial Makeup   Beginning in the antebellum period and continuing through the 1930s, most inhabitants of the state were African American. The first decennial census to report a white majority was in 1940, when whites composed 50.7 percent of the total population. In the following decades, large numbers of blacks continued to emigrate from the state, their proportion steadily declined to 35.2 percent in 1980, and at the end of the century it was 36.3 percent.

In "A Poem for Myself (or Blues for a Mississippi Black Boy)"[2] Etheridge Knight relates his experience of being "born black in Mississippi." In the rhythm of the blues, he remembers leaving then returning to the place where he had walked "barefooted thru the mud."

> Going back to Mississippi
> This time to stay for good—
> Gonna be free in Mississippi
> Or dead in the Mississippi mud.

The first drop in the number of black residents occurred in the 1910s (7.4 percent), contributing to the state's overall population decline that decade. But between 1940 and 1970 the number of African Americans in the state fell by 259,000 persons, a 24 percent rate of decline, while the number of whites increased by 26 percent. During the final three decades of the century, however, the number of blacks rose by 28 percent, whites by 25 percent.

1 See Appendix IV, Total Population, 1800–2000.
2 Etheridge Knight, "A Poem for Myself (or Blues for a Mississippi Black Boy)," as quoted in Dorothy Abbott, ed., *Mississippi Writers: Reflections of Childhood and Youth*, vol. 3, *Poetry* (Jackson: University Press of Mississippi, 1988), 163.

The fastest population increases in the twentieth century were among persons of other races (predominately Asian Americans and American Indians), whose numbers rose steadily from 2,026 in 1930 to 64,750 in 2000, when they composed 2.3 percent of the total population. Of the nearly 19,000 Asian Americans in Mississippi at the end of the twentieth century, those of Vietnamese descent comprised the largest group (28 percent), having begun to enter the state in the 1980s. Most first- and second-generation Vietnamese Americans resided in the Gulf Coast counties and engaged primarily in the fishing industry, one of the popular occupations of their homeland. The other two largest groups of Asians were the Chinese (16 percent) and the Asian Indians (20 percent). The former people, whose ancestors had first come to Mississippi more a century earlier, lived mainly in the Delta, where many of them operated mercantile businesses. Asian Indians resided in urban centers throughout the state and engaged in commercial and professional pursuits.

American Indians in Mississippi, virtually all of whom were Choctaws, numbered only about 12,000 persons in 2000. More than 170 years earlier, after the federal government forcibly removed the Choctaws to present-day Oklahoma, a number of them—perhaps as many as six thousand of the tribes' total population of 20,000—had remained in their historic homeland, primarily Winston and Neshoba counties in east central Mississippi. But the government failed to fulfill the terms of the removal treaty (Dancing Rabbit Creek), which promised parcels of land to Choctaws who stayed in the state. The ensuing economic hardships, social isolation, discrimination, and civil disfranchisement caused their numbers to decline steadily, as groups migrated to Oklahoma. Finally, in the early twentieth century, following a disastrous outbreak of influenza, the Federal Bureau of Indian Affairs established the Choctaw Indian Agency in Neshoba County to provide

Family vacation on the Gulf Coast. Courtesy Mississippi Development Authority/Division of Tourism.

Choctaw women and children in traditional dress. Courtesy Mississippi Department of Archives and History. Photograph by D. C. Young.

health and educational assistance. During World War II the federal government established the Choctaw Reservation and officially recognized the Mississippi Band of Choctaws as a legal entity with an elected tribal council. Despite their long-lasting tribulations, the Choctaws preserved their rich culture, including their original language, which is still spoken by most members of the tribe, traditional crafts featuring weaving and quilting, and even their historic dances and games. And beginning in the 1980s under the leadership of Chief Philip Martin, the Choctaws launched several successful business enterprises, including two casinos in Neshoba County, projects further described in Chapter Twenty-Seven.

A summary of these twentieth-century population trends reveals that the net increase for the total population was 1,293,388 (83.4 percent); for African Americans it was 126,179 (13.9 percent), for whites it was 1,104,899 (172.3 percent), and for other races 62,310 (2,553.7 percent). The average per-decade increase for the total population was 7.7 percent, including 3.6 percent for African Americans, 11.3 percent for whites, and 45.6 percent for the other races.[3]

Redistribution-Urban Growth   During the twentieth century the population was redistributed in two significant ways. One was the rise of an urban population, and the other involved regional shifts. The proportion of Mississippians residing in urban places increased from 7.7 percent in 1900 to almost 49 percent in 2000. The fastest urban development occurred in the first half of the century, rising more than 400 percent. The rate of growth in the second half slowed to 128 percent, but in this period four major metropolitan areas developed.[4]

Beginning with the 1950 census, Jackson was designated as the state's first "metropolitan statistical area" (MSA) with a population of about 100,000 residents in the city and adjacent parts of Hinds County. When outlying areas of Rankin County were included, the total Jackson MSA population rose to 259,000 in 1970 and to 362,000 in 1980. The neighboring community in Madison County was added to the Jackson MSA in the next decade, raising the entire MSA to 395,000 in 1990 and 441,000 by the end of the century.

In the meantime, a second MSA emerged along the Gulf Coast, with Biloxi-Gulfport qualifying as one by 1970. Including adjacent parts of Harrison County, Biloxi-Gulfport reported a population of 135,000, which rose to 192,000 by 1980, with the inclusion of communities in Hancock and Stone counties. Pascagoula–Moss Point in Jackson County, with a population of 118,000, was designated as a separate MSA in 1980. But after this area experienced no gains in the 1980s, Pascagoula was put into the Biloxi-Gulfport MSA, and with outlying communi-

3 See Appendix V, Racial Population Changes, 1800–2000.
4 See Table 24.1, Urban Population, 1890–2000.

TABLE 24.1 Urban Population, 1890–2000

YEAR	MISSISSIPPI URBAN POPULATION	PERCENT OF TOTAL POPULATION	CHANGE	UNITED STATES PERCENT OF TOTAL POPULATION
1890	69,966	5.4%		
1900	120,035	7.7	71.6%	39.6%
1910	207,311	11.5	72.7	45.6
1920	240,121	13.4	15.8	51.2
1930	338,850	16.9	41.1	56.1
1940	432,882	19.8	27.8	56.5
1950	607,162	27.9	40.3	64.0
1900–1950			405.8	
1960	820,805	37.7	35.2	69.9
1970	986,642	44.5	20.2	73.6
1980	1,192,805	47.3	20.9	73.7
1990	1,210,729	47.1	1.5	75.2
2000	1,387,351	48.8	14.6	
1950–2000			128.5	

SOURCE: *United States Bureau of the Census, Urban and Rural Population, 1995 (census.gov/ population/censusdata/urbpop0090.txt); Mississippi Official and Statistical Register [various dates]; Mississippi Statistical Abstract [various dates].*

ties in Hancock, Harrison, and Jackson counties, this metropolitan area had a total population of 364,000 residents in 2000.

Two other metropolitan centers were De Soto County, which became part of the Memphis MSA in 1973, and Hattiesburg with adjacent places in Forrest and Lamar counties, which were added to the Hattiesburg MSA in 1994. Though relatively small, De Soto County—mainly the town of Southhaven, a suburb of Memphis—was the state's fastest growing county at the end of the century, having doubled its population in twenty years. The Hattiesburg MSA reported 112,000 residents in 2000. In the 1990s the number of people residing in all metropolitan areas increased by 32 percent, reaching 36 percent of the state's total population by 2000.

Despite the growth of such metropolitan areas, however, Mississippi remained less urban than most other states. Less than half of the state's inhabitants occupied urban places, in contrast to more than 75 percent of the total United States population at the end of the century. Mississippi had only thirty-seven municipalities with more than 10,000 residents, and fourteen of them were adjacent to or within the four Metropolitan Statistical Areas, including the state's four largest cities—Jackson (184,256), Gulfport (71,127), Biloxi (50,644), and Hattiesburg (44,779). The largest towns outside the MSAs were Greenville, which ranked fifth in the state (41,633), followed by Meridian (39,968), Tupelo (34,211), Vicksburg (26,407), and Columbus (25,944).

One reason for the lack of noticeable growth by many of these leading towns was the movement of many of their residents to the county suburbs. Although this "flight" was mostly white, urban populations remained predominately white until late in the century due to the earlier exodus of blacks from the state. In most towns with populations greater than 2,500, whites retained majorities, although African Americans averaged higher percentages in towns (42 percent) than they did statewide (36 percent). The rising number of urban blacks rendered important changes in Mississippi. On the positive side, African Americans now had greater opportunities for economic advancement and independence. Not only did they move to higher positions in white-owned businesses, often reaching managerial levels, but black entrepreneurs now began to open their own companies. They bought homes, and their children attended better schools. An increasing number of African Americans won municipal elections, and many accepted appointments to leadership positions in city governments. On the other hand, de facto racial segregation became even more entrenched in neighborhoods and schools, as whites moved to suburbs and sent their children to private schools. Reminiscent of nineteenth-century patterns, whites sometimes stereotyped African American officials as incompetent and fraudulent administrators who could not control crime and resolve other urban problems.

Regional Redistribution   In addition to urban growth, another population trend in the late twentieth century redistributed the numbers of inhabitants among the three traditional geographic regions of the state—the southern, central, and northern counties. Between 1970 and 2000 the southern third of the state had the highest growth rate, about 36 percent, rising to almost 975,000. Led by the Gulf Coast area counties of Harrison, Jackson, Pearl River, and Hancock, and by Forrest, Jones and Lamar counties, this region moved ahead of the other sections of the state in total population.

The central group of counties, which had the largest population in 1970, developed at a slower rate than did the other sections, and it fell to second place. Led by Hinds, Rankin, Lauderdale, Madison, and Washington counties, this section's population increased to 950,000, a rate of 21.5 percent, well below the state's overall growth rate of 28.3 percent. Hinds County, for example, had increases in the 1970s and 1980s but declined in the 1990s.

The northern section had the second biggest increase, as its population rose to more than 920,000, a growth rate of 28 percent. The leading counties in this section were De Soto, Lee, Lowndes, and Oktibbeha.

HEALTH CARE

State Agencies

From its limited functions in the late nineteenth century, the state Board of Health acquired virtual independence from political interference, exercised regulatory powers, and oversaw a major, multilevel state agency, the state Department of Health. As executive officer of the board for thirty-four years, from 1924 until his death early in 1959, Dr. Felix J. Underwood was the principal leader in the expansion of the state's public health services. Inducted posthumously into the Mississippi Hall of Fame in 1996, Dr. Underwood, recognized as "perhaps the most outstanding physician Mississippi has ever produced," was praised for his many accomplishments, including free immunizations, the fluoridation of public drinking water, and substantial strides in the state's battle against such diseases as syphilis, tuberculosis, malaria, polio, and diphtheria.

During his tenure public health services were established in every county. By the 1950s the county health departments provided comprehensive services in the areas of communicable diseases, sanitation, maternal and pediatric care, vital statistics, medical laboratories, health education, and chronic diseases. In succeeding decades the state Department of Health steadily extended its programs to virtually every community in the state. The growing list of its functions included the licensure and certification of health professionals and health facilities, family planning services, the genetic screening of newborns, and well-child health services.

Institutions   A century after their founding, the state institutions for sightless and deaf persons, the "School for the Blind" and the "School for the Deaf," were moved into adjoining campuses in the northeastern part of Jackson at Highway 51 and Eastover Drive. Construction of the new facilities began with an appropriation of $2.4 million in 1946, and the new facilities opened in 1951. By the end of the century each institution provided accredited programs and other services for more than 150 children from preschool through high school.

The state also expanded its facilities for the treatment of persons with mental illnesses. Through the first half of the twentieth century the major facilities were the State Hospital at Whitfield in Rankin County, which had its origins in the antebellum era, and East Mississippi State Hospital in Meridian, established in 1928. By the late twentieth century inpatient services were provided through two regional comprehensive psychiatric hospitals (Whitfield and Meridian) and two new regional acute psychiatric hospitals for adults, the North Mississippi State Hospital in Tupelo and the South Mississippi State Hospital in Purvis. A fifth regional facility was the Ellisville State School in Jones County, originally founded as the "Mississippi School and Colony for the Feebleminded" in 1920. Renamed in 1929, this institution's mission was to serve "individuals with mental retardation and/or developmental disabilities." Including these hospitals, the Department of Mental Health, created in 1974, operated a total of eleven facilities throughout the state.

Another state institution, the Tuberculosis Sanatorium hospital in Simpson County, under the effective leadership of Dr. Henry Boswell until 1956, expanded its mission in the 1970s. With the decline of tuberculosis and improved treatment for those it afflicted, the facility began to accept patients with other upper-respiratory illnesses. In the final decades of the century the legislature authorized the establishment of a nursing home for mentally retarded persons on the Sanatorium site. Named the Boswell Regional Center, this facility operated under the jurisdiction of the state Board of Mental Health.

Charity and General Hospitals   The state operated several "charity" hospitals throughout the nineteenth and twentieth centuries, which were closed by the legislature in the late 1980s. The closures came as a move to reduce state expenditures and rely on federal assistance programs, such as Medicare and Medicaid, for funds to treat needy patients in the larger medical centers. Most of the older charity hospitals originally had been small, local infirmaries, such as the Natchez Charity Hospital and Matty Hersee Hospital in Meridian, which had been transferred to state ownership.

The mid-twentieth century saw a sharp increase in the number of general hospitals, but their patient capacities did not rise at the same rate. By 1946 there were 114 hospitals with a total capacity of 4,200 beds, representing about only one-third of the recommended minimum for the state's population.

In the last half of the century small hospitals gradually declined in number and began to be replaced by larger and more comprehensive facilities; institutions for the aged also increased rapidly in number and total capacity. By 1970 the total number of hospitals had increased only slightly to 122, but their total capacity had risen substantially, to more than 17,000 beds. While most hospitals were owned and operated by private groups, churches, or municipalities and counties, the post–World War II establishment of the Veterans Administration hospitals in Jackson, Biloxi, and Gulfport, and the University Medical Center in Jackson were important additions to the state's health services.

A survey of licensed hospitals by the State Department of Health in 2000 reported 105 establishments, not including federal hospitals and the Whitfield and East Mississippi facilities. Altogether they provided a total of 13,251 licensed beds in four categories—acute care, psychiatric, chemical dependency, and rehabilitation. This number of beds did not include those in nursing-home facilities, which reported separately beginning in the 1980s. Licensed hospitals were distributed roughly according to population density. Nine counties reported no licensed hospitals; fifty-one counties had one each; sixteen counties had two each; and four counties—Hinds, Rankin, Harrison, and Lauderdale—reported six each.

Institutions for the Aged or Infirm   Reflecting the aging population generally, the number of long-term-care or nursing facilities rose faster than the number of hospitals during the last three decades of the century. In 2000 there were 402 licensed "skilled nursing facilities," an increase of 530 from the previous year and more than three and one third times the number (120) reported in 1970. With a total of more than 18,000 beds and an occupancy rate of 91 percent in 2000, there was at least one licensed facility in every county except Carroll and Issaquena.

Accomplishments   There were many examples of progress in the improvement of Mississippi's pubic health during the twentieth century. In the 1950s, following epidemics of poliomyelitis, the Salk vaccine was administered as a pilot project in Hinds, Jones, and Warren counties, and the state Board of Health subsequently distributed it to all first and second graders in the state. Later in the century county health departments provided comprehensive services to thousands of Mississippians, including immunizations against contagious diseases like rubella and influenza and emergency assistance in the wake of natural disasters like hurricane Camille. In 1996 the first single survey to compare state immunization levels ranked Mississippi sixth nationally, in a tie with New Hampshire. To its credit, Mississippi had fully immunized 83 percent of all two-year-olds against diphtheria, tetanus, pertussis, polio, measles, mumps, and rubella.

Shortcomings   In general health care, however, the state's progress did not match that of most other states. By the end of the century the infant mortality rate stood at 10.6 per 1,000 live births, a drop of 84 percent since 1922; however, only Alabama and the District of Columbia had higher infant mortality rates than Mississippi. Over the same period the maternity mortality rate fell by 74 percent to 1.8 per 10,000 live births, but this rate was still considerably higher than the national average. While the state's birth rate in the 1990s exceeded the national average,[5] the

5 See Table 24.2 Infant & Maternity Mortality Rates, 1922, 1968, 2000.

TABLE 24.2 Infant & Maternity Mortality Rates, 1922, 1968, 2000

INFANT MORTALITY RATES
(INFANTS UNDER ONE YEAR PER 1,000 LIVE BIRTHS)

YEAR	TOTAL	NONWHITE	WHITE
1922	64.6	78.4	50.1
1968	35.3	47.8	22.7
2000	10.6	15.1	6.7

MATERNITY MORTALITY RATES
(PER 10,000 LIVE BIRTHS)

YEAR	TOTAL	NONWHITE	WHITE
1922	6.8	8.5	5.0
1968	4.6	7.8	1.3
2000	1.8	2.9	0.9

SOURCE: *Mississippi Statistical Abstract, 1971; Statistical Abstract of the U.S., 2001; Vital Statistics, Mississippi State Department of Public Health.*

TABLE 24.3 Poverty Levels by County, 2000

COUNTIES WITH HIGHEST POVERTY

COUNTIES	POVERTY LEVELS*	RACIAL PERCENTAGES OF TOTAL POPULATION		
		BLACK	WHITE	OTHER
Holmes	41.1%	79%	20%	0.9%
Sharkey	38.3	69	29	1.3
Humphreys	38.2	72	27	1.3
Wilkinson	37.7	68	31	0.6
Jefferson	36.0	86	13	0.5
Coahoma	35.9	69	29	1.5
Leflore	34.8	68	30	2.3
Bolivar	33.3	65	33	1.6
Issaquena	33.2	63	36	0.9
Tunica	33.1	70	28	2.3
Quitman	33.1	69	30	0.9
Totals		70	28	1.5

COUNTIES WITH LOWEST POVERTY

De Soto	7.1%	11.4%	86%	2.8%
Rankin	9.5	17.1	81	1.9
Union	12.6	14.9	83	1.6
Jackson	12.7	20.9	75	3.8
Lamar	13.3	12.9	85	1.8
Lee	13.4	24.5	74	1.8
Tate	13.5	31.0	68	1.1
Pontotoc	13.8	14.0	84	1.6
Madison	14.0	37.5	60	2.2
Itawamba	14.0	6.5	92	1.1
Tishomingo	14.1	3.1	95	2.0
Totals		19.4	78	2.4
Mississippi	19.9	36.3	61	2.3

Percent of population in poverty.
SOURCE: *United States Bureau of the Census, 2000 Population by Poverty Status for Counties (www.census.gov.hhes/poverty/2000census/poppvstat00).*

COUNTIES

0   80

Miles

state's average lifetime ranked last among the fifty states, and its mortality rate ranked forty-seventh. Based on a comprehensive study of health risk factors and outcomes, the United Health Foundation rated the state forty-ninth in the nation.

As in the case of the public schools, through the 1960s the state's health services (both public and private) were racially segregated, and programs for African Americans were substantially inferior. This system was not only blatantly inequitable and inherently inefficient, but it resulted in long-lasting ill effects for the state generally and for its black residents in particular. Combined with the high poverty levels, deficient health care for African Americans resulted in higher mortality rates throughout the twentieth century. Both the infant and the maternity mortality rates for nonwhites were consistently and substantially higher than those for whites. Recognizing the need to address the long-standing existence of "racial health disparities," the state Department of Health in March 2000 organized a statewide conference of health care providers, government officials, community organizations, and other diverse groups. The outcome was the development of a plan to eliminate disparities by identifying and removing barriers to minorities' access and usage of health care resources.

OTHER SOCIAL CHALLENGES

Poverty

Based on the United States Census Bureau's determination of poverty levels, the proportion of Mississippians living in poverty declined from 55 percent in the late 1950s to 35 percent in 1969. During the last three decades of the twentieth century that percentage dropped to 17 percent of the total population below the federally established thresholds of $17,603 annual income for a family of four persons or $8,800 for an individual.

Although this record showed significant improvement, especially in the 1990s when the poverty rate fell by 27 percent, Mississippi remained one of the poorest states in the nation. More than one-fourth of all persons below the age of eighteen years still lived in poverty, and the numbers were higher for African Americans and single-parent families. Although this rather bleak picture was modified somewhat by the relatively low cost of living in the state, the annual per capita personal income was lower in Mississippi than in any other state.[6]

The eleven counties with the greatest levels of poverty—more than one-third of their respective populations—in descending order were Holmes, Sharkey, Humphreys, Wilkinson, Jefferson, Coahoma, Leflore, Bolivar, Issaquena, Quitman, and Tunica. The counties with the lowest poverty rates, in ascending order, were DeSoto, Rankin, Union, Jackson, Lamar, Lee, Tate, Pontotoc, Itawamba, Madison, and Tishomingo. Black residents composed 70 percent of the population of the counties displaying the highest poverty rates but only 19 percent of the counties with the least poverty.[7]

Single Parents Among the factors closely related to the high poverty statistics was the changing nature of the traditional family, particularly the rising number of single-parent families. The number of such families—predominately female-headed households, rose by 350 percent in the thirty-year period beginning in the 1960s, and in 1990 the number of single-parent homes in Mississippi composed 32 percent of all households with children.

Teenage Mothers One important aspect of this single-parent phenomenon was the state's unusually high number of teenage mothers. Although the incidence of births to teenagers declined somewhat during the 1990s, as a percentage of

6 If the three-year-median household income for 1998–2000 is used as a measure, the state ranked forty-seventh.
7 See Table 24.3 Poverty Levels by County.

all births they remained significantly higher than national levels. In Mississippi births to teens ranged from 22 to 19 percent of all births, while nationally they declined slightly from 13 to 12 percent. By the end of the century, the state ranked first in the nation in this category and twelfth in births to unmarried teenagers.

Even worse, the number of births to unmarried teenagers rose sharply. In the 1970s almost half of teenage mothers were unmarried at the time of delivery. That proportion rose to an exceedingly high 82 percent by the end of the century. Unfortunately, this proliferation of births to unmarried teens reflected the national trend, which rose from 68 to 80 percent in the 1990s.

Although composing a smaller group, the number of unmarried white teenaged mothers increased rapidly, rising from 524 in 1974 to 1,586 in 1994. In the same twenty-year period, the already high number of births to African American teens also increased, though at a much slower rate, from 5,458 to 5,797. In 2000 the total number of teenagers giving birth was 8,266, including 3,189 whites (58 percent of whom were unmarried) and 5,077 nonwhites (97 percent of whom were unmarried).

Human Services   To address the prevalence of poverty, low educational levels, and other social and economic problems afflicting a large proportion of the population, the state reorganized its assistance programs late in the twentieth century. The Department of Human Services (DHS) was established by the legislature in 1989 to provide help for "needy and disadvantaged individuals and families" throughout the state. Originally, the agency included offices of Family and Children's Services, Youth Services, Economic Assistance, and Child Support.

Intended to administer all human services more efficiently and provide easier access for clients, DHS quickly became one of the state's largest and most expensive bureaucracies. Emphasizing the importance of integrating many existing programs, the legislature transferred to the department several state agencies, including the Department of Public Welfare and various programs within the Division of Federal-State Programs—such as the Office of Energy and Community Services, the Juvenile Justice Advisory Committee, and the Council on Aging. For more effective administration of its comprehensive programs, DHS was required to plan its services in coordination with the Board of Health and the Board of Mental Health.

The agency, moreover, was authorized to establish "family resource centers" to help distribute information and facilitate the delivery of such government welfare benefits as Food Stamps and Temporary Assistance for Needy Families. Another major assistance program was the Children's Health Insurance Program which began in 1998 for "targeted, uninsured, low-income children." DHS determined children's eligibility for federal and state funds, which were then received and disbursed by the Division of Medicaid and the Department of Finance and Administration.

Despite the initial objectives of efficient service delivery to all eligible clients, the success of DHS soon became questionable. A key obstacle was the political character of the agency. With many high-paying positions and an increasingly large budget, decisions about personnel—as well as policy—often depended on the outcome of elections. The executive director of DHS was appointed by the governor with the advice and consent of the senate and served "at the will and pleasure" of the governor. This official, however, was also answerable to a Joint Oversight Committee regarding all matters within the agency's jurisdiction. The committee was composed of eight legislators, including four who served by virtue of their positions as key committee chairpersons, two who were appointed by and served "at the will and pleasure" of the lieutenant governor, and two who were appointed by and served "at the will and pleasure" of the speaker of the house.

In this environment there were repeated changes in leadership, frequent disagreements over policy, and questions about the agency's effectiveness, particularly in view of the enormous budget and the number of employees. With expenditures rising from $530.8 million to $671 million in the final years of the century, DHS had a reported staff of more than three thousand persons. In 2000 Governor Musgrove appointed and then dismissed Executive Director Bettye Ward Fletcher for "philosophical differences." He then appointed Janice Broome Brooks, who served two years before resigning amidst "budget and personnel troubles" that included a reported deficit of $19.8 million.

CONCLUSION

During the twentieth century Mississippians witnessed major social progress. The state's stagnant population growth, however, revealed major problems. Alienated by the continuing plague of racial discrimination and related factors, great numbers of African Americans left the state for good. There also was a gradual population shift into urban areas, including four major metropolitan areas, but in increasing numbers whites moved from town centers to the suburbs. Nevertheless, Mississippi remained a predominantly rural state in an age of rapid urbanization nationwide. Access to health care improved generally, but considerable numbers of people in rural communities still lived in poverty and received only minimal medical services.

Despite Mississippi's failure to compete successfully with most other states in the standard of living of most of its residents, enormous social improvements were made. The fundamental disadvantage was that in many arenas the state had a lower point from which to start. But at the beginning of the twenty-first century Mississippi was poised to accelerate its recent progress in achieving a healthier and more prosperous society. The question, then, is can its people overcome historic obstacles in order to achieve greater economic diversity, genuine racial reconciliation, and substantial educational improvements?

SELECTED SOURCES

Harrell, Laura D. S., "Medical Services in Mississippi, 1890–1970," in Richard Aubrey McLemore, ed., A *History of Mississippi*, 2 vols. (Hattiesburg: University & College Press of Mississippi, 1973), 2: 516–569.

Mississippi, *Annotated Code of 1972.*

———. *General Laws of Mississippi* [various dates].

Mississippi Center for Public Policy, Mississippi Family Council Report (www. mspolicy.org).

Mississippi Official and Statistical Register [various dates].

Mississippi State Department of Health, 1996 Report (www.msdh.state.ms.us).

————. "2000 Annual Report on Institutions for the Aged or Infirm Licensed by Mississippi Department of Health" (www.msdh.state.ms.us).

————. "2000 Report on Hospitals Licensed by Mississippi State Department of Health" (www.msdh.state.ms.us).

————. Office of Minority Affairs, "Mississippi's Plan to Eliminate Racial & Ethnic Health Care Disparities," 2000 (www.msdh.state.ms.us).

————. "Selected Facts About Teenage Pregnancy, 1994" (www.msdh.state. ms.us).

————. "Teenage Vital Statistics Data by Race of Mother, 2000" (www.msdh.state. ms.us).

————. Vital Statistics (www.msdh.state.ms.us).

Mississippi Statistical Abstract [various dates].

United Health Foundation, State Health Rankings, 2002 (www.unitedhealth foundation.org).

United States Bureau of the Census, *1990 Census of Population*.

————. Current Population Survey, Poverty 2000.

————. Income 2000 (www.census.gov/hhes/income/income00/statemhi.html).

————. *Statistical Abstract of the United States: 2001*.

United States Department of Commerce, Bureau of Economic Analysis, *Regional Accounts Data: Annual State Personal Income. SA05 Personal Income by Major Source and Earnings by Industry—Mississippi* (www.bea.gov/bea/regional/spi/ action.cfm).

CHAPTER TWENTY-FIVE

Recent Political Trends

A New Day Dawns

Governor William Forrest Winter, 1980–1984

The election of William Winter in 1979 represented an acceleration of political changes that had begun, even if only haltingly, a decade earlier. New trends in the final years of the twentieth century would include transitions from reluctant acquiescence to willing compliance to civil rights legislation and a rapidly rising number of African Americans elected to public office. On the other hand, the black-white coalition in the Democratic party would become increasingly unreliable, as many whites conservatives crossed over to join an expanding Republican party.

In the first Democratic party primary in August 1979 the best-known candidate and frontrunner was William Winter. A respected lawyer known for his interest in the study of history and other scholarly pursuits, he had already held three statewide offices. As lieutenant governor during Governor Waller's administration, Winter had received regional recognition for supporting public access to all government processes. Then, after failing in his second gubernatorial campaign in 1975, he had practiced law in Jackson during the Finch administration.

Elections of 1979   In his third gubernatorial campaign Winter faced five Democrats, Lieutenant Governor Evelyn Gandy, Jim Herring, Richard Barrett, the intransigent segregationist lawyer,[1] Charles Deaton, a lawyer and state representative from Greenwood, and John Arthur Eaves. When the votes were counted it appeared that

Governor Winter speaking at the Neshoba County Fair. Courtesy Mississippi Department of Archives and History.

1 A native of New York, Barrett had served in the United States Army during the Vietnam War before moving to Mississippi in 1966. A resident of Learned, a small town in southern Hinds County, he practiced law, having received his degree from Memphis State University, but devoted increasing attention to supporting and organizing white supremacist groups. He attracted only 14,550 votes in the 1979 primary.

Winter was again in trouble, having received 183,944 votes to Gandy's 224,714. But in the second primary, Winter received 57 percent of the votes to become the party's nominee. He won the general election by a comfortable margin (61 percent) over Republican Gil Carmichael.

Winter agreed with former congressman Frank Smith, who became the governor's special assistant, that his election proved the presence of a "moderate underground" in the state. In other words, they were optimistic that most voters now understood, at least privately, that Mississippi's welfare required a change in traditional attitudes regarding race relations, including the wisdom of supporting desegregation and equal opportunities in public schools.

Given the Republicans' recent successes in federal elections, it was surprising that the party nominated candidates in only four statewide races in 1979. In the legislative elections Republicans were on the ballots in 18 of 52 senate districts and 37 of 122 house districts but won only four seats in each house. Thus, the traditional Democratic party control on the state and local levels continued during Winter's administration.

As the lieutenant governor's office was now open with Gandy in the gubernatorial campaign, former state treasurer Brad Dye was nominated in the first primary and ran unopposed in the general election. Three other statewide offices were available due to the resignations of long-time Secretary of State Heber Ladner, Attorney General Albioun F. Summer, and State Treasurer Edwin Pittman, who won election to the secretary of state office. William A. "Bill" Allain became the new secretary of state, and William J. Cole took the office of state treasurer.

Voters in 1979 also approved two constitutional amendments, one authorizing the legislature to reapportion itself following every federal census (Sections 254–255) and another to create a Commission on Judicial Performance (Section 177a).

African American Legislators   During Governor Winter's administration the state witnessed increasing numbers of American Americans elected to public office. Due in part to the governor's enlightened leadership, this progress was primarily the result of federal courts' earlier reapportionments of the legislature, forming single-member districts among which an appropriate number contained majorities of voting-age African Americans. Designed to end the state's policy of diluting black voting strength, these court orders—first by federal district Judge William Barbour, Jr., in *Connor v. Finch* (1976) then by the United States District Court for the Southern District of Columbia in *Mississippi v. United States* (1979)—gradually resulted in the election of a rising number of black legislators. In 1968 Representative Robert Clark had been the first and only African American to enter the legislature in the twentieth century, and by 1976 only three additional blacks had been elected to the state house of representatives and none to the senate.

However, after the federal redistricting plans took effect, the number of African American legislators rose to eighteen representatives and two senators by the end of Winter's term. Black persons' opportunity to participate in state government was not only incredibly late in coming, but it was disproportional to the number of African American residents, less than 9 percent of the legislators to more than 35 percent of the total population. The role of black legislators, moreover, was carefully controlled by the powerful white conservative leaders like Clarence D. "Buddie" Newman. Elected speaker of the house in 1976, Newman, according to colleagues, aimed to follow in the footsteps of his mentor, Speaker Walter Sillers, a defender of racial segregation who had controlled the house from 1944 until his death in 1966. Newman had entered the legislature in 1948 as a senator and four years later had become a representative. He succeeded Speaker John Junkin (1966–76) and presided over the house until 1988.

The Congressional Elections of 1980   In the 1980 Democratic primaries for Congress, incumbents Whitten, Bowen, Montgomery in the first three districts respectively were nominated without opposition. In the Fourth and Fifth districts, which were represented by Republicans, several Democrats contended for their party's nomination. In the Fourth District Henry Kirksey led in the first primary but lost to Britt Singletary in the runoff, and Jimmy McVeay won the Fifth District nomination.

In the general election Democratic Congressmen Whitten and Bowen easily defeated Republicans, while Montgomery ran unopposed. In the Fifth District Republican Congressman Lott was reelected by a wide margin, but the Fourth District again hosted a very competitive election, with Republican Jon Hinson being reelected with only 39 percent of the total number of votes cast. A sizable majority of the electorate opposed Hinson but divided its vote equally between Singletary, the Democratic party's candidate, and Lester Burl McLemore, an African American independent. This election was an example of occasional racial divisions among Democrats, who split their larger vote between the party's nominee and an independent. The same phenomenon sometimes afflicted the Republicans, particularly in legislative contests, but the causes were different. Because local elections were always held in odd-numbered years, not during the congressional and presidential elections, they were insulated somewhat from national politics. Elections in counties and towns, moreover, still fell under the powerful legacy of the old Southern Democratic party; in other words, to win the contest for sheriff or county supervisor one had to be a "Democrat." Some Republicans, therefore, chose to run for office as "Independents," believing the label might better their chances of winning, not necessarily because they disagreed with their party's platform.

The Presidential Election of 1980   President Jimmy Carter, who had narrowly carried the state four years earlier, received 429,281 votes (48 percent of all votes cast) but lost Mississippi's electoral votes to Republican Ronald Reagan, who won with 441,089 votes (49.4 percent). Four candidates of independent or "third" parties, including John B. Anderson, received a total of only 22,250 votes. Winning many other states by a similarly close margin, Reagan received less than 51 percent of the nation's popular vote but received 91 percent of the electoral college.

A Republican Setback   Recent successes of Mississippi Republicans were significantly tarnished when, following published reports of his homosexual activities in Washington, Congressman Hinson resigned. In the summer of 1981 a special election to fill his position attracted a total of eight candidates representing both parties, with Republican Liles B. Williams, a Hinds County businessman, receiving the most votes but not the required majority. In the runoff the Republicans lost the seat they had held for eight years, as Democrat Wayne Dowdy, a lawyer and the mayor of McComb, defeated Williams by a very narrow margin, one of less than one thousand votes. Dowdy's victory was due primarily to the absence of black independent candidates, a fatal factor for Democrats in previous elections, and his campaign promise to support the extension of the Voting Rights Act in Congress. The latter position, in sharp contrast to Williams's declarations, secured for Dowdy a strong turnout of black voters.

The Congressional Elections of 1982   In the 1982 senatorial election Senator Stennis was nominated without serious opposition, while Haley Barbour, a lawyer from Yazoo City and future governor, won the Republican primary, in which only about 41,000 total votes were cast. Reelected for his seventh and last time, Stennis defeated Barbour who received 36 percent of the total votes.

The Democrats nominated incumbent congressmen Whitten, Montgomery, and Dowdy. In the Second District state representative Robert Clark was nominated following Congressman Bowen's decision not to run for reelection, and in the Fifth District Arlon Coate was chosen to challenge Congressman Lott.

The Republicans held primaries in the First and Second districts nominating Fran Fawcett and Webster "Webb" Franklin. Although the outcome was never in question, the primary in the latter Delta district was historically interesting due to the candidacy of Clennon King, an African American who had challenged the state's policy of racial segregation in education during the early 1950s. Without opposition Liles Williams was nominated in the Fourth District and incumbent Trent Lott in the Fifth, but no Republican chose to challenge Montgomery in the Third.

In the general election all incumbent congressmen were reelected, but the Republicans won in the vacant Delta district. Despite the margin being rather narrow, Webb Franklin prevailed over Clark and an independent candidate. In the Fourth District Dowdy received 53.5 percent of the votes to defeat Republican Williams for a second time. If anyone was naive enough to believe that race was no longer a major aspect of Mississippi politics, this contest should have opened their eyes. Franklin's campaign used images of a Confederate monument as well as carefully placed pictures of Clark to emphasize the racial as well as political differences between the candidates.

Governor Winter's Key Accomplishment   In July 2001, some seventeen years after he left the governor's office, Winter was honored nationally for his contributions to civil rights. Presenting him with the prestigious Martin Luther King, Jr., Memorial Award, the National Education Association acknowledged his leadership in persuading the legislature to adopt the Education Reform Act of 1982, widely recognized as a turning point in the state's official policy towards public education.[2] Robert Clark, the African American chairman of the Education Committee at the time, recalled that Winter's leadership made reform possible after years of legislative resistance. The governor said this legislation ". . . advances the rights for all people regardless of class, race, where they live or what they do."

2 For more information on the Educational Reform Act, see Chapter Twenty-Six: Tumultuous Trends in Education.

Governor William A. Allain, 1984–1988

The Elections of 1983 During his final year in office, Governor Winter witnessed what seemed to be the state's stamp of approval for his administration through the sweeping election victories of Democratic party candidates, even in the face of rising Republican opposition. Of the five Democratic party candidates in the gubernatorial contest of 1983, the leaders were former lieutenant governor Evelyn Gandy, Attorney General William A. "Bill" Allain, and in third place Mike Sturdivant, a successful businessman and Delta planter. After winning the first primary by about 23,000 votes, Gandy was defeated in the runoff by Allain, who received more than 52 percent of the votes. In the general election Allain won 55 percent of the total votes, defeating Republican Leon Bramlett (39 percent) and three independents including Charles Evers. Despite an allegation by some Jackson Republicans late in the campaign that he was a homosexual, Allain won convincingly, carrying 74 of the 82 counties. In perhaps a more direct reflection of the electorate's endorsement of the Winter years, two staff members of the former governor won election to state executive offices: Secretary of State Dick Molpus and State Auditor Ray Mabus.

Governor Bill Allain A native of Washington in Adams County, Allain earned his law degree at the University of Mississippi before serving in the United States Army during the Korean War. He practiced law in Natchez until he became an assistant attorney general in 1962, and in his first political campaign he had been elected attorney general in 1979.

The Allain years were characterized by significant political developments, including steady increases in the number of African American and women officeholders as well as in the Republican party's appeal, despite its lingering inability to win elections. To help with fundraising and to boost party officeholders and potential candidates, President Reagan visited Jackson in June 1983. The tradition of all-white male supreme court judges would end with the entrance of the state's first female judge, Lenore Prather, and the first African American judge, Reuben Anderson. Major changes in Mississippi's representation in the Congress would occur with the election of Mike Espy, the first African American of the twentieth century to represent the state in Washington and with Senator Stennis's announcement in 1987 that he would not seek reelection after a tenure of forty years.

Administratively, Governor Allain renewed historic attempts to reorganize state government agencies and rewrite the constitution through the establishment of a constitutional study commission. Drawing from the commission's report, the legislature proposed eighteen constitutional amendments that contained fundamental changes in several important categories. The voters approved amendments that modified or removed some of the existing restrictions on corporations, added protections for the state retirement program, and created, expanded, and safeguarded trust funds derived from taxes and other sources for public education. A major structural amendment to Section 116 allowing the governor's reelection to one successive term was approved by the voters in 1986 and became effective in the next administration. Two amendments regarding race in 1987 repealed the sections added in the 1950s allowing the legislature to abol-

Senator Thad Cochran.
Courtesy Senator Cochran.

ish the public schools and the original 1890 Section 263 outlawing interracial marriages. Seventy-one percent of the voters favored the former proposal, while the latter passed by only 52 percent.

The Congressional Elections of 1984   The Democratic party victories in statewide and legislative races did not carry over into the senatorial election of 1984. Four Democrats entered the campaign to vie for the U.S. Senate seat held by Republican Thad Cochran. Former Governor William Winter won the nomination but was soundly defeated in the general election by Cochran, who received 61 percent of the votes.

But the state's tradition of returning incumbents to office continued in the elections for the United States House of Representatives. As in 1982, the closest contests were in the Second and Fourth districts, where Republican Congressman Franklin received less than 51 percent of the votes to defeat Robert Clark, and Congressman Dowdy won 55 percent of the vote to overcome Republican David Armstrong.

The Presidential Election of 1984   Despite its internal political party competition and local loyalty to the Democrats, Mississippi continued to vote Republican and with the nation in presidential elections. Besides the Democratic and Republican tickets in the 1984 presidential election, the Libertarians and five independent parties had candidates on the ballot. President Ronald Reagan won 62 percent of the total votes cast, easily defeating Democrat Walter Mondale and the six other candidates. The Republican victory was almost as overwhelming nationally as Reagan won 59 percent of the popular vote and 98 percent of the electoral college.

The Congressional Elections of 1986   The Democrats gained one seat in the U.S. House of Representatives in the mid-term elections of 1986. In the Delta, Democrats Hiram Eastland, Mike Espy, and Pete Johnson entered the first primary seeking the opportunity to unseat Congressman Franklin. A major surprise occurred when Espy, an African American, won the nomination over rivals with such well-known Mississippi political family names. Eastland, a lawyer and planter, was a second cousin of former Senator Eastland, and Johnson, also a lawyer, was a grandson of former Governor Paul B. Johnson and a nephew of former Governor Paul B. Johnson, Jr. Espy, who accomplished another upset by winning 52 percent of the votes in the general election, had been an assistant to Edwin Pittman in the secretary of state's office and was working as his assistant attorney general at the time of the election. The other congressional elections were dull by comparison, as all four incumbents retained their seats without facing serious opposition.

Governor Raymond E. "Ray" Mabus, 1988–1992

The Elections of 1987   With the attention he attracted for his work on Governor Winter's staff and his accomplishments as state auditor since 1984, Ray Mabus entered his second political campaign in 1987. Only thirty-eight years old, he faced several more experienced and well-known candidates, including former Governor Bill Waller, Attorney General Pittman, former gubernatorial candidates Mike Sturdivant, Maurice Dantin, and John Arthur Eaves, plus two other lesser-known opponents. In the first Democratic primary Mabus led the field, followed by Sturdivant, whom Mabus defeated by a three-to-one vote in the runoff.

In November Mabus faced Republican Jack Reed. Having won the Republican gubernatorial primary in which only 18,853 votes were cast, Reed campaigned as a Tupelo businessman, former president of the Mississippi Economic Council, longtime supporter of public education, rare voice for moderation in the 1960s, defender of traditional family values, and harsh critic of governmental corruption and inefficiency. With this record his candidacy was not only appealing in the traditionally pro-Republican urban counties but also in rural areas. Nevertheless, Reed could not prevail against Mabus's Democratic organization, which not only had the full support of prominent state politicians and African American leaders but reached to powerful party figures in Washington. Mabus captured 53 percent of the votes to become the next governor.

The only other contest attracting as much attention as the gubernatorial race—and having longer lasting consequences—brought thirty-five-year-old Michael "Mike" Moore into the office of attorney general. In a hotly contested, widely publicized Democratic primary Moore defeated former Jackson mayor Dale Danks. Attorney General Moore served in the office sixteen years, attracted national attention for his successful lawsuit against giant tobacco companies that garnered Mississippi a $4.1 billion settlement, and left office in 2004 with a 65 percent favorable-opinion rating in the state.

Governor Mabus   The youngest governor in the nation, Mabus was a native of Ackerman in Choctaw County and had earned a Master's degree from Johns Hopkins University and a law degree from Harvard University before serving in the United States Navy. He had served as legal counsel to Governor Winter and had contributed to the adoption of several reforms measures, including the Education Reform Act of 1982 and an open public records law. As state auditor during the Allain administration, Mabus's aggressive investigation of county supervisors' handling of public funds had uncovered widespread waste and fraud.

Mabus's administration reflected former Governor Winter's progressive approach to social and economic affairs and encouraged greater participation in local and state government by African Americans and women. By the end of Mabus's term, Mississippi led all other states in the number of elected African American officials with more than seven hundred in local positions and forty-two elected to the legislature. Now composed of members representing a new generation of constituents who understood that fundamental changes were essential to the welfare of the state, the house of representatives challenged the old establishment. This shift in direction was best illustrated in the downfall of Speaker Newman. In 1988 the house discarded Newman in favor of thirty-seven-year-old Timothy Alan "Tim" Ford of Prentiss County in the state's northeastern Tennessee Hills region.

Such changes, however, did not mean the legislature would turn its back on all traditions. For example, it resisted Mabus's efforts to reorganize the state's cumbersome administrative structure, blocked higher appropriations for higher education, defeated a lottery plan proposed to help fund public schools, and remained firmly opposed to change on such issues as abortion and gun control. But the governor was successful in obtaining some progressive legislation. Pursuant to discoveries of corruption in county governments during his tenure as auditor, Mabus recommended that counties be required to change from the traditional "beat system" to a more centralized administration, the "unit system." In the former practice, counties were divided into five separate districts, each with its own elected supervisor to administer its roads and perform other public duties. In the "unit system," the districts still elected supervisors, but the districts no longer served as separate administrative entities. Instead, the supervisors, meeting together as a board, elected a county administrator to manage the county as a whole. Legislation in 1988 allowed voters in each county to switch to the unit system of governance but required all counties to centralize their budgetary and personnel functions, thus reducing opportunities for corruption and redundant positions.

From 1984 through 1987, as state auditor Mabus had cooperated with an undercover investigation by the FBI known as "Operation Pretense." Ultimately fifty-five county supervisors in twenty-six counties, one county road foreman, two state highway commissioners, and thirteen vendors were convicted of bribery, extortion, or other felonies.

The Presidential Election of 1988   As had been the case for nearly three decades, most voters were willing to support conservative Democrats within the state, but they were reluctant to support national party candidates whom they considered too liberal. Pursuant to this customary inclination, 60 percent of Mississippi voters in 1988 preferred Republican nominee George Bush, who had served as vice president during Reagan's two terms, over Governor Michael Dukakis of Massachusetts, who received 39 percent of all votes cast, or the three independent and third-party candidates. Again, the state was in line with the national vote, which gave Bush 53 percent of the popular votes and 79 percent of the electoral college.

The Congressional Elections of 1988 and 1990   The elections of 1988 produced three important changes in the state's congressional delegation. While incumbents Whitten, Espy, and Montgomery were reelected in the first three congressional districts, Dowdy and Lott decided to enter the race for Senator Stennis's seat instead of trying to retain their positions in the House of Representatives. In the Democratic party primary Dowdy defeated Secretary of State Molpus, while Lott was unopposed in his nomination. The hard-fought general election resulted in Lott receiving 54 percent of the votes and Mississippi having two Republicans in the U.S. Senate for the first time since 1877.

Senator Trent Lott. Courtesy Senator Lott.

Mississippi state capitol building. Courtesy Mississippi Development Authority/Division of Tourism.

Out of the scramble by nine Democrats in Dowdy's Fourth District and six in Lott's Fifth District, Mike Parker and Gene Taylor were finally nominated in second primaries. In the general election they faced Republican candidates Thomas Collins and Larkin Smith, who had won their nominations among groups of six and five hopefuls respectively. Parker received 55 percent of all votes cast to defeat Collins in the fourth district, while Smith, the sheriff of Harrison County, garnered 55 percent to win over Taylor. The result, therefore, was the state's continuing ratio of four Democrats to one Republican in the U.S. House.

An unexpected change occurred in August 1989, however, as the result of the tragic death of Congressman Larkin Smith in a private airplane crash in south Mississippi. Three candidates, Taylor, Tom Anderson, a lawyer on Trent Lott's staff, and Attorney General Mike Moore entered a special election in October. Even though President Bush visited Gulfport to speak on behalf of Anderson, Taylor won 65 percent of the votes in the runoff against Anderson. The Democrats now controlled, albeit temporarily, the state's entire House delegation, a century-old tradition that had been interrupted in 1973.

In 1990 Senator Cochran was reelected without opposition, and all five Democratic congressmen were returned to the House of Representatives. Except for the Third District, where Montgomery had no opposition, Republican candidates competed in each district but with disappointing results; their best performance was Bill Bowlin's 36 percent of the votes in northeast district, where eighty-year-old Congressman Whitten was reelected for the twenty-sixth time.

Governor Kirk Fordice, 1992–2000
Historic Gubernatorial Election of 1991   For the first time since Governor Adelbert Ames in 1873, Mississippians elected a Republican governor in 1991. Not only was Kirk Fordice's election historic in that sense, but his victory over an incumbent Democrat shocked contemporary political observers, as it would have been unthinkable just a few years earlier. Virtually unknown politically outside Republican party leadership circles, Fordice had to win his nomination in a second primary against former Democrat Pete Johnson, who had both campaign experience and name recognition.

Fordice was a native of Memphis, Tennessee, and had earned the bachelor's and master's degrees at Purdue University. Never having been elected to a public office, he owned and operated a construction company in Vicksburg that specialized in big commercial projects, including road and bridge construction along the Mississippi River. One of Fordice's key advantages was his ability to identify with ordinary working people, folks who generally distrusted professional politicians and respected the candidate's plain, straight talk and common-sense ideas for economic improvements.

In the campaign Fordice portrayed himself as a conservative, experienced businessman whose hero was President Ronald Reagan, an image that contrasted starkly with the Mabus Democrats. In fact, Governor Mabus's vulnerability had been exposed in the first Democratic primary, which he barely won; the combined votes for former Congressman Wayne Dowdy and George Blair had almost forced a runoff. In the general election Fordice received 51 percent of all votes cast and defeated Mabus by 23,041 votes.

A variety of factors underlay Mabus's defeat, including his active support of the national Democratic party, which attracted African American voters but failed to secure a sufficient number of their white counterparts. Besides the popularity of the Reagan Republicans among Mississippians, other potent factors influencing white Democrats were Mabus's "meddling" with county supervisors, his inability or refusal to deal with the legislature bosses, and his liberal image in general. Finally, another obstacle to his future aspirations for public office lay on the horizon—marital difficulties leading ultimately to divorce and a lawsuit filed by his former wife, Julia Hines Mabus, regarding the custody of their two children.

Other Statewide Elections in 1991   The Democrats also lost the office of lieutenant governor, as state Senator Eddie Briggs, a lawyer from Kemper County, received 59.5 percent of the total votes cast to defeat incumbent Brad Dye and state Senator Henry Kirksey, who ran again as an independent. Five of the other six statewide offices were retained by the incumbent Democrats, all of whom ran unopposed in the general election except Commissioner of Insurance George Dale, who easily defeated his Republican opponent. To succeed Auditor Pete Johnson, the Democrats nominated Steve Patterson, who also faced no opposition in the general election.

Fordice's first term was marked by rising numbers of African Americans, women, and Republicans participating in local and legislative campaigns, although the governor himself was an outspoken advocate of only the latter group. The number of black legislators rose to thirty-two representative and ten senators, an overall increase of 91 percent since the last election, while thirty-two of the sixty-seven Republican legislative candidates were elected to the legislature in 1991. Though both groups remained distinct minorities, they began to play significant political roles in contrast to their virtual nonexistence (though for different reasons) just twenty years earlier. The number of woman legislators rose from only two representatives elected in 1981 to fifteen representatives and four senators in 1991, of which totals eight were African American. During the final years of the 1990s, Mississippi continued to lead the nation in the total number of black elected officeholders, which had risen to more than eight hundred persons, including a substantial number of women.

The Presidential Election of 1992   In the presidential election of 1992 President George Bush again won the state's seven electoral votes with 49.7 percent of the popular vote. Arkansas Governor Bill Clinton got 40.1 percent, while independent Texas businessman H. Ross Perot captured 8.7 percent, and five other independent or third-party candidates received the remaining 1.5 percent. Possibly due to Perot's ability to capture 19 percent of the national popular votes, Clinton won the election with only 43 percent of the popular votes but 69 percent of the electoral college.

The Congressional Elections of 1992 and 1994   During Fordice's first term two changes occurred in the state's delegation to the U.S. House of Representatives. In 1992 Republican candidates tried in vain to unseat the incumbents, and although no Democrat encountered a serious threat, Clyde Whitaker in Whitten's northeastern district and Paul Harvey in Taylor's southern district attracted the most support. Early in 1993 after Delta Congressman Espy resigned from Congress upon his appointment as secretary of agriculture in President's Clinton cabinet, eight candidates entered a special election to fill the vacancy. Bennie Thompson, an African American who had served as mayor of Bolton and Hinds County supervisor, received 55 percent of the votes in the runoff to defeat Hayes Dent, a former Democrat who had switched to the Republican party.

In the mid-term congressional elections of 1994 three incumbents defeated their Republican challengers by wide margins, and Congressman Thompson received 54 percent of the votes to overcome a significant challenge by Republican Bill Jordan, an African American. An important change occurred, however, in the First District on the retirement of Congressman Whitten. Democrat William R. Wheeler, Jr., won the Democratic party's nomination, defeating speaker of the state house of representatives, Tim Ford, but lost in the general election to former state senator Roger F. Wicker, a lawyer from Pontotoc. There was no change in the state's U.S. Senate membership, as Trent Lott received more than two-thirds of the votes to defeat Democrat Ken Harper.

Fordice's Reelection, 1995   Under Section 116 of the Constitution of 1890 governors had been ineligible for election to successive terms, but with the approval of an amendment to that section in 1986, Fordice became the first governor to succeed himself in office since Governor Robert Lowry did so in 1885. After having been nominated by 94 percent of the votes in the Republican primary, Governor Fordice engaged in a rather dramatic and sometimes personal reelection contest with Secretary of State Molpus, the Democratic nominee in 1995. Evidently satisfied with Fordice's first-term performance and influenced by his broad base of support among prominent leaders like former governor Bill Waller, 55 percent of the voters decided to break tradition and return Fordice to office. Apparently the governor's support for income-tax reductions and conservative social and business policies outweighed

Congressman Bennie Thompson.
Courtesy Congressman Thompson.

his opposition to higher appropriations for education, which contrasted sharply with Molpus's active support for the public schools.

Other Statewide Elections in 1995   Fordice's success had little effect on the other seven statewide elections, which were all won by Democrats, although the Republicans fielded credible candidates in every contest, including Lieutenant Governor Briggs. But, in somewhat of a surprise, Democratic state Senator Ronnie Musgrove, a lawyer from Panola County, received 53 percent of the votes to upset Lieutenant Governor Briggs's reelection bid. The race for the secretary of state's office, now open with Molpus's exit to the gubernatorial campaign, attracted a number of candidates from both parties. After narrowly defeating state Senator Amy Tuck in the second primary (a difference of only 2,375 votes out of 425,581 total votes cast), Democratic nominee Eric Clark received 61 percent of the votes in the general election to defeat Republican nominee Barbara Blanton.

The Presidential Election of 1996   The Democratic party's sweep of the elections of 1995 did not carry over into the presidential election of 1996. Republican nominee Robert Dole received a plurality of 49 percent of all votes cast and secured the state's seven electoral votes, while President Clinton got 44 percent, and five independent and third-party candidates shared the remaining 7 percent. Democrats took notice that although the turnout was considerably lower than it had been in 1992, Clinton's share of all votes cast was higher in this election, and nationally he was reelected with 49 percent of the popular votes and 70 percent of the electoral college.

Congressional Elections of 1996 and 1998   Mississippi Democrats, however, could take little comfort in the steadily increasing numbers of Republican state legislators and congressional representatives. On the eve of Governor Fordice's second term, just three days after the November 1995 general election, Congressman Parker announced that he was changing his party affiliation from Democrat to Republican. Moreover, following Congressman Montgomery's retirement announcement in 1996, this after thirty years in the House, the Democrats failed to elect his successor. Their nominee, Jackson attorney John Arthur Eaves, Jr., was overwhelmingly defeated by Republican Charles W. "Chip" Pickering, Jr., of Laurel, who received 61 percent of all votes. Hoping to unseat Fourth District Congressman Parker, who had switched parties, the Democrats nominated Kevin Antoine, an African American from Jackson who received 54 percent of the votes in the second primary against Margaret Barrett, a member of the Jackson city council. In the general election, however, Parker was reelected with 61 percent of all votes cast. With the reelection of the other three incumbents, the Mississippi Republicans now had a three-to-two majority in the U.S. House of Representatives.

Perhaps a reflection of the rising conservative sentiment among Mississippi voters during Fordice's second term, the Libertarian party exhibited a surge of activity and placed candidates in all congressional elections as well as in many state and local contests. Their campaigns, however, had little if any impact on election results, and in 1998 all congressional incumbents were reelected, save Parker, who decided not to run so that he could launch a gubernatorial campaign. In the contest for Parker's Fourth District seat, the Democrats nominated Clifford Ronald

"Ronnie" Shows, former state senator from Jefferson Davis County and a member of the state Transportation Commission. Portraying himself as a rural, conservative or "blue dog" Democrat and his Republican opponent, Delbert Hosemann, as a wealthy tax attorney from Jackson, Shows was elected with 53 percent of the votes in the general election.

Governor Ronnie Musgrove, 2000–2004

The Controversial Gubernatorial Election of 1999   The gubernatorial election of 1999 was both historic and bizarre. Conducted in the aftermath of President Clinton's impeachment and in the midst of Governor Fordice's marital problems, this state contest as well as the following year's presidential election would have unprecedented outcomes. Reports of Fordice's extramarital affair had surfaced during his first term and became indisputable by 1999. Just weeks after he left office in January 2000, his divorce from his wife of forty-four years was finalized. (Interestingly, five of the seven married Mississippi governors between 1968 and 2004 had marital strife while in office that led to threats of divorce or separation!) His own transgressions, notwithstanding, Fordice had consistently proclaimed support for "family values" and issued public denunciations of President Clinton's alleged illicit sexual behavior. In Washington, a Republican-controlled House of Representatives approved two articles of impeachment, charging Clinton with perjury and obstruction of justice, but the Senate declined to remove him from office in January 1999.

In the summer of 1999 Lieutenant Governor Musgrove won the Democratic party's nomination with 58 percent of the votes in the first primary, which included seven other candidates. His Republican opponent, former congressman Mike Parker, was also nominated in his party's first primary, although a runoff with former lieutenant governor Eddie Briggs was very narrowly avoided by the scattering of votes among four other candidates, including longtime state Representative Charlie Williams.

In the general election Musgrove received 49.6 percent of all votes cast, while Parker got 48.5, with the small balance going to a third-party candidate and an independent. Musgrove and Parker each won 61 of the state's so-called "electoral votes" (majorities in the house of representatives districts), but neither candidate met the constitution's requirements for election (Section 140) which included winning a majority of both the popular votes and the electoral votes. So, for the first time under the Constitution of 1890 and pursuant to its provision in Section 141, the house of representatives was required to break the impasse. In January 2000 the newly elected representatives voted along party lines rather than in response to the majority vote in their districts when they elected Musgrove by a vote of 86 to 36.[3]

Other Elections in 1999   The other statewide elections were not afflicted with such complications, and following tradition all incumbents were reelected except in the lieutenant governor's office, which was now vacant. Seeking that office,

---

3 An illustration of the partisan, personal nature of the political climate was the legislators' refusal to allow Governor Fordice to make the traditional farewell address to a joint session of the legislature. The usual resolution inviting him to speak died when the house failed to take action on it.

Democrat Amy Tuck, who had come very close to the 1995 secretary of state nomination, won the first primary by capturing 52 percent of the votes. Only the second woman to hold an elected statewide office, Tuck received 53 percent of the votes in the general election against the Republican candidate Bill Hawks. A native of Maben in Oktibbeha County, Tuck had earned a master's degree at Mississippi State University and a law degree at the Mississippi College School of Law. She had been a teacher rather than an attorney before being elected to the state senate in 1990 as Amy Tuck Powell. Following her unsuccessful campaign in 1995, Tuck had become secretary of the senate. The lone successful Republican in a statewide contest in 1999, State Auditor Phil Bryant, became just the third member of that party to win such an election to state office since Reconstruction.

The Elections of 2000   After the explosive gubernatorial election of 1999, the elevation of a woman to the office of lieutenant governor, and the election of another Republican to statewide office, the 2000 contests may have seemed routine, except for the presidential election and the Democrats' nomination of a candidate to oppose Senator Trent Lott. From an original field of five hopefuls, Troy D. Brown won the Democratic nomination over Ricky L. Cole in the second primary but could attract only 31.6 percent of all votes cast in the general election. Along with Senator Lott, all five congressional incumbents were reelected by wide margins.

In the presidential election of 2000 Mississippians cast 58 percent of their votes for Republican George W. Bush and 41 percent for Democrat Albert Gore, Jr., who had been vice president during President Clinton's two terms. Nationally, the disputed results of the election, centering on Florida's electoral votes, finally had to be decided by the U.S. Supreme Court. When Florida's electoral votes were counted by the Congress, Bush was declared the president elect with 271 electoral votes, only 5 more than Gore received, although Bush had received fewer popular votes than Gore, 47.9 and 48.4 percent respectively.

Into the Twenty-First Century

State politics would be almost as explosive in the first years of the new century. The loss of one congressional seat following the 2000 census resulted in a controversial district reapportionment and the loss of a Democratic member of the House of Representatives in the 2002 election. Ultimately the Third and Fourth congressional districts were combined, but the legislature failed to resolve differences between house and senate configurations, which reportedly favored Democratic incumbent Ronnie Shows over Republican incumbent Chip Pickering. Rather frantic litigation ensued, beginning with a Hinds County Chancery Court ruling that pleased Democrats and ending with the United States Supreme Court's refusal to reverse a district map put forth by a panel of three federal judges—the plan preferred by Republicans.[4]

The redistricting controversy and Pickering's election with 64 percent of the total vote in the new Third District overshadowed news of other election results, including Senator Thad Cochran's landslide reelection to a fifth term.[5] Parallel-

4 The federal judges were E. Grady Jolly of the 5th Circuit Court of Appeals and District Court judges David C. Bramlette and Henry T. Wingate.

5 House incumbents, Wicker and Taylor, were re-elected without significant opposition, but Thompson encountered a surprisingly strong African American Republican challenger, Clinton B. LeSueur, who received 43 percent of the total vote.

Governor Haley Barbour. Courtesy Mississippi Development Authority/Division of Tourism.

ing these Republican victories, the trend of switching from the Democratic to the Republican party gained momentum among state officeholders.

There was public speculation that Senator Trent Lott's insensitive comments in December 2002 would damage the Republicans' chances in state elections of the following year. At Senator Strom Thurmond's (South Carolina) 100th birthday party, Lott reminded the senator and a group of well-wishers that Mississippi had supported Thurmond's "Dixiecrat" presidential candidacy in 1948, adding that had Thurmond prevailed in that election the nation would have been better off today. Under attack for the remarks, which were labeled "racially divisive" by his critics and "offensive" by members of his own party, Lott apologized and resigned his majority leadership position in the Senate but not his seat.

The effect the incident had on state politics is difficult to gauge, but most voters either sympathized with Lott's behavior or did not consider it a factor in 2003. In the legislative contests Republicans made no significant gains, but they prevailed in key statewide elections. Democrats retained their 56 percent majority in the senate with 29 members, but they suffered a net loss of 5 seats in the house, from 81 to 76 (62 percent of the total membership). Alternatives of gridlock or cooperation faced the new 2004 legislature, given the presence of a strong black caucus, rising Republican minorities, the retirement of Speaker Ford, a Republican president of the senate (the lieutenant governor), and a Republican governor. A notable milestone in the house of representatives was the retirement of Speaker Pro Tempore Robert G. Clark, Jr., who had paved the way for African American legislators in 1968.

After a campaign characterized by negative attacks by both sides and record-setting expenditures, the Republicans elected a governor, lieutenant governor, treasurer, and auditor. Haley Barbour of Yazoo City, a lobbyist in Washington, D.C., and former chairman of the Republican National Committee, received 53 percent of the total vote to defeat incumbent Musgrove. Lieutenant Governor Tuck, who had switched to the Republican party in December 2002, was re-elected with 61 percent of the total vote, winning over African American state senator Barbara Blackmon. Another black candidate, Democrat Gary Anderson, was narrowly defeated by Tate Reeves in the race for treasurer.

The twentieth century had ended in political controversy and change in Mississippi with the resurrection of two-party competition after many decades of dominance by the Democrats. Reversals had occurred in the traditional competition between the Delta and the Hills, as increasing participation by African Americans in western counties supported the national Democratic party and mounting numbers of Republicans in eastern counties and suburban areas favored the advocates of more conservative policies. In 1964 the state had no black officeholders, except for the city council in the all-black town of Mound Bayou, but thirty years later, in 1994, Mississippi had led all other states with at least 750 African Americans elected to public office. At the beginning of the twenty-first century the number was approaching 900, including a 45-member black caucus in the state legislature.

Political scientists observed, however, that African American candidates had not been elected to statewide offices since the Reconstruction era. Their exclusion was a consequence of increasing numbers of whites leaving the Democratic party, a trend that raised questions about the extent of voters' lingering racial considerations. Many observers may have doubted Barbara Blackmon's opinion "that if my [skin] pigmentation were different, I would be the lieutenant governor of this state." But even the most conservative commentators suggested that the outcome of the Anderson-Reeves contest indicated that race still remained a key issue in Mississippi.

SELECTED SOURCES

Biographical Directory of the United States Congress, 1774 to Present (Washington, D.C.: Government Printing Office, 2003, http://bioguide.congress.gov).

Campbell, Will D., *Robert G. Clark's Journey to the House: A Black Politician's Story* (Jackson: University Press of Mississippi, 2003).

Historical Statistics of the States of the United States: Two Centuries of the Census, 1790–1990, comp. Donald B. Dodd (Westport, Conn.: Greenwood Press, 1993), Population.

Lamis, Alexander P., *The Two-Party South* (New York: Oxford University Press, 1984).

Minor, [Wilson] Bill, *Eyes on Mississippi: A Fifty-Year Chronicle of Change* (Jackson, Miss.: J Prichard Morris Books, 2001).

Mississippi Official and Statistical Register, 1984–1988, 1988–1992, 1992–1996, 1996–2000, 2000–2004.

Mitchell, Dennis J., *Mississippi Liberal: A Biography of Frank E. Smith* (Jackson: University Press of Mississippi, 2001).

Parker, Frank R., *Black Votes Count: Political Empowerment in Mississippi after 1965* (Chapel Hill: University of North Carolina Press, 1990).

Parker, Joseph B., ed., *Politics in Mississippi*, 2d ed. (Salem, Wisc.: Sheffield Publishing Company, 2001).

Yoste, Elizabeth, "Winter Civil-Rights Award Choice," *The Clarion Ledger*, June 28, 2001, 1B.

CHAPTER TWENTY-SIX

Tumultuous Trends in Education

The new speaker of the state house of representatives in 2004, Democrat William Joseph "Billy" McCoy, a twenty-four-year veteran of the house from Alcorn County, has declared that education is one of his highest priorities. Given Mississippi's tradition of tumultuous and woeful experiences in this arena, tackling educational issues will not only be the most challenging but also the most important task of state government.

BACKGROUND: THE FINAL YEARS OF SCHOOL SEGREGATION

The Funding Problem

In their tenacious struggle to maintain separate schools for whites and blacks through the middle decades of the twentieth century, white Mississippians encountered virtually insurmountable challenges. Unable to fund adequately the dual system, the state could not provide appropriate facilities and sufficient numbers of well-trained teachers. The legislature's limited appropriations for the schools amounted to less than half the needed funds and had to be supplemented by county and local district revenues. Not surprisingly, such local contributions went primarily to white schools and teachers, while paltry amounts found their way to schools for blacks.

Teacher Education

Through the early decades of the twentieth century, most teachers had no professional training, their educational experiences quite often limited to rural high school attendance. Due to substandard salaries, few college graduates opted for careers in teaching in Mississippi's public schools. White enrollment in professional education programs began with the opening of the Mississippi Normal College (present-day University of Southern Mississippi) in 1912 and Delta State Teachers College (present-day Delta State University) in 1924. In succeeding decades other institutions of higher learning added education courses to their curricula and created departments of education.

Meanwhile, the first major action by the state in support of the training of African American teachers had to wait until 1940. That year the legislature established the "State Teachers College for Negroes" (present-day Jackson State University), which had operated earlier as Jackson College, a private institution maintained primarily through private, out-of-state donations until it closed in the 1930s.

Old one-room schoolhouse. Courtesy Mississippi Department of Archives and History.

School Consolidation

In their attempts to improve public education through a more efficient use of limited funds, state leaders promoted the process of consolidating school districts. During the early years of public education, virtually autonomous county school boards made frequent changes in district lines and relocated many schoolhouses at their whim. In many small communities students ranging in age from five to twenty years old attended one-teacher, one-room, wood-frame schools that were barely equipped and poorly maintained. Attendance had been irregular, and under the circumstances it was not surprising that the state had continued to suffer high illiteracy rates.

School consolidation had begun in 1910 during Governor Noel's administration, and it continued rather irregularly for decades. Having fewer but larger schools in broader geographic areas made the system more efficient academically and economically; nevertheless, the consolidation process became difficult and erratic due to persisting local opposition, changing population patterns, and social considerations, including racial attitudes.

Transportation

Other major obstacles to consolidation had been inferior roads and unreliable means of student transportation. At first, families had received little or no public help, and as late as the 1940s some children still had to be taken to distant schools aboard trucks that were also used to haul farm products, including pigs and other livestock. But as school consolidations continued, some state and county provisions were made. By 1948 there were about 1,600 county-owned school buses and about 500 district or privately owned school buses. That year these vehicles transported about 155,000 children over 3,900 routes to and from schools.

TABLE 26.1 Selected Data for Public Schools

AVERAGE SALARIES FOR TEACHERS IN MISSISSIPPI

YEARS	MISS.	BLACK	WHITE
1948	$1,189	$599	$1,637
1969	5,760	5,643	5,846
1980	11,851		
1990	24,364		
2000	31,857		

COMPARISONS WITH OTHER STATES, 2000

MS	$31,857	
U.S.	41,754	48th
SREB*	37,362	15th
SE**	35,651	8th

EXPENDITURES PER STUDENT IN MISSISSIPPI

1950	$75
1969	466
1980	1,603
1990	3,229
2000	5,014

COMPARISONS WITH OTHER STATES, 2000

MS	$5,014	
U.S.	6,911	48th
SREB*	6,200	16th
SE**	5,689	8th

FUNDS RECEIVED FOR EDUCATION

YEAR	TOTAL AMOUNT	STATE		FEDERAL & LOCAL	
		AMOUNT	PERCENT	AMOUNT	PERCENT
1950	$35,207	$17,500	49.7%	$17,707	50.3%
1960	93,013	50,657	54.5	42,356	45.5
1969	252,810	132,870	52.6	119,940	47.4
1970	263,681	134,465	51.0	129,216	49.0
1979	664,464	316,109	47.6	348,355	52.4
1980	780,518	414,387	53.1	366,131	46.9
1990	1,625,790	896,328	55.1	729,462	44.9
2000	2,887,005	1,607,484	55.7	1,279,521	44.3

*Sixteen states that compose the Southern Regional Education Board.
**Eight southeastern states: Alabama, Arkansas, Florida, Georgia, Louisiana, Mississippi, South Carolina, and Tennessee.
SOURCE: *Statistical Abstract of the United States, 2001*, 154. SREB *Educational Data*, www.sreb.org. National Center for Educational Statistics, 2002. http://nces.ed.gov/programs/digest/d02/tables'dt169B.asp. Mississippi Department of Education, www.mde.k12.ms.us.

School Attendance

It was impossible to achieve acceptable educational goals without regular attendance, longer school terms, some degree of curriculum uniformity and academic standards. Although the first compulsory attendance law had been enacted

TABLE 26.2 Enrollment in Institutions of Higher Learning, 1970–2000

	1970	1980	1990	2000	CHANGE 1970–2000
PUBLIC TWO-YEAR COLLEGES					
Full-time Enrollment	21,190	36,757	50,257	61,361	190%
Percent/Rank in SREB*	4.6/8th	3.4/10th	3.3/10th	3.5/10th	
NON-PUBLIC TWO-YEAR COLLEGES					
Full-time Enrollment	1,979	2,351	3,205	895	-55
Percent/Rank in SREB*	4.4/10th	3.8/10th	5.0/11th	1.4/12th	
ALL TWO-YEAR COLLEGES					
Full-time Enrollment	23,169	39,108	53,462	62,256	169
Percent/Rank in SREB*	4.6/7th	3.4/11th	3.4/11th	3.4/12th	
PUBLIC FOUR-YEAR INSTITUTIONS					
Full-time Enrollment	43,778	53,904	58,781	63,994	46
Percent/Rank in SREB*	3.5/13th	3.1/15th	2.9/15th	2.9/15th	
NON-PUBLIC FOUR-YEAR INSTITUTIONS					
Full-time Enrollment	7,020	9,352	10,640	11,139	59
Percent/Rank in SREB*	5.2/9th	4.3/10th	4.5/9th	4.2/9th	
ALL FOUR-YEAR INSTITUTIONS					
Full-time Enrollment	50,798	63,256	69,421	75,133	48
Percent/Rank in SREB*	3.1/14th	2.9/15th	2.7/15th	2.5/15th	
ALL INSTITUTIONS OF HIGHER EDUCATION					
Full-time Enrollment	73,967	102,364	122,883	137,389	86
Percent/Rank in SREB*	3.5/12th	3.1/12th	2.9/13th	2.9/13th	

*Percentage of full-time enrollment and rank within the 16 states that compose the Southern Regional Education Board. For example, in 1970 enrollment in Mississippi's public two-year colleges was 4.6 percent of the total enrollment in the SREB, and Mississippi's enrollment ranked 8th from the top among the sixteen states.
SOURCE: SREB Educational Data, www.sreb.org/main/EdData/FactBook/indexoftables03. asp#Enrollment.

in 1918, it was virtually impossible to enforce, and great numbers of children—including most blacks in some counties—did not attend school regularly if at all. There were great variances in school schedules among the various districts, depending on the size of the district's school fund as well as the local farmers' labor needs. Most country schools had short terms of four months, while town districts and others attempted to extend classes to eight months. Not until 1958 did nine-month terms become standard.

Curriculum and Textbooks

At first there had been no statewide understanding about curriculum, and individual teachers had taught the "three Rs" and whatever else their own educational and life experiences would allow. For their textbooks pupils usually had to rely on materials the teachers and the community were able to supply. Except for recommendations by the state superintendent of education, there had been no enforceable state policy about books for subjects or class levels. Attempting to acquire some degree of uniformity in the selection of textbooks and to break an alleged monopoly of the American Book Company, the legislature had established a textbook commission in 1904. Founded by New York publisher Alfred C. Barnes in the late nineteenth century, the American Book Company, a consortium of several leading publishers of schoolbooks, supplied texts throughout the Southern states, including about 80 percent of those adopted in Mississippi.

Thereafter, progress had been made in the selection of books, but uniformity had been difficult to achieve, as many pupils' families could not afford to buy the selected texts. A proposal that the state provide free school books for all students had been repeated through the decades, but not until 1940 was it enacted by the legislature. This law also created the state Textbook Rating and Purchasing Board, members of which were appointed by the governor until 1946, when the state superintendent was given appointment authority. Opponents of the law went to court, objecting to free books for black students and for Roman Catholic students attending parochial schools. They argued that most blacks did not pay taxes and that assistance to church-related schools violated the principle of church-state separation. But in 1941 the state supreme court in *Chance et al.* v. *Mississippi State Textbook Rating and Purchasing Board* upheld the state's distribution of free texts to students in all schools, public, private, and parochial. But controversies over who controlled the book selection process continued, and a 1960 law provided the appointment of four board members by the governor and the other three by the state superintendent of education.

Accreditation

While providing free textbooks was the state's most progressive educational achievement at the time, slowness in attaining a process for school accreditation remained one of its serious shortcomings. Action had begun rather late, and sporadic efforts undertaken over half a century had failed to produce viable accrediting procedures for black schools. The origin of school accreditation was a program designed at the University of Mississippi in 1898 for white high school students to complete for admission to the university. Twenty years later the Mississippi Education Association created a high school accrediting commission, and in 1926 an elementary accrediting commission was established. Finally in the 1940s the two groups joined to form the Mississippi Commission on School Accreditation for white schools. At that time only 17 percent of the state's white high schools were accredited by the Southern Association of Secondary Schools and Colleges (SACS), the respected regional agency.

Accreditation for black schools came much later. In 1945 the Mississippi Association for Teachers and Colored Schools (which became the Mississippi Teachers' Association in 1947) formed a "Negro Accrediting Commission." In 1959 this agency became the "State Accrediting Commission" for black schools and adopted the same criteria as those held by the Mississippi Commission on School Accreditation for white schools. These dual commissions continued to accredit public schools until 1970, when the legislature shifted the responsibility for all schools to the state Board of Education.

Illiteracy Rates

Progress in reducing the number of illiterate persons was a more realistic measurement of the performance of the public education system than the status of school accreditation. During the first two decades of the twentieth century the illiteracy rate declined slowly among native males twenty-one years of age and older. Among blacks it declined from 53 to 36 percent; among whites from 8 to 5 percent; and among all men from 34 to 21 percent. Another criterion reveals minimal improvements during the 1940s. There were only slight rises in the percentage of persons twenty-five years of age and older who had completed four years of high school. For females the numbers rose from 10 to 14 percent; for males, from 7 to 10.5 percent; and for all persons, from 8.5 to 12 percent.

While these numbers indicated some improvements, the reality was that far too many Mississippians were under educated. In actual numbers, for example, almost 941,000 adult residents had not completed four years of high school in 1950—eighty years after public education began in the state. Not surprisingly, African Americans composed a large majority of this group. These facts were not only shocking and alarming but indictments of the state leadership and its system of public education.

PUBLIC SCHOOL DESEGREGATION AND BEYOND

Separate and Unequal Schools

The State's Dilemma   In spite of the United States Supreme Court's "separate-but-equal doctrine" of 1896, Mississippi's separate schools for whites were clearly

Early integrated classroom. Courtesy Mississippi Department of Archives and History.

superior to those for African American children, who comprised a majority of the state's youth. Failing to meet the high court's standard, the white chiefs of public education showed little interest in the deplorable conditions of black schools until the federal government finally intervened in the 1950s.

Some state leaders saw the "handwriting on the wall" early, and in 1949 Superintendent of Education Jackson M. Tubb warned the legislature that action was necessary to "insure a greater degree of comparable educational opportunities for all the children of all the people." On the race issue Tubb announced a program of adult education through a contract with the Veterans Administration "for the benefit primarily of Negro service men." And he appealed for white and "Negro" leaders to work together for the improvement of "Negro" education. "Negro boys and girls," he maintained, "are entitled to maximum opportunities in developing their abilities to the fullest usefulness. . . ." Anticipating that obviously unequal school conditions might result in federal court orders to desegregate, white leaders sought preventive actions. With one eye on national civil rights developments and the other on white citizens' agitation, Governor White called extraordinary sessions of the legislature in three successive years beginning in 1953.

Now the legislature voted record-setting increases in educational appropriations, mainly to address the problem of inferior black school facilities. In 1953 it established the Educational Finance Commission to disburse funds for buildings and approve plans for school locations and district reorganization and consolidation. But because the largest share of all educational costs still had to be paid by counties and districts, support for black schools remained deficient. To strengthen the state's contribution to local school districts, the "Minimum Foundation Program" was begun in 1954. But in spite of the rise of expenditures per pupil from $75 to $175 during the 1950s, state appropriations increased no higher than about 55 percent of total school expenditures.

Hoping to somehow put off the inevitable, recalcitrant white legislators continued to raise funding to maintain a dual system of public schools. Appropriations grew by almost 180 percent during the 1950s and by 162 percent in the following decade. Total expenditures in this twenty-year period jumped from $75 to $466 per student. Now, however, state leaders were caught in the paradox of justifying more money for education as the means for economic advancement while paying for a redundant, uneconomical program.

Teachers' salaries remained woefully low, and the difference between what white and black teachers took home was glaringly unequal as the state approached desegregation. The legislature steadily worked to accomplish equitable pay, but it proved to be a costly and unobtainable task, partly because of the higher number of teachers needed in the dual system. In 1948 the average annual salary had been $1,637 for white teachers and $599 for their black counterparts, and through the next two crucial decades the average pay increased by 257 percent for whites and 842 percent for blacks, but whites were still receiving more money than blacks. By 1969 there were 22,327 teachers in the state earning an average of $5,760 a year, the lowest pay in the southeastern states and far below the national average of $10,114.

Because their attempts to equalize funding for black schools were too little and too late, white leaders resorted to an extreme strategy. Reacting to the first

Brown ruling, the special session of the legislature in 1954 proposed, as mentioned, a constitutional amendment to abolish the state's public schools as a last resort for the preservation of segregation.

Although the voters overwhelmingly ratified the amendment, the state's teachers were not happy about the prospect. Addressing the Mississippi Education Association, Superintendent Tubb agreed that the dual, segregated system was "best for us" but argued against abolishing the public school system. The following year the legislature employed another strategy. By repealing the requirement for separate districts for blacks and whites, the state might desegregate school districts but continue segregated schools. A further safeguard for whites came with the repeal of the compulsory attendance law in 1956.

In a series of speeches around the state, Thomas P. Brady, a state circuit court judge, declared that the date of the 1954 *Brown* decision would be remembered as "Black Monday." He blamed the school desegregation order on a Communist plot designed to "mongrelize our children and grandchildren." White people in Mississippi and throughout the nation, he proclaimed, should resist such racial "amalgamation" by abolishing public schools and forcing the creation of a separate state for blacks, whom he viewed as inferior to white persons.

Representing hundreds of black leaders in the state, T. R. M. Howard, an African American physician and successful businessman, presented the opposite point of view. He called on the governor and legislators to implement the Supreme Court's ruling by improving the public schools and ending legal segregation. Instead of seeking ways to evade the law, Howard declared, the state should act to end "all the injustices that you have heaped upon the Negro in Mississippi."

Transitions, the 1960s and 1970s

Forced Compliance   For more than a decade the state managed to avoid compliance with the federal court's mandate. Not until the enactment of the Civil Rights Act of 1964 was Mississippi forced to begin desegregating public schools, a process that would require six more years. In the midst of these transitions, a new state superintendent of education took office in 1968. Garvin Johnston, the state's first superintendent with an earned doctorate, the Ed. D. from the University of Southern Mississippi, described the first three and one half years of his tenure as the most critical time for public education in the twentieth century. In 1969 the Supreme Court ended the "all deliberate speed" doctrine when it ordered thirty-three school districts in Mississippi to desegregate immediately. The Department of Heath, Education and Welfare had asked that the districts be granted more time to desegregate, the first time HEW had sought a delay in integration. But in *Alexander* v. *Holmes County Board of Education* the Supreme Court ordered that integration proceed "at once."

In the summer of 1970 school districts that had not yet adopted acceptable desegregation plans were placed under federal court orders to integrate all their schools. Superintendent Johnston reported that although many whites enrolled in "hastily-established private schools," the public school enrollment of 534,000 students in September was 92 percent of the previous year's number. He believed, therefore, that statewide the great majority continued to support public schools. Such confidence, Johnston opined, was further reflected in the 1971 legislature's

State Superintendent of Education Garvin Johnston. Courtesy Pearl River Community College.

10 percent increase in appropriations for teachers' salaries, with an average raise of $1,825 per teacher since 1968. In the same period appropriations for elementary and secondary schools were increased by 59 percent. In his article, "Johnston Saved Public Education," veteran journalist Bill Minor includes Johnston among his Mississippi "heroes"— individuals such as Aaron Henry, Willie Morris, Claude Ramsay, the spokesman for organized labor, and William Winter. Minor recalls that when most state leaders, including by Governor John Bell Williams, reacted to the *Alexander* decision by encouraging—whether by implication or through unequivocal statements—whites to move their children to private schools, Johnston "assumed the full burden at the state level to defend the public schools."

EDUCATIONAL TRENDS IN THE LATE TWENTIETH CENTURY

A Different Kind of School Segregation

Superintendent Johnston's confidence in public education may have been better defined as hope. Like him, a growing number of state leaders understood that better schools were essential for economic growth, which had been obstructed by the continuing blight of illiteracy among a large portion of the state's population. Many whites, however, reasoned that private or home schooling was an acceptable alternative to the racially integrated public system.

This inclination produced a fast rise in the number of private schools, which jumped from 95 in 1968 to 289 in 1971. Their enrollment rose quickly from 25,747 in 1969 to 65,707 in 1971, which was 11 percent of the state's total enrollment in elementary and secondary schools. After this first spurt, however, the number of private schools dropped about as fast as it had risen. By the end of the century the state Department of Education reported fewer than fifty private schools.

Although the number of well-established, accredited private schools declined, the size of non-public school enrollment actually increased at a faster pace than the growth rate of the state's total population. Even with the addition of kindergartens, the total public school enrollment of 496,558 students at the end of the twentieth century was lower than it had been for at least fifty years. Many white families sent their children to private and parochial schools and to scores of small nursery-kindergartens and elementary schools provided by their local churches. Moreover, dissatisfaction with both public and private schools led many parents to educate their children at home. By 2000 the estimated private school enrollment was more than forty thousand, while the number of home-schooled students may have exceeded ten thousand.

The reasons given publicly for not having one's children attend public schools shifted gradually away from racist attitudes of earlier decades. Most major parochial institutions and a few private schools opened their doors to persons of color, although very few African Americans entered the latter institutions. Whites increasingly blamed their lack of faith in the public schools on worries about the quality of public education generally and desires to integrate religion with the school curriculum following federal court rulings related to church-state separation. A serious problem with the fragmented system of public, private, parochial, and home schools was the absence of accreditation consistency.

The Educational Reform Act of 1982

The turning point in Mississippi's struggle to attain quality and equity in public education came with the election of Governor William Winter in 1979 and the enactment of the Educational Reform Act of 1982. Following a prolonged struggle to make the state's educational leadership less political and more professional, this law and a constitutional amendment in 1982 produced fundamental changes in the state organization.

More authority was given to a new state Board of Education composed of nine members who did not hold political office and who were appointed to nine-year, staggered terms. The governor's five appointments would include one person from each of the three supreme court districts, a school administrator, and a teacher, while the lieutenant governor and the speaker of the house would appoint two members each from the state at large. Selected on the basis of appropriate qualifications and experience in public education, this board exercised final policy-making authority over the state Department of Education, which implemented the board's policies under the direction of the state superintendent of education. Primarily a planning and service organization, the Department of Education supervised local school operations from kindergartens through junior colleges and was required to formulate and publish ongoing "five-year plans" with specific objectives as bases for budget requests to the legislature.

Garvin Johnston (1968–76) and Charles E. Holladay (1976–84) were the last state superintendents of education to be elected, as the new legislation authorized the board to select the superintendent with the advice and consent of the senate. Under this new system, three superintendents would serve "at the board's will and pleasure," Richard A. Boyd (1984–92), Tom Burnham (1992–2000), and Richard Thompson (2000–02), who was succeeded by the first African American to hold that office, Henry L. Johnson.

Within this structure, however, local officials exercised the primary administrative duties within three main types of school districts: county, municipal separate, and consolidated. The county district encompassed an entire county; the municipal separate district included a large town and, in "special" cases, extended into the suburbs of that town; and the consolidated district comprised different parts of a county (but not the entire county) or covered areas in more than one county. In the latter case, that of crossing county lines, the consolidated district was called a "line" district. In each district a board of education and superintendent oversaw public school funding and operations and thus had far-reaching influence in community affairs generally.

General Funding and Teachers' Salaries

The new state leadership in education inherited a seriously underfinanced system despite substantially higher appropriations in the 1970s: state funding rose to more than $316 million and total expenditures from all sources exceeded $664 million by 1979. In that decade spending per student increased by 244 percent, but Mississippi still lagged behind the national and southeastern averages. Accompanying the reform measures in the early 1980s, appropriations rose during that decade by 116 percent and total spending per student by 101 percent, reaching $3,229 by 1990. This momentum, however, did not continue through the final decade of the century, when state appropriations grew at a rate of 79 percent and total spending per student 55 percent.

At the end of the century Mississippi was spending more on education than on any other function of state government, except for health and social services. Representing more than one-fourth of all expenditures, the state reported $1.6 billion for education in 2000 ($2.9 billion from all sources). Total spending per pupil that year was $5,014, and the average salary for teachers was $31,857, more than five-and-one-half times the 1969 level. But impressive as these gains were, the state still could not overcome the burdens it carried from the past. In both categories, teachers' salaries and spending per student, Mississippi ranked forty-eighth among the fifty states and last among its neighboring southeastern states.[1]

Consolidation and Transportation

Notwithstanding these low national and regional standings, the state did achieve some important internal progress. School consolidation was finally accomplished in the post–World War II years. During the 1950s and 1960s, as segregation ended, the number of school districts dropped from 1,003 to 150, and the total number of schools fell from almost 5,800 to 1,043. At the end of the century there were 1,028 schools and 152 districts.

Consolidation required public transportation, and in spite of early concerns about cost and safety, school buses became the most visible symbols of public education. The number of buses increased from about 1,600 in 1948 to almost 7,200 in 2000. State costs for the transportation of students rose from $16.9 million in 1973 to $113.7 million in 1999, remaining through the years at about 5 percent of total public school expenditures. The number of students transported grew from an estimated 31 percent of enrolled students in 1948—when the buses were primarily for whites and before consolidation had made much headway—to 83 percent in 2000. Except for the brief period when it was identified with forced segregation in the early 1970s, the school bus remained a popular, relatively safe and economical way to facilitate consolidation and improve school attendance.

The Question of Quality

Although Mississippi did not rise in the national and regional ranks for financing teachers and students, the state did began to improve substantially the

1 See Table 26.1, Selected Data for Public Schools, p. 369.

quality of public education in the 1980s. This accomplishment was truly a daunting task, for past mistakes haunted a system burdened with massive, firmly entrenched problems. Aiming to hold students, teachers, and administrators accountable to higher standards and expand opportunities for learning, the Reform Act of 1982 launched a more effective program for accreditation, which was now mandatory for all public school districts and voluntary for private schools. The process involved systematic planning, setting uniform criteria and goals, and assessing performance. The extent to which a school district fulfilled performance and process standards determined the district's accreditation status. Using these objective measurements, the Commission on School Accreditation assigned districts to accredited levels ranging from five for "excellent" to one for "probation" or "withdrawn" for failing districts.

Upon the implementation of this new program a number of school districts failed to meet the standards and were designated as "warned," "on probation," or "withdrawn." For the purpose of helping all districts achieve at least accreditation level three, "successful," the legislature enacted the "Adequate Education Program" of 1997, which increased funding to schools based on their average daily attendance.

Teacher Qualifications and Student Competency

Other major reforms aimed to ensure classroom teachers' instructional skills and subject competency. A commission was established to set new standards for teachers' preparation, licensure, and continuing professional development. State certification that these standards were fulfilled, including successful completion of the National Teacher Examination, was required for all teachers. To attract more qualified persons, salary levels were raised to reflect the four teacher certification levels. For the 2000–01 school year, however, more than 70 percent of all teachers were certified at the lowest level, and less then 3 percent had attained the two highest levels.

Statewide tests were administered for pupils in the third grade and higher to determine their competency levels in the core curriculum. Test results were used to improve instruction and reduce dropout rates. High school graduation requirements were imposed beginning in 1985, including the completion of a minimum number of academic credits and the attainment of satisfactory scores on performance tests in reading, writing, and mathematics.

Compulsory Attendance and Early Childhood Education

Since the state's efforts to dodge racial integration in the 1950s, there had been no requirement for school attendance. Now, more than a quarter century later, the reform measures reestablished compulsory attendance for children six and seven years of age beginning in 1983 and extended the minimum age for required school attendance to sixteen in succeeding years. These reforms also extended educational opportunities to preschool and early elementary children, as provisions were made for teaching assistants in all classrooms for grades 1–3 by 1985 and for public kindergartens in all school districts by 1986.

The Dropout Problem and Adult Illiteracy

A persisting obstacle was the excessive number of youths who did not finish their basic schooling. During the 1960s less than 60 percent of all fifth graders had continued in school through the twelfth grade, and on the eve of racial desegregation in 1969 that completion rate had been 62 percent, including 74 percent of the white students and 50 percent of black students. There had been virtually no change in the following decade, and by 1980 the rate had risen only one point to 63 percent.

During the 1971–72 school year, a tumultuous time for the public schools, a total of 19,512 students had dropped out of school. This attrition rate of 3.6 percent had remained constant through the 1970s but declined gradually in the next two decades as a consequence of retention programs initiated in the early 1980s. The Department of Education provided assistance to local schools for "dropout prevention" programs, and federal funds became available for after-school tutorial sessions. During the 1990s the attrition rate dropped from 2.61 percent of enrolled students to 1.8 percent during the 1999–2000 school year, when 8,178 students withdrew.

Although the student attrition rate had declined, the cumulative effect of large numbers of dropouts over many years was excessive illiteracy among the state's adult population. Calling attention to the negative consequences of adult illiteracy and proposing remedies, the Mabus administration established an Office for Literacy and requested special state funding and private business support for a high-profile literacy campaign for adults. In 1988 Governor Mabus ". . . vowed that nine out of ten Mississippians would be functionally literate by the year 2000, a monumental task that amounts to a holy war on illiteracy." According to columnist Jonathan Maslow, the governor "staked his political future on a comprehensive education-reform program, including a proposed $13.5 million in new state funds . . . for adult-literacy programs." In 1990, 46 percent of the state's adult population had not graduated from high school, and about 400,000 adults were classified as "functionally illiterate," having less than nine years of schooling. In spite of Governor Mabus's efforts, adult illiteracy persisted; at the start of the twentieth-first century more than one-fourth of all Mississippi adults had not completed four years of high school. Indeed, Mississippi still ranked last among the fifty states in this category, substantially above the national illiteracy rate of 16 percent.

A study by the Friedman Foundation, an organization established by economists Milton and Rose D. Friedman to promote educational reform, concluded that Mississippi public schools in the 1990s wasted 21 percent of the tax money they spent by failing to reduce levels of basic illiteracy in reading, writing, and computing, the worst state record in the nation. Echoing similar concerns about illiteracy, the publisher of the *Mississippi Business Journal* in 2001 bemoaned the fact that 30 percent of the state's adults were unable to read simple instructions and argued that illiteracy was a major factor in the loss of manufacturing jobs and sluggish economic growth. In his view the state's top priority should be to lower Mississippi from its position of highest illiteracy ranking in the United States except for the District of Columbia. Acknowledging the problem and seeking to help find solutions, early in 2000 Mississippi native James Barksdale, former head of Netscape Communications, and his wife Sally donated $100 million to the University of Mississippi for the establishment of an institute that would aim to reduce the rate of illiteracy by teaching children to read.

"The Report Card"

Based on troublesome evaluations of the public schools' performances such a contribution and other actions were sorely needed. As in the area of state funding, the state's internal progress was notable but still lagged behind that of other states. One national organization of professional educators assessed the state's public school system as barely average at the start of the twenty-first century, citing some progress in early childhood education but noting low scores by fourth and eighth graders on competency tests in reading, mathematics, and science, and high adult illiteracy rates. Such concerns were reflected in the state's struggle to extend the education of high school graduates to higher levels.

HIGHER EDUCATION

Junior Colleges

The fastest growing college enrollment in the late twentieth century was in the state's system of junior colleges, which had begun in the 1920s. The trend of junior colleges separating from their agricultural high school forebears gained momentum with increasing public support, and in the 1950s the legislature began to organize the state into geographic districts for junior colleges to serve.

One example of the institutions' evolution was the history of the Mississippi Gulf Coast Community College, which began as the Harrison-Stone-Jackson Agricultural High School and Junior College in 1925. Its name changed to Perkinston Agricultural High School and Junior College in 1942, to Perkinston Junior College when the agricultural high school was discontinued, to the Mississippi Gulf Coast Junior College in 1962, and, finally, to the Mississippi Gulf Coast Community College in the late 1980s, by which time it was operating eight campuses and centers.

Until 1986, when the state Board for Community and Junior Colleges was established, the state Department of Education and the Junior College Commission

were jointly responsible for overseeing the system. Reflecting a more appropriate description of the institutions' role in the state, by 1987 the term *community* replaced *junior* in the colleges' titles except for Jones County, which chose to re-

Perkinston campus of the Mississippi Gulf Coast Community College. Courtesy Mississippi Gulf Coast Community College.

Mississippi State University's school of veterinary medicine. Courtesy Mississippi State University.

tain its original name. At the end of the twentieth century there were fifteen public community and junior colleges with twenty-three campuses and nine vocational-technical centers operating in fifteen districts throughout the state. All the institutions were governed locally by district boards of trustees, who were appointed by county boards of supervisors, but the entire system was coordinated by the ten-member state board, which was appointed by the governor with the advice and consent of the senate. Two board members were named from each of the five congressional districts, and their six-year terms overlapped.

If judged by its popularity, the state's community college system was a successful means of expanding educational opportunities. Not until the 1970s, however, did it provide equal access for African Americans. Prior to desegregation, only three black schools offered the thirteenth and fourteenth grades, and they were not developed until the late 1940s.

Total community college enrollment rose from 1,600 in 1931 to 44,000 in 1969 (full-time enrollment was substantially lower). During the final three decades of the century, the number of students attending these institutions increased to a total headcount of more than 123,000. Funds for this expanding system came from four sources, which varied in proportion over the decades; in 2001 state appropriations provided 61 percent, students' tuition 20 percent, local tax revenues 13 percent, and federal assistance 6 percent.

Public Universities

In increasing numbers community college graduates continued their education in the state's eight universities. Racially segregated until 1962, there were three historically black institutions, Alcorn State University, Jackson State University, and Mississippi Valley University. The latter institution's origin dates to 1946, when the legislature approved the establishment of a vocational school for African Americans. After a four-year delay, the Mississippi Vocational College opened at Itta Bena in Leflore County with the critical support of Governor Wright and Speaker Walter Sillers. Their efforts were influenced by the desire to maintain racially segregated colleges in the face of mounting challenges to the "separate but equal" doctrine in federal courts. The college's initial mission was to prepare students for employment and train teachers, but reflecting the growth of its liberal arts curriculum the name was changed to Mississippi Valley State College in 1964. Four years later the college was accredited by SACS, and in 1974 it was granted university status. Four other institutions elevated to university status in 1974 were Alcorn Agricultural and Mechanical College, Delta State College, Jackson State College, and Mississippi State College for Women. Mississippi Southern College became the University of Southern Mississippi in 1962.

Despite financial difficulties and troublesome racial and political issues, the state's universities made significant progress in the late twentieth century. The institutions gained accreditation by SACS in the following order: University of Mississippi, 1895; Mississippi University for Women, 1921; Mississippi State University, 1926, University of Southern Mississippi, 1929; Delta State University, 1930; Alcorn State University, 1948; Jackson State University, 1948; Mississippi Valley State University, 1968. The University of Mississippi medical school became a full, four-year program in 1955, when it was moved to Jackson upon the opening of the university medical center that in succeeding decades would include the schools of nursing, health related professions, and dentistry. The university's repeated attempts to acquire a chapter of Phi Beta Kappa, a national academic honor society, finally succeeded in April 2001.

The State Agricultural and Mechanical College was accredited by SACS in 1926, and by 1932, when it was renamed Mississippi State College, its programs

had expanded to include the Agricultural Experiment Station, the state Agricultural Extension Service, the college of business and industry, and other curricula. After the addition of the graduate school, the school of forest resources, and the college of arts and sciences, the legislature designated the institution Mississippi State University in 1958. In the following decades the schools of architecture and accountancy, and the college of veterinary medicine were established.

The Mississippi University for Women, which had been recognized for its superior academic program, admitted male students for the first time in 1982, pursuant to the United States Supreme Court's ruling in *Mississippi University for Women* v. *Hogan*. In this case, Joe Hogan, an experienced registered nurse who did not have a baccalaureate degree in nursing, applied for admission to MUW's recently established School of Nursing. After the university refused to

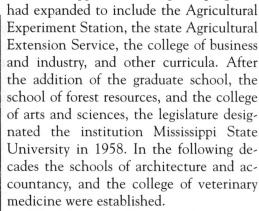

Belhaven College. Courtesy Belhaven College.

admit him soley on the basis of his sex—he was otherwise qualified—Hogan filed a law suit in federal court, claiming MUW's single-sex admissions policy violated the equal protection clause of the Fourteenth Amendment to the United States Constitution. Ultimately, the Supreme Court agreed with Hogan, who was admitted to the School of Nursing. Thereafter, the school's mission was adjusted to affirm "MUW as an institution of quality academic programs for all qualified students with emphasis on distinctive opportunities for women." Somewhat ironically given its heritage, the university did not install its first female president until 1988; however, alumnae and supporters resisted pressures to adopt a nongender specific institutional title.

Private Colleges

The state's seven leading private colleges, all of which were related to various religious denominations, attracted fewer students than did the public institutions of higher education. By the 1960s the private colleges had discontinued admissions policies based on race and gender: Rust and Tougaloo colleges were historically African American institutions, Mississippi College and Millsaps had been founded for white males, and Belhaven, Blue Mountain, and William Carey were originally for white females.

With liberal arts and religious curricula initially, most of these institutions expanded their arts and sciences core and developed programs in business and professional education.[2] By the late twentieth century some of them began graduate studies, special programs for adults, and off-campus branches in Mississippi and other states. In the 1970s, for example, the Mississippi College curriculum was expanded to include a law school through the acquisition of the Jackson School of Law, a private institution located in Jackson. Signs of academic achievement included Millsaps College's acquisition of the state's first chapter of Phi Beta Kappa in 1989. Ahead of other private, white institutions, in 1965 the Millsaps trustees approved a policy of admissions without regard to race.

Accreditation and Racial Issues

The path traveled by institutions of higher education in Mississippi lay strewn with more than the ordinary obstacles. Among the highest hurdles in the twentieth century were instances of political manipulation that threatened the institutions' chances for accreditation and perpetuated racist practices. The best-known events related to the former problem involved actions by Governor Bilbo during his second administration and by Governor Johnson in the early 1940s. Both instances prompted the legislature to reorganize the governance of the state's institutions of higher education. The state's intransigent stance against admitting African Americans to all public colleges and universities finally culminated at the doors of Ole Miss in 1962, when James Meredith finally broke through the barriers on the shoulders of federal marshals.

The Ayers Case Meredith's admission, however, ended neither the state's policy of racial segregation in higher education nor its maintenance of a dual system in

2 The private colleges were accredited by SACS in the following order: Millsaps College, 1912; Mississippi College, 1922; Blue Mountain College, 1927; Belhaven College, 1946; Tougaloo College, 1955; William Carey College, 1958; Rust College, 1970.

which historically black institutions remained inferior to white institutions due to discrimination in funding and other state practices. Remedies for such inequities were claimed in 1975 by Jake Ayers, Sr., who filed a lawsuit against the state in the northern district federal court in Oxford. After twenty-seven years of litigation involving appeals and counter appeals to the Fifth Circuit Court and the United States Supreme Court, District Court Judge Neal B. Biggers finally approved a settlement agreement favoring the plaintiffs and ordering the state to appropriate for the black institutions more than $500 million, to be used to expand their academic programs, and recognize Jackson State University as a "comprehensive university." As late as 2004, however, disbursement of the money was not forthcoming due to continuing appeals by some of the plaintiffs, who argued that the settlement was inadequate.

Enrollment

In spite of the increasing number of public and private two-year and four-year colleges, student enrollment advanced at a relatively slow rate through the first half of the twentieth century. Between 1900 and 1950 the number of college students rose from 2,700 to 22,700, representing an increase from 2 to 15 percent of the traditional college-age population on those dates. In the next two decades the rate of growth increased, and by 1970 almost 74,000 students were enrolled, representing about 43 percent of the college-age population. But throughout this period of racial segregation, African Americans continued to be denied equal access, and the great majority of college students were white. In the late 1960s, when a small number of blacks were just beginning to enter the state's all-white institutions, only 15 percent of all college students attended the black colleges. In 1970 their numbers rose to more than 15,000 students, a record high but less than 21 percent of total college enrollments—this at a time when blacks composed 37 percent of the state's population.

During the last three decades of the century the total number of students enrolled full time in public and private institutions of higher learning rose to more than 137,000. In the late 1990s, 29 percent of all persons aged eighteen to twenty-four years attended college, a rate of enrollment just below the national average of 32 percent and even with the Southern Regional Educational Board average. In the year 2000, 62,256 students enrolled for full-time studies in the community colleges, while 75,133 entered the four-year institutions.[3]

Leading in the state's overall increase in student population during the 1990s were women, who accounted for 58 percent, and minorities, who composed 33 percent of the total enrollment in 1998. Women earned about three-fifths of all associate's, bachelor's, and master's degrees awarded in 1998, while blacks earned about one-fourth of these degrees. Even though the number of adults with a bachelor's degree or higher edged up from 8 percent in 1970 to 19 percent in 2000, the state remained far below the national average of 26 percent and failed to rise above 47th nationally in this category.

Funding

Notwithstanding the other manifold obstacles in the progress of higher education, the highest hurdle had been inadequate funding. Until the 1920s there was

3 See Table 26.2, Enrollment in Institutions of Higher Learning, p. 370.

only minimum state support for the public institutions, and most expenses were paid from student fees and local contributions. In response to reports of insufficient funds for academic programs and deplorable physical conditions, in 1928 the legislature adopted record appropriations of $1.6 million for the University of Mississippi and $2.15 million for the five state colleges. This level of funding, however, was short-lived, as appropriations declined sharply during the Depression years.

Factors demanding larger appropriations in the post–World War II years included growing enrollments, expanding curricular offerings, inflation of the dollar's value, and the founding of new institutions. The total 1950–51 biennial appropriation of $18.3 million (including funds for junior colleges) rose to an annual appropriation totaling $87.2 million in 1974. In spite of what appeared to be substantial increases, the state still trailed the other southeastern states, except Arkansas, by considerable margins.

Notwithstanding occasional efforts to change the situation, appropriations for higher education continued to rise, but not to the level needed to improve the state's inferior regional and national standing. During the final three decades of the twentieth century state funding rose by 1,044 percent, reaching $824 million for 2000–01, but increases by the other southeastern states, except Arkansas, were as much or more.

State support was only part of the challenge of financing higher education. Because operating costs greatly exceeded tax revenues, the institutions had to depend on other sources for about half their budgets. Income from nonstate sources, including student tuition and fees, federal assistance, private contributions, and various grants, amounted to 46.5 percent of total expenditures in 1980 and 54 percent in 1997.

Faculty Salaries

The best example of adequate funding as an absolute requirement for the maintenance of higher education was the state's struggle to attract and retain able college faculties. During the 1990s salaries at Mississippi's public four-year institutions rose by 40 percent, a slower rate than the national average but even with the regional average. Though the state's increases were praiseworthy, they were based on meager salary levels in previous years and did not result in totals that compared favorably with those in most other states. In 1999 the average annual salary of $48,600 for a college professor at a four-year institution in the state ranked forty-sixth nationally and twelfth in the sixteen-state SREB region. (It was $8,300 below the national average and $4,400 behind the regional average.) And the average salaries for faculty members at community colleges and private colleges were even lower. In 2001 the state's University Faculty Senate Association reported that "college and university faculty salaries have not grown at rates as high as those of all workers over the past 25 years."

SELECTED SOURCES

Bond, Bradley G., *Mississippi: A Documentary History* (Jackson: University Press of Mississippi, 2003).

Brieger, James F., *Hometown, Mississippi*, 3rd ed. (Jackson: Town Square Books, Inc., 1997).

The Constitutions of Mississippi as Originally Adopted (University, Miss.: Bureau of Governmental Research, 1982).

Griffith, Reuben W., "The Public School, 1890–1970," in Richard Aubrey McLemore, ed., *A History of Mississippi*, 2 vols. (Hattiesburg: University & College Press of Mississippi, 1973), 2: 392–414.

Holland, Robert and Don Soifer, "Waste in Education Public Schools Produce Low Literacy Return for the Dollars Spent," Milton and Rose D. Friedman Foundation, *Latest News* (www.friedmanfoundation.org).

Jones, Joe D., "As I See It," *Mississippi Business Journal*, October 22, 2001 (www.msbusiness.com).

Kirwan, Albert D., *Revolt of the Rednecks, Mississippi Politics: 1876–1925* (Lexington: University of Kentucky Press), 1951.

Maslow, Jonathan, "Mississippi: Literate at Last," *The Atlantic Monthly*, August, 1990, 28–33.

McLemore, Richard Aubrey, "Higher Education in the Twentieth Century," in Richard Aubrey McLemore, ed., *A History of Mississippi*, 2 vols. (Hattiesburg: University & College Press of Mississippi, 1973), 2: 415–445.

Mississippi, *Annotated Code of 1972*. See Title 37 for education statutes.

———, Mississippi Department of Education, Mississippi Public Education, Quick Facts, 2000; 2000 Annual Report, 2000–2001 (www.mde.k12.ms.us).

———, State Board for Community and Junior Colleges, Fall 2000, Preliminary Enrollment Report, Statistical Data, 2000–2001 (www.sbcjc.cc.ms.us).

Mississippi Community Colleges (www.50states.com/cc/miss).

Mississippi Home Educators Association (www.mhea.net).

Mississippi Official and Statistical Register [various dates].

Mississippi Private School Association (www.mpsa.org).

Mississippi Statistical Abstract, 1971, 1974, 1981, 1991.

National Center for Education Statistics, 1999 (www.nces.ed.gov).

"Quality Counts 2002," *Education Week* (www.edweek.org/sreports/qc02).

Sansing, David G., *Making Haste Slowly: The Troubled History of Higher Education in Mississippi* (Jackson: University Press of Mississippi, 1990).

Southern Literary Communications Consortium (slincs.coe.utk.edu).

The Southern Regional Education Board. Benchmarks 2000: Faculty Salaries (www.sreb.org).

United States Bureau of the Census, Profile of Selected Social Characteristics: 1990, 2000 (factfinder.census.gov).

———, *Statistical Abstract of the United States*, 2001.

University Faculty Senate Association. Position Statement, February 27, 2001 (www.olemiss.edu/orgs/faculty).

University of Virginia Geospatial and Statistical Data Center. United States Historical Census Data Browser (http://fisher.lib.virginia.edu/census).

Young, James B., and James M. Ewing, *The Mississippi Public Junior College Story: The First Fifty Years, 1922–1972* (Jackson: University Press of Mississippi, 1978).

CHAPTER TWENTY-SEVEN

Recent Economic Trends

CAPITAL INVESTMENTS AND BANKING

Background

During the last three decades of the twentieth century Mississippians witnessed fundamental economic changes that introduced new employment choices and opportunities to enjoy a higher standard of living. But to achieve sustained economic progress the state had to attract more capital investment, a task long encumbered by Mississippi's persisting antibank attitude and credit problems, along with its legacy of racial prejudice and educational inadequacies. Not until 1914, following a serious banking crises and the enactment of the national Federal Reserve Act, did the legislature finally create a state banking department and a plan for maintaining banking standards and deposit security. Such action, however, hardly ameliorated the flagging economy, as declining land values and cotton prices in the 1920s made capital even scarcer, and many banks could not guarantee their deposits even before the great stock market crash of 1929.

But as was the case in other areas of the state's economy, the real turning point for banking in Mississippi came during the Great Depression. By 1933, 127 banks in the state had failed, and total banking assets fell to $138 million, the 1917 level. The potential for recovery depended to a major extent on federal New Deal relief and reform measures, particularly the Federal Deposit Insurance Corporation (FDIC) program, and the 1934 state banking law. This legislation, which imposed tighter regulations and created the state Department of Bank Supervision headed by a state comptroller, continued as the basis for state banking regulation until 1980.

Under this system, banking assets and the ratio of cash (deposits) to assets gradually increased, and by 1940 all but eleven of the more than two hundred state banks were members of FDIC; only two banks, however, were members of the Federal Reserve System. During World War II deposits and assets rose faster, and a new trend saw fewer but bigger parent banks, more branch offices, and more federal reserve and FDIC memberships. By 1955 bank assets reached the landmark level of $1 billion, primarily because of earnings from loans, which increased by 170 percent during that decade. As in so many other economic areas, however, this growth lagged behind progress made in other states, where the average bank assets were twice those in Mississippi.

Mississippi banking entered a new era in the 1960s, when new computer technology, devices like credit cards, and long-sought gains in the state's crusade to attract outside investment capital reshaped the industry. By 1970 bank assets reached $3.3 billion, as income from loans continued to surpass investment earnings. Now, all commercial banks became members of FDIC, and bank mergers continued. The two largest banks at the time were Deposit Guaranty National Bank and the First National Bank, both in Jackson. Beginning in 1969, for the first time a state law allowed the state treasury to deposit certain funds into interest-earning accounts in banking institutions in Mississippi.

Recent Banking Trends

Until the 1980s banking conditions remained healthy. The total number of banks declined from almost 200 in 1955 to 177 in 1981, but the 704 branch offices represented a substantial expansion in operations, and total bank assets rose to $12 billion. In 1980 the legislature attempted to improve banking accountability by making all financial institutions in the state answerable to the new Department of Banking and Consumer Finance, which included a state Board of Banking Review. Managed by a commissioner (formerly titled state comptroller) appointed by the governor, the department was required to examine each bank at least once during each eighteen-month period but was allowed to accept examinations by the FDIC or the Federal Reserve Board.

Financial Difficulties: The S&L Crisis   These reforms, however, did not usher in a brighter financial future. On the contrary, in the early 1980s mortgage interest rates climbed to a record high of 21 percent, the annual rate of inflation rose to 14 percent, the value of farmland dropped, and the growth of bank assets and deposits virtually stalled. Between 1980 and 1994, three banks in the state with total assets worth $339 million failed. But the greatest financial catastrophe, practically a fatal one, was the collapse of the savings and loan (S&L) associations. These institutions differed from banks in that their primary business was to make long-term loans (mortgages) for housing. Chartered by the state legislature, S&Ls offered attractive interest rates to investors and used those deposits as the basis for lending money. But unlike commercial banks in the state, Mississippi S&Ls did not federally insure their deposits, a mistaken practice that would devastate the finances of thousands of investors.

Taking on an increasing share of the mortgage business, the S&Ls had experienced steady growth in the 1960s. By the end of that decade assets of the state's seventy-seven S&Ls had risen to $777 million. Despite such expansion, Mississippi remained behind all other southeastern states, and the number of associations dropped to fifty-nine by 1981, as a national banking crisis had already bloomed. By 1990 Mississippi S&Ls had lost an estimated $139 million. By this time customers were moving their loans and investments to banks and mutual funds, and the "thrift" institutions were simply collapsing. Nationally almost one-third of all S&Ls failed between 1980 and 1994, and the FDIC estimated the cost of this "debacle" at $160.1 billion, of which about $132.1 billion was borne by American taxpayers. Most Mississippi investors, however, did not directly benefit from the federal bail out, as the state S&Ls had not become members of the Federal Savings and Loan Insurance Corporation (FSLIC).

Financial difficulties persisted into the 1990s. Suddenly, for the first time since the Great Depression, national banks in the state experienced losses in assets and deposits, with ratios of deposits to assets dropping 20 percent, and state chartered banks realized their smallest gains ever. These negatives would have been worse except for an economic recovery during the final years of the century. For example, from the beginning of 1999 to the end of 2000, the banking deposits increased by 43 percent, but the ratio of deposits to assets was still lower than it had been in more than thirty years.

Mergers and Acquisitions   From 1980 through 1998 there were eighty-six bank mergers and acquisitions worth $15,431 million in Mississippi. The trend was strongest after 1994, and by the end of the century many of the state's major banks, including the largest, Deposit Guaranty, were acquired by regional holding companies with out-of-state home offices.

RECENT TRENDS IN AGRICULTURE

The longstanding emphasis on agricultural diversification, the application of new scientific methods, and technological advances produced a new farming culture. The principal trends during the last three decades of the twentieth century included a declining rural population, fewer but larger farms, the production of greater volumes and varieties of commodities, and an increase in net profits.

Rural Population Decline

In the late twentieth century rising numbers of people moved away from farms and into towns where they entered nonfarming occupations. The state still had an image of being rural, and farming was still a basic part of its economy, but major changes were occurring. By the end of the century most people lived in urban settings and were no longer associated with the farmland on which their parents and grandparents had lived. The rural population had declined to 55.5 percent of all Mississippians by 1970, and in the following decades it dropped to 51 percent.

Labor Changes and Costs

Technology had a revolutionary impact on farming as tractors and mechanized equipment greatly reduced the need for fieldhands. Now a farmer and his or her family, perhaps with one part-time hand, could use machines to accomplish jobs that a generation earlier had required dozens of workers. In 1970 the number of hired farm laborers had declined to about 41,000, a total not inclusive of farmer families, who actually composed the majority of agricultural workers. Thirty years later the number of hired farm workers had dropped to only 10,300.

But having to hire fewer hands did not necessarily reduce operational costs, and during the last three decades of the twentieth century, total farm expenses rose by 579 percent. The costs of buying, maintaining, and operating tractors and other equipment were greater than the wages paid for hired laborers. As a portion of the farmers' total expenses, these wages declined 13 to 10 percent, and as a portion of all wage and salary disbursements in the state, farm wages dropped from 2.5 percent in 1970 to 0.05 percent in 2000.

Farm Consolidation

Throughout most of its history Mississippi was a state of numerous small farms, but beginning in the mid-twentieth century that configuration, as men-

TABLE 27.1 Personal Income, 1929–2000 (Millions of Dollars)

YEAR	1929	1932	1940	1950	1960	1970	1980	1990	2000	CHANGE SINCE 1970
Total Income	$563	$251	$461	$1,685	$2,680	$5,768	$17,500	$33,928	$59,545	932%
Per Capita (dollars)	$282	$125	$212	$774	$1,228	$2,597	$6,926	$13,156	$20,900	705%

SOURCES OF INCOME (MILLIONS OF DOLLARS AND PERCENT OF TOTAL)										
Farm	$225 40%	$61 24%	$123 27%	$388 23%	$280 10%	$414 7%	$315 2%	$329 1%	$712 1%	72%
Services	$46 8%	$26 10%	$41 9%	$133 8%	$298 11%	$643 11%	$1,946 11%	$4,037 12%	$9,323 16%	1350%
Retail / Wholesale Trade	$75 13%	$31 12%	$67 15%	$253 15%	$388 14%	$725 13%	$2,084 12%	$3,366 10%	$5,703 10%	687%
Finance, Insurance, and Real Estate	$12 2%	$6 2%	$9 2%	$32 2%	$79 3%	$179 3%	$536 3%	$1,012 3%	$1,866 3%	942%
Construction	$13 2%	$3 1%	$22 5%	$76 5%	$120 4%	$291 5%	$902 5%	$1,161 3%	$2,461 4%	746%
Manufacturing	$61 11%	$22 9%	$49 11%	$201 12%	$446 17%	$1,137 20%	$3,179 18%	$5,653 17%	$7,524 13%	562%
Transportation and Public Utilities	$39 7%	$20 8%	$27 6%	$80 5%	$139 5%	$263 5%	$874 5%	$1,526 4%	$2,563 4%	875%
All Government	$30 5%	$30 12%	$68 15%	$187 11%	$395 15%	$908 16%	$2,470 14%	$5,302 16%	$8,686 15%	857%
Mining / Oil and Gas Extraction			$2 0.4%	$13 0.8%	$76 2.8%	$109 1.9%	$474 2.7%	$388 1.1%	$515 0.9%	372%
Forestry, Fisheries	$2 0.4%	$2 0.8%	$1 0.2%	$7 0.4%	$18 0.7%	$40 0.7%	$86 0.5%	$161 0.5%	$324 0.5%	710%

SOURCE: *United States Department of Commerce, Bureau of Economic Analysis, State Personal Income, 1929–87* (Washington, D.C.: U.S. Government Printing Office, July 1989), 170–173; United States Department of Commerce, Bureau of Economic Analysis, *State Personal Income, 1970, 1980, 1990, 2000, www.bea.doc.gov/ bea/regional/spi/action.cfm.*

TABLE 27.2 Top Jobs in the 1990s

JOBS	ESTIMATED EMPLOYMENT 1994
Salespersons (Retail)	33,320
Cashiers	29,460
Truck Drivers	21,800
Supervisors and Managers	19,440
General Office Clerks	19,370
Registered Nurses	16,730
Janitors and Cleaners	15,940
Waiters and Waitresses	14,870
Nursing Aides and Orderlies	13,680
Teachers—Elementary School	13,410
Teachers—Secondary School	13,310
Meat, Poultry, and Fish Cutters	11,300
Maintenance Repairers	10,050
Licensed Practical Nurses	9,600
Food Preparation Workers	9,120
Guards and Watch Guards	7,490
Cooks—Restaurants	6,520
Teacher Aides	5,210
Teachers—Special Education	3,530
Home Health Aides	3,170

SOURCE: *United States Department of Labor, Bureau of Labor Statistics, November 1995.*

tioned, changed rapidly. Small farmers no longer could compete with the larger operators, those able to bear the costs of using the latest methods and equipment to cultivate more acreage and produce a greater volume of commodities. Between 1950 and 1970 the total farm acreage had remain relatively stable, but the number of farms had dropped by 58 percent.

During the following three decades the number of farms continued to plummet, and by 2000 it had fallen to 43,000, less than 60 percent of the 1970 number. This trend was paralleled by a decrease of agricultural acreage from 16 million in 1970 to 11.1 million acres in 2000, placing the state twenty-ninth nationally in that category and resulting in much larger farms. The average size was 258 acres at the end of the century, having expanded by 18 percent in this period, but about 10,000 farms in the state averaged more than 650 acres.

Diversification: The Livestock Business

Since the Civil War state leaders had talked about the advantages of crop diversification, but that goal was not actually accomplished until the late twentieth century. A major indication of this change was the emergence of livestock products as more important sources of income than traditional crops. By the 1970s the sales of poultry and eggs, cattle and calves, and other products brought farmers as much cash as cotton and all other crops. Beginning in the 1980s receipts from livestock sales exceeded crop income, and the difference grew larger each year. In 1989 livestock receipts were 56 percent of total farm receipts, and by 1997 they represented more than 60 percent.

Catfish farm. Courtesy Mississippi Development Authority/Division of Tourism.

The principal reason for this development was the rapid increase in production of poultry and eggs. Although hardly a new farm activity, poultry enterprises advanced rapidly in the late twentieth century. In the mid-1950s they had produced only about 9 percent of all farm receipts, and as recently as 1970 broilers brought farmers $109 million and eggs $85 million, together about 19 percent. Thirty years later, total receipts for these products ($1.6 billion) had increased by almost 800 percent to contribute almost half of all farm receipts. Broilers alone brought more than $1.3 billion or 62 percent of total receipts from livestock sales and 42 percent of all farm receipts in 1999. Other important livestock products in the 1990s included farm-raised catfish and cattle and calves, but two traditional livestock businesses, hog production and dairies, failed to keep pace with these growing enterprises.

The newest phenomenon was "aquaculture." By the end of the century the state ranked first among all states in the production of catfish and other aquaculture commodities. State public relations publications in 2000 claimed that more commercial catfish were raised and sold in Mississippi than in any other nation in the world. The estimated 1990 payroll in farm-raised, grain-fed catfish production was $81.6 million. By 1999 the average per acre production was 5,000 pounds annually, with about 103,000 acres of ponds operating mainly in the Delta. In southern counties other expanding aquaculture businesses produced striped bass, shrimp, and tilapia, a tasty freshwater fish that was the most recent addition to this kind of commercial activity.

Traditional Crops

While advances were occurring in livestock production, crop farming witnessed persisting practices as well as innovations. Cotton remained a popular cash crop, and Mississippi continued to lead all other southeastern states in its production and value. In 1970 cash receipts for cotton amounted to one-fifth of the state's total farm income and ranked third behind poultry and cattle receipts. At the end of the century, in spite of some decline in cotton prices, Mississippi farmers produced 1.74 million bales annually on about 1.2 million acres. In total farm marketing receipts, cotton ranked second to broilers but ahead of aquaculture and soybeans.

Thus, cotton, though still a principal crop, no longer dominated the state's agriculture as it had up until the recent past. Back in the mid-1950s cotton had accounted for 57 percent of the total cash receipts on farms, but a generation later other crops were rapidly emerging to challenge the cotton tradition. By 1970 the soybean had begun to compete as a major crop, and during the following ten years soybean receipts rose dramatically ahead of cotton, amounting to 31 percent of total farm receipts and 55 percent of all crop receipts. Following this highpoint, when the state ranked eighth in the nation in soybean production, the crop fell back to a position below cotton in the 1990s. At the end of the century the state's soybean farmers ranked fourteenth nationally, producing 34.8 million bushels on 1.6 million acres at a total value of more than $239 million, 8 percent of total farm receipts.

Another major crop gaining a bigger share of farm production and value was rice. By 1999 Mississippi ranked fifth nationally in rice production with cash receipts of $110.5 million for about 500 producers harvesting a total of 218,000 acres, almost all of which were in Delta counties. This crop had developed rapidly since 1970, when it brought only $13 million.

Other Crops

Farmers also devoted large numbers of acres to the production of corn, wheat, hay, sorghum, and other traditional crops. In terms of production, corn was considered one of Mississippi's biggest crops, leading most southeastern states. Most of this crop, however, was used on the same farm on which it was produced (85 percent in 1980), the surplus selling for only about $3 per bushel. Corn was produced in virtually every county, but the leading areas were in the north, northeast, and the Delta.

Among states that produced sweet potatoes, Mississippi ranked third in the number of acres planted (10,000) by the end of the century. The town of Vardaman in Calhoun County, which claimed to be the "sweet potato capital of the world," hosted an annual National Sweet Potato Festival each November. In spite of such colorful publicity, however, this commodity did not produce large enough cash receipts to rank as a major farm crop.

In an effort to increase the production of fruits, vegetables, and nuts (mainly pecans), Mississippi farmers in 1948 opened the Central Farmers' Market in Jackson, which became a popular destination for many thousands of fresh-food shoppers. By the late 1960s about $2.25 million worth of fruits and vegetables were sold annually through this market. The leading commodities included watermelons, tomatoes, peaches, cantaloupes, and lima beans.

Statewide, the value of all fruits and vegetables increased from about $13 million in 1970 to an estimated $52 million in 1999, when approximately 55,000 acres were devoted to commercial production. Although these crops did not make major contributions to the state's overall agricultural economy, they did provide income opportunities for thousands of small "truck farmers."

Farm Income

In the late twentieth century farmers' overall net income increased in Mississippi but not at a rate comparable to that in other agricultural states. Between 1950 and 1970 farmers' income had remained stagnant, and in the latter year they earned slightly less than they had twenty years earlier. During the 1970s net farm income rose to $702 million, an increase of more than 54 percent, but in spite of this increase the average farm owner netted only $12,887. By the end of the century total farm income reached almost $1 billion, ranking Mississippi twenty-fifth nationally, with the bulk of the net receipts coming from the sale of broilers, cotton, catfish, and soybeans.

Even with the significant changes in farming and the advances of other industries and businesses, Mississippi remained an agricultural state at the start of the twenty-first century, as a major portion of the state's economy continued to depend on agriculture, directly or indirectly. But this historic aspect of Mississippi life now appeared to be fading fast, with an ever-increasing number of persons seeking their livelihoods in occupations and professions unrelated to the farm.

INDUSTRIAL DEVELOPMENT

Manufacturing

Attracting industrial jobs had long been the primary objective of the state's historic goal for economic diversification, and in the last half of the twentieth century increasing numbers of Mississippians finally began to draw wages or salaries from a variety of new or expanded plants. Personal income earned in manufacturing saw its fastest rate of growth in the 1950s and 1960s, when it climbed from 12 percent of the state's total to 20 percent in 1970. Although actual dollar increases continued at a rapid pace, manufacturing income's share of the state's total gradually declined to 13 percent by 2000.

The number of manufacturing establishments also declined after 1970. As a proportion of the total number of businesses in the state, the number of manufacturing plants dropped from more than 7 percent in the 1970s to less than 5 percent in 2000. Average annual employment followed the same pattern, declining from almost one-third of the state total to one-fifth in 2000. But reports on the value of manufacturing's gross products were more positive, indicating growth at a rate of 237 percent between 1970 and 2000, rising steadily to rank first among all businesses and remaining at least one-fourth of the state's total gross product.

Analysis of census data shows that the leaders in manufacturing produced lumber, foods, furniture, paper, textiles, metals, transportation equipment, industrial machinery, and electronics. It is noteworthy that the first five of these industries had a relationship with agricultural activity in the state, because they used raw materials produced from the land.

Furniture   Furniture-making plants led in rate of growth and had the biggest payroll ($841 million) by 2000. Some examples of leading companies included La-Z-Boy in Newton with 1,400 employees, Franklin Corp in Houston with 1,200 employees, Quartet Manufacturing Company in Booneville with 1,200 employees, and Chromcraft Furniture in Senatobia with 875 employees.

Lumber   The lumber industry data, which excluded logging, showed steady increases, and this business remained first in value of gross state product, $1.46 billion in 2000. In addition to sawmills, which dominated the industry, other plants manufactured plywood, fiberboard, and mobile homes. Closely related to the lumber business, paper mills produced cardboard, paperboard, fiber boxes, as well as various types of paper goods. Some examples of leading companies included International Paper Company with sawmills, papermills, and lumber-treating plants in Moss Point, Morton, and Wiggins; Georgia-Pacific Corp with sawmills and plywood and particleboard plants in Bay Springs, Roxie, Taylorsville, Grenada, Louisville, and Oxford; Weyerhaeuser Forest Products Company with sawmills and plywood plants and with its main location in Philadelphia; and Hood Industries with sawmills and plywood plants in Hattiesburg, Beaumont, Wiggins, and Waynesboro.

Textiles   The textile industry experienced a decline, but it still had an annual payroll of $423 million. Examples of leading plants, which produced various fabrics and clothing, included Ashley Company in Ecru with 1,400 employees and Burlington Industries in Stonewall with 977 employees.

Food Products   Food manufacturing ranked second in gross state product with $1.29 billion in 2000. The vanguards in this industry were the animal, poultry, and seafood processing plants. Examples of leading plants included Bryan Foods in West Point with 2,500 employees; Choctaw Maid Farms (poultry) in Carthage and three other locations with 2,800 employees and an annual payroll of more than $49.5 million; and Sanderson Farms (poultry and other foods) in Laurel, Summit, McComb, Hazelhurst, and two out-of-state plants, with a total of 8,500 employees and sales of $606 million in 2000. Others included B. C. Rogers, which would soon be bought by Koch Foods (poultry and other foods), in Forest and Morton with more than 2,200 employees; Tyson Foods in Jackson and Forest with more than 2,100; Peco Foods in Bay Springs and Scott County with about 1,500; and Wayne Farms (poultry) in Laurel with 1,200. Delta Pride Catfish in Indianola employed 950 persons, and other catfish processors included America's Catch in Itta Bena, Confish in Isola with 700 workers, Pride of the South Catfish in Brooksville with 200, and Simmons Farm Raised Catfish in Yazoo City with 200.

Electrical Equipment   A late-developing industry that experienced fast growth involved the manufacture of various kinds of electrical equipment. Personal income derived from this business rose from $21 million in 1960 to $707 million in 2000. The leading products included household appliances, lighting fixtures, and transformers, as well as computer products and electronic instruments. Examples of major companies were Howard Industries in Laurel with 3,700 employees, Heatcraft in Grenada with 2,500, and Viking Range Corporation (appliances and equipment for kitchens and bathrooms) in Greenwood with 850 workers. Other key businesses were Peavey Electronics (sound systems and musical instruments) in Meridian with 1,800 employees; Cooper Lighting in Vicksburg with 1,200; Quebecor World (digital products) in Corinth with 1,100; and ACT Global Electronics in Corinth with 850 persons on the payroll.

Transportation Equipment   The manufacture of transportation equipment ranked second in personal income in 2000 ($834 million) and was one of the fastest growing industries. The production of various motor vehicle parts and the building and repairing of ships were the leading activities. Ingalls Shipbuilding in Pascagoula was the biggest employer with a workforce of 12,000. Friede Goldman Offshore in Pascagoula hired 3,500 workers. Other examples of major industries included Delphi Automotive Systems in Clinton with 1,800 employees; Cooper Tire and Rubber in Tupelo with 1,500; and Borg-Warner Automotive in Water Valley with 800.

Nonmanufacturing Businesses

In 1970 the leading sources of personal income in descending order were manufacturing (20 percent of the state's total), federal and state governments (17 percent), wholesale and retail trade (12 percent), services (11 percent), and farming (7 percent). In the next three decades changes in the economy resulted in service-related businesses providing the most personal income (16 percent) followed

WorldCom headquarters in Clinton. Courtesy Westley F. Busbee, Jr.

by government (15 percent), manufacturing (13 percent), and wholesale and re-tail trade (10 percent).

Services

The only source of income that increased in this period was the service cat-egory. Overtaking manufacturing as the state's leader during the 1990s, services became the fastest growing businesses in the late twentieth century. For example, total personal income derived from services in 2000 was 14.5 times greater than the 1970 amount; in the same period the number of establishments almost doubled, the average annual employment grew by four times, and the gross prod-uct was 7.5 times larger. Within this sphere of the economy, the biggest increases were in health care and various business and legal services. Based on the annual payrolls in 2000, the leaders in descending order were hospitals, physicians' of-fices, employment agencies, business management, lawyers' offices, nursing-care facilities, educational services, engineering, and dentists' offices.

WorldCom

An important albeit short-lived business in the service category, WorldCom, Inc., with headquarters in Clinton, rose to national prominence and then fell into notoriety and bankruptcy at the turn of the century. Tracing the story of this busi-ness, which provided long-distance and other telephone services, is like riding a roller coaster at the state fair. Early in March 2004, Mississippians saw the head-lines that a federal court in New York had indicted former WorldCom Chief Ex-ecutive Officer Bernard J. Ebbers for securities fraud and other crimes related to false accounting practices amounting to $11 billion and described as the biggest corporate fraud case ever prosecuted in the United States.

The story began in 1983, when Ebbers and three friends around a cafe table in Hattiesburg formulated plans to start a new business, Long Distance Discount Service (LDDS). Under Ebbers's leadership over the next seventeen years, what began as a small operation became a telecommunications monster through acquisitions of some seventy-five companies, culminating in a merger with MCI in 1997. Renamed WorldCom in 1995, the company's reported assets rose to more than $100 billion. Its stock climbed to $64.50 per share in 1999, then plummeted to six cents within three years in the wake of news that a proposed merger with Sprint had failed and that false accounting practices had been used to balloon profits and mislead stockholders.

The fallout was earthshaking in the financial world: Ebbers and other executives resigned or were fired, thousands of employees nationwide—including hundreds in Mississippi—lost their jobs and retirement funds, and the company filed for bankruptcy in July 2002. Although the Clinton office remained open, it was merely a shell of earlier times, and in 2003 the headquarters of the company, now renamed MCI, moved to Virginia. The ongoing WorldCom debacle not only cost Mississippians jobs and fortunes in stock investments, but it sullied the state's business reputation generally. For example, in August 2003 MCI's "Restoring Trust" report to the federal court in New York stated that the newly organized company had "closed the finance and accounting department located in the Company's former Clinton, Mississippi headquarters where most of the fraudulent activities were conducted."

The Gaming Business

In contrast to the WorldCom disaster, another major venture begun in the late twentieth century, the gaming business, displayed enormous economic health. In one of the most colorful paradoxes in state history, hundreds of thousands of Mississippians and persons from other states flocked monthly to casinos, notwithstanding the state's long-held opposition to gambling on moral and religion grounds. By 2004, thirty-one casinos operated in nine Mississippi towns, and investors in Las Vegas and other places scrambled to build more of them. Except for the two establishments in Neshoba County, owned by the Mississippi Band of Choctaw Indians (and exempt from state taxes), the casinos were out-of-state operations, located along the Gulf Coast and the Mississippi River, and regulated by the state.

The industry began in 1992 after Governor Fordice signed a bill creating the Mississippi Gaming Commission and allowing counties on the designated waterways to vote on whether to accept "dockside gambling." As mentioned, the laws' local-option provision weakened the impact of statewide opposition from churches and other antigambling groups. Persuaded by promises of new employment opportunities, economic development generally, and tax revenues for public schools and highways, voters in seven counties ultimately overcame any reservations they might have had about gambling and voted to approve casinos that would, after all, be located "offshore." (The latter requirement, however, became a laughable technicality, one that most patrons could not detect upon entering any casino.)

During the first three months of 2004, about 30,000 employees earned $219 million in the state-regulated casinos. Almost 14 million patrons, with Mississippi-

Roulette at Harrah's Casino. Courtesy Mississippi Development Authority/Division of Tourism.

ans comprising one-fourth of that number, visited the establishments and left some $900 million behind. In addition to the benefits represented by new jobs, gaming made other significant contributions to the state's economy. The millions of people who traveled to Mississippi to gamble spent money not only at casinos but at restaurants, hotels, shopping malls, and other businesses along the way. Finally, state tax revenue from gaming mounted annually, rising from $44.4 million in fiscal year 1993 to $329.4 million in 2003 and adding a grand total of more than $2 billion to state coffers through the casinos' twelve-year history in Mississippi.

ENERGY RESOURCES

Oil and Gas Businesses

Overall economic growth continued to depend on the availability of energy resources. After their speedy expansion at mid-century, the state's oil and gas extracting operations did not experience sound gains in the final three decades. The number of these businesses declined to only 102, a fall of 67 percent, and the average annual number of employees dropped to around 5,000, a decline of almost 50 percent.

Although the value of gross product in oil and gas almost doubled during this period, reaching $725 million, its proportion to the state total dropped sharply, from about 5 percent in 1980 to 1 percent in 2000. Because of the huge rise in oil and gas prices, personal income in the industry rose from $51 million to $229 million in 2000. In spite of such an increase, however, the proportion of personal income from oil and gas extraction operations to the state total declined from 1.9 to 1.1 percent.

Annual oil production declined steadily to 20 million barrels in 2000, only 31 percent of the 1970 record amount. In national rankings the state dropped two places to a tie for tenth in production volume and three places to twelfth in production value ($277 million). The five leading oil-producing counties were Clarke, Lamar, Jasper, Adams, and Wayne.

Natural gas extraction experienced a brief revival in the 1980s, but by the end of the century it had declined to 113.5 billion cubit feet, which was only 45 percent of the mid-1950s high point and 47 percent of the 1980s levels. Mississippi fell from tenth to sixteenth place nationally in production volume and value ($181million). The leading gas-producing counties were Jefferson Davis, Walthall, Marion, Smith, and Forrest.

After rising rapidly earlier, total natural gas consumption declined by about 7 percent during the final three decades. While most customers continued to be residential, the trend saw industries consume greater quantities of gas (45 percent) and electric utilities (36 percent) than residential customers. The largest distributor was Mississippi Valley Gas Company, which served about 250,000 customers in 108 communities throughout 33 western counties in 2000, numbers that represented 36 percent fewer customers than reported in the 1970s. In 2001 this company announced that it would be acquired by Atmos Energy Corporation, the nation's fifth-largest gas distributor, with headquarters in Dallas, Texas. Other distributors included several regional companies, such as Reliant Energy in Rankin County, and 30 municipal utilities.

Electric Power

In contrast to the lower levels of natural gas usage, electric power consumption continued to rise dramatically. The relevance of this energy source to economic development is indicated by the increasing proportion of electricity demanded by nonresidential customers. By the end of the century, the state's leading electric utilities sold more megawatt hours to industrial and commercial establishments (69 percent) than to residences. The biggest users of electricity were industries (41 percent).

By the end of the century, homes and businesses throughout most regions of the state were supplied by 28 electric power associations (EPAs) and 15 public, municipal utilities. The municipalities and 14 of the EPAs received wholesale power from TVA and supplied electricity to more than 305,000 customers in 36 counties. Led by Southern Pine EPA in Taylorsville in Smith County, and Coast EPA in Bay St. Louis in Hancock County, the "rural" associations alone served at least 600,000 customers, more than double their 1968 number.

Mississippi Power and Light (MP&L), which became a part of Entergy Corporation in the 1990s, was the state's leading and fastest-growing supplier of electric power. Between 1970 and 2000 its number of customers increased by 87 percent to almost 404,000. Even though it had fewer individual customers than the rural associations, MP&L provided a much greater amount of electricity, for more than four-fifths of its power went to commercial and industrial consumers. The most important factor in this company's growth was its 90 percent ownership of the nuclear-generating station at Grand Gulf near Port Gibson in Claiborne County. This $3 billion facility began operations in November 1984 and was operating with full capacity, producing 10.69 billion kilowatts, by 2000.

The second largest distributor of electric power was Mississippi Power Company, which became a subsidiary of Southern Company, an energy supplier to Mississippi and three other southeastern states. This company expanded its service to 191,000 Mississippi customers, a 45 percent growth rate since 1968. It sold 46 percent of its power to industries, making Mississippi Power the leader in this category.

The Role of State Government

Probusiness policies of state government played an important role in Mississippi's changing economy in the late twentieth century. Starting with the "Balance Agriculture with Industry" program in 1936 and continuing throughout the twentieth century, the legislature pursued an increasingly active part in the promotion of economic diversification, an overall strategy of attracting new industries to Mississippi. First implemented by the Agricultural and Industrial (A&I) Board, this policy became even more comprehensive in the 1980s, after the legislature established the Department of Economic Development. Through this agency and its successor, the Mississippi Development Authority (MDA), organized in 2000, the state offered new and expanded businesses wide-ranging incentives, including various tax exemptions and easier access to low-interest loans and federal grant programs. The legislature, moreover, raised appropriations to pay for job-training, market research, and advertising programs.

THE SYSTEM OF TRANSPORTATION

Highways

But state government's support for improvements in the transportation system had perhaps the greatest impact on Mississippi's economic growth. Other than heavy, interstate and international commerce, the great bulk of travel and freight activity now moved over the highways rather than rails and water. In 1969 and 1972 the legislature adopted several highway measures. The 1969 "Overlay" program increased the gasoline tax by one cent per gallon to finance $300 million in bonds for reconstruction of 2,300 miles of two-lane highways and for the construction of 300 miles of new four-lane highways.

The "Corridor" Program   The 1972 "Corridor" program authorized additional tax revenues to finance $600 million in bonds for 1,200 additional miles of four-lane construction. Seven corridors were planned, including two north-south routes, Highway 61 paralleling the Mississippi River in the western counties and Highway 45 paralleling the Alabama border in the east; two east-west routes, Highway 82 linking the Columbus and Greenville areas in the north and Highway 84 connecting the Waynesboro and Natchez areas in the south; and three diagonal routes, Highway 49 connecting Jackson with the Delta, Highway 25 linking Jackson with the northeast, and Highway 78 running between Memphis and the Tupelo area.

Expenditures   In the brief period between 1969 and 1972, therefore, the state substantially increased its total investment in highways from $169 million to more than $1 billion. Most of this increase came from state and federal taxes on gasoline and state taxes on cigarettes and commercial trucks.

During the 1970s the state's total investment in highways more than doubled, rising to $2.34 billion. Construction on all but 430 miles of the state highway system was completed, and the number of unpaved roads in this 10,140-mile system declined from approximately 500 to 170. The length of four-lane (divided) highways increased from 881 to 1035 miles. County road mileage increased by more than 500 miles for a total of 15,446, and the state's investment in these roads totaled almost $300 million.

Interstates   By the early 1970s more than 530 miles of the federal interstate system were open for traffic. This construction, 90 percent of which was federally funded, continued on the following highways: I-55 paralleling U.S. Highway 51, a north-south route from Memphis through Jackson to New Orleans; I-59 paralleling U.S. Highway 11, a north-southwest route from Birmingham through Meridian, Laurel, Hattiesburg and into Louisiana; I-20 paralleling U.S. Highway 80, an east-west route from Alabama though Meridian, Jackson, and Vicksburg; I-220 connecting I-20 and I-55 northwest of Jackson; I-10 paralleling U.S. Highway 90 from Mobile along the Gulf Coast and into Louisiana; and I-110 linking I-10 with Biloxi on the Gulf. By 1980 only 29 of the 685 miles of interstate system remained incomplete in the state. (See map on inside front cover.)

Four-Lane Program   The state abandoned its "Corridor" program, as "the expected funding did not materialize," and 1981 legislation placed the highest priority on road maintenance. The legislature, however, did adopt a new $1.6 billion program in 1987 with the goal of adding 1,077 miles of four-lane highways for a total of almost 2,500 total miles by the end of the century. Various motor-fuel tax increases, fees for license plates, and the Mississippi Department of Transportation's bond retirement fund were the main "pay as you go" revenue sources for the program. In another program designed specifically to stimulate industrial growth, the legislature approved the "Access Road Program" in 1988, which helped defray construction expenses for roads that linked qualified companies to existing highways.

The Department of Transportation (MDOT)   The old highway department was restructured and named the Department of Transportation in 1992. The new agency incorporated offices of Public Transit, Weight Enforcement, Rail Planning and Safety, Aeronautics, and State Aid. It remained under the authority of the three commissioners of transportation, who continued to be elected within the three supreme court districts.

The Gaming Road Program   In the mid-1990s the legislature created the "Gaming Road Program" that empowered MDOT to issue bonds to pay for the construction and improvement of access roads to the state's new gaming establishments. MDOT also received appropriations funded mainly by motor fuel taxes for the expansion of the 1987 four-lane program and for a county bridge replacement program through its State Aid Division.

End-of-the-Century State Road Mileage and Expenditures   By the end of the century the entire state system, including fourteen U.S. highways plus state and county highways and roads, had expanded to 37,700 miles of paved roads, including 18,848 miles of county-administered roads. This total mileage was a remarkable increase from the 26,600 total mileage reported in 1980. All 685 miles of the six interstate highways were complete and carrying about 17 percent of the state's total highway traffic.[1]

1 According to the census bureau, in 1999 the state had an overall total of 73,318 miles of functional highways and roads, including 65,385 miles of rural roads. The state and counties were responsible for only a certain "designated" portion of this total.

Truck stop along Interstate at Jackson. Courtesy Westley F. Busbee, Jr.

According to reports of the Federal Highway Administration, the state's total disbursements from current revenues or loans for highways rose from $662 million in 1995 to $968 million in 1999. Based on an analysis of the state's annual expenditures on highway improvements and new construction, which exceeded the national average, a 2002 study at the University of North Carolina ranked Mississippi highways as the fourth best in the nation and best in the South—an assessment that many drivers might dispute.

Numbers of Cars and Trucks   Highway expansion was driven by the rapidly rising numbers of cars and trucks in the state. During the 1970s the numbers of registered automobiles jumped to 1,124,059, an increase of more than 30 percent, while trucks and buses increased by more than 50 percent to an estimated 470,000 vehicles. The numbers continued to escalate in the following decades, reaching totals of 1,299,000 cars and 1,018,000 trucks and buses in 1999. During the last three decades, therefore, the number of all vehicles operating on state highways and roads had doubled. Trucks and buses increased at the fastest rate, 228 percent, while car numbers rose by 51 percent.

Railroads

Decline of Passengers   With the sharp rise in highway travel, passenger travel by rail declined substantially and was limited primarily to interstate travel aboard Amtrak, the federally owned and funded passenger railroad. There were two main Amtrak routes traversing the state: one running from Memphis southward through Greenwood, Yazoo City, Jackson, Hazelhurst, Brookhaven, McComb, to New Orleans. The other line operated from New Orleans northeastward through Hattiesburg, Laurel, and Meridian. Amtrak reported no significant growth in passenger miles during the final decades of the century.

Freight Trains   Virtually all profitable railroad operations, therefore, were freight carriers. By 2000 the number of freight railroads had declined to five "Class I" companies, fourteen local roads, and five switching and terminal railroads. The total track mileage in operation was 2,590 miles, 29 percent fewer than the late 1960s total.

Illinois Central Merger   The most important railroad news in the late twentieth century was the merger of the Canadian National and the Illinois Central railroads in 1999. With its combined 844 miles of in-state track and alliances with many local railroads, the new company, which retained the name Canadian National (CN), was the largest system in the state. Through these connections businesses in most sections of the state gained direct access to markets from Canada to Mexico and to points from coast to coast in the United States. The MDA reported an example of steel pipe shipped from Brazil to Gulfport and then transported through CN lines to Canada at a cost of $6.50 per ton, the lowest freight rate available. Jackson was designated as the headquarters of the railroads' new Gulf Division. Soon thereafter, CN announced plans to spend $1.7 million to modernize and improve the Jackson rail yard, making it a major center of rail commerce.

The Kansas City Southern Railway Company   CN had a marketing alliance with the Kansas City Southern Railway Company, the second largest railroad in the state with 681 miles of track. Known as a "NAFTA"[2] railway, the KC Southern was part of a system connecting midwestern and eastern states with the Southwest. In Mississippi its main lines connected Vicksburg, Jackson, and Meridian and extended from Jackson southward to Mobile and Gulfport.

Other Railroads   The other three major lines were the Norfolk Southern, with 213 track miles running from Meridian southwestward through Laurel and Hattiesburg to New Orleans; the Burlington, Northern and Sante Fe, with 179 track miles running southeastward out of Memphis through towns like Holly Springs, Amory, Aberdeen, and Columbus; and CSX Transportation, with facilities at Gulfport and Pascagoula on its 94 miles of track along the Gulf Coast.

Railroad Operations and State Incentives   The positive moves by the CN and KC Southern, notwithstanding, by 2000 the entire freight rail business employed only 1,833 persons in Mississippi, a decline of 332 employees since 1997. The state ranked thirty-second nationally in both the total volume of railroad freight exported and the total imported. In actual numbers, the former total of 14.7 million tons exported—7.5 percent less than in 1997—exceeded the later total of 17.8 million tons imported—almost the same as in 1997. Wood and lumber products led the list of exported and imported commodities, although chemical products and coal were also major imports. In increasing volume, agricultural commodities, which historically composed a leading share of the state's railroad freight, now moved primarily via water transports and trucks.

Even though the heyday of active rail service for passengers and freight had long since left the station, the state development agency tried to revitalize local railroad traffic in the 1990s by offering loans and grants. For projects to improve freight rail service, eligible county or municipal governments could borrow as much as $1 million for a term of fifteen years at low interest rates. Grants of $250,000 were available to communities for upgrading railroad grade crossings.

Waterways

Similar inducements were offered to expand other transportation facilities, as the MDA offered loan programs to local communities for the construction and improvement of port and airport authorities. For each qualified project 100 per-

2 The North American Free Trade Agreement had been enacted in 1994.

cent financing was available for a loan up to $750,000 at an annual interest rate of 3 percent for a ten-year term.

Mississippi River and Interior Ports   Almost eight hundred miles of navigable waterways with sixteen strategically located ports provided access to national and international markets. The major ports on the Mississippi River were Natchez, Vicksburg, Greenville, and Rosedale, while an interior port was located on the Yazoo River at Yazoo City. The leading cargo commodities in 2000 included such bulk commodities as various wood and lumber products, fertilizers, rice, corn, wheat, and other agricultural products.

The "Tenn-Tom Waterway"   Construction on the Tennessee-Tombigbee Inland Waterway system of canals and locks by the United States Corps of Engineers began late in 1972 and was completed early in 1985. The linking of the two rivers provided a new avenue for commerce between the Gulf at Mobile and midwestern points in the Ohio and upper Mississippi River valleys. The six ports built along this 234-mile system of canals and locks in northeast Mississippi were Yellow Creek (Iuka), Itawamba (Fulton), Amory, Aberdeen, Clay County (West Point), and Lowndes County (Columbus). The major cargos were wood and lumber products, farm products like soybeans and corn, steel products, crude oil and petroleum products, and various chemicals. In 1997 the total volume of freight transported on this waterway was 8 million tons, most of which was outbound southward.

The Gulf Intracoastal Waterway and Gulf Ports   The Intracoastal Waterway, a federally maintained channel between the mainland and barrier islands in the Gulf, served as a commercial route running from Texas to Florida along the Gulf Coast. In Mississippi, barge facilities were located at Pascagoula, Moss Point, Biloxi, Gulfport, and Port Bienville. The state's two deepwater international ports were Pascagoula, the largest industrial tonnage port in the state, and Gulfport, a state-owned port. In 2000 the latter facility handled more bananas and other tropical fruit than any port in the United States and was the terminus for the Kansas City Southern Railroad. Other major cargos reported by the Gulf ports included petroleum products, wood and lumber products, refrigerated meat, iron and steel products, chemicals, machinery and equipment, and bulk grains and other agricultural products. According to MDOT reports, by the end of the century the state ports contributed a total of $1.4 billion to the gross state product, provided about 34,000 jobs, and disbursed $765 million in wages and salaries.

Aviation

In the last thirty years of the twentieth century, the number of public airports increased from sixty-seven to seventy-six, but the number of private airports declined sharply. Scheduled commercial airline service was available at the state's seven major airports, and the number of enplaned passengers was 1.3 million in 2000, an increase of 48 percent in three years. The 231 million pounds of arriving cargo, however, represented a 39 percent decline during the 1990s. Federal assistance to the state's airports continued to rise, with Airport Improvement Program grants and other funding reaching $25 million by 2000.

The busiest airport was Jackson International (Allen C. Thompson Field), which experienced rapid growth in passenger and cargo service between 1970 and

2000. With the number of commercial airlines providing service to and from Jackson rising to eleven by 2000, the number of enplaned passengers rose by more than five times to reach 662,052 persons, representing 58 percent of the state total. In addition, almost all the air freight and mail in the state passed through this facility.

But even as operations at Jackson International expanded, the recent trend in aviation evidenced a decline in the number of full-service airports and the development instead of large, regional centers. At the beginning of the twentieth-first century 95 percent of the state's enplaned passengers boarded at Jackson International and the Gulfport-Biloxi Regional airport, which experienced fast growth in the late 1990s as a result of the casino attractions on the Gulf Coast. The five other regional airports were the Golden Triangle Regional serving Columbus, West Point, and Starkville; the Hattiesburg-Laurel Regional in Jones County; the Mid-Delta Regional near Greenville in Washington County; the Tupelo Regional; and Meridian's historic Key Field.

Commercial service at these five airports was provided by subsidiaries of the major airlines. Two examples were the Golden Triangle, which announced flight schedules by Northwest's Airlink and Atlantic Southeast Airlines, a subsidiary of Delta Airlines, and Meridian, which provided a schedule of six ASA flights daily and served as headquarters for the Air National Guard 186th Air Refueling Wing.

CONCLUSION

No one can dispute that the economic condition of the state greatly improved during the twentieth century. Agriculture and industry had finally achieved the long-sought "balance," and major advances had been made in both sectors. Diversification brought new opportunities for prosperity, and public attitudes became more supportive of government programs to promote and aid both agriculture and industry. Capital investments increased, per capita income rose, and the state's gross product posted gains. Overall, conditions within the state showed signs of progress.

Optimism soared at the beginning of the Musgrove administration when, in the fall of 2000, the mammoth, international manufacturer of automobiles, Nissan Motor Company, announced its decision to establish a huge production plant near Canton in Madison County. The action was preceded by an extraordinary legislative session that provided for infrastructure improvements and tax incentives to attract the project. Initially planned as an $930 million, 4,000-employee operation, within two years Nissan declared its intention to make an additional $500 million investment that would expand the plant's size to 3.4 million square feet, increase annual production capacity from 250,000 vehicles to 400,000, and add approximately 1,300 new workers.

There were a number of other positive indicators. Northrop Grumman Ship Systems in Pascagoula announced an expansion that would require 2,000 new employees in addition to the existing workforce of about 11,000 persons. The MDA circulated similar reports of anticipated growth in investments and employment by such major businesses as La-Z-Boy Furniture Company in Newton, Ashley Furniture in Ecru, Lockheed Martin at the Stennis Space Center in Hancock County, Alcoa (American Aluminum Company) in Hernando, and Whirlpool (maker of household appliances) Corporation in Oxford.

Despite the sanguine outlook at the beginning of the twenty-first century, Mississippi could not escape the troublesome consequences of the national economic recession of 2000. Blaming the recession, frivolous liability lawsuits, the lure of cheap labor in other countries because of NAFTA, and other factors, a growing number of manufacturing operations closed in the next three years. A significant number of new jobs that did survive were taken by a new workforce, including thousands of Hispanic workers, who arrived in Mississippi with keen aptitudes for arduous labor, capacities to perform skillfully, and a willingness to work for what employers considered reasonable wages.[3] Governor Musgrove's opponents in the 2003 gubernatorial campaign pointed to the state's loss of more than 40,000 jobs, hoping potential voters would believe the governor's policies were responsible.

The economic downturn of the first three years of the twenty-first century, however, did not represent a fall from the mountain heights of prosperity! In spite of Mississippi's overall growth during the last three decades of the twentieth century, the rate and quantity of advancement had not compared favorably with most other states. The standard of living for the average Mississippian still stood well below the national average. Although between 1970 and 2000 per capita income rose from $2,641 to $21,017, it remained the lowest in the nation, and the wide gap between the state figure and the national average closed only slightly, from 64 to 71 percent. The estimated three-year median household income for 1998 to 2000 was $31,963, ranking forty-eighth among all states. Also reflecting unsatisfactory progress was the rate of growth in the value of gross state product. Through the 1990s the value of the gross state product increased from $45 billion to $61 billion, a seemingly healthy increase rate of 36 percent, but Mississippi remained in thirty-second place among the fifty states, and in the Southeast, only Arkansas ranked lower.

Reasons for this condition included the state's heritage of interracial strife and an inadequate system of public education. Other obstacles were the state's long history of dependence on agriculture and its sluggishness in adopting probusiness attitudes, which prevented early and efficient leadership by state government. Even after the change of policy beginning in the 1930s, state efforts to accomplish economic diversification and growth were inconsistent and subject to the winds of politics.

3 During the 1990s, Mississippi's Hispanic population increased from 15,931 persons to 39,569, a growth rate of 148 percent.

SELECTED SOURCES

Bond, Bradley G., *Mississippi: A Documentary History* (Jackson: University Press of Mississippi, 2003).

McNew, Ben B., "Banking, 1890–1970," in Richard Aubrey McLemore, ed., *A History of Mississippi*, 2 vols. (Hattiesburg: University & College Press of Mississippi, 1973) 2: 312–333.

Most information in this chapter is based on various state and federal documents and other primary sources. Several prominent sources include the following:

Federal Deposit Insurance Corporation (www.fdic.gov).

Federal Reserve Board (www.federalreserve.gov).

Mississippi, *Annotated Code of 1972.*

————, *General Laws of Mississippi* [various dates].

————, *Journal of the House of Representatives* [various dates].

————, *Journal of the Senate* [various dates].

Mississippi Statistical Abstract [various dates].

United States Bureau of the Census, *1990 Census of Population.*

————, *Current Population Survey*, Poverty 2000.

————, *Income 2000* (www.census.gov/hhes/income/income00/statemhi.html).

————, *Statistical Abstract of the United States* [various dates].

United States Department of Commerce, Bureau of Economic Analysis, *Regional Accounts Data: Annual State Personal Income. SA05 Personal Income by Major Source and Earnings by Industry—Mississippi* (www.bea.gov/bea/regional/spi/action.cfm).

EPILOGUE

As Mississippians begin their journey into the twenty-first century, they remain inextricably connected to the past. Critical choices about whether to continue along old paths or take new directions will determine the quality of life for generations to come. If the stewards of state affairs understand the lessons of history and use them properly in decision making, then Mississippi's prospects for a positive future are indeed hopeful. Thus, the destiny of the state rests on the resolutions of the perennial, interrelated problems of race, education, and economy.

At the start of the century, debates over the best pubic policy for the state have produced intense competition among various political groups, each one purveying its own unique proposals. Republican Governor Haley Barbour, who wants to balance the budget by reducing expenditures rather than increasing taxes, has met keen opposition in the legislature, which now contains three rather divergent groups—the black caucus of forty-five Democrats; sixty white Democrats, including "blue dog" conservatives[1] who might vote across party lines; and sixty-nine white Republicans. Unusually strong rivalry also exists between the house, firmly controlled by Democrats who disagree with many of Barbour's proposals, and the senate, with its large Republican minority led by Lieutenant Governor Amy Tuck.

Disagreements among these elements of state government that have attracted the most attention involve such issues as tort reform (limits on jury awards in liability lawsuits) and appropriations for public schools and institutions of higher education. While the legislators finally adopted the former measure, believing it would improve business prospects, they failed to increase spending for education. In additional haggling over the budget, the legislature has authorized the governor to reduce state spending for Medicaid benefits and adjourned without passing appropriations for the Department of Human Services.

Long accustomed to economic shortages, however, many Mississippians remained undaunted, hoping that the election campaigns of 2004 would produce progressive ideas. They anticipated that congressional candidates, spokespersons for the presidential candidates, as well as many state officials would offer solutions for the state's problems at the historic Neshoba County Fair, where for more than a century thousands have gathered every summer to hear the "political speaking."

On a brighter note, the state can boast about its relatively clean environment. Because Mississippi remains primarily rural with expansive woodlands and few

---

1"Blue dog" Democrats say they were once "yellow dogs"—Southerners so loyal to the party that they would rather vote for a yellow dog than a candidate of another party—but their conservative views have been "choked blue" by the national Democratic party.

major industries, it has experienced less environmental damage than most other states. By the mid-twentieth century, however, the accumulated applications of agricultural pesticides and other chemicals, as well as the transportation of hazardous materials through waterways and ports, polluted the state's air and water in some areas. Further environmental degradation resulted from the rapid growth of commercial poultry farming and the expansion of suburban housing, neither of which fell under strict waste management requirements until late in the century. Popular acknowledgement of the serious consequences of these problems became widespread only in the 1970s, after the federal Environmental Protection Agency (EPA) started its program to stop pollution and clean up the environment. Warnings about the dangers of asbestos and lead poisoning quickly caught the public's attention, as these hazardous substances actually affect folks where they live and work.

With a longstanding awareness of the importance of the land to their livelihood and with keen interests in outdoor pursuits such as hunting and fishing, Mississippians took action to protect the environment. In 1989 the legislature created the Department of Environmental Quality (DEQ), which replaced the Department of Natural Resources that had begun operations in the 1970s. Under the supervision of the Commission on Environmental Quality, the DEQ continues to enforce the various state and federal environmental laws, monitor pollution levels, and perform a wide variety of other tasks designed to protect Mississippi's air, land, and water. One example of the agency's aggressive enforcement approach was its lawsuit (joined by the EPA) in the 1990s against an international chemical company with a facility in Moss Point, Jackson County. Accused of violating clean air, clean water, and other environmental regulations by dumping hazardous wastes into landfills and deep wells and discharging pollutants into the air and a nearby river, the company paid fines of more than $20 million, equally divided between the state and federal governments.

But even with cleaner air and water than most other states, Mississippi forged ahead in the environmental crusade. In 2001 only two Mississippi counties, Harrison (thirty-seventh) and Warren (eighty-sixth), ranked in the top one hundred counties most polluted by toxic chemicals and other industrial wastes throughout the nation.

The resurgence of the Choctaw Indians represents another positive development. Under the leadership of Chief Philip Martin, chairman of the Tribal Council of the Mississippi Band of Choctaw Indians, the Choctaws developed the Pearl River Resort in Neshoba County, which includes the "Silver Star" and "Golden Moon" casinos, the "Dancing Rabbit Creek" golf course, a water park, and other entertainment facilities. These and other economic advances parallel educational and cultural revivals, illustrated by the displays of crafts (highlighted by woven cane baskets), traditional dress, music, dance, and stickball games at the annual Choctaw Indian Fair. Retaining their ancient language and folkways, the Choctaws, among Mississippi's earliest inhabitants, have overcome centuries of oppression to become a vibrant part of the state's diverse culture.

African Americans also made significant progress, overcoming generations of slavery, segregation, and discrimination. Finally obtaining equal standing under federal and state laws, black Mississippians have taken full advantage of their hard-won civil rights. They not only continue to make remarkable contributions

Gulfport Shrimpboats. Courtesy Kirk Irwin.

in the arts but win elections to hundreds of local and state offices and attain notable successes in business and educational endeavors. Like the Choctaws, however, African Americans understand that their forward progress still depends on
their perseverance in the struggle against Mississippi's legacy of racism. Signs of
success include the state's ongoing investigations (and criminal prosecutions) of
persons accused of past crimes against blacks. Many white and black leaders agree
that while further progress requires such legal action, it also demands changes in
deep-rooted attitudes. But even if obstacles remain, the rise in the number of interracial groups committed to genuine racial reconciliation signal important advances in Mississippi over the last forty years.

Finally, a brighter future for Mississippians requires careful long-range planning—including the rewriting of the 1890 state constitution—that would substantially reorganize the cumbersome network of unwieldy state agencies, eliminating bureaucratic redundancies and excessive political interference. Overarch-
ing such reforms, the single most important prerequisite for success in Mississippi
involves making substantial improvements in public education.

Although they may disagree on how to achieve these goals, the people of Mississippi are optimistic about the future of their state. With a diverse racial and ethnic heritage, which includes descendants of African, American Indian, Asian,
and European ancestors, the people of Mississippi now demonstrate their common dedication to a new, positive era of unity and growth. The widespread and
enthusiastic support for the United States military in Iraq, notwithstanding disagreements over whether the war itself was justifiable and Mississippi's relatively
high number of casualties, illustrates not only the strong national patriotism of
the state but its sense of internal unity on basic values. When Thomas Hamill, a
dairy farmer from Macon who drove trucks in Iraq to support his family's troubled
business, was taken hostage by an insurgent militant group, Mississippians held
nightly prayer vigils for three weeks. His escape and return home in May 2004 oc-
casioned statewide celebrations, culminating in parades on the Fourth of July.

SELECTED BIBLIOGRAPHY
OF MISSISSIPPI HISTORY

SECONDARY SOURCES

Books

Abbott, Dorothy, ed., *Mississippi Writers: An Anthology* (Jackson: University Press of Mississippi, 1991). This volume contains selections from the substantial four-volume anthology of Mississippi literature, including fiction, nonfiction, poetry, and drama, compiled at the Center for the Study of Southern Culture at the University of Mississippi.

Akin, Edward N., and Charles C. Bolton, *Mississippi: An Illustrated History* (Sun Valley, Calif.: American Historical Press, 2002).

Andrews, Kenneth T., *Freedom is a Constant Struggle: The Mississippi Civil Rights Movement and Its Consequences* (Chicago: University of Chicago Press, 2004).

Ballard, Michael B., *Civil War Mississippi: A Guide* (Jackson: University Press of Mississippi, 2000).

————, *Pemberton: A Biography* ((Jackson: University Press of Mississippi, 1991).

Barry, John M., *Rising Tide: The Great Mississippi Flood of 1927 and How It Changed America* (New York: Simon & Schuster, 1997).

Bettersworth, John K., *Mississippi: A History* (Austin, Tex.: The Steck Company, 1959). A textbook used for decades in Mississippi's secondary schools.

————, and James W. Silver, eds., *Mississippi in the Confederacy* (Jackson: Mississippi Department of Archives and History, 1961).

Biographical Directory of the United States Congress, 1774 to Present (Washington, D.C.: Government Printing Office, 2003, http://bioguide.congress.gov).

Black, Patti Carr, *Art in Mississippi, 1790–1980*, Vol. 1, Heritage of Mississippi Series (Jackson: University Press of Mississippi for the Mississippi Historical Society and the Mississippi Department of Archives and History, 1998).

————, and Marion Barnwell, *Touring Literary Mississippi* (Jackson: University Press of Mississippi, 2002).

Blumberg, Rhoda L., *Civil Rights: The 1960s Freedom Struggle* (Boston: Twayne Publishers, 1984).

Bond, Bradley G., Political Culture in the Nineteenth Century South: Mississippi, 1830–1900 (Baton Rouge, La.: Louisiana State University Press, 1995).

Brieger, James F., *Hometown, Mississippi*, 3rd ed. (Jackson, Mississippi: Town Square Books, Inc., 1997).

Buchanan, Minor Ferris, *Holt Collier: His Life, His Roosevelt Hunts, and the Origin of the Teddy Bear* (Jackson: Centennial Press of Mississippi, Inc., 2002).

Burner, Eric R., *And Gently He Shall Lead Them: Robert Parris Moses and Civil Rights in Mississippi* (New York: New York University Press, 1994).

Bynum, Victoria E., *The Free State of Jones: Mississippi's Longest Civil War* (Chapel Hill: The University of North Carolina Press, 2001).

Cagin, Seth, and Philip Dray, *We Are Not Afraid: The Story of Goodman, Schwerner, and Chaney and the Civil Rights Campaign for Mississippi* (New York: Macmillan Publishing Company, 1988).

Campbell, Will D., *Robert G. Clark's Journey to the House: A Black Politician's Story* (Jackson: University Press of Mississippi, 2003).

Carson, James Taylor, *Searching for the Bright Path: The Mississippi Choctaws from Prehistory to Removal* (Lincoln: University of Nebraska Press, 1999).

Cobb, James C., *The Most Southern Place on Earth: The Mississippi Delta and the Roots of Regional Identity* (New York: Oxford University Press, 1992).

Cresswell, Stephen, *Multiparty Politics in Mississippi, 1877–1902* (Jackson: University Press of Mississippi, 1995).

Dittmer, John, *Local People: The Struggle for Civil Rights in Mississippi* (Chicago: University of Illinois Press, 1994).

Erenrich, Susie, ed., *Freedom Is a Constant Struggle: An Anthology of the Mississippi Civil Rights Movement* (Montgomery, Ala.: Black Belt Press, 1999).

Fabel, Robin F. A., *Colonial Challenges* (Gainesville: University Press of Florida, 2000).

———, *The Economy of British West Florida, 1963–1783* (Tuscaloosa: The University of Alabama Press, 1988).

Galloway, Patricia, *Choctaw Genesis, 1500–1700*, Indians of the Southeast Series, Theda Perdue and Michael D. Green, eds. (Lincoln: University of Nebraska Press, 1995).

———, ed., *Native, European, and African Cultures in Mississippi, 1500–1800* (Jackson: Mississippi Department of Archives and History, 1991).

Green, A. Wigfall, *The Man Bilbo* (Baton Rouge: Louisiana State University Press, 1963).

Harris, William C., *The Day of the Carpetbagger: Republican Reconstruction in Mississippi* (Baton Rouge: Louisiana State University Press, 1979).

———, *Presidential Reconstruction in Mississippi* (Baton Rouge: Louisiana State University Press, 1967).

Henry, Aaron, with Constance Curry, *Aaron Henry: The Fire Ever Burning*, Margaret Walker Alexander Series in African American Studies (Jackson: University Press of Mississippi, 2000).

Holmes, William F., *The White Chief: James Kimball Vardaman* (Baton Rouge: Louisiana State University Press, 1970).

Hudson, Charles, and Carmen Chaves Tesser, eds., *The Forgotten Centuries: Indians and Europeans in the American South, 1521–1704* (Athens: The University of Georgia Press, 1994).

Johnston, Erle, *Mississippi's Defiant Years 1953–1973: An Interpretive Documentary with Personal Experiences* (Forest, Miss.: Lake Harbor Publishers, 1990).

———, *I Rolled with Ross: A Political Portrait* (Baton Rouge, La.: Moran Publishing Corporation, 1980).

Katagiri, Yasuhiro, *The Mississippi State Sovereignty Commission: Civil Rights and States' Rights* (Jackson: University Press of Mississippi, 2001).

Kidwell, Cara Sue, *Choctaws and Missionaries in Mississippi, 1818–1918* (Norman: University of Oklahoma Press, 1995).

Kirwan, Albert D., *Revolt of the Rednecks, Mississippi Politics: 1876–1925* (Lexington: University of Kentucky Press, 1951).

Lamis, Alexander P., *The Two-Party South* (New York: Oxford University Press, 1984).

Lee, Chana Kai, *For Freedom's Sake: The Life of Fannie Lou Hamer* (Urbana: University of Illinois Press, 1999).

Loewen, James W., and Charles Sallis, eds., *Mississippi: Conflict and Change* (New York: Random House, 1974).

Marsh, Charles, *God's Long Summer: Stories of Faith and Civil Rights* (Princeton, N.J.: Princeton University Press, 1997). This book presents accounts in the lives of "five religious persons": Fannie Lou Hamer, Sam Holloway Bowers, Jr., William Douglas Hudgins, pastor of Jackson's First Baptist Church, Edwin King, white chaplain at Tougaloo College, and Cleveland Sellers, SNCC staff member and an early advocate of "Black Power."

Mason, Nina, and Charlene Barr, comps., *History of the Mississippi Poetry Society, Inc., 1932–1995* (Privately published by The Mississippi Poetry Society, Inc., 1995).

May, Robert E., *John A. Quitman: Old South Crusader* (Baton Rouge: Louisiana State University Press, 1985).

McAdam, Doug, *Freedom Summer* (New York: Oxford University Press, 1988).

McKee, Jesse O., *The Choctaw*, Indians of North America Series, Frank W. Porter III, ed. (New York: Chelsea House Publishers, 1989).

———— and Jon A. Schlenker, *The Choctaws, Cultural Evolution of a Native American Tribe* (Jackson: University Press of Mississippi, 1980).

————, et al., *Mississippi: Portrait of an American State* (Montgomery, Ala.: Clairmont Press, 1995).

McLemore, Richard Aubrey, ed., *A History of Mississippi*, 2 vols. (Hattiesburg: University & College Press of Mississippi, 1973).

McMillen, Neil R., *The Citizens' Council: Organized Resistance to the Second Reconstruction, 1954–64* (Urbana: University of Illinois Press, 1994).

————, *Dark Journey: Black Mississippians in the Age of Jim Crow* (Urbana: University of Illinois Press, 1989).

————, ed., *Remaking Dixie: The Impact of World War II on the American South* (Jackson: University Press of Mississippi, 1997).

Mills, Kay, *This Little Light of Mine: The Life of Fannie Lou Hamer* (New York: E. P. Dutton, 1993).

Minor, [Wilson] Bill, *Eyes on Mississippi: A Fifty-Year Chronicle of Change* (Jackson: J. Prichard Morris Books, 2001).

Mitchell, Dennis J., *Mississippi Liberal: A Biography of Frank E. Smith* (Jackson: University Press of Mississippi, 2001).

Morgan, Chester M., *Redneck Liberal: Theodore G. Bilbo and the New Deal* (Baton Rouge: Louisiana State University Press, 1985).

O'Brien, Greg, *Choctaws in a Revolutionary Age, 1750–1830* (Lincoln: University of Nebraska Press, 2002).

Olsen, Christopher J., *Political Culture and Secession in Mississippi: Masculinity, Honor, and the Antiparty Tradition, 1830–1860* (New York: Oxford University Press, 2000).

Oshinsky, David M., *"Worse Than Slavery": Parchman Farm and the Ordeal of Jim Crow Justice* (New York: The Free Press, 1997).

Parker, Frank R., *Black Votes Count: Political Empowerment in Mississippi after 1965* (Chapel Hill: University of North Carolina Press, 1990).

Parker, Joseph B., ed., *Politics in Mississippi*, 2d ed. (Salem, Wisc.: Sheffield Publishing Company, 2001).

Payne, Charles M., *I've Got the Light of Freedom: The Organizing Tradition and the Mississippi Freedom Struggle* (Berkeley: University of California Press, 1995).

Prenshaw, Peggy W., and Jesse O. McKee, eds., *Sense of Place: Mississippi* (Jackson: University Press of Mississippi, 1979).

Rowland, Dunbar, *History of Mississippi: The Heart of the South*, 4 vols. (Chicago-Jackson: The S. J. Clarke Publishing Company, 1925). Volume 1 is a narrative from geography and Indians through Civil War battles. Volume 2 continues the narrative to the mid-1920s and includes various topical chapters. The final two volumes are biographical.

Sansing, David G., *Making Haste Slowly: The Troubled History of Higher Education in Mississippi* (Jackson: University Press of Mississippi, 1990).

Shirley, Aleda, Susan M. Glisson, and Ann J. Abadie, eds., *Mississippi Writers: Directory and Literary Guide* (University, Miss.: The Center for the Study of Southern Culture, 1995). This source contains basic facts about 130 Mississippi authors.

Skates, John Ray, Jr., *A History of the Mississippi Supreme Court, 1817–1948* (Jackson: Mississippi Bar Foundation, Inc., 1973).

———, *Mississippi: A Bicentennial History*, The States and the Nation Series, James Morton Smith, ed. (New York: W.W. Norton & Company, Inc., 1979).

———, *Mississippi's Old Capitol: Biography of a Building* (Jackson: Mississippi Department of Archives and History, 1990).

Sparks, Randy J., *On Jordan's Stormy Banks: Evangelical Religion in Mississippi, 1773–1876* (Athens: University of Georgia Press, 1994).

———, *Religion in Mississippi*, Vol. 2, Heritage of Mississippi Series (Jackson: University Press of Mississippi for the Mississippi Historical Society, 2001).

Starkville [Mississippi] High School Department of English, Mississippi Writers and Musicians Project (shs.starkville.k12.ms.us/mswm/MSWritersAndMusicians). This site also includes artists.

Sumners, Cecil L., *The Governors of Mississippi* (Gretna, La.: Pelican Publishing Company, 1981).

Swain, Martha H., Elizabeth Anne Payne, and Marjorie Julian Spruill, eds., *Mississippi Women: Their Histories, Their Lives*, foreword by Anne Firor Scott (Athens: The University of Georgia Press, 2003).

Thompson, Julius, *Hiram R. Revels, 1827–1901: A Biography* (New York: Arno Press, 1982).

Trigger, Bruce G., and Wilcomb E. Washburn, eds., *North America*, Vol. 1, *The Cambridge History of the Native Peoples of the Americas* (Cambridge: Cambridge University Press, 1996).

University of Mississippi Department of English, *The Mississippi Writers Page* (www.olemiss.edu/mwp).

Usner, Daniel H., Jr., *Indians, Settlers, and Slaves in a Frontier Exchange Economy: The Lower Mississippi Valley Before 1783* (Chapel Hill: The University of North Carolina Press, 1992).

Weber, David J., *The Spanish Frontier in North America* (New Haven, Conn.: Yale University Press, 1992).

Wells, Mary Ann, *Native Land: Mississippi, 1540–1798* (Jackson: University Press of Mississippi, 1994).

Wharton, Vernon L., *The Negro in Mississippi, 1865–1890* (Chapel Hill: The University of North Carolina Press, 1947).

Young, James B., and James M. Ewing, *The Mississippi Public Junior College Story: The First Fifty Years, 1922–1972* (Jackson: University Press of Mississippi, 1978).

Articles

The *Journal of Mississippi History*, sixty-six volumes published to date, is a veritable goldmine for students of the state's history. Only a few examples of the numerous helpful articles are included here.

Barnett, Jim, and H. Clark Burkett, "The Forks of the Road Slave Market at Natchez," *Journal of Mississippi History* 63 (Fall 2001): 169–87.

Bigelow, Martha M., "Mississippi Progessivism," *Journal of Mississippi History* 27 (May 1965): 202–205.

Bond, Bradley G., "Edward C. Walthall and the 1880 Senatorial Nomination: Politics of Balance in the Redeemer Era," *Journal of Mississippi History* 50 (February 1988): 1–20.

Clark, Eric C., "Legislative Apportionment in the 1890 Constitutional Convention," *Journal of Mississippi History* 42 (November 1980): 298–315.

———, "Regulation of Corporations in the Mississippi Constitutional Convention of 1890," *Journal of Mississippi History* 48 (February 1986): 31–42.

Holmes, William, "James K. Vardaman and Prison Reform in Mississippi," *Journal of Mississippi History* 27 (May 1965): 229–236.

James, D. Clayton, "Mississippi Agriculture, 1861–1865," *Journal of Mississippi History* 24 (July 1962): 129–141.

Jenkins, Robert L., "The Development of Black Higher Education in Mississippi, 1865–1920," *Journal of Mississippi History* 45 (November 1983): 272–86.

Libby, Billy W., "Senator Hiram Revels of Mississippi Takes His Seat, January–February, 1870," *Journal of Mississippi History* 37 (November 1975): 381–394.

Lowery, Charles D., "The Great Migration to Mississippi Territory, 1798–1819," *Journal of Mississippi History* 30 (August 1968): 173–92.

Skates, John Ray, Jr., "World War II as a Watershed in Mississippi History," *Journal of Mississippi History* 37 (May 1975): 135–141.

Swain, Martha, "A New Deal for Mississippi Women, 1933–1943," *Journal of Mississippi History* 46 (August 1984): 191–212.

Upchurch, Thomas Adams, "Why Populism Failed in Mississippi," *Journal of Mississippi History* 65 (Fall 2003): 249–276.

Vogt, Daniel C., "Government Reform, 1890 Constitution, and Mike Conner," *Journal of Mississippi History* 48 (February 1986): 43–56.

Winter, William F., "Mississippi's Civil War Governors," *Journal of Mississippi History* 51 (May 1989): 77–88.

Mississippi History Now, an Online Publication of the Mississippi Historical Society (mshistory.k12.ms.us) offers numerous articles including bibliographies written by contemporary historians about wide-ranging topics.

Publications of the Mississippi Historical Society, fourteen volumes published from 1898 to 1914 and five volumes published as the Centenary Series from 1916 to 1925, contain numerous articles by historians of the era, as well as many writers' recollections.

Primary Sources

American Religious Data Archive, Religious Congregations (www.thearda.com/RCMS/2000/State/28.htm).

American Religious Identification Survey 2001, The Graduate Center of the City University of New York (www.gc.cuny.edu/studies/aris.pdf).

Bond, Bradley G., *Mississippi: A Documentary History* (Jackson: University Press of Mississippi, 2003).

Claiborne, J. F. H., *Mississippi as a Province, Territory and State, with Biographical Notices of Eminent Citizens,* Vol. 1 (Jackson: Power & Barksdale, Publishers and Printers, 1880).

Clayton, Lawrence A., et al., eds., *The DeSoto Chronicles: The Expedition of Hernando De Soto to North America in 1539–1543,* 2 vols. (Tuscaloosa: University of Alabama Press, 1993).

Constitution and Form of Government for the State of Mississippi, 1817.

The Constitution of the State of Mississippi, 1890.

The Constitutions of Mississippi as Originally Adopted (University of Mississippi: Bureau of Governmental Research, 1982).

Federal Deposit Insurance Corporation (www.fdic.gov).

Federal Reserve Board (www.federalreserve.gov).

Historical Statistics of the States of the United States: Two Centuries of the Census, 1790–1990, comp. Donald B. Dodd (Westport, Conn.: Greenwood Press, 1993), Population.

Hogan, William Ransom, and Edwin Adams Davis, eds., *William Johnson's Natchez: The Ante-Bellum Diary of a Free Negro* (Baton Rouge: Louisiana State University Press, 1951).

————, *The Barber of Natchez; Wherein a Slave Is Freed and Rises to a Very High Standing; Wherein the Former Slave Writes a Two-Thousand-Page Journal About His Town and Himself; Wherein the Free Negro Diarist is Appraised in Terms of His Friends, His Code, and His Community's Reaction to His Wanton Murder* (Baton Rouge: Louisiana State University Press, 1973).

Mississippi, *Annotated Code of 1972*.

————, *General Laws of Mississippi* [various dates].

————, *Journal of the Senate* [various dates].

————, *Journal of the House of Representatives* [various dates].

————, Mississippi Arts Commission (www.arts.state.ms.us).

————, Mississippi Development Authority (www.mississippi.org).

————, Mississippi Department of Agriculture and Commerce (www.mdac.state.ms.us).

————, Mississippi Department of Education (www.mde.k12.ms.us).

————, *Mississippi Official and Statistical Register* [various dates].

————, Mississippi State Department of Health (www.msdh.state.ms.us).

————, Mississippi Secretary of State (www.sos.state.ms.us).

————, State Board for Community and Junior Colleges (www.sbcjc.cc.ms.us).

————, Other state government agencies provide general information and statistical data through their official Web sites.

Mississippi Art Colony (www.msartcolony.com).

Mississippi Baptists (www.mbcm.org).

Mississippi Center for Public Policy, Mississippi Family Council Report (www.mspolicy.org).

Mississippi Home Educators Association (www.mhea.net).

Mississippi Museum of Art (www.msmuseumart.org).

Mississippi Private School Association (www.mpsa.org).

Mississippi Statistical Abstract [various dates], Office of Business Research & Services, College of Business and Industry, Mississippi State University.

Mississippi Symphony Orchestra (www.msorchestra.com).

The United Methodist Church, Mississippi Conference (www.mississippi-umc.org).

The United Pentecostal Church International (wec.upci.org/churches).

United States Bureau of the Census [various dates].

————, *Statistical Abstract of the United States* [various dates].

United States Department of Commerce, Bureau of Economic Analysis, *Regional Accounts Data: Annual State Personal Income, SA05 Personal Income by Major Source and Earnings by Industry–Mississippi* (www.bea.gov/bea/regional/spi/action.cfm).

University of Virginia Geospatial and Statistical Data Center, *United States Historical Census Data Browser* (http://fisher.lib.virginia.edu/census).

APPENDIX I

EUROPEAN RULERS WITH RELATION TO MISSISSIPPI
DURING THE COLONIAL AND TERRITORIAL PERIODS

Spain

Charles I	1516–1556
Philip II	1556–1598
Philip III	1598–1621
Philip IV	1621–1665
Charles II	1665–1700
Philip V	1700–1746
Ferdinand VI	1746–1759
Charles III	1759–1788
Charles IV	1788–1808
Ferdinand VII	1808
Joseph Bonaparte	1808–1813
Ferdinand VII (restored)	1813–1833

France

Louis XIV	1643–1715
Louis XV	1715–1774
Louis XVI	1774–1793
The Convention	1793–1795
The Directory	1795–1799
The Consulate	1799–1800
Napoleon as First Consul	1800–1804
Napoleon as Emperor	1804–1814

England

William and Mary	1689–1702
Anne	1702–1714
George I	1714–1727
George II	1727–1760
George III	1760–1820

Key Military Commandants And Governors in Mississippi during the French Period[1]

Pierre le Moyne, Sieur d'Iberville, Commandant	1699–1706
Jean Baptiste le Moyne, Sieur de Bienville, Commandant	1706–1713
Antoine Laumet de la Mothe Cadillac, Governor	1713–1716
Jean Baptiste le Moyne, Sieur de Bienville, Commandant / Governor	1716–1725
Étienne Boucher de la Périer, Governor / Commandant	1727–1733
Jean Baptiste le Moyne, Sieur de Bienville, Governor	1733–1743
Philippe de Rigaud, Marquis de Vaudreuil, Governor	1743–1753
Louis Billouart de Kerlerec, Governor	1753–1763

Governors during the British Period

George Johnstone	1764–1767
Montfort Browne, Acting Governor	1767–1769
John Eliot (Died in office.)	1769
Elias Durnford	1769–1770
Peter Chester	1770–1781

Governor-Generals during the Spanish Period[2]

Bernardo de Gálvez	1777–1785
Esteban Miró	1785–1791
Francisco Luis Hector de Carondelet	1791–1797
Manuel Gayoso de Lemos	1797–1799

Governors during the Territorial Period

Winthrop Sargent	1798–1801
William C. C. Claiborne	1801–1803
Robert Williams	1805–1809
David Holmes	1809–1817

Governors of the State of Mississippi

David Holmes	1817–1820	Jeffersonian Republicans[3]
George Poindexter	1820–1822	Jeffersonian Republicans
Walter Leake (Died in office.)	1822–1825	Jeffersonian Republicans
Gerard C. Brandon (As lieutenant governor, succeeded Leake.)	1825–1826	Jeffersonian Republicans
David Holmes (Resigned.)	1826	Jeffersonian Republicans

1 Until 1763, Mississippi was part of the French colony of Louisiana.
2 Spanish Governors of Louisiana exercised authority over the Mississippi area, 1781–1798.
3 Jeffersonian Republicans were forerunners of the Democratic-Republicans, the Jacksonian Democrats, and the Democrats.

Gerard C. Brandon	1826–1832	Democratic
(As lieutenant governor, succeeded Holmes.)		
Abram M. Scott	1832–1833	Whig
(Died in office.)		
Charles Lynch	1833	Whig
(As president of the senate, succeeded Scott.)		
Hiram G. Runnels	1833–1835	Democratic
(Term ended before the governor-elect could be inaugurated, pursuant to the Constitution of 1832.)		
John A. Quitman	1835–1836	States Rights[4]
(As president of the senate, succeeded Runnels.)		
Charles Lynch	1836–1838	Whig
Alexander G. McNutt	1838–1842	Democratic
Tilghman M. Tucker	1842–1844	Democratic
Albert G. Brown	1844–1848	Democratic
Joseph W. Matthews	1848–1850	Democratic
John A. Quitman (Resigned.)	1850–1851	Democratic
John I. Guion	1851	Democratic
(As president pro tempore of the senate, succeeded Quitman.)		
James Whitfield	1851–1852	Democratic
(As president of the senate, succeeded Guion, who vacated the governor's office.)		
Henry S. Foote	1852–1854	Union
(Resigned ten days before the end of his term.)		
John J. Pettus	1854	Democratic
(As president of the senate, succeeded Foote.)		
John J. McRae	1854–1857	Democratic
(Term ended early due to a constitutional amendment changing the dates for general elections and gubernatorial inaugurations.)		
William McWillie	1857–1859	Democratic
John J. Pettus	1859–1863	Democratic
Charles Clark	1863–1865	Democratic
(Arrested and removed from office by U. S. Army.)		
William L. Sharkey	1865	Whig Unionist
(Appointed provisional governor by President Andrew Jackson.)		
Benjamin G. Humphreys	1865–1868	Whig
(Removed from office by U.S. Army.)		
Adelbert Ames	1868–1870	Republican
(Military and provisional governor)		
James L. Alcorn	1870–1871	Republican
(Resigned.)		
Ridgley C. Powers	1871–1874	Republican
(As lieutenant governor, succeeded Alcorn.)		
Adelbert Ames	1874–1876	Republican
(Resigned to avoid removal by impeachment.)		

4 Quitman was also known as a "Nullifier."

John M. Stone (As president pro tempore of the senate, succeeded Ames, because the lieutenant governor had been impeached and removed from office.)	1876–1882	Democratic
Robert Lowry	1882–1890	Democratic
John M. Stone	1890–1896	Democratic
Anselm J. McLaurin	1896–1900	Democratic
Andrew H. Longino	1900–1904	Democratic
James K. Vardaman	1904–1908	Democratic
Edmond F. Noel	1908–1912	Democratic
Earl L. Brewer	1912–1916	Democratic
Theodore G. Bilbo	1916–1920	Democratic
Lee M. Russell	1920–1924	Democratic
Henry L. Whitfield (Died in office.)	1924–1927	Democratic
Dennis Murphree (As lieutenant governor, succeeded Whitfield.)	1927–1928	Democratic
Theodore G. Bilbo	1928–1932	Democratic
Martin S. (Mike) Conner	1932–1936	Democratic
Hugh L. White	1936–1940	Democratic
Paul B. Johnson, Sr. (Died in office.)	1940–1943	Democratic
Dennis Murphree (As lieutenant governor, succeeded Johnson.)	1943–1944	Democratic
Thomas L. Bailey (Died in office.)	1944–1946	Democratic
Fielding L. Wright (As lieutenant governor succeeded Bailey.)	1946–1952	Democratic
Hugh L. White	1952–1956	Democratic
James P. (J. P.) Coleman	1956–1960	Democratic
Ross R. Barnett	1960–1964	Democratic
Paul B. Johnson, Jr.	1964–1968	Democratic
John Bell Williams	1968–1972	Democratic
William L. Waller	1972–1976	Democratic
Charles C. (Cliff) Finch	1976–1980	Democratic
William F. Winter	1980–1984	Democratic
William A. (Bill) Allain	1984–1988	Democratic
Raymond E. (Ray) Mabus	1988–1992	Democratic
Daniel Kirkwood (Kirk) Fordice	1992–2000	Republican
David Ronald (Ronnie) Musgrove	2000–2004	Democratic
Haley R. Barbour	2004–	Republican

APPENDIX II

MEMBERS OF THE U.S. CONGRESS, 1817–1861

The House of Representatives

One Seat, At-Large, 1817–33
George Poindexter, 1817–19
Christopher Rankin, 1819–26,
    died in office
William Haile, 1826–28, resigned
Thomas Hinds, 1828–31
Franklin Plummer, 1831–35
Two Seats, At–Large, 1833–43
Harry Cage, 1833–35
J. F. H. Claiborne, 1835–38,
    seat declared vacant
David Dickson, 1835–36, died in office
Samuel J. Gholson, 1836–38,
    seat declared vacant
Seargent S. Prentiss, 1838–39
Thomas J. Word, 1838–39
Albert G. Brown, 1839–41
Jacob Thompson, 1839–47
William M. Gwin, 1841–43
Four Seats, At-Large, 1843–47
William H. Hammett, 1843–45
Robert W. Roberts, 1843–47
Tilghman M. Tucker, 1843–45
Stephen Adams, 1845–47
Jefferson Davis, 1845–46, resigned
Henry T. Ellett, 1847
Four Seats, Districts, 1847–53
Jacob Thompson, 1847–51, 1st
Winfield S. Featherston, 1847–51, 2nd
Patrick W. Tompkins, 1847–49, 3rd
Albert G. Brown, 1847–53, 4th
William McWillie, 1849–51, 3rd
Benjamin D. Nabers, 1851–53, 1st
John A. Wilcox, 1851–53, 2nd
John D. Freeman, 1851–53, 3rd
**Five Seats, Four Districts Plus One
    At-Large, 1853–55**
William Barksdale, 1853–55, At-Large
Daniel B. Wright, 1853–57, 1st
William T. S. Barry, 1853–55, 2nd
Otho R. Singleton, 1853–55, 3rd
Wiley P. Harris, 1853–55, 4th

Five Seats, Districts, 1855–61
Hendley S. Bennett, 1855–57, 2nd
William Barksdale, 1855–61, 3rd,
    Withdrew
William A. Lake, 1855–57, 4th
John A. Quitman, 1855–58, 5th,
    died in office
Lucius Q. C. Lamar, 1857–60, 1st,
    resigned
Reuben Davis, 1857–61, 2nd, withdrew.
Otho R. Singleton, 1857–61, 4th
    withdrew
John J. McRae, 1858–61, 5th, withdrew

The Senate

Walter Leake, 1817–20
Thomas Hill Williams, 1817–29
David Holmes, 1820–25
Powhatan Ellis, 1825–26
Thomas B. Reed, 1826–27
Powhatan Ellis, 1827–32
Thomas B. Reed, 1829
Robert H. Adams, 1830
George Poindexter, 1830–35
John Black, 1832–38
Robert J. Walker, 1835–45
James F. Trotter, 1838
Thomas Hickman Williams, 1838–39
John Henderson, 1839–45
Jesse Speight, 1845–47
Joseph W. Chalmers, 1845–47
Henry S. Foote, 1847–52
Jefferson Davis, 1847–51
John J. McRae, 1851–52
Walker Brooke, 1852–53
Stephen Adams, 1852–57
Albert G. Brown, 1854–61, withdrew
Jefferson Davis, 1857–61, withdrew

SOURCE: Biographical Directory of the United
States Congress, 1774–Present, *bioguide.
congress.gov.*

MEMBERS OF THE U.S. CONGRESS, 1870–2004

The House of Representatives

1870
George E. Harris (1st Dist.)
Joseph L. Morphis (2nd)
Henry W. Barry (3rd)
George C. McKee (4th)
LeGrand W. Pierce(5th)
1871
George E. Harris (1st Dist.)
Joseph L. Morphis (2nd)
Henry W. Barry (3rd)
George C. McKee (4th)
LeGrand W. Pierce(5th)
REDISTRICT **1873**
Lucius Q. C. Lamar
  (1st Dist.)
Albert R. Howe (2nd)
Henry W. Barry (3rd)
Jason Niles (4th)
George C. McKee (5th)
John R. Lynch (6th)
1875
Lucius Q. C. Lamar
  (1st Dist.)
Guilford W. Wells (2nd)
Hernando D. Money (3rd)
Otho R. Singleton (4th)
Charles E. Hooker (5th)
John R. Lynch (6th)
1877
Henry L. Muldrow
  (1st Dist.)
Van H. Manning (2nd)
Hernando D. Money (3rd)
Otho R. Singleton (4th)
Charles E. Hooker (5th)
James R. Chalmers (6th)
1879
Henry L. Muldrow
  (1st Dist.)
Van H. Manning (2nd)
Hernando D. Money (3rd)
Otho R. Singleton (4th)
Charles E. Hooker (5th)
James R. Chalmers(6th)
1881
Henry L. Muldrow
  (1st Dist.)

Van H. Manning (2nd)
Hernando D. Money (3rd)
Otho R. Singleton (4th)
Charles E. Hooker (5th)
James R. Chalmers/
John R. Lynch(6th)
REDISTRICT **1883**
Henry L. Muldrow
  (1st Dist.)
Van H. Manning / James R.
  Chalmers (2nd)
Elza Jeffords (3rd)
Hernando D. Money (4th)
Otho R. Singleton (5th)
Henry S. Van Eaton (6th)
Ethelbert Barksdale (7th)
1885
John M. Allen (1st Dist.)
James B. Morgan (2nd)
Thomas C. Catchings (3rd)
Frederick G. Barry (4th)
Otho R. Singleton (5th)
Henry S. Van Eaton (6th)
Ethelbert Barksdale (7th)
1887
John M. Allen (1st Dist.)
James B. Morgan (2nd)
Thomas C. Catchings (3rd)
Frederick G. Barry (4th)
Chapman L. Anderson (5th)
T. R. Stockdale (6th)
Charles E. Hooker (7th)
1889
John M. Allen (1st Dist.)
James B. Morgan (2nd)
Thomas C. Catchings (3rd)
Clarke Lewis (4th)
Chapman L. Anderson (5th)
T. R. Stockdale (6th)
Charles E. Hooker (7th)
1891
John M. Allen (1st Dist.)
John C. Kyle (2nd)
Thomas C. Catchings (3rd)
Clarke Lewis (4th)
Joseph H.Beeman (5th)
T. R. Stockdale (6th)

Charles E. Hooker (7th)
1893
John M. Allen (1st Dist.)
John C. Kyle (2nd)
Thomas C. Catchings (3rd)
Hernando D. Money (4th)
John Sharp Williams (5th)
T. R. Stockdale (6th)
Charles E. Hooker (7th)
1895
John M. Allen (1st Dist.)
John C. Kyle (2nd)
Thomas C. Catchings (3rd)
Hernando D. Money (4th)
John Sharp Williams (5th)
Walter M. Denny (6th)
James G. Spencer (7th)
1897
John M. Allen (1st Dist.)
William V. Sullivan /
  Thomas Spight (2nd)
Thomas C. Catchings (3rd)
Andrew F. Fox (4th)
John Sharp Williams (5th)
William F. Love / Frank A.
  McLain (6th)
Patrick Henry (7th)
1899
John M. Allen (1st Dist.)
Thomas Spight (2nd)
Thomas C. Catchings (3rd)
Andrew F. Fox (4th)
John Sharp Williams (5th)
Frank A. McLain (6th)
Patrick Henry (7th)
1901
Ezekiel S. Candler (1st
  Dist.)
Thomas Spight (2nd)
Patrick Henry (3rd)
Andrew F. Fox (4th)
John Sharp Williams (5th)
Frank A. McLain (6th)
Charles E. Hooker (7th)
REDISTRICT **1903**
Ezekiel S. Candler (1st
  Dist.)

Thomas Spight (2nd)
Benjamin Humphreys (3rd)
Wilson S. Hill (4th)
Adam M. Byrd (5th)
Eaton J. Bowers (6th)
Frank A. McLain (7th)
John Sharp Williams (8th)
1905
Ezekiel S. Candler (1st Dist.)
Thomas Spight (2nd)
Benjamin Humphreys (3rd)
Wilson S. Hill (4th)
Adam M. Byrd (5th)
Eaton J. Bowers (6th)
Frank A. McLain (7th)
John Sharp Williams (8th)
1907
Ezekiel S. Candler (1st Dist.)
Thomas Spight (2nd)
Benjamin Humphreys (3rd)
Wilson S. Hill (4th)
Adam M. Byrd (5th)
Eaton J. Bowers (6th)
Frank A. McLain (7th)
John Sharp Williams (8th)
1909
Ezekiel S. Candler (1st Dist.)
Thomas Spight (2nd)
Benjamin Humphreys (3rd)
Thomas U. Sisson (4th)
Adam M. Byrd (5th)
Eaton J. Bowers (6th)
William A. Dickson (7th)
James W. Collier (8th)
1911
Ezekiel S. Candler (1st Dist.)
Hubert D. Stephens (2nd)
Benjamin Humphreys (3rd)
Thomas U. Sisson (4th)
Samuel A. Witherspoon (5th)
Pat Harrison (6th)
William A. Dickson (7th)
James W. Collier (8th)
1913
Ezekiel S. Candler (1st Dist.)

Hubert D. Stephens (2nd)
Benjamin Humphreys (3rd)
Thomas U. Sisson (4th)
Samuel A. Witherspoon (5th)
Pat Harrison (6th)
Percy E. Quin (7th)
James W. Collier (8th)
1915
Ezekiel S. Candler (1st Dist.)
Hubert D. Stephens (2nd)
Benjamin Humphreys (3rd)
Thomas U. Sisson (4th)
Samuel A. Witherspoon / William W. Venable (5th)
Pat Harrison (6th)
Percy E. Quin (7th)
James W. Collier (8th)
1917
Ezekiel S. Candler (1st Dist.)
Hubert D. Stephens (2nd)
Benjamin Humphreys (3rd)
Thomas U. Sisson (4th)
William W. Venable (5th)
Pat Harrison (6th)
Percy E. Quin (7th)
James W. Collier (8th)
1919
Ezekiel S. Candler (1st Dist.)
Hubert D. Stephens (2nd)
Benjamin Humphreys (3rd)
Thomas U. Sisson (4th)
William W. Venable (5th)
Paul B. Johnson, Sr. (6th)
Percy E. Quin (7th)
James W. Collier (8th)
1921
John E. Rankin (1st Dist.)
Bill G. Lowery (2nd)
Benjamin Humphreys (3rd)
Thomas U. Sisson (4th)
Ross A. Collins (5th)
Paul B. Johnson, Sr. (6th)
Percy E. Quin (7th)
James W. Collier (8th)
1923
John E. Rankin (1st Dist.)
Bill G. Lowery (2nd)

William Y. Humphreys (3rd)
T. Jeff Busby (4th)
Ross A. Collins (5th)
T. Webber Wilson (6th)
Percy E. Quin (7th)
James W. Collier (8th)
1925
John E. Rankin (1st Dist.)
Bill G. Lowery (2nd)
William M. Whittington (3rd)
T. Jeff Busby (4th)
Ross A. Collins (5th)
T. Webber Wilson (6th)
Percy E. Quin (7th)
James W. Collier (8th)
1927
John E. Rankin (1st Dist.)
Bill G. Lowery (2nd)
William M. Whittington (3rd)
T. Jeff Busby (4th)
Ross A. Collins (5th)
T. Webber Wilson (6th)
Percy E. Quin (7th)
James W. Collier (8th)
1929
John E. Rankin (1st Dist.)
Wall Doxey (2nd)
William M. Whittington (3rd)
T. Jeff Busby (4th)
Ross A. Collins (5th)
Robert S. Hall (6th)
Percy E. Quin (7th)
James W. Collier (8th)
1931
John E. Rankin (1st Dist.)
Wall Doxey (2nd)
William M. Whittington (3rd)
T. Jeff Busby (4th)
Ross A. Collins (5th)
Robert S. Hall (6th)
Percy E. Quin / Lawrence R. Ellzey (7th)
James W. Collier (8th)
REDISTRICT **1933**
John E. Rankin (1st Dist.)
Wall Doxey (2nd)

William M. Whittington
(3rd)
T. Jeff Busby (4th)
Ross A. Collins (5th)
William M. Colmer (6th)
Lawrence R. Ellzey (7th)
1935
John E. Rankin (1st Dist.)
Wall Doxey (2nd)
William M. Whittington
(3rd)
Aaron Lane Ford (4th)
Aubert C. Dunn (5th)
William M. Colmer (6th)
Dan R. McGehee (7th)
1937
John E. Rankin (1st Dist.)
Wall Doxey (2nd)
William M. Whittington
(3rd)
Aaron Lane Ford (4th)
Ross. A. Collins (5th)
William M. Colmer (6th)
Dan R. McGehee (7th)
1939
John E. Rankin (1st Dist.)
Wall Doxey (2nd)
William M. Whittington
(3rd)
Aaron Lane Ford (4th)
Ross. A. Collins (5th)
William M. Colmer (6th)
Dan R. McGehee (7th)
1941
John E. Rankin (1st Dist.)
Wall Doxey (2nd)
William M. Whittington
(3rd)
Aaron Lane Ford (4th)
Ross A. Collins (5th)
William M. Colmer (6th)
Dan R. McGehee (7th)
1943
John E. Rankin (1st Dist.)
Jamie L. Whitten (2nd)
William M. Whittington
(3rd)
Thomas G. Abernethy (4th)
W. Arthur Winstead (5th)
William M. Colmer (6th)
Dan R. McGehee (7th)

1945
John E. Rankin (1st Dist.)
Jamie L. Whitten (2nd)
William M. Whittington
(3rd)
Thomas G. Abernethy (4th)
W. Arthur Winstead (5th)
William M. Colmer (6th)
Dan R. McGehee (7th)
1947
John E. Rankin (1st Dist.)
Jamie L. Whitten (2nd)
William M. Whittington
(3rd)
Thomas G. Abernethy (4th)
W. Arthur Winstead (5th)
William M. Colmer (6th)
John Bell Williams (7th)
1949
John E. Rankin (1st Dist.)
Jamie L. Whitten (2nd)
William M. Whittington
(3rd)
Thomas G. Abernethy (4th)
W. Arthur Winstead (5th)
William M. Colmer (6th)
John Bell Williams (7th)
1951
John E. Rankin (1st Dist.)
Jamie L. Whitten (2nd)
Frank E. Smith (3rd)
Thomas G. Abernethy (4th)
W. Arthur Winstead (5th)
William M. Colmer (6th)
John Bell Williams (7th)
REDISTRICT **1953**
Thomas G. Abernethy (1st
Dist.)
Jamie L. Whitten (2nd)
Frank E. Smith (3rd)
John Bell Williams (4th)
W. Arthur Winstead (5th)
William M. Colmer (6th)
1955
Thomas G. Abernethy (1st
Dist.)
Jamie L. Whitten (2nd)
Frank E. Smith (3rd)
John Bell Williams (4th)
W. Arthur Winstead (5th)
William M. Colmer (6th)

1957
Thomas G. Abernethy (1st
Dist.)
Jamie L. Whitten (2nd)
Frank E. Smith (3rd)
John Bell Williams (4th)
W. Arthur Winstead (5th)
William M. Colmer (6th)
1959
Thomas G. Abernethy (1st
Dist.)
Jamie L. Whitten (2nd)
Frank E. Smith (3rd)
John Bell Williams (4th)
W. Arthur Winstead (5th)
William M. Colmer (6th)
1961
Thomas G. Abernethy (1st
Dist.)
Jamie L. Whitten (2nd)
Frank E. Smith (3rd)
John Bell Williams (4th)
W. Arthur Winstead (5th)
William M. Colmer (6th)
REDISTRICT **1963**
Thomas G. Abernethy (1st
Dist.)
Jamie L. Whitten (2nd)
John Bell Williams (3rd)
W. Arthur Winstead (4th)
William M. Colmer (5th)
1965
Thomas G. Abernethy (1st
Dist.)
Jamie L. Whitten (2nd)
John Bell Williams (3rd)
Prentiss Walker (4th)
William M. Colmer (5th)
1967
Thomas G. Abernethy (1st
Dist.)
Jamie L. Whitten (2nd)
John Bell Williams (3rd)
G. V. Sonny Montgomery
(4th)
William M. Colmer (5th)
1969
Thomas G. Abernethy (1st
Dist.)
Jamie L. Whitten
(2nd)

Charles H. Griffin (3rd)
G. V. Sonny Montgomery (4th)
William M. Colmer (5th)
1971
Thomas G. Abernethy (1st Dist.)
Jamie L. Whitten (2nd)
Charles H. Griffin (3rd)
G. V. Sonny Montgomery (4th)
William M. Colmer (5th)
REDISTRICT **1973**
Jamie L. Whitten (1st Dist.)
David R. Bowen (2nd)
G. V. Sonny Montgomery (3rd)
Thad Cochran (4th)
Trent Lott (5th)
1975
Jamie L. Whitten (1st Dist.)
David R. Bowen (2nd)
G. V. Sonny Montgomery (3rd)
Thad Cochran (4th)
Trent Lott (5th)
1977
Jamie L. Whitten (1st Dist.)
David R. Bowen (2nd)
G. V. Sonny Montgomery (3rd)
Thad Cochran (4th)
Trent Lott (5th)
1979
Jamie L. Whitten (1st Dist.)
David R. Bowen (2nd)
G. V. Sonny Montgomery (3rd)
Jon C. Hinson (4th)
Trent Lott (5th)
1981
Jamie L. Whitten (1st Dist.)
David R. Bowen (2nd)
G. V. Sonny Montgomery (3rd)
Wayne Dowdy (4th)
Trent Lott (5th)
1983
Jamie L. Whitten (1st Dist.)
W. Webster Franklin (2nd)

G. V. Sonny Montgomery (3rd)
Wayne Dowdy (4th)
Trent Lott (5th)
1985
Jamie L. Whitten (1st Dist.)
W. Webster Franklin (2nd)
G. V. Sonny Montgomery (3rd)
Wayne Dowdy (4th)
Trent Lott (5th)
1987
Jamie L. Whitten (1st Dist.)
Mike Espy (2nd)
G. V. Sonny Montgomery (3rd)
Wayne Dowdy (4th)
Trent Lott (5th)
1989
Jamie L. Whitten (1st Dist.)
Mike Espy (2nd)
G. V. Sonny Montgomery (3rd)
Mike Parker (4th)
Larkin I. Smith / Gene Taylor (5th)
1991
Jamie L. Whitten (1st Dist.)
Mike Espy (2nd)
G. V. Sonny Montgomery (3rd)
Mike Parker (4th)
Gene Taylor (5th)
1993
Jamie L. Whitten (1st Dist.)
Bennie G. Thompson (2nd)
G. V. Sonny Montgomery (3rd)
Mike Parker (4th)
Gene Taylor (5th)
1995
Roger Wicker (1st Dist.)
Bennie G. Thompson (2nd)
G. V. Sonny Montgomery (3rd)
Mike Parker (4th)
Gene Taylor (5th)
1997
Roger Wicker (1st Dist.)
Bennie G. Thompson (2nd)
Charles W. (Chip)

Pickering, Jr. (3rd)
Mike Parker (4th)
Gene Taylor (5th)
1999
Roger Wicker (1st Dist.)
Bennie G. Thompson (2nd)
Charles W. (Chip) Pickering, Jr. (3rd)
C. Ronald Shows (4th)
Gene Taylor (5th)
2001
Roger Wicker (1st Dist.)
Bennie G. Thompson (2nd)
Charles W. (Chip) Pickering, Jr. (3rd)
C. Ronald Shows (4th)
Gene Taylor (5th)
REDISTRICT **2003**
Roger Wicker (1st Dist.)
Bennie G. Thompson (2nd)
Charles W. (Chip) Pickering, Jr. (3rd)
Gene Taylor (4th)

Members of the U.S. Senate

Class 1

Adelbert Ames	1870–1874
Henry R. Pease	1874–1875
Blanche K. Bruce	1875–1881
James Z. George	1881–1897
Hernando D. Money	1897–1911
John Sharp Williams	1911–1923
Hubert D. Stephens	1923–1935
Theodore G. Bilbo	1935–1947
John C. Stennis	1947–1989
Trent Lott	1989–

Class 2

Hiram R. Revels	1870–1871
James L. Alcorn	1871–1877
Lucius Q. C. Lamar	1877–1885
Edward C. Walthall	1885–1894
Anselm McLaurin	1894–1895
Edward C. Walthall	1895–1898
William V. Sullivan	1898–1901
Anselm McLaurin	1901–1909
James Gordon	1909–1910
LeRoy Percy	1910–1913
James K. Vardaman	1913–1919
Byron P. (Pat) Harrison	1919–1941
James O. Eastland	1941–1941
Wall Doxey	1941–1943
James O. Eastland	1943–1978
Thad Cochran	1978–

SOURCE: *Biographical Directory of the United States Congress, 1974–Present.bioguide.congress.gov/ biosearch/biosearch.asp;* The United States Senate, *www.senate.gov.*

APPENDIX III

MISSISSIPPI SYMBOLS AND FACTS

Flower and Tree	Magnolia
Bird	Mockingbird
Motto	*Virtute et Armis* ("by valor and arms")
Stone	Petrified wood
Beverage	Milk
Fossil	Prehistoric whale
Land mammals	Red fox (*Vulpes vulpes*) and White-tailed deer (*Odocoileus virginianus*)
Waterfowl	Wood duck (*Aix sponsa*)
Fish	Largemouth or black bass (*Micropterus salmoides*)
Insect	Honeybee (*Apis mellifera*)
Shell	Oyster shell (*Crassostrea virginica*)
Water mammal	Bottlenosed dolphin (*Tursiops truncatus*)
Butterfly	Spicebush swallowtail (*Pterourus troilus*)
Wildflower	Coreopsis
Dance	Square dance
Language	English
Grand Opera House	Grand Opera House of Meridian
Song	"Go Mississippi"
Toy	Teddy bear
Land area	46,914 square miles, making Mississippi the thirty-first largest state in land area
Population	2,844,658 (as of 2000), making Mississippi the thirty-first most populous state
Counties	82 counties, ranging in land area size from Yazoo County, the largest, to Alcorn County, the smallest
Capital	Jackson, the largest city
Highest Point	Woodall Mountain, Tishomingo County, 806 feet above sea level

Total Population, 1800–2000

YEAR	MS TOTAL	CHANGE	% OF U.S.	U.S. TOTAL	CHANGE
1800	7,600			5,308,483	
1810	31,306	311.9%		7,239,881	36.4%
1820	75,448	141.0	.78%	9,638,453	33.1
1830	138,621	81.1	1.06	12,866,020	33.5
1840	375,651	175.0	2.20	17,069,453	32.7
1850	606,528	61.5	2.62	23,191,876	35.9
1860	791,305	30.5	2.52	31,443,321	35.6
1870	827,922	4.6	2.15	38,558,371	22.6
1880	1,131,597	36.7	2.25	50,189,209	30.2
1890	1,289,600	14.0	2.05	62,979,766	25.5
1900	1,551,270	20.3	2.04	76,212,168	21.0
1910	1,797,114	15.8	1.95	92,228,496	21.0
1920	1,790,618	-0.4	1.69	106,021,537	15.0
1930	2,009,821	12.2	1.63	123,202,624	16.2
1940	2,183,796	8.7	1.65	132,164,569	7.3
1950	2,178,914	-0.2	1.44	151,325,798	14.5
1960	2,178,141	-0.0	1.21	179,323,175	18.5
1970	2,216,912	1.8	1.09	203,302,031	13.4
1980	2,520,638	13.7	1.11	226,542,199	11.4
1990	2,573,216	2.1	1.03	248,709,873	9.8
2000	2,844,658	10.5	1.01	281,421,906	13.2

Average Growth per Decade, 1900–2000

Mississippi	6.4%
U.S.	14.0

Twentieth-Century Growth

Mississippi	6.4%
U.S.	14.0

SOURCE: Historical Statistics of the States of the United States: Two Centuries of the Census, 1790–1990. Compiled by Donald B. Dodd (Westport, Connecticut: Greenwood Press, 1993). Population. United States Bureau of the Census, 2000, www.census.gov.

APPENDIX V

Racial Population Changes, 1800–2000

YEAR	AFRICAN AMERICANS TOTAL NO.	% OF TOTAL*	CHANGE	WHITES TOTAL NO.	% OF TOTAL*	CHANGE	OTHER RACES** TOTAL NO.	% OF TOTAL	CHANGE
1800	3,154	41.5%		4,446	58.5%				
1810	14,704	47	366%	16,602	53	273%			
1820	33,272	44	126	42,176	56	154			
1830	66,178	48	99	70,443	52	67			
1840	196,577	52	197	179,074	48	154			
1850	310,808	51	58	295,718	49	65			
1860	437,404	55	41	353,899	45	20			
1870	444,201	54	2	382,896	46	8		0.1	
1880	650,291	57	46	479,398	42	25	825	0.2	131%
1890	742,559	58	14	544,851	42	14	1,908	0.2	15
1900	907,630	59	22	641,200	41	18	2,190	0.2	11
1910	1,009,487	56	11	786,111	44	23	2,440	0.1	-38
1920	935,184	52	-7	853,962	48	9	1,516	0.1	-3
1930	1,009,718	50	8	998,077	50	17	1,472	0.1	38
1940	1,074,578	49	6	1,106,327	51	11	2,026	0.1	43
1950	986,494	45	-8	1,188,632	55	7	2,891	0.2	31
1960	915,743	42	-7	1,257,546	58	6	3,788	0.2	28
1970	815,770	37	-11	1,393,283	63	11	4,852	0.4	62
1980	887,206	35	9	1,615,190	64	16	7,859	0.7	132
1990	915,057	36	3	1,633,461	63	1	18,242	1.0	35
2000	1,033,809	36	13	1,746,099	61	7	24,698	2.3	162
							64,750		

Twentieth-Century Growth

TOTAL	AFRICAN AMERICANS	WHITES	OTHERS
83.4%	13.9%	172.3%	2553.7%

*Percentages are rounded to whole numbers.
**In 2000, "Other Races" include 11,652 American Indians, 18,626 Asians, and 34,472 other races. After whites and African Americans, the largest group was Hispanics, numbering 39,569.

SOURCE: Historical Census Statistics on Population Totals by Race, 1790 to 1990, and by Hispanic Origin, 1970 to 1990. For the United States, Regions, Divisions, and States. www.census/gov/population/www/documentation/twps0056.html
U.S. Census Bureau, Census 2000, factfinder.census.gov.

Racial Composition of Population, 2000
Counties Ranked in Descending Order Based on African-American Percentages*

COUNTIES	BLACK	OTHER	WHITE	COUNTIES	BLACK	OTHER	WHITE
Jefferson	86%	0.5%	13%	Leake	37%	6.4%	56%
Claiborne	84	0.7	15	Benton	37	1.5	62
Holmes	79	0.9	20	Carroll	37	0.7	63
Humphreys	72	1.3	27	Franklin	36	0.9	63
Tunica	70	2.3	28	Covington	36	1.0	63
Sunflower	70	1.3	29	Clarke	35	0.7	64
Sharkey	69	1.3	29	Simpson	34	1.3	64
Noxubee	69	1.2	29	Forrest	34	2.1	64
Coahoma	69	1.5	29	Lawrence	32	1.0	67
Quitman	69	0.9	30	Marion	32	1.2	67
Wilkinson	66	0.6	31	Tate	31	1.1	68
Leflore	68	2.3	30	Monroe	31	0.9	68
Bolivar	65	1.6	33	Choctaw	31	1.3	68
Washington	65	1.5	34	Newton	30	4.6	65
Issaquena	63	0.9	36	Lincoln	30	1.0	69
Hinds	61	1.6	37	Calhoun	29	1.9	69
Tallahatchie	59	1.0	40	Jones	26	2.8	71
Kemper	58	2.8	39	Greene	26	1.0	73
Jeff. Davis	57	1.0	42	Lafayette	25	3.1	72
Clay	56	0.9	43	Lee	25	1.8	74
Yazoo	54	1.3	45	Smith	23	0.8	76
Jasper	53	0.7	46	Perry	23	1.2	76
Adams	53	1.2	46	Harrison	21	5.8	73
Copiah	51	1.2	48	Webster	21	1.5	78
Marshall	50	1.3	48	Jackson	21	3.8	75
Panola	48	1.2	50	Neshoba	19	15.2	65
Pike	48	1.2	51	Stone	19	1.4	79
Montgomery	45	0.8	54	Rankin	17	1.9	81
Walthall	44	1.3	55	Tippah	18	2.2	82
Winston	43	1.5	55	Union	15	1.6	83
Warren	43	1.8	55	Pontotoc	14	1.6	84
Amite	43	0.9	56	Prentiss	13	1.2	86
Lowndes	42	2.0	56	Lamar	13	1.8	85
Chickasaw	41	1.9	57	Pearl River	12	2.3	86
Grenada	41	1.1	58	DeSoto	11	2.8	86
Attala	40	1.7	58	Alcorn	11	1.6	87
Scott	39	3.9	57	George	9	1.8	89
Yalobusha	39	0.9	60	Hancock	7	3.0	90
Lauderdale	38	1.7	60	Itawamba	6	1.1	92
Wayne	38	0.7	61	Tishomingo	3	2.0	95
Madison	37	2.2	60	State	36	2.3	61
Oktibbeha	37	3.9	59				

*Percentages for blacks and whites rounded to the highest number.
SOURCE: U.S. Census Bureau, Census 2000

INDEX

Abernethy, Thomas G., 260, 266, 277, 330
abolitionist movement, 111, 116, 125, 127
accreditation, 114, 202, 221, 229–30, 371, 378, 382
Ackia, Battle of, 33
Adam, Bidwell, 220
Adams County, formation of, 56; division of, 58
Adams, John, 54, 89
Adams, John Q., 80
Adams, Robert H., 82
Advertising Commission, 236
African Americans: in the antebellum era, 108–109; and church membership, 284–287, *passim*; churches of, 193–94; civil rights of, 150, 151, 153, 155, 158, 172, 199, 266–67, 272; and constitutional Convention of 1868, 155; and Constitution of 1868, 156; and Democratic Party, 314; demographics, 7, 93, 101, 125, 130, 211, 227, 297, 316, 338, 342; disenfranchisement, 164, 172, 176; during post–Reconstruction period, 170–71; and education, 189, 191–92, 384; and the elections of 1873, 160; and healthcare, 346–47; and flood of 1927, 218–220; intimidation of, 156, 162, 267, 300; as musicians, 247–50; in politics, 352–57 *passim*, 360; and public school enrollment, 159; and religion, 114–16; and the Republican Party, 154–55, 220, 278; as sharecroppers, 184; social

progress of, 409–10; violence against, 278, 280, 291, 298–300, 302, 306, 308, 314, 410; and voter registration, 298, 300–304, 308, 310; as voters, 153, 162; as writers, 239–40, 244–45
African Methodist Episcopal Church, 154
African slaves, 2, 13, 30, 33; agrarian movement, 165; and Civil War effort, 143; and demand for new constitution, 170; demographics, 34, 48, 50; during British colonial period, 41. *See* slavery.
Agricultural Adjustment Administration (AAA), 232
Agricultural and Industrial Board (A&I Board). *See* Mississippi Development Authority
Agricultural and Mechanical College. *See* Mississippi State University
Agricultural Stabilization and Conservation Service, 232
Agriculture: diversification, 101, 143, 152, 158, 182, 184–85, 202, 235, 270, 317–20; during the early twentieth century, 182; during latter twentieth century, 389–93; during mid-twentieth century, 317–20; experiment stations, 20, 184, 233; and farm acreage, 106, 108, 112, 182, 216, 218, 262, 270, 317, 389–91; and farm income, 393–94; lien law of 1876, 183; modernization of, 184, 216, 262, 270, 320

Air National Guard, 405
Alabama and Vicksburg Railroad, 188
Alabama Territory, 70
Alcorn Agricultural and Mechanical College. *See* Alcorn University
Alcorn College. *See* Alcorn University
Alcorn University, 113, 157, 175, 185, 191, 221
Alcorn, James Lusk, 127, 151, 53–54, 157, 160, 164; and Ku Klux Klan, 159–60
Alexander v. *Holmes County Board of Education*, 374
Alexander, Margaret Walker, 239–40, 243, 245
Allain, William A. "Bill," 352, 355–56
Allison's Wells, 251
American Family Association, 293
American Independent Party, 313
American Missionary Association of New York, 192
American Party, 126, 131
American Red Cross, 209, 218
American Revolution, 42–43, Ames, Adelbert, 149, 157–58, 160–62, 165
Amite County, formation of, 66
Amory, 12
Anderson, Reuben, 355
Anderson, Walter Inglis, 252
Anglican Church (Church of England), 42
anti-bank movement, 76
Anti-Semitism, and the civil rights movement, 287
anti-trust laws, 180, 200

Mississippi: A History
Developmental editor and copy editor: Andrew J. Davidson
Production editor: Lucy Herz
Proofreader: Claudia Siler
Indexer: Maragaret Root
Cartographer: Jason Casanova, Pegleg Graphics
Cover designer: DePinto Graphic Design
Printer: McNaughton & Gunn, Inc.